Oscar Wilde: The Complete Interviews

Volume Two

Oscar Wilde
the Complete Interviews

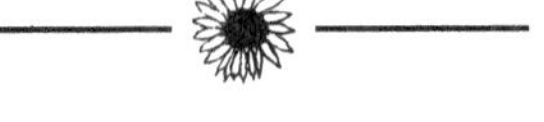

Volume Two

Edited by
Rob Marland

Little Eye

First published in 2022 in Jena, Germany by Little Eye

A CIP catalogue record for this book is available from the British Library

Hardcover ISBN 978-3-9824134-1-9
Paperback ISBN 978-3-9824134-3-3

Front cover: Oscar Wilde in New York City, plate 14
Photograph by Napoleon Sarony, 1882. Colourisation by Rob Marland, 2021.
Library of Congress, LC-DIG-ppmsca-40827

For errata and updates see https://robmarland.co.uk/wildeints

Contents

Figures   512

Abbreviations   513

The Interviews (1883–1900)   515

[Robert Batho], "An Interview with Oscar Wilde," *Liverpool Daily Post* (Liverpool, UK), 8 Jan. 1883, 7   517

"Oscar Wilde at Home," *The Times* (Philadelphia, PA), 28 Jan. 1883, 2   523

"The Talk of Paris," *The Evening Telegram* (New York, NY), 17 Apr. 1883, 3   527

"Paris Gossip," *The Chicago Daily Tribune* (Chicago, IL), 17 Apr. 1883, 7   529

"London Gossip," *The Sunday Herald* (Boston, MA), 17 June 1883, 3   533

"The Poet of the Intense," *The Brooklyn Daily Eagle* (Brooklyn, NY), 12 Aug. 1883, 1   534

"Return of the Aesthete," *The Sun* (New York, NY), 12 Aug. 1883, 5   536

"Bunthorne Transformed," *The Evening Telegram* (New York, NY), 11 Aug. 1883, 3rd ed., 1   538

"Return of Oscar Wilde," *The Cincinnati Commercial Gazette* (Cincinnati, OH), 12 Aug. 1883, 1   540

[Frank George Carpenter], "Carp", *The Cleveland Leader* (Cleveland, OH), 16 Aug. 1883, 4   542

"Oscar Wilde's Ambition," *New York Tribune* (New York, NY), 12 Aug. 1883, 12   543

"Mr. Oscar Wilde's Hair," *The New York Herald* (New York, NY), 12 Aug. 1883, 10   545

"Oscar Wilde Returns," *The World* (New York, NY), 12 Aug. 1883, 5   547

"Theatrical World," *Truth* (New York, NY), 12 Aug. 1883, 5   551

"Brought Across the Sea," *The New York Times* (New York, NY), 12 Aug. 1883, 7   554

"Mr. Wilde Sanguine About Vera," *The New York Mirror* (New York, NY), 18 Aug. 1883, 7   555

"Oscar Wilde on 'Vera'," *The Evening Telegram* (New York, NY), 21 Aug. 1883, 4th ed., 1   557

"Oscar's Opinion of 'Vera'," *Philadelphia Press* (Philadelphia, PA), 22 Aug. 1883, 3   558

"Gossip from Gotham," *The News and Courier* (Charleston, SC), 30 Aug. 1883, 1   561

"The Failure of 'Vera'," *New York Tribune* (New York, NY), 28 Aug. 1883, 5   562

"'Vera' Killed by Critics," *The Sun* (New York, NY), 28 Aug. 1883, 3   564

"Amusements," *The New York Herald* (New York, NY), 28 Aug. 1883, 4   567

"Oscar Wilde's Views," *The Morning News* (Paris, France), 20 June 1884, 1   569

"Mr. Oscar Wilde Interviewed in Glasgow," *Evening News and Star* (Glasgow, UK), 22 Dec. 1884, 4   574

"Oscar Wilde," *The Montgomery Advertiser* (Montgomery, AL), 31 Jan. 1886, 3   580

[Robert Batho], "Shakespeare's Statue," *The New York Herald, European Edition* (Paris, France), 11 Oct. 1888, 1   583

"Oscar Wilde's Hair Cut," *The Brooklyn Daily Eagle* (Brooklyn, NY), 20 Oct. 1889, 14   589

Jacques Daurelle, "Un Poète Anglais a Paris," *L'Écho de Paris* (Paris, France), 6 Dec. 1891, 2 — 593

The Pictorial World (London, UK), 19 Dec. 1891 — 600

"Mr. Oscar Wilde and the Lord Chamberlain," *The Pall Mall Gazette* (London, UK), 28 June 1892, 4 — 601

[Maurice Sisley], "Courrier des Spectacles," *Le Gaulois* (Paris, France), 28 June 1892, 4 — 602

"The Censure and 'Salome'," *The Pall Mall Gazette* (London, UK), 29 June, 1892, 1–2 — 603

Maurice Sisley, "La Salomé de M. Oscar Wilde," *Le Gaulois* (Paris, France), 29 June 1892, 1 — 607

Henry Bauer, "La Ville et le Théâtre," *L'Écho de Paris* (Paris, France), 2 July 1892, 1 — 612

"Les Théatres," *Le XIXe Siècle* (Paris, France), 6 July 1892, 3 — 616

William Theodore Peters, "Oscar Wilde at Home," *The Sunday Inter Ocean* (Chicago, IL), 16 Dec. 1894, 31 — 617

Percival H. W. Almy, "New Views of Mr. Oscar Wilde," *Theatre* (London, UK), Vol. 23, Mar. 1894, 119–27 — 622

"Un Referendum Artistique et Social," *L'Ermitage* (Paris, France), July 1893, 1–24 — 632

"Mr. Oscar Wilde the Lion of Dinard," *The New York Herald, European Edition* (Paris, France), 3 Sep. 1893, 5 — 633

"Mr. Oscar Wilde's Philosophy," *The New York Herald, European Edition* (Paris, France), 9 Sep. 1893, 1 — 635

"The Dramatic Week," *The Press* (New York, NY), 7 Jan. 1894, 4 — 636

"Local Stage Gossip," *The Philadelphia Inquirer* (Philadelphia, PA), 4 Feb. 1894, 10 — 637

F. E. McKay, "A Clever Dramatist's Eccentric Views," *Kate Field's Washington* (Washington, DC), Vol. 9, 4 Apr. 1894, 220–1 — 638

"News From Afar," *The Press* (New York, NY), 8 July 1894, 7 — 640

"News From Afar," *The Press* (New York, NY), 15 July 1894, 3 — 640

"At the Play," *Hearth and Home* (London, UK), 30 Aug. 1894, 553 — 641

"Théatres," *Le Temps* (Paris, France), 5 Jan. 1895, 4 — 642

Gilbert Burgess, "An Ideal Husband at the Haymarket Theatre," *The Sketch* (London, UK), 9 Jan. 1895, 495 — 643

[Robert Ross], "Mr. Oscar Wilde on Mr. Oscar Wilde," *St. James's Gazette* (London, UK), 18 Jan. 1895, 4–5 — 648

Frank Marshall White [and Robert Batho], "Oscar Wilde to Write," *The Chicago Daily Tribune* (Chicago, IL), 17 May 1897, 2 — 655

A.-F. Lugné-Poé, "M. Oscar Wilde en France," *La Presse* (Paris, France), 28 May 1897, 2 — 660

Gedeon Spilett [Louis Sérizier], "Une Entrevue avec M. Oscar Wilde," *Gil Blas* (Paris, France), 22 Nov. 1897, 3 — 663

[Eugenio Zaniboni], "Un' intervista con Oscar Wilde," *Il Pungolo Parlamentare* (Naples, Italy), 9–10 October 1897, 1 — 670

[Clifford Millage], "The Late Oscar Wilde," *The Daily Chronicle* (London, UK), 3 Dec. 1900, 5 — 679

Appendix A: Untraced Interviews — **681**

Appendix B: Articles Not Original Interviews — **687**

Appendix C: Other Articles of Interest — **689**

"Oscar Wilde," *The New York World, Semi-Weekly Edition* (New York, NY), 6 Jan. 1882, 2 — 691

"Oscar Wilde Sees 'Patience'," *New York Tribune* (New York, NY), 6 Jan. 1882, 5 — 694

"Sunbeams," *The Sun* (New York, NY), 10 Jan. 1882, 2 — 695

Hall-Haynes, "Art's Apostle," *The Sunday Herald* (Boston, MA), 15 Jan. 1882, 8 — 696

"Wilde's Lecture," *Philadelphia Press* (Philadelphia, PA), 18 Jan. 1882, 5 — 700

"New York Gossip," *The Sunday Herald* (Boston, MA), 22 Jan. 1882, 4 — 700

"The Aesthete Entertained," *The Washington Post* (Washington, DC), 23 Jan. 1882, 4 — 703

"Oscar Wilde a Guest of the Wednesday Club," *The Sun* (Baltimore, MD), 26 Jan. 1882, 4 — 704

"The Aesthete on His Travels," *Truth* (London, UK), 2 Feb. 1882, 175–7 — 705

Lilian Whiting, "They Will Show Him," *The Daily Inter Ocean* (Chicago, IL), 10 Feb. 1882, 2 — 708

"Oscar's Departure," *Buffalo Commercial Advertiser* (Buffalo, NY), 9 Feb. 1882, 3 — 711

"Oscar Wilde," *The Chicago Daily Tribune* (Chicago, IL), 14 Feb. 1882, 7 — 711

"Decorative Art," *The Milwaukee Sentinel* (Milwaukee, WI), 6 Mar. 1882, 5 — 712

"Wilde Under Ground," *Denver Tribune* (Denver, CO), 15 Apr. 1882 — 713

The Evening Item (Richmond, IN), 2 May 1882, 4 — 714

"Oscar at the Art Gallery," *Toronto Evening Telegram* (Toronto, ON), 25 May 1882, 4 — 715

"Oscar Wilde," *The Globe* (Toronto, ON), 26 May 1882, 6 — 716

"Homicide at Vicksburg," *The Daily Picayune* (New Orleans, LA), 15 June 1882, 2 — 716

"Over the Breakfast Table," *The Times-Democrat* (New Orleans, LA), 26 June 1882, 2 — 717

"The State Camp," *The New York Herald* (New York, NY), 31 July 1882, 3 — 719

"The Saratoga Season," *The Times* (Philadelphia, PA), 13 Aug. 1882, 6 — 720

"The Jersey Lily," *The Boston Herald* (Boston, MA), 24 Oct. 1882, 4 — 721

"New York," *Boston Evening Transcript* (Boston, MA), 18 Nov. 1882, 10–11 — 725

"New York City Life," *The Brooklyn Daily Eagle* (Brooklyn, NY), 26 Nov. 1882, 1 — 726

"Farewell to Oscar Wilde," *New York Tribune* (New York, NY), 28 Dec. 1882, 4 — 727

"Keswick," *Cumberland and Westmorland Advertiser* (Penrith, UK), 26 Feb. 1884 — 729

"Mr. Oscar Wilde," *The Standard* (London, UK), 30 June 1892, 5 — 730

Arthur Howard Pickering, "Unknown Wives of Well-Known Men," *The Ladies' Home Journal* (Philadelphia, PA), Oct. 1892, 11 — 731

"'Five o'Clock' Played at Dinard," *The New York Herald, European Edition* (Paris, France), 8 Sep. 1893, 3 — 734

"To Champion Sin," *The Clinton Public* (Clinton, IL), 6 Oct. 1893, 5 — 735

"Oscar Wilde Scandal," *South Wales Daily News* (Cardiff, UK), 8 May 1895, 5 — 737

"Oscar Wilde Released," *The Pall Mall Gazette* (London, UK), 19 May 1897, 7 — 739

"Oscar Wilde Released," *The Times* (Philadelphia, PA), 20 May 1897, 1 — 743

Appendix D: Interviews about Wilde — **745**

"Return of Miss Blanche Roosevelt," *The New York Herald* (New York, NY), 10 Oct. 1881, 4 — 747

"Mr. Boucicault's Return" *The New York Herald* (New York, NY), 23 Dec. 1881, 4 — 748

"A Chat with Genevieve Ward," *The Daily Picayune* (New Orleans, LA), 27 Dec. 1881, 8 — 748

"Oscar Wilde's Visit," *The Scranton Republican* (Scranton, PA), 3 Jan. 1882, 2 — 749

"Preparing the Poet for Work," *New York Tribune* (New York, NY), 5 Jan. 1882, 3 — 751

"Oscar, The Aesthete," *Philadelphia Press* (Philadelphia, PA), 7 Jan. 1882, 8 — 752

"D'Oyly Carte and His Plans," *New York Tribune* (New York, NY), 12 Jan. 1882, 8 — 755

"Wilde and Whitman," *The Philadelphia Press* (Philadelphia, PA), 19 Jan. 1882, 8 — 757

"Wilde's Experience," *The Topeka Daily Capital* (Topeka, KS), 23 Jan. 1882, 3 — 760

"Oscar and the Barber," *The New York World, Semi-Weekly Edition* (New York, NY), 24 Jan. 1882, 2 — 763

"Not Too Aesthetic to Eat," *New York Tribune* (New York, NY), 28 Jan. 1882, 8 — 764

"Boucicault at Home," *The Sunday Herald* (Boston, MA), 29 Jan. 1882, 2 — 764

"Miss Genevieve Ward," *Cincinnati Daily Gazette* (Cincinnati, OH), 3 Feb. 1882, 5 — 765

"The Question of the Hour," *The New York Herald* (New York, NY), 4 Mar. 1882, 9 — 766

"Gotham Gossip," *The Tribune* (Minneapolis, MN), 5 Mar. 1882, 1 — 767

"An Interview with Oscar Wilde's Brother," *The New Zealand Herald* (Auckland, NZ), 8 Apr. 1882, Supp. 2 — 769

"The New Costume," *The New York World, Semi-Weekly Edition* (New York, NY), 5 May 1882, 6 — 771

"Oscar Wilde," *The Atlanta Constitution* (Atlanta, GA), 27 June 1882, 5 — 773

"Theatrical World," *Truth* (New York, NY), 17 Sep. 1882, 5 — 774

"Madame Christine Nilsson," *The New York Herald* (New York, NY), 25 Oct. 1882, 5 — 775

"Mrs. Langtry's Visit," *The New York Herald* (New York, NY), 26 Oct. 1882, 6 — 776

"Mme. Christine Nilsson," *The Chicago Daily Tribune* (Chicago, IL), 5 Dec. 1882, 5 — 777

"Lily Langtry's Friend," *Buffalo Evening News* (Buffalo, NY), 15 Dec. 1882, 3 — 778

"How They Took Oscar In," *The Sun* (New York, NY), 29 Dec. 1882, 1 — 779

"Oscar Fleeced at Banco," *The New York Times* (New York, NY), 29 Dec. 1882, 5 — 784

"Theatrical World," *Truth* (New York, NY), 11 Feb. 1883, 5 — 786

"D'oyley Carte," *The Chicago Daily Tribune* (Chicago, IL), 27 Feb. 1883, 5 — 788

"Oscar Wilde's Play Withdrawn," *The New York Times* (New York, NY), 28 Aug. 1883, 8 — 788

"'Vera' Withdrawn," *Truth* (New York, NY), 28 Aug. 1883, 1 — 790

"A Crushed Author," *Morning Journal and Courier* (New Haven, CT), 28 Aug. 1883, 3 — 791

"Mrs. Langtry in Paris," *Birmingham Daily Mail* (Birmingham, UK), 12 Sep. 1883, 4 — 793

"Matthew Arnold's Opinions," *The Detroit Free Press* (Detroit, MI), 26 Oct. 1883, 7 — 793

[John Black], "Interview with a Theatrical Manageress," *The South Australian Advertiser* (Adelaide, SA), 4 Aug. 1885, 6 — 794

"An Amazon of Journalism," *The Pall Mall Gazette* (London, UK), 28 Aug. 1886, 1–2 — 795

"Here and There," *The Omaha Daily Herald* (Omaha, NE), 4 May 1888, 4 — 796

"Chats With Celebrities," *Hearth and Home* (London, UK), 30 June 1892, 219–20 — 797

"The Censorship and 'Salome,'" *The Pall Mall Gazette* (London, UK), 6 July 1892, 1–2 — 801

Adele Marroc, "Oscar Wilde's Children," *The Philadelphia Inquirer* (Philadelphia, PA), 5 Nov. 1893, 23 — 803

"Mrs. Oscar Wilde at Home," *To-day* (London, UK), 24 Nov. 1894, 93–4 — 810

Baroness von Zedlitz, "Some Famous Stage Lovers: No. 1.—Mr. George Alexander at Home," *The Englishwoman* (London, UK), Mar. 1895, 33–8 — 814

"Lord Queensberry in the Dock," *The New York Herald, European Edition* (Paris, France), 3 Mar. 1895, 1 — 816

"Finished!" *The Sun* (London, UK), 5 Apr. 1895, 3 — 817

"Oscar Wilde Imprisoned," *The New York Times* (New York, NY), 6 Apr. 1895, 5 — 819

"Mr. Oscar Wilde in a Cell in Bow Street," *The New York Herald, European Edition* (Paris, France), 6 Apr. 1895, 1 — 821

"Charge Against Oscar Wilde," *The Birmingham Daily Post* (Birmingham, UK), 8 Apr. 1895, 8 — 823

"His Oscars," *The Cincinnati Enquirer* (Cincinnati, OH), 8 Apr. 1895, 1 — 824

"Oscar Wilde," *Le Gaulois* (Paris, France), 10 Apr. 1895, 1–2 — 827

"Marquis and Son Come to Blows," *The New York Herald, European Edition* (Paris, France), 22 May 1895, 1 — 833

Ballard Smith, "Father and Son Fight," *The Philadelphia Inquirer* (Philadelphia, PA), 23 May. 1895, 1 — 837

Georges Docquois, "Entretien avec Lord Alfred Douglas," *Le Journal* (Paris, France), 25 May 1895, 1–2 — 838

"O. Wilde is Guilty," *The Sunday Tribune* (Minneapolis, MN), 26 May 1895, 1 — 844

"Oscar Wilde in Prison," *Reynolds's Newspaper* (London, UK), 9 June 1895, 5 — 845

Georges Docquois, "Les Poèmes de Lord Alfred Douglas," *Le Journal* (Paris, France), 8 May 1896, 2 — 846

Adolphe Possien, "Oscar Wilde," *Le Jour* (Paris, France), 28 May 1897, 2nd ed., 1 — 852

Robert Sherard, "At Oscar Wilde's Grave," *Reynolds's Newspaper* (London, UK), 21 Jun. 1903 — 855

Desda Cornish, "Oscar Wilde Redivivus," *Boston Evening Transcript* (Boston, MA), 16 Dec. 1908, 22 — 858

Hayden Church, "The Facts About Oscar Wilde Scandal Are Coming Out at Last," *The Atlanta Constitution* (Atlanta, GA), 3 Aug. 1913, G6 — 861

Appendix E: Burlesque Interviews — **869**

"Wilde Interviewed," *The Daily Graphic* (New York, NY), 31 Dec. 1881, 422 — 871

"Our New York Letter," *The Philadelphia Inquirer* (Philadelphia, PA), 4 Jan. 1882, 7 — 874

"After an Interview," *The Brooklyn Daily Eagle* (Brooklyn, NY), 8 Jan. 1882, 4 — 876

"Where the Poet is Kept," *Truth* (New York, NY), 8 Jan. 1882, 4 — 878

"Fitznoodle in America," *Puck* (New York, NY), 11 Jan. 1882, 295 — 881

"Oscar Interviewed," *Punch* (London, UK), Vol. 82, 14 Jan. 1882, 14 — 883

"Oscar Wilde Interviewed," *The Stage* (London, UK), 20 Jan. 1882, 12 — 886

"The Latest," *Moonshine* (London, UK), 21 Jan. 1882, 34 — 887

W. T. Mercer, "The Aesthetic Gospel," *New York Tribune* (New York, NY), 23 Jan. 1882, 5 — 888

"The Stage," *Bell's Life in London* (London, UK), 28 Jan. 1882, 11 — 890

"Oscar Wilde," *The Sunday Oregonian* (Portland, OR), 19 Feb. 1882, 6 — 891

"Oscar Wilde," *The Saturday Review* (Indianapolis, IN), 11 Mar. 1882, 7 — 893

Kate Crombie, "Aunt Ruth Goes to Hear Oscar Wilde," *Godey's Lady's Book and Magazine* (Philadelphia, PA), Apr. 1882, 352–4 — 896

"Oscar," *The Idaho Avalanche* (Silver City, ID), 1 Apr. 1882, 2 — 901

"A Distinguished Arrival," *The Daily Picayune* (New Orleans, LA), 1 Apr. 1882, 3 — 902

"Bill Nye and Oscar Wilde," *The Daily Inter Ocean* (Chicago, IL), 8 Apr. 1882, 11 — 906

"Oscar Wilde," *The Denver Republican* (Denver, CO), 13 Apr. 1882, 4 — 907

"Oscar Wilde in Atchison," *The Atchison Globe* (Atchison, KS), 22 Apr. 1882, 1 — 908

"The Two Too," *The Topeka Sunday Capital* (Topeka, KS), 23 Apr. 1882, 2 — 911

"Wilde Witticisms," *The Daily Nonpareil* (Council Bluffs, IA), 27 Apr. 1882, 5 — 915

"Aestheticism," *Georgia Weekly Telegraph and Journal & Messenger* (Macon, GA), 14 July 1882, 5 — 916

"Eli Perkins in Saratoga," *Nashville Banner* (Nashville, TN), 16 Aug. 1882, 3 — 917

"Mrs. Langtry in America," *Funny Folks* (London, UK), 25 Nov. 1882, 372 — 918

"The O. W. Vade Mecum," *Punch* (London, UK), 23 Feb. 1895, 85 — 919

Index — **923**

Figures

16. Oscar Wilde photographed by Napoleon Sarony, 1883   535
17. Marie Prescott photographed by Benjamin J. Falk, 1883   559
18. Sarah Bernhardt as Lady Macbeth   571
19. The Gower Monument, Stratford-upon-Avon   585
20. Wilde and Lord Alfred Douglas in Naples, 1897   675
21. *Legend of the Blush Roses*, by Beatrice and Walter Crane   805
22. Constance, Cyril, and Vyvyan Wilde   807
23. Drawing, iguanodon, by Alice B. Woodward   835

Credits: 16, oscarwildeinamerica.org; 17, Harvard Theatre Collection, TCS 2, Box 382; 18, Paris Musées, PH24479; 19, Warwickshire County Record Office, PH130/40; 20, British Library, Add MS 81783 A; 21, 22, editor's collection; 23, Jissen Women's University Rare Books, Honma Hisao Collection, Oscar Wilde Scrapbook Vol. 5, No. 268.

Abbreviations

Listed here are all works cited more than once, and volumes of the OET *Complete Works* cited at least once, in either Volume One or Two. The details of other works cited only once are given in full in the relevant notes.

Archer	Archer. W. (1896). *The Theatrical 'World' of 1895*. Walter Scott.
Bisch	Bisch, M. C. (1996). *Oscar Wilde in Indiana*. [Unpublished master's thesis]. Indiana State University.
Chesson	Chesson, W. H. (1912). A Reminiscence of 1898, *The Bookman*, *34*, 389–94.
CL	Holland, M., & Hart-Davis, R. (Eds.). (2000). *The Complete Letters of Oscar Wilde*. Fourth Estate.
Cooper	Cooper, J. *www.oscarwildeinamerica.org*. Accessed October 2019 – December 2021.
CW i	Fong, B., & Beckson, K. (Eds.). (2000). *The Complete Works of Oscar Wilde, Vol. 1: Poems and Poems in Prose*. Oxford University Press.
CW iii	Bristow, J. (Ed.). (2005). *The Complete Works of Oscar Wilde, Vol. 3: The Picture of Dorian Gray: The 1890 and 1891 Texts*. Oxford University Press.
CW iv	Guy, J. M. (Ed.). (2007). *The Complete Works of Oscar Wilde, Vol. 4: Criticism: Historical Criticism, Intentions, The Soul of Man*. Oxford University Press.
CW v	Donohue, J. (Ed.). (2013). *The Complete Works of Oscar Wilde, Vol. 5: Plays, Vol. 1: The Duchess of Padua; Salomé: Drame en Un Acte; Salome: Tragedy in One Act*. Oxford University Press.
CW vi	Stokes, J., & Turner, M. W. (Eds.). (2013). *The Complete Works of Oscar Wilde, Vol. 6: Journalism, Vol. 1*. Oxford University Press.
CW vii	Stokes, J., & Turner, M. W. (Eds.). (2013). *The Complete Works of Oscar Wilde, Vol. 7: Journalism, Vol. 2*. Oxford University Press.
CW x	Donohue, J. (Ed.). (2019). *The Complete Works of Oscar Wilde, Vol. 10: Plays, Vol. 3: The Importance of Being Earnest; 'A Wife's Tragedy' (fragment)*. Oxford University Press.
CW xi	Guy, J. M. (Ed.). (2021). *The Complete Works of Oscar Wilde, Vol. 11: Plays, Vol. 4: Vera; or The Nihilist and Lady Windermere's Fan*. Oxford University Press.
Dearinger	Dearinger, K. L. (2009). *Marie Prescott: A Star of Some Brilliancy*. Fairleigh Dickinson University Press.
Dibb	Dibb, G. (2013). *Oscar Wilde: A Vagabond with a Mission*. The Oscar Wilde Society.
Douglas (1914)	Douglas, A. B. (1914). *Oscar Wilde and Myself*. Duffield & Company.
Douglas	Douglas, A. B. (1929). *The Autobiography of Lord Alfred Douglas*. Martin Secker.
Ellmann	Ellmann, R. (1987). *Oscar Wilde*. Hamish Hamilton. / Ellmann, R. (1988). *Oscar Wilde*. Knopf.
Fitzsimons	Fitzsimons, E. (2015). *Wilde's Women: How Oscar Wilde Was Shaped by the Women He Knew*. Duckworth Overlook.

Friedman	Friedman, D. M. (2014). *Wilde in America*. WW Norton & Co.
Gide	Gide, A. (1905). *Oscar Wilde: A Study*. The Holywell Press.
H & S	Hofer, M., & Scharnhorst, G. (Eds.). (2010). *Oscar Wilde in America: The Interviews*. University of Illinois Press.
Hamilton	Hamilton, W. (1882). *The Aesthetic Movement in England* (3rd ed.). Reeves & Turner.
Harris	Harris, F. (1918). *Oscar Wilde: His Life and Confessions*. Frank Harris.
Holland	Holland, M. (2003). *Irish Peacock & Scarlet Marquess*. Fourth Estate.
Hyde (1963)	Hyde, H. M. (1963). *Oscar Wilde: The Aftermath*. Methuen & Co. Ltd.
Hyde	Hyde, H. M. (1976). *Oscar Wilde*. Eyre Methuen.
Keller–Farmer	Keller-Farmer Co. (1907). *The Writings of Oscar Wilde: His Life, with a Critical Estimate of His Writings*. A. R. Keller & Co.
Langtry	Langtry, L. (1925). *The Days I Knew*. George H. Doran Company.
Mason	Mason, S. (1914). *Bibliography of Oscar Wilde*. T. Werner Laurie Ltd.
Melville	Melville, J. (1994). *Mother of Oscar*. John Murray.
Mendelssohn	Mendelssohn, M. (2018). *Making Oscar Wilde*. Oxford University Press.
Mikhail	Mikhail, E. H. (Ed.). (1979). *Oscar Wilde: Interviews and Recollections*. Macmillan.
Miscellanies	Ross, R. B. (Ed.). (1908). *The Collected Works of Oscar Wilde: Miscellanies*. Methuen and Co.
Moyle	Moyle, F. (2011). *Constance: The Tragic and Scandalous Life of Mrs Oscar Wilde*. John Murray.
Munby	Munby, A. N. L. (Ed.). (1971). *Sale Catalogues of Libraries of Eminent Persons: Poets and Men of Letters*. Mansell.
Nordau	Nordau, M. (1895). *Degeneration*. William Heinemann.
O'Brien	O'Brien, K. (1982). *Oscar Wilde in Canada*. Personal Library.
OED	*Oxford English Dictionary Online*. December 2021. Oxford University Press.
OWDA	Lewis, L., & Smith, H. J. (1936). *Oscar Wilde Discovers America: 1882*. Harcourt, Brace & Co.
Page	Page, N. (1991). *An Oscar Wilde Chronology*. Macmillan.
Pearson	Pearson, H. (1946). *The Life of Oscar Wilde*. Methuen & Co.
Ricketts	Ricketts, C. (1932). *Recollections of Oscar Wilde*. Nonesuch.
Schroeder	Schroeder, H. (2002). *Additions and Corrections to Richard Ellmann's Oscar Wilde*. 2nd ed. Privately printed.
Seaside Library	Wilde, O. (1882). *Poems by Oscar Wilde, and His Lecture on The English Renaissance*. The Seaside Library.
Seeley	Seeley, P. (2019). *Richard D'Oyly Carte*. Routledge.
Sherard	Sherard, R. H. (1902). *Oscar Wilde: The Story of an Unhappy Friendship*. Privately Printed.
Small	Small, I. (1993). *Oscar Wilde Revalued*. ELT Press.
Stratmann	Stratmann, L. (2013). *The Marquess of Queensberry: Wilde's Nemesis*. Yale University Press.
Sturgis	Sturgis, M. (2018). *Oscar: A Life*. Head of Zeus. / Sturgis, M. (2021). *Oscar Wilde: A Life*. Knopf.
Sturgis (2020)	Sturgis, M. (2020). *Wildeana*. Riverrun.
Sutherland	Sutherland, L. (2020). *George Alexander and the Work of the Actor-Manager*. Palgrave Macmillan.
Woman	Ross, R. B. (Ed.). (1908). *The Collected Works of Oscar Wilde: A Woman of No Importance*. Methuen and Co.
Wright	Wright, T. W. (2008). *Oscar's Books*. Chatto & Windus.

The Interviews (1883–1900)

[Robert Batho], "An Interview with Oscar Wilde," *Liverpool Daily Post* (Liverpool, UK), 8 Jan. 1883, 7[1]

HIS AMERICAN TOUR AND OPINIONS ON THE ATLANTIC.

However strange Mr. Oscar Wilde may have appeared to American eyes, he needs very little introduction to English newspaper readers. His form and features, as seen through the lens of the caricaturist, have been as familiar in the illustrated comic journals as those of the Prime Minister, and he became in the pages of *Punch* the type of a class which is destined, perhaps, to divert the current of English society. He is a practical illustration of the teaching of the Neo-romantic school of Swinburne and Rossetti: he is the concentration of that "sweetness and light" which are the leading characteristics of the new "English Renaissance." He has been called the Apostle of Aestheticism, not in admiration of the sentiment but in derision of the sentimentality of what was thought to be the craze of an hour; and it is not generally or popularly conceded that he is the leader of a movement which has already vastly affected every branch of art that is associated with our daily lives and the comfort and beauty of our homes, and which may in future develop into a complete revolution of our ideas and methods of existence.

Such is the lofty aim of the aesthetic school, and though we may not all be so enthusiastic as to realise such a Utopia, many will recognise some possibilities of good in the teachings of the school. Mr. Oscar Wilde was not the first to don knee-breeches and velvet jackets and wear long hair, but he was the cleverest and boldest of his class, and instead of being the presentiment and embodiment of that sickly sentimentality and languid effeminacy which are supposed to be the characteristic qualities of the aesthetes, he inherits in no small degree the penetrative appreciation of the distinguished archaeologist Sir William Wilde, as

---

1. Quoted in OWDA, 33, 445; and Pearson, 77. Robert Batho later claimed that he had conducted this interview: see Frank Marshall White [and Robert Batho], "Oscar Wilde to Write," *The Chicago Daily Tribune* (Chicago, IL), 17 May 1897, 2, p. 657. Robert Batho, the son of a warehouse keeper, was born in 1856 in Birkenhead, across the Mersey River from Liverpool. At 15 he was working as a railway clerk and in 1881, aged 25 and still living in Birkenhead, as a shorthand writer. The 1891 census lists him as a "chartered journalist, author" in Rugby; his son had been born in Birmingham a year earlier (this perhaps explains why he was on hand to interview Wilde in nearby Stratford-upon-Avon in 1888; [Robert Batho], "Shakespeare's Statue," *The New York Herald, European Edition* (Paris, France), 11 Oct. 1888, 1, pp. 583–8). In 1901 Batho was living in Hackney, London and working as an "advertising agent"; his second wife had given birth to a son in Hackney four years earlier. In 1911 Batho was still in London, now listed as an "author and journalist". According to "Solved, as Reporter, Jack-the-Ripper Mystery," *Buffalo Evening News* (Buffalo, NY), 8 Oct. 1920, 1, an article evidently based on information provided by Batho himself, he began his journalistic career in 1879, solved the Jack the Ripper mystery after sleeping in the Ripper's bed for thirteen nights, and in the 1910s worked for various Canadian newspapers before returning to England in 1920. He died in 1928.

well as the courageous enthusiasm and imaginative fervour of his mother, Lady Wilde—the "Speranza" of Irish song—"the Madame Roland of the Irish Gironde." It was Lady Wilde, we are told by Mr. A. M. Sullivan in "New Ireland," who, at the trial of Gavan Duffy, when a fiery revolutionary article was read in court, rose up in the ladies' gallery and, acknowledging the authorship, said "I am the culprit, if crime it be."[1] Mr. Oscar Wilde has none of this kind of heroism, but in his own theme he is an enthusiast quite as extravagant; and perhaps all the more reckless because of a certain mocking humour in which he would sometimes seem to treat his own professions as a sort of joke. Unquestionably he has a "mission," and on the whole perhaps—rightly or wrongly—he is none the less sincere because he assumes to laugh at a scoffing audience quite as much as they laugh at him.

It is well known that he has been educating the Yankees. If he had never attained celebrity for anything else he would have immortalised himself by the one observation which he made to an interviewer on his arrival in America—that "he was disappointed with the Atlantic."[2] It seemed so perfectly preposterous that of all things in nature the Atlantic Ocean should have failed to come up to the expectations of Mr. Oscar Wilde that the majority of people didn't believe the report, but rather supposed the idea to be another example of sardonic Yankee humour. The author himself, however, has more than verified the accuracy of the report, and in a few words of a brief interview with our reporter on Saturday— when he arrived in Liverpool by the Cunard steamer Bothnia—he even justified the conclusion to which he had come on the subject of the Atlantic as an artistic failure.[3]

The vessel arrived in the river soon after seven o'clock in the morning, and the handful of cabin passengers she brought came ashore in a grey and very murky dawn, which must have been unfavourable to the impressions of so sensitive an observer as Mr. Oscar Wilde, although he was complimentary enough to describe it shortly afterwards as a "good grey" in colour. As Mr. Wilde came on

1. Lady Wilde's affiliation with *The Nation* and her role in the trial for seditious conspiracy of its co-founder and editor Charles Gavan Duffy (1816–1903) is related on pages 109–10 of Sullivan's *New Ireland* (1878). In brief, Jane Francesca Elgee, as she then was, had penned an anonymous article titled *Jacta Alea Est*: this was the article read out in court. Jane did not stand up in court and claim authorship (Melville, 39). The comparison here of Lady Wilde with Madame Roland is taken from Sullivan. Madame Roland (1754–1793) was a French writer and salonnière. During the revolution she was affiliated with the Girondins, a moderate faction. She fell afoul of more hard-line revolutionaries and was guillotined. In his prison text, *De Profundis*, Wilde repeated this flattering comparison, writing that his mother "intellectually ranks with Elizabeth Barrett Browning, and historically with Madame Roland," (CL, 762).
2. See e.g., "Oscar Wilde's Arrival," *The New York World, Semi-Weekly Edition* (New York, NY), 3 Jan. 1882, 4, p. 35.
3. Saturday 6 January.

the saloon deck among the other passengers preparatory to crossing the gang-
way to the Satellite tender, he stood out prominently as the central figure of the
group. He appears at least five feet eight inches or six feet in height, and is broad
in proportion. Physically, therefore, he is the antithesis of the ethereally-
attenuated creatures of the Du-Maurier–Gilbert ideal, of which he is supposed to
be the type, and there is nothing very "intense" about him, excepting the colour
of his clothes, which, though widely differing from the sombre hues of ordinary
every-day costume, is exceedingly harmonious and tasteful. Anyone who expected to see in him a lanky "foot-in-the-grave young man," dressed in velvet and
posing rapturously over a lily, must have been perfectly shocked by the contrast.
He is a rather robust young man, apparently about thirty-four or thirty-five years
of age, and his dress was a modernised copy of the picturesque pattern of the
French Revolution of "Directoire," with the exception of the sash and hessian
boots—the coat buttoning high across his breast, disclosing a cream-coloured
vest and massive watch seals.[1] Both the undercoat and trousers were of a chocolate brown colour, harmonising with the sage-green of a greatcoat in the French
style, with collar and cuffs of light sealskin, and sloping pockets, out of one of
which hung about a yard of a deeply-fringed silk handkerchief of an amber
brown or "gold" colour. Mr. Wilde wore a loosely turned-down collar of the
Byron pattern and a sage-green scarf tie, and the edifice was crowned by a
brown felt hat of a slightly "sugar-loaf" form, so as to match the undercoat and
complete the revolutionary aspect of a figure that would otherwise have been a
consummate study in green, brown, and amber. Mr. Wilde has a round, full face,
dreamy blue eyes of a gazeful character, and long hair of a sandy yellow, which is
sometimes called "no colour at all," and which is not nearly so pronounced in
dullness of hue as the red-raddle and brick-dust tresses of the ineffable young
ladies in Mr. Rossetti's pictures.[2] The hair falls in a thick curve almost to his
shoulders, and lends to the cherub-like face—which is clean-shaven; or rather
not shaven at all, for it has no appearance even of incipient growth of beard—
that semi-poetic aspect which would be beautiful if it were not infantile. To sum
up, Mr. Wilde's features are like a very commonplace and badly-executed print of
a portrait of Raphael.[3] He, however, unpoetised himself for the purposes of de-
barkation, and puffed rakishly at a huge unlit cigar, while he smilingly nodded his
adieux and shook hands with the officers of the ship. Mr. Wilde's smile is one of

1. Directoire style was a neoclassical style popular in France in the last years of the eighteenth-
century. In Britain a similar style was adopted by the dandies. Men wore high-collared tailcoats
of a dark colour, tight-fitting knee-breeches or trousers of a lighter material, and long flowing
neckties.
2. Wilde's hair is generally described as brown, and this is how it appears in Pennington's portrait and in Frith's *A Private View at the Royal Academy, 1881* (but see p. 676, note 1).
3. Resemblance to portrait of Raphael: see p. 49, note 1.

his strong points. It is always unexpected, and it is so beamingly beatific that it is quite irresistible to the beholder. In comparison, Mr. Whitley's seraphic efforts are tame and meaningless.[1] Mr. Wilde's smile is a perfect symphony of harmonious changes, and he punctuates every sentence with a ray of joyous brilliancy which is quite contagious for a fitful interval, though it relapses again into a repose which seems altogether melancholy by contrast.

It was with one of his most bewitching wreaths of smiles that he informed our representative of his "astonishment" at being interviewed. He thought this deplorable custom was indigenous to America, and while gently, and with evident satisfaction, deprecating the custom, modestly suggested that he was the first great man who had ever been "interviewed" in this country.

Briefly to indicate the drift of Mr. Wilde's few observations, and without attempting the inquisitorial process of giving them verbatim, it may be recorded on his own good authority that his lecturing tour was the most successful undertaking of the kind that has ever been known, and that he has "lectured to more people than anyone else who has visited that country." He left England nearly twelve months ago, but his tour, which was extended over nearly the whole of America and Canada, only occupied seven months. He visited, among many other places, Chicago, and San Francisco, and Colorado; west to Salt Lake city, where he lectured and was entertained by the Mormon President Taylor; lectured to the miners at Leadville; went through Texas to New Orleans;[2] back through Virginia and the Southern States, taking Savannah and Richmond, back to Philadelphia. Here he lectured twice, in Boston twice, in New York three times, and in Chicago twice.[3] He then journeyed through Canada and lectured in Montreal, Quebec, Toronto, Ottawa, &c., visited Nova Scotia and Prince Edward's Island, and experienced an "interesting storm" on the way. In Chicago he had an audience of 4,000 persons, and in Boston he spoke to 3,500.[4]

When asked as to the character of the American audiences, Mr. Wilde displayed some slight reticence, and, after duly thinking the matter over, said he had come to the conclusion that his audiences generally were "very attentive, but entirely undemonstrative." There was probably, therefore, an absence of that

1. Edward Whitley (1825–1892) was an English Conservative politician who served as a Member of Parliament for Liverpool and, later, for Everton (a constituency in Liverpool), from 1880 until his death.

2. Wilde did not travel to New Orleans via Texas but vice versa.

3. Wilde omits the two times he lectured in Brooklyn, a city independent of New York until 1898.

4. Wilde is exaggerating: his first audience in Boston was over 1,000 (Sturgis, 225/216); in Chicago, it was around 2,000 to 2,500 (Friedman, 159; Sturgis, 236/226). Alternatively, he may be estimating the total number of people he lectured to in each city (he lectured twice in both Chicago and Boston).

enthusiasm which the nobility of his theme might have been expected to inspire, and doubtless the explanation rests in the circumstance that this lecturer was regarded to some extent, from the reputation that preceded him, as somewhat of a curiosity in himself. He had, he states, a variety of three or four lectures, one being on "Decorative Art," another on the "English Renaissance," and another detailed lecture called "The House Beautiful." It would be difficult to suggest which of these he selected for the instruction and edification of the "miners of Leadville." A fourth lecture breathed the general spirit of romanticism and beauty pervading Europe—particularly France and England—as preached by Byron and Goethe.[1]

Mr. Wilde is of the opinion that "there is some very fine decorative art at New York and some of the other large cities in the States, but it is of the most modern kind." There is no semblance of mediaevalism, and "the general character of the furniture, wall papers, and decorations, from the ordinarily well-to-do American household to that of the millionaire, is commonplace." In some of the best houses, however, "there are many fine specimens of modern French art, but the pictures are almost exclusively French, and therefore the French school will form and influence the American taste." "It is astonishing," continued Mr. Wilde, "how totally unacquainted the Americans are with English art of any kind. They know nothing of Millais or Leighton; but they have many examples of Corot, Daubigny, and of the French school generally.[2] They are not at all influenced by English art. The best collections are those in the Boston and Philadelphia museums."

Mr. Wilde was then questioned on the crucial point—the report that had been spread regarding his expression of opinion on the subject of the Atlantic Ocean. Had he been accurately reported in the statement that he was "disappointed with the Atlantic?" Was our cherished regard and veneration for the stupendous element that separates the hemispheres to be dissipated at one fell swoop? "Certainly I was disappointed," said Mr. Wilde, with an imperturbable gravity, relieved only by the faintest glimmer of a smile. "The Atlantic," he proceeded to explain, "is greatly misunderstood." His questioner ventured to hint

1. *The English Renaissance, The Decorative Arts,* and *The House Beautiful* were the three lectures Wilde gave with any regularity in North America. He gave *Irish Poets and the Poetry of the Nineteenth Century* (5 April 1882, San Francisco) and *The Relation of Art to Other Studies* (31 May 1882, Hamilton) once each. Byron and Goethe are referenced in *The English Renaissance.* In Leadville Wilde gave *The Decorative Arts,* but in *Personal Impressions of America* he would claim that he lectured the miners on "the Ethics of Art" and Benvenuto Cellini (Dibb, 242; see also p. 382, note 3).

2. Sir Frederic Leighton (1830–1896) was a British painter and sculptor, and President of the Royal Academy between 1878 and 1896. Jean-Baptiste-Camille Corot (1796–1875) was a French landscape and portrait painter. Charles-François Daubigny (1817–1878) was a French landscapist of the Barbizon school.

that the mysterious phrase in which he had expressed his disappointment did not help to clear away the misunderstanding that existed with respect to this particular ocean. "Everything one says," added Mr. Wilde, looking far away into the bank of smoke that hung over Liverpool, "should be in mystery, more or less."

After this oracular statement, the unhappy interrogator saw no means of pursuing the argument; but in a moment or two the philosophical cloud that was gathering was cleared away by a sunshiny smile, and Mr. Wilde continued—"The Atlantic, as I first saw it, was wanting in all the elements of grandeur; it was a monotonous and uninteresting grey." We inquired whether that opinion had been modified since, and he said, "Yes, considerably, for we had one very fine storm on the way home." "But, after all," he proceeded, with a tinge of sadness, "one's scope of vision is very limited. You see no more on the Atlantic than you do on a lake—less, in fact; for on the Atlantic you get a dreadful monotony of colour. You cannot have fine colour except in water which is more or less shallow. The splendid colours you see in lake water come from the ground; but when you come to water which is three miles deep you have nothing but a very dirty grey."

On the tender, and while approaching the Landing-stage, Mr. Wilde subsided into contemplative silence, which was only broken when the foghorn of the Satellite emitted a shriek close to his ear. He naturally started, and shrank from the deafening sound, and when it ended he sighed and said, "We live in a century of hideous noises," and then went on puffing at the unlit cigar.

He was much interested in some information given him on the subject of the exhibition of Rossetti's pictures at Burlington House and the rehanging of them that had been arranged, and was glad to hear that one of Rossetti's most important works—"Dante's Dream"—had been acquired for the permanent collection by the Liverpool Corporation. He asked what was thought of this picture by the public generally—"was it appreciated?" He was told that it was not popularly appreciated; that its symbolism was perhaps a trifle too profound for the general public in the present neglected condition of their art education. "Ah," he said, with another smile that was half a sigh, "Rossetti was not a painter in the vulgar or conventional sense; he was a poet who expressed himself in colours." Then he asked, "Whether Ruskin had written anything yet on the subject of the Rossetti exhibition," and thought that Ruskin's comments would be eagerly looked for.[1]

---

1. The Royal Academy's 14th Winter Exhibition of Works by the Old Masters, and by Deceased Masters of the British School had opened at Burlington House on 1 January. Some 83 works by Rossetti were exhibited, including *Dante's Dream at the Time of the Death of Beatrice* (1871). Rossetti's largest painting, it was bought from the artist in 1881 for £1,575 by the Liverpool Corporation and displayed in the Walker Art Gallery, where it remains. It depicts Dante at the deathbed of Beatrice Portinari, the object of his unrequited love. The green clothes of Beatrice's attendants are supposed to symbolise hope; the flowers spread on the floor, purity; and two red

Mr. Wilde bestowed a rapturous smile upon his interviewer at parting, and expressed his intention of visiting the Walker Art Gallery if it was open before he left for London, which he intended to do by the eleven o'clock train from Lime-street the same morning. His travelling companions stated that he was a great favourite with everyone on board the Bothnia. On the voyage he usually dressed in the familiar costume of velvet coat and knee breeches and silk stockings, and in the evenings he frequently entertained the company in the saloon with recitations. He was asked to deliver one of his lectures on the voyage, but declined.

On the whole the impression formed of the now famous exponent of aestheticism is that he certainly believes in his mission, and that he is sincere in the worship of his ideal. He has lived through a period of scoffing scepticism and has been ridiculed into renown. It will be strange if, with his serene self-reliance and enthusiasm, he does not make use of his personal notoriety to advance the doctrines of his school, and to realise to a large extent the vision the contemplation of which has raised him above the level of conventionality. Good has been and will be done by the promotion of views which are included in the aesthetic curriculum, even though some of the methods employed for the promulgation and the personal idiosyncrasies of such men as Oscar Wilde may be open to severe and serious criticism.

"Oscar Wilde at Home," *The Times* (Philadelphia, PA), 28 Jan. 1883, 2[1]

The Aesthete's Opinion That the Average American is Narrow-Minded and Ignorant.

HIS IDEAS OF ART VERY CRUDE

An Egotist and Without Veneration—A Foundation for a School of Literature.

Special Correspondence of THE TIMES.

---

doves, love. In an article for *The Pall Mall Gazette* Wilde would refer to Rossetti as "the poet of the Blessed Damozel, the painter of Dante's Dream." (18 Apr. 1887; CW vi, No. 62, lines 10–11.)

1. Reprinted as Oscar Wilde at Home," *The Washington Post* (Washington DC), 29 Jan. 1883, 1; "Oscar Wilde at Home," *The Chicago Daily Tribune* (Chicago, IL), 30 Jan. 1883, 3; and "Oscar Wilde at Home," *The Courier-Journal* (Louisville, KY), 31 Jan. 1883. Excerpted in "The Point of View," *The Boston Daily Globe* (Boston, MA), 29 Jan. 1883, 1; and "Wilde on Americans," *The Daily American* (Nashville, TN), 31 Jan. 1883, 6. Quoted in Cooper ("I Can Wait," 28 Dec. 2015); and Sturgis (2020), 92.

London, January 9.

The Troubadour of Aestheticism has returned from American shores and today made his first appearance in streets and clubs. He is sad and depressed. The English people, having been instructed by their American cousins how to "guy" a public character such as Mr. Wilde, have begun already and "skits" are being made in the public prints and club sarcasm is rife in every direction. As a consequence Oscar Wilde had already announced his intention to leave England for the south of France, to spend the summer, and Willie Wilde, his brother, proposes to go with him, as he too has been the object of a raillery rather malicious than good-natured.[1] Oscar did not care to talk about his experiences in the United States, but said, with some bitterness, that he had been treated so badly by many people and a part of the newspaper press that he could not refrain from saying that he was much disappointed. Yes, really disappointed. He was not angry, but disappointed.

THE AMERICANS NARROW-MINDED.

"When I first came to America I was received with a warmth of welcome that bespoke no end of future pleasure. I was led to be too enthusiastic and hopeful. The better class of people were pleasant, and I found some society the equal of our best society here, but not much. The average American is narrow-minded and ignorant. He is self-assertive. He is more opinionated than his English cousin, whom he resembles in all of the bad points and is equal to in none of the good. The average American I found to be without respect or veneration, consequently he has no desire to acquaint himself with the canons of art. He is the most splendid egotist, and frequently demonstrates qualities as the most magnificent liar, the world produces. He regards the size of his country as a personal compliment of nature to himself. Having no respect nor veneration and being accustomed to exaggeration, he sneers at what he does not understand and scorns to learn that which does not immediately return a reward."[2]

"Mr. Wilde, you appear to have some special cause of complaint."

---

1. Wilde went to Paris for three months at the end of January, without his brother William "Willie" Charles Kingsbury Wilde (1852–1899).

2. See also "The American Man": "To him the greatness of a country consists in the number of square miles that it contains; and he is never tired of telling the waiters at his hotel [in Europe] that the State of Texas is larger than France and Germany put together. [...] For him art has no marvel, and Beauty no meaning, and the Past no message. [... T]he only thing that can console him for having wasted a day in a picture-gallery is a copy of the New York Herald or the Boston Times. Finally, having looked at everything, and seen nothing, he returns to his native land. There he is delightful. [...] At home, the American man is the best of companions, as he is the most hospitable of hosts." (CW vi, No. 60, lines 35–65.)

"Not so. I have no cause of complaint, and only speak as every gentleman must who visits the States and spends, as I have done, a considerable time there. Let me continue. You have no idea, on the other hand, what intellects are to be found there, what wit, elegance, taste and female beauty in the first grade of society. They have artists in painting and sculpture; they have a good social life, which has nothing of the Republic about it, but yet a quiet American dignity at once charming and befitting. There are picture galleries and churches which are very fair. There is some good architecture in the cities, but as a rule it is crude and new. The city of New York is cosmopolitan in its population, and its dwellings and public places reflect that mixture of nationalities in which, as a rule, the elements were not originally the best."

THAT BUNKO MAN.

"You came away rather unexpectedly, did you not?"

"Yes—no—I was preparing to go when an unexpected call from England accelerated my preparations."

"The cable brought word that you had met a 'bunko' man and that you were his."

"Ah, that is a very absurd story, which has such a little bit of foundation that I won't deny it or explain it. I may say, however, that I did meet 'Mr. Drexel's son,' as clever Americans had done before me. If that industrious young man has accomplished all the knavery with which he is so liberally credited, his wealth will soon exceed that of his putative father."

"Was your lecturing tour a financial success?"

"Yes, quite so. It was very successful. I was somewhat startled by the attitude of the newspapers toward me and they ran amuck with their usual graceful and witless criticism. They attracted the public attention to me."

"What was your opinion of the newspapers?"

"Full of news, but edited without judgment, written with a minimum amount of brains and good English and put together without regard to truth and decency."

"Perhaps the newspaper press is responsible for your somewhat obvious ill-will against Americans?"

"Do you think it obvious? It is only in appearance, for I adore America and Americans as I would any other curiosity. I have nothing but the kindliest feelings for the Americans, and the newspapers are full of interest and monstrously enterprising. If they spared themself effort and sought to be polished with the same assiduity they seek to be sensational they would be much improved. What I complain of, to be particular, is the fact that they are written by incompetent men, or rather certain subjects are handled by incompetent pens. The man who excels as a descriptive writer on subjects such as fires and arrests in gaming houses is

525

not the man to write intelligently about a statue from the hand of a great sculptor—at least not always—and how can the man whose musical ear has the training only of street music write fairly or well of Berlioz's Damnation of Faust?[1] As for art, the ordinary newspaper writer in America gained his knowledge of it by studying art through the glass panes of a print shop and his knowledge of architecture in enforced contemplation of the walls of jails."

Here somebody said that the newspapers in America had credited Mr. Wilde with having created a sensation in the Lotus Club [*sic*] when he made that remark before.[2] Mr. Wilde said: "I did say so before and it is none the less true in that I have repeated it."

Then he went on: "What impresses itself upon the unprejudiced observer is that the newspapers are stamped with incompetency. They do lots of great big things, but nothing is rounded in and completed. They are loose and flying, like a silken scarf torn and waved by unsteady hands."

ART NOT STRONGLY ROOTED.

"What art did you find in America?"

"What you might expect in a new country. The art idea is not strongly rooted in their character. The Catholic religion has fostered a love for Madonnas and altar studies. The vast sweeps of prairie, the grand mountain and landscape scenery, the tumbling falls of Niagara, than which nothing is grander in the world, have not, as one might have thought, impressed an artistic sentiment. The fact is that art-love has not yet a permanency in America. That has got to be created. There are some magazines and periodicals that make very nice pictures and print them, but that kind of picture, while requiring some skill, is not art. It is elementary only."

"And the literature?"

"There is, it seems to me, the foundation for an excellent school of literature in the States. It is marked by many signs of promise. It is too clannish, however. There are half a dozen or so who are active workers in the field of literature who monopolize the seats in its highest places. These are Mr. Howells, James, Aldrich, Mrs. Burnett, Mrs. Stuart Phelps, Cable and one or two others."[3]

1. *The Damnation of Faust* is an oratorio by French composer Hector Berlioz (1803–1869), first performed at Paris's Opéra Comique in 1846.

2. Wilde had attended a dinner at The Lotos Club on 28 October. In a speech he criticised the American press, saying that he had more than once met with interviewers "whose ideas of painting had evidently derived from the chromos in the stationers' shop windows, their ideas of sculpture from the figures in front of tobacconists' shops, and their ideas of architecture from the local jail" ("Items," *The Chicago Daily Tribune* (Chicago, IL), 30 Oct. 1882, 5).

3. Elizabeth Stuart Phelps (1844–1911) was an American author of spiritual novels and, like Wilde, an advocate for clothing reform.

"And do you not think they are entitled to their high position?"

"Most assuredly, for if they were not they could not hold it. There are among them, as a leaven to their protective system of maintaining the best places, a goodly number of women, who share their honors."

"Are you going back to America?"

"Not I, indeed."[1]

"They made it pretty warm for you, did they not?" asked a friend.

"I was very comfortable. But there begins the music." Mr. Wilde came forward from the mantelpiece, and taking the arm of his brother Willie sauntered out of the lounging room into the large hall of Raleigh House, where a smoking concert was just beginning.

The half-dozen who had gathered about him in the manager's lounging parlor were his acquaintances and friends. Among them was THE TIMES correspondent. When Mr. Wilde had gone a gentleman said: "I fear Oscar is very much embittered by the loss of his money. The fact is, they got nearly $7,000 from him, and one check only did he succeed in stopping. A chap calling himself A. J. Drexel's son called on him, wanted him to see a picture by Millet, led him into a confidence game and then, when he remonstrated, he was thrown out. The whole story was told by a friend of his to a British Consular officer, from whom I have it. Then he was very much involved in the Langtry esclandre. He had espoused her too warmly and made some enemies by trying to bring her into a dinner party. He was curtly written to and told that the dinner would be postponed."[2]

PILGRIM.

"The Talk of Paris," *The Evening Telegram* (New York, NY), 17 Apr. 1883, 3[3]

French and Chinese Civilization Compared.

ECHOES OF THE BIGGAR CASE.

The Excitement About the American Duty on Pictures Cooling Down.

DRAMATIC AND LITERARY GOSSIP.

1. Wilde sailed on the *Brittanic* for New York on 11 August 1883.

2. The American press had reported that Wilde's praise of Langtry at the Lotos Club dinner displeased his fellow guests, who had insisted that what Wilde saw as her "elegance," they saw as "gall" (see e.g., "Oscar and the Lily," *Buffalo Express* (Buffalo, NY), 7 Nov. 1882, 2).

3. Quoted in "Oscar Wilde," *The Chicago Daily Tribune* (Chicago, IL), 18 Apr. 1883, 5.

SPECIAL CORRESPONDENCE OF THE EVENING TELEGRAM.
Paris, March 30.—

✂ *Several paragraphs that are unrelated to Wilde.*

OSCAR WILDE'S NEW PLAY.

Oscar Wilde, having now quite finished revising his Russian play "Vera," is now at work on a five-act drama for Mary Anderson, entitled "The Duchess of Padua."

"I have laid the plot at Padua," said he, "chiefly on account of the opportunity it gives of introducing gorgeous and delightful costumes. I should like to see my characters attired in raiment as glorious as that in Paul Veronese's 'Marriage at Cana.'"[1] And from this the conversation drifted off to an interchange of opinion with respect to the charms and virtues of Mary Anderson. Mr. Wilde, without a touch of his usual languor, unhesitatingly proclaimed that lady "the most exquisite and beautiful thing yet produced by America."

As soon as he has finished his "Duchess of Padua" Mr. Wilde will fix his powerful mind upon his promised "Souvenirs of America."[2] They will, I am inclined to think, be written in a less foppish and self-conceited spirit than might be imagined. "I shall always regard my journey to America," remarked Mr. Wilde, "as having formed a most important part of my education; and I hope to return to the States again—in September, probably—to superintend the production of my play."[3]

✂ *Several paragraphs that are unrelated to Wilde.*

1. *The Wedding Feast at Cana* (1863), by Italian Renaissance painter Paulo Veronese (1528–1588), depicts the celebration at which Christ transformed water into wine. The guests at the feast wear luxurious clothing of the period the picture was executed. The picture is the largest in the collection of the Louvre Museum, which Wilde is known to have visited in the spring of 1883 (see "Mr. Oscar Wilde's Hair," *The New York Herald* (New York, NY), 12 Aug. 1883, 10, p. 545).

2. The book was never written. Instead, Wilde toured the United Kingdom with his lecture *Personal Impressions of America.*

3. Wilde had evidently agreed with the producers of *Vera* that he would return. See "Theatrical World," *Truth* (New York, NY), 11 Feb. 1883, 5, p. 786.

"Paris Gossip," *The Chicago Daily Tribune* (Chicago, IL), 17 Apr. 1883, 7[1]

Oscar Wilde Engaged in Writing His Book on the United States.

His Views on This Country and its Various Phases of Life.

What He Thinks of the Chicago Water-Works and the Large Balance Wheel.

Paris, April 2.—(Special Correspondence.)
—Have you quite forgotten the memorable visit paid to the City of Chicago last year by that astonishing and eccentric young man, Oscar Wilde? Or does an amused smile still flit over some Chicago faces as they conjure up his esthetic image and think of the novel theories, sartorial and artistic, which he expounded in America? In either case Oscar is, with all his absurdities (and perhaps a good deal on account of them), a sufficiently interesting character to deserve reverting to now and then, as occasion offers; and, the occasion having offered itself to me several times lately in Paris, I took it. I had various reasons for doing so. First and foremost, a very natural desire to see a man who had so audaciously run the gauntlet of popular prejudice and convention; secondly, professional curiosity— a wish to learn something about the work on America which rumor said he had come to Paris to write, far from the madding crowd of adoring virgins that beset him in his native Kensington; and thirdly—but the two reasons I have given already are sufficient.

He has been here for at least two months already, but curiously enough has attracted very little attention. Not a single French paper has, so far as I have heard, thought it worth its while to send a man to interview him, and though he has been seen daily on the Boulevard de Capucines and in the Avenue de l'Opera his coming and going have made no more stir amongst the Parisians than if he had been a mere Roumanian Minister or a Turkish Pasha. From this my intelligent readers, even though they should not happen to have crossed the briny ocean, will at once perceive that Paris is a very much more cosmopolitan and blasé city than New York or Chicago.

To some extent, no doubt, this absence of excitement may be accounted for by the comparative quiet and simplicity of the esthete's demeanor here. Having no particular object to gain by cutting any ultra-esthetic capers on the boulevard,

---

1. Excerpted in "Mr. Oscar Wilde and the Unutterable Wheel," *The Pall Mall Gazette* (London, UK), 7 May 1883, 11 (which is H & S, b99). *The Pall Mall Gazette* version was reprinted as "Oscar Wilde on Wheels and Things," *The New York Times* (New York, NY), 24 May 1883, 5 (quoted in Ellmann, 185/194); "Oscar Wilde on Wheels and Things," *The Courier-Journal* (Louisville, KY), 27 May 1883, 10; and "Oscar Wilde on Wheels and Things," *The Boston Daily Globe* (Boston, MA), 4 June 1883, 5.

and, wishing to be allowed to work at his book and his plays undisturbed, he has put away much of his bombast and absurdity for a season; dropped the knee-breeches, discarded all thought of lilies or sunflowers, trimmed his hair carefully, and, in short, has discreetly toned himself down into something not *very* unlike the objectionable and detestable bourgeois against whom he points so much satire.

At home, however, that is to say, in his rooms at the Hotel Voltaire, and at night, when, responsive to the invitations liberally showered upon him by the Americans and English in Paris, he condescends to shine at a stray soirée or dinner, he becomes the Oscar you have seen and I had read of—a glorious creature, all harmonious color and intensity; a gentle dogmatist, a High Priest, and Prophet of the Beautiful. The other day, for instance, when I called upon him, I found him lounging luxuriously in an arm-chair and attired in a green velvet jacket, salmon-colored neckcloth, burnt sienna "inexpressibles," red silk stockings, and pumps. At the back of his head he had artfully disposed a tiger or a leopard skin, and round him, strewn about with a great appearance of elaborate disorder, were fifteen or twenty half-read and half-cut yellow-covered novels.[1]

He rose with real though languid courtesy, and begged me to be seated. I must say his face pleased me. Effeminate it is, of course, but decidedly clever and refined. His conversation, of which I had heard so much, pleased me less. He seemed to have an almost insuperable difficulty in being natural, and the tritest remark set him pompously digressing for full five minutes. "I believe you frequent the same café as I do?" was, for instance, replied to by an exhaustive dissertation (suspiciously like a bit of an old lecture) on the important part the café played in the social economy of the Greeks. Gradually, however, I led him from the ancients to the moderns, and at last we fell into what I found a very enjoyable, gossipy discussion of America. Mr. Wilde spoke of the land of liberty in a kindly and almost a regretful tone; vowed he had learned much from his short trip from the Atlantic to the Pacific, and hinted that the day might not be far distant when he would return to the West. But he had no illusions about the reception he might expect there. "Even Sarah Bernhardt," said he, "would not have any success if she were to go back.[2] See how indifferently it has fared with Rossi,[3] and many another."

Soon after I made some reference to the book he was supposed to be writing and inquired what scope and character he intended to give it. "Well," he re-

1. French novels were often published in yellow paper covers.
2. Bernhardt embarked on a further eight successful American tours between 1887 and 1917.
3. Ernesto Rossi (1827–1896) was an Italian actor.

plied, "it will probably be issued in two volumes, and be ready this year. As to its character, I shall not go into very deep criticism. Neither shall I say much about Boston jails and Philadelphia sanitation or things of that sort, which are, of course, of no importance. I shall try to set down what I have heard Americans say of life and art—and I have heard much that was of deep interest—and I shall especially consider what life is to young men in America, what they can hope to do there, and what they do."

"You must have found yourself very little in sympathy with America and Americans, surely?" I remarked after a pause.

"Oh, no," condescendingly replied the generous Oscar. "I feel an interest in—er—all humanity. Even in Chicago I found much—much—of intensest interest—beauties—wonderful beauties. One day as I sojourned in that city I came upon—er—the water-works. A sort of—er—castellated atrocity, with pepper-box turrets and absurd portcullises. How came they (thought I, with amazement)—how came they to erect this hideous building in this most modern and utilitarian of cities? I must have a closer look at this horror. Perchance I shall find some beauty even here, I murmured, for we cannot live without Beauty, you know. We can do without food and—er—things of that sort, but not without Beauty..... Then it occurred to me that perhaps I might discover this Beauty I had sought for in vain so long in—American machinery. A wheel is in itself a very beautiful object. All the noblest forms of the ceramic art are derived from the potter's wheel. And yet in England I had always found machinery such a pitiful and ugly thing; a jumble of cranks and cogs and petty pieces, you know, without a touch of grandeur about them. So I entered that castellated horror at Chicago, and there at last I came upon a wheel—the wheel of the Chicago Water-Works— a mighty, majestic, unutterably harmonious wheel. I saw the beauty and the poetry of America in that revolving wonder; and I said to myself if ever America produces a great musician let him write a Machinery Symphony. He could have no more worthy subject.

"But of course they never will have a great musician out there," continued Oscar, dropping from the clouds to earth with singular suddenness, "until they have abolished the shrieking steam whistle. Their tympanums have all been ruined by those whistles."[1]

---

1. *Personal Impressions of America*: "It is surprising that the sound practical sense of the Americans does not reduce this intolerable noise. I fail to see why these whistles could not be set to very beautiful notes of music. It might not be possible to treat the hearers to a symphony of Beethoven's played by them—I have to acknowledge that would be *too* elaborate—but at least the whistle might play some form of musical sound somewhat less harrowing." (Dibb, 234.)

We left Chicago at this point and drifted into art. Oscar professed immense admiration for much of the decorative art he had seen in America, and spoke in glowing terms of Chase, "who has done more for art in his country than any one living," said he, and Lafarge, "who has made quite a new departure in the art of manufacturing stained-glass." Tiffany's centrepieces, too, he pronounced "finer than anything of the sort we can show in England." And he regretted very much that art was such a rarity in America still despite the example set by these three reformers, Chase, Lafarge, and Tiffany.[1]

"But, after all," he went on, "the stage will afford Americans the greatest scope. The actor's art is the best for them, because it is the most democratic."

This brought us to a discussion on transatlantic actresses, one or two of whom appear to have made a deep impression upon our young esthete. From this again we rambled on to American women in general, and American love, on which subject I found Oscar rather shy of expressing an opinion for some time. Why, I know not. He said at last, however, that he thought American love on the whole a very innocent, boy-and-girlish, brotherly and sisterly affair.

"You do not seem to believe in its being profound," said I, half hoping to hear a burning confession. "Well, no," replied Oscar, with a smile. "You see there can be no question of deep love where it is of the slightest consequence to a man whether he catches his train or loses it. Every one is anxious to catch trains in America, you know."[2]

And now, fair American maidens, I leave the esthete to your tender charity.

DESDICHADO.

1. William Merritt Chase (1849–1916) was an American painter and teacher. John La Farge (1835–1910) was an American painter, muralist, and stained glass window maker. Louis Comfort Tiffany (1848–1933) was an American artist and designer, best known for his work in stained glass.

2. *Personal Impressions of America*: "There was an absence of romantic unpunctuality in America, everybody seems in a hurry to catch a train, it was a sort of national amusement. This is a state of things which is not favourable to poetry or romance. Had Romeo or Juliet been in a constant state of anxiety about trains, or had their minds been agitated by the question of return-tickets, Shakespeare could not have given us those lovely balcony scenes which are so full of poetry and pathos." (Dibb, 234.)

"London Gossip," *The Sunday Herald* (Boston, MA), 17 June 1883, 3

Two Cardinals—Gladstone and Wales—A Ruskinesque Criticism.

(*From our Special Correspondent.*)
LONDON, June 5, 1883.

✂ *Several paragraphs that are unrelated to Wilde.*

A CLASSIC "FREAK."

The ladies, especially of Boston, may be especially interested in the series of classical dramatic performances at Lady Freake's, Kensington.[1] This was given in the private theatre where Mrs. Langtry first learned to fret and strut her little hour upon the stage. The "Story of Troy" was enacted, and on certain evenings in Greek. Mr. Gladstone was among the audience on the first "Greek" night; and the sweet, aesthetic youths and maidens became possessed with a sudden fear when they beheld the stern features of the "Grand Old Man" who had informed the hostess that he "trusted due regard would be paid to the qualities of the classic verse."[2] Mr. Gladstone expressed himself, on the whole, as well pleased. Not so the Prince of Wales, who put in an appearance at one of the charity rehearsals, but never came again, giving as his reasons that the "Kensington Belles" were not good looking enough. With Kit Marlowe, he might have exclaimed—only in derision:

> "Is this the face that wrecked a thousand ships
> And turned the topmost towers of Ilium?"[3]

On the following evening the performance was in English, and among the audience I noticed Browning and Ruskin. Oscar Wilde, too, was there with his locks pruned. He says that the statue of Nero, with its cropped hair, determined him to sacrifice the aesthetic redundancy of his wavy curls, because it was "the statue of the wickedest man, modelled by the greatest sculptor."[4] Poor Oscar! He

---

1. Sir Charles James Freake (1814–1884), an architect and builder, and his wife Eliza, Lady Freake, née Pudsey (d. 1900), regularly staged theatrical entertainments at their South Kensington home.

2. In the source, "qualities" is given as "quantities"—surely a typo.

3. Christopher "Kit" Marlowe (1564–1593) was an Elizabethan dramatist and poet. He wrote *Tamburlaine the Great* (c. 1587), *The Jew of Malta* (c. 1592), and *Edward II* (c. 1592). The lines quoted, which refer to the beauty of Helen of Troy, are from *Doctor Faustus* (c. 1588), and should read: "Was this the face that launch'd a thousand ships, | And burnt the topless towers of Ilium".

4. There were several sculptures in the Louvre that, in 1883, were identified as Nero. Whether Wilde copied the hairstyle of one of them is a moot point. See Marland, R. (2021). Imitatio Neronis: Oscar Wilde's 'Neronian coiffure'. *The Wildean*, *59*, 3–56. Wilde repeated the story in interviews in New York in August.

may be weak, but he is not wicked, and it is too bad of him to cast ridicule on a really stupendous ruffian by such puerile imitation.

✂ *Several paragraphs that are unrelated to Wilde.*

"The Poet of the Intense," *The Brooklyn Daily Eagle* (Brooklyn, NY), 12 Aug. 1883, 1[1]

Oscar Wilde Returns to America Looking Very Much Like a Commonplace Young Man.[2]

"It is a little thing of my own. I will not publish it," murmured a tall, graceful looking young man as he stepped from the gang plank of the Britannic of the White Star line yesterday morning, and looked about him for a four wheeler to take him to a hotel. The young gentleman was no other than Oscar Wilde, the original Bunthorne and leader of the aesthetic order of sunflower dudes.[3] "I have come back again to America for the express purpose of looking after the production of my new play, 'Vera,'" said Mr. Wilde, slowly swaying his body in an artistic curve toward one of his lady acquaintances, who had come down to the steamer to meet him. "I will not publish my play and I intend to strictly guard the copyright. It will be produced at the Union Square Theater one week from next Monday night. The public is my critic. It is often unreasonable but usually just," continued Oscar, as he left the reporter and mixed with the many friends assembled on the wharf to welcome him back to this "horribly new country." A change has come over the spirit of the poet of the intense since he left these shores a few months ago. In appearance he has become "a matter of fact young man," and following the example of Reginald in the concluding act of "Patience," he has cut his hair, thrown off his eccentric style of costume, and resolved himself into a fearfully ordinary looking individual, comparatively speaking. "Alas, Mr. Wilde, you are no longer Early English," sighed a fair worshiper at the shrine of the too too utter, as she gazed despondingly upon the poet. In fact, Mr. Wilde looked much the same in dress as his fellow passengers on the steamer. He wore a black

---

1. H & S, b101.

2. "Commonplace": an allusion to *Patience.* See p. 32, note 1.

3. The "dude" was a new type of man that New Yorkers were noticing in 1883. There was much debate over what the term meant exactly, but it tended to describe a young man who banged his hair and parted it in the middle, grew a moustache, affected either haughtiness or a "lack-a-daisy air", incessantly smoked cigarettes, carried a silver-headed cane, and wore fancy waistcoats, skin-tight trousers, and pointed shoes.

Figure 16. Wilde, photographed by Napoleon Sarony with the short hair he wore in the summer of 1883.

broadcloth sack coat, somewhat the worse for the ocean trip it had taken; a black vest, cut high, and showing very little of his linen, and a pair of badly cut light colored cassimere trousers, which were strapped down to a pair of patent leather shoes. An Alpine slouch hat rested upon all that remained of his erstwhile flowing locks, and, horror of horrors, it was slightly tipped over his left ear, giving him a tinge of the old Fire Department air. His hair was cut close to his head, and altogether he might easily have been mistaken for an English commercial traveler of some cloth or fancy goods house in London. The hard practical world had at last succeeded in brushing off the poetic gloss from the former brilliant butterfly of the ethereal aesthetic world, and Oscar Wilde has tacitly resigned the leadership of the intense school of philosophy and gone into the show business. Early on Monday morning Mr. Wilde will commence superintending the rehearsal of his new play at the Union Square Theater, and he seems to wish it to be distinctly understood that his second visit to America is purely one of business.

"Return of the Aesthete," *The Sun* (New York, NY), 12 Aug. 1883, 5[1]

Mr Wilde Explains that he Had to Cut his Hair when he Changed his Breeches.

Oscar Wilde arrived in this city today on the White Star steamer Britannic. Mr. and Mrs. John T. Raymond and M. B. Curtis were among his fellow passengers.[2] As Mr. Wilde tripped smilingly down the gangplank to the pier he was, to all appearance, a commonplace young man.[3] He wore a dark sack coat, a pair of light-colored trousers, tight above the knee and rather loose below, a white waistcoat, patent leather shoes, and a high-crowned, broad-brimmed, dove-colored felt hat. His face was very full, and seemed to be running over with good humor. It had been burned red by the sun. Everybody noticed at once that Mr. Wilde had cut his hair, and that the back of his neck was visible for the first time in America. He had not adopted the State prison cut. His locks were now three or four inches long. He wore a turn-down collar and turn-up cuffs, and a cravat of mauve silk caught together by a cameo ring. His handkerchief was of mauve silk.

1. Printed simultaneously with slight variations as "Oscar Wilde in New York," *The Sunday Herald* (Boston, MA), 12 Aug. 1883, 6.
2. John O'Brien (1836–1887) was an American comic actor who appeared under the name John T. Raymond. Maurice Curtis (1849–1920) was a Hungarian-born American comic actor.
3. "Commonplace": an allusion to *Patience*. See p. 32, note 1.

Mr. Wilde was driven at once to the Hotel Brunswick, where he will remain for the present. He has a pleasant room in the rear of the hotel on the third floor.

"I have been just seven months away from this country," he said to a reporter of THE SUN, "and have been planning for months past to come over at this time. We left Liverpool on Thursday a week ago, and had a delightful passage. Mr. Raymond was a most amusing companion. On Thursday evening last a charity entertainment was given on board ship, and Mr. Raymond and I assisted. I read my poem, 'Ave Imperatrix.'"

"What is the purpose of your visit this time?" asked the reporter.

"It is solely to superintend the rehearsals and production of my play, 'Vera, the Nihilist,' at the Union Square Theatre. It will be produced on Monday, Aug. 20. All the scenery and costumes have been made in this country. 'Vera' is the first play I have written. We have taken the theatre for a month—taking the time for which Mr. Joseph Jefferson had engaged it."

"Did you bring no properties or costumes with you?"

"Only a peculiar shade of vermillion silk, which could not be found in this country. It will be worn by Miss Prescott in the last act."[1]

"What have you done since you left New York in January last?"

"I went at once to Paris, and remained there for four months working at my new play, and when I had finished it I returned to London. The play is called 'The Duchess of Padua.' It deals with Italian life of the sixteenth century. On my return to London I lectured on art before the students of the Royal Academy.[2] In July I delivered a public lecture on America, and passed the month in lecturing."[3]

"How do English theatre audiences compare with American audiences?"

"On the whole, American audiences are more sympathetic and quicker to catch a point. They respond more readily to what appeals to their intelligence; whereas the English are affected to a greater extent through the eye. Americans are more affected by epigram, and the English by beauty of color and fine scenery. In the present advanced condition of art there is naturally an immense sense of joy in the skilful grouping of color. For this reason it is difficult for a play to succeed in England unless it is magnificently mounted."

1. Prescott was photographed in this dress and the monochrome prints were hand-coloured. See the dust jacket of Dearinger.

2. Wilde delivered *Modern Art Training* on 30 June 1883 (for the text see Dibb, Appendix A). Johnston Forbes-Robertson chaired the event.

3. *The Sunday Herald* ends this sentence with "in the provinces." Wilde spoke about his American experiences at a dinner at the Paris Pen and Pencil Club in early March 1883. He delivered *Personal Impressions of America* for the first time on 10 July 1883 at Princes' Hall, Piccadilly. Before leaving for America Wilde gave the lecture in Margate, Ramsgate, Southampton, Southport, and possibly Brighton. He would go on to deliver the lecture at least 56 times across Great Britain and Ireland, with the last known performance in London on 28 December 1885.

"It was reported here that you had abandoned knee breeches and cut your hair?"

"Indeed? I suppose the news sent a thrill of excitement through the country. I have given up knee breeches for a time, and did put myself in the hands of the hair dresser. Everything has changed. Art has not one form only. It is only necessary to follow the essence of art, and one may dress beautifully without wearing knee breeches. That style of dress was worn when long, flowing wigs were in vogue. Removing the knee breeches necessitated a curtailment of the hair. Many forms of dress are beautiful if the laws of art and color are observed. For the present I shall not wear my hair long—not, at least, until I have thoroughly thought the matter over."

"Did you wear knee breeches when you were lecturing in England?"

"No, I did not. The London papers said that I dressed like Count D'Orsay.[1] I followed the prevailing fashion—as it is generally best to do—and dressed in black and white. My lectures were quite successful, and I made many engagements for others in the fall.[2] I don't know whether I shall get back to fulfil them. I never make a plan except for the pleasure of breaking it."

"Bunthorne Transformed," *The Evening Telegram* (New York, NY), 11 Aug. 1883, 3rd ed., 1[3]

Oscar Wilde Returns with Short Hair and Baggy Trousers.

THE OBJECT OF HIS VISIT

Mr. John T. Raymond on the Apostle, Henry Irving and Lillian Russell.

HIS EXPERIENCES IN LONDON

As the steamer Britannic, of the White Star Line, from Liverpool, touched her wharf this morning the tall, commanding form of Oscar Wilde, the apostle of aestheticism, emerged from the cabin and glided down the gangplank. A number of his English friends were on hand to receive him, and the demonstrative greet-

1. Alfred Guillaume Gabriel, Comte d'Orsay (1801–1852), was a French dandy and amateur artist. In Sir George Hayter's portrait (1839), D'Orsay is depicted wearing a black tailcoat and flowing black scarf with a white shirt.
2. Wilde's first lecture upon his return to the United Kingdom was at Wandsworth on 24 September. Thereafter he toured the United Kingdom, lecturing almost daily until late April 1884.
3. Excerpted in "Bunthorne Transformed," *The Boston Sunday Globe* (Boston, MA), 12 Aug. 1883, 2; "World of Amusement," *New York Dispatch* (New York, NY), 12 Aug. 1883, 4; and "Bunthorne Transformed," *Burlington Free Press and Times* (Burlington, VT), 14 Aug. 1883, 3.

ings on their part were returned by the sunflower worshipper with an equal amount of enthusiasm. Among those who were on the pier to receive their friends or relations was a young society lady, who, as her eyes followed the apostle, expressed great disappointment at his personal appearance. "Just to think," she said, "he has cut off his lovely curls, and the symmetry of his Apollo-like limbs is concealed by a pair of baggy trousers."

A COMPLETE TRANSFORMATION.

If, as Mr. Labouchère of the London *Truth* maintains, the only things that ever elevated Oscar Wilde above ordinary mortals were a three cornered handkerchief, a sunflower and a pair of knee breeches, he was certainly mingled with the herd again, as these were missing this morning.[1] His hair was closely cut in the ordinary style. His head was graced by a sweeping Alpine slouch hat that concealed his hair almost entirely and rested on his ears for support. He wore a black broadcloth sack coat and vest and a pair of light colored cassimere trousers that were held down to his patent leather shoes by straps.

HE TALKS ABOUT HIS PLAY.

To a TELEGRAM reporter Mr. Wilde said that his present trip to America had been taken solely for the purpose of superintending the rehearsal and presentation of his play "Vera," which will be put upon the boards for the first time at the Union Square Theatre Monday next week. "In regard to its merits," he continued, "it would be useless for me to express an opinion. You know the author looks at the children of his brain as the parent does upon his offspring—through the colored glasses of affection and love, and either may overlook imperfections or faults which the disinterested must discern at once. If my play possesses merit it will succeed exactly in proportion to its worth."

AN INEXORABLE CRITIC.

"The public," continued Mr. Wilde, "while it is unreasonable in a great many respects and is often imposed upon in a great many ways, is an inexorable but just critic of the drama. The reputation, no matter how great, that a playwright may have obtained in other fields of art or literature does not assist him in the

---

1. Labouchère's *Truth* had been supportive of Wilde during his 1882 tour, but the review of *Personal Impressions of America* was scathing. Labouchère had described Wilde as an "effeminate phrase-maker" and a "temporary jest in London drawing rooms, the butt of American lecture halls, and a failure in Bohemian Paris" who had lectured "to empty benches at the height of the season [....] The joke is played out; the soap bubble of prismatic hues blown from a clay pipe has burst," ([Henry Labouchère], "Exit Oscar," *Truth* (London, UK), 19 July 1883, 86–7). For Wilde's response to the article, see "Mr. Oscar Wilde's Hair," *The New York Herald* (New York, NY), 12 Aug. 1883, 10, pp. 546–7.

539

slightest in the theatre. His verses or the production of his brush may be eagerly sought for, whether good or bad, as long as he creates them, once his reputation is acquired; but his histrionic work will have to bear the unbiased criticism of the herds which must needs pronounce its doom, or sustain it. As an illustration of this, take, for instance, the presentation of Tennyson's 'Promise of May.'[1] Now, while all his late lines have been flashed over the cables of the world and eagerly read throughout all nations where literature is loved, his 'Promise of May' was put upon the stage, with the disastrous result with which all are familiar."

✂ *A paragraph about John T. Raymond.*

RAYMOND ON WILDE.

In speaking of Oscar Wilde Mr. Raymond said that he had been the life of the ship during her passage, and had entertained the ladies with the reading of some of his poems at entertainments gotten up on board. "Upon Mr. Wilde's last visit to this country he came as a 'poser,'" said Mr. Raymond. "It was a business enterprise, and the idea was an exceedingly brilliant one in my mind. He came, he saw, he conquered, and he left with a good bank account. He comes now as a dramatist and his worth in that field will soon be known."

✂ *Several paragraphs about John T. Raymond's experiences in London.*

"Return of Oscar Wilde," *The Cincinnati Commercial Gazette* (Cincinnati, OH), 12 Aug. 1883, 1[2]

He Is to Produce His New Play and Pays America the Usual Compliment.

Special to the Commercial Gazette.

New York, August 11.—Oscar Wilde, the great apostle of aestheticism, arrived in this city from Liverpool on the steamship Britannic, of the White Star Line, today and registered at the Hotel Brunswick. Mr. Wilde has undergone a complete transformation since his former visit to this country. The long and flowing locks have been discarded and given over to the shears, and Oscar looks, in the language of a fellow-passenger, "like a rational being." His front hair—in

---

1. Tennyson's play, his only prose work, had flopped in November 1882.
2. Reprinted as "Oscar, Dear," *The Courier-Journal* (Louisville, KY), 12 Aug. 1883, 2; "Return of Oscar Wilde," *The Daily American* (Nashville, TN), 13 Aug. 1883, 8; "Return of Oscar Wilde," *The Atlanta Constitution* (Atlanta, GA), 14 Aug. 1883, 1; and, in abbreviated form, as "Oscar Wilde's Return," *Fort Worth Daily Gazette* (Fort Worth, TX), 18 Aug. 1883, 7 (which is referenced in Sturgis, 292/277).

spite of Mrs. Langtry's edict—is cut squarely across in the most approved style of "bang."[1]

On being asked the purpose of his visit to New York the poet aesthete said: "I come to attend the rehearsals of my play, 'Vera,' which is to be produced at the Union Square Theater on August 20. There were some details in regard to colors, dresses and scenery that I wanted to look after myself, so I just ran over for a few weeks. I cannot remain long in this country, for I have several engagements to lecture in England."

"Your new play has a political aspect, I believe?" said the reporter.

"Yes, and that is the reason it was not produced in England, because they said it trenched on political subjects. So here I am coming to America to produce my play, instead of bringing it out in my native land. Americans are without prejudices, and it can be produced here without fear or favor. 'Vera' is a five-act play in prose.[2] It is my first attempt at dramatic prose of any kind."

"On your return to England, did you not find that the aesthetic school had proved a failure?" asked the reporter.

"Oh, dear no. On the contrary, it has been a great success. A careful inspection will show that the whole scheme of color is altered. If we hear less of the movement just at present, it is because the victory has been already won."

"What practical result has been brought about by your school?"

"An entire alteration of our domestic decorations and the elevation of the artisan into an artist. Thus we find that handicraft has been given an increased dignity. Besides the general feeling was produced among the public that art is the chief joy and delight in life, and so we find daily delight in the household."

"But knee-breeches have not yet come in vogue to any great extent?"

"No; and for the reason that an alteration of men's dress is the most difficult reform to make in the sphere of fashion, which is another name for stupidity. On this point fashion still holds its ground. But after all what does it matter? A man can be a poet and wear any style of coat; indeed he need not wear a coat at all to be a poet. But in the dress of females there is a change, and also in the dress of children. The books of Kate Greenaway and Walter Crane have greatly aided in

1. Langtry wore a fringe, or "bangs", and, along with fellow actress Lotta Crabtree, was held responsible for the popularity of the style among women in 1883 ("All About Hair," *The Bloomington Daily Pantagraph* (Bloomington, IL), 6 Aug. 1883, 3). The "edict" referred to was Langtry's announcement that she was growing out her bangs: "Yes, bangs must go" ("Mrs. Langtry Speaks Her Mind," *New York Herald* (New York, NY), 24 July 1883, 5).

2. The 1882 privately printed edition of *Vera* is described on the title page as "A Drama | IN A PROLOGUE AND FOUR ACTS", but Wilde, Prescott, and journalists often referred to the play as having five acts.

the latter reform.[1] Once it was tried, it was found to be inexpensive and made the children look very charming and made them feel comfortable. So you see that the aesthetic school has not been a failure."

[Frank George Carpenter], "Carp", *The Cleveland Leader* (Cleveland, OH), 16 Aug. 1883, 4[2]

Oscar Wilde and His New Play—How the Poet Looks

Something From the Inside on Ohio Politics—The Hoadly-Payne Combination.

Central Park on Sunday—The Happy Children and the Obelisk.

Special Correspondence of the Leader.

NEW YORK, August 14.—Oscar Wilde is again in New York. He came in Saturday by a Cunard steamer, and lolled in his cab in an aesthetic attitude, as he was driven to the Brunswick. He says he has come to America for a stay of two weeks, to superintend the putting on the stage of his play, 'Vera, or the Nihilist,' which is to open at the Union Square on next Monday. Oscar is looking well. He is fatter than when he left America, and his dress is more like that of a civilized being. He has cut his long flowing locks, and long pantaloons have taken the place of his knee breeches. He wore this afternoon a soft black hat, slouched like that of a brigand. His trousers were almost as tight as his skin, and his cuffs were rolled back over his coat. Speaking of his short hair, he said: "Its present cut is modeled after that of a bust of Nero in the Louvre. Having had my hair cut short I was forced, you know, to give up my knee breeches, for knee breeches only go with long hair. Short hair and knee breeches are an absurdity."

Mr. Wilde says he has written much new poetry, and he will issue a second volume of his poems this fall.[3] He thinks America is on the road to a proper appreciation of art, which, he says, in America should be of the simple nature of the days of the Revolution. Mr. Wilde's play,

1. Kate Greenaway (1846–1901) and Walter Crane (1845–1915) were British artists and writers, known for their children's book illustrations (Crane provided illustrations for Wilde's 1888 collection of short stories, *The Happy Prince and Other Tales*). In her book, *Under the Window* (1879), Greenaway depicted children wearing costumes inspired by the Queen Anne style. The images were popular, and Liberty's produced clothing to her designs.
2. Frank George Carpenter (1855–1924), an American journalist, wrote for newspapers under the name "Carp".
3. Wilde is either exaggerating the amount of poetry he had written, or poems from this period have been lost. It is known that in Paris in 1883 Wilde had worked on his long poem *The Sphinx* (CW i, No. 118). He did not publish a second volume of poetry.

is much talked of here, and its first night will be before a full house. Marie Prescott will be its heroine, and the elegant costumes which she is to wear are on exhibition in the corner window of Lord & Taylor's on Broadway. Four costumes are shown on wax lay figures, and in each case the face is hidden by a mask. The dresses comprise a peasant's costume, a fine gold-brocaded silk trimmed with pearls, and a striking costume of black and gold plush. A magnificent crown, a facsimile in paste of the one worn by Alexander III at his coronation, is also exhibited.[1] A letter to Marie Prescott from Oscar Wilde concerning the play was published here today. It is full of good sense about the success of plays in general. A part of it reads as follows:

✂ *Wilde's letter to Prescott, as printed in* The New York Herald *(New York, NY), 12 Aug. 1883, 10, from "I think we must remember that no amount of advertising will make a bad play succeed, if it is not a good play well acted," (CL, 203–4).*

"Oscar Wilde's Ambition," *New York Tribune* (New York, NY), 12 Aug. 1883, 12[2]

AN ABSTRACTION TO BE DRAMATIZED.

THE MUSIC OF YEARNING CRIES FOR LIBERTY—THE MOTIVE OF HIS PLAY.

"Mr. Wilde?" said the clerk at the Brunswick Hotel to a Tribune reporter yesterday. "Yes, there he is sitting on that bench." The reporter gazed in the direction indicated, but thought the clerk must have been mistaken. In place of the rather gaunt, long-haired and sallow-faced Oscar of a few months ago, he saw a rosy-cheeked, cherry-faced individual whose close-cropped hair was almost hidden in the shade of a broad-brimmed, peaked felt hat. But on drawing close Mr. Wilde's identity became apparent, and holding out his hand he gave a cordial greeting. He had only been in the city for a few hours, having arrived on the Britannic early in the morning.

"I suppose I am looking well," assented he; "you see a sea voyage does one a tremendous lot of good. Besides the invigorating air there is the absence of all petty annoyances such as inquisitive callers, letters that have to be answered and—"

---

1. The coronation of Alexander III of Russia (1845–1896) took place on 27 May 1883.
2. Excerpted in "World of Amusement," *New York Dispatch* (New York, NY), 19 Aug. 1883, 4.

"Interviews?"

"Oh, no, I really think that is too bad. I never object to talking with newspaper men, and, in fact, generally enjoy it. What have I been doing since I left America? Resting chiefly. As soon as I reached the other side I went to Paris and, shutting myself up there, I devoted myself to writing a new play which I have with me here. Its scene is laid in Europe in the sixteenth century. I stopped in Paris till the Salon was opened and then went to London.[1] I was so importuned by the students of the Royal Academy to give them a lecture on painting, that I consented, and I guess what I told them must have roused the ire of their several preceptors and instructors, to whom my ideas are as "caviar to the general."[2] Then everyone was always asking me my opinion of America, so I lost patience and told them to wait till they heard my lecture on America. I was in for it then, you see, and had to lecture in London. I had heaps of offers for the provinces, of course, but I only repeated it five or six times, for I had to hurry to America.

"Now, I suppose you want to know what I have come over for specially. Well, first and foremost, it is to superintend the production of 'Vera,' but there is a motive behind that. Last year I told the people of America, or rather as many as would come to hear me, what my views of art were. This year I want them to see those ideas put into practice. In 'Vera' I am making a bold experiment. I am trying to see whether the love of an abstract idea cannot be made as dramatically interesting as the love of an individual.[3] I am trying, too, whether the hoarse cry of the yearners after liberty, which rose above the din around the barricades in Paris, and still is heard not quite drowned by the drum-taps of the Russian soldiery as they beat at the executions of the Nihilistic martyrs, whether that hoarse, harsh cry, which has never ceased in Europe for ninety years, cannot be reduced to music, and thus become a work of art. That my scene is laid in Russia is a mere accident, due to the fact that Russia is the only country where tyranny is ever grinding the people, and where that dull, unromantic, unemotional Philistine 'middle class' does not exist. In Russia there are only two degrees—the masters and the slaves.[4]

1. Wilde was spotted at the Paris Salon in May in the company of Whistler, who was exhibiting his portrait of his mother ("Personal," *New York Tribune* (New York, NY), 26 May 1883, 4).

2. "Caviar to the general": p. 402, note 1.

3. Constance to her brother Otho, 23 and 24 November 1883: "I have just read *Vera* through again, and I really think it very fine. Oscar says he wrote it in order to show that an abstract idea such as liberty could have quite as much power and be made quite as fine as the passion of love." (Moyle, 71–2.)

4. Wilde here echoes his letter to Marie Prescott, which appeared as a puff for *Vera* on the same day as this interview: "As regards the play itself, I have tried in it to express within the limits of art that Titan cry of the peoples for liberty, which in the Europe of our day is threatening thrones, and making governments unstable from Spain to Russia, and from north to southern seas. [....] modern Nihilistic Russia, with all the terror of its tyranny and the marvel of its

"Now for the first time I am really on my trial before the American public. Anyone can talk about art, but to talk well one must be able to do well. It is only the creator who can analyze his own creations.[1] There are few exceptions to this. Edgar Allan Poe carried the analytical faculty to the utmost, and thus became the exquisite critic as well as the original creator. Keats was an analyst. Byron was not, and to this most of his shortcomings are due. But I must not bore you. I can only add that I shall take the greatest pains to have my costumes and setting as harmonious as I can, though the question of expense has hampered me materially. Miss Prescott seems thoroughly enthusiastic, and if anyone can make my play a success, I am sure she will."

"Mr. Oscar Wilde's Hair," *The New York Herald* (New York, NY), 12 Aug. 1883, 10[2]

HE EXPLAINS WHY HE CUT IT OFF AND ALSO DISCUSSES OTHER ARTISTIC
EVENTS.

Oscar Wilde arrived in New York yesterday on the steamer Britannic. He sat in the lobby of the Brunswick Hotel late in the afternoon. A HERALD reporter was received courteously and had a long chat with Mr. Wilde, who spoke with the peculiar ladylike drawl which is familiar to all who have heard him.

"I see you've had your hair cut," observed the reporter.

"Oh, yes," said the poet, "to the amazement of Europe I cut off my locks. I never had my hair cut in my life until last March."

"Do you really mean to say that people abroad were amazed?"

"Positively amazed, I assure you. They have not quite recovered. It was a bold act."

"How did it happen?"

"It's rather interesting I think. You see, I was in the gallery of the Louvre in Paris, and I saw the bust of a young Roman Emperor. It was very beautiful, in-

---

martyrdoms, is merely the fiery and fervent background in front of which the persons of my dream live and love." ("Amusement Notes," *The World* (New York, NY), 12 Aug. 1883, 5; CL, 214–15.)

1. But see *The Critic as Artist*: "GILBERT. [....] Indeed, so far from its being true that the artist is the best judge of art, a really great artist can never judge of other people's work at all, and can hardly, in fact, judge of his own." (CW iv, 197.25–198.2.)

2. Reprinted as "Bunthorne is Back," *Daily Illinois State Register* (Springfield, IL), 18 Aug. 1883, 4; and "Mr. Oscar Wilde's Hair," *The Courier-Journal* (Louisville, KY), 19 Aug. 1883, 15. Excerpted in "Return of a Foreign Nuisance," *The Cleveland Leader* (Cleveland, OH), 17 Aug. 1883, 4; "Oscar Back Again," *The Irish Nation* (New York, NY), 18 Aug. 1883, 5. Quoted in Ellmann, 226/240; and Sturgis, 291/276.

deed. As soon as I saw that the young Emperor had his hair cut short, I wanted to be like him."

"Are you?"

"So far as the hair is concerned, I think I am. I got a hairdresser—and the French hairdressers are artists—to come with me to the Louvre and I showed him the young Emperor's bust. He cut my hair after the fashion he saw there—as nearly as he could. I afterward found that the bust represented Nero, one of the worst behaved young men in the world, and yet a man of strong artistic passion. I thought it just suited my case."

SHORT HAIR AND ART.

"Speaking of my hair," he resumed, "the trouble is that people mistake the forms of art for the principle. There is only one principle in art and yet millions of forms. The majority of people think that one cannot admire art unless one's hair falls below one's collar. I want to show them that they are mistaken. I wore my hair long because I think that long hair is beautiful when it is properly cut."

"Cut off?"

"No, when it is properly trimmed; but so is short hair."

"You have given up knee breeches?"

"For the present, yes. You see, one's taste changes; and, besides, one must suit one's trousers to the cut of one's hair. I think there is really a strong desire among young men to wear knee breeches, but it requires great courage to be-gin—it does, indeed. But they were invented for a period when people wore wigs. We cannot wear short breeches and short hair. That would be absurd."

"Don't you find it hard to get knee breeches on?

"Not very. Then they are so comfortable, and they give play to the grace and joy and poetry of one's physical being."

"Have you changed your opinion about the ugliness of the Atlantic ocean?"

"No; I must still quarrel with the Atlantic. It is not beautiful at all. There are no objects to give it distance; nothing but gray, gray sky and gray, gray sea. It is simply monotonous."

MR. LABOUCHÈRE'S POINTED FUN.

"Mr. Labouchère says in *Truth* that your lecture on America was a failure, and that your audience laughed at you. Is it true?"[1]

"Labouchère made a most brilliant attack on me. It was a rare, brilliant thing, and do you know he is one of the most able men in England and has a great future before him. But the lecture charmed the English people and was well re-ceived. To call anything published in Labouchère's paper 'truth' is only a bit of

1. Labouchère's criticism of *Personal Impressions of America*: see p. 539, note 1.

546

fun on his part. Everybody knows that. It is the pride of the paper that nothing published in it is consistent with fact. If it took Labouchère three columns to prove that I was forgotten, then there is no difference between fame and obscurity."

"Have you written any new poems?"

"Yes, I will publish a new volume before Christmas."[1]

In conclusion, Mr. Wilde said that he would not make a comparison between the artistic tastes of Londoners and New Yorkers, because such a comparison would not be fair. He said that he was more than ever convinced that the French art imported into the United States after the Revolution was suited only for a king's court and not for the people of a republic. It should be costly or it would not be pretty. The Americans were, he said, going back to the real, simple art which flourished in the colonial days. This, he said, was the only genuine American art, and would be the art of the Republic in the future.

Mr. Wilde has grown quite plump. He wore a black slouch hat, tight trousers, a black waistcoat and coat and white cuffs rolled back. He said he was accompanied on his voyage from England by several old classmates, who were going West to rid the country of wild animals, if they could find any to shoot at.[2] He will be in the city for two weeks, and will then visit several watering places, after which he will go home.

"Oscar Wilde Returns," *The World* (New York, NY), 12 Aug. 1883, 5[3]

IN COMMONPLACE CLOTHING AND SHORN OF HIS GLORIOUS LOCKS.

He Will Superintend the Production of His New Play and Will Not Lecture.

In the café of the Hotel Brunswick yesterday afternoon a tall, athletic young man sat smoking cigarettes and gazing dreamily out upon Fifth avenue. He wore a new, shiny, black high hat and a short black coat. A white vest enveloped the stout body and a pair of very light cassimere trousers fitted closely to well-

1. "New poems": see p. 542, note 3.
2. See "Brought Across the Sea," *The New York Times* (New York, NY), 12 Aug. 1883, 7, p. 555.
3. H & S, b100. Reprinted as "Oscar Wilde Returns," *Daily Patriot* (Harrisburg, PA), 13 Aug. 1883, 2; and "Oscar Wilde Returns," *The Evening Star* (Kansas City, MO), 15 Aug. 1883, 4; without the final paragraph, in Mikhail, 114–17; and without the final five paragraphs as "Without Knee-Breeches," *Denver Republican* (Denver, CO), 18 Aug. 1883, 7. Quoted in *Buffalo Morning Express* (Buffalo, NY), 21 Aug. 1883, 2; Ellmann, 185/195; and Sturgis, 293/277. The interview also appeared, with some differences, as "Oscar Wilde's 'Vera'," *The Chicago Daily News* (Chicago, IL), 18 Aug., Evening Edition, 1883, 2.

formed legs. A light, olive-green scarf nearly hid the immaculate shirt-front. Unaesthetic as this garb was, its wearer was none other than the very standard-bearer of aestheticism—Mr. Oscar Wilde. The hat was bad and the trousers worse, but the saddest thing of all was the absence of the long, cowboy locks which of yore fell about Mr. Wilde's broad shoulders. They have gone, but a square bang still droops dreamily across the dome-like forehead. Few who entered the hotel recognized the eminent guest.

When a WORLD reporter called upon him Mr. Wilde led the way to a leather-covered settee near the office door. Then he lighted another cigarette and began talking in a quiet manner, entirely free from affectation. He is much tanned and looks more like a robust farmer than a poet.

"I arrived this morning in the Britannic, of the White Star line, after a charming passage," he said. "My only errand here is to superintend the production of my play, 'Vera,' which will be brought out at the Union Square Theatre Monday week. I don't think I shall stay here more than three months."[1]

"Please tell me something about your play?"

Mr. Wilde blew a little cloud of smoke into the air and watched it silently until it disappeared. Then he continued:

HIS FIRST DRAMA.

"'Vera' is a prose play in five acts, which I wrote seven years ago.[2] It was not produced in England because its political sentiments would not have found favor there. Heretofore the passion portrayed in the drama has been altogether personal, like the love of a man for a woman, or a woman for a man. I have tried to show the passion for liberty. For this purpose I have chosen the most extreme expression of liberty, the Nihilism of Russia, which is akin to the anarchism of old France. All art takes an aristocratic view of life, for civilization belongs to the higher classes. I want to show how far the aspirations of an uncultivated people can be made a subject for art. Life under a good government is rarely dramatic; life under a bad government is always so."

Here the clatter of vehicles interrupted the speaker for a moment. He went on in a clear, deliberate voice, pausing long between the sentences, like one dictating to an amanuensis:

1. Given that Wilde stressed in other interviews that his second visit to America would be brief, it seems likely that "three months" is an error and that Wilde said, or intended to say, "three weeks".

2. As Josephine Guy (CW xi, 42) points out, it is not possible to know how long it took Wilde to write *Vera*, but it seems unlikely that he began as early as the mid-1870s. *The World* here omits a sentence retained in *The Chicago Daily News:* "The prevailing idea is the conflict between liberty and love."

"I have gone to Greek and Gothic life for subjects for most of my poems, but my drama is from modern life. The incidents are purely imaginary, with modern Russia as the realistic background. When I saw Miss Marie Prescott playing Emilia to Salvini's Othello, I felt that she was the artist I wanted to create the heroine of my play.[1] Most of the arts, poetry in particular, are to a certain degree isolated, but the drama is the meeting-place of art and life. It is the one art which is criticised as though it were reality. It is the great democratic art. I wanted to see if I could write a play which would satisfy not merely artists but the people."

THE PEOPLE MUST BE CRITICS.

Here the poet paused to light another cigarette. After a few pensive whiffs he went on:

"And the people are the sternest and most just of dramatic critics. A man's play is judged regardless of his reputation in other branches of art. So far as my own work is concerned, I am sure that its politics will not prejudice it in the eyes of Americans."[2]

"Are you satisfied with the cast of 'Vera'?" asked the reporter.

"Perfectly. All the artists are Americans, and, although I have not seen them rehearse, I am much pleased with them. We shall have a rehearsal in the theatre on Monday. I designed the scenery and costumes myself. A crown used in one of the acts is a reproduction of the crown used at the recent coronation of Alexander III. I wish to have as much fact as will convey the impression of reality, and as much beauty as the artist can create. The decorations of a stage should be not merely true, but beautiful. A scene is a work of art, not a piece of archaeology.[3] I have lectured so much in America upon the principles of art, that science of beauty which is aestheticism, that I feel anxious to show the flower that may grow from such a root. It is one thing to talk of the principles of art and quite another to create a piece of artistic work."[4]

1. Prescott appeared as Emilia with Salvini a number of times, but Wilde must have seen the performance in New York on 1 November 1882.

2. *The World* here omits a section that *The Chicago Daily News* retains, taken from Wilde's letter to Marie Prescott: CL, 214–15, from "I have tried in it to express [...]" to "[...] the persons of my drama live and love." There then follows: "When I saw Miss Marie Prescott playing Emilia to Salvini's Othello, I felt that she was the artist I wanted to create the heroine of my play." Note that this sentence does appear in *The World* version, but earlier, and that *The World* printed Wilde's letter to Prescott in full, separately from the interview.

3. Wilde's views on archaeological realism in stage design and costumes were complex. He addressed the topic in *The Truth of Masks*.

4. *The Chicago Daily News* omits from "The decorations of a stage [...]" up to this point. It includes a sentence here, adapted from the letter to Prescott, that is omitted from *The World:* "There is, I think, no country in the world where there are such appreciative theatrical audiences as in America."

549

"Can you give me a sketch of the plot of 'Vera'?"

Mr. Wilde smiled as he said:

"No, I don't care to do that. The prevailing idea is a conflict between liberty and love."

"Which passion triumphs?"

"That's my fifth act," replied the aesthete, smiling again.

"Have you altered the play much since you wrote it?"

"Well, a good play is hardly ever finished, you know. It must be fitted to the stage. It is not enough to make music; one must make music that the instruments can play."[1]

HE WILL NOT LECTURE.

"Shall you lecture while in this country?"

"I think not. My stay will be shortened, because I have so many engagements to lecture in England."

"Do you intend to publish any poems?"

"Possibly. The students of the Royal Academy invited me to lecture to them on painting a while ago, and I should like very much to publish that lecture in America."[2]

"You feel at home in New York, do you not?"

"Oh, yes; New York is very cosmopolitan."

"Do you consider aestheticism a success?"

"Altogether. It has changed the whole plan of domestic decoration, and if we hear less of it now than formerly, it is because its position is assured. By bringing the delights of art into the household we have elevated the artisan into the artist."

"To return to your play; is 'Vera' your first prose drama?"

"It is."

When the reporter hinted that American patriotism had been grievously wounded by Mr. Wilde's criticism upon Niagara, the poet laughed and said modestly:

"Niagara will survive any criticisms of mine. I must say this, however, that it is the first great disappointment in the married life of many Americans who spend their honeymoon there."[3]

In the basement of Clarendon hall, in Thirteenth street, "Vera" was rehearsed yesterday. Some of the scenery designed by Mr. Wilde is made of papier-

---

1. Wilde had added a prologue to the 1880 text for the 1882 edition. He later added to the prologue and revised the final act, with many of the changes following discussions with Prescott (CW xi, 71–3).

2. Wilde did not publish *Modern Art Training*.

3. Wilde's statement echoes *Personal Impressions of America*: see p. 150, note 2.

550

maché instead of canvas. From a distance it presents the appearance of metalwork. The costumes which Miss Prescott is to wear as Vera are on exhibition in a shop-window on Broadway, together with the glittering fac-simile of the Russian crown.

"Theatrical World," *Truth* (New York, NY), 12 Aug. 1883, 5

When I saw Oscar Wilde in the lobby of the Brunswick yesterday afternoon he was lolling upon one of the settees smoking a cigarette, and talking in a measured, easy manner to a new reporter, who was making desperate efforts with pencil and note book to record every word the apostle of aestheticism uttered. Mr. Wilde appeared to understand his visitor's tribulation, and exhibited a commendable sympathy by speaking slowly and quietly.

As he half reclined there in the most Democratic fashion I had an excellent opportunity of studying the man, and I was struck by the change that had come over him. I remembered him as he appeared on the lecture stand, at the Wyndham breakfast,[1] and on one or two other occasions, when his long hair and knee breeches were his principal means of attracting attention. Then he posed continually. He was playing a role for notoriety and money, and he played it well. What is more, he won the stakes.

But yesterday there was nothing extraordinary in Mr. Wilde's appearance unless it was the breadth and depth of his mouth and, possibly, the peculiarly olive-green tint of his necktie. It was clear that the former devotee to the sunflower had cast aside his peculiarities, not only of dress but of speech and the subject of speech.

His coat and vest were of dark color and of ordinary fashion, while his trousers were of light cassimere, and fitted him almost with the exactness of dudeism.[2] His hair was cut short and a soft black felt hat covered his head.

To the new reporter he was immensely amiable, pleasantly answering the most irrelevant questions and laughing quite heartily at anything and everything the former said that possibly would admit of laughter. Even at parting, when the reporter handed him a copy of the morning paper which the reporter represented, Mr. Wilde accepted it with the most profuse thanks.

---

1. Wyndham breakfast: see "New York," *Boston Evening Transcript* (Boston, MA), 18 Nov. 1882, 10–11, pp. 725–6.
2. "Dudes": see p. 534, note 3.

When the opportunity offered, I presented myself, and encountered the same admirable amiability. Mr. Wilde assured me that although he had already been interviewed many times that day, he was nevertheless not in the least tired. I cut short any further protestations by asking him if any other cause than the production of his play, "Vera," had brought him back to America.

He replied that there was no other cause. He had come back partly at the request of Miss Prescott and partly at his own desire. He sincerely wished his play to prove a success, and he felt that he should do all in his power to achieve that end. As to the capacity in which he should act with Miss Prescott, he was not definitely certain. He felt that a great deal depended upon a proper presentation of the play, upon the harmony and arrangement of colors not only in the costumes but in the scenery, and in the costumes and scenery together. He had spent much time upon this subject, and had studied it thoroughly. Therefore he felt that the play could not be a failure in this particular.

As to the other qualities of the play, he would not then speak. He had a good opinion of them, but he preferred to leave the verdict to the public. He had endeavored to exemplify art in the highest form in "Vera," but there were so many exterior considerations and so many attendant circumstances that it was quite beyond him to predict the result.

Mr. Wilde then entered upon a short discourse concerning the relative merits of dramatic and musical art and painting and sculpture, which was highly instructing and entertaining, but rather too long for a place here. He said that he longed for the first night of "Vera" to come. He had an ardent desire to stand somewhere and watch the effect of the play upon the audience. Even if they received it indifferently, or absolutely refused it, he wished to experience the sensation. This thing of presenting a play was novel and fascinating to him. Hitherto he had been an observer, a critic, but now he was a creator. The change quite transported him.

When he had enthused considerably upon his new condition, I ventured to remark on his altered personal appearance. At this he laughed heartily and replied that he had cut his hair in Paris and thereby offended all England, which had decreed that he should never approach a hairdresser's establishment. But he himself could see no reason why a man should not wear his hair short as well as long, provided the cutting conformed to the rules of beauty.

I did not ask Mr. Wilde what the rules of beauty in hair cutting consisted of, but made some allusion to his being quite an every-day young man.[1] To this he instantly demurred, saying that he could not conceive of himself in such a state under any circumstances. I apologized at once, and our cordiality was re-established.

He then began to question me closely as to the probable condition of the weather a week from tomorrow night,[2] as to the theatrical taste of our public, and finally as to the histrionic abilities of the several people whom Miss Prescott has chosen to form her company. In all this he impressed me as being particularly shrewd, and as having an eye to the profits of the venture.

Indeed, from this interview with Oscar Wilde, I conclude that he recognizes the fact that the aesthetic racket is played out, but that the notoriety which he has already attained may be utilized advantageously as a means of advertising "Vera," and for that purpose he has come back to America. He began well yesterday, for I think he was interviewed by a representative of every daily newspaper in New York. This may not be particularly agreeable to Mr. Wilde's aesthetic qualities and artistic culture, but as an advertisement it will be of vast use to Miss Prescott and her energetic husband and manager, Mr. William Perzel.[3] And from the way in which Mr. Wilde submitted to the ordeal yesterday, I fancy that every word that fell from his lips had been paid for beforehand with Prescott gold.

Oscar Wilde has not cut off his hair for nothing, you may be sure. He has squeezed the milk out of the old cocoanut and he is casting about for fresh fruit. Whether he will find it or not remains to be seen. But whether he does or does not, the man who sets Oscar Wilde down for a fool is himself not the wisest of men.

Apropos of Wilde, I notice that Mr. Perzel is now exhibiting the costumes, which Miss Prescott is to wear in "Vera," in the windows of Lord & Taylor's dry goods establishment on Broadway. They attract considerable attention and present quite a novelty in the matter of advertising, surpassing even the paintings of "Francesca da Rimini," which Mr. Lawrence Barrett is "borrowing from wealthy friends" and distributing about the town.[4]

1. "Every-day": an allusion to *Patience.* See p. 32, note 1.
2. On the day that *Vera* opened the temperature in New York reached 93°F / 33.9°C; it remained high for the rest of the week.
3. Prescott claimed that she had married William Perzel (1844–1907) in 1881; ten years later, after she filed for divorce, he insisted that they had never been wed (Dearinger, 87, 210). Perzel was the proprietor of a delicatessen's store and not an experienced theatrical manager.
4. George Henry Boker's *Francesca da Rimini* (1856) opened at New York's Star Theatre on 27 August 1883, with Lawrence Barrett in the role of Lanciotto, Francesca's brother. Wilde saw this

Mr. Wilde told me that he designed these costumes, as well as all the scenery in the play, but, for all that, I do not think them very beautiful. Still, I suppose we must wait for the ensemble to judge correctly, and even then the art displayed may be above American comprehension.

"Brought Across the Sea," *The New York Times* (New York, NY), 12 Aug. 1883, 7[1]

OSCAR WILDE'S PLAY AND LILIAN RUSSELL'S DEBUT.

THE HISSES FOR MR. SOLOMON—EDWARD SOLOMON NOT A MASCOTTE—A NEW COMIC OPERA BY AN ASPIRING COMPOSER.

Oscar Wilde arrived in this City by the steamer Britannic yesterday, and is stopping at the Hotel Brunswick. His visit at this time, as he stated to a reporter of THE TIMES last evening, is made for the purpose of personally superintending the mounting of his new play, "Vera," which is to be produced at the Union-Square Theatre Monday evening, Aug. 20 and to attend the rehearsals by the company which is to render the piece. He brought with him designs for the scenery and the costumes. He did not, as reported, however, bring any scenery with him. "I have been told," he said, "that the announcement had been made that I had my scenery painted abroad, and had brought it all with me, corn-field and all. That is a mistake. I think your scene-painters are quite as good as ours, and I have simply prepared the designs, as the architect, in fact." Mr. Wilde also brought some dress stuffs to be made into costumes for Miss Prescott, such materials as he feared could not readily be procured here. The first rehearsal of the play will take place in the Union Square Theatre tomorrow.

Mr. Wilde's personal appearance is greatly changed. He has substituted regulation trousers for knee-breeches, and his leonine mane has been "cut down." He wears his hair "banged" on the forehead, but in other respects its style is only a trifle different from that prevailing among business men. He wore, last evening, a cutaway velvet coat, drab pantaloons, of the prevailing style, and closely fitting patent-leather boots, a Byron collar, and scarf with diamond pin. He smoked cigarettes constantly, but apparently did not inhale the smoke, as habitual cigarette smokers do. Since he left New York, he said, he had delivered several lec-

---

production and in a letter to Barrett several years later declared it "one of the best modern productions of our stage."(CL, 406.)

1. Reprinted, without the last paragraph, as "He Comes Again," *The Wheeling Intelligencer* (Wheeling, WV), 14 Aug. 1883, 1. Excerpted in "Oscar Wilde," *The Chicago Sunday Tribune* (Chicago, IL), 12 Aug. 1883, 7. Quoted in Ellmann, 227/241; and Sturgis, 292–3/277.

tures in England, and he had spent four months in Paris writing a new play, called the "Duchess of Padua." It is an Italian play, of a poetical nature, and is founded upon life in Padua in the sixteenth century. It is in five acts, and will depend for its success more upon the passions depicted than upon the scenery and costumes. "Of course," said Mr. Wilde, "I shall mount it handsomely. The best of pictures require suitable frames." Mr. Wilde said he thought the American public cared less for scenery, however, than the English. If a play possessed merit it was more likely to have a long run here, even if the scenery were susceptible of improvement, than it was in England. As long as costumes were not grotesque in the display of color the public would not find fault. Mr. Wilde said he had not yet made any attempt to introduce his new play.[1]

He said he enjoyed his recent voyage across the Atlantic very much. The weather was delightful, and the company was pleasant. The customary entertainment for the benefit of the Liverpool Orphans' Asylum was given aboard the steamer Thursday night, when he read his poem, "Ave Imperatrix," and Mr. Raymond contributed his specialities. Mr. Wilde was accompanied by Sir Saville Crossley, Mr. Cresswell, Mr. Hanbury, and the Hon. St. John Brodrick, member of Parliament from Surrey.[2] "He sits on the Conservative side of the House," said Mr. Wilde, referring to Mr. Brodrick. Sir Saville Crossley and the other two gentlemen are going out West "to hunt buffaloes, providing there are any to hunt, and—they can shoot them," said Mr. Wilde, significantly. "After 'Vera' is fairly under way," he continued, "I shall visit Newport and some other watering-places, and I must not forget my friend, the Rev. Mr. Beecher, at Peekskill."

✄ *Several paragraphs that are unrelated to Wilde.*

"Mr. Wilde Sanguine About Vera," *The New York Mirror* (New York, NY), 18 Aug. 1883, 7

A MIRROR reporter, disappointed in not seeing a dress rehearsal of Vera at the Union Square Theatre yesterday, it being postponed until Friday evening, called on Oscar Wilde at the Brunswick in hopes of obtaining some interesting details regarding the production. After being assured that a regular cut-and-

---

1. This is not strictly true as Wilde had written the play under contract with Mary Anderson. Since she had refused it, he was seeking other parties who might be interested in producing it (Sturgis, 284/271).

2. Sir Savile Brinton Crossley (1857–1935), 2nd Baronet of Halifax, was later a Liberal Member of Parliament and Paymaster General. William St John Fremantle Brodrick (1856–1942) had been elected Conservative Member of Parliament for West Surrey in 1880 and later served as the Secretary of State for War and for India. His name is given in the source as "Broderick".

dried interview was not to be inflicted upon him, Mr. Wilde launched into a confidential chat, something as follows:

"There is nothing much new that I can tell you. You see, I've been interviewed so much, that the story must be familiar."

A question was hazarded as to what would be the result should Vera prove unsuccessful. "Oh, now, I don't wish to entertain such a possibility. It cannot fail, but must be a success. Mounted as it will be and in the hands of such a good company, I cannot see how it can be otherwise than a success. Yet while attending rehearsals I find each time so many new things to learn. Really, we should all be stage carpenters; then we would understand all the minute details which most managers are unacquainted with, until they are brought face to face with them at rehearsals. Dramatists and actors are on the same level—neither one below or above that line. The dramatist writes his best thoughts into a play and the actor endeavors by facial expression and action to present the same to his audience, which is quite as important."

"Then you claim that the success of a piece is in the acting?"

"When the play is not really bad—yes. In olden times fine things were written, but principally intended to be uttered by mouth alone. Now we write to have our ideas acted. In old French plays you will find between each line large gaps. These admit of proper action. A person feels pain and shows the feeling before it can be told of in words. Hence the pauses between sentences, if in the hands of artists, can be made exceedingly interesting, and that is the beauty of successful play-writing, and in your own line—brevity—doing away with and cutting out all superfluous matter."

"Of course you are pleased with your company?"

"Very much. Miss Prescott's Emilia, in her support of Salvini, decided me to give my play to her. That was a great performance. In case Vera should prove a failure it will further teach me and give rise to the question, 'Why is it?'"

"But haven't you another play to follow Vera?"

"Yes, I have; but it has not been announced. It is a story of the Sixteenth century, and I've named it The Duchess of Padua. I began writing it while here before, but found myself unable to make headway while rushing around the country in trains. So when I went home I spent three months in Paris, and if Vera is a success I should like very much to put it on here. Unlike England, you have no provinces; but with Boston, Philadelphia, Chicago and other large cities, you have distinct and great audiences."

At this juncture a salver of mail matter was brought to Mr. Wilde, and the reporter withdrew.

"Oscar Wilde on 'Vera'," *The Evening Telegram* (New York, NY), 21 Aug. 1883, 4th ed., 1[1]

What He Says of the Play and His Opinions of the Critics.

Mr. Oscar Wilde, the distinguished apostle of aestheticism, was found this morning by a TELEGRAM reporter enjoying a cigarette in the cafe of the Hotel Brunswick. He was clad in a mixed woollen short coat and spotless white trousers and vest. A light and airy straw hat crowned his wealth of dark hair. Mr. Wilde greeted the reporter very pleasantly, and in answer to a question, said, laughingly:—"Considering the high pressure that the clerk of the weather has seen fit to put on the thermometer I was rather agreeably surprised last night at the extent, respectability, and the decided enthusiasm of the audience that greeted the first production of 'Vera.' The play received applause at points that I did not expect, and was watched with strict, almost breathless attention where I thought applause would be given. The first production of a play is little more than a rehearsal in public, the writer and actors concerned being always anxious to see how the play will be received. I am very well satisfied, however."

"What do you think of the criticisms in the morning papers?" queried the reporter.[2]

With another light laugh Mr. Wilde replied:—"Well, I have been subjected to all sorts of criticism during my last visit to your beautiful country. No matter where I went it was the same thing over and over, so that I have ceased to pay any attention to critics. There is one thing, however, that the critics should learn, and that is to pay more attention to the actors and less to the writers of plays."

"What were your own impressions from witnessing the first representation of 'Vera?'"

"I am satisfied that the play is too long. There is also too much delay between the acts and in the setting of the scenery. I will attend the rehearsal today and cut down the play as much as possible without destroying the sense of the representation or impairing its worth. The next play I write shall have but one scene."

"Have you anything under way at present?" again asked the reporter.

"You are inquisitive," answered Mr. Wilde, "but I will say that I have. I must look for my leading lady first, though, before mentioning the title."[3]

---

1. Reprinted with slight variations as "Oscar Wilde," *The Daily Inter Ocean* (Chicago, IL), 22 Aug. 1883, 6; and "Oscar Wilde on his New Play," *The Cincinnati Enquirer* (Cincinnati, OH), 22 Aug. 1883, 8. This article did not appear in earlier editions of *The Evening Telegram*. The 4th edition was issued at 17:00.

2. The negative reaction of the press to *Vera* is summarised in Mason, 273–4.

3. Wilde is being unnecessarily coy here. He first shared the title of *The Duchess of Padua* with the author of "The Talk of Paris," *The Evening Telegram* (New York, NY), 17 Apr. 1883, 3, p. 528.

"Will you stop here long?"

"Probably ten days. I want to see 'Vera' in proper working order before I leave. I have engagements to fill in September, and must be back before the 10th."[1]

"Oscar's Opinion of 'Vera,'" *Philadelphia Press* (Philadelphia, PA), 22 Aug. 1883, 3[2]

He Regards the Play as Successful, but Will Trim it—He Ignores Criticism.

The first appearance of Mr. Oscar Wilde as a dramatic author, which event took place at the Union Square Theatre last night,[3] seems to have been taken advantage of by numerous dramatic critics to make an onslaught that would daunt anyone but the placid Oscar himself, who comes up smiling this morning. Shortly after 9 o'clock the newly-fledged dramatist was met on Fifth Avenue by a reporter for the *Mail and Express.* Oscar looked jaunty, dressed in a short seersucker coat, light trousers and a small straw hat.

"What are your impressions of the first night of 'Vera?'" inquired the reporter.

"I consider that the play was a success. Of course it has some faults, but I will correct them. For one thing, 'Vera' is too long. I shall cut it judiciously. The first night of a play is nothing more or less than a full-dress rehearsal, and the audience is always a peculiar one. Last night the actors did not act so well, because it was a first night. But, take it altogether, I was quite satisfied. When I have altered the play and shortened the last act a great deal; it will be more successful."

"The critics seem to be unanimous in speaking of 'Vera' as a failure."

"Ah, well, now, I make it a rule, you know, never to take seriously what newspaper writers say. Oh, dear, no, not at all. If people like my play, why they will go to see it; that's all there is to it. Otherwise all the papers in the country cannot make them come, you know. Besides, I was surprised to see people come out in this hot weather."

"Will you remain here to improve the play?"

He also mentioned it to several interviewers on 11 August. It was public knowledge that Wilde had offered the play to Mary Anderson, who had "decided not to appear in it," (see e.g. "Amusement Notes," *The Boston Herald* (Boston, MA), 14 June 1883, 2).

1. *The Inter Ocean* has "before the 12th."

2. Reprinted in abbreviated form in "Our New York Letter," *The Philadelphia Inquirer* (Philadelphia, PA), 22 Aug. 1883, 7. Quoted in "The United States," *The Standard* (London, UK), 22 Aug. 1883, 5 (which is quoted in Sturgis, 295/279), and in Dearinger, 143.

3. The opening night was on 20 August and not the 21st as this implies.

Figure 17. Marie Prescott photographed by Benjamin J. Falk in a costume Wilde designed for Act I of Vera; or, The Nihilists.

"I shall stay for a few weeks to see how it goes after pruning. I think that it is just that people who were there last night should come again next week to note the improvement, don't you know."

"Did the actors portray the characters to suit you?"

"Yes, indeed. Mr. Lamb in particular was very good; very good, indeed. Mr. Boniface looked splendid, and Mr. Morrison was exceedingly fine.[1] Miss Prescott was too nervous. She will surprise the public after that wears off. Why, bless me, she acted much better at rehearsal. But she did do some fine work last night, and several of her speeches she gave in a manner to win applause. Yet she gave the same speeches infinitely better at rehearsal. But, as I said before, a first-night audience is an abnormal one, composed mostly of actors and critics. They do not make a play. It is the mere passer-by, who drops into the theatre, who makes a play successful."

"The critics say there is too much poetry in the play?"

"I presume they think so. Well, the last act does pass into poetry and the prose becomes rhythmic. That is in the nature of things. One could not for a moment imagine the balcony scene from 'Romeo and Juliet' rendered in prose. Always passion passes into music at a certain altitude."

"If 'Vera' is a success, will you write another play to afflict a long-suffering public?"

"'Vera' is a success," said Mr. Wilde, smiling blandly. "You ask if I will write another play. I have one already written. It is in my room. Come up and I will read it to you."[2]

The reporter excused himself.

"Well, I will tell you, then, that I have a five-act drama, entitled 'The Duchess of Padua.' The period is of the fifteenth century, and the scene is laid in Italy. It is in blank verse and prose mixed. The prose is the comedy portion, and the blank verse is the dramatic parts. I have not yet offered it to a manager. Goodbye; I shall go to a rehearsal shortly," said Mr. Wilde, as he started down Fifth Avenue.

1. George Boniface (1832–1912) played the Czar. Edward Lamb (c. 1819–1887) played Prince Paul Maraloffski. Lewis Morrison (1844–1906) played the Czarevich.

2. It was customary for authors to read unproduced scripts to small groups or individuals. Wilde read a draft of *Salomé* to the theatrical manager Paul Fort (CW v, 342–3), the last act of *A Woman of No Importance* to a party of friends (Sturgis, 466/436), and *The Importance of Being Earnest* to the cast (CW x, 613–14).

"Gossip from Gotham," *The News and Courier* (Charleston, SC), 30 Aug. 1883, 1

THE COMPLETE FIASCO OF OSCAR WILDE'S 'VERA.'

Critics Sit on it and Play-goers Ignore it—Lord Chief Justice Coleridge Arrives
and is Promptly Captured by the Vanderbilts.

(FROM OUR OWN CORRESPONDENT.)

New York, August 25.—

✂ *A review and synopsis of Vera.*

On Tuesday morning Oscar was found by an enterprising reporter soon after he had gone through the newspapers. He was not downcast; he was defiant and inclined to be haughty. "I never pay any attention to what newspapers say," he remarked. "The public must be the judge, and when the public crowd to see my piece the critics will begin to find good things in it." Poor Oscar has since been doomed to disappointment in one respect at least. The public upon whom he counted have shown a decided indifference about going to find out whether the critics were right or wrong. Appalled by accounts of the heat in the theatre and the badness of the play people have stayed away and 'Vera' has been given at a loss all the week. The piece first saw the light on Monday; here we are on Saturday and yet the public outside of theatrical and literary circles has shown a growing indifference. It had been the intention to begin in New York by a season of a month or two. But unless business should pick up there must be a change of plan and it would surprise no one to hear that 'Vera' had been shelved *sine die*. This morning Marie Prescott succeeds in getting some of the newspapers to print a piteous letter, in which she begs New Yorkers not to judge 'Vera' by what the critics have said of it, but to go and see it for themselves.[1] The critics, she hints, have damned the piece because Oscar wrote it. They were jealous of Oscar's fame and success, and took this occasion to pull him down. If, she says, no one had known that Oscar Wilde had written 'Vera,' it would have been received with enthusiasm by the critics. No letters from Marie Prescott will save 'Vera' from oblivion. The simple truth is that it is a poor play, and no extraneous features of merit, such as remarkable acting or stage-setting, diverted attention from this central and prominent fact.

✂ *Several paragraphs that are unrelated to Wilde.*

1. Prescott's letter was printed as "Newspaper Nihilism," *Truth* (New York, NY), 24 Aug. 1883, 2; and "'Vera' and its Critics," *The New York Times* (New York, NY), 24 Aug. 1883, 3.

"The Failure of 'Vera,'" *New York Tribune* (New York, NY), 28 Aug. 1883, 5[1]

MR. PERZEL ANNOUNCES THE WITHDRAWAL OF THE PLAY—OSCAR WILDE'S COOLNESS.

The rumor as to the withdrawal of Oscar Wilde's play, of which mention was made in yesterday's TRIBUNE, proves to have been well founded, for yesterday the Union Square actors were paid their week's salary and discharged, and the theatre is for the present tenantless. William Perzel is Marie Prescott's husband. He is also her business manager, and has been as enthusiastic over the unappreciated beauties of the play as the exponent of *Vera* herself. The following letter was received from him last night:

The papers of New York city have condemned Oscar Wilde's play, "Vera." They have made an impression on the theatregoing public that "Vera" is an unattractive play. It is not in my power to correct this impression. I have neither time nor inclination to make any complaints against the critics; I only wish to state that the attitude of the press toward "Vera" keeps the people from the theatre, and consequently I am the principal sufferer. There is no doubt that "Vera" will be more popular in other cities. I have the assurance from managers out of town who have seen the play. But for the present I am obliged to withdraw "Vera" in New York city and dismiss my company. My losses are very large so far, and I am unable to incur further risks. My dates out of town are cancelled up to October, when I shall reorganize a company for Miss Prescott.[2]

W. PERZEL.

Mr. Perzel was found yesterday afternoon busily engaged in paying off the rather discontented actors who were flocking round the box office of the theatre. "Yes," said he, "'Vera' is withdrawn and I have just sent a card to the papers stating my reasons for the sudden move. The piece was killed by the newspapers and the hot weather combined. I do not think one without the other would have proved powerful enough to crush it, for I am convinced of its merits and feel sure it will be successful on the road. We have another play in preparation in which Miss. Prescott could have appeared, but we have lost so much money already that I thought it better to stop at once."

---

1. Excerpted in "Oscar Wilde's 'Vera,'" *The Boston Daily Globe* (Boston, MA), 28 Aug. 1883, 1; and Dearinger, 145–6.

2. In some other papers the letter is addressed "To the Public:" and ends "She will play 'Vera' together with 'Czeka,' a drama by Alexander Gautier, which she made a success in Brooklyn and Philadelphia" (e.g. "A Crushed Author," *Morning Journal and Courier* (New Haven, CT), 28 Aug. 1883, 3).

Alfred Joel, who was business manager of the combination, was clear and concise in his utterances: "Perzel had lost as much money as he could afford and had to stop. That is all there is about it. I agree with him—the newspapers killed the play. I imagine Perzel and his wife have lost about $10,000. There was a nominal $5,000, paid to Oscar of which I guess he received about $3,000 cash and a royalty of $50 a night; advertising, say $1,000 at least; rent of the theatre for one week, $1,800; forfeit deposited on signing the lease, $1,000; dresses and scenery about $1,500 or $2,000, with the salary list and incidental expenses. All these make up pretty much the sum I mentioned. I believe they intend to take the play on the road with a cheaper company about October 1."

Busily engaged in dispatching a telegram from the office in the Brunswick Hotel the reporter found Mr. Wilde. "There is a rumor that you are going to appear as the *Czarevitch* in your own play, Mr. Wilde. Is there any truth in it?"

Mr Wilde carefully counted his change, apostrophized a dollar gold piece as being a "little darling," placed it in his waistcoat pocket for safe keeping and blandly remarked:

"Who said so?"

"Mr. Perzel hinted it, I believe."[1]

Mr. Wilde slowly shook his head from side to side, emitted a sibilant sound from his pursed-up lips, and murmured: "How interesting!"

"But have you any such idea?"

"Not the faintest," said Mr. Wilde, at last waking up. "My play has proved a failure in New York and they wisely have taken it off. After the harsh treatment it received at the hands of the critics it had no chance of success. But New York is not the world, it is not even America, and I am convinced that if the play is produced in other cities the verdict will be a different one. The failure here will not tell against it in Boston or Chicago, rather the contrary, I think, for there is a feeling of rivalry and independence between the larger cities of this country. It is not as it is in England, where if a play is damned in London it is useless for provincial purposes."

"You are satisfied with the course pursued by Miss Prescott?"

"I have nothing to say in the matter. It was not I that produced the play, though of course it is to my interest to have it played as often as possible. I am sorry Miss Prescott has lost money by it, but that is not my fault, you know, and I think she will do well by producing it in Chicago or Boston, even if it is only for

---

1. "Whether or not the play [Vera] would be withdrawn tonight depended upon the result of an interview with Oscar Wilde, who was at Coney Island, and to whom a proposition, artistic rather than financial, would be presented. Mr. Perzel would not say whether Mr. Wilde would be asked to act in the play or lecture between the acts, but a surprise might perhaps be in store for the public." ("Losing Money on 'Vera,'" *The New York Times* (New York, NY), 27 Aug. 1883, 5.)

one night. As I said, however, she brought the play out and not I." And Mr. Wilde strolled away with a friend after stowing away in his wallet a bulky roll of bills with which he had been toying during the conversation.

Sheridan Shook was found at the Morton House discussing the situation with Mr. Collier.[1] "'Vera' has been played for the last time in this theatre," he said. "The matter is simple enough as far as I am concerned. When I asked for my rent this morning it was not forthcoming, so I declined to allow the play to be produced. Mr. Perzel endeavored to make an arrangement with me, but as he had absolutely no money to put up or any reasonable expectation of having it in the near future, I was obliged to decline. I want it to be distinctly understood that I have in no way been mixed up in this. The contract was made by Mr. Palmer and we had to assume it when we took the theatre. The scenery was painted outside the theatre. I was not even asked to attend any of the rehearsals. I have never spoken to Mr. Wilde in my life and don't want to. I knew the thing was a failure on the first night and expected this would be the end of it."

"Are you going to engage any other attraction?"

"No. The theatre will remain idle until the Wyndham Company comes, which will be in two weeks from today. I have had several offers but do not care to accept any of them."

"'Vera' Killed by Critics," *The Sun* (New York, NY), 28 Aug. 1883, 3[2]

OSCAR WILDE SURE THAT HIS PLAY WAS NOT A SUICIDE.

Withdrawn After Six Nights—Mr. Perzel has Faith in the Piece and will Resurrect it on the Road—Mr. Wilde Appeals to Boston.

"Will 'Vera' be given tonight?" asked a reporter of THE SUN at the ticket office of the Union Square Theatre yesterday afternoon.

"I don't know for sure, but I don't think so," was the reply. "Mr. Perzel is on the stage, and can tell you. He is the manager. We merely let the theatre to him. We have nothing whatever to do with the play. He can run it the three weeks for which he engaged the theatre, or withdraw it and lose the forfeit."

1. Sheridan Shook (1828–1899) was an American theatre manager. He built the Union Square Theatre, which he managed with A. M. Palmer for ten years. Palmer had recently taken a sabbatical from the theatre business and Shook and James W. Collier had entered into partnership in the management of the Union Square Theatre. The Morton House, of which Shook was also proprietor, was a hotel in Union Square that adjoined the theatre.

2. Excerpted in "'Vera' Withdrawn," *The Boston Herald* (Boston, MA), 28 Aug. 1883, 1.

"The loss," said an actor, who was standing by, "must have been about $1,200 on the seven performances, counting only the running expenses, without considering the plant. I doubt if there was more than forty dollars in the house Saturday afternoon or a hundred in the evening. But I think Perzel will make a mistake if he withdraws the play. He ought to give it a chance to pick up."

The reporter found Mr. Perzel on the stage.

"Will you continue 'Vera' for another week?" he was asked.

"I have decided to withdraw the play," he said, "and have just prepared this letter to the public," handing the reporter the following written statement:

✂ *The letter that also appeared in "The Failure of 'Vera,'"* New York Tribune *(New York, NY), 28 Aug. 1883, 5, p. 562.*

"So you still have faith in the play, Mr. Perzel."

"'Vera' is a great play, notwithstanding the critics. As far as I can see from the criticisms, they ignored the play and confined themselves to the annihilation of Mr. Wilde. Unfortunately, they annihilated my funds at the same time. The uniformly adverse opinions must have staggered even those who had fully made up their minds to see 'Vera,' if only out of curiosity."

"Why do you consider it a great play?"

"Because on the opening night, when the house was jammed, hardly a person left before the play was over, in spite of the intense heat; because such audiences as have come after the stunning criticisms of last Tuesday have been very enthusiastic; because, moreover, Mr. Lawrence Barrett, Mr. Steele Mackaye, and other competent authorities consider the play a great play."

"With so much faith, why don't you keep the play on the boards, in the hope that it will pick up?"

"Because I have more faith than money. The plant cost me about $12,000, and my loss during the week has been considerable. I wanted to mount the play artistically, in keeping with Mr. Wilde's aesthetic tastes, and I engaged a good company at good salaries. I shall pay my company's salaries and my forfeit money, but I can't afford to risk more money in the hope that the play will pick up. Mr. Wilde is entitled to a royalty of $50 a performance in addition to the $2,500 paid for the play, and he will of course receive the royalties from the performances we give on the road."

"Will you take the same company on the road with you?"

"I do not know."

"Is there any chance of Mr. Wilde's appearing in the play?"

"Not in this city. He may appear in one of the cities where we propose to give it, though nothing is definitely settled as yet. But there is Mr. Wilde; why don't you ask him?"

"Where?" asked the reporter. There was a third person present, but he was only a young man in a light sack suit and an ordinary crop of hair crowned by a straw hat.

"Mr. Wilde," asked the reporter, "to what do you attribute the failure of 'Vera?'"

"'Vera' is not a failure," said Mr. Wilde. "It may be financially, but not otherwise."

"Then you do not agree with the critics?"

"The critics," continued Mr. Wilde, "do not understand that art is abstract; that it is, for instance, as abstract as a mathematical problem. They do not seem to understand that my having cut my hair has nothing to do with the value of 'Vera' as a work of art; that my wearing long trousers does not necessarily imply that the dramatic situations are spun out.

"I know a great deal more about my play that the critics do," continued Mr. Wilde with the same serenity. "I am sure it is a good play, and confident that it will ultimately succeed. I am glad that it is to be taken on the road. All the provincial criticisms I have seen have been highly favorable. I should like it to be heard in other cities, especially in Boston."

"Are you satisfied with the manner in which it is acted?"

"Perfectly. I would not have sold the play to an actress who could not realize my ideal."

"Was the play studied under your directions?"

"No. Every playwright has pet points of his own which he wishes to have brought out. In regard to these I made suggestions. I am not disposed to teach people who have made acting the study of their lives. I don't expect actors to teach me how to write poetry, and I am sure actors don't expect a poet to teach them how to act."

"Do you think of appearing in 'Vera?'"

"I have no intention of the kind. It is my business to write plays, and the business of others to act them. I have another play completed, and am about to begin a third.[1] I assure you I have perfect confidence in 'Vera' as it now stands with the cuts made after the first performance. Most of my confidence is derived from observing the audiences. I have observed that the small audiences we succeeded in drawing, in spite the unfavorable notices, have been deeply impressed, and very enthusiastic. I have been called out every night. I believe it is a great mistake to withdraw the play. I think it would have picked up if the people who liked it had time enough to speak to their friends."

---

1. Wilde would not write a third play until *Lady Windermere's Fan* (1892). He may have been thinking of *The Cardinal of Avignon*, a tragedy he sketched out in the early 1880s but never completed.

The usual crowd of actors who find employment in second-class combinations on the road was standing near the Union Square Theatre. The failure of "Vera" was earnestly discussed.

"It affects us quite as much as it does Miss Prescott or Mr. Wilde," said one of them to a reporter. "A failure at the outset of the season is apt to frighten off managers who organize companies to take on the road, and until the managers recover we shall be out in the cold. I wish Perzel would keep on. Plays have sprung into popularity after worse setbacks than 'Vera' got."

"Amusements," *The New York Herald* (New York, NY), 28 Aug. 1883, 4[1]

Lawrence Barrett's Success in 'Francesca da Rimini.'

WITHDRAWAL OF 'VERA.'

The Coming Opera Season—A Brilliant Prospect.

CHATS WITH AIMEE, GRAU AND STRAKOSCH.

✂ *Several paragraphs that are unrelated to Wilde.*

THE UNION SQUARE THEATRE CLOSED.

The Union Square Theatre was closed yesterday and will not be reopened until September 10, when Mr. Charles Wyndham and his company begin an engagement. Mr. Perzel, the husband of Miss Marie Prescott, had reflected on the financial failure of Mr. Oscar Wilde's play, 'Vera,' and yesterday morning decided finally to discontinue the performances. The members of Miss Marie Prescott's company were engaged on terms which provided that the engagement could be broken by one week's notice.

Mr. Lewis Morrison said that he had not the least idea that 'Vera' was to be withdrawn until he arrived at the theatre yesterday. The whole affair was very unfortunate, to the members of the company especially. He personally had spent $500 in costumes, which was rather a heavy outlay for an engagement of only one week's duration.[2]

Mr. Perzel said he had lost about $15,000 on the production and was not prepared to risk any more at present. The company was dismissed and a new

1. Excerpted in "Record of the Week," *The Irish Nation* (New York, NY), 1 Sep. 1883, 3. Quoted in Dearinger, 145.
2. It was customary at this time for actors to pay for their own costumes.

company would be organized for an autumn and winter season, for which some of the 'Vera' company would perhaps be engaged.[1] Mr. Wilde received a certain sum down for the play and was to have a royalty of $50 a performance for 100 performances, which Mr. Perzel considered were extraordinarily high priced terms. Miss Marie Prescott has agreed to play it 100 times within a year. Both Miss Prescott and Mr. Wilde were very anxious to continue the engagement at the Union Square Theatre, but Mr. Perzel thought it best to close. Mr. Wilde, Mr. Perzel said, had said to him, "The great mistake I made was in not appearing as Alexis myself."[2] The company assembled at the Union Square Theatre yesterday afternoon and received their salaries for last week. Miss Marie Prescott will rest until October 15, when she will begin a season on the road, playing 'Vera' and Ghautier's 'Czeka,' which she played with success last spring in Brooklyn and Philadelphia. Mr. Perzel, in a letter to the HERALD, makes the following re-marks:—

✂ *The letter that also appeared in "The Failure of 'Vera,'"* New York Tribune *(New York, NY), 28 Aug. 1883, 5, p. 562.*

WHAT MR. WILDE SAYS.

Mr. Wilde was in the Union Square Theatre during the afternoon. In speaking to a HERALD reporter about the sudden withdrawal of 'Vera' he said it was very unfortunate, and that he was convinced the play would have succeeded if the management and the company could have given it a longer trial. "I," he added, "have done my part well. I have written a good play, and that is all I pretended to do; I did not engage the company nor hire the theatre. I simply wrote a good play which has pleased the audience. Every night it has been well received by those in the house. In fact, the audiences have appeared to be keenly interested and pleased with the play. The curtain has frequently been raised, and Miss Prescott has been recalled every night. I was very anxious that the play should have been given in Boston, but as it has been decided to withdraw it I must bear my disappointment."

"What are your future plans?" the reporter asked.

"I shall return to England next week," Mr. Wilde answered.

"Then you will not appear on the American stage just yet?"

"No."

1. Prescott did not engage any of the *Vera* company for her touring company.
2. Alexis, the Czarevich, is the play's male romantic lead.

When Mr. Sheridan Shook was asked the reason of the withdrawal of 'Vera' from the stage of the Union Square Theatre he said:—

"The enterprise was not undertaken by this house nor did we have anything to do with it. The very contract for playing here had been signed before I bought Mr. Palmer's interest in the theatre. According to the arrangement he made the company appeared here. Today I asked them to comply with the conditions agreed to. They complained that they were short of funds and had only enough money to pay the performers. They broke the terms of the agreement, and that was the end of it. As to the play itself the Union Square Theatre had nothing to do with it. The scenery was painted outside, the business was done outside, the whole affair was an outside matter."

✂ *Several paragraphs that are unrelated to Wilde.*

"Oscar Wilde's Views," *The Morning News* (Paris, France), 20 June 1884, 1[1]

WHAT HE THINKS OF PARIS, ITS THEATRES AND PICTURES

Enthusiastic Concerning Sarah Bernhardt and Richepin's Translation of "Macbeth"—His Own Experiences as a Playwright.

Mr. Oscar Wilde is in Paris, on his wedding tour,[2] "too happy to be interviewed," as he himself pleaded in a letter that would have melted any heart but that of a representative of THE MORNING NEWS. He was seen at the Hôtel Wagram, stretched on a sofa amid a heap of books, in a room overlooking the spacious Gardens of the Tuileries.

"You are reading, Mr. Wilde?"—not exactly a brilliant opening: but how to begin.

"Yes, I am dipping; I never read from the beginning, especially with novels. It is the only way to stimulate the curiosity that books, with their regular openings, always fail to rouse. Have you ever overheard a conversation in the street, caught the fag end of it, and wished you might know more? If you 'overhear' your

1. Excerpted in "Literature and Art," *The Nottinghamshire Guardian* (Nottingham, UK), 20 June 1884, 3 (supplement); and "Our London Looking-Glass," *The New York Mirror* (New York, NY), 28 June 1884, 3. Quoted in Ellmann, 235–6/250–1, 237/252; and Sturgis, 293/278, 309–10/292–3.
2. Constance and Oscar were married at St. James's, Paddington, on 29 May 1884 (Page, 28).

books in that way, you will go back to the first chapter, and on to the last naturally, as soon as the characters 'bite.'"[1]

"Huysmans and Stendhal are, I see, in your collection."

"Stendhal, of course;" and Mr. Oscar Wilde held up "Le Rouge et le Noir" as some people hold up their Bibles. "As for Huysmans, this last book of his is one of the very best things I have seen."[2]

"You go to Stendhal again and again?"

"Yes; and he is one of the few. For my part, I think the most exquisite thing in reading is the pleasure of forgetfulness. It is so nice to think there are some books you cared for so much at a certain epoch in your life and do not care for now. There is to me a positive delight in 'cutting' an author and feeling I have got beyond him."

"And do you extend that observation to persons?"

"Undoubtedly; so we all do only I would make it a positive satisfaction instead of a regret. Why should we not joyfully admit that there are some people we do not want to see again? It is not ingratitude; it is not indifference; they have simply given us all they have to give."

"You do not feel in that way about Paris, I suppose? You were here last year for a long time, and this season brings you here again."

"No; it is not easy to exhaust the message of Paris, especially when Sarah Bernhardt is playing."[3]

"You have seen 'Macbeth'?"

1. Wilde expressed a similar opinion in a book review for *The Pall Mall Gazette*: "There is a great deal to be said in favour of reading a novel backwards. The last page is as a rule the most interesting, and when one begins with the catastrophe or the dénouement one feels on pleasant terms of equality with the author." (5 June 1889; CW vii, No. 129, lines 2–5.)

2. Marie-Henri Beyle (1783–1842) was a French novelist who wrote under the pen name Stendhal. His novel *Le Rouge et le Noir* (1830) is a Bildungsroman that follows the protagonist Julien Sorel's attempts to rise from poverty to the Parisian elite. Wilde may have been especially taken by the climax of the book, when Sorel is guillotined and his lover kisses his severed head. The scene evokes the story of Salomé and St. John the Baptist, which Wilde would later dramatise (*Salomé*; 1892). Charles-Marie-Georges Huysmans (1848–1907) was a French novelist and art critic who wrote as Joris-Karl Huysmans. Wilde refers to Huysmans's *À rebours* (*Against the Grain* or *Against Nature*; May 1884), in which the Duc Jean Des Esseintes, the last scion of a noble family, renounces society and becomes a recluse. The novel is essentially plotless, and describes Des Esseintes's musings on literature and art and his other attempts to stimulate his senses. It was one of Wilde's favourite books and he often returned to it, even taking it as the inspiration for the "poisonous" book that corrupts Dorian Gray (CW iii, 362–3; Holland, 94–100; Wright, 214–15).

3. Sarah Bernhardt was playing Lady Macbeth at the Théâtre de la Porte Saint-Martin. Constance commented on the production in a letter to her brother, describing Bernhardt's performance as "the most splendid acting I ever saw [....] she simply stormed the part." (CL, 227–8.) Bernhardt later took the play to London, opening at the Gaiety Theatre on 4 July.

Figure 18. Sarah Bernhardt as Lady Macbeth. "She brings all her fine intelligence to the part."

"Over and over again; there is nothing like it on our stage, and it is her finest creation. I say her creation, deliberately, because to my mind it is utterly impertinent to talk of Shakespeare's 'Macbeth' or Shakespeare's 'Othello.' Shakespeare is only one of the parties; the second is the artiste through whose mind it passes. When the two together combine to give me an acceptable hero, that is all I ask. Shakespeare's intentions were his own secret; all we can form an opinion about is what is actually before us."[1]

"And Sarah satisfies you?"

"There is absolutely nothing like her. She brings all her fine intelligence to the part, all her instinctive and acquired knowledge of the stage. Her influence over Macbeth's mind is just as much an influence of womanly charm as of will—with us they only accentuate the last. She holds him under a spell; he sins because he loves her; his ambition is quite a secondary motive. How can he help loving her? She binds him by every tie, even by the tie of coquetry. Look at her dress; the tight-fitting tunic and the statuesque folds of the robe below.

"The whole piece is admirably done. Richepin's translation is perfect in its way.[2] He has put it into rude, majestic prose, the very language of the epoch, as one might conceive it—it is almost literal in parts. Intelligent minds have worked over the whole play in this French rendering. The very ghost is Elizabethan. Remember, in Shakespeare's day ghosts were not shadowy, subjective conceptions, but beings of flesh and blood, only beings living on the other side of the border of life, and now and then permitted to break bounds. The ghosts of the Porte-Saint-Martin are men; you could pinch them and run them through and through; they are not mere things of gauze, like our English stage figures of the kind, elaborated, apparently, from some programme of the Psychical Society."

"You have seen the 'Maître de Forges!'"[3]

1. Gilbert in *The Critic as Artist*: "People sometimes say that actors give us their own Hamlets, and not Shakespeare's; [....] In point of fact, there is no such thing as Shakespeare's Hamlet. If Hamlet has something of the definiteness of a work of art, he has also all the obscurity that belongs to life. There are as many Hamlets as there are melancholies." (CW iv, 165.29–166.5.)

2. Jean Richepin (1849–1926) was a French poet and dramatist.

3. *Le Maître de forges* (*The Ironmaster*; 1882) is a novel by Georges Ohnet (1848–1918). It is about a rich ironworker whose aristocratic wife treats him coldly because of his inferior beginnings. Ohnet adapted the novel for the Parisian stage; it opened at the Théâtre du Gymnase Marie Bell on 15 December 1883. The version Wilde saw in London was adapted by Arthur Wing Pinero (1855–1934) and opened at the St. James's Theatre on 17 April 1884. As to the interviewer's suggestion that London might be shocked by the play, the *Standard* had this to say: "*Le Maître de Forges* [...] is now in the midst of a success in Paris, where, however, stories which turn on the delicacies of conjugal relationship [*sic*] are more popular than they are in England, and possess, indeed, a peculiar attraction. [...] Having selected the piece, however, the management [of the St. James's Theatre] has at least taken a judicious step in preserving French names and a French *locale*, thus to a great extent mitigating criticisms which would have been obvious" ("St. James's Theatre," *The Standard* (London, UK), 18 Apr. 1884, 3).

"Not here; we have it in London, you know."

"And London is not 'shocked?'"

"Oh, London is improving; and besides it will take anything from the French. Of course, if an English writer had done anything of the sort, there would have been one loud shriek."

"So you might consider yourself a Frenchman—if you meant to go on writing plays?"

"In one respect, certainly; for the sake of the interpretation. What a gulf there is between the character as you conceive it and the character as it comes out on the stage. I admit, after what I said just now, that the author has no right to complain where the result is artistic; but with us that is so often not the case. I speak from experience: I shall never forget the two hours and a half I passed in the playhouse at New York on the first night of my piece. It was the sharpest agony of my life."[1]

"But you will write another play of course?"

"Undoubtedly; but just now I am laying myself out for a novel.[2] Plays and novels, I think, ought to go together in a man's practice, if only to make one bear in mind what I consider the cardinal principle of all good style, that writing is something meant to be said aloud—to be spoken, in fact. With the multiplication of books we have got into the habit of merely writing for the eye, and that is fatal to all rhythm and music. Shakespeare's music came naturally from his habit of writing for the voice and the ear. I care little for archaism, for the nice choice of words of this or that epoch; please the mind through the ear—that is the all in all."

"You have seen the Salon?"

"Yes; I have seen the work of 'the trade,' matchless work a good deal of it; if you like but still that."

"And Sargent's portrait?"[3]

"Oh, that is altogether on a higher level: like everything he does, it shows the influence of his fine nature and fine taste. Who but he would have ventured

1. Wilde refers to the staging of *Vera; or, The Nihilists* at New York's Union Square Theatre on 20 August 1883. On the first night the play began at about 20:00 and ended at 23:45, so Wilde's estimate of "two hours and a half" is rather low.

2. Wilde's only novel, *The Picture of Dorian Gray*, did not appear until July 1890. Joseph Bristow (CW iii, xxxii) suggests that Wilde began writing it in the autumn of 1889.

3. John Singer Sargent (1856–1925) was an American artist. His portrait of Virginie Amélie Avegno Gautreau (1859–1915) was exhibited at the Paris Salon under the title *Portrait de Mme *** (later retitled *Portrait of Madame X*). Gautreau, a Parisian socialite, was immediately identified as the model. The public was shocked by the portrait, and particularly by the loose shoulder strap on Gautreau's dress, which Sargent would later repaint as more securely fastened. Sargent moved from Paris to London and, as Wilde predicted, was successful there, though he would later concede that *Madame X* was "the best thing I have done." (Davis, D. (2003). *Strapless: John Singer Sargent and the Fall of Madame X*. Jeremy P. Teacher/Penguin. 236.)

to outline that head as he has done, and yet you feel that was just the way to treat it. It is a pictorial reminiscence of the earlier grand art."

"Will he succeed in England, do you think? He is going to paint there."

"Beyond question. England is in a better condition to understand him than France. There is more individuality with us, less of that respect for tradition, good tradition though it be. Everybody there is a law unto himself. Even in such a thing as costume we revive the earlier styles or invent new ones, just because we think them good. He may treat his sitters according to his fancy; he will be sure to find people ready to judge him and them on their merits."

"So his Salon picture is the one righteous work that saves the city?"

"Not the one; you forget the Whistlers. Was anything more beautiful ever done than the portrait of the child—more tender and simple and finely true? It ought to be a revelation to the art world on this side."[1]

"Mr. Oscar Wilde Interviewed in Glasgow," *Evening News and Star* (Glasgow, UK), 22 Dec. 1884, 4

HIS OPINIONS ON UGLY DRESS. TIGHT WAISTS, TIGHT BOOTS AND GLOVES.
LOW-NECKED DRESSES, THE LAND QUESTION, ORNAMENTS, THE PROGRESS
OF DRESS REFORM.

OSCAR WILDE.

"Good evening," said Mr. Wilde, with a pleasant smile, as he shook hands with our representative in the smoking-room of the Central Hotel last night. "Just draw your chair in here." Mr. Oscar Wilde is a young man, tall and well formed, with a pleasant face and a heavy head of dark curling hair. There was nothing extraordinary in his dress. He wore a plain orthodox evening suit, with the cuffs of his shirt turned up in order to give his hands free play. He chatted with our representative quite freely.

---

1. Wilde refers to Whistler's *Harmony in Grey and Green: Miss Cicely Alexander* (1872–1873), exhibited in Paris as *Portrait de Miss Alexander*. Wilde may have seen it before when it was exhibited at the Grosvenor Gallery in 1881. Whistler also exhibited his *Arrangement in Grey and Black, No. 2: Portrait of Thomas Carlyle* (1872/1873) under the title *Portrait de Carlyle*. Wilde had reviewed this picture positively when it was exhibited at London's Grosvenor Gallery in 1877: "the expression on the old man's face, the texture and colour of his grey hair, and the general sympathetic treatment, show Mr. Whistler to be an artist of very great power when he likes." (CW vi, No. 1, lines 345–8.)

"This reminds me of being in America," said Mr. Wilde, throwing himself back in his chair with a fragrant cigar in his hand; "I used to have them (interviewers) coming to my rooms five or six times a day, and I rather liked it. By the way," he asked, "how long is it since you commenced your interviews?" Our representative explained that the "Evening News" had interviewed all the distinguished people who had visited the city within the last six months. "Yes," said Mr. Wilde. "I think it is a capital feature of the paper. It gives a man an opportunity of saying and explaining things which he could not do as satisfactorily in an ordinary speech."

DRESS.

"Now," said Mr. Oscar Wilde, "what do you want me to talk about—dress?[1] Well I think all ugly dress has been made and worn by the most useless people in the world, and all beautiful dress by people who had something to do and knew how to do it. The only well-dressed people are the classes like the fisher people and the peasants. In the peasant, the dress has been without a change for centuries. The French workman and the English ploughboy of the present day wear respectively the short tunic, and the long tunic of the thirteenth century—the dress they wore—once adorned kings. I do not mean, of course, that the king should adopt the peasant's costume, but the principle—comfort, utility—ought to be the same.[2] Why," continued Mr. Wilde smiling, "when I was in France I wore a blouse for three months, and I was never more comfortable in my life." Naturally we come now to

TIGHT LACING.

"I say at once that the shoulder is the natural place from which to hang anything. Nature gives no opportunity to suspend articles of clothing from the waist, and it has therefore to be compressed.[3] I am quite sure that the reason of tight

1. Since returning from America Wilde had toured Great Britain and Ireland with *The House Beautiful, Personal Impressions of America,* and *The Value of Art in Modern Life.* He first gave his new lecture on *Dress* in late September or early October 1884; this was the lecture he gave most frequently during the winter season. He gave it on 21 December 1884 at Glasgow's St. Andrews Hall (Dibb, 163–5).

2. Comfort and utility in dress: see also "Wilde," *The Evening Telegram* (Providence, RI), 26 Sep. 1882, 1, p. 464. In *Dress* Wilde noted that the blouse then worn by French workmen had been worn in the fourteenth-century "by kings and princes." (Dibb, 274.)

3. Wilde had recently made the same point in a letter to the editor of *The Pall Mall Gazette,* printed on 14 Oct. 1884: "Now it is quite true that as long as the lower garments are suspended from the hips, a corset is an absolute necessity; the mistake lies in not suspending all apparel from the shoulders. In the latter case a corset becomes useless, the body is left free and unconfined for respiration and motion, there is more health, and consequently more beauty." (CL, 233;

lacing is not so much the desire to have a tiny waist as the necessity there is for some strong compression in order to keep the clothes on at all. Yes, as you may say, small waists and tight lacing are fashionable, but fashion is folly, and it has always been the greatest enemy of art. The waist, naturally, is a very delicate and very beautiful curve, not a triangle. I know

A FAMOUS ACTRESS

who has a beautiful waist simply because she never makes it unnaturally small. I mean Miss Ellen Terry. She does not make herself like an hour-glass. Then, there is Sara Bernhardt, she never compresses her waist, and the result is she shows a figure with the most beautiful lines imaginable."

TIGHT GLOVES AND BOOTS.

"The same remarks" continued Mr. Wilde, "apply also to the foot and the hand. A foot is not beautiful because it is small, but just as it is in proportion to the rest of the figure. And so also with the hand. A hand is not beautiful because it is small, but just as it is in proportion, and as its lines and curves are clearly shown. To crowd a hand into a glove many sizes too tight for it does not make the hand look smaller. It really makes it apparently larger—a shapeless, useless mass. This is not beauty, for beauty consists in the sense of power that it gives you, and a tightly-gloved hand is of no practical use at all. Beauty does not go by size. If you go to China you will get both the smallest foot and the smallest hand, and consequently the ugliest."[1]

THE PROGRESS OF DRESS REFORM.

"But," protested our representative, "you speak against modern dress, and hold up the Greek costume as the most perfect of all, yet do not advocate its adoption. What would you have us do?"

"Why," replied Mr. Wilde, "take their principle—comfort and utility. No good is got by imitation, but we can follow their principles. The principles of Greek art are beauty of line and symmetry and proportion. These are principles

---

CW vi, No. 8, lines 10–15.) See also *Dress* (Dibb, 268–9) and Wilde's essay *The Philosophy of Dress*: "The first and last rule is this, that each separate article of apparel is to be suspended from the shoulders always, and never from the waist. Nature, it should be noted, gives one no opportunity at all of suspending anything from the waist's delicate curve." (*New York Tribune* (New York, NY), 19 Apr. 1885, 9; CW vii, Appendix 2, lines 138–41.)

1. *The Philosophy of Dress*: "Size is a mere accident of existence, it is not a quality of Beauty ever. A great cathedral is beautiful, but so is the bird that flies round its pinnacle, and the butterfly that settles on its shaft. A foot is not necessarily beautiful because it is small. The smallest feet in the world are those of the Chinese ladies, and they are the ugliest also." (Lines 42–6.) See also *Dress* (Dibb, 264).

that are eternal. You ask if reform in dress is progressing? Look at the societies and institutions we have in London. Apart from them there is Jaeger, who began by simply having two houses for the sale of sensible articles of dress. Now he has several large shops in the West End, and they are always crowded. His woollen dresses are more comfortable than you can imagine—cool in summer, and warm in winter. I wear mine constantly in London. Others are buying them, too, for people wouldn't keep their shops open if they weren't selling their goods.[1] And now," said Mr. Wilde, "I want you to let me say something about

THE LAND QUESTION.

"In consequence of the land coming to be the property of private persons, most towns are becoming spoiled. The immense price which has to be paid for land necessitates people building monstrously high houses. The houses of our great towns are so absurdly high that the sunlight is never able to enter. The proper proportions should be fixed by law as they are by art—they ought never to be higher than the width of the street. As it is, they shut out the light of the sun. In London, for instance, they have pulled down Northumberland House in Tra- falgar Square, and such an enormous price has been asked for the land that the people who bought it have erected unusually high houses, with the result that the sun-light will only be able to enter the street for one hour during the day. Consequently, the streets will always be grim and dark. There ought to be none of this. In every town there should be trees and gardens, places for pretty walks, and open spaces here and there. The fact, however, that the land is in the hands of private individuals prevents all this. They want what they can get out of the property, and consequently, our towns are not what they ought to be—a combi- nation of town and country. Moreover," continued Mr. Wilde, "we can never have any beautiful architecture in these narrow streets, and if we had we could not appreciate it. How can you see a beautiful building by standing on the other side

---

1. Dr. Gustav Jaeger (1832–1917) was a German naturalist. He wrote *Die Normalkleidung als Gesundheitsschutz (Standardised Apparel For Health Protection*; 1880), in which, for health rea- sons, he advocated wearing wool rather than fabrics made from plant fibres. British business- man Lewis Tomalin translated Jaeger's *Health Culture* into English and obtained the rights to Jaeger's name in the United Kingdom. He opened his first shop near Moorgate, central London, in February 1884, under the name of "Dr. Jaeger's Sanitary Woollen System". The company proved successful. It was awarded a gold medal at the International Health Exhibition in South Kensington, London, in the summer of 1884, and was the subject of a leading article in *The Times* (London, UK), 4 Oct. 1884, 4. *The Philosophy of Dress*: "And one of the chief errors in modern costume comes from the particular material which is always selected as the basis for dress. We have always used linen, whereas the proper material is wool. [....] I would like to refer my read- ers to a little hand-book on 'Health Culture,' by Dr. Jaeger, the Professor of Physiology at Stutt- gart." (Lines 224–38.) See also *Dress* (Dibb, 272–3, 281–2).

of the street? You are too close to it. Even if you want to look at a picture you must stand back from it."

MR. OSCAR WILDE AS A PAINTER.

"Do I paint? Well, sometimes—for my own pleasure. When I am travelling I find it easier and more pleasant to use my sketch-book than keep a diary."[1]

ORNAMENTS.

"I think," continued Mr. Wilde, "the whole face of England has been changed within the last ten years. You could not enter the humblest house now without finding something pretty about the room. In decorative art, ornament should be suggested either by the manufacture or the material. Nobody, for instance, would think of painting on a mat. In the case of the material, take the difference between wrought iron and cast iron. Wrought iron, which is beaten out at the anvil, gives us delicacy of curve and beauty, and immense strength. If you have a cast-iron ornament in the round, you would require to have three or four times the bulk. The best form of ornament is that suggested by the material. You ought to look also at the utility of a thing. The use of a mirror is that people should see themselves in it, and that it should reflect things. To paint anything on a mirror is, of course, to spoil its use. The beauty of a jug or vase is simply the beauty of its curves and the utility of it. The ornament ought never to interfere with it. To stick on it, for instance, great roses as big as life, and twice as natural, is to spoil entirely its beauty, and make it useless. In this way we get no beauty and no utility. The Greeks, in decorating a vase, would mark it first with circles to show the curves, then round the neck, and then perhaps put a little leaf ornament to emphasise its delicacy. Apart from the question of decoration, we should consider the value of ornaments. Once a thing like an ornament ceases to be useful, we demand from it the highest possible beauty. Coming short of this, it falls under the double damnation of being useless and ugly. Art is primarily a question of construction, use, and proportion. Art is not ornamentation—a thing can be quite beautiful without an atom of ornament. In the present day people are always imagining that art means decoration, and so covering everything with foolish designs. An 'ornament' is a dangerous thing, because when a thing is useless we demand from it the highest beauty. Bad ornaments are the worst things in the way."

---

1. Wilde had won a prize for drawing at Portora School and, as a teenager, painted watercolours of Lough Corrib in the west of Ireland. Examples of his work can be seen in White, H. (2019). The curious case of the Lough Corrib watercolour. *The Wildean, 54*, 3–15.

LOW-NECKED DRESSES.

"You want me back to dress—low-necked dresses? Well, if a person wears a dress from the shoulder to shoulder a harsh line is produced, which at once diminishes the height. No dress of the kind is beautiful. A well-constructed dress ought to go right up to the neck, and hang from the shoulders—not by the ridiculous things called shoulder straps.[1] Apart from the question of health, there ought to be an equal temperature over the whole body, whereas the most delicate part of the body is neglected, and left exposed. Wherever you find anything ugly, either in dress or in anything else, you may be quite certain that some mistake has been committed—that somebody has been impractical. Ugliness is thus a sign by which we may judge that a mistake has been committed."

DINNER AND SUPPER.

"I think," said Mr. Wilde, incidentally, "people who wanted to go to the theatre, could have supper afterwards. Undoubtedly, the best time to appreciate art is before eating."

MR. WILDE'S KNEE-BREECHES.

"Yes," concluded Mr. Wilde smiling, "I have discarded my knee-breeches. I found them a little too tight, both at and above the knee. Knickerbockers would, I think, be better. They are comfortably loose above the knee, and tight enough below it not to allow of the air passing up. What, are you going now? Well, good night," and our representative left.

Mr. Oscar Wilde was born in Dublin on the 16th October, 1856, and is consequently now 28 years of age.[2] His father was Sir. W. R. Wilde, who arranged the Art Museum in Dublin. Mr. Wilde went in 1874 to Magdalen College, Oxford, where he obtained the first scholarship, two first classes, and the Newdigate Prize for poetry. He has travelled all over Greece and Italy, and about eighteen months ago he returned from a tour in America. He is married to Constance Lloyd, daughter of the late Horace Lloyd, Q. C.

---

1. Wilde was willing to compromise on this point in *The Philosophy of Dress*: "If some support is considered necessary, as it often is, a broad woollen band, or band of elastic webbing, held up by shoulder straps, will be found quite sufficient." (Lines 177–9.)
2. Wilde was born on 16 October 1854 and so was 30 years of age.

"Oscar Wilde," *The Montgomery Advertiser* (Montgomery, AL), 31 Jan. 1886, 3[1]

HIS OPINION OF AMERICA AND THE HOSPITABLE AMERICANS.

Kind Words of all Sections—Various Literary Notes Picked up Here and There Beyond the Atlantic.

Correspondence of the Advertiser.

DUNFERMLINE, SCOTLAND, Jan. 10.—
Oscar Wilde was in Dunfermline a little while back, and lectured on "Dress" to a very large audience.[2] In this country, as was the case in the States, he draws well as a lecturer. While here he was the guest of Mr. and Mrs. Kenneth Mathieson, Jr., a charming newly married couple who have a delightful home.[3] They have fine literary tastes, and had several friends at their house to meet Mr. Wilde. It was my good fortune to be one of the number, and a more enjoyable evening I do not remember to have spent. Socially Mr. Wilde is a most agreeable gentleman. And he is an ardent friend of America. When he learned of my connection with Montgomery, he immediately asked about the late Mrs. Henry D. Clayton, whom he knew as Miss Allen, and whose recent untimely death was so profoundly regretted throughout Alabama.[4] When I told him of her death he was greatly shocked,

1. I am grateful to John Cooper for identifying this article.

2. Wilde lectured in St. Margaret's Hall in Dunfermline on 10 December 1885. He was reported to be "in bad 'form,'" with his voice and "fervour" adversely affected by the severe weather (*Fifeshire Advertiser* (Kirkcaldy, UK), 12 Dec. 1885, 3).

3. Kenneth Mathieson Jr. (1847–1924) and Sarah M. Robertson (1863–1943) had married on 2 June 1885. The 1891 Scottish Census shows the Mathiesons living in Park Avenue, Dunfermline, with Kenneth's occupation listed as "ironfounder". His father appears to be the Kenneth Mathieson of Dunfermline who wrote *How We Saw the United States of America* (1883), a memoir of his 1882 visit to the United States at the invitation of Scottish–American steel magnate Andrew Carnegie (1835–1919). Mathieson Sr. was accompanied on the trip by several family members and friends, including Sarah and her father.

4. Virginia Ball Allen and Henry DeLamar Clayton, Jr. (1857–1929), whose fathers had both been generals in the Confederate Army, were married in Montgomery on 22 November 1882. Virginia died after a brief illness on 29 September 1883 ("Death of Mrs. Clayton," *The Daily Times* (Eufaula, AL), 29 Sep. 1883, 4). In 1882 Wilde was reported to have declared "Miss Alsatia Allen" the most beautiful woman in America ("Loveliness and Politeness," *The Sun* (New York, NY), 20 Aug. 1882, 5, pp. 454–5). Another report suggested that Jennie Allen was meant ("Personal Intelligence," *The New York Herald* (New York, NY), 3 Aug. 1882, 6), and Lewis and Smith (OWDA, 369) make a case that it was Lila Allen, who had played Lady Angela in a pirated production of *Patience*. However, Wilde was almost certainly referring to Virginia, none of whose sisters were named Alsatia, Jennie, or Lila (Banta, T. M. (1901). *Sayre Family: Lineage of Thomas Sayre, a Founder of Southampton.* De Vinne Press. 503–4). A report of the Clayton–Allen marriage suggests that Virginia may have gone by Jennie: "Miss Jennie Allen, of Montgomery, Ala, pronounced by Oscar Wilde to be the most beautiful woman in America, was recently married to

and expressed the deepest regret. "She was a beautiful woman," he said, "I may say she was perfect," and he went on to speak at length of her many charms. "I thought Miss Allen," said he, "and a young lady in California, and one in Boston, were the most beautiful women I saw in America, and your American women are marvellously lovely.[1] There is a spirit and a dash, and withal a delicacy, about them charming to behold." Mr. Wilde was warm in his praises of our country, and he was quite enthusiastic about the Southern people. He had been delighted with a visit to Mr. Jefferson Davis, at Beauvoir, and referred to the famous chieftain as "that grand old man living with his books and fighting battles with his pen that he was powerless to win with his sword." He referred at length to other distinguished Americans whom he had met, among them being Mr. Beecher, Mr. Whittier, Harriet Beecher Stowe, Mark Twain, Mr. Pendleton and Mr. Bayard, for all of whom he entertained a lively appreciation.[2] In reference to Bret Harte, he said: "Why did your government remove him from the consularship at Glasgow?[3] I think you should pay him a good salary to represent American literature in London. He is a great pet at all the clubs; we are all very fond of him. He is a very charming companion."

Mr. Wilde, like many other of his countrymen, cannot appreciate or comprehend the social gulf between the white and black races in the States. He thinks that political equality should beget some measure of social equality; which opinion seems very absurd to an American. And upon this point, strange to say, the unthinking millions in this country have an idea that there are no social distinctions of any nature in the Land of the Free. They suppose that men who meet upon a common level at the ballot-box do not change their relation when they come to the drawing room. As they see it, the social and political world of America blend in the utmost harmony, and the man who has the right to aspire to the

---

Mr. Henry D. Clayton, Jr., of Enfauls [*sic*], in the same state." (*Daily State Gazette* (Trenton, NJ), 19 Dec. 1882, 2.)

1. The Californian woman may be Hattie Crocker; the Bostonian, Maud Howe.

2. John Greenleaf Whittier (1807–1892) was an American poet and abolitionist. Samuel Langhorne Clemens (1835–1910), better known by his pen name Mark Twain, was an American lecturer, humourist, and author. There is no evidence that he and Wilde met in America in 1882, though they did meet in Bad Nauheim in 1892, attending a luncheon at which "both were delightfully amusing" (Vranken, T. L. (2014). Transatlantic relations—The convergence of Oscar Wilde and Mark Twain. *The Wildean*, *45*, 113–20; "Homburg Looks Happy," *The New York Herald, European Edition* (Paris, France), 31 July 1892, 2). Harriet Beecher Stowe (1811–1896) was an American author and abolitionist, best known for her novel *Uncle Tom's Cabin* (1852). She was the sister of Henry Ward Beecher. George H. Pendleton (1825–1889) served as United States Senator from Ohio from 1879 to 1885. Wilde attended a reception at Senator Pendleton's residence after his lecture in Washington, D. C. on 23 January 1882.

3. Harte took up the role of United States Consul in Glasgow in 1880. In 1885 he settled in London.

Senate, carries a passport to the parlors of the upper-ten thousand, which he can use if he has but one coat to his back and no learning in his head.

Mr. Wilde had a colored valet whom he picked up in New York, and he never saw a servant his equal for intelligence and reliability. This model valet always carried his master's cash, and with great satisfaction the poet lecturer related that whenever he desired a little pocket change, he had to go to his colored valet for it. But something he couldn't understand, was why his valet was not permitted to travel in the sleeping-car with the master. Once in North Carolina, his servant came into the car to bring some books, when the conductor peremptorily ordered him out.[1] "We British know nothing of good servants," he said. "The colored people of the United States are the model servants of the earth."

"But," said Mr. Wilde, "I have no quarrel to make with Southern people on the race question. They are a high-minded, intelligent, hospitable, Christian people; they are simply delightful. Richard Henry Wilde, the Southern poet, was my blood relation, and my family had other kins-people who emigrated from the old country to the South.[2] So I feel that the Southern people are, to some extent, my own people."

"Take America as a whole," continued Mr. Wilde, warming up on what was evidently a pleasant subject, "and it is a grand country. It is a marvel of progress and development. New York is a garden of delight, Boston is unsurpassed, New Orleans is most charming. Madison Square is one of the most beautiful spots I ever beheld; and, do you know, the statue of Farragut in New York is a finer work of art than anything of the kind we have in London.[3] A desire to live in New York is not an unworthy ambition of any man."

1. When a rail employee at Atlanta realised that one of the sleeping car tickets he had sold to Wilde's agent was intended for Wilde's valet, he requested the return of the ticket "as it was against the rules of the company to sell sleeping-car tickets to colored persons". (Mendelssohn, 211, notes that the 1875 Civil Rights Act granted all Americans equal rights to access public facilities, including transportation.) The agent refused, as did Wilde: "Mr. Wilde said that he had never been interfered with before, and persisted in having his darkey retain his sleeping car ticket." The porter of the sleeping car informed Wilde's valet that the train would pass through Jonesboro, "and if the people saw a negro in the sleeper they would mob him." The ticket was returned and Wilde's valet vacated the berth. ("Oscar Wilde's Valet," *The Atlanta Constitution* (Atlanta, GA), 6 July 1882, 7.) Either Wilde is mistaken in locating the story in North Carolina, or he is recalling a different incident.

2. Richard Henry Wilde (1789–1847) was a Dublin-born lawyer who served as a Member of the House of Representatives from Georgia. His best known poem is the posthumously published *Hesperia*, "a nationalistic poem in four cantos". Wilde also refers to his uncle, Judge John Kingsbury Elgee.

3. *Personal Impressions of America*: "Madison Square, in New York, lit by a great mast from which the electric light hung in lanterns, was one of the most beautiful sights one could see." (Dibb, 235.) David Glasgow Farragut (1801–1870) was an admiral in the United States Navy. A bronze statue of Farragut, by sculptor Augustus Saint-Gaudens, stands in Madison Square Park and was dedicated in 1881.

Something was said about the statement of a leading London journal to the effect that England is becoming Americanized. "So it is," said Mr. Wilde, "and to me it is far from being a cause of regret. The world will probably become Americanized some day, which is so much the better for mankind. The Americans are so far-sighted, shrewd and energetic. There was one thing that struck me very forcibly: Your people are born orators. Any and every man can speak well in public. Just before Matthew Arnold left home for his lecturing tour of the States he asked me if I had any advice to offer him. 'Commit your lectures to memory,' said I. 'If you use manuscript the people won't listen to you. They are all orators.' And after Mr. Arnold reached New York he felt obliged to employ a teacher and go through a regular course of study in elocution. It would strike you as a trifle odd that an Englishman of such conspicuous ability as Matthew Arnold should feel called upon to study that which is taught to all your school boys before they are taught to read!"[1]

✂ *Several paragraphs that are unrelated to Wilde.*

[Robert Batho], "Shakespeare's Statue," *The New York Herald, European Edition* (Paris, France), 11 Oct. 1888, 1[2]

Unveiling Lord Ronald Gower's Monument at Stratford.

OSCAR WILDE SPEAKS.

Literature the Medium by which England Has Expressed Itself.

(BY TELEGRAPH TO THE HERALD.)

STRATFORD-ON-AVON, October 10, 1888.

1. Arnold's tour of North America was managed, as Wilde's had been, by Richard D'Oyly Carte. He delivered his first lecture, *Numbers*, in New York's Chickering Hall on 30 October 1883, later visiting cities on the Eastern seaboard and in the Midwest and Canada. He sailed for Liverpool on 8 March 1884 (Seeley, 65–7). In Chicago he admitted to an interviewer that the rhythm of his voice was unfamiliar to Americans and that he did not speak loud enough ("Matthew Arnold," *The Sunday Inter Ocean* (Chicago, IL), 20 Jan. 1884, 5).

2. Robert Batho (see p. 517, note 1) later claimed that he had conducted this interview: see Frank Marshall White [and Robert Batho], "Oscar Wilde to Write," *The Chicago Daily Tribune* (Chicago, IL), 17 May 1897, 2, pp. 657–8. Wilde wrote to Robert Ross c. 13 October 1888, "I have been speaking at Stratford about Shakespeare, but in spite of that enjoyed my visit immensely. My reception was semi-royal, and the volunteers played God Save the Queen in my honour" (CL, 360).

The several thousand Americans who yearly visit Stratford-on-Avon have now an extra attraction. This morning at noon was unveiled the new Shakespeare monument, presented to Stratford-on-Avon by Lord Ronald Gower.[1] The work consists of an exceedingly artistic statue in bronze of the bard seated reclining on a chair reading a book. The pose is graceful, natural and easy. This forms the centre and is elevated on a stone pedestal about 10ft. high. At the sides, elevated some distance from the ground are the figures in bronze of Lady Macbeth, Hamlet, Prince Hal and Falstaff. At the corners of the upper portion of the pedestal are hung laurel wreaths of bronze. The statue faces the old church where Shakespeare was buried, and looks over the placid Avon as the bard so often did in life. The back is towards the Memorial Theatre and within thirty yards of it.[2]

At noon a large crowd had gathered about the monument. The people had come in crowds from the surrounding country. Stratford was gaily decorated with flags and the people turned out *en masse*. Among those within the inner circle around the statue were the Duke of Manchester, Lord Leigh, Lord Lieutenant of the County, Oscar Wilde, Sir Philip Cunliffe Owen, George A. Sala, Sir Arthur and Lady Hodgson, the Mayor and Mayoress, Mr. and Mrs. Charles Flower, Mr. and Mrs. Edgar Flower, the Rev. Mr. Propert, the Rev. R. S. de C. Laffan and Mrs Laffan (Mrs. Leith Adams), Dr. and Mrs. Nason, Lord and Lady Lifford and Lord Ronald Gower.

UNVEILING THE STATUE.

To Lady Hodgson, the Mayoress of Stratford-on-Avon, fell the duty of unveiling the statue. She gave a pull and the Union Jack which covered the bronze was drawn back leaving the face exposed and the bunting forming itself over the head like a Capuchin cape. Another pull and the whole veil went flying away, and the statue was exposed to view. The people cheered and the volunteer band played. Sir Philip Owen made a brief speech, and Oscar Wilde, the orator of the day, also spoke. There was quite a little scene at this time among the staunch Shakespearean devotees of Stratford. It came about thus:—Oscar Wilde, in the course of his oration, said:—"Shakespeare was born here; here he passed his sweet boyhood, and here he died. But he saw what made his great impressions of life in London. I doubt whether London has not some right to a monument also." (Here the people yelled and howled "No! No!") The speaker smiled and said:—"I

---

1. Lord Ronald Gower (1845–1916) was a British sculptor and author. He and Wilde met in Oxford in June 1876 (Sturgis, 90/90).

2. The Shakespeare Memorial Theatre was built in 1879 and destroyed by fire in 1926. The Gower Monument was then moved to its present location in Bancroft Gardens, with the four statues at a remove from the main monument.

Figure 19. The Gower Monument in its original location and arrangement outside the Shake-speare Memorial Theatre.

regret having put in any claim for the monument, and I trust you will not proceed to violence. If you do I feel sure the gallant Stratford Volunteers will rescue me."[1] He then read the following ode by Mr. Laffan, of Stratford, to Lord Ronald Gower:—

> Aye so, methinks, by the red embers glare,
> Silent he sat with eagle eyes astrain,
> And saw the myriad children of his brain
> Take form and semblance on the midnight air;
> Heard Royal Henry chide his self crowned heir,
> The guilty Queen moan for her white hand's stain,
> Or Falstaff troll some roystering refrain,
> Or Hamlet play with his own soul's despair.
> And as his soul thrilled to their changing tone
> Thy hand, O sculptor, in that hour supreme
> Smote with swift strokes his being into stone.
> We, too, have dreamt beside our Avon's stream
> Of this great haunting presence—thou alone
> Could'st give it substance worthy of our dream!

Then Lord Ronald Gower spoke a few words, saying how pleased he was to be able to donate the statue to Stratford.

DONNELLY AND SHAKESPEARE.

Luncheon was the next move. Places were laid for seventy persons in the picture gallery. It may be said that Miss Ada Rehan dominated the proceedings, for her grand life size picture recently added to the collection, excited the admiration of all the company.[2] Sir Arthur Hodgson proposed the health of the Queen and Prince of Wales. Then that of the Lord Lieutenant of the county. Lord Leigh replied and among other things said:—"The visit of Mr. Ignatius Donnelly had made people read Bacon more and love Shakespeare better."[3] In reply to the

---

1. Wilde's speech at the unveiling was longer than the version given here. A fuller version can be found in "Unveiling of the Gower Memorial at Stratford," *The Birmingham Daily Post* (Birmingham, UK), 11 Oct. 1888, 5. That version has Wilde delivering his remark about the Stratford Volunteers during his later speech at the luncheon, in response to Lord Leigh saying that Wilde should "esteem himself fortunate that there were not some bold Warwickshire men to have ducked him in the Avon".

2. Ada Rehan (1860–1916) was an Irish-born American actress who interpreted many Shakespearian roles. The picture referred to depicts her in the role for which she was most famous: Katherine in *The Taming of the Shrew*.

3. Ignatius L. Donnelly (1831–1901) was an American Congressman and writer, known for his fringe theories. In *The Great Cryptogram* (1888) he argued that Shakespeare's plays had been written by Francis Bacon. He visited England in 1888, where he debated his theory at Oxford

586

toast of the drama, George Augustus Sala spoke. He drew attention to the cere-mony they had just witnessed, done in a style that the bard himself would have liked, within sight of his favourite woods, the Avon and the church, and sur-rounded by the peasants he loved so well. Mr. Sala said he had learnt his Shake-speare from the stage and told of the various great actors he had seen in Shakes-pearian parts.

ENGLAND'S MEDIUM OF EXPRESSION.

Then came the toast, "The Health of Lord Ronald Gower," and everybody applauded. To Oscar Wilde was given the duty of replying to this, the toast of the day, and he delighted his audience. He said:—

Literature has always been the true medium by which the English nation has expressed itself. Long before we had any painters and sculptors we had great poets, and that while other nations like Greece and Italy had found a medium of expression in marble and color, we in England had always spoken in words. In Shakespeare's days and the time immediately following him, we had imported our painters. Architecture in Shakespeare's days had come to us through the classical revival, what we called the Renaissance. Even when we had painters of our own, such as Turner and Constable, their influence was shown not in the creation of schools of art, but in the creation of an entirely new form of literature, of which art was the subject matter. The glorious color of Turner's sunsets was to be found in the prose of John Ruskin, and Constable's truth to nature in the ex-traordinarily developed descriptive power of modern writers of fiction. There-fore there was something particularly fascinating about the monument made by Lord Ronald Gower. He was an artist who had taken the creations of a poet and shown them in visible form through the medium of bronze. He had produced a work entirely ideal and imaginative in character. Looking at the characters in Shakespeare with their constant change, their quick movement and their never ceasing development, one might wonder how they possibly could be adequately mirrored by an art that took merely a single moment of expression.[1] But in the present instance, so subtle had been the perception of the sculptor that he had seized upon the moments in each character that might be termed moments of

---

and Cambridge (he lost the vote in both instances) and visited the grave of Shakespeare. Asked on his return to America if he had wept there, he replied, "No, sir, not by a — sight!" ("He Wouldn't Weep," *Sunday Truth* (Buffalo, NY), 26 Aug. 1888, 5). The Mayor of Stratford-upon-Avon, in his speech at the unveiling of Gower's monument, declared Donnelly's theory "wild and fanciful [...] a collossal monument of wasted energy", but reflected that "[t]hanks to that idle and absurd controversy there had been a larger influx of strangers to visit Shakespeare's birthplace during the last summer than on any previous occasion." ("Unveiling of the Gower Memorial at Stratford," *The Birmingham Daily Post* (Birmingham, UK), 11 Oct. 1888, 5).

1. The source has "single movement", presumably an error.

psychological revelation. He has shown us Falstaff making merry at the tavern; Hamlet brooding over life's tragedy, the graveyard; Lady Macbeth trying to wipe from her hand the stain that was upon her soul; Prince Hal forgetting the dying king while he sought to place upon his head the crown upon which England's rose and the lilies of France were emblazoned. In this way the sculptor has shown us the heart and nature of each character, and has concentrated into one moment of visible beauty the gradual psychological creation of the mind of the great dramatist. This monument might therefore serve as a symbol of perfect unity of art, and as an expression of the great truth "that though beauty has but one soul, she has many faces."[1]

Lord Ronald Gower replied. He said that his two ideas when he came to Stratford were to erect a monument to Shakespeare and found a Shakespearian scholarship. He had done the first and hoped some day he might do the second. The proceedings then closed.

OSCAR WILDE'S OPINION.

I asked Oscar Wilde what he thought of the figures. He said:—"Prince Hal is the best, next Lady Macbeth. It is difficult to give in bronze the humor and vivacity of Falstaff, but the figure of Hamlet is exceedingly beautiful. I consider the statue of Shakespeare graceful and dignified."

I may mention that the general opinion was one of entire approval and admiration.

✂ *An interview with Lord Ronald Gower.*

1. Wilde's speech at the luncheon was longer than the version given here. A fuller version can be found in "Unveiling of the Gower Memorial at Stratford," *The Birmingham Daily Post* (Birmingham, UK), 11 Oct. 1888, 5.

"Oscar Wilde's Hair Cut," *The Brooklyn Daily Eagle* (Brooklyn, NY), 20 Oct. 1889, 14[1]

He is No Longer a Lackadaisical Man in Knee Breeches.

A Straight, Strong Shouldered Athletic Fellow Who is Bent on Making Fame and Money. The Subsiding of the Aesthetic Craze.

The Oscar Wilde who made himself famous in America a few years ago is not the Oscar Wilde of today. The long hair has been cut and is now short and curly. The knee breeches have been put away carefully, the lackadaisical air is no longer worn, and the Oscar Wilde of London today is a straight, strong, broad-shouldered, athletic fellow, with no nonsense about him and an evident determination on his face to make fame and money. The Wilde craze, so far as England is concerned, is over. Mr. Wilde will question this—yet there are thousands of people, men and women, who believe that Wilde did much good in his late crusade, and he has still a very respectable following, but nothing like what one would be led to believe from a perusal of the satirical Gilbert's "Patience." I saw Oscar on Fleet street today, and would not have known him had not an English friend pointed him out to me. He looked as English in his dress as in his manner, and conducted himself as thousands of other broad-shouldered young fellows whom you will find at Oxford or Cambridge, or in the big commercial houses of London and Liverpool. He was looking in the window of a second hand book store. He carried an armful of papers and a thick blackthorn stick in his hand. There was nothing about him to attract attention. He might perhaps be picked out of a crowd for a professional man. In a recent newspaper article it was reported that Mr. Wilde had grown very stout and very inartistic looking in the matter of dress. This does him a great injustice. As all the world knows, he has an artistic cast of countenance, and his proportions are massive. He is not a favorite among men. Englishmen seem to look upon him as something of a curiosity. Women take more kindly to him. He is chiefly known now by his contributions to magazines,

1. I am grateful to John Cooper for identifying this article. A shorter version (400 fewer words, dated "London, Oct. 12 1889") was printed simultaneously as "The New Oscar Wilde," *The Times* (Philadelphia, PA), 20 Oct. 1889, 12. A longer version (see the footnote below for the two paragraphs omitted in the *Eagle* version) was printed as "Oscar Wilde," *The Weekly Times Democrat* (New Orleans, LA), 26 Oct. 1889, 12; "A Chat With Wilde," *The Kalamazoo Gazette* (Kalamazoo, MI), 26 Oct. 1889, 7; "A Chat With Wilde," *The Weekly Teller* (Lancaster, WI), 31 Oct. 1889, 3; "A Chat With Wilde," *The Sunday Ledger* (Topeka, KS), 3 Nov. 1889, 2; "A Chat With Wilde," *The Maryville Times* (Maryville, TN), 6 Nov. 1889, 3; and "A Chat With Wilde," *The Kansas Democrat* (Topeka, KS), 2 May 1890, 2. Excerpted (all text after "[...] your correspondent had a brief chat with him" excluded) in "The Oscar Wilde of Today," *The Kansas City Star* (Kansas City, MO), 31 Oct. 1889, 4. Excerpted (all text after "It pervades his conversation and his articles alike" excluded) in "A Chat With Wilde," *The Kansas City Gazette* (Kansas City, KS), 10 Jan. 1890, 3.

work in which he is most assiduous. *Punch* calls his latest article "Oscar Wilde's Mad Fancy."[1] His time is entirely occupied. He lectures now and then, writes special articles occasionally, does a book review once in a while, and every other day spends a couple of hours or so editing the *Ladies' World*, or the *Woman's World* as he now calls it, and performs the difficult task of managing a large staff of feminine contributors in a masterly fashion.[2] He frequently drops in at the Lyric Club, although he belongs to half a dozen others in London, and it was there over a cigarette and a straw drink that your correspondent had a brief chat with him.

"Your school of aestheticism, Mr. Wilde" I began, "seems to have died out?"

"Oh, no," was the quick rejoinder, "it has not. There does not seem to be the interest in aesthetic matters that there was some years ago, but the school has not died out—not by any means."

"Then the progress has been satisfactory to you?"

"Oh, yes, yes," was the reply, "perfectly satisfactory;" and then he added after a puff at his cigarette, "perfectly; how could it be otherwise?"

"It was said in a leading newspaper not long since that you had grown tired of what was called 'the aesthetic fad' and did not desire to be identified with the movement any longer."

To this view of the matter Mr. Wilde offered a distinct, implicit and somewhat contemptuous denial—one of those denials which are far better expressed by looks and gesticulations than by words. It meant that such an idea was ridiculous. "Of course things change," he said. "They have their various stages, they develop, and require different treatment. But I have not changed, as my articles in the late magazines on the subject will show."

"Has the progress of aestheticism been more marked in this country or America?"

"Oh, it is difficult to draw any hard and fast lines where the change everywhere has been so great," was the reply. "For the same reason it is perhaps hard to note the advance. Everything is different and no comparison can be drawn. Both countries have made satisfactory progress."

"Do you think the poor people have benefited equally with the rich in the development of artistic grace?"

"Well, of course, the rich can have their artistic hangings, their fringes, their tapestry and very many things which the poor cannot have. Still, they have

---

1. Wilde's story *The Portrait of Mr. W. H.*, about the identification of the dedicatee of Shakespeare's sonnets as the boy actor William Hews, appeared in *Blackwood's Edinburgh Magazine*, July 1889, 146, 1–21. *Punch* described Hews as "Oscar Wilde's Mad Fancy" (13 July 1889, 24).

2. Wilde edited *The Woman's World* between 1887 and 1889. His assistant would later recall that Wilde's editorship "incurred his attendance at the office only twice a week—on the mornings of Tuesday and Thursday" (Fish, A., "Oscar Wilde as Editor," *Harper's Weekly*, 4 Oct. 1913, 18–20).

gained much recently. They have their People's Palace, their music and the like, and this all through our endeavors.[1] I think on the whole you may safely say that the common people have benefited very much."

"What are some of the benefits afforded by the Renaissance school?"

"Look at color. The new colors in dress, in tapestries and in fringes. It is beautiful."

"What about dress?"

"Well, you may change the Englishman's religion, but you must not change his dress. In other countries it is different. In your own it is different. No court dress, no traditional uniform which extends everywhere in this country. There is, of course, some hope for a change of beauty in America."

"Speaking of America, American people took well to your plans, did they not, and your visit there was agreeable?"

"Quite so," replied Mr. Wilde, "the Americans are charming people. They treated me very generously."[2]

"Do you think the Americans adopted your ideas with more eagerness than the English people?"

"No; I did not imply that. I like the Americans. It is a pleasure to lecture to them. The American audience is all attention. It sees your ideas and it grasps your points at once. The people are smart, quick-witted, and if they like a thing they warmly express their approbation."

"You lecture occasionally now, Mr. Wilde?"[3]

"Yes," was the reply, "and I have received a great many letters from all parts of America and from England on the subject. None of these letters are of much importance. Many of them contain words of hearty praise. These I remember. There are a few others not so pleasant, but I have forgotten them."

He lighted a fresh cigarette, crossed his legs in a comfortable sort of way, was lost in silence for a moment, and when he spoke his thoughts were apparently running on literature. He introduced the subject by saying that a nation had

1. The People's Palace was opened in 1887 as an educational and cultural venue for the East End of London. In 1886 Wilde had unsuccessfully applied for the Secretaryship of the Beaumont Trust Fund, which funded the building of the Palace (CL, 278–9). In considering the application, the Palace's designer, Edward Robert Robson (1836–1917), noted that Wilde "is a high-class university man with some experience of technical instruction, but I wonder if he is an organizer & can talk to working men." (Queen Mary University of London, QMC/PP/8/5.)

2. Later versions of this article retain two paragraphs here that were omitted by the *Eagle* editor, presumably so that the article would fit into one column: "Then he repeated the word charming half a dozen times, which I learned afterwards is a pet word of his. It pervades his conversation and his articles alike. 'Americans are so quick to catch a point,' he went on. 'I like them very much. They treated me better than I had expected. They are charming people.'"

3. Wilde had by this time ceased lecturing entirely: he is known to have given four or five lectures in 1887 and only two—his final lectures—in 1888.

only one way of expressing its better instincts. "England expresses hers through her literature, Greece did the same, and the literature of these two nations stands forth incomparable," he said.

"And America?"

"Oh, America expresses hers by energy. What marvelous workers the Americans are. No wonder they all make money so rapidly. Yours, indeed, are a wonderful people."

He rose to go. He explained that he had to dine out, which he does very often, by the way, and that he had first of all to see his mother and wife. It may interest American readers to know that the leader of the aesthetes takes a great deal of pleasure in his home life, that he is comfortably if not luxuriously situated and that he is much sought after by good company. He is an inveterate first-nighter, and when he has nothing else to do he spends an hour or two to great advantage in the British Museum scanning some of the treasures of that wonderful collection. He is making money and those who ought to know say he has a comfortable bank account. Lady Wilde, his mother, is often seen in London. She is an inveterate diner out, believes in the opera and the theatres, and is often seen at late dances. She is still a beautiful woman, well preserved, has splendid mental capabilities, writes pretty verses and is evidently proud of her big son. She is an ardent Home Ruler. She is also the mother of another son not so well known as Oscar—Willie Wilde—a man who has the money making instinct more thoroughly developed than any other member of the Wilde family.

Mrs. Oscar Wilde is a lovable woman who has a large circle of acquaintances, and who entertains in a small, but very satisfactory manner. She is a charming figure in the ball room, which her talented mother-in-law frequents, and many of the leading lights of art, literature and science crowd her snug little drawing room on a reception night. There is always music, some good readings, singing and light refreshments. It is a place worth going to if you get an invitation. Mr. Wilde made so many friends in America that you are almost certain to meet one or two American men and women there. The hours are late, but every moment is enjoyable.

Jacques Daurelle, "Un Poète Anglais a Paris," *L'Écho de Paris* (Paris, France), 6 Dec. 1891, 2[1]

Oscar Wilde

Un de ces derniers soirs, dans un café de la rive gauche, nous étions en train de deviser de choses diverses, lorsque les poètes Stuart Merrill et Henri de Régnier entrèrent, accompagnés d'un jeune homme taillé en Hercule, vêtu d'une façon élégante et correcte, sauf un plastron rose de chemise qui s'avivait dans le noir du pardessus.

Stuart Merrill nous présenta M. Oscar Wilde, que la plupart d'entre nous connaissaient seulement de réputation. L'aspect vigoureux de sa personne, la rougeur de son visage glabre, qui évoquait la vision d'une lune rousse, surprenaient un peu. Ce n'est pas ainsi qu'on se représentait le poète raffiné, le critique subtil et délicat dont Stuart Merrill et Stéphane Mallarmé parlaient souvent avec une vive admiration.

Tandis que, dans les nuages de fumée, les conversations s'animaient, M. Stuart Merrill me dit tout à coup:

— Savez-vous que c'est un homme extraordinaire que cet écrivain anglais, ignoré à Paris de presque tout le monde ? Je vous assure que son premier livre, *Poèmes*, publié vers 1876, est un pur chef-d'œuvre. Et rien n'est plus délicieux que ses volumes de contes, le *Prince Heureux*, et la *Maison des Grenades*, parue la semaine dernière. Quel dommage que je n'aie pas le temps de les traduire en français ! J'ai aussi recueilli sur Wilde un tas d'anecdotes charmantes qui doivent nous le rendre tout à fait intéressant. Quand il étudiait à Oxford, il s'habillait en culottes courtes, avec un pourpoint de velours et des manches de dentelle. Il paraît même qu'il sortait avec un lys ou un tournesol à la main.

Un jour, des étudiants le trouvent chez lui absorbé dans la contemplation d'un vase de porcelaine. Comme ils lui demandent ce qu'il fait en cette attitude.

— « J'essaie de me rendre digne de ma porcelaine, » répond gravement Oscar Wilde.

---

1. See below for an annotated English translation. An English translation is given in Mikhail, 169–71. Referenced in Sturgis, 437/405 (where it is noted that Lady Wilde wrote approvingly to Oscar of the interview: she thought that Daurelle had approached him with "a kind of awe"). Other profiles of Wilde that appeared in the French press at this time but, despite their evident basis in encounters with Wilde, fall short of qualifying as interviews, include Hugues Le Roux, "Oscar Wilde," *Le Figaro* (Paris, France), 2 Dec. 1891, 3; and Robert Sherard, "Oscar Wilde," *Le Gaulois* (Paris, France), 17 Dec. 1891, 1–2. Towards the end of October Wilde was invited by Princess Alice of Monaco to visit her and meet Le Roux (1860–1925), an author and journalist (CL, 492). Sherard showed Wilde the text of his article and Wilde suggested corrections, which Sherard adopted (CL, 504).

Un autre jour, en Amérique, Marion Crawford lui demande pourquoi il semble triste.

Et Wilde de répondre :

« Je suis triste parce que la moitié du monde ne croit pas en Dieu et l'autre moitié ne croit pas en moi. »

Et je vous affirme qu'il ne fait pas cela par pose. Il est d'une sincérité exquise; et les particularités de son costume, — le gilet rouge qu'il exhibe parfois, les chemises de couleur qu'il se plaît à porter, — ne doivent pas du tout nous le faire comparer au sâr Péladan. Par son allure, par ses goûts et par son talent, il rappelle assez exactement Théophile Gautier. »

En cet instant, Oscar Wilde nous offrit des cigarettes. Et il nous dit d'un air flegmatique, sans le moindre sourire sur les lèvres :

— Ce sont des cigarettes d'Egypte. Elles sont excellentes. D'ailleurs, les Anglais ne gardent l'Egypte que parce que c'est le pays d'où nous viennent les meilleures cigarettes.

Je désirais vivement m'entretenir en tête-à-tête avec M. Oscar Wilde. Hier au soir, aux environs de cinq heures, j'ai pu satisfaire ma curiosité. J'ai trouvé M. Oscar Wilde dans un petit salon d'hôtel du boulevard des Capucines, fumant des cigarettes d'Egypte sur un divan. J'aperçois, encombrant une table, des livres que nos écrivains se sont empressés de lui adresser avec des dédicaces admiratives, des revues, des photographies d'amis.

M. Oscar Wilde me parle tout d'abord de Paris et de son séjour parmi nous:

— « Paris est une ville où je me plais beaucoup. Tandis qu'à Londres on cache tout, à Paris on montre tout. On peut aller où l'on veut et personne ne songe à vous critiquer. Moi je vais en tous les endroits où je pourrais éprouver une émotion. Je fréquente aussi bien le Château-Rouge que le café Anglais. Quoi de plus charmant que ces visites à des poètes, avec lesquels on cause au gré de la pensée ?

» Du reste, j'aime infiniment votre littérature. Il y a dans votre histoire littéraire une époque qui me ravit tout particulièrement. C'est l'époque des Cours d'amour. La poésie sensuelle et mystique des troubadours est délicieuse. Elle a exercé une grande influence sur les Préraphaëlites, sur Dante Rossetti, sur Swinburne et sur moi-même.

» Vos jeunes poètes d'aujourd'hui sont également très curieux. Il me semble qu'ils reviennent au romantisme en apportant à cet art plus de souplesse, plus de tact et de nervosité. »

Notre conversation fut interrompue plusieurs fois par l'arrivée de visiteurs, de lettres, de dépêches. Je demandais cependant à M. Oscar Wilde quelle religion artistique il avait prêchée dans ses nombreuses conférences et dans ses articles réunis en volume sous ce titre : *Intentions*. D'une voix traînante et douce, avec des gestes lents il me dit :

— « *J'ai toujours prêché que l'art était un mensonge, et le mensonge c'est la vérité idéale.* C'est la nature qui imite l'art et non pas l'art qui imite la nature. C'est pourquoi un historien qui veut écrire l'histoire d'un siècle ne doit jamais étudier les manifestations artistiques de ce siècle. D'où il faut conclure que les Grecs, qui ont exprimé la Beauté, n'étaient pas beaux, que les gens du moyen-âge n'étaient pas grotesques, n'étaient pas tels que les représentent les artistes de ce temps-là.

» Je soutiens aussi que l'artiste ne prend pas son inspiration dans la nature, mais dans le « matériel », dans l'instrument qu'il emploie. Un peintre ne doit pas faire un paysage avec le paysage qu'il a devant les yeux, mais avec les couleurs qui sont sur sa palette. L'art, c'est le parfait emploi d'un « matériel » qui n'est pas parfait. J'ai écrit et prêché des idées. Et les journaux m'ont beaucoup raillé et critiqué. C'est qu'en Angleterre les journalistes sont toujours du côté du public c'est-à-dire du côté de la bêtise et de l'ignorance. En France les journalistes sont plutôt du côté des novateurs et des artistes. »

De temps à autre M. Oscar Wilde buvait une gorgée d'une boisson à l'eau de seltz. Je remarquai que peu à peu il s'énervait.

— « Oh! me dit-il, cela m'agace de chercher les mots pour m'exprimer. »

Toutefois il voulut bien continuer à parler. Il me résuma, à propos de ses théories sur le roman, son livre *Dorian Gray*, dont le thème est en effet excessivement curieux. Comme je le priais de me conter un ou deux souvenirs recueillis dans ses voyages, il me répliqua :

— « Je ne me souviens de rien. L'artiste doit détruire la mémoire, et ne s'intéresser qu'au moment, qu'à l'heure qui passe. L'homme qui pense à son passé n'a pas de futur. Moi, je me donne au présent d'une façon absolue. »

Je voulais savoir aussi si les anecdotes racontées sur M. Oscar Wilde étaient exactes.

— « Sachez, me répondit-il en souriant, que ce qu'il y a de vrai dans la vie d'un homme, ce n'est pas ce qu'il fait, mais la légende qui se crée autour de lui. Je ne me suis jamais promené dans les rues de Londres avec un lys à la main, parce qu'un concierge ou un cocher de fiacre pourraient en faire autant. Cette légende indique seulement l'impression que j'ai produite sur la foule, et elle indique, mieux que ce que j'ai fait, les tendances de mon tempérament. »

En me reconduisant, M. Oscar Wilde ajouta :

— « Il ne faut jamais détruire les légendes. Ce sont elles qui nous font entrevoir la véritable physionomie d'un homme. »

Je puis apprendre aux admirateurs de M. Oscar Wilde une nouvelle inédite. Un de ses amis a eu l'heureuse imprudence de me confier que Oscar Wilde avait écrit pendant son séjour à Paris une piécette en français, *Salomé*, il publiera en outre dans quelques mois un volume de contes fantastiques, l'*Auberge des Songes*, et prochainement on jouera de lui, à Londres, un drame en quatre actes sur la vie moderne.

JACQUES DAURELLE.

An English Poet in Paris

Oscar Wilde

On a recent evening, in a cafe on the left bank, we were chatting about various things, when the poets Stuart Merrill and Henri de Régnier entered,[1] accompanied by a young man built like Hercules, elegantly and properly dressed, except for a pink shirt front that enlivened his black overcoat.

Stuart Merrill introduced us to Oscar Wilde, whom most of us only knew by reputation. The vigorous aspect of his person and the redness of his beardless face, which evoked the vision of a red moon, was a little surprising. This is not how we imagined the refined poet, the subtle and delicate critic of whom Stuart Merrill and Stéphane Mallarmé often spoke with great admiration.[2]

As the conversation sparkled amongst the clouds of smoke, Mr. Stuart Merrill suddenly said to me:

"Do you know that this English writer, almost unknown in Paris, is an extraordinary man? I assure you that his first book, *Poems*, published around 1876,[3] is a pure masterpiece. And nothing is more delicious than his volume of tales, *The Happy Prince,* and the *House of Pomegranates*, published last week.[4] What a pity that I don't have time to translate them into French! I have also collected a lot of charming anecdotes about Wilde that make him quite interesting to us. When he studied at Oxford, he dressed in knee-breeches, with a velvet waistcoat and lace sleeves. It even seems that he went out with a lily or a sunflower in his hand.

"One day, his fellow students found him in his rooms, absorbed in the contemplation of a china vase. They asked him what he was doing.

"'I'm trying to live up to my china,' Oscar Wilde replied gravely.

"Another day, in America, Marion Crawford asked him why he seemed sad.[5]

"And Wilde answered:

1. Stuart Fitzrandolph Merrill (1863–1915) was an American poet who wrote mostly in French. Like Henri de Régnier (1864–1936), a French poet, he was a symbolist.

2. Stéphane Mallarmé (1842–1898) was a French symbolist poet.

3. Wilde's *Poems* was published in 1881.

4. Wilde's collections of fairy tales: *The Happy Prince and Other Tales* (1888), and *A House of Pomegranates* (1891).

5. Francis Marion Crawford (1854–1909) was an American novelist. He was the nephew of Julia Ward Howe. In the source his name is given as "Mario Crawford".

"'I am sad because half the world does not believe in God and the other half does not believe in me.'

"And I assure you that he doesn't do these things as a pose. He is exquisitely sincere; and the peculiarities of his costume—the red waistcoat he sometimes exhibits, the colored shirts he likes to wear—should not lead us to compare him to Sâr Péladan.[1] By his looks, his tastes, and his talent, he brings to mind Théophile Gautier quite clearly."

At that moment, Oscar Wilde offered us cigarettes and told us with a phlegmatic air, without the slightest smile on his lips:

"These are cigarettes from Egypt. They are excellent. By the way, the English keep Egypt only because it is the country that produces the best cigarettes."[2]

I very much wanted to have a one-on-one conversation with Mr. Oscar Wilde. Yesterday evening, around five o'clock, I was able to satisfy my curiosity. I found Mr. Oscar Wilde in a small hotel lounge on the boulevard des Capucines, smoking Egyptian cigarettes on a couch. I saw, cluttering a table, books that our writers had hastened to send him with admiring dedications, along with magazines and photographs of friends.

Mr. Oscar Wilde first told me about Paris and his stay with us:[3]

"Paris is a city that pleases me greatly. Whereas in London we hide everything, in Paris we show everything. We can go wherever we want and nobody thinks of criticizing us. I go to all the places I can experience an emotion. I frequent the Château-Rouge as well as the Café Anglais.[4] What could be more charming than these visits to poets, with whom we chat freely?

"Besides, I love your literature very much. There is an era in your literary history that particularly delights me. It is the era of courtly love. The sensual and mystical poetry of the troubadours is delightful.[5] It had a great influence on the Pre-Raphaelites, on Dante Rossetti, on Swinburne and on myself.

---

1. Joséphin Péladan (1858–1918) was a French novelist who was interested in spirituality and mysticism and who had an unconventional fashion sense. He claimed that a Babylonian king had conferred the title of "Sâr" on his family.

2. *The Critic as Artist*: "ERNEST. Cigarettes have at least the charm of leaving one unsatisfied. | GILBERT. Try one of mine. They are rather good. I get them direct from Cairo. The only use of our attachés is that they supply their friends with excellent tobacco." (CW iv, 142.8–12.)

3. Wilde visited Paris for about two months from late October 1891.

4. The Château-Rouge was known as a district favoured by criminals. Large dormitories—the "Halls of the Dead"—were the resting places of men who had neither the money nor the papers necessary for admission to more reputable lodgings. Wilde visited such a dormitory with friends (Sturgis, 431/399–400). The Café Anglais was a restaurant that was frequented by the wealthy and aristocracy of Paris.

5. The troubadours were composers and performers of lyric poetry, active during the High Middle Ages.

"Your young poets today are also very intriguing. It seems to me that they are returning to romanticism by bringing to their art more flexibility, more delicacy and tension."

Our conversation was interrupted several times by the arrival of visitors, letters, telegrams. However, I asked Mr. Oscar Wilde what artistic religion he had preached in his numerous lectures and in his articles collected under the title *Intentions*.[1] In a soft and languid voice, accompanied by slow gestures, he said to me:

"I have always preached that art is a lie, and a lie is the ideal truth. It is nature that imitates art, not art that imitates nature.[2] That is why a historian who wants to write the history of a century should never study the artistic creations of that century. From such study it must be concluded that the Greeks, who expressed Beauty, were not beautiful, and that the people of the Middle Ages were not grotesque, that they were not as represented by the artists of that time.[3]

"I also argue that the artist does not take his inspiration from nature, but from the 'material', from the instrument he uses. A painter should not make a landscape from the landscape he has before his eyes, but from the colours that are on his palette. Art is the perfect use of a material that is not perfect. I have written and preached ideas. And the newspapers have mocked and criticized me often. It's because in England journalists are always on the side of the public, that is to say on the side of stupidity and ignorance. In France, journalists are more on the side of innovators and artists."

Occasionally Mr. Oscar Wilde took a sip of soda water. I noticed that he was gradually becoming angry.

"Oh!" he said to me, "it annoys me to look for words to express myself."

However, he was willing to continue speaking. So as to explain his theories on the novel, he summarized his book *Dorian Gray*, the theme of which is indeed excessively intriguing. I asked him to tell me one or two memories collected during his travels, and he replied:

---

1. *Intentions*, a collection of essays and dialogues, was published in 1891.

2. Vivian in *The Decay of Lying*: "Paradox though it may seem—and paradoxes are always dangerous things—it is none the less true that Life imitates art far more than Art imitates life." (CW iv, 90.25–7.)

3. Vivian in *The Decay of Lying*: "Do you think that Greek art ever tells us what the Greek people were like? Do you believe that the Athenian women were like the stately dignified figures of the Parthenon frieze, or like those marvellous goddesses who sat in the triangular pediments of the same building? If you judge from the art, they certainly were so. But read an authority, like Aristophanes for instance. You will find that the Athenian ladies laced tightly, wore high-heeled shoes, dyed their hair yellow, painted and rouged their faces, and were exactly like any silly fashionable or fallen creature of our own day. The fact is that we look back on the ages entirely through the medium of Art, and Art, very fortunately, has never once told us the truth." (CW iv, 98.24–99.4.)

"I do not remember anything. The artist must destroy memory, and only be interested in the moment. The man who thinks about his past has no future. I give myself to the present absolutely."

I also wished to know whether the anecdotes told about Mr. Oscar Wilde were accurate.

"Know," he replied with a smile, "that what is true in the life of a man is not what he does, but the legend that is created around him. I have never walked the streets of London with a lily in my hand, because a porter or a cab driver could do the same. This legend only shows the impression that I made on the masses, and it reveals, better than what I did, the tendencies of my temperament."[1]

While he was accompanying me back, Mr. Oscar Wilde added:

"You should never destroy legends. They are what make us see the true face of a man."

I can inform admirers of Mr. Oscar Wilde of his as yet unpublished works. One of his friends fortunately was imprudent enough to confide in me that Oscar Wilde had written during his stay in Paris a small piece in French, *Salomé*;[2] that he will also publish in a few months a volume of fantastic tales, l'*Auberge des Songes*;[3] and soon a four-act drama of his on modern life will be produced in London.[4]

JACQUES DAURELLE.

1. Carrying a flower: see p. 44, note 1.

2. Shortly after his arrival in Paris Wilde had told the English poet Wilfrid Scawen Blunt (1840–1922), and possibly others, that he was writing a play in French (Ellmann, 320/339). Wilde claimed that he drafted *Salomé* in a frenzy of inspiration, after recounting his version of the story to a group of young writers (Sturgis, 436/404).

3. Wilde did not publish a collection titled l'*Auberge des Songes* (*The Inn of Dreams*). In 1942 René Guillot de Saix published *Les Songes merveilleux du Dormeur éveillé. Le Chant du Cygne – contes parlés d'Oscar Wilde* (*The Wonderful Dreams of the Awakened Sleeper. Swan Song – Spoken Stories by Oscar Wilde*). The book is divided into three parts, the titles of which de Saix claimed in his preface had been chosen by Wilde. Part three, "L'Auberge des Songes", begins with Daurelle's interview. See also Mead, D. (2015). Swan Song: spoken stories by Oscar Wilde collected by Guillot de Saix. *The Wildean*, 47, 101–8.

4. Rehearsals for Wilde's first society comedy, *Lady Windermere's Fan*, began in February 1892 and the play premiered on the 20th.

The Pictorial World (London, UK), 19 Dec. 1891[1]

Mr. Oscar Wilde gives himself away to a press representative here on the subject of things French, mainly upon the drama. He says that he is now writing a one-act tragedy in French and a four-act comedy in English.[2] The tragedy is mediaeval and the comedy is *fin de siècle*, and he wants to see both plays produced in Paris because he says French taste for the theatre is far superior to that of England. In England, according to the Apostle of Aesthetics, the stage is greatly influenced by the "whims and rulings of the public." Along with other misguided individuals, I was under the impression that the French stage is also greatly influenced by the whims and rulings of the public, but Mr. Wilde won't have it. Mr. Wilde loves to indulge in paradoxes, often highly ingenious and clever, and he has delivered himself of a *mot* on this subject which I am sure is rightly delightful to himself. The English public, he says, has but little taste for poetry; consequently that art has shaped an original course and developed great excellence. If the English public had been as indifferent to the drama as it is to poetry, the British stage [?w]ould certainly have taken a more original form and possessed greater merit. "The public is a modern invention," he cries, "and it scarcely existed until it found a voice—the newspaper. In the Middle Ages, prince and Court gave a standard for art, and all three were in sympathy. Courts and princes are of the past—at least, such Courts and princes as guide a nation's art. The public has developed a taste for the arts—yes; but that taste is often so perverted that when it dictates it misleads. If the dramatist does not find a public which can appreciate his work, he must live for his art. It is no sacrifice to follow a high standard of art and miss the public's approval, but it is a sacrifice to listen and to shape one's work according to a false appreciation."

Mr. Wilde did not hesitate to express himself freely as to the novels of Zola. Zola seems to him one of the greatest writers of our times, and is even greater as a poet in his thought than a romancer. He animates lifeless subjects and makes them the leading characters of his stories. The earth in *La Terre* and the mine in *Germinal* are huge monsters which appeal to us like the heroes of some great epic.[3] It is the Earth which is so cruel, so relentless, so monstrous in *La Terre*. In

---

1. The copy text is a clipping in a scrapbook once owned by Stuart Mason (No. 227, Oscar Wilde Scrapbook Vol. 2, Honma Hisao Collection, Jissen Women's University Rare Books). The newspaper title and the date are written at the top of the clipping, presumably by Mason. It is unclear whether Wilde spoke to a representative of *The Pictorial World* or if this article quotes an earlier, unidentified interview.

2. *Salomé* and *Lady Windermere's Fan*.

3. *La Terre* (*The Soil*; 1887) is the fifteenth novel in Zola's Rougon–Macquart cycle. It chronicles the disintegration of a family of farmers. *Germinal* (1885) is the thirteenth novel in the cycle. It follows a young man who begins working in a coal mine and embraces socialist politics. In *The Decay of Lying* Vivian interrupts his criticism of Zola to concede that: "He is not without power.

Germinal the great dark mine seems to realise the awful *rôle* it plays in the destinies of men.

"Mr. Oscar Wilde and the Lord Chamberlain," *The Pall Mall Gazette* (London, UK), 28 June 1892, 4[1]

Mr. Wilde to Change his Nationality.

The Lord Chamberlain's refusal to license Mr. Oscar Wilde's new play, "Salomé," will deprive London play-goers of the advantage of seeing Mdme. Sarah Bernhardt in the title rôle.[2] There is nothing to prevent Mr. Oscar Wilde from producing his French play at an invitation performance in London—and possibly he will do so[3]—but, unfortunately, the engagements of Mdme. Bernhardt and M. Albert Darmont will not admit of their taking the parts for which they were cast, and which they have already rehearsed.[4]

Mr. Oscar Wilde has been interviewed by a representative of the *Pall Mall Gazette*. The prohibition of "Salomé" is the source of intense disappointment to the talented author; and naturally so, for his work had commanded remarkable interpretation at the hands of Mdme. Bernhardt and her colleagues. Mr. Wilde informed our representative of his intention to leave England and settle in France, where he will take out letters of naturalization as soon as the necessary formalities and terms of residence have been completed.[5]

Indeed at times, as in *Germinal*, there is something almost epic in his work." (CW iv, 79, lines 1–2.) See also "Newport Gossip," *The Sunday Herald* (Boston, MA), 23 July 1882, 9, p. 443.

1. This is the first published account of the interview given in more detail in "The Censure and 'Salome'," *The Pall Mall Gazette* (London, UK), 29 June, 1892, 1–2, pp. 603–6. It is one of the three interviews referred to by Wilde in his letter to the artist William Rothenstein (CL, 531).

2. The Lord Chamberlain, who had the authority to veto performance of any play, was E. F. S. Pigott. He thought *Salome* "half Biblical, half pornographic," (Sturgis, 455/423). His refusal to license the play had been announced in "London Day by Day," *The Daily Telegraph* (London, UK), 27 June 1892, 5.

3. That is, a performance to which the public would not be admitted. There was no performance in London, invitation or otherwise, during Wilde's lifetime.

4. Auguste Albert Darmont (1863–1913) was a playwright as well as Bernhardt's newest leading man. He had recently toured with her in Australia and North America and was appearing alongside her in a season at the Royal English Opera House. Rehearsals for *Salomé* took place during June (CW v, 341).

5. Wilde did not take out letters of naturalisation in France. On 11 July he wrote to Arthur Fish, who had apparently inquired about the plan: "As regards the idea of my becoming a French citizen, I have not yet decided. I am very much hurt not merely at the action of the Licenser of Plays, but at the pleasure expressed by the entire Press of England at the suppression of my work." (CL, 531.)

[Maurice Sisley], "Courrier des Spectacles," *Le Gaulois* (Paris, France), 28 June 1892, 4[1]

✂   *Several paragraphs that are unrelated to Wilde. In the copy text the first three lines of the relevant section are obscured by tape.*

être reprentée pour la première fois lundi prochain au Royal English Opera, avec Mme Sarah Bernhardt comme principal interprète, a été interdite par la censure.

  » L'auteur me déclare qu'en présence de cette mesure maladroite et injuste il va se faire naturaliser Français et que *Salomé* sera jouée à Paris et à Saint-Pétersbourg par la tournée Sarah Bernhardt. »

✂   *Several paragraphs that are unrelated to Wilde.*

Entertainments Letter

✂   *Several paragraphs that are unrelated to Wilde. In the copy text the first three lines of the relevant section are obscured by tape.*

to be performed for the first time next Monday at the Royal English Opera, with Mme Sarah Bernhardt as principal performer, has been banned by the censorship.[2]

  The author tells me that in the face of this clumsy and unfair measure he will become naturalised French and that *Salomé* will be performed in Paris and St. Petersburg on Sarah Bernhardt's tour.[3]

✂   *Several paragraphs that are unrelated to Wilde.*

1. See below for an annotated English translation. This is the first published account of the interview given in more detail in Maurice Sisley, "La Salomé de M. Oscar Wilde," *Le Gaulois* (Paris, France), 29 June 1892, 1, pp. 607–12. It is one of the three interviews referred to by Wilde in his letter to the artist William Rothenstein (CL, 531).

2. The next Monday was 4 July. Advertisements for Bernhardt's season that appeared before the announcement of the censorship did not project as far as 4 July. The first advertisements that did appeared in the morning papers on 27 June and listed *La Tosca* for 4 July. Either there had been no plans to stage *Salomé* on 4 July or Bernhardt was made aware of Pigott's decision by the 26 June at the latest.

3. After the close of her London season in July Bernhardt had plans to tour in Belgium, the Netherlands, Austria, and Russia (*L'Écho de Paris* (Paris, France), 26 July 1892, 4). She never appeared as *Salomé*. For the play's premiere in Paris see p. 660, note 1.

"The Censure and 'Salome'," *The Pall Mall Gazette* (London, UK), 29 June, 1892, 1–2[1]

The Lord Chamberlain has declined to authorize the representation of Mr. Oscar Wilde's French play, "Salomé," so the *première* will probably be given in Paris instead of London.[2]

I should show (writes a representative of the *Pall Mall Gazette*) but small appreciation of Mr. Wilde's courtesy were I to describe the piece, or do more than refer incidentally to a conversation that would have appeared in this column on the eve of the first performance had "Salomé" been licensed for representation. I may, however, be permitted to say that, judging from what I saw at rehearsal, Art has suffered by the Lord Chamberlain's action, for with such interpreters as Mdme. Sarah Bernhardt and M. Albert Darmont there was no danger that the author's dignified treatment of the Biblical story would be degraded. I have had the advantage of reading a great many forbidden plays, for in Paris the Censure is applied more frequently than in London, and I have no hesitation in saying that in nine cases out of ten the prohibitive measure is a mistaken policy. It is not pretended that there is any religious or moral gain to compensate for the wrong done to Art. Diametrically opposed standards seem to be set up by the Censure in passing judgment on religious and social dramas. If Justice does not suffer every time some monstrous injustice is handled by the playwright, why should Religion suffer when the acts of its oppressors are made the subject of artistic treatment by the dramatic author? The public can be trusted to save Religion from insult.

This is, of course, but the expression of my own opinion. It was with these thoughts running in my mind that I called on Mr. Oscar Wilde yesterday to beg him to modify an earlier interview he had given me in such particulars as might be important in view of the Lord Chamberlain's decision.[3]

---

1. H & S, b103. Reprinted with minor variations as "The Censure and 'Salome'", *The Pall Mall Budget* (London, UK), 30 June, 1892, 947 (which is reprinted in Mikhail, 186–9; excerpted in Mason, 370–74; and Hyde, 140; and quoted in Ellmann, 351–2/372–3). Quoted in Pearson, 228; and Sturgis, 455/423–4. Ellmann, 351/372, attributes the article to Robert Ross but, as Schroeder, 129, points out, there is no proof that Ross was the interviewer and it is likely that Ellmann is thinking of [Robert Ross], "Mr. Oscar Wilde on Mr. Oscar Wilde," *St. James's Gazette* (London, UK), 18 Jan. 1895, 4–5, pp. 648–54. This is one of the three interviews referred to by Wilde in his letter to the artist William Rothenstein (CL, 531). The author was accompanied for the second part of his interview by Maurice Sisley (see Maurice Sisley, "La Salomé de M. Oscar Wilde," *Le Gaulois* (Paris, France), 29 June 1892, 1, pp. 607–612).

2. Salomé would not be staged in Paris until 1896. See p. 660, note 1.

3. The first brief account of the interview had been printed the day before ("Mr. Oscar Wilde and the Lord Chamberlain," *The Pall Mall Gazette* (London, UK), 28 June 1892, 4, p. 601), but "yesterday" may still be correct as *The Pall Mall Gazette* was an evening paper.

"Personally," said Mr. Wilde, "to have my *première* in Paris instead of London is a great honour, and one that I appreciate sincerely. The pleasure and pride that I have experienced in the whole affair has been that Mdme. Bernhardt, who is undoubtedly the greatest artist on any stage, should have been charmed and fascinated by my play and should have wished to act it."

I could not help feeling that Mr. Wilde's pride was justified. It is the fashion today to write single-rôle pieces for Mdme. Bernhardt. The talents of several authors have been almost exclusively devoted to the task of fitting the talents of the artist. "Salomé" is not a one-rôle drama: it was not written for Mdme. Bernhardt; indeed, it had been in manuscript nearly six months before it was submitted to her.

"Every rehearsal," continued Mr. Wilde, "has been a source of intense pleasure to me. To hear my own words spoken by the most beautiful voice in the world has been the greatest artistic joy that it is possible to experience. So that you see, as far as I am concerned, I care very little about the refusal of the Lord Chamberlain to allow my play to be produced. What I do care about is this, that the Censorship apparently regards the stage as the lowest of all the arts, and looks on acting as a vulgar thing. The painter is allowed to take his subjects where he chooses. He can go to the great Hebrew and Hebrew–Greek literature of the Bible and can paint Salomé dancing, or Christ on the cross, or the Virgin with her child. Nobody interferes with the painter. Nobody says painting is such a vulgar art that you must not paint sacred things. The sculptor is equally free. He can carve St. John the Baptist in his camel-hair, and fashion the Madonna or Christ in Bronze or in marble as he wills. Yet nobody says to him sculpture is such a vulgar art that you must not carve sacred things. And the writer—the poet—he also is quite free. I can write about any subject I choose. For me there is no Censorship. I can take any incident I like out of sacred literature and treat it as I choose, and there is no one to say to the poet, 'Poetry is such a vulgar art that you must not use it in treating sacred subjects.' But there is a Censorship over the stage and acting, and the basis of that Censorship is that, while vulgar subjects may be put on the stage and acted, while everything that is mean and low and shameful in life can be portrayed by actors, no actor is to be permitted to present, under artistic conditions, the great and ennobling subjects taken from the Bible. The insult in the suppression of 'Salomé' is an insult to the stage as a form of art, and not to me."[1]

1. Wilde expressed himself similarly in a letter to the artist William Rothenstein, and then complained that "not one single actor has protested against this insult to the stage – not even Irving, who is always prating about the Art of the Actor. This shows how few actors are artists." (CL, 531–2.)

"I understand that Mdme. Bernhardt's engagements will not allow her to play 'Salomé' at an invitation performance. We shall not see your play in London, then?"

"I shall publish 'Salomé.'[1] No one has the right to interfere with me, and no one shall interfere with me. The people who are injured are the actors; the art that is vilified is the art of acting. I hold that this is as fine as any other art, and to refuse it the right to treat great and noble subjects is an insult to the stage. The action of the Censorship in England is odious and ridiculous. What can be said of a body that forbids Massenet's 'Hérodiade,' Gounod's 'Reine de Saba,' Rubinstein's 'Judas Maccabaeus,' and allows 'Divorçons' to be placed on any stage?[2] The artistic treatment of moral and elevating subjects is discouraged, while a free course is given to the representation of disgusting and revolting subjects."

"How came you to write 'Salomé' in French?"

"My idea of writing the play was simply this: I have one instrument that I know I can command, and that is the English language. There was another instrument to which I listened all my life, and I wanted once to touch this new instrument to see whether I could make any beautiful thing out of it. The play was written in Paris some six months ago, where I read it to some young poets, who admired it immensely. Of course there are modes of expression that a French man of letters would not have used, but they give a certain relief or colour to the play. A great deal of the curious effect that Maeterlinck produces comes from the fact that he, a Flamand by grace, writes in an alien language.[3] The same thing is true of Rossetti, who, though he wrote in English, was essentially Latin in temperament."

During this part of our interview the correspondent of the *Gaulois* was present. The conversation was consequently carried on in French, and my colleague remarked on the admirable way that Mr. Wilde spoke the language. This elicited from him a splendid tribute to Paris, "the centre of art, the artistic capital of the world."

1. *Salomé* was published simultaneously in Paris and London on 22 Feb. 1893 (CW v, 351).

2. Jules Émile Frédéric Massenet (1842–1912) was a French composer. His opera, *Hérodiade*, which told the story of Salomé and John the Baptist, was first performed in Brussels in 1881 after the manager of the Paris Opera House, Auguste Vaucorbeil, refused it because he thought the libretto underdeveloped. Charles-François Gounod (1818–1893) was a French composer whose opera, *La reine de Saba* (*The Queen of Sheba*), was premiered in Paris in 1862. Anton Grigoryevich Rubinstein (1829–1894) was a Russian pianist and composer who wrote several operas on biblical themes, including *Judas Maccabaeus*. Wilde saw him perform in London in 1877 (Sturgis, 109/108). All three of the operas Wilde mentions here were censored by the Lord Chamberlain. *Divorçons* was not.

3. Maurice Polydore Marie Bernard Maeterlinck (1862–1949) was a Belgian writer who was Flemish but wrote in French.

"If the Censure refuses 'Salomé,'" said Mr. Wilde, for at the time of my first interview the decision of the Lord Chamberlain had not been announced, "I shall leave England and settle in France, where I will take out letters of naturalization. I will not consent to call myself a citizen of a country that shows such narrow mindedness in its artistic judgments."

My colleague of the *Gaulois* made a movement of surprise....

"I am not English, I'm Irish, which is quite another thing."

"To continue the story of 'Salomé'—"

"A few weeks ago," said Mr. Wilde, "I met Mdme. Sarah Bernhardt at Mr. Henry Irving's. She had heard of my play and asked me to read it to her. I did so, and she at once expressed a wish to play the title-rôle. Of course it has been a great disappointment to her and to her company not to have played this piece in London. We have been rehearsing for three weeks, the costumes, scenery, and everything has been prepared, and we are naturally disappointed. Still all are looking forward now to producing it for the first time in Paris, where the actor is appreciated and the stage is regarded as an artistic medium. It is remarkable how little art there is in the work of dramatic critics in England. You find column after column of description, but the critic rarely knows how to praise an artistic work. The fact is, it requires an artist to praise art; any one can pick it to pieces. For my own part, I don't know which I despise most, blame or praise. The latter, I think, for it generally happens that the qualities praised are those one regards with the least satisfaction oneself."

Just as I was taking leave of Mr. Oscar Wilde the conversation went back to the question of prohibition:—

"What makes the Lord Chamberlain's action to me most contemptible, and the only point in which I feel at all aggrieved in the matter, is that he allows the personality of an artist to be presented in a caricature on the stage,[1] and will not allow the work of that artist to be shown under very rare and very beautiful conditions."

1. Wilde refers to *The Poet and the Puppets*, a parody of *Lady Windermere's Fan* by Charles Brookfield (1857–1913) and James Mackey Glover (1861–1931), premiered on 19 May 1892. Charles Hawtrey (1858–1923) played a version of Wilde. Wilde also complained about this seeming double-standard in his letter to William Rothenstein: "He [Pigott] even allows the stage to be used for the purpose of the caricaturing of the personalities of artists, and at the same moment when he prohibited *Salomé*, he licensed a burlesque of Lady Windermere's Fan in which an actor dressed up like me and imitated my voice and manner!!!" (CL, 531–2.)

Maurice Sisley, "La Salomé de M. Oscar Wilde," *Le Gaulois* (Paris, France), 29 June 1892, 1[1]

CONVERSATION AVEC L'AUTEUR

(De notre correspondant ordinaire)

Londres, 28 juin.

La *Salomé* de M. Oscar Wilde ne sera pas jouée à Londres; ainsi l'a décidé la censure anglaise.

La raison donnée par la censure, c'est que les personnages de la pièce sont bibliques: Hérode, Salomé, Tocanahan.

Ce dernier masque, dit-elle, le personnage de saint Jean-Baptiste.

Dans une scène qui est le point culminant de la pièce, Salomé exprime à Tocanahan l'amour qu'il lui a inspiré. Elle le fait en termes passionnés. Tocanahan repousse Salomé, qui ordonne alors qu'il soit tué.

Dans la scène suivante on apporte à Salomé la tête de Tocanahan.

Ivre de fureur et d'amour, elle prend cette tête qu'elle couvre de baisers. Hérode a assisté à cette scène et ordonne que Salomé soit tuée à son tour.

Ce sont ces situations, qui forment un ensemble d'études psychologiques d'une rare puissance et le dialogue nerveux qu'elles ont inspiré à l'auteur, qui sont la cause de l'interdiction de *Salomé*.

M. Oscar Wilde répond à cet acte quelque peu *sommaire* en déclarant qu'il va se faire naturaliser Français.

Je dois ajouter que M. Wilde a sollicité de M. Bemberg, l'auteur d'*Elaine*, de faire pour *Salomé* une musique de scène. M. Bemberg a accepté. Il se mettra à l'œuvre dès le lendemain de la première représentation d'*Elaine*.

Les faits que je vous ai fait connaître hier, par dépêche, ont besoin de quelques commentaires, et j'ai été les prendre chez l'auteur lui-même.

M. Oscar Wilde me fait le plus aimable des accueils, je lui expose le but de ma visite et, immédiatement, il me dit:

— Oui, ma résolution est bien prise. Puisque, en Angleterre, il est impossible de faire jouer une œuvre d'art, je vais entrer dans une nouvelle patrie que

---

1. See below for an annotated English translation. H & S, b102. Excerpted in "Les Théatres," *Le XIXᵉ Siècle* (Paris, France), 1 July 1892, 3. Translated into English and excerpted in "Mr. Oscar Wilde," *The Standard* (London, UK), 30 June 1892, 5, pp. 730–731; "The Rage of Bunthorne," *The New York Times* (New York, NY), 18 July 1892, 2; Glaenzer, R. B. (1906). *Decorative Art in America*. Brentano's. 147–8; and Mikhail, 189–90. Quoted in Ellmann, 352/373. Sisley was accompanied by the author of "Mr. Oscar Wilde and the Lord Chamberlain," *The Pall Mall Gazette* (London, UK), 28 June 1892, 4, p. 601 / "The Censure and 'Salome'," *The Pall Mall Gazette* (London, UK), 29 June, 1892, 1–2, pp. 603–6. This is one of the three interviews referred to by Wilde in his letter to William Rothenstein (CL, 531).

j'aime déjà depuis longtemps. Il n'y a qu'un Paris, voyez-vous, et Paris est en France; c'est la ville des artistes, je dirais volontiers: c'est la ville... artiste.

» J'adore Paris. J'adore aussi votre belle langue française, qui, avec la grecque, sont les deux langues par excellence, pour moi du moins.

» Ici, on a l'esprit essentiellement anti-artistique et d'une étroitesse dont les exemples sont malheureusement trop nombreux.

» L'ostracisme dont vient d'être frappée *Salomé* vous donnera une idée des mœurs anglaises. Impossible de mettre à la scène des personnages bibliques ou touchant à la Bible.

» La censure a interdit *Samson et Dalila*, de Saint-Saëns, *Hérodiade*, de Massenet. On ne pourrait jouer *Athalie*, la « superbe *Athalie* », de Racine, sur une scène anglaise. Je ne sais vraiment ce qui l'emporte, de l'odieux ou du ridicule, dans la mesure prise.

— Avez-vous donc une aussi mauvaise opinion de vos compatriotes ?

— Oh! ils ont des qualités... pratiques, je ne le nie pas; mais, en ma qualité d'artiste, ce n'est pas celle — loin de là — que j'admire le plus. Je ne suis pas d'ailleurs, à l'heure où je vous parle, Anglais, je suis encore *Irlandais*, ce qui n'est pas du tout le même chose. Certes, j'ai des amis anglais que j'aime beaucoup. Mais je n'aime pas la *race anglaise*.

» Je vous disais tout à l'heure que les sujets bibliques ou s'y rattachant étaient interdits : en revanche, la censure permettra sur toutes les scènes anglaises *Divorçons*. Bien plus, elle permettra toute pièce même *Salomé*, à condition que je la fasse jouer devant une salle d'invités. Par conséquent, si j'étais riche, je pourrais me payer le plaisir de faire entendre ma pièce à tous ceux qu'il me plairait.

» Voilà l'hypocrisie anglaise, que très justement vous critiquez en France. *L'Anglais en général, mais c'est Tartufe assis dans une boutique!* « Les nombreuses exceptions, ajoute en souriant mon interlocuteur, prouvent la règle. »

Ici je demande à M. Oscar Wilde quelle a été la genèse de sa *Salomé*, comment l'idée lui est venue, d'écrire une pièce en français.

— Il y a trois mois, dit-il, que j'ai écrit *Salomé*. Votre belle langue française m'a séduit. J'ai tenté d'exprimer ce que je sentais... en français. Et un jour j'ai lu en petit comité à quelques-uns de mes bons amis de France, de vrais artistes, l'acte que j'avais composé.

» Ils l'apprécièrent et me donnèrent ainsi du courage. Je revins en Angleterre presque au même moment où Mme Sarah Bernhardt y arrivait. Je la rencontrai un soir au « Lyceum ». Elle me parla de ma pièce, dont elle avait entendu dire du bien par des amis communs, et me demanda de lui confier le manuscrit. Elle le lut, s'en montra très éprise et me demanda de jouer Salomé. Je ne pouvais espérer une plus grande artiste — Sarah Bernhardt est la plus grande artiste du monde — pour interpréter Salomé.

» J'acceptai avec grand plaisir, et aussitôt on se mit à répéter. Malgré moi, je voulais espérer dans un peu de justice et de bon sens de la part de la censure, et la représentation était fixée au lundi 4 juillet.

» Maintenant tout est changé. Je pourrais faire jouer la pièce devant un public d'invités, mais je ne pourrais avoir ni Mme Sarah Bernhardt, ni M. Darmont, un jeune acteur de grand avenir, pour jouer les deux rôles principaux, car ils sont engagés par des directeurs qui ne pourraient — et je le comprends parfaitement — perdre une ou deux soirées de recettes.

» Par conséquent, vous n'entendrez pas *Salomé*, à Londres, mais vous pourrez l'entendre à Paris, au retour de Mme Sarah Bernhardt.

» Certes, j'ai certains tours de phrase, certaines expressions que n'emploierait pas un auteur français; mais il est des originalités qui, peut-être, donneront du relief au style. Maeterlinck n'a-t-il pas, lui aussi, des expressions à lui, à lui seul, qui produisent leur effet, l'effet que l'auteur ou l'écrivain veut atteindre ?

» En Angleterre, Rossetti, le poète que tout le monde littéraire admire, a des expressions qu'aucun auteur anglais n'oserait employer et qui, cependant, ont à la fois et une force et une grâce particulières qui frappent les Anglais eux-mêmes.

Il ne me restait plus qu'à remercier M. Oscar Wilde de ses intéressantes explications. Comme lui, je trouve inique la décision de la censure, mais le résultat produit n'est pas pour me déplaire. C'est Paris qui, le premier, applaudira *Salomé*, qui sera pour M. Oscar Wilde, je l'espère, la meilleure lettre de naturalisation.

Maurice SISLEY.

The Salomé of Mr. Oscar Wilde

A CONVERSATION WITH THE AUTHOR

(*From our ordinary correspondent*)

London, 28 June.

Mr. Oscar Wilde's *Salomé* will not be played in London; so decided the English censor.

The reason given by the censor is that the characters in the play are biblical: Herod, Salomé, Jokanaan.

This last is a disguise for the person of Saint John the Baptist.

In a scene that is the highlight of the play, Salomé expresses to Jokanaan the love he inspired in her. She does so in passionate terms. Jokanaan rebuffs Salomé, who then orders that he be killed.

In the following scene, Jokanaan's head is brought to Salomé.

Drunk with fury and love, she takes that head and covers it with kisses. Herod witnesses this scene and orders that Salomé be killed as well.

It is these situations, which form a psychological study of rare power, combined with the tense dialogue which they have inspired the author to produce, which are the reasons for the ban of Salomé.

Mr. Oscar Wilde responds to this somewhat capricious act by declaring that he will become a naturalized Frenchman.

I should add that Mr. Wilde asked Mr. Bemberg, the author of *Elaine*, to compose music for *Salomé*. Mr. Bemberg accepted. He will get to work the day after the first performance of *Elaine*.[1]

The facts that I made known to you yesterday, by dispatch,[2] require some comment, and I went to seek such from the author himself.

Mr. Oscar Wilde gave me the most kind welcome, I explained the purpose of my visit to him, and immediately he said to me:

"Yes, I have made my decision. Because, in England, it is impossible to deliver a work of art, I will enter a new homeland that I have loved for a long time. There is only one Paris, you see, and Paris is France; it is the city of artists, I would gladly say the artist's city.

"I love Paris. I also love your beautiful French language, which, along with Greek, are the two languages above all others, at least for me.

"Here, we have an essentially anti-artistic spirit of restrictiveness, the examples of which are unfortunately too numerous.

"The snubbing of *Salomé* will give you an idea of English manners. It is impossible to put on the stage characters that are biblical or that touch the Bible.

"The censor has banned *Samson and Delilah* by Saint-Saëns, and Massenet's *Hérodiade*. We could not play *Athalie*, the "superb *Athalie*", by Racine, on an English stage.[3] I do not really know who wins by these measures, the odious or the ridiculous."

"Do you have such a bad opinion of your compatriots?"

"Oh! they are… practical, I do not deny it; but, as an artist, it is not that quality—far from it—that I admire the most. As a matter of fact, at present I am not English, I am Irish, which is not at all the same thing. Certainly, I have English friends whom I love dearly. But I do not love the English race.

1. Herman Emanuel Bemberg Ocampo (1859–1931) was a Paris-born composer. The premiere of his grand opera *Elaine* at Covent Garden was scheduled for 2 July 1892 but postponed to the 5th.

2. See [Maurice Sisley], "Courrier des Spectacles," *Le Gaulois* (Paris, France), 28 June 1892, 4, p. 602.

3. Charles-Camille Saint-Saëns (1835–1921) was a French composer and pianist. The French public reacted negatively to the prospect of his opera, *Samson and Delilah*, being performed, and he abandoned work on it for several years. It was premiered in Weimar in 1877. Racine's *Athalie* (1691) could not be licensed for production in the United Kingdom because it was drawn from the Bible.

"I told you earlier that biblical or related subjects were prohibited: however, the censor will allow *Divorçons* to play on the English stage. What is more, it will allow any piece, even *Salomé*, provided that I produce it for invited guests. Therefore, if I were rich, I could afford the pleasure of making my piece heard by anyone I like.

"This is English hypocrisy, which you quite rightly criticize in France. *The typical Englishman is Tartuffe seated in a shop!*[1] The numerous exceptions," added my smiling interviewee, "prove the rule."

Here I asked Mr. Oscar Wilde about the genesis of his *Salomé*, and how he came up with the idea to write a play in French.

"It's been three months," he said, "since I wrote *Salomé*. Your beautiful French language seduced me. I tried to express what I felt... in French. And one day I read to a small group of some of my good friends from France, real artists, the act that I had composed.

"They liked it and gave me courage. I returned to England almost at the same time as Mme. Sarah Bernhardt arrived here. I met her one evening at the Lyceum.[2] She spoke to me about my play, of which she had heard good things from mutual friends, and asked me to give her the manuscript. She read it, was very taken by it, and asked me if she could play Salomé. I could not have hoped for a greater artist—Sarah Bernhardt is the greatest artist in the world—to interpret Salomé.

"I accepted with great pleasure, and immediately we started rehearsing. In spite of myself, I hoped for a little justice and common sense on the part of the censor, and the premiere was fixed for Monday, July 4.[3]

"Now everything is changed. I could have the play performed in front of an audience of guests, but I could have neither Mme. Sarah Bernhardt nor Mr. Darmont, a young actor with a great future, to play the two main roles, because they are hired by directors who could not—and I understand it perfectly—lose one or two evenings of receipts.[4]

"Therefore, you will not hear *Salomé* in London, but you will be able to hear her in Paris, when Mme. Sarah Bernhardt returns.

"Of course, I use certain phrases, certain expressions, that a French author would not use; but there are originalities which, perhaps, will give relief to the style. Does not Maeterlinck, too, have expressions of his own which have their effect, the effect that the author or the writer wants to achieve?

1. The eponymous character in Molière's comedy, *Tartuffe* (1664), is a hypocritical religious devotee.
2. A theatre in London's West End under the management of Henry Irving.
3. Planned premiere on 4 July: see p. 602, note 2.
4. Darmont was cast as Jokanaan ("The Censorship and 'Salome,'" *The Pall Mall Gazette* (London, UK), 6 July 1892, 1–2, p. 802), suggesting that Wilde saw this as one of the two main roles.

"In England, Rossetti, the poet whom the entire literary world admires, has expressions which no English author would dare to use and which, however, have both a particular force and a grace which are striking to the English."

It only remained for me to thank Mr. Oscar Wilde for his interesting explanations. Like him, I find the censorship decision unfair, but the result does not displease me. It is Paris that will be the first to applaud *Salomé*. This will, I hope, be for Mr. Oscar Wilde the best letter of naturalisation.

Maurice SISLEY.

Henry Bauer, "La Ville et le Théâtre," *L'Écho de Paris* (Paris, France), 2 July 1892, 1[1]

✂ *Several paragraphs about Sarah Bernhardt's successful London season.*

M. Oscar Wilde, littérateur et poète anglais, dont en ce moment même un drame obtient au Saint-James-Theater un très vif succès, eut récemment la fantaisie d'écrire, en français, une *Salomé* d'après « Hérodias », la nouvelle de Gustave Flaubert. Quand il eut achevé sa pièce, il la lut à Sarah Bernhardt qui immédiatement décida de la jouer et commença les répétitions. Elle avait accepté de créer le personnage de Salomé et c'eût été un régal pour le public anglais de la voir en costume de princesse des Hébreux *danser* le pas des sept voiles devant Hérode, étaler ses séductions pour Siocacanahan [*sic*] et lancer au prophète une

1. See below for an annotated English translation. This is one of the three interviews referred to by Wilde in his letter to William Rothenstein (CL, 531). Rothenstein wrote to Wilde shortly after the censoring of *Salomé*, evidently to ask his friend for further details. Wilde replied: "The *Gaulois*, the *Echo de Paris*, and the *Pall Mall* [*Gazette*] have all had interviews. I hardly know what new thing there is to say." It is possible that Wilde was referring to the article by Jacques Daurelle, "Un Poète Anglais a Paris," *L'Écho de Paris* (Paris, France), 6 Dec. 1891, 2, pp. 593–9. However, that article had been published several months earlier and only made passing reference to Salomé. Instead, it seems likely that Wilde was referring to a more recent article, published about the same time as the interviews in *Le Gaulois* and *The Pall Mall Gazette* (28 and 29 June). Although this article is not formatted as a verbatim interview, the reporter (French theatre critic Henri François Adolphe Bauër; 1851–1915) claims to have attended rehearsals and spoken with Wilde. Wilde wrote to Rothenstein from Bad Homburg, where he was undergoing a rest cure. He arrived on 7 July and left before 12 August (Hamann, C. (1997). Oscar Wilde in Bad Homburg. *The Wildean*, *11*, 39–41). No other articles about Wilde that could be construed as interviews were printed in *L'Écho de Paris* between 27 June, when the censorship of *Salomé* was announced in the British press, and 11 August. Bauer's positive review of the eventual premiere of *Salomé* appeared as "Les Premières Représentations," *L'Écho de Paris* (Paris, France), 13 Feb. 1896, 3.

brûlante déclaration d'amour sensuel. Déjà les décors étaient préparés, une magnifique tunique orientale commandée sur dessin à l'un des plus habiles costumiers de Paris, quand, à la dernière heure, la pièce fut interdite. Il existe à Londres, en ce pays de liberté, une censure, et plus ridicule et plus intraitable que la nôtre, parce qu'elle invoque les principes religieux. Je ne sais pas si le fanatisme catholique, la momerie juive et ses accessoires l'emportent sur l'hypocrisie protestante, sur cette intolérance haineuse cachée derrière l'affirmation du libre examen. C'est elle qui prohibe au théâtre les sujets religieux et les personnages bibliques ; c'est elle qui défendit l'*Hérodiade* de Massenet comme elle avait longtemps empêché l'approche de *la Dame aux Camélias* ; c'est elle qui, personnifiée en une sire Piggot [*sic*] chambellan de la reine et censeur qualifié, supprima *Salomé*. Cette prohibition ne surprit guère ici ; je dirais même qu'elle avait été un peu prévue.

Aussi n'avais-je pas manqué d'assister à quelques répétitions. Hélas ! j'ai à peine vu Sarah Bernhardt indiquer la danse des sept voiles, esquisser ces attitudes hiératiques et les poses voluptueuses sous les gazes polychromes tendues par un chœur de ballerines, au-dessus de sa tête ; mais j'ai attentivement écouté l'acte du débutant en prose française. M. Oscar Wilde n'ignore assurément pas Maiterlinck [*sic*] et il a approprié son dialogue au procédé de répétition de la *Princesse Maleine* ; il a lu Flaubert, Hugo, Huysmans, et il y paraît ; mais sa forme, en dépit de l'imitation, garde une couleur originale, une saveur littéraire très personnelle et sa Salomé est bien une fille légitime de son imagination d'artiste.

Le piquant c'est qu'avant et après l'interdiction, Sarah Bernhardt fut assaillie par tous les auteurs anglais en disponibilité, armés de manuscrits en français. Il y eut plusieurs essais de lectures à l'accent baroque, d'un comique achevé. N'y cherchons point malice.

M. Oscar Wilde, dépossédé de la scène et de son unique interprète, a manifesté une irritation véhémente de la mise à l'index de *Salomé* [*sic*]. Il a secoué la poussière de ses souliers sur l'Angleterre et m'a déclaré qu'il allait se faire naturaliser Français. Certes il n'est pas inconnu sur les rives de la Seine et son exode, à la fin de l'an dernier, par les salons parisiens, fut très brillant. Même nos lecteurs se souviennent peut-être d'une lettre de fort bonne tournure qu'il publia en ce journal, à propos de son appréciation motivée de Swinburne, rapportée dans le mémorial d'Edmond de Goncourt. Mais la mystification est devenue un procédé littéraire de quelque ragoût et l'excentricité semble, au pays de lord Byron, comme un défi jeté à une société de pharisiens, une pierre lancée aux vitraux du tabernacle des préjugés stupides et des conventionnelles servitudes. Déjà le spirituel cavalier, le subtil écrivain avait bravé ses compatriotes, au sortir d'Oxford, par un dandysme bizarre à la Barbey d'Aurevilly, par le costume de des Esseintes. Volontiers, il entrait un lys à la main au bar, au café, demandait un verre d'eau, y mettait une feuille de rose et buvait le verre d'idéal. Plus tard, à cette originalité un peu voulue et hautainement affirmée, à sa causerie d'esprit étincelant et de finesse pénétrante, il ajouta les qualités d'écrivain raffiné et de subtil analyste ; il est même allé jusqu'à l'extrême audace dans le portrait de *Dorian Grey* [*sic*], un roman qui a fait scandale et dont la combinaison de Vautrin et de Rubempré, dans Balzac, peut seule donner une idée.

HENRY BAUER

The City and the Theatres

Mr Oscar Wilde, English writer and poet, whose drama is at this very moment achieving a very great success at the St. James's Theatre,[1] recently had the notion of writing, in French, a *Salomé* taken from "Herodias", the short story by Gustave Flaubert.[2] When he had finished his play, he read it to Sarah Bernhardt, who immediately decided to play it and began rehearsals. She had agreed to create the character of Salomé and it would have been a delight for the English public to see her in the costume of a princess of the Hebrews dancing the dance of the seven veils before Herod, displaying her seductions for Jokanaan and hurling at the prophet a burning declaration of sensual love. The sets had already been prepared, a magnificent oriental tunic ordered from one of the most skilful costume designers in Paris, when, at the last hour, the play was banned. There exists in London, in this country of freedom, a censorship, and one more ridiculous and more intractable than ours, because it invokes religious principles. I don't know if Catholic fanaticism, or Jewish mummery and its paraphernalia, outweigh Protestant hypocrisy, that hateful intolerance hidden behind the assertion of free inquiry. It is this that prohibits religious subjects and biblical characters from the theatre; it was this that forbade Massenet's *Hérodiade* as it had long prevented the appearance of the *Dame aux Camélias*; it was this that, personified in one Sir Pigott [*sic*], chamberlain of the queen and proficient censor, suppressed *Salomé*. The prohibition hardly came as a surprise here; I would even say that it had been somewhat planned.

Therefore I had not failed to attend a few rehearsals. Alas! I have barely seen Sarah Bernhardt outline the dance of the seven veils, sketch the hieratic attitudes and the voluptuous poses under the polychrome gauzes stretched, by a

1. *Lady Windermere's Fan.*

2. Gustave Flaubert (1821–1880) was a French novelist, best known for *Madame Bovary* (1857); Wilde preferred *Salammbô* (1862) and *La Tentation de Saint-Antoine* (*The Temptation of Saint Anthony*; 1874; see also p. 662, note 4) (Wright, 126). Wilde claimed that "Flaubert is my master" (CL, 372), and described the author as France's "one great artist, [...] who is the impeccable master of style." (*The Woman's World*, Jan. 1888; CW vii, No. 91, lines 246–7.) In prison Wilde requested the *Temptation* and *Trois Contes* (*Three Tales*; 1877), a collection of stories that includes *Hérodias* (Wright, 321).

614

chorus of ballerinas, above her head;[1] but I listened attentively to the one act play of the beginner in French prose. Mr Oscar Wilde is certainly not unaware of Maeterlinck and he has adapted his dialogue to the repetitions of *Princess Maleine*;[2] he has read Flaubert, Hugo, Huysmans, and it shows; but his play's form, despite the imitation, retains an original colour, a very personal literary flavour, and his Salomé is indeed a legitimate daughter of his artistic imagination.[3]

The spicy point is that before and after the ban, Sarah Bernhardt was besieged by all the out-of-work English authors, armed with manuscripts in French. There were several attempts at readings in outlandish accents: a sheer comedy. But there was no malice in it.

Mr Oscar Wilde, dispossessed of the stage and of its sole interpreter, expressed vehement irritation at the prohibition of *Salomé*. He shook the dust off his shoes over England and told me he was going to become a naturalised Frenchman. Certainly he is not unknown on the banks of the Seine and his sojourn, at the end of last year, through the Parisian salons, was very brilliant. Even our readers may remember a letter of very good character which he published in this paper, concerning his reasoned appreciation of Swinburne, recorded in the journal of Edmond de Goncourt.[4] But myth has become a stimulating literary device, and eccentricity seems, in the country of Lord Byron, like a challenge cast at a society of Pharisees, a stone thrown at the stained-glass windows of the tabernacle of stupid prejudices and conventional servitudes. Already the witty knight, the subtle writer, had defied his compatriots, on leaving Oxford, with a bizarre dandyism à la Barbey d'Aurevilly, by the costume of des Esseintes.[5] Willingly, lily in hand, he entered the bar, the café, asked for a glass of water, put a rose leaf in it and drank the glass of his ideals. Later, to this somewhat haughtily asserted and quite intentional originality, to his talk with its sparkling wit and penetrating finesse, he added the qualities of a refined writer and a subtle critic; he even went to lengths of extreme audacity in *The Picture of Dorian Gray*, a

1. The description of the dance in Wilde's script is famously brief: "SALOMÉ danse la danse des sept voiles" ("SALOMÉ dances the dance of the seven veils"; CW v, 549.804). An earlier stage direction describes slaves carrying on perfumes and the seven veils and taking off Salomé's shoes (547.774). These may be the ballerinas seen by Bauer.

2. Maeterlinck's first play, printed in 1889 but not performed in the author's lifetime, makes extensive use of repetition (CW v, 406–7).

3. Wilde would later admit that Hugo and Maeterlinck had "interested" him, but denied that they had influenced his work: see [Robert Ross], "Mr. Oscar Wilde on Mr. Oscar Wilde," *St. James's Gazette* (London, UK), 18 Jan. 1895, 4–5, pp. 652–3.

4. Edmond de Goncourt (1822–1896) was a French author. *L'Écho de Paris* was serialising his diaries from 1883. On 17 December 1891 an entry was published in which Wilde was represented as having criticised Swinburne. Wilde's letter correcting what he felt was an error attributable to his imperfect French was printed on 19 December (CL, 504–6).

5. Jules Barbey d'Aurevilly (1808–1889) was a French Decadent novelist and critic. Des Esseintes is the aesthetic protagonist of *À rebours*: see p. 570, note 2.

novel that caused a scandal and of which the combination of Vautrin and Rubempré, in Balzac, can alone give an idea.[1]

HENRY BAUER

"Les Théatres," *Le XIXᵉ Siècle* (Paris, France), 6 July 1892, 3[2]

Nouvelles de la *Salomé* de M. Oscar Wilde.

Le jeune et célèbre esthète anglais vient de passer par Paris, se rendant à Hambourg. Il a en le temps d'annoncer à un reporter que *Salomé* serait donnée ici avec Sarah Bernhardt au mois d'octobre. Et il a ajouté qu'il n'y avait à ses yeux que deux pays artistes, la France… et le Japon. Mais il n'a pas eu jusqu'ici la curiosité d'écrire en japonais.

The Theatres

News of Mr. Oscar Wilde's *Salomé*.

The young and famous English aesthete has just passed through Paris, on his way to Hamburg.[3] He had time to announce to a reporter that *Salomé* will be given here with Sarah Bernhardt in October. And he added that in his eyes there were only two artistic countries, France… and Japan. But thus far he has not had the curiosity to write in Japanese.

---

1. Vautrin and Lucien de Rubempré are characters in Balzac's *Comédie Humaine*. Vautrin, a criminal mastermind, promises to make the younger Rubempré wealthy and powerful if he obeys him. Elsewhere in the cycle Vautrin attempts to exercise a similar influence over another young man, urging him to cure himself of the wicked ideas that torment him by succumbing to them, a moment echoed in Lord Henry's advice to Dorian that: "The only way to get rid of a temptation is to yield to it." (CW iii, 21.22, 377.) Wilde's novel received a number of adverse reviews, including one in the *Scots Observer* that suggested that it had been written for "outlawed noblemen and perverted telegraph boys", a reference to the Cleveland Street Scandal of 1889, when a male brothel was discovered by the police. Wilde responded to this and other reviews; the correspondence is collected in Mason, S. (1908). *Art and Morality*. J. Jacobs. See also CL, 438–9, and CW iii, xliii–xlix.

2. See below for an annotated English translation. Printed simultaneously as "Théâtres," *Le Courrier du Soir* (Paris, France), 7 July 1892, 2. It seems likely that this article was cribbed from a longer untraced interview printed elsewhere.

3. The reporter appears to have misunderstood Wilde, whose destination was not Hamburg but the spa town of Bad Homburg, near Frankfurt.

William Theodore Peters, "Oscar Wilde at Home," *The Sunday Inter Ocean* (Chicago, IL), 16 Dec. 1894, 31[1]

An Impression.

"It is necessary to have an interior where one never is," observed the wicked old Duke, in that witty play, "Paris Fin de Siecle."[2] Nothing if not paradoxical, Mr. Oscar Wilde has a most attractive home at No. 16 Tite street, and it was there that his charming wife presented me to him. Mrs. Wilde receives during the season on Wednesday afternoons, in a drawing-room decorated in white and harmonizing shades of blue and green. If one has the privilege of being admitted to it, the "interior" of No. 16 Tite street is well worthy inspection, for apart from its aesthetic beauty it contains many interesting literary and artistic souvenirs. In Mr. Wilde's study, which is littered with books, pamphlets, and manuscripts, a place for everything and nothing in its place, a veritable paradise for a man of letters, I remarked hanging upon the wall the original manuscript of Keats' "blue" sonnet and looking calmly down from its pedestal, beautiful and "forever young," a life-size bust of the Hermes of Praxiteles.[3] Near by, on a chair, stood a clever imitation of an old Elizabethan painting by Mr. Charles Ricketts, a portrait of the "incomparable Mr. W. H."[4] Leaning against the wall, on the floor

1. William Theodore Peters (1862–1905) was a Brooklyn-born poet and actor. According to Sherard a portrait of Peters was displayed in the Wildes' drawing room (Sherard, R. H. (1905). *Twenty Years in Paris.* Hutchinson & Co. 392). Peters attended Wilde's funeral service. It seems unlikely that Wilde was aware that Peters would publish their conversation. Peters's visit to the Wildes' home must have taken place between late June 1892 (when it was announced that the Lord Chamberlain had refused to license *Salomé*) and February 1893 (when the French edition of *Salomé* was published). Peters states that "Mrs. Wilde receives during the season on Wednesday afternoons", which would seem to fix his visit to a Wednesday between June and August 1892. Wilde was in Bad Homburg for most of July and early August. This suggests that Peters's visit occurred on 10 or 17 August. By the following Wednesday Oscar and Constance had already arrived in Felbrigg for a late summer holiday (*Norwich Mercury* (Norwich, UK), 24 Aug. 1892, 6).
2. An 1890 comedy by French dramatists and journalists Ernest Blum (1836–1907) and Raoul Toche (1850–1895).
3. Keats manuscript: see p. 326, note 4. The Hermes of Praxiteles is a statue that was discovered among the ruins of Ancient Olympia shortly after Wilde visited the diggings in 1877. Wilde's bust was a plaster cast. Wilde told Charles Ricketts that "the plaster did not retain the beauty and transparency of the marble, which is like ivory lit by the sun." (Ricketts, 35.) The 1895 auction catalogue incorrectly describes it as a "colossal bust of Apollo" (Munby, 386).
4. *The Portrait of Mr. W. H.*: see p. 590, note 1. Wilde commissioned Charles Ricketts to paint the portrait of Willie Hughes. Ricketts painted it on "a decaying piece of oak and framed it in a fragment of worm-eaten moulding" (Ricketts, 35–6).

was a nude study of a woman by Mr. Charles Shannon.[1] "What does Cook think of it?" asked Mr. Wilde with a twinkle in his eye.[2]

In the drawing-room is a full-length portrait of the author of "Lady Windermere's Fan," by Mr. Harper Pennington;[3] an etching by Whistler, and a good reproduction of Bastien le Page's portrait of Bernhardt, underneath which is a note in uncertain English by the divine one to Mr. Wilde.[4] Here is also to be seen a portrait of Lady Mount Temple and a graceful drawing by Mr. Graham Robertson of Miss Ellen Terry.[5] The room is filled, but not overcrowded, with bibelots, silver dragee-boxes, silver photograph frames, flowers, rare first editions, pretty lamps, silken cushions—all the usual adjuncts of a smart London drawing-room.

Mrs. Wilde sits on a low couch by the fire, pouring out tea from an old Georgian teapot with a malachite green handle. Cyril, the elder of her two sons, a fine little boy, is perhaps aiding his mother in dispensing hospitality to her guests. Mr. Oscar Wilde has named the two characters in his essay on "The Decay of Lying" after his two children, Cyril and Vivian.[6] Mrs. Wilde, who is one of the London beauties, has a blooming complexion and an abundance of gold-brown hair. She is always tastefully and modishly dressed. On the first night of "Lady Windermere's Fan" she made a very attractive picture in one of the stage boxes, wearing a blue silk gown copied from the style of dress worn by Henrietta Maria in Van Dyck's portrait.[7]

It is easy to be seen that among Mr. Wilde's most ardent admirers not the least is his wife, whose devotion is indeed charming. She has made a complete collection of his journalistic work in a large scrap book, in which I noticed an appreciative review of one of Mr. Richard Le Gallienne's earlier books and an

1. *Ashtoreth*, exhibited at the Grosvenor Gallery in 1888. See Wilson, S. C. (2021). 'Dangerous to chambermaids': *Ashtoreth*, a controversial early work by Charles Shannon, owned by Oscar Wilde. *The Wildean*, *59*, 72–88; and Maier-Sigrist, W. (2022). Where was *Ashtoreth*? *The Wildean*, *60*, 120–1.

2. Perhaps a reference to Edward Tyas Cook (1857–1919), editor of *The Pall Mall Gazette* between 1889 and 1892. The meaning of the reference is unclear.

3. R. G. Harper Pennington (1854–1920) was an American artist. His full length portrait of Wilde was painted as a wedding present.

4. Jules Bastien-Lepage (1848–1884) was a French naturalist painter. His painting of Sarah Bernhardt (1879) won him the cross of the Legion d'Honneur. The etching (1879) was executed by Eugène André Champollion (1848–1901).

5. Georgina, Lady Mount-Temple née Tollemache (1822–1901) was a close friend of Constance. Walford Graham Robertson (1866–1948) was a British painter, illustrator, and author. Robertson's picture of Terry may be the drawing that was reproduced in her autobiography. The engraving Robertson made of Terry as Rosamund in c. 1893 is another possibility.

6. The Wildes' second son was christened, and preferred, Vyvyan, but his parents usually spelt his name "Vivian" (CL, 330).

7. Anthony Van Dyck (1599–1641) was a Flemish artist. He painted many portraits of Queen Henrietta Maria, the wife of Charles I, in several of which she wears blue silk gowns.

article on Mrs. Brown Potter's and Buffalo Bill's first season in London.[1] In this paper he says: "Formerly we sent the Americans the pilgrim fathers; now at length in revenge they send us every spring the pilgrim mothers."[2] "Mr. Wilde hates journalistic work," said Mrs. Wilde. I was likewise permitted to turn the leaves of a very interesting book of autographs, which contains specimens of the writings of almost every living famous English author, artist, statesman, actor, and actress, most of whom Mrs. Wilde has personally known. Among these I observed the "sentiments" (in prose or verse) of Mr. Henry Irving, Miss Ellen Terry, Mr. Burne Jones, Mr. George Meredith, Mr. Ruskin, Mr. Archibald Balfour, and Miss Marie Corelli.[3]

Late in the afternoon, but before his wife's guests have departed, a step is heard on the stair, the portiere is pushed aside by a large, smooth, white hand, and Mr. Oscar Wilde, in a fashionable frock coat and irreproachable trousers, his silk scarf fastened with the very latest style of pin, wearing a "carefully thought out buttonhole,"[4] and carrying a pair of spotless gloves, enters his wife's drawing-room smiling.

1. Richard Le Gallienne (1866–1947) was an English poet whom Wilde befriended in 1888. Wilde reviewed his *Volumes in Folio* for *The Pall Mall Gazette* (12 July 1889, 3; CW vii, No. 132). Cora Urquhart Brown-Potter (1857–1936) was an American actress who made her stage debut in 1887 in Brighton. Buffalo Bill brought his Wild West Show to London in 1887. Wilde wrote about both in "The American Invasion" (CW vi, No. 55).

2. Peters quotes from memory. Wilde wrote: "Dreary as were those old Pilgrim Fathers, who left our shores more than two centuries ago to found a New England beyond seas, the Pilgrim Mothers, who have returned to us in the nineteenth century, are drearier still." (CW vi, No. 55, lines 70–3.)

3. Irving, Terry, and Burne-Jones inscribed their autographs in 1887, 31 March 1887, and 26 December 1888, respectively. George Meredith (1828–1909) was an English novelist (and, in youth, the model for Wallis's painting of Chatterton). In an editorial for *The Woman's World* Wilde wrote: "As for George Meredith, who could hope to reproduce him? His style is chaos illumined by brilliant flashes of lightning. As a writer he has mastered everything, except language; as a novelist he can do everything, except tell a story; as an artist he is everything, except articulate." (January 1888; CW vii, No. 91, lines 256–60; echoed in *The Decay of Lying*, CW iv, 81.7–8.) In prison Wilde requested his *Essay on Comedy* and his novel *Amazing Marriage* (Wright, 320–1). Meredith's inscription is dated Box Hill, 30 November 1891. Ruskin's inscription is dated Sandgate, 28 January 1888. Peters is mistaken in naming Archibald Balfour (1840–1922), a British businessman: Constance's autograph book was inscribed by Arthur James Balfour (1848–1930), the Conservative politician and future Prime Minister, on 2 August 1891. Marie Corelli (1855–1924) was a popular English novelist. A prison warder asked Wilde for his opinion of her and he replied: "Now don't think I've anything against her moral character, but from the way she writes she ought to be here." (CL, 905.) For more on Constance's autograph album, see "Mrs. Oscar Wilde at Home," *To-day* (London, UK), 24 Nov. 1894, 93–4, pp. 812–13.

4. Cecil Graham to Lord Darlington in *Lady Windermere's Fan*: "My dear fellow, what on earth should we men do going about with purity and innocence? A carefully thought-out buttonhole is much more effective." (CW xi, 427.256–8.)

He seats himself before the open fireplace on an elegant lacquered settee, upholstered with blue silken cushions (a present from Mrs. Bloomfield Moore).[1] Cyril offers him a plate of tea-cakes and a cup of freshly made tea.

Some one remarks on the vigor and beauty of his eldest little boy, who is truly a handsome child, reminding one, in spite of his chocolate-colored jersey suit and stockings, of Andrea Verrochio's boy with the dolphin in the Ducal Palace at Florence.[2]

"Yes," replied Mr. Wilde, "he is filled with the wine of life and he will suffer superbly."

Mr. Wilde having recently returned from France, I ventured to ask him about his play of "Salome," which Mr. Pigott had prohibited in England on account of the chief character having been taken from the New Testament.[3]

"It is not yet ready for publication," Mr. Wilde answered. "I have brought it back in order to put a few more little gilt things in it—a few more little Oscarisms."

From "Salome" the conversation naturally drifted to the Jewish question.

"The Jews are a wonderful race," said Mr. Wilde. "They are the only people who have ever appreciated the romance of commerce."[4]

Speaking of a mutual acquaintance, a young American painter, he said: "Yes, yes, he has talent, but at present he is too troubled about life."

"What a pity it is," I said, "that no artist, however great, ever 'arrives' altogether. There will always be some one who will deny his right to exist as an artist." "You are mistaken in that," replied Mr. Wilde. "No audience can be exclusive enough. The most exclusive audience will always include some one who ought not to be there.

"It is for the artists to ask the questions, and for the others to answer them.

"There is the genius and the artist. The genius, like Keats or like Chatterton, who gives birth to some great book and then dies;[5] the artist, like Shakespeare,

1. Clara Jessup Bloomfield-Moore (1824–1899) was an American philanthropist, poet, and philosopher.

2. *Putto with Dolphin* by Andrea del Verrocchio (1435–1488), a Florentine sculptor, was commissioned by Lorenzo de Medici around 1470 for the Villa Medici at Careggi, near Florence. It was moved by Cosimo I to the Palazzo Vecchio in 1557.

3. Wilde had stopped in Paris on his way to Bad Homburg ("Les Théatres," *Le XIXᵉ Siècle* (Paris, France), 6 July 1892, 3, p. 616), and presumably did the same on his return.

4. For more on Wilde's attitude to Jews, see Nassaar, C. S. (2003). The problem of the Jewish manager in "The Picture of Dorian Gray". *The Wildean*, *22*, 29–36.

5. Thomas Chatterton (1752–1770) was an English poet, known for forging the works of an imaginary fifteenth-century poet and as the subject of a painting by Henry Wallis: *The Death of Chatterton* (1856). Wilde delivered a lecture about the poet to the Birkbeck Literary & Scientific Institution on 24 November 1886. The notes for the lecture, and for the unpublished essay on which it was based, are reproduced in Dibb, 295–328. See also Bristow, J. & Mitchell, R. N. (2015). *Oscar Wilde's Chatterton*. Yale University Press.

who begins by writing such poorly constructed comedies as 'Love's Labor Lost' [*sic*] and the 'Comedy of Errors,' and then becomes gradually more and more of a sublime artist, until he finally produces a 'Hamlet' and a 'Tempest.'"

"It is sinning against art," I observed, "for an artist to conceive of a work and not to produce it."

"Ah, yes," he answered, "there is a certain poem that I have in my mind ('The Sphinx') which I mean to have sumptuously published in gold and purple.[1] I could not help thinking what a curious thing it would be if I died before it was written without ever having produced it. I am such a Hedonist I have to shut myself up or else go away by myself in order to write; but I find the country life by wood and stream more complex than life in town."

Then the inevitable question rose to my lips: "And what do you think of America?" I asked.

Mr. Wilde turned upon me fiercely.

"I do not think of America," he replied, "any more than I think of my school Latin prose exercises."

Whereupon I bowed my adieus and departed.

If not always as clever in his talk as the conversations in his comedies, at least it cannot be denied that Mr. Wilde is an amusing man, in spite of the accusation that like Moliere he takes his own wit where he finds it. But, to echo Jean Jacques Rousseau, "Better a man with paradoxes than a man with prejudices,"[2] or, as Trublet said, "To select well among old things is almost equivalent to inventing new ones."[3]

WILLIAM THEODORE PETERS.
Paris, Aug. 10. 1894.

1. Wilde had begun writing *The Sphinx* in 1877–1878 and continued working on it in Paris in April 1883 (CW i, No. 118). It was finally published in June 1894 in gilt vellum boards with designs by Charles Ricketts and printed in black, red, and green ink.

2. Accused of peddling paradoxes, Rousseau wrote: "Vulgar readers, excuse my paradoxes. For someone who reflects they are unavoidable, and whatever you may say, I should rather be a man of paradoxes than a man of prejudices."

3. Nicholas Charles Joseph Trublet (1697–1770) was a French clergyman and writer. The source has "Grublet".

Percival H. W. Almy, "New Views of Mr. Oscar Wilde," *Theatre* (London, UK), Vol. 23, Mar. 1894, 119–27[1]

A rambling fishing village on the western shore of Torbay, with a rugged range of cliffs sloping down to the water's edge—such is Babbacombe.

An old-world place, with its cluster of decaying cottages at the cliff's foot, the thresholds of which are washed by the incoming tides; with its deeply indented harbour, its tiny fleet of boats, its chaos of tattered nets and broken oars, its everlasting odour of ozone and fish and tar—an old-world place it is—or *was*. For that ubiquitous spirit, *Modernity*, has found Babbacombe out, and in its dilettante attempts to improve, has already more than half destroyed the air of quaintness that so long brooded over the little village, and Babbacombe the quaint is fallen—is fallen.

But still it is a lovely spot. Nothing can destroy the beauty of its situation—the grandeur of its coasts—the placid azure of its bay. It is a dwelling place for a poet still, and it was here that I sought and found the poet Oscar Wilde.

He was spending a few weeks at "Babbacombe Cliff," a picturesque old manor house of 16th century date, whose mullioned windows glance down across a wooded slope within murmuring distance of the sea.[2]

I found him seated at an open window, for although the month was December, the air of this delightful place is mild as that of the Riviera.

Luxuriously ensconced in a deep armchair, with eyes slightly elevated, and head thrown carelessly back, his appearance suggested the idea of indolence or ennui, but it was the abstraction of a thoughtful mind, rather than the inertia of a vacant one that produced this result. Poetry is from within; it is produced by the action of external scenes and circumstances on the sensitive plate [*sic*] of a poet's soul. Hence the most important action of a poetic mind consists of absolute passivity—a complete abandonment of the soul to the inspiration of chance or surrounding influences. It was in such a mood that Oscar Wilde seemed to be indulging at the moment of my entry; he was as one who waited for inspirations. He rose as I approached, and I had an opportunity of making a mental note of his chief personal characteristic. I never saw a face so garrulous of the inner mind; it

1. H & S, b104. Reprinted in Mikhail, 228–35. Excerpted in "New Views," *The Westminster Budget* (London, UK), 23 Mar. 1894, 18. Quoted in Ellmann, 273/290, 310/328, 482/513, 548/583. Percival Henry William Almy (1871–1962), the son of a Baptist minister, was an English solicitor and poet. The 1891 census found him living in Brixham, a town in Devon some ten miles from Babbacombe. In 1895 he published *Scintillae Armenis*, a collection of poetry. Almy notes that his interview with Wilde was conducted in December. Wilde arrived at Babbacombe on 3 December 1892 (Sturgis, 468/438), so the interview was printed after a considerable delay.

2. Babbacombe Cliff was the home of Lady Mount-Temple. Photographs of the exterior and interior of Babbacombe Cliff are reproduced in Moyle, plate opposite 246.

is such as is best described as a "speaking countenance"—one that cannot keep a secret. In manner he is refined, not without a suspicion of aestheticism, and there is an engaging charm in his personality that would win him many friends and not a few disciples.

He plunged at once into poets and poetry. "A glorious passion is poetry." Keats is his favourite; "he is the greatest artist of them all." He is prepared to admit, however, that there is "often more colour than congruity in the creations of that remarkable genius; with ability so great and judgment so immature, this is naturally to be expected." I find, although he did not mention the fact, that the celebrated letter from Keats to Fanny Brawne, in which the poet recants his late rhapsodies with regard to the sex, was, in 1885, purchased by Mr. Wilde for £18.[1]

Shelley is "a magnificent genius," but as far as his own personal taste is concerned he prefers Keats. He likes a poet that "walks on the ground;" Shelley is "too ethereal."

He has no great regard for the Brownings—there is too much effort with them. Mrs. Browning is "a dear good soul," but he allots her a very secondary place. Her rhymes are shocking. "She rhymes 'moon' with 'table'!" he exclaimed. He wishes "Aurora Leigh" has been written in prose.[2]

Robert Browning is too diffuse. It is a pity he did not concentrate more. "I can revel in four of the closely compressed lines of Herrick,"[3] Mr. Wilde observed, "but I cannot tolerate dross in poetry." Poetry should be absolutely without a moral. "That is a great thing in its favour," Mr. Wilde writes, in a letter now be-

---

1. The children of Fanny Brawne had permitted the publication in 1878 of the letters Keats wrote to their mother, to whom he was secretly betrothed. The letters were sold at Sotheby's on 2 March 1885. The letter to which Almy refers is presumably the last of the Keats letters in the auction catalogue (lot 35; letter 37 in the 1878 edition), in which Keats writes: "Shakespeare always sums up matters in the most sovereign manner. Hamlet's heart was full of such Misery as mine is when he said to Ophelia 'Go to a Nunnery, go, go!' Indeed I should like to give up the matter at once—I should like to die." It is described in the catalogue as "a most interesting but most painful letter, evidently written in the greatest agony of mind." Wilde's poem *Sonnet. On the Sale by Auction of Keats' Love Letters* was published in the *Dramatic Review* on 23 Jan. 1886 (CW 1, No. 103). It begins: "These are the letters which Endymion wrote | To one he loved in secret, and apart. | And now the brawlers of the auction mart | Bargain and bid for each poor blotted note".

2. Elizabeth Barrett Browning (1806–1861) was an English poet, married to Robert Browning. She described her epic poem *Aurora Leigh* (1856) as "a novel in verse". In his January 1888 editorial for *The Woman's World* Wilde stated that: "Mrs. Browning, the first great English poetess, was also an admirable scholar, though she may not have put the accents on her Greek, and even in those poems that seem most remote from classical life, such as 'Aurora Leigh,' for instance, it is not difficult to trace the fine literary influence of a classical training." (CW vii, No. 91, lines 150–5.) Elsewhere he was less equivocal in his praise: "Mrs Browning is unapproachable by any woman who has ever touched lyre or blown through reed since the days of the great Aeolian poetess [Sappho]." (*The Queen*, 8 Dec. 1888; CW vii, No. 108, lines 21–3.)

3. Robert Herrick (1591–1674) was an English poet and cleric.

fore me, of a poem of which it had been stated that it did not strive to inculcate any particular moral. "A poet should not think." "Poetry is not the place for thought; we must have beauty, and beauty and thought are incoalescent." He recalled that passage in "The Excursion," in which the poet,[1] discoursing of the effects of natural beauty on the soul of the youthful herdsman, says:—

> "They were his life;
> In such access of mind, in such high hour
> Of visitation from the living God
> Thought was not; in enjoyment it expired."

Thought and beauty cannot occupy the mind at the same time.

Mr. Wilde is not a great Shakespearean; he likes Ford and Marlowe, and Jonson and Massinger, and the Elizabethan dramatists generally, but he does not rave over Shakespeare.[2]

"Lady Windermere's Fan" has sometimes been paralleled with "The School for Scandal;"[3] it is, therefore, interesting to know what are Mr. Wilde's opinions of Sheridan. He is by no means enthusiastic over the author of "The Rivals." "I do not rate Sheridan very high," he writes in another letter; "I consider Congreve far beyond him."[4]

Milton is sometimes heavy; but "Paradise Lost" is "undoubtedly the grandest organ-music we have." "Very sober" is Thomson. There is one line in "The Seasons," however, that he greatly admires—that in which the poet compares the colour of the wallflower to iron-rust; "the simile is perfect."[5]

The life and fate of Chatterton is "the most tremendous tragedy in history." Wordsworth is sometimes fine; but, as a whole, "The Excursion" is "Decidedly tedious." Tennyson is "a supreme artist." "The music of Swinburne is perfect." "What all-seeing eyes William Morris has!" Austin Dobson is "very delightful"—

---

1. William Wordsworth.

2. All the men named were English playwrights. John Ford (bap. 1586–c. 1639) wrote during the Jacobean and Caroline eras; his most famous play is *'Tis Pity She's a Whore* (c. 1626). Benjamin Jonson (1572–1637) is known for his plays *Volpone* (c. 1606) and *Bartholomew Fair* (1614), among others. Philip Massinger (1583–1640) collaborated with numerous other playwrights; his most popular play is *A New Way to Pay Old Debts* (1625).

3. E.g. in the review of *Lady Windermere's Fan* in *The Pall Mall Gazette*: "we were listening to more of 'deliberate wit' and finished epigram than any play has contained since the day of Sheridan's 'School for Scandal.'" (22 Feb. 1892, 2.)

4. William Congreve (1670–1729) was an English playwright and poet of the Restoration period. His plays, such as *The Way of the World* (1700), were early examples of the comedy of manners genre.

5. James Thomson (1700–1748) was a Scottish poet and playwright, best known for his sequence of poems, *Seasons* (1726–1730). Wilde refers to a line from *Spring*: "The yellow wallflower, stain'd with iron-brown;". He had earlier included *Seasons* in his list of books not to read at all (CL, 276).

"you *must* get Austin Dobson." "The other Austin is vulgar—'The Season' execrable."[1] "There is not enough fire in William Watson's poetry to boil a tea-kettle."[2]

He wishes that it were always possible to convey poetry to the mind by some means other than print. "Print is by no means the proper purple for Poetry to show herself in," he says.

The conversation turned to prose writers. He is a great novel reader. Amongst English novelists, he prefers George Meredith. "The Egoist" is "a terrible book for human nature. Every sentence tells—every line is an arrow in one's own soul."[3] R. L. Stevenson is very fine.[4] Some people would rather have Rider Haggard; "that is because they are insane."[5] The two are not to be compared. "Rider Haggard writes like a man playing football, and as long as he confines himself to blood and bruises he does well; but immediately he begins to moralise, he gets outside his natural sphere and becomes absurd." He is not enthusiastic over Scott. He is able to read Thackeray's "Esmond."[6] Charlotte Brontë is "often quite charming."[7] "Robert Elsmere" "everyone should read."[8]

1. Henry Austin Dobson (1840–1921) was an English poet. "The other Austin" is Alfred Austin (1835–1913), an English poet who served as Poet Laureate from 1896 until his death, and who wrote *The Season: A Satire* (1861).

2. William Watson (1858–1935) was an English poet who wrote celebratory and political poems. Wilde had been annoyed by Watson's comic poem, printed in the *Spectator* on 9 July 1892, about Wilde's intention to leave England for France in the wake of the censorship of *Salomé* (CL, 531, note 2; 541, note 3). It ended: "Would any but a stupid race | Have made the fuss about you *we* did?"

3. Meredith's *The Egotist* (1879) is about a self-absorbed knight who cannot understand why the various women whom he pursues do not want to marry him.

4. Robert Louis Stevenson (1850–1894) was a Scottish novelist, best known for his adventure novels *Treasure Island* (1881–1882) and *Kidnapped* (1886) and his gothic novella *Strange Case of Dr Jekyll and Mr Hyde* (1886). Wilde later described him as "the humane artist" (*The Queen*, 8 Dec. 1888; CW vii, No. 108, line 160). Constance listed *Treasure Island* among the favourite books of her and Oscar's first son, Cyril (Adele Marroc, "Oscar Wilde's Children," *The Philadelphia Inquirer* (Philadelphia, PA), 5 Nov. 1893, 23, p. 808). Wilde requested that *Treasure Island* and other of Stevenson's novels be added to the prison library at Reading, and was glad to learn that they were "much appreciated" by his fellow inmates (Wright, 271–2).

5. Henry Rider Haggard (1856–1925) was an English writer of adventure stories and novels, including *King Solomon's Mines* (1885), *She* (1887), and the Allan Quatermain series. In *The Decay of Lying* Vivian states that: "As for Mr. Rider Haggard, who really has, or had once, the makings of a perfectly magnificent liar, he is now so afraid of being suspected of genius that when he does tell us anything marvellous, he feels bound to invent a personal reminiscence, and to put it into a footnote as a kind of cowardly corroboration." (CW iv, 77.19–24.)

6. Thackeray's *The History of Henry Esmond* (1852) tells the story of a colonel in the service of Queen Anne, and has him participate in a number of historical events of the English Restoration.

7. Charlotte Brontë (1816–1855) was an English novelist, best known for *Jane Eyre* (1847). Wilde thought her style "too exaggerated" (*The Woman's World*, Jan. 1889; CW vii, No. 112, line 9).

8. *Robert Elsmere* (1888), an immensely popular novel about the religious struggles of an Oxford clergyman, was written by Mrs Humphry (Mary Augusta) Ward (1851–1920). Robert Sher-

He is thoroughly steeped in French literature. Indeed, he is more conversant with French than with English, and spends some months of each year in France. The French novel is "a miracle." "They have brought the art of fiction to a point beyond which human genius cannot go."

The English stage is in "a shocking condition;" this is rather the fault of the public; "nothing but comedy and farcical comedy go down with an English house; the French are far ahead of us in matters theatrical."

On matters of English history he discoursed much and curiously.

He likes the Puritans "for their thoroughness;" they are the only people he would burn—"they really deserve burning—it is a great honour to a man to burn him." But "when the faith of the Puritan begins to broaden, that which constituted his greatest charm is gone; he is no longer a Puritan, and forthwith he becomes unworthy of the honours of faggot and stake." There is much in the character of the Stuart Kings that he admires. William III he detests.[1] "Kings ought not to be 'ower gude.'"[2] His ideal king is "a man of high artistic sensibilities; one who can write beautiful poetry; who can appreciate good music; who is charmed with the beauties of painting and sculpture." "Not one who goes about with a swallow-tail coat on, laying foundation stones and doing little goodnesses." "In matters of taste" our present Royal Family is "shockingly deficient."

---

ard wrote that Wilde "found everybody in the States reading 'Robert Elsmere,' and during a luncheon party in Dublin after his return from the States he described how in the trains every passenger seemed to have a cheap edition of this book in his or her hands. 'As each page is finished it is torn out and flung through the window,' he said, 'So that in the end the American prairie will get a top-dressing of Robert Elsmere,'" (Sherard, R. H. (1907). *The Life of Oscar Wilde.* Mitchell Kennerley. 221). Wilde's tour of America took place six years before the publication of that book, so the story, like many of Wilde's American anecdotes, must be apocryphal. In *The Decay of Lying*, Wilde had his character Vivian remark that "Robert Elsmere is of course a masterpiece—a masterpiece of the 'genre ennuyeux [tedious type],' the one form of literature that the English people seems thoroughly to enjoy. A thoughtful young friend of ours once told us that it reminded him of the sort of conversation that goes on at a meat tea in the house of a serious Nonconformist family, and we can quite believe it." (CW iv, 78.13–17.) Vivian's friend Cyril later says that he is devoted to the book: "Not that I can look upon it as a serious work. As a statement of the problems that confront the earnest Christian it is ridiculous and antiquated. It is simply Arnold's *Literature and Dogma* with the literature left out." (CW iv, 80.25–8.) After his dialogue was published Wilde wrote to Mrs George Lewis: "I have blown my trumpet against the gates of dullness, and I hope some shaft has hit *Robert Elsmere* between the joints of his nineteenth edition." (CL, 389).

1. William of Orange (1650–1702) invaded England in 1688–1689, deposed James II of England and Ireland (who was also James VII of Scotland), and thereafter reigned as William III of England, Scotland, and Ireland until his death. James attempted to regain his crown, but was defeated by William's forces at the Battle of the Boyne in Ireland in 1690. James was the last of the Stuart kings and the last Catholic monarch of England, Scotland, and Ireland.

2. Scots dialect, "too good". Wilde may be recalling the use of the phrase by James I of Scotland in that king's poetry.

Theology was the next subject touched upon. He reads Theology every day; "the history of Theology is the history of madness." He much laments that religious literature is of so poor a quality. Dante is the only Christian writer of supreme merit. Wordsworth's was the religion of nature rather than the religion of Christ; he is pantheistic rather than Christian. "I do not altogether believe in bringing children up on the Bible," Mr. Wilde observed. By the time they arrive at an age to appreciate the Book, it has lost, to them, much of its charm. Anyone taking up the Gospels for the first time at or about the age of 18 would be enchanted. "'What a marvellous personality!' they would exclaim, 'what a remarkable story!'" "But when their infancy has been surfeited with it, their manhood revolts at it. Their eyes have become blind by gazing at the sun before their minds are strong enough to comprehend and appreciate its vastness and meaning." He has a profound admiration for the character and personality of Christ, but he cannot accept the doctrine of his Divinity; "it would place too broad a gulf between Him and the human soul."[1] I suggested that the humanity of Christ bridges over the gulf that his Divinity creates, but in his opinion such bridgement is not adequate for the purpose. It is in the milder aspects of the Christ character that he most delights: teaching the poor, tending the sick, discoursing of a marvellous and ideal Faith with a few uncultured fishermen on the margin of Galilee.[2] "In His utmost humanity, He approaches nearest the Divine." Those scathing words that He uttered at Jerusalem on the eve of His betrayal—in which, in the divine consciousness of innocence and right, He hurls anathema and defiance in the teeth of the Pharisees who were clamouring for His blood, Mr. Wilde considers rather as an outburst of spleen consequent upon the disappointment of cherished hopes and the defeat of a high and generous ambition.[3] He discovered a certain partiality for the Pharisees; "they were the repositories of all the learning and culture of their times."

"Creeds are very personal things," continued Mr. Wilde. "Most of us believe in the great cardinal religious doctrines. That God made the Heaven and the Earth, and is the preserver and ruler of all things, few of us are prepared to deny: but when it gets beyond that, it becomes a merely personal matter." "The same reasoning applies to matters of secular history: Henry VIII reigned, granted; but if we proceed further, if we commence to tell how he reigned and to pass judgment on his commissions, omissions, and permissions as a King, we get out of

1. A favourite book of Wilde's—he read it early in life and requested it when he was imprisoned—was *Vie de Jésus* (1863) by the French philosopher Joseph Ernest Renan (1823–1892), in which Christ is depicted as entirely human. Wilde referred to it as "that gracious fifth Gospel," (Wright, 126).
2. "And he saith unto them, Follow me, and I will make you fishers of men." (Matthew 4:19.)
3. The Woes of the Pharisees: Luke 11:37–54 and Matthew 23:1–39.

history into personal opinion." "History ends with a few bare facts; Religion with a few undeniable Doctrines—beyond that all is invention."

"Prayer is a splendid privilege, but it is the utmost presumption for a man to expect or suppose that his petition will be granted." "What a funny world it would be, to be sure, if the Almighty answered every prayer that is offered up to him! As though the All-Father does not know what is best for us!"

From Theology to Thieves is a long leap. But it is like the man to take it. He feels "considerable sympathy" with Burglars. "In nine cases out of ten they only take what we really do not want." "That only may be accounted a loss that is something gone from our own persons, or that it is impossible to do without." "The loss of a finger *is* a loss; the loss of our last guinea is a loss; but the loss of a thousand pounds when we have a hundred thousand in the bank is *not* a loss." Burglars broke into the house of a friend of his and made off with all they could lay their hands to. Mr. Wilde called; everybody was in hysterics. He administered to them the consolations of this unique philosophy; he assured them that inasmuch as human nature is constituted to be capable, in certain contingencies, of dispensing with silver spoons and Japanese curiosities, a visitation of burglars is really a matter of very small moment indeed. "Now, had someone fallen downstairs and broken a limb, it would have been a reasonable cause for distress; but really, silver spoons! Japanese curiosities! what good are they?"

He is "very sorry Smugglers have gone out of fashion." "What glorious places the creeks and caves of Babbacombe would be for smuggling enterprise, and what a pity it is that such fine natural advantages have to be disregarded." Adam Smith (he believes it is) somewhere says that "if it had not been for Smugglers in the last century, the commercial property of this country would have become extinct!"[1]

Pirates, too, are "very fine fellows." It was they who established the maritime reputation of England. What was his friend Sir Francis Drake, but a pirate?[2] "Every profession in which a man is in constant danger of losing his life has something rather fine about it." He would "infinitely rather" see one of his boys a

---

1. Adam Smith (1723–1790) was a Scottish economist and philosopher. His *An Inquiry into the Nature and Causes of the Wealth of Nations* (1776), most commonly referred to as *The Wealth of Nations,* contains, if not exactly a defence of smuggling, an explanation for its allure and the injustice associated with its punishment: "An injudicious tax offers a great temptation to smuggling. But the penalties of smuggling must arise in proportion to the temptation. The law, contrary to all the ordinary principles of justice, first creates the temptation, and then punishes those who yield to it; and it commonly enhances the punishment, too, in proportion to the very circumstance which ought certainly to alleviate it, the temptation to commit the crime." In 1778 Smith was appointed Scottish commissioner of customs, with part of his remit the enforcement of laws against smuggling.

2. Sir Francis Drake (c. 1540–1596) was an English privateer and explorer of the Elizabethan era.

smuggler "than a grocer serving up sugar, or a stock-broker baiting traps for people, and keeping himself secure beyond the reach of law."

Beggars are remarkable people. He greatly wonders that no one has undertaken to write the history of beggars. He is sure the subject is full of capabilities. "The life of an Italian beggar is one of the jolliest that can be imagined." "They have no need of homes who can live in the open air; their only requirement is food." "The climate of England is a great hardship to the poor of this country."[1]

He likes Jews. He has many friends among the Hebrews. He thinks Spinoza a very fine character. He seems to have some doubt as to whether Spinoza was really the founder of the Pantheistic sect.[2]

The conversation drifted into politics. "We are all of us more or less Socialists now-a-days," he remarked. "Our system of government is largely socialistic." "What is the House of Commons but a socialistic assembly?" "I think I am rather more than a Socialist," he added, laughingly; "I am something of an Anarchist, I believe; but, of course, the dynamite policy is very absurd indeed."

"What a perfect fiasco is our system of penal administration!" "To punish a man for wrong-doing, with a view to his reformation, is the most lamentable mistake it is possible to commit." "If he has any soul at all, such procedure is calculated to make him ten times worse than he was before." "It is a sign of a noble nature to refuse to be broken by force." "Never attempt to reform a man," he said; "men never repent."[3]

He loves true ignorance. He has not much faith in our modern system of educating everybody. "A truly ignorant and unsophisticated man is the noblest work of God."[4]

And so he reasoned on; the range of subjects, the diversity of interests, that his conversation represented was truly surprising. He does not weary with profundity, nor bore with unnecessary detail. No arm-chair lecturer he. Like a bee, he flits from flower to flower, just tastes the sweets and passes on. His style is fluent and animated, like a sort of gentle insistence not infrequently found in men of strong mind. He avoids hackneyed terms and commonplace phrases; his words are choice and ready; he takes the lead in all topics of discussion, and ini-

1. Wilde's short story *The Model Millionaire*, first published in *The World* in June 1887, is about a wealthy man who models as a picturesque beggar for a portrait painter.

2. Baruch Spinoza (1632–1677) was a Dutch philosopher of Portuguese Sephardi origin. He is considered by some to be an exponent of pantheism because of his equating God with Nature, although he complained that his readers took him too literally.

3. Wilde's own imprisonment did not change his attitude. After his release he wrote to the editor of the *Daily Chronicle*: "It is not the prisoners who need reformation. It is the prisons." (CL, 852.)

4. Lady Bracknell in *The Importance of Being Earnest*: "I do not approve of anything that tampers with natural ignorance. Ignorance is like a delicate exotic fruit: touch it and the bloom is gone." (CW x, 780.415–17.)

tiates all new departures in the conversation. His opinions are convincingly expressed, but not oracularly delivered. His conversation is entirely free from that ipse-dixitical "cocksurishness" so often assumed by people on pedestals. I noticed one peculiarity: he makes very frequent use of one or two select words—"artist" is one, "culture" another, "fascinating" another, and so on.

To accurately gauge the character of the man is a task for which I feel myself incompetent. Words are to him a means whereby he may disguise his own personality. He never allows us to see the real emotions of his heart; his object seems to be to cast a glamour over us with the brilliance of his mind; he appears to sacrifice sentiment on the altar of analysis. He is a moral acrobat of a most extraordinary description. He stands before us a sane, plain gentleman of the nineteenth century, but in a moment, "Εια άγε!"[1] he is on his head, gazing up at us solemn as a Sphinx, declaring that up to this moment humanity has been labouring under a ridiculous delusion, that *this* is the natural gait of a man, and that God Almighty never ordained that he should go otherwise. He is so solemn, so composed, so self-possessed, wonder seizes us—is the man schooling us in a great fact, or fooling us with a great farce!

To deny everything that is generally credited, and credit everything that is generally denied, seems to be the first article of literary faith. The world has long enough been dominated by a parcel of shaky old moralities. There is a proverb—so Trench would assure us—for every emergency in life.[2]

These proverbs have assumed oracular pretensions. They usurp the place of argument, they override precedent, they hold philosophy in scorn. To the vulgar they are invincible, indisputable, final. How can they be combated? Logic and learning are alike powerless. There is one way, and one way only; it is this: set a proverb to overthrow a proverb—meet maxim with maxim—combat saw with saw. It is a trick of the tongue. Set up a counter-glitter of words; out-sophisticate sophistry. Truth lies between the two extremes of falsehood. Oscar Wilde has found his vocation. It is his to restore the balance of Truth disturbed by the falsely-named "philosophy" of proverbs. He does it well. His veracity is terrible—and all the more terrible because it is implied rather than direct. He leaves us not a lie to cover us. He strips our vices of their last concealing falsehood. He tears the rags from the gangrene we had been so careful to disguise, and beholds, with a malicious laugh, our consternation at the rude discovery. Oh, he is a grim physician! He applies no soothing emollient to the wound he has so ruthlessly unwrapped. Exposure is the only remedy he prescribes; let others find a better. Hence—because of the terrible truthfulness of the man—he is called a satirist—

---

1. εἶα άγε, a colloquialism meaning "come on!"
2. Richard Chenevix Trench (1807–1886) was a Church of Ireland archbishop of Dublin. Almy refers to his *On the Lessons in Proverbs: Five Lectures* (1853).

"satire" being the name we have given to truths that are not pleasant to hear. By those who do not take him seriously—who regard his truths as jokes—he is called Humourist.

It appears somewhat strange that a writer of this description should be so largely popular; but the cause is not far to seek. His admirers are divided into two classes: first, those who do not believe a word he says—who call him humourist; and secondly, those who are perfectly satisfied with the truthfulness of his statements as applied to their neighbours—who call him Satirist; and as these two classes constitute a very large proportion of Society, the secret of Mr. Wilde's popularity as a writer is at once proclaimed.

But Mr. Wilde is not a moralist in the highest sense of the word. There are two sorts of morality; or rather, morality has two sources. There is the morality of the taste, which is inspired by imagination; and there is the morality of the soul, which is dictated and governed by the Decalogue.[1] Mr. Wilde's morality is of the first order. I never knew a man whose actions and beliefs are so controlled by taste as in his case. Taste, it may be said, is the conscience of the aesthetic nature; and a well-regulated taste is as sensitive in artistic matters as a well-balanced conscience in matters of morality. But in the case of Mr. Wilde the moral conscience is merged and extinguished in the aesthetic conscience. He attacks the vices—they are so out of taste; he extols the virtues—they have so picturesque an effect.

Finally, the New Humour of which Mr. Wilde is said to be the great exponent, consists, I think, not in saying funny things, but in making funny discoveries. Dickens was a great humourist; he was constantly discovering and proclaiming some little idiosyncrasy in human nature that, by an inexplicable oversight, had never been observed by us before. In this respect, Oscar Wilde is the Dickens of the moral character. He is ever discovering some peculiarity in our moral constitution that, strange as it seems, had never occurred to ourselves. The new light that these discoveries let in upon the soul strikes us with a strange sense of humour. It is not the sort of humour to keep an audience screaming. It fills us with a singular elation that often breaks into a chuckle, but never into a roar. This is the new humour.

Percival H. W. Almy.

---

1. The Ten Commandments.

"Un Referendum Artistique et Social," *L'Ermitage* (Paris, France), July 1893, 1–24[1]

Quelle est la meilleure condition du Bien social, une organisation spontanée et libre, ou bien une organisation disciplinée et méthodique ? Vers laquelle de ces conceptions doivent aller les préférences de l'artiste ?

Les réponses que l'on va lire n'émanent que d'écrivains de la génération nouvelle, c'est-à-dire ayant moins de trente-cinq ans.

Cette première consultation dont on trouvera plus loin les résultats sera suivie et complétée par une seconde série donnant les opinions sur le même sujet des principaux écrivains de la génération antérieure, tant français qu'étrangers. Pour l'Italie notamment, nous possédons déjà, grâce à l'obligeant concours de nos confrères de l'*Idea libérale*, les réponses de MM. Carducci, Lombroso, Amicis, Graf. Fogazzaro, Ferri, Morselli et plusieurs autres.

✂ *Responses of various artists, listed in alphabetical order.*

Wilde (Oscar), de Londres. — Autrefois, j'étais poète et tyran. Maintenant je suis artiste et anarchiste.

✂ *An epilogue in which the authors sum up the results of their investigation.*

An Artistic and Social Referendum

What is the best condition of social good: a spontaneous and free organisation, or a disciplined and methodical organisation? Which of these notions should the artist prefer?

The answers that we are going to read come only from writers of the new generation, that is to say, those under thirty-five.[2]

This first consultation, the results of which will be found below, will be followed and completed by a second series giving the opinions on the same subject of the main writers of the previous generation, both French and foreign. For Italy in particular, we already have, thanks to the obliging support of our colleagues

---

1. See below for an annotated English translation. Referenced in Hyman, E. W. (2008). Salomé as bombshell, or how Oscar Wilde became an anarchist. In J. Bristow (ed.) *Oscar Wilde and Modern Culture*. Ohio University Press. 96–109.
2. At the time of publication Wilde was 38.

from l'*Idea liberale*, the responses of MM. Carducci, Lombroso, Amicis, Graf. Fogazzaro, Ferri, Morselli and several others.

✂   *Responses of various artists, listed in alphabetical order.*

Wilde (Oscar), of London. — In the past, I was a poet and a tyrant. Now I am an artist and an anarchist.

✂   *An epilogue in which the authors sum up the results of their investigation.*[1]

"Mr. Oscar Wilde the Lion of Dinard," *The New York Herald, European Edition* (Paris, France), 3 Sep. 1893, 5[2]

The Robust Apostle of Aestheticism Made Much of at the Channel Resorts.

ON THE "QUICKSILVER."

Last Run of the Season to Dinan—The Hon Mrs. Marshall's Ball.

(FROM OUR SPECIAL CORRESPONDENT.)

DINARD, Sept. 1.

✂   *Several paragraphs about a coaching trip from Dinard to Dinan. Wilde is listed among the passengers.*

MR. OSCAR WILDE LIONIZED.

Mr. Oscar Wilde arrived on Tuesday morning,[3] and was dined that evening by Dr. and Mrs. Manley Sims. Later he went to the Hon. Mrs. Marshall's ball for a short time.

On Wednesday evening, Mrs. Hughes Hallet gave a party at the Villa Cristal, followed by a supper at her own house, in honor of Mr. Oscar Wilde, Mrs. Orville Horwitz, the Marquis and Marquise San Carlos de Pedrosa and Miss Martindale. It was a merry and congenial party of thirty or forty guests. At Mrs. Hughes Hallett's table were Mr. Oscar Wilde, with Mrs. Orville Horwitz at his right, the Hon. Arthur Cadogan, Lady Seymour, the Marquis San Carlos de Pedrosa, Comte

---

1. The respondents are categorised as "supporters of restrictions," "intermediate opinions," and "supporters of liberty," with Wilde in the third group. This group is again split into three—"mixed liberals," "liberals pure and simple," and "liberal anarchists"—with Wilde in the third group.

2. Wilde spent the first half of September holidaying alone in Dinard, a town on the coast of Brittany.

3. Tuesday 29 August.

Blome, Chancellor of the Emperor of Austria; Mrs. Goodriche, Mr. Codman, of Boston; and Miss Martindale.

At the end of the supper Miss Aimée Lowther arose and said: "I propose the health of the guest of the evening, Mr. Oscar Wilde"; and after some moments' hesitation, Mr. Wilde responded by saying: "I propose the health of Miss Aimée Lowther, the guest *par excellence:* Miss Lowther."[1]

Then M. Jean de Grandmaison said that, as a Frenchman, he had the honor of welcoming to these shores "England's great poet and dramatist, Mr. Oscar Wilde." To which Mr. Oscar Wilde replied: "Unworthy as I am to drink the toast, the dramatic talent now at Dinard is centred in Miss Aimée Lowther."

Lady Seymour then proposed the health of the charming hostess, Mrs. Hughes Hallett, who replied in a graceful and appropriate speech.

✂ *A list of guests at the party.*

Very few young people had been invited, but the assembly was most agreeable and enjoyable.

AN "AL FRESCO" ENTERTAINMENT.

A very charming *al fresco* party was given on Wednesday afternoon at the cricket ground, a beautiful expanse of lawn, where music and tea were provided by Mrs. Spencer Chapman and Mrs. Goodriche. On Thursday night Mrs. Goodriche gave a small dinner to meet Mr. Oscar Wilde. The guests included Lady Berkeley Paget, Sir Richard Shaw, Miss Aimée Lowther, the Hon. Arthur Cadogan and others.

This evening there will be a fancy dress ball at the Ladies' Club; but as Mr. Oscar Wilde said to me: "It is distressing that the Dinard people keep such late hours. I rather prefer Homburg, with its 'early to bed and early to rise.'"

'Tis true, Dinard has room for many improvements, among which the keeping of earlier hours and the watering of the streets to lay the dust may be specially mentioned.

✂ *Several paragraphs about the movements of other visitors to Dinard.*

---

1. Aimée Constance Anne Lowther (1869–1935) was a playwright and amateur actress. She claimed that as a young girl Wilde had told her: "Aimée, Aimée, if you had been a boy you'd have wrecked my life." (CL, 583.) She met Wilde for the last time in Paris in 1900, when she and Ellen Terry saw him in the street and invited him to eat with them. In 1912 she published her versions of four of Wilde's spoken stories (Fitzsimons, 174, 303).

"Mr. Oscar Wilde's Philosophy," *The New York Herald, European Edition* (Paris, France), 9 Sep. 1893, 1[1]

"Forget Everything Unpleasant in the Past, Live for the Present and the Future."

DINARD HAS AN ACHING VOID

A Theory, Based on Colors, As to What Women Should Be Avoided.

(FROM OUR SPECIAL CORRESPONDENT)

DINARD, Sept. 7.

Mr Oscar Wilde left Dinard today on the steamer for St. Helier, where he will surprise the audience at the theatre there by appearing unexpectedly at the performance of his play, "A Woman of No Importance."

I met him on the beach this morning previous to his departure.

"I came to Dinard," he said, "upon the advice of Dr. Manley Sims, for seclusion and rest, but I have not found either; and I must go away. Dinard is a delightful spot and filled with most charming people, but for summer life the hours are too late, if one follows the round of gaiety here; and I prefer rest and repose.

"I am not only engaged in writing a new play, but I am thinking of publishing a book of maxims, called *Oscariana*, which may or may not be acceptable to the thinking world.[2]

"My idea is that every day should begin a new thought, a fresh idea, and that 'yesterday' should be a thing of the past. Forget everything unpleasant in the past, and live for the present and the future."

"What was your idea when in your book *Dorian Gray* you said, 'Beware of women who wear violet?'" I asked.[3]

"Ah!" Mr. Wilde replied, "I cannot tell you that without giving you the story of my life, and that would take too long. But truly, it is my theory to *beware of women who wear mauve.* It is a dangerous colour, and therefore most attractive,

---

1. Reprinted (without the paragraphs about social events in Dinard here omitted) in "Oscar Wilde's Philosophy," *The New York Herald* (New York, NY), 20 Sep. 1893, 9. Excerpted in "Interview with Oscar Wilde," *South Wales Echo* (Cardiff, UK), 14 Sep. 1893, 3; and "Oscar Wilde's Philosophy," *The Weekly Standard and Express* (Bradford, UK), 16 Sep. 1893, 7 (which is quoted in Sturgis, 489/456).

2. Wilde was supposed to be writing a new comedy. He may also have been working on *La Sainte Courtisane*, which he never finished (Sturgis, 493/459). *Oscariana*, with selections from Wilde's writings made by Constance, did not appear until January 1895 (Mason, 555).

3. In *The Picture of Dorian Gray* Lord Henry advises Dorian: "Never trust a woman who wears mauve, whatever her age may be, or a woman over thirty-five who is fond of pink ribbons. It always means that they have a history." (CW iii, 79.12–14.)

for to be fascinating one must be the least bit dangerous. And apart from this, there are psychological reasons for the warning."

AN ACHING VOID.

And now that the apostle of aestheticism has departed there will be a great void, for as a young lady remarked the other evening at the Casino to Mr. Wilde, who was surrounded by a crowd of ladies: "You remind me of 'Patience' and the 'twenty love-sick maidens.'"[1]

At the balls and dinners given for Mr. Wilde there has been a run on sunflowers for decorations, and today there is scarcely a sunflower left in the gardens of the working classes, for every *soleil* has been plucked to adorn the tables at which "Oscar" has been a guest.

✂ *Several paragraphs about social events in Dinard. Wilde is listed among the guests at an "evening entertainment" and a yachting party.*

"The Dramatic Week," *The Press* (New York, NY), 7 Jan. 1894, 4

✂ *Several paragraphs about American and British theatrical news.*

When the English feel hard times they generally blame America for their troubles. In this instance, while the commercial people were abusing Governor McKinley, professionals were wrathful at Miss Rehan. Every manager in London has a leading woman whom he considers a British Bernhardt, and from Mrs. Bernard-Beere to Ellen Terry these ladies were in arms against our actress for monopolizing the praises of the critics and the discussions of the feuilltonists. But in London the big newspapers are wholly uninfluenced by the theatrical advertisements, which form merely an infinitesimal portion of their income, and the critic notices or leaves unnoticed anything he pleases. As a sop to the Garrick Club Cerberus,[2] however, the London writers have decided that Ada Rehan is an Irish, not an American product. This assumption was carried out to some degree by the policy of Daly's new theater in engaging only English players.[3] At present almost half the company at Leicester Square is composed of London actors. The audi-

1. "Love-sick maidens": see "Oscar Dear, Oscar Dear!" *The News and Courier* (Charleston, SC), 8 July 1882, 4, p. 439.

2. The Garrick Club is a gentlemen's club in London, founded in 1831. Members have included actors and artists, such as Herbert Beerbohm Tree, Henry Irving, John Everett Millais, and Dante Gabriel Rossetti.

3. John Augustin Daly (1838–1899) was an American theatre manager. Ada Rehan had laid the foundation stone for Daly's Theatre in Leicester Square in 1891 and the theatre opened on 27 June 1893.

636

ences of that city do not like our American accent, and have no hesitation in saying so. I came across Oscar Wilde sitting in deshabille and dejection one night in the stalls of the Empire Music Hall, and in a discussion of the subject he said lazily: "Your American women are like cockatoos—beautiful only in silence.[1] For example, the most successful of your exportations is Loie Fuller, whose fame depends wholly on the fact that she talks with her legs instead of her lips."[2]

✂ *Several paragraphs about American and British theatrical news.*

"Local Stage Gossip," *The Philadelphia Inquirer* (Philadelphia, PA), 4 Feb. 1894, 10[3]

✂ *Several paragraphs that are unrelated to Wilde.*

People who admired Oscar Wilde's epigrams in "Lady Windermere's Fan" during its recent engagement at the Chestnut Street Theatre, and those who will admire them when that play returns to the Park, February 26, will be interested in learning that most of them go through a process of evolution. Wilde told one of his recent interviewers that he keeps a note-book in which he jots down a promising epigram, or the material for one, and when he had nothing better to do he takes it out and polishes it and sand-papers it.[4]

1. Wilde had expressed a similar sentiment in "The American Invasion": "Still, they [American girls] never really lose their accent, it keeps peeping out here and there, and when they chatter together they are like a bevy of peacocks." (CW vi, No. 55, lines 51–3.)
2. Marie Louise "Loie" Fuller (1862–1928) was an American actress, dancer, choreographer, and stage lighting pioneer. In 1892 she relocated to Paris.
3. Reprinted in "Gossip of the Foyer," *The Indianapolis News* (Indianapolis, IN), 10 Feb. 1894, 12; and "Personal and Other Jottings," *The Morning Call* (San Francisco, CA), 18 Feb. 1894, 16. Both of these articles append an additional sentence: "The most famous epigram of the play, 'A cynic is a man who knows the price of everything and the value of nothing,' was the result of a whole week's tinkering." The epigram appears in act 3 (CW xi, 428.278–9). The *Inquirer's* source is untraced.
4. Wilde did keep notebooks containing draft epigrams (Small, 127–31).

F. E. McKay, "A Clever Dramatist's Eccentric Views," *Kate Field's Washington* (Washington, DC), Vol. 9, 4 Apr. 1894, 220–1[1]

I called lately upon Oscar Wilde at his apartments in St. James [*sic*] Place.[2] It is here he receives those whom he wants to spare the long drive to Tite Street, where he has a charming house, over whose aesthetic penates,[3] Mrs. Wilde, his beautiful wife, presides.

Mr. Wilde, it is well known, has abandoned his "Fauntleroy" costumes and now dresses, as he imagines, in *fin-de-siecle* fashion.[4] He wears a long sack coat. It is of gray Scotch cloth. It reaches nearly to his knees. His cravat is enormous. His hair is long and parted on the side. His cuffs are many sizes too large for him and are fastened with links. He wears a golden chain bracelet. Attached to it is a heart-shaped locket. The little finger of his left hand is covered, to the nail, with conspicuous rings.

I asked Mr. Wilde if he will ever go again to America. He said he had not decided. "I had fully intended to be present at a performance of my comedy, 'A Woman of No Importance,' by Rose Coghlan at the Fifth Avenue Theatre,"[5] said he, "but the dislike I have to be interviewed by inquisitive reporters, who make no allowances for moods, has kept me from making trips. I shall go to France soon. I am content in its atmosphere. It is sympathetic."

I asked Mr. Wilde how he works.

1. H & S, b105. Reprinted as "Eccentric Oscar Wilde," *New York Tribune* (New York, NY), 8 Apr. 1894, 15; "Eccentric Oscar Wilde," *Worcester Daily Spy* (Worcester, MA), 20 Apr. 1894, 3; and in Welhausen, C., & Scharnhorst, G. (2008). A recovered interview with Oscar Wilde. *The Wildean*, *32*, 2–5. Frederic Edward McKay was an American theatrical producer and author. In 1890 he edited *Vignettes: Real and Ideal*, a collection of stories by American authors, one of whom was Clyde Fitch (see p. 733, note 2), and in 1896 *Famous American Actors of To-Day*, with profiles written by, among others, Harrison Grey Fiske, Stephen Fiske, and A. M. Palmer (McKay wrote a profile of Rose Coghlan).

2. Wilde kept rooms at 10 St. James's Place for the purpose of writing (CL, 585). According to the testimony of a former employee of the establishment, Wilde also met young men there "of quite inferior station" (Hyde, 246).

3. In ancient Roman religion the Penates were household gods.

4. *Little Lord Fauntleroy* is a children's novel by Frances Hodgson Burnett about an American boy who inherits a British title. The little lord's costume—a black velvet suit with knee breeches and a lace collar—became fashionable attire for children in Europe and America. The book was serialised between 1885 and 1886, and so postdates Wilde's aesthetic costume of 1882.

5. Rosamond Marie "Rose" Coghlan (1851–1932) was an English actress who worked in England and America. *A Woman of No Importance* was first performed in London on 19 April 1893 and had its American premiere on 11 December. *The Sun* (New York, NY; 12 Dec. 1893, 5) judged that "Rose Coghlan distinguished herself by a touching, moving, pitiful, and tender portrayal of [Mrs. Arbuthnot]", but also suggested that the play was "not fit to be performed in the presence of assemblages of both sexes."

"I am not able to write a line," he said, "unless I feel inspired. In order to evolve anything I consider worthy of myself, I must feel that I am 'possessed' of my subject. I seldom write during the day; it is at night, when all is still, dead almost to the writer, that the mind may soar above earthly considerations. In this I follow the maxims of Gustave Flaubert."

"Does this apply to everyone?" I asked.

"I do not believe in equality," he replied. "The world would be far better off if only few were in command and the masses were reduced to slavery—mentally as well as bodily.

"In each century only three or four men should rule; men of genius, and these men should be allowed to do exactly as they please."

"Why?"

"Because they have genius. That is superior to anything human. It is a subtle something that is a spark of divinity. It should excuse vagaries, faults, weaknesses, even crimes."

When asked whether he applied his theory to women, too, Mr. Wilde said: "I like to detect intelligence in men; I do not like to find it in women—their mission in life is to be beautiful—that is all!"

Beautiful women, in Wilde's mind, ought to have the same privilege that men of genius would possess in the ideal world he describes. That is to say, there should be no restraint put upon them. No laws of country, conventions of society of prejudices of class should hamper them.

With regard to the drama, Wilde declares it one of the most wonderful achievements of modern civilization. "The stage," he told me, "should be neither a battlefield nor a mere place for amusement. All plays should contain morals. The stage should not teach a stratum of society, but all humanity. It ought to hold before the public's eyes all the vices. It should not stay there. It should reveal the consequences of an evil life, so that the audience be thoroughly impressed and prevented from doing likewise.[1]

"Before all, and above all, the characters that interpret a play should be true to life. Whether they are types of people the author has met in different epochs of his life or in different countries, he should be permitted to combine them in one drama."[2]

Wilde says he never writes a line in a play or a book without supposing himself the person he makes talk. This applies with equal force, of course, to

1. This opinion contrasts with Wilde's oft-stated aversion to moralising and improving works of fiction.

2. Compare Wilde's opinion here with that expressed in Gilbert Burgess, "An Ideal Husband at the Haymarket Theatre," *The Sketch* (London, UK), 9 Jan. 1895, 495, p. 645.

Dorian Gray, Lady Windermere, Mrs. Erlynne, Lord Illingworth or "A Woman of No Importance."[1]

F. E. McKay.

"News From Afar," *The Press* (New York, NY), 8 July 1894, 7

✂ *Several paragraphs that are unrelated to Wilde.*

During Beerbohm Tree's absence on tour next autumn the Haymarket will pass into the hands of Lewis Waller, who intends to produce there a new comedy by Oscar Wilde.[2] In connection with the above forthcoming production, a characteristic correspondence has passed by wire between Oscar Wilde and a writer. Lewis Waller is at present out of town, and in order to obtain particulars about the new play the writer telegraphed to Oscar Wilde, asking him to grant an interview. This was the reply, received about an hour or so later:

"Very many thanks, but quite impossible. No one should read newspapers. Oscar."

A second telegram was sent to the literary esthete, reading: "Many thanks for your wire. What should one read?"

"My own books, of course," was the prompt response.

✂ *Several paragraphs that are unrelated to Wilde.*

"News From Afar," *The Press* (New York, NY), 15 July 1894, 3[3]

✂ *Several paragraphs that are unrelated to Wilde.*

Oscar Wilde is pleased to continue to be interviewed by telegraph. Last week people were recommended to read his books instead of the daily newspa-

---

1. Lady Windermere and Mrs. Erlynne are characters in *Lady Windermere's Fan*; Lord Illingworth in *A Woman of No Importance*.

2. Herbert Beerbohm Tree (1852–1917) and Lewis Waller (1860–1915) were English actors and theatre managers. Tree had, in 1893, staged *A Woman of No Importance* at the Theatre Royal, Haymarket, creating the role of Lord Illingworth. Later that year Waller played Illingworth in the touring production. In 1894 Waller leased the Haymarket while Tree was touring in the United States, and *An Ideal Husband* was his first production. He played Sir Robert Chiltern.

3. Printed simultaneously in "London Theatricals," *The Daily Picayune* (New Orleans, LA), 15 July 1894, 8.

pers. This, naturally, called for some explanation, and the following wire was sent to the author of "Dorian Gray:"

"What is the difference between your books and newspapers?"

The question proved a poser to the maker of epigrams who begged it, thus: "The difference between literature and journalism is that journalism is unreadable and literature is not read. Oscar Wilde."[1]

An hour later he was asked: "Is not the unread only known through the unreadable?"

To this he replied: "Of course; that is why the world has still to be civilized."

✂   *Several paragraphs that are unrelated to Wilde.*

"At the Play," *Hearth and Home* (London, UK), 30 Aug. 1894, 553

✂   *Several paragraphs that are unrelated to Wilde.*

Mr. Oscar Wilde tells me that his new play is in the hands of Mr. Lewis Waller, who hopes to bring it out at the Haymarket Theatre on or about New Year's Day.[2] Mr. Waller will play the principal man's part, but who will be his leading lady is not quite decided yet. Negotiations are proceeding with a very great actress indeed, and one who is exceptionally popular just now, but whether they will come to anything remains to be seen.[3] The play is not a costume piece, as has been rumoured, but is quite modern, and no doubt stuffed with epigrams. Mr. Lewis Waller made a very great hit in "The Woman of No Importance," [*sic*] with which he made the tour of the provinces, and his ambition now is to establish himself in London as a popular actor-manager. I hear that his wife, Miss Florence West, has been unwell lately, and has been travelling in Switzerland, where she has gained much good from the glacier air.

PIERROT.

1. *The Critic as Artist*: "ERNEST. But what is the difference between literature and journalism? | GILBERT. Oh! journalism is unreadable, and literature is not read. That is all." (CW iv, 135.11–13.)
2. *An Ideal Husband* opened at the Haymarket on 3 January 1895.
3. Lady Chiltern was played by Julia Neilson (1868–1957).

"Théatres," *Le Temps* (Paris, France), 5 Jan. 1895, 4[1]

✂ *Several paragraphs that are unrelated to Wilde.*

— Hier soir a eu lieu à Londres, au théâtre de Haymarket, la première représentation d'une nouvelle pièce de cet esthète attardé que tout Paris connaît, M. Oscar Wilde. Titre : *The Ideal Husband* (l'*idéal mari*). Le public a fait à cette œuvre un accueil si enthousiaste que M. Wilde a daigné paraître en personne devant lui pour le féliciter de son bon goût et déclarer « que la soirée lui avait, quant à lui, beaucoup plu ».

À un reporter qui l'avait interviewé avant la représentation, M. Wilde avait fait cette confidence : « Il n'y a rien dans ma pièce, mais elle est bonne, elle est très bonne. »

Theatres

Last night there took place in London, at the Haymarket Theatre, the first performance of a new play by this backward aesthete that all Paris knows, Mr. Oscar Wilde. Title: *The Ideal Husband* [*sic*]. The public gave this work such an enthusiastic reception that Mr. Wilde deigned to appear in person in front of them to congratulate them on their good taste and to declare "that he had enjoyed the evening very much".[2]

To a reporter who interviewed him before the performance, Mr. Wilde confided: "There is nothing in my play, but it is good, it is very good."[3]

1. See below for an annotated English translation. Printed simultaneously in "Courrier des théatres," *Journal des débats* (Paris, France), 5 Jan. 1895, 3. Reprinted in "Derriere la toile," *Le Rappel* (Paris, France), 6 Jan. 1895, 4; and "Les Théatres," *le XIXᵉ siècle* (Paris, France), 6 Jan. 1895, 3.
2. Wilde was reported to have said: "Ladies and Gentlemen,—I thank you very much for the charming reception you have given to my play. I thank the company for the very careful way in which they have acted it, and I have enjoyed my evening immensely." ("The New Management at the Haymarket," *The Daily News* (London, UK), 4 Jan. 1895, 3.)
3. Wilde's comment "There is nothing in it; but it is good—very good" was also reported in the British press, including a day earlier in *The Glasgow Herald* (Glasgow, UK), 4 Jan. 1895, 5, although with no reference to the interviewer.

Gilbert Burgess, "An Ideal Husband at the Haymarket Theatre," *The Sketch* (London, UK), 9 Jan. 1895, 495[1]

A TALK WITH MR. OSCAR WILDE

On the morning following the production of "An Ideal Husband" I met Mr. Oscar Wilde as he came down the steps of a club at the top of St. James's Street, and I took advantage of the occasion to ask him what he thought of the attitude of the critics towards his play. "Well," he replied, as we walked slowly down the street, "for a man to be a dramatic critic is as foolish and as inartistic as it would be for a man to be a critic of epics or a pastoral critic, or a critic of lyrics. All modes of art are one, and the modes of the art that employs words as its medium are quite indivisible. The result of the vulgar specialization of criticism is an elaborate scientific knowledge of the stage—almost as elaborate as that of the stage-carpenter and quite on a par with that of the call-boy—combined with an entire incapacity to realize that a play is a work of art, or to receive any artistic impressions at all."

"You are rather severe upon dramatic criticism, Mr. Wilde."

"English dramatic criticism of our own day has never had a single success, in spite of the fact that it goes to all the first nights."

"But," I suggested, "it is influential."

"Certainly; that is why it is so bad."

"I don't think I quite—"

"The moment criticism exercises any influence it ceases to be criticism. The aim of the true critic is to try and chronicle his own moods, not to try and correct the masterpieces of others."

"Real critics would be charming in your eyes, then?"

"Real critics? Ah, how perfectly charming they would be. I am always waiting for their arrival. An inaudible school would be nice. Why do you not found it?"

I was momentarily dazed at the broad vista that had been opened for me, but I retained my presence of mind, and asked—

"Are there absolutely no real critics in London?"

"There are just two."

"Who are they?" I asked eagerly.

---

1. H & S, b106. Reprinted in "Wilde Paradoxes," *New York Tribune* (New York, NY), 27 Jan. 1895, 23; Mikhail, 239–43; and Seeney, M. (2014). An Ideal Husband: the first night. *The Wildean*, 44, 14–18. Excerpted in Mason, 439–42; and Pearson, 250–1. Quoted in "In a Storm of Hisses," *The Chicago Sunday Tribune* (Chicago, IL), 27 Jan. 1895, 38; Pearson, 235; Hyde, 159; Ellmann, 348/368; and Sturgis, 527/491, 533/496–7. Gilbert Burgess (1868–1911) was an English author and journalist. In a letter to Robert Ross dated 6 April [1897], Wilde listed a few friends who might give him books upon his release from prison; Burgess was one of them (CL, 790).

Mr. Wilde, with the elaborate courtesy for which he has always been famous, replied, "I think I had better not mention their names; it might make the others so jealous."[1]

"What do the literary cliques think of your plays?"

"I don't write to please cliques; I write to please myself. Besides, I have always had grave suspicions that the basis of all literary cliques is a morbid love of meat-teas. That makes them sadly uncivilized."

"Still, if your critics offend you, why don't you reply to them?"

"I have far too much time. But I think some day I will give a general answer in the form of a lecture in a public hall, which I shall call 'Straight Talks to Old Men.'"

"What is your feeling towards your audiences—towards the public?"

"Which public? There are as many publics as there are personalities."

"Are you nervous on the night that you are producing a new play?"

"Oh, no, I am exquisitely indifferent. My nervousness ends at the last dress rehearsal; I know then what effect my play, as presented upon the stage, has produced upon me. My interest in the play ends there, and I feel curiously envious of the public—they have such wonderfully fresh emotions in store for them."

I laughed, but Mr. Wilde rebuked me with a look of surprise.

"It is the public, not the play, that I desire to make a success," he said.

"But, I'm afraid I don't quite understand—"

"The public makes a success when it realizes that a play is a work of art. On the three first nights I have had in London, the public has been most successful, and, had the dimensions of the stage admitted of it, I would have called them before the curtain. Most managers, I believe, call them behind."

"I imagine then, that you don't hold with the opinion that the public is the patron of the dramatist?"

"The artist is always the munificent patron of the public. I am very fond of the public, and, personally, I always patronize the public very much."

"What are your views upon the much-vexed question of subject-matter in art?"

"Everything matters in art except the subject."

When I recovered I said, "Several plays have been written lately that deal with the monstrous injustice of the social code of morality at the present time."

"Ah," answered Mr. Wilde, with an air of earnest conviction, "it is indeed a burning shame that there should be one law for men and another law for women.

---

1. One of the unnamed critics was William Archer (1856–1924). See [Robert Ross], "Mr. Oscar Wilde on Mr. Oscar Wilde," *St. James's Gazette* (London, UK), 18 Jan. 1895, 4–5, p. 651.

I think"—he hesitated, and a smile as swift as Sterne's "hectic of a moment" flitted across his face—"I think that there should be no law for anybody."[1]

"In writing, do you think that real life or real people should ever give one inspiration?"

"The colour of a flower may suggest to one the plot of a tragedy; a passage in music may give one the sestet of a sonnet; but whatever actually occurs gives the artist no suggestion.[2] Every romance that one has in one's life is a romance lost to one's art. To introduce real people into a novel or a play is a sign of an unimaginative mind, a coarse, untutored observation, and an entire absence of style."[3]

"I am afraid I can't agree with you, Mr. Wilde; I frequently see types and people who suggest ideas to me."

"Everything is of use to the artist except an idea."

After this I was silent, until Mr. Wilde pointed to the bottom of the street and drew my attention to the "apricot-coloured palace" which we were approaching. So I continued my questioning.

"The enemy has said that your plays lack action."

"Yes; English critics always confuse the action of a play with the incidents of a melodrama. I wrote the first act of 'A Woman of No Importance' in answer to the critics who said that 'Lady Windermere's Fan' lacked action. In the act in question, there was absolutely no action at all. It was a perfect act."

"What do you think is the chief point that critics have missed in your new play?"

"Its entire psychology—the difference in the way in which a man loves a woman from that in which a woman loves a man, the passion that women have for making ideals (which is their weakness) and the weakness of a man who dare not show his imperfections to the thing he loves. The end of Act I., and the end of Act II., and the scene in the last act, when Lord Goring points out the higher importance of a man's life over a woman's—to take three prominent instances—seem to have been missed by most of the critics. They failed to see their meaning;

1. Burgess's reference is to *A Sentimental Journey Through France and Italy* (1768), a novel by Laurence Sterne (1713–1768): "The poor Franciscan made no reply: a hectic of a moment pass'd across his cheek, but could not tarry—Nature seemed to have done with her resentments in him;—he showed none:—but letting his staff fall within his arms, he pressed both his hands with resignation upon his breast, and retired."

2. Gilbert in *The Critic as Artist*: "Whatever actually occurs is spoiled for art." (CW iv, 195.25–6.) Compare Wilde's opinion here with that expressed in "Oscar Wilde," *The Cheyenne Daily Leader* (Cheyenne, WY), 13 Apr. 1882, 1, p. 333.

3. Compare Wilde's opinion here with that expressed in Percival H. W. Almy, "New Views of Mr. Oscar Wilde," *Theatre* (London, UK), Vol. 23, Mar. 1894, 119–27, p. 639.

they really thought it was a play about a bracelet.[1] We must educate our critics—we must really educate them," said Mr. Wilde, half to himself.

"The critics subordinate the psychological interest of a play to its mere technique. As soon as a dramatist invents an ingenious situation they compare him with Sardou.[2] But Sardou is an artist not because of his marvellous instinct of stagecraft, but in spite of it: in the third act of 'La Tosca,' the scene of the torture, he moved us by a terrible human tragedy, not by his knowledge of stage methods. Sardou is not understood in England because he is only known through a rather ordinary travesty of his play 'Dora,' which was brought out here under the title of 'Diplomacy.'[3] I have been considerably amused by so many of the critics suggesting that the incident of the diamond bracelet in Act III. of my new play was suggested by Sardou. It does not occur in any of Sardou's plays, and it was not in my play until less than ten days before production. Nobody else's work gives me any suggestion. It is only by entire isolation from everything that one can do any work. Idleness gives one the mood in which to write, isolation the conditions. Concentration on oneself reveals the new and wonderful world that one presents in the colour and cadence of words in movement."

"And yet we want something more than literature in a play," said I.

"That is merely because the critics have always propounded the degrading dogma that the duty of the dramatist is to please the public. Rossetti did not weave words into sonnets to please the public, and Corot did not paint silver and grey twilights to please the public. The mere fact of telling an artist to adopt any particular form of art, in order to please the public, makes him shun it. We shall never have a real drama in England until it is recognised that a play is as personal and individual a form of self-expression as a poem or a picture."

"I'm afraid you don't like journalists?" I remarked nervously.

"The journalist is always reminding the public of the existence of the artist. That is unnecessary of him. He is always reminding the artist of the existence of the public. That is indecent of him."

"But we must have journalists, Mr. Wilde."

"Why? They only record what happens. What does it matter what happens? It is only the abiding things that are interesting, not the horrid incidents of everyday life. Creation, for the joy of creation, is the aim of the artist, and that is why the artist is a more divine type than the saint. The artist arrives at his moment, with his own mood. He may come with terrible purple tragedies, he may come

---

1. In *An Ideal Husband* Lord Goring confronts Mrs Cheveley about a bracelet he suspects she has stolen.

2. Victorien Sardou (1831–1908) was a successful and influential French playwright. His works include the opera *La Tosca* (1887) and *Dora* (1877).

3. *Diplomacy* (1878) was adapted by B. C. Stephenson (1839–1906) and Clement Scott (1841–1904).

with dainty rose-coloured comedies—what a charming title!" added Mr. Wilde, with a smile. "I must write a play and call it 'A Rose-Coloured Comedy.'"

"What are the exact relations between literature and the drama?"

"Exquisitely accidental. That is why I think them so necessary."

"And the exact relations between the actor and the dramatist?"

Mr. Wilde looked at me with a serious expression which changed almost immediately into a smile, as he replied, "Usually a little strained."

"But surely you regard the actor as a creative artist?"

"Yes," replied Mr. Wilde, with a touch of pathos in his voice; "terribly creative—terribly creative!"

"Do you consider that the future outlook of the English stage is hopeful?"

"I think it must be. The critics have ceased to prophesy. That is something. It is in silence that the artist arrives. What is waited for never succeeds; what is heralded is hopeless."

We were nearing the sentries at Marlborough House, and I said—

"Won't you tell me a little more, please? Let us walk down Pall Mall— Exercise is such a good thing."

"Exercise!" he ejaculated, with an emphasis which almost warrants italics, "the only possible form of exercise is to talk, not to walk."

And as he spoke he motioned to a passing hansom. We shook hands, and Mr. Wilde, giving me a glance of approval, said—

"I am sure that you must have a great future in literature before you."

"What makes you think so?" I asked, as I flushed with pleasure at the prediction.

"Because you seem to me such a very bad interviewer. I feel sure that you must write poetry. I certainly like the colour of your necktie very much. Good-bye."

GILBERT BURGESS

[Robert Ross], "Mr. Oscar Wilde on Mr. Oscar Wilde," *St. James's Gazette* (London, UK), 18 Jan. 1895, 4–5[1]

AN INTERVIEW.

I found Mr. Oscar Wilde (writes a Representative) making ready to depart on a short visit to Algiers,[2] and reading—of course, nothing so obvious as a time-table, but a French newspaper which contained an account of the first night of "The Ideal Husband" [*sic*] and its author's appearance after the play.

"How well the French appreciate these brilliant wilful moments in an artist's life," remarked Mr. Wilde, handing me the article as if he considered the interview already at an end.

"Does it give you any pleasure," I inquired, "to appear before the curtain after the production of your plays?"

"None whatsoever. No artist finds any interest in seeing the public. The public is very much interested in seeing an artist. Personally, I prefer the French custom, according to which the name of the dramatist is announced to the public by the oldest actor in the piece."

"Would you advocate," I asked, "this custom in England?"

"Certainly. The more the public is interested in artists, the less it is interested in art. The personality of the artist is not a thing the public should know anything about. It is too accidental." Then, after a pause—

"It might be more interesting if the name of the author were announced by the *youngest* actor present."

"It is only in deference, then, to the imperious mandate of the public that you have appeared before the curtain?"

1. H & S, b107. Reprinted in Mikhail, 246–51. Excerpted in Hyde, 175–6. Quoted in "Theatrical Gossip," *The Era* (London, UK), 26 Jan. 1895, 12; Pearson, 255–6; Ellmann, 347/367; and Sturgis, 532–3/496. This article has been attributed to Robert Ross (Mason, 438; Mikhail, 246; Pearson, 255; Ellmann, 347/367; in the copy at No. 181, Oscar Wilde Scrapbook Vol. 2, Honma Hisao Collection, Jissen Women's University Rare Books, somebody, presumably Mason—the scrapbook's former owner—has written "R. Ross" above "a Representative"). The interview was critiqued in *The Globe* on 19 January 1895 and a letter to the editor in defence of Wilde and signed "R." appeared soon after: "will you allow me to state as a personal friend of his that it was only at the earnest and importunate solicitation of another friend that he consented to be interviewed at all." ("Wilde Words," *The Globe* (London, UK), 25 Jan. 1895, 3.) Holland and Hart-Davis (CL, 629) suggest that Wilde's letter from Algiers thanking Ross for the "most brilliant and delightful" interview implies that it was a collaborative effort. Joseph Donohue (CW x, 928) refers to the article as "a mock interview written by Robert Ross, possibly with W[ilde]'s collaboration" (see also CW x, 1012).

2. Wilde departed for Algiers on 15 January for a two week holiday with Lord Alfred Douglas (Page, 61).

"Yes; I have always been very good-natured about that. The public has always been so appreciative of my work I felt it would be a pity to spoil its evening."[1]

"I notice some people have found fault with the character of your speeches."[2]

"Yes, the old-fashioned idea was that the dramatist should appear and merely thank his kind friends for their patronage and presence. I am glad to say I have altered all that. The artist cannot be degraded into the servant of the public. While I have always recognized the cultured appreciation that actors and audience have shown for my work, I have equally recognized that humility is for the hypocrite, modesty for the incompetent. Assertion is at once the duty and privilege of the artist."

"To what do you attribute, Mr. Wilde, the fact that so few men of letters besides yourself have written plays for public presentation?"

"Primarily the existence of an irresponsible censorship. The fact that my 'Salome' cannot be performed is sufficient to show the folly of such an institution. If painters were obliged to show their pictures to clerks at Somerset House, those who think in form and colour would adopt some other mode of expression.[3] If every novel had to be submitted to a police magistrate, those whose passion is fiction would seek some new mode of realization. No art ever survived censorship; no art ever will."

"And secondly?"

"Secondly to the rumour persistently spread abroad by journalists for the last thirty years, that the duty of the dramatist was to please the public. The aim

---

1. Wilde appeared before the curtain and spoke at the opening nights of *Vera; or The Nihilists*, *Lady Windermere's Fan*, and *An Ideal Husband*. Hyde, 158, reports that, at the opening night of *A Woman of No Importance*, Wilde replied to calls for the author by standing up in his box and announcing: "Ladies and gentlemen, I regret to inform you that Mr Oscar Wilde is not in the house." He then appeared before the curtain but did not speak. During the first performance of *The Importance of Being Earnest* Wilde is supposed to have told actor Franklin Dyall that he did not think he would take a curtain call: "I took one only last month at the Haymarket [after *An Ideal Husband*], and one feels so much like a German Band!" (Hyde, 180.)

2. After *Lady Windermere's Fan* Wilde had told his audience: "I think that you have enjoyed the performance as much as I have, and I am pleased to believe that you like the piece almost as much as I do myself." ("London's Theatres," *The Stage* (London, UK), 25 Feb. 1892, 12.) He was criticised in the press for the speech, not only for its content but because he was smoking when he made it. After *An Ideal Husband* he said: "I thank you very much for the charming reception you have given to my play. I thank the company for the very careful way in which they have acted it, and I have enjoyed my evening immensely." ("The New Management at the Haymarket," *The Daily News* (London, UK), 4 Jan. 1895, 3.) Even critics hostile to the play tended not to take Wilde to task for this speech.

3. Somerset House had previously hosted the annual Royal Academy Exhibition; at this time it was the headquarters of various government departments.

of art is no more to give pleasure than to give pain. The aim of art is to be art. As I said once before, the work of art is to dominate the spectator—the spectator is not to dominate art."[1]

"You admit no exceptions?"

"Yes. Circuses where it seems the wishes of the public might be reasonably carried out."

"Do you think," I inquired, "that French dramatic criticism is superior to our own?"

"It would be unfair to confuse French dramatic criticism with English theatrical criticism. The French dramatic critic is always a man of culture and generally a man of letters. In France poets like Gautier have been dramatic critics. In England they are drawn from a less distinguished class. They have neither the same capacities nor the same opportunities. They have all the moral qualities, but none of the artistic qualifications. For the criticism of such a complex mode of art as the drama the highest culture is necessary. No one can criticise drama who is not capable of receiving impressions from the other arts also."

"You admit they are sincere?"

"Yes; but their sincerity is little more than stereotyped stupidity. The critic of the drama should be versatile as the actor. He should be able to change his mood at will and should catch the colour of the moment."

"At least they are honest?"

"Absolutely. I don't believe there is a single dramatic critic in London who would deliberately set himself to misrepresent the work of any dramatist—unless, of course, he personally disliked the dramatist, or had some play of his own he wished to produce at the same theatre, or had an old friend among the actors, or some natural reasons of that kind. I am speaking, however, of London dramatic critics. In the provinces both audience and critics are cultured. In London it is only the audience who are cultured."

"I fear you do not rate our dramatic critics very highly, Mr. Wilde; but, at all events, they are incorruptible?"

"In a market where there are no bidders."

"Still their memories stand them in good stead," I pleaded.

"The old talk of having seen Macready: that must be a very painful memory.[2] The middle-aged boast that they can recall 'Diplomacy:' hardly a pleasant reminiscence."

---

1. *The Soul of Man Under Socialism*: "If a man approaches a work of art with any desire to exercise authority over it and the artist, he approaches it in such a spirit that he cannot receive any artistic impression from it at all. The work of art is to dominate the spectator: the spectator is not to dominate the work of art. The spectator is to be receptive. He is to be the violin on which the master is to play." (CW iv, 258.4–8.)

2. William Charles Macready appeared on the London stage between 1816 and 1851.

"You deny them, then, even a creditable past?"

"They have no past and no future, and are incapable of realizing the colour of the moment that finds them at the play."

"What do you propose should be done?"

"They should be pensioned off, and only allowed to write on politics or theology or bimetallism, or some subject easier than art."

"In fact," I said, carried away by Mr. Wilde's aphorisms, "they should be seen and not heard."

"The old should neither be seen nor heard" said Mr. Wilde, with some emphasis.

"You said the other day there were only two dramatic critics in London.[1] May I ask"—

"They must have been greatly gratified by such an admission from me; but I am bound to say that since last week I have struck one of them from the list."

"Whom have you left in?"

"I think I had better not mention his name. It might make him too conceited. Conceit is the privilege of the creative."

"How would you define ideal dramatic criticism?"

"As far as my work is concerned, unqualified appreciation."

"And whom have you omitted?"

"Mr. William Archer, of the *World*."[2]

"What do you chiefly object to in his article?"

"I object to nothing in the article, but I grieve at everything in it. It is bad taste in him to write of me by my Christian name, and he need not have stolen his vulgarisms from the *National Observer* in its most impudent and impotent days."

"Mr. Archer asked whether, if it was agreeable to you to be hailed by your Christian name when the enthusiastic spectators called you before the curtain."

"To be so addressed by enthusiastic spectators is as great a compliment as to be written of by one's Christian name is in a journalist bad manners. Bad manners make a journalist."

"Do you think French actors, like French criticism, superior to our own?"

---

1. See Gilbert Burgess, "An Ideal Husband at the Haymarket Theatre," *The Sketch* (London, UK), 9 Jan. 1895, 495, pp. 643–4.

2. Archer judged *An Ideal Husband* to be "a very able and entertaining piece of work [....] but there are times when the output of Mr. Wilde's epigram-factory threatens to become all trademark and no substance. *An Ideal Husband*, however does not positively lack good things, but simply suffers from a disproportionate profusion of inferior chatter." (Archer, 18.) Archer had defended Wilde when *Salomé* was refused a licence (William Archer, "Mr. Oscar Wilde and the Censorship," *The Pall Mall Gazette* (London, UK), 1 July 1892, 3), and positively reviewed *A Woman of No Importance*. (Sturgis, 478–9/448). He later raved about *The Importance of Being Earnest*, describing it as "a sort of *rondo capriccioso*, in which the artist's fingers run with crisp irresponsibility up and down the keyboard of life." (Archer, 57.)

"The English actors act quite as well; but they act best between the lines. They lack the superb elocution of the French—so clear, so cadenced, and so musical. A long sustained speech seems to exhaust them. At the Théâtre Français we go to listen, to an English theatre we go to look. There are, of course, exceptions. Mr. George Alexander, Mr. Lewis Waller, Mr. Forbes Robertson, and others I might mention, have superb voices and know how to use them.[1] I wish I could say the same of the critics; but in the case of the literary drama in England there is too much of what is technically known as 'business.' Yet there is more than one of our English actors who is capable of producing a wonderful dramatic effect by aid of a monosyllable and two cigarettes."[2]

For a moment Mr. Wilde was silent, and then added, "Perhaps, after all, that is acting."

"But are you satisfied with the interpreters of the 'Ideal Husband?'"

"I am charmed with all of them. Perhaps they are a little too fascinating. The stage is the refuge of the too fascinating."

"Have you heard it said that all the characters in your play talk as you do?"

"Rumours of that kind have reached me from time to time," said Mr. Wilde, lighting a cigarette, "and I should fancy that some such criticism has been made. The fact is that it is only in the last few years that the dramatic critic has had the opportunity of seeing plays written by anyone who has a mastery of style. In the case of a dramatist also an artist it is impossible not to feel that the work of art, to be a work of art, must be dominated by the artist. Every play of Shakespeare is dominated by Shakespeare. Ibsen and Dumas dominate their works.[3] My works are dominated by myself."

"Have you ever been influenced by any of your predecessors?"

"It is enough for me to state definitely, and I hope once for all, that not a single dramatist in this century has ever in the smallest degree influenced me. Only two have interested me."

"And they are?"

1. George Alexander (1858–1918) was an English actor and theatre manager who appeared in and produced *Lady Windermere's Fan* and *The Importance of Being Earnest*. Wilde is probably referring to Johnston Forbes-Robertson, Norman Forbes-Robertson's older and more successful brother.

2. Joseph Donohue suggests the possibility that Wilde may have had in mind Allan Aynesworth (1864–1959), creator of the role of Algernon Moncrieff in *The Importance of Being Earnest* (CW x, 928).

3. Henrik Ibsen (1828–1906) was a Norwegian dramatist; the author of *Peer Gynt* (1867), *A Doll's House* (1879), and *Hedda Gabler* (1891). Several of his plays were translated into English by the critic, William Archer. Alexandre Dumas *père* (1802–1870) was a French novelist and dramatist, but Wilde is probably referring to his son, Alexandre Dumas *fils* (1824–1895), also a novelist and dramatist, but better known than his father for his plays, which include *La Dame aux Camélias* (1852).

"Victor Hugo and Maeterlinck."

"Other writers surely have influenced your other works?"

"Setting aside the prose and poetry of Greek and Latin authors, the only writers who have influenced me are Keats, Flaubert, and Walter Pater;[1] and before I came across them I had already gone more than halfway to meet them. Style must be in one's soul before one can recognize it in others."

"And do you consider the 'Ideal Husband' the best of your plays?"

A charming smile crossed Mr. Wilde's face.

"Have you forgotten my classical expression—that only mediocrities improve?[2] My three plays are to each other, as a wonderful young poet has beautifully said,

> as one white rose
> On one green stalk to another one.[3]

They form a perfect cycle, and in their delicate sphere complete both life and art."

1. Walter Pater was an English literary and art critic, a classics professor at Brasenose College, Oxford, and a mentor to Wilde from autumn 1877. His *Studies in the History of the Renaissance* (1873), was one of Wilde's favourite books: he would request a copy in prison (Wright, 319). In it, Pater argued for an art that was more about style than message, thus allying himself to the nascent aesthetic movement. In the conclusion to the book (which he omitted in the second edition because "it might possibly mislead some of those young men into whose hands it might fall"), he made the case for a philosophy of life that appealed to the young Wilde:

> Not the fruit of experience, but experience itself, is the end. A counted number of pulses only is given to us of a variegated, dramatic life. How may we see in them all that is to be seen in them by the finest senses? How shall we pass most swiftly from point to point, and be present always at the focus where the greatest number of vital forces unite in their purest energy? To burn always with this hard, gemlike flame, to maintain this ecstasy, is success in life. (210)

On their first meeting, Pater asked Wilde: "Why do you always write poetry? Why do you not write prose? Prose is so much more difficult." (*The Speaker*, 22 Mar. 1890; CW vii, No. 134, lines 5–6.) Wilde thought Pater ranked "amongst our century's most characteristic artists" (ibid, lines 173–4), and was one of the "very few masters" of English prose (*The Queen*, 8 Dec. 1888; CW vii, No, 108, lines 155–6). Wilde testified at the Queensberry libel trial that Pater pointed out to him that "a certain passage [of the *Lippincott's* version of *The Picture of Dorian Gray*] was liable to misconstruction", and that he had consequently modified the text for the 1891 version to avoid conveying "the impression that the sin of Dorian Gray was sodomy." (Holland, 78–9.)

2. In August 1894 a poem titled *The Shamrock* had been printed in the *Sunday Sun* above Wilde's name. Wilde protested that he had not written these "doggerel verses". The editor of the *Sun* disingenuously claimed to have thought the poem a piece of Wildean juvenilia. Wilde responded that this "showed a lamentable ignorance of the nature of the artistic temperament. Only mediocrities progress. An artist revolves in a cycle of masterpieces, the first of which is no less perfect than the last." (CL, 611, 613–5.)

3. Wilde quotes *Jonquil and Fleur-de-lys*, a poem by Lord Alfred Douglas (1870–1945). A "shepherd lad" and prince talk of their different lives and decide to swap roles: "Whereon they stripped off all their clothes, | And when they stood up in the sun, | They were as like one white rose | On one green stalk, to another one." Fleur-de-Lys was one of Wilde's nicknames for Douglas (CL, 648). The three plays Wilde refers to are presumably his society comedies.

"Do you think that the critics will understand your new play, which Mr. George Alexander has secured?"[1]

"I hope not."[2]

"I dare not ask, I suppose, if it will please the public?"

"When a play that is a work of art is produced on the stage what is being tested is not the play, but the stage; when a play that is not a work of art is produced on the stage what is being tested is not the play, but the public."

"What sort of play are we to expect?"

"It is exquisitely trivial, a delicate bubble of fancy, and it has its philosophy."

"Its philosophy!"

"That we should treat all the trivial things of life very seriously, and all the serious things of life with sincere and studied triviality."[3]

"You have no leanings towards realism?"

"None whatever. Realism is only a background; it cannot form an artistic motive for a play that is to be a work of art."

"Still I have heard you congratulated on your pictures of London society."

"If Robert Chiltern, the Ideal Husband, were a common clerk, the humanity of his tragedy would be none the less poignant. I have placed him in the higher ranks of life merely because that is the side of social life with which I am best acquainted. In a play dealing with actualities to write with ease one must write with knowledge."

"Then you see nothing suggestive of treatment in the tragedies of every-day existence?"

"If a journalist is run over by a four-wheeler in the Strand, an incident I regret to say I have never witnessed, it suggests nothing to me from a dramatic point of view. Perhaps I am wrong; but the artist must have his limitations."

"Well," I said, rising to go, "I have enjoyed myself immensely."

"I was sure you would," said Mr. Wilde. "But tell me how you manage your interviews."

"Oh, Pitman," I said carelessly.[4]

"Is that your name? It's not a very *nice* name."

Then I left.

---

1. *The Importance of Being Earnest.*

2. This sentiment echoes an article by Wilde for the *Saturday Review*: "it is only mediocrities and old maids who consider it a grievance to be misunderstood" (7 May 1887; CW vi, No. 71, lines 133–4.) Also, Lord Darlington in *Lady Windermere's Fan*: "Now-a-days, to be intelligible, is to be found out." (CW xi, 358.166–7.)

3. The subtitle of the play is "A Trivial Comedy for Serious People" (CW x, 855). Wilde also referred to the play as "trivial" in letters to friends (CL, 630, 1124).

4. Pitman is a system of shorthand developed by Sir Isaac Pitman (1813–1897).

Frank Marshall White [and Robert Batho], "Oscar Wilde to Write," *The Chicago Daily Tribune* (Chicago, IL), 17 May 1897, 2[1]

TELLS OF HIS PLANS WHEN RELEASED FROM PRISON.

Will Live in Seclusion at Some Place Near London and Do Literary Work Soon—But at Present He Says His Brain is "Too Weak, Too Worn, Too Tired"—Will Leave the Prison on Wednesday.

(SPECIAL CABLE BY FRANKLIN WHITE.)

LONDON, May 16.—(Copyright, 1897)—Oscar Wilde has broken his long enforced silence. In Reading Prison today he announced to me his plans for the future. The terrible punishment he has suffered has not broken his spirit nor impaired his strength. He will try to live down the shame he has brought on himself and will not flee from his country and his enemies.[2] Frank Harris of the Saturday Review remains his friend through his humiliation and disgrace.[3] These are the questions put to Wilde and his answers:[4]

---

1. I am grateful to John Cooper for identifying this and other related articles. Printed simultaneously with variations as "Oscar Wilde Breaks Silence," *Buffalo Evening News* (Buffalo, NY), 17 May 1897, 5. Abbreviated versions (without reference to Batho[s]) were printed as "Oscar Wilde's Release," *New York Journal and Advertiser* (New York, NY), 17 May 1897, 1; and "Oscar Wilde to Write Again," *The Examiner* (San Francisco, CA), 17 May 1897, 3. Robert Batho (see p. 517, note 1) and Frank Marshall White probably collaborated on the article, with Batho conducting the interview and White cabling it to his employers in America. White (1861–1906) had previously worked as a reporter for the *New York Times* (1882–1885) and as the London correspondent of the New York *Sun* (1889–1893). He had been in Reading for at least a week, seeking information about Wilde's imprisonment and his impending release. An American reporter, possibly White, had written to Major James Osmond Nelson (1859–1914), the governor of HM Prison Reading, offering to pay any sum for an interview with Wilde. Wilde was appalled by the idea (CL, 829; Hyde (1963), 138). However, Wilde and Nelson may have been more willing to agree to an interview prior to Wilde's release if Nelson acted as intermediary, perhaps hoping that this would dissuade the interviewers from ambushing Wilde later. If Batho had been granted a face-to-face interview, or if he had fabricated the interview, it seems very likely that he would have given a physical description of Wilde, which the article lacks. Wilde does not appear to have been paid for the interview. He later told Leonard Smithers that a representative of the *New York Journal* had "offered £1,000" (CL, 937), and Lord Alfred claimed that he knew "that within three months of his release Wilde regretted bitterly that he had not closed with the American gentleman's proposition." (Douglas (1914), 141.)

2. *The Examiner* also has "and his enemies"; the *Buffalo Evening News* instead has "and his friends."

3. Frank Harris (1855–1931) was an Irish–American journalist. In April 1897 he visited Wilde in prison and promised to give him £500, a promise he later rescinded (Sturgis, 620–1/579). Wilde was annoyed and wrote to other friends accusing Harris of blowing "lying trumpets" and posing as generous (CL, 829).

4. In other versions of the interview fewer of the questions are given and Wilde's responses are phrased such that it appears that he introduced topics rather than being asked about them.

"Tell me the condition of your health?"

"My health, physically, is good, but my brain is weary."

"Have you formulated any plans for your future?"

"Yes, and now I am in the hands of a few faithful friends and my own dearest friend. To them I will deliver myself up, and with them chiefly lies my destiny. To them alone will I communicate my dearest desires."[1]

"But I ask for the public, the myriad admirers of your genius as poet, dramatist, and author. Are they to lose the benefit of your gifts? Is the world to have no more masterpieces from your pen?"

His Brain is Tired.

"At present my brain is too weak, too worn, too tired, but the power that is in me will sway.[2] I shall write again soon, but not yet. I am too tired, too distressed."

"You will write in English or in French exclusively?"

"I will write in English."

"Do you propose leaving England?"

"Not at present. As I have told you I am in the hands of a few friends. They will decide for a while."

"Allow me to ask bluntly, you do not intend to efface yourself?"

"I do not. I shall get to work again before long, the moment I feel well enough."

"And for the present?"

"For the present, thanks to the friends to whom I have alluded, I shall retire into absolute seclusion. I shall see no one, speak to no one but them."

"When may I tell the public they may expect to hear of you?"

"The public will hear from me through my next work, not before it is ready and not by any other means."

"Will it bear your name?"

"Most assuredly, as I am at present disposed."

"Can you not give me some approximate idea of when that will be?"

"No, I cannot tell until I have rested. I do not intend to work until my brain has recovered its balance."

"And you seek to recover your equanimity in absolute seclusion?"

"In absolute seclusion."

Will Go Into Seclusion.

"Of course, you decline to name the whereabouts of your seclusion?"

1. Other versions have "ambition" instead of "desires".
2. Other versions have "but the power that is in me will resume its sway."

"Most assuredly. The place will not, however, be far from London."[1]

Maj. Nelson, Governor of Reading Prison, here abruptly terminated the interview, as the limit of time under the Home Office regulations had expired. Robert Batho, who obtained the interview today, is a London journalist, who has won Wilde's confidence by accurately reporting him on previous occasions.[2] His account of three previous interviews with Wilde only accentuates the terrible tragedy in the life of this gifted man. Mr. Batho writes: "This is the fourth time in Wilde's career that I have interviewed him. Each time marked an epoch in his remarkable history. The first occasion was on his landing in Liverpool when he was returned from his first memorable visit to New York.[3] He was young then, full of good spirits, and intensely satisfied with himself. His large oval face was youthful and handsome. He was wearing a costume which, from his necktie to his boots, was a consistent gradation of blending tints of his 'green and gold and yellow.' He spoke of the monotony of the ocean and its inartistic coloring and assured me that 'the American people are the greatest people of all ages. You know not life, you know not existence, until you have known the Americans. Old England is asleep.'[4]

Wilde at Stratford on Avon.

"The next important occasion of my interviewing him was at Stratford-on-Avon, about eight years ago, when, in company with Henry Irving, George Augustus Sala, Lord Leigh, and a host of literary and artistic eminences, he supported Lord Ronald Gower at the ceremony of the unveiling of the beautiful Gower group of Shakespearean statuary.[5] Wilde was then matured, grave, and fault-

1. The *Buffalo Evening News* adds here "More than that, I canot [*sic*] say."

2. Batho's name is spelt "Bathos" throughout this article and in the *Buffalo Evening News*.

3. [Robert Batho], "An Interview with Oscar Wilde," *Liverpool Daily Post* (Liverpool, UK), 8 Jan. 1883, 7, pp. 517–23. A "representative of the *Evening News*", almost certainly Batho, made this same claim shortly after Wilde's conviction ("Wilde in Prison," *Western Mail* (Cardiff), 28 May 1895, 3, quoting an article in the *Evening News* of Monday, i.e. 27 May).

4. The description of Wilde's dress and his comments about the Atlantic are consistent with the Liverpool interview, but the quotation about the American people does not feature there. Instead Wilde criticised American culture. Batho seems to have tailored his 1897 account to suit an American audience. In an article for the 27 May 1895 edition of the *Evening News* that was reprinted as "Wilde in Prison," *Western Mail* (Cardiff, UK), 28 May 1895, 3, Batho wrote: "I met Wilde in his youth after he made his first memorable visit to America. His attire then was eccentric, but a justification of his doctrines. No man was more perfectly, more beautifully dressed. There was not a tinge in the colours of his apparel but completed the harmony. His long hair became him; his face was an oval, youthful, fresh, and bright with intelligence."

5. [Robert Batho], "Shakespeare's Statue," *The New York Herald, European Edition* (Paris, France), 11 Oct. 1888, 1, pp. 583–8. Sala and Lord Leigh were present at the unveiling of the monument, but Henry Irving sent apologies for his absence ("Unveiling of the Gower Memorial at Stratford," *The Birmingham Daily Post* (Birmingham, UK), 11 Oct. 1888, 5). In 1895 Batho wrote: "[...] I met him [Wilde], sat with him at dinner in the library of the Shakspeare [*sic*] Me-

657

lessly dressed in black. He delivered an address on the art of sculpture which for learning and eloquence was worthy of being placed on the level of the classics in criticism.

"His leaning was now towards France. Yet, with the throwing off of his Della Cruscan insanity,[1] he had discovered something good in England. He then assured me he had hopes for the old country.[2] The third time I interviewed him he was in Room No. 14 Holborn Viaduct Hotel, London, on the day of the sensation of the collapse of his action against Queensberry. A few hours after his arrest he assured me he was 'sore distressed.' He had refused to speak to scores of newspaper men who had besieged the hotel, because 'the reporters have reproduced my remarks in the witness box most inaccurately.' As to the trial, he would have made me take a shorthand note of his statement and got Lord Douglas of Hawick, who was present, to write out a longhand copy of the same, and this he signed.

Took the Blame Himself.

"The statement was that he could prove his innocence by placing Lord Alfred Douglas in the box as a witness against his father,[3] the noble Marquis,[4] but 'rather than put Lord Alfred in so painful a position I determined to bear on my own shoulders whatever ignominy and shame might result from my prosecuting Lord Queensberry.'[5] He has borne the ignominy and shame, and now, three days

---

morial Theatre at Stratford-on-Avon. Mr. Henry Irving and the veteran journalist, Mr. George Augustus Sala, were also there."

1. The Della Cruscans were a group of English and Italian poets of the late eighteenth-century, criticised for their artificial, sentimental, and overly elaborate verse. Batho is perhaps alluding to *Patience*, in which Lady Saphir, one of the "rapturous maidens", rejects the unaesthetic Colonel Calverley: "It can never be. You are not Empyrean. You are not Della Cruscan. You are not even Early English."

2. No such assurance features in the Stratford interview.

3. The *Buffalo Evening News* has "The statement was that he *could have proved* his innocence by placing Lord Alfred in the box as a witness against his father" (emphasis added).

4. "Marquis" is the French spelling of the title; in Great Britain the title is traditionally spelt "marquess". Holders of the Marquessate of Queensberry are usually referred to as the Marquess of Queensberry. However, John Sholto Douglas signed himself "Marquis of Queensberry" and this is how the title was printed on his visiting cards (The National Archives, CRIM 1/41/6).

5. The statement to which Batho refers was written in the hand of Robert Ross on two envelopes from the Holborn Viaduct Hotel, signed by Wilde, and printed in the London *Evening News*, 5 Apr. 1895, 3. A facsimile is reproduced on the inside front cover of Hyde. It reads:

> It would have been impossible for me to have proved my case without putting Lord Alfred Douglas in the witness-box against his father. Lord Alfred Douglas was extremely anxious to go into the box, but I would not let him do so. Rather than put him in so painful a position I determined to retire from the case, and to bear on my own shoulders whatever ignominy and shame might result from my prosecuting Lord Queensberry. (CL, 637.)

Batho appears to be claiming that he was the reporter who took Wilde's letter to the newspaper offices for publication in that afternoon's edition. A later article about Batho's career, no

before the completion of his two years' martyrdom, I have interviewed him for the fourth time under weird conditions while he still wears the degrading costume of the convict."[1]

In consenting to Mr. Batho's interview with Oscar Wilde today Maj. Nelson, Governor of Reading Prison, explained:[2]

"I can be your mouthpiece and Wilde's. You may frame your sentences. Such questions as the laws of the Home Office will permit me to transmit to my prisoner I will transmit and you shall have his replies."

Wilde was sent for, and he in one room and Batho in another carried on the interview as published above, Maj. Nelson being the medium of communication. Wilde will be released from prison, according to present arrangements, between 6:30 and 7 o'clock on Wednesday morning, when he will be met by Frank Harris, who intends to take him in a cab to Windsor, fourteen miles distant, for breakfast.[3]

---

doubt including information he himself furnished, boasts that "Batho's story of the prison life of Oscar Wilde [...] is said to have doubled the circulation of Lord Northcliffe's Evening News" ("Solved, as Reporter, Jack-the-Ripper Mystery," *Buffalo Evening News* (Buffalo, NY), 8 Oct. 1920, 1), presumably a reference to the article for the *Evening News* that was reprinted as "Wilde in Prison," *Western Mail* (Cardiff), 28 May 1895, 3. Lord Northcliffe was raised to the peerage in 1904 and, with his brother Harold, had bought the *Evening News* in 1894. Lord Alfred Douglas and his brother Percy Sholto Douglas (1868–1920), who had been styled Lord Douglas of Hawick until the death in 1894 of his elder brother Francis Archibald Douglas, Viscount Drumlanrig, were also at the Holborn Viaduct Hotel with Wilde on 5 April 1895. A reporter for the *Sun* sought an interview with Wilde, and Percy came out to answer his questions, making the same points as in Wilde's statement (see "Finished!" *The Sun* (London, UK), 5 Apr. 1895, 3, pp. 817–19). If Batho had really taken down Wilde's statement as he describes, one would expect him to remember that Robert Ross wrote the longhand version rather than Percy Douglas, and to have quoted Wilde in the *Evening News* (the report of the collapse of the libel trial does not include quotations or any other evidence that an interview took place). It should also be noted that Batho, in his article for the *Evening News* on 27 May 1895, gives his impressions of Wilde in the witness box under the heading "AND A THIRD", the implication being that this is the third time he "met" Wilde, after Liverpool and Stratford-upon-Avon. If Batho had met Wilde at the Holborn Viaduct Hotel as he claimed in 1897, he would surely have mentioned the fact in 1895.

1. Wilde's prison clothing was printed with the broad arrow to indicate it was government property; Batho would have known this without having to see Wilde. The *Buffalo Evening News* here begins a new section with the subheading "A Mild Governor", which reads: "The Governor of Reading Prison is externally the mildest and kindest hearted man ever placed in authority. It is an act of Governmental philanthropy to place in the hands of such a man the lash which controls the criminal." This appraisal accords with Wilde's. He later spoke of Nelson as "such a delightful man" (Mikhail, 342), and "the most Christ-like man I ever met" (Chesson).

2. The *Buffalo Evening News* has "commenting on" instead of "consenting to".

3. Wednesday was 19 May. It seems likely that, if it was Nelson who gave Batho/White this information, it was with the intention of confounding the efforts of journalists to ambush Wilde upon his release. Wilde left Reading Prison on the evening of 18 May in a closed carriage in the company of the deputy governor and a warder. He was taken to Pentonville Prison and released at 06:15 on the following morning. He was met not by Frank Harris but by his friend More Adey

Reporters were swarming in Reading today, as it is rumored that Wilde's friends will obtain permission from the Home Office to remove him secretly from the prison before his term has entirely expired.

A.-F. Lugné-Poé, "M. Oscar Wilde en France," *La Presse* (Paris, France), 28 May 1897, 2[1]

Voici le mot que je trouvai, hier, à mon hôtel, dans le petit port français où M. Oscar Wilde se remet des souffrances que lui a fait endurer, si l'on veut se servir du vieux mot de Goethe, le *pédantisme* de ses inexorables compatriotes :

« L'auteur de *Salomé* prie le tétrarque de *Judée* de lui faire l'honneur de déjeuner avec lui demain matin, à midi. »

Sous un nom d'emprunt très balzacien, M. Wilde est, en effet, notre hôte depuis quelques jours. Mais comme il désire, avant tout, la paix et le repos, on comprendra qu'il tienne à rester inconnu sur une petite plage où son nom même est ignoré, n'admettant, depuis sa sortie de prison, aucun interviewer et ne recevant que quelques amis très intimes. Ces quelques mots seulement pour tranquilliser ceux-là que le sort ou l'infortune de l'écrivain anglais a pu toucher.

Bien que M. Wilde m'ait paru très maigri, sa santé ne semble pas avoir été trop atteinte par sa longue incarcération les tortures morales non plus n'ont pas métamorphosé son esprit si paradoxal. Ironique comme autrefois; il ressemble à un voyageur revenant à nos pays après une longue absence, s'émerveillant comme un enfant de la « beauté terrible » des moindres choses.

Pour l'instant, il lit le plus possible tout ce qui a paru dans ces deux dernières années; sur sa table, je n'ai remarqué qu'un livre anglais, les deux autres étaient l'*Orme du Mail*, d'Anatole France, et l'*Imitation de notre maître Napoléon*, d'Ernest la Jeunesse. Pendant de longs mois, étranger à la vie littéraire, avide de

---

(1858–1942) and the Reverend Stewart Duckworth Headlam (1847–1924), an English Anglican priest (Sturgis, 627/585).

1. See below for an annotated English translation. Aurélien-Marie Lugné, known by the pen name Lugné-Poe, was a French actor and director. He had staged Wilde's *Salomé* in his Théâtre de l'Œuvre on 11 February 1896, playing the part of Herod himself. When news of the production reached Wilde in prison he is supposed to have remarked: "France understands the value of an artist for what he is, not for what he may have done." (Ricketts, 47.) Wilde wrote to More Adey of his meeting with Lugné-Poe: "I earnestly impressed on him the importance of writing no interview, and giving no details of my strange name, my place of sojourn, my altered appearance, and the like: but I know how tempted people are to write for their own pleasure about others, thoughtlessly and without care. So would you see him, if possible, and impress on him that ten lines on me will be enough?" (CL, 847.) The letter is post-marked 25 May 1897 and Wilde refers to having breakfasted with Lugné-Poe "this morning".

nouvelles et d'impressions, il a paru très surpris d'apprendre l'abandon peu à peu sensible en France de la forme symbolique.

C'est à peine si, dans sa prison, la deuxième année, quelques livres purent lui parvenir; on lui avait permis *En Route!* de Huysmans, sans doute parce que M. Gladstone l'avait presque préfacé en Angleterre ; l'*Enfer*, du Dante. On lui refusa la *Tentation de saint Antoine*, de Flaubert. C'était le secret absolu, sans nouvelles, sans permission d'écrire, de parler, et des punitions cellulaires très pénibles, s'il enfreignait les règlements.

Un jour qu'ainsi puni pour avoir hasardé quelques mots, on l'avait laissé avec une Bible entre les mains (on sait qu'en Angleterre la Bible reste toujours le viatique des suppliciés), il conçut, en la feuilletant, le projet d'un drame intitulé *Pharaon*, qu'il écrit aujourd'hui pour le théâtre de l'Œuvre.

Il ne sait de quelle manière remercier les nombreuses sympathies qui ne l'abandonnèrent jamais à Paris. — Elles eurent, en effet, un contre-coup inattendu auprès de ses bourreaux : *un mois après la représentation de Salomé, son régime lui fut très adouci*, et depuis on s'efforça de lui rendre la prison moins rigoureuse. Aussi, M. O. Wilde veut obtenir de nouveaux suffrages dans les lettres françaises pour forcer les hésitations de ses compatriotes, reprendre la situation méritée qu'il occupait et que la lâcheté commune lui a fait perdre.

A.-F. Lugné-Poé.

P.-S. — M. O. Wilde, depuis qu'il a quitté Londres, n'est pas venu à Paris, et il n'est plus à l'heure présente a Dieppe, qu'il a quitté pour une autre plage du littoral. — L.P.

Oscar Wilde in France

Here is the note I found yesterday at my hotel in the small French port where Mr. Oscar Wilde is recovering from the suffering he was made to endure, to use Goethe's old phrase, the pedantry of his ruthless compatriots:

"The author of *Salomé* begs the Tetrarch of *Judea* to do him the honor of having lunch with him tomorrow morning at noon."[1]

Under a very Balzacian assumed name,[2] Mr. Wilde has indeed been our host for a few days. But as he wishes, above all, peace and quiet, we understand that he wants to remain unknown in a small seaside resort where even his name is

1. "Tetrarch of *Judea*": i.e. Herod. Wilde's letter was dated 24 May 1897, Hôtel Sandwich, Dieppe (CL, 846).
2. On arriving in France Wilde had adopted the name Sebastian Melmoth, in homage to Saint Sebastian and the eponymous character in *Melmoth the Wanderer*, an 1820 gothic novel by his great-uncle Charles Maturin (1780–1824).

unknown, admitting, since his release from prison, no interviewer and only a few very close friends. I share these few words only to reassure those who may feel touched by the unfortunate fate of the English writer.

Although Mr. Wilde appeared very thin, his health does not seem to have been affected too much by his long incarceration, nor have the moral tortures altered his paradoxical mind. He is as ironic as he was before; he seems like a traveler returning to our country after a long absence, marvelling like a child over the "terrible beauty" of the smallest things.

For the moment, he reads as much as possible of everything that has appeared in the last two years; on his table I noticed only one English book, the two others being l'*Orme du mail*, by Anatole France, and l'*Imitation de notre maître Napoléon*, by Ernest la Jeunesse.[1] For many months he has been a stranger to literary life, eager for news and impressions, and he seemed very surprised to learn of the gradual abandonment of the symbolic form in France.

In the second year of his imprisonment only a few books reached him; he was allowed *En Route!* by Huysmans, presumably because Mr. Gladstone nearly wrote a preface for it in England,[2] and Dante's *Inferno*.[3] He was refused *The Temptation of Saint Anthony* by Flaubert.[4] He lived in absolute isolation, without

1. Anatole France, born François-Anatole Thibault (1844–1924), was a French poet, journalist, and novelist. l'*Orme du mail* (*The Elm-Tree on the Mall*; 1897) was the first of four volumes in his novel series, l'*Histoire contemporaine* (*A Chronicle of Our Own Times*). Ernest La Jeunesse (1874–1917) was a French literary critic and cartoonist. Wilde, in a letter written during the final weeks of his imprisonment to Robert Ross, had requested La Jeunesse's novel, l'*Imitation de notre maître Napoléon* (*The Imitation of our Master Napoleon*; 1897), Anatole France's latest works, and other books in French and English (CL, 791–3).

2. *En Route* (1895) is the second in a series of four novels about the conversion to Catholicism of a protagonist who is a thinly veiled portrait of the author. Wilde requested it from the prison governor in July 1896 ("I would of course prefer it in the French if it would be allowed. If not I would like to read it in the translation. It is a book on modern Christianity;" CL, 660). The request was denied, probably for reasons of expense (the governor also denied many uncontroversial titles on Wilde's long list). In March 1897 Wilde requested the book again, noting: "This is the religious novel of which Mr Gladstone wrote in terms of such high commendation." This time the request was approved (CL, 682). C. Kegan Paul, the translator of *En Route*, had sent the former prime minister a copy of the book, and Gladstone had replied in complimentary terms (*The Academy*, Vol. 53, 28 May 1898, 587). Wilde, however, was disappointed with the book, writing to Robert Ross: "*En Route* is most over-rated. It is sheer journalism. It never makes one hear a note of the music it describes. The subject is delightful, but the style is of course worthless, slipshod, flaccid," (CL, 790).

3. As well as *The Divine Comedy*, Wilde requested books about Dante (Wright, 320). He told several of his friends that, in prison, Dante had been his greatest consolation (Chesson; Harris, 357; CL, 669; Wright, 264).

4. *The Temptation of Saint Anthony* was among Wilde's favourite books. He told one friend that he began each working day by reading a few pages of it (Wright, 182), and another that "I never read Flaubert's *Tentation de St Antoine* without signing my name at the end of it," (Wright, 184). He asked the publisher Alfred Nutt: "Do you think (this is private) that a translation of that

news, without permission to write or speak, and was subjected to very harsh cell punishments if he broke the rules.

One day, thus punished for venturing a few words and left with a Bible in his hands (we know that in England the Bible is always the viaticum of the tortured), he conceived, by leafing through it, the outline of a drama entitled *Pharaoh*, which he is writing now for the Théâtre de l'Œuvre.[1]

He does not know how to thank the many sympathetic persons in Paris who never abandoned him.— In fact, they struck an unexpected blow against his persecutors: a month after the performance of *Salomé*, his regime was very much softened, and from that time efforts were made to lessen the harshness of the prison.[2] Also, Mr. O. Wilde hopes to win new support from French men of letters to force the hesitation of his compatriots, and to resume the deserved position he occupied and that common cowardice made him lose.

A.-F. LUGNÉ-POÉ.

P.-S.— Mr. O. Wilde, since he left London, has not come to Paris, and is no longer present in Dieppe, having left for another resort on the coast . —L.P.[3]

Gedeon Spilett [Louis Sérizier], "Une Entrevue avec M. Oscar Wilde," *Gil Blas* (Paris, France), 22 Nov. 1897, 3[4]

La scène est à Dieppe, où le romancier anglais a passé les derniers beaux jours avant de s'embarquer pour Naples qu'il a choisi, croyons-nous, comme station d'hiver.

---

amazing book of Flaubert's 'La Tentation de St. Antoine' would be a success[?] I want to do it" (not included in CL; Sotheby's sale n09920, lot 311). The translation did not appear. Wilde requested Ross purchase the book for him before his release from prison (CL, 791).

1. Wilde projected several theatrical works after his release from prison, none of which he realised. For the synopsis of *Pharaoh* see Ellmann, 487–8/519.

2. In a letter to Lord Alfred Douglas dated [? 2 June 1897], Wilde wrote: "The production of *Salomé* was the thing that turned the scale in my favour, as far as my treatment in prison by the Government was concerned, and I am deeply grateful to all concerned in it." (CL, 872.) Wilde also told the French author André Gide (1869–1951): "You cannot imagine how much good it did me in prison that *Salomé* was being played in Paris just at that time. In prison it had been entirely forgotten that I was a literary person, but when they saw that my play was a success in Paris, they said to one another, 'Well, but that is strange; he has talent, then.' And from that moment they let me have all the books I wanted to read." (Gide, 70.)

3. Wilde arrived in Dieppe on 20 May 1897 and moved to Berneval, a village ten kilometres distant, on 26 May (Page, 75).

4. See below for an annotated English translation. An English translation is also given in Mikhail, 354–8. Quoted in Ellmann, 508/541. Gedeon Spilett was a pseudonym of Louis Sérizier: he took it from Jules Verne's 1875 novel, *The Mysterious Island*, in which Spilett is a journalist. Wilde sent a copy of this interview to Robert Ross (CL, 992).

Un groupe de jeunes poètes et littérateurs parisiens entoure M. Oscar Wilde, qui répond avec une bonhomie teintée d'ironie ou d'amertume aux questions plutôt indiscrètes que nous lui posons.

Oscar Wilde s'exprime avec aisance, en un français coloré, moderne, mâtiné d'un léger accent britannique qui n'est pas sans charme.

Quoi qu'il nie être Anglais et qu'il se targue de son origine irlandais et de son catholicisme, il faudrait être aveugle pour ne pas reconnaître de suite, dans sa contexture physique, un représentant authentique de la race anglo-saxonne. Sa haute et corpulente stature, le bleu gris de ses yeux, ses cheveux blonds, les maxillaires puissants qui terminent le bas du visage ne laissent aucun doute à ce sujet.

Quand il rit — il rit souvent, d'un rire d'ogre satisfait — ses dents apparaissent, redoutables, longues, larges, les brèches comblées de lingots d'or.

Wilde, très fataliste, porte, au petit doigt de chaque main, une bague enchâssée d'une émeraude. Ces pierres précieuses, gravées de signes cabalistiques, proviennent d'une pyramide égyptienne. Il attribue à l'émeraude de la main gauche la cause efficiente de tous ses bonheurs, et celle de ses malheurs à celle de la main droite. Sur mon observation — assez logique, crois-je — qu'il eût dû se défaire de la bague maléfique, il répondit d'une voix changée : « Il faut du malheur dans la vie pour vivre heureux. »

Du reste, le vert est la couleur favorite d'Oscar Wilde : il la prône et en fait le symbole de l'enfer. Il a une opinion toute spéciale à propos d'enfer. Il dit que le ciel est fait pour les braves gens, les honnêtes bourgeois et, en général, pour toute la médiocratie qui ignore les Vouloirs neufs. Le bon Dieu est bon, il est miséricordieux, il l'est trop ; saint Pierre a le cordon facile, mais Satan exige beaucoup plus de ses fidèles: avec lui il faut des formalités.

« Pour entrer au paradis, on n'a qu'à frapper un coup, mais il faut frapper trois fois pour entrer en enfer. Croyez-moi, aimez le vert, aimez l'enfer : le vert et l'enfer sont faits pour les voleurs et les artistes. »

Oscar Wilde aime la France, parce qu'elle est, seule, la courageuse du Dire, parce qu'elle est l'Aide du plus faible et qu'elle seule détient l'Aspiration vers les justices. Interrogé si l'on pourrait jouer devant un public anglais tel vaudeville français médiocre qu'il est inutile de nommer, il dit (et je donne cet avis à méditer aux auteurs qui travaillent pour l'exportation) : « On peut tout jouer devant les Anglais, tout... excepté *Tartuffe* ! »

Cependant, son âme est vierge de rancune; il admet, telle une Rédemption, sa condamnation et ses deux années de *hard-labour*, qu'il dénomme poétiquement son Exil. « C'est le péché d'orgueil qui perdit toujours les hommes : j'étais monté trop haut et je me vautrai dans la boue. » Il a une grande reconnaissance pour la Presse française qui plaida si chaleureusement sa cause. Sa gratitude va surtout à ceux qui prirent sa défense sans la connaître. A l'entendre, ce qu'il regretterait le plus, c'est de n'avoir pu assister à la représentation de la *Salomé* que le théâtre de l'Œuvre joua lors de son internement. Il parle de bonne grâce de deux années perdues pour lui et des remarques faites sur ses codétenus dont il s'appliquait à mettre au point l'état d'âme. Il ne semble pas avoir beaucoup souffert physiquement, mais sa grand torture a dû être celle de l'esprit et du cœur ; il a dû traverser toutes les phases et les angoisses de *la nuit de l'âme* dont parle Huysmans d'après saint Jean de la Croix. Comme nous lui demandions de dire toutes les souffrances de sa détention, il répondit avec une épouvante dans la voix : « Excusez-moi, je ne parle jamais de cela. »

A le voir si gai, si lucide, si vif à la riposte, nous finissions par oublier les terribles épreuves qu'il avait traversées.

Il connaît à merveille l'évolution littéraire moderne et ses facteurs, il en est même déconcertant: il nous citait des jeunes de demain que nous connaissions à peine de nom.

Wilde fut, comme l'on sait, très lié avec Verlaine, qu'il considère comme un des plus magnifiques écrivains du dix-neuvième siècle, tant pour son œuvre poétique que pour l'évolution qu'il sut imprimer à narrer les entretiens esthétiques qu'il eut avec lui au café François-Ier, sous l'œil bénévole de l'ineffable Bibi-la-Purée. Il voudrait que la statue du pauvre Lélian fût érigée non au Luxembourg, ni dans la rue, mais dans un des cafés où Verlaine passa sa vie, afin que son image fût soustraite aux intempéries, surtout à la pluie que le poète craignait tant :

Il pleure dans mon cœur comme il pleut sur la ville.

« La statue du héros doit être sur le champ de bataille de sa vie », nous a-t-il dit à ce sujet.

Quant à M. Stéphane Mallarmé, M. Oscar Wilde préfère ce poète lorsqu'il écrit en français, — on sait que M. Mallarmé écrit également en anglais, — « parce qu'au moins, en français, Mallarmé est incompréhensible, et que, hélas! en anglais, il ne l'est pas ». Et Wilde ajoute, comme un correctif peut-être de ce que sa critique peut avoir d'amer : « C'est un don que celui de l'incompréhensibilité, tout le monde ne l'a pas. Ainsi, tenez, ce pauvre Moréas ne l'a pas, mais Moréas existe-t-il vraiment ? »

Et, sur notre affirmation que le poète Moréas existait bien en chair et en os, Wilde ajoute avec un sourire : « J'ai toujours cru que c'était un mythe. » Et il nous cite deux ou trois autres écrivains français dont l'existence lui avait toujours paru une légende, peut-être même une mystification.

L'auteur du *Portrait de Dorian Gray* loue sans réserve *Aphrodite*, et, comme nous faisions un parallèle entre les romans de Pierre Louÿs et *Salammbô,* il nous interrompit, avec une sorte d'extase dans le regard : « Rien n'est beau comme ce livre ! ... Et les Goncourt, quels artistes! et fiers, et orgueilleux, et jaloux, à juste titre, de leur renommée ! ... »

Peu à peu, s'éteignit le critique, et Oscar Wilde nous parla de ses projets, de ses livres. Il doit en écrire un directement en français ; puis, il fera comme Mallarmé, il le traduira en anglais. Il dit le théâtre qu'il rêve, les pièces qu'il veut faire, et le culte sans pareil qu'il voua à la « *princess du beau geste et des attitudes* », à Sarah Bernhardt, sur qui il compte pour incarner une de ses héroïnes.

Il nous conte ensuite, avec verve, le scénario d'une pièce ironiste en trois scènes, qu'il projetait, mais qu'il a renoncé à écrire, pour l'instant du moins.

Ici, nous lui laissons la parole :

« L'Evangile parle souvent de malades que le Christ guérit ; nulle part, dans les livres saints, il n'est fait mention de ce qu'ils devinrent. C'est une lacune que l'imagination d'un nouvelliste ou d'un auteur dramatique devrait essayer de combler.

» Voici une idée à moi :

» A la première scène, on voit un jeune homme couronné de roses s'enivrer de vin. Vient à passer le Christ, qui lui reproche son intempérance. Le jeune homme le reconnaît et, lui rendant hommage, dit : « Maître, je suis le paralytique que tu guéris. »

» Le Christ arrive, à la deuxième scène, en un lieu où autre homme se livre à la débauche avec des courtisanes. Il lui reproche son vice. L'homme le reconnaît et, se prosternant, lui dit : « Maître, je suis le lépreux que tu guéris. »

» Alors le Christ, très triste, alla vers le désert (troisième scène) et voyant un jeune homme qui pleurait, lui dit doucement : « Pourquoi pleures-tu ? » Et le jeune homme, le reconnaissant, de répondre : « Maître, j'étais mort, et tu m'as ressuscité ! »

— Mais, a ajouté Oscar Wilde, en terminant, je ne crois pas que je donnerai suite à ce projet, car il faut respecter la majesté du Christ.

M. Jules Lemaître ne partage pas les mêmes scrupules, car il a, si nous avons bonne mémoire, écrit, sur une donnée analogue, un *Conte de Noël*, paru l'an dernier dans une revue politique et littéraire.

GEDEON SPILETT.

An Interview with Mr. Oscar Wilde

The scene is Dieppe, where the English novelist spent the last beautiful days before departing for Naples, which he has chosen, we believe, as a winter resort.[1]

---

1. Wilde was in Rouen until at least 6 September, arrived in Dieppe by 13 September, and left for Paris on or about 15 September. Once he had secured funds from a friend he made his way to Aix-le-Bains, where he met up with Lord Alfred Douglas. The pair continued on to Naples and rented the Villa Giudice in Posillipo. By December Douglas had departed; Wilde was back in Paris by mid-February 1898 (CL, 941–2; Page, 78–82).

A group of young Parisian poets and literary men surrounds Oscar Wilde, who responds with a good humour tinged with irony or bitterness to the rather indiscreet questions that we ask him.

Oscar Wilde is fluent in colorful, modern French, with a light British accent that is not without charm.

Although he denies that he is English and prides himself on his Irish origins and his Catholicism, one would have to be blind not to immediately recognise at first sight, from his physical appearance, an authentic representative of the Anglo-Saxon race. His height, portly build, the grey blue of his eyes, his fair hair, and the powerful jaw that rounds off the lower face leave no doubt about it.

When he laughs—he often laughs, with the laugh of a contented ogre—his teeth appear: dreadful, long, wide, with the gaps filled with gold.

Wilde, quite the fatalist, wears, on the little finger of each hand, a ring set with an emerald. These gemstones, engraved with cabalistic symbols, are from an Egyptian pyramid. He attributes to the emerald of the left hand the cause of all his happiness, and that of his misfortunes to the emerald of the right hand. To my observation—logical enough, I think—that he should have ridden himself of the evil ring, he replied in a changed voice: "It takes misfortune in life to live happily."

Besides, green is Oscar Wilde's favourite colour: he advocates it and says it is the symbol of Hell. He has a very special idea about Hell. He says that Heaven is made for the good people, the honest bourgeois and, in general, for all the mediocrities who ignore the new Desires. The good Lord is good. He is merciful, he is too merciful; Saint Peter allows easy entry, but Satan demands much more from his followers: with him formalities are required.

"To enter Paradise, you only have to knock once, but you have to knock three times to enter Hell. Trust me, love green, love Hell: the colour green and Hell are made for thieves and artists."

Oscar Wilde loves France, because she alone is for freedom of speech, because she helps the weakest, and she alone aspires towards justice. Asked if we could stage for an English public French vaudeville pieces so mediocre that it would be pointless to name them, he said (and I state his opinion for the benefit of those authors who work for the export market): "We can stage anything for the English, anything... except *Tartuffe!*"

However, his soul is devoid of resentment; he confesses that he has experienced a Redemption through his sentence and his two years of hard labour, which he poetically calls his Exile. "It is always the sin of pride that wrecks men: I had climbed too high and now I will wallow in the mud." He is very grateful for the French Press which has so warmly argued for his cause. His gratitude goes especially to those who took up his defence without knowing him. To hear him, what he regrets most is that he was unable to attend the performance of his *Salomé* at the Théâtre de l'Œuvre during his imprisonment. He speaks with good grace of the two years lost to him and in his remarks about his fellow prisoners, whose state of mind he set out to define. He does not seem to have suffered much physically, but his great torture must have been that of the mind and the heart; he had to go through all the phases and anxieties of the night of the soul, which Huysmans speaks of befalling St. John of the Cross. When we asked him to talk about all he suffered during his imprisonment, he replied with horror in his voice: "Excuse me, I never talk about that."

To see him so cheerful, so lucid, so quick with the repartee, we ended up forgetting the terrible trials he had gone through.

He is very familiar with modern literary movements and their proponents, to the extent that he confounded us: he quoted from the young up-and-comers whom we hardly knew by name.

Wilde was, as we all know, very close to Verlaine,[1] whom he considers to be one of the most magnificent writers of the nineteenth century, as much for his poetic work as for the changes he wrought and for the aesthetic talks Wilde had with him at the Café François I, under the benevolent eye of the ineffable Bibi-la-Purée.[2] He would like Poor Lélian's statue to be erected not in the Luxembourg nor in the street, but in one of the cafes where Verlaine spent his life, so that his image would be sheltered from the weather, especially from the rain that the poet feared so much:[3]

It rains in my heart as it rains on the city.[4]

"The hero's statue must be on the battlefield of his life," he told us, when speaking of this subject.

As for Mr. Stéphane Mallarmé, Mr. Oscar Wilde prefers this poet when he writes in French—we all know that Mr. Mallarmé also writes in English—"because at least in French Mallarmé is incomprehensible; Alas! in English he is not." And Wilde adds, perhaps to remedy his harsh criticism: "incomprehensibility is a gift, not everyone has it. Poor Moréas doesn't have it, but does Moréas really exist?"[5]

And, upon our assertion that the poet Moréas really existed in the flesh, Wilde added with a smile: "I always thought he was a myth." And he quoted us

1. Paul-Marie Verlaine (1844–1896) was a French poet.
2. André-Joseph Salis (1848–1903), known as Bibi-la-Purée, was a French actor and iconic figure of bohemian Paris.
3. Verlaine's nickname for himself was Pauvre Lélian. A public subscription to fund a monument to Verlaine was announced in February 1897. A statue was unveiled in the Jardin du Luxembourg in 1911. Time has perhaps proved Wilde right, as the marble of the statue is now visibly weathered.
4. The opening of Verlaine's poem, *Il Pleure dans mon Cœur*, or *It Rains in My Heart*.
5. Jean Moréas (1856–1910), born Ioannis A. Papadiamantopoulos, was a Greek symbolist poet and art critic who wrote mostly in French.

two or three other French writers whose existence had always seemed to him a legend, perhaps even a hoax.

The author of *The Picture of Dorian Gray* praises *Aphrodite* without reservation, and, as we drew a parallel between the novels [*sic*] of Pierre Louÿs and *Salammbô*,[1] he interrupted us, with a sort of ecstasy in his gaze: "Nothing is as beautiful as this book! ... And the Goncourts, what artists![2] and proud, and conceited, and jealous, justifiably, of their fame!..."

By and by, Oscar Wilde ceased his criticisms, and spoke instead of his own projects, of his books. He will write one directly in French; then, he will do as Mallarmé did, and translate it into English. He told us about the theatre he dreams of, the plays he wants to write, and the unparalleled worship he dedicates to the "princess of beautiful gesture and attitudes," Sarah Bernhardt, on whom he counts to embody one of his heroines.[3]

He then told us, with verve, the scenario of an ironic play in three scenes, which he projected but gave up writing, at least for the moment.

Here we give him the floor:

"The Gospel often speaks of the sick whom Christ healed; nowhere in the holy books is there any mention of what happened to them afterwards. This is a gap that the imagination of a short story writer or a playwright should try to fill.

"Here is my idea:

"In the first scene, we see a young man crowned with roses getting drunk on wine. Christ passes by and reproaches him for his intemperance. The young man recognises him and, paying homage to him, says: 'Master, I am the paralysed man whom you healed.'

"Christ arrives, in the second scene, in a place where another man is engaging in debauchery with courtesans. He blames him for his vice. The man recognises him and, bowing down, says to him: 'Master, I am the leper whom you healed.'

"Then Christ, very sad, goes to the desert (third scene) and, seeing a young man who was crying, says to him softly: 'Why do you weep?' And the young man, recognising him, replies: 'Master, I was dead, and you resurrected me!'[4]

---

1. Pierre Louÿs (1870–1925) was a French writer and the dedicatee of the French edition of *Salomé*. His first—and, at the time this interview was given, his only—novel *Aphrodite: Mœurs Antiques* (*Aphrodite: Ancient Manners*; 1896) is about a sculptor who attempts to win the love of a courtesan by committing theft and murder for her. In prison Wilde requested a copy (Wright, 321).

2. Jules de Goncourt (1830–1870), like his brother Edmond, was a French author. All of their novels, plays, and non-fiction works published before Jules's death were written collaboratively.

3. None of these projects was realised.

4. Around the time of the production of his play *The Land of Heart's Desire* (premiered 29 March 1894), William Butler Yeats heard that Wilde was telling this story and had described it

"But," added Oscar Wilde, in closing, "I don't think I will follow through on this project because one has to respect the majesty of Christ."

Mr. Jules Lemaître does not share the same scruples, because he has, if we remember correctly, written a *Christmas Tale* along the same lines, which was published last year in a political and literary review.[1]

GEDEON SPILETT.

[Eugenio Zaniboni], "Un' intervista con Oscar Wilde," *Il Pungolo Parlamentare* (Naples, Italy), 9–10 October 1897, 1[2]

La notizia che Oscar Wilde—colui che mancò poco non fosse nominato il poeta laureato della Corte d'Inghilterra a le cui teorie estetiche invece ebbero la loro conclusione in una condanna ai lavori forzati, duramente scontata,—fosse, da varie settimane, qui a Napoli, in una remota e deliziosa villa a Posillipo, si era sparsa in qualche crocchio artistico e giornalistico, ed era stata commentata un pò soverchiamente, con sottintesi e allusioni fatte di reminiscenze platoniche e socratiche.

Quest'esteta contro cui si scatenò ferocemente l'ipocrisia inglese con un accanimento speciale dei giudici, dei giornali della pubblica opinione,—per quanto vizioso e corrotto—è finito per diventare un tipo interessante ed acquistare quella celebrità che fuori della patria non gli avevano procurato i suoi drammi e i suoi romanzi meravigliosi per finezzo stilistiche e per finzioni artistiche. Colui che si macchiò d'un peccato, tanto più mostruoso, in quanto che alcuni pervertiti hanno voluto idealizzarlo quasi come un canone estetico della vita—ha sofferto ed espiato. Si è emendato?

Egli è sceso in italia insieme a qual lord Douglas il cui nome venne spesso a galla durante lo svolgersi del processo e la loro unione, ahimè! fa a monti

---

as "the best story in the world". Yeats reproduced it in his *Autobiographies*, and this is the version reprinted in Wright, T. (Ed.). (2000). *Table Talk: Oscar Wilde.* Cassell & Co.

1. François Élie Jules Lemaître (1853–1914) was a French critic, playwright, and author of stories.

2. See below for an annotated English translation. Printed in the combined Saturday/Sunday edition, dated 9–10 October. An English translation is given in Miracco, R. (2020). *Oscar Wilde's Italian Dream 1875–1900.* Damiani. 74–7. Referenced in Sturgis, 655/611. There is no byline but Miracco identifies the author as Eugenio Zaniboni (1871-1926), a Dante scholar, teacher and translator of German and, under the pseudonym Cino Spada, the editor of *Il Pungolo Parlamentare.* This two column interview was presumably that referred to by Wilde in his letter to Ernest Dowson dated Monday [?11 October 1897]: "The Neapolitan papers have turned out to be the worst form of American journalism. They fill columns with me, and write interviews of a fictitious character. I wish the world would let me alone, and really I thought that at Naples I would be at peace. I dare say they will tire of this nonsense soon." (CL, 958.)

670

supporre che i lavori forzati non abbiano spento nel celebre scrittore il vizio estetico, che gl'inglesi considerano come una doppia incarnazione del male.

Io, che ho avuto la strana curiosità di avvicinare questo superuomo e di tentare con lui un' intervista, non so immaginare la grandezza incommensurabile del suo egoismo, che lo rende estraneo a tutto ciò che non abbia rapporto alla sua persona, cercando, come meglio può, di realizzare un ideale di vita, che la gente sana ed equilibrata non può che giudicare mostruosa.

Il Wilde è alla villa del Giudice a Posillipo: questo lo sapeva come gran parte dei lettori: il difficile era di giungere a lui avendo egli date delle severe disposizioni per non essere avvicinato.

Egli è dunque a Napoli da circa un mese; prese prima stanza all'*Hotel Royal* passò a villa del Giudice ove sona degli splendidi appartamenti mobiliati.

Ma come venir meno alle severe disposizioni date?...

La custode—alla quale confessai lealmente il desiderio mio—non seppe rispondermi.

—*Signorino mio,* disse la buona donna, *milord nun vò vedè nisciuno!*

Ma questo primo inciampo non mi sconvolse, misi fuori tutta la mia dialettica e finalmente riuscii a far breccia nell'animo della custode.

—*Mo facimmo na cosa, ve chiammo'oservitore 'e milord, isso ve po' fa trasì.*

—E chiamatemi il servitore di milord annuii entrando nella villa e scendendo il bel viale ombroso che porta agli appartamenti.

La buona donna mi fece segno di aspettare presso una porta a pianterreno, una porta a vetri *bleu* e bianchi, opachi; era lì l'appartamento di Oscar Vylde.

—*Aspettate nu momento.*

Attesi. Il luogo era bellissimo; intorno aiuole di fiori tenute con cura grandissima; più lungi viali ombrosi, tra gli alberi la vastità del mare calmo, d'una tinta livida che si slargava fino all'orizzonte. Un silenzio profondo.

—Chi desidera il signore? Era il servitore che mi toglieva dalla mia contemplazione.

—Vorrei sapere chi è in casa, il signor Wilde o lord Douglas?

—Lord Douglas è fuori, vi è il signor Wilde; io sono il suo servitore.

—Mi ci vorreste annunziare?

—Ma... nessuno può essere ricevuto, gli ordini sono rigorosi.

E qui una nuova dose di dialettica per convincere quest' altro che non dimostrava affatto l'intenzione d'essere convinto.

Il servitore a poco a poco si persuase, lasciò un vassoio che avea tra le mani ed entrò dal suo padrone, qualche minuto dopo la porta a vetri si riapriva e il servitore mi faceva cenno di entrare,

---

Entrai e mi sedetti.

O numi del cielo! chi aveva mai annunziato quel cane di servitore? vidi una massa bianca che si dirigeva affettuosamente verso di me e quel saluto che si annunziava troppo cordiale—vi giuro, o lettori—non mi produsse un grande piacere.

Ma ad un tratto l'affettuosità del primo momento disparve completamente, il Wilde si avvicinò ancora a me con passo lento e con uno sguardo glaciale ed interrogativo.

E allora io potetti vederlo bene.

È un uomo sui quarant'anni, alto, dalla complessione vigorosa, l'occhio chiaro dell'inglese, dal volto accentuatamente colorito, il labbro ed il mento rasi con grandissima cura. I capelli d'un biondo splendido tenuti con cura straordinaria gli scendono intorno al volto molto allungato, uno di quei volti cavallini che nel tipo inglese si incontrano sovente.

Lo strano di quell'uomo è quando egli dirige la parola: uno dei denti incisivi superiori, e propriamente l'incisivo medio di sinistra è un sol pezzo d'oro assicurato nella gengiva, dell'oro chiude qualche altro dente corroso; quando l'esteta apre la bocca, quel metallo luccica stranamente.

Ma la nota particolare del Wilde è l'eleganza del vestire.

Aveva un perfetto vestito di lana bianca, di quelle lane inglesi insuperabili, una ricca camicia di seta dai risvolti a ricami, sotto il collo della camicia una cravatta a nocca, una striscia, vermiglia sul biancoro del vestito.

—Signor Wilde, cominciai, tanto per pigliar tempo—le chiedo scusa; forse il suo servitore non le avrà ripetuto bene il mio nome.

—Infatti... credevo...

—Ma in tutti i modi, giacché la sua venuta in Napoli è già conosciuta, vuole avere la cortesia di dirmi da quanto tempo è qui?

—Io e il mio amico venimmo a Napoli da circa un mese; pigliammo alloggio all'*Hotel Royal des Etrangers;* giovedì scorso venimmo qui.

—E si tratteranno molto?

—Ma..... non sappiamo. Il luogo è delizioso, forse resteremo qualche tempo ancora, almeno....

—E lei, signor Wilde, si occuperà di arte; avrà forse—non è vero?—preferito questa dolce solitudine per acquistare quella calma dello spirito tanto necessaria allo scrittore?

—Ma... per ora... no, veramente.

Non ho ancora deciso quel che farò, dipende dal tempo che ancora resterò qui.

E della vita attuale ne sapevo abbastanza. Qualche domanda sulle precedenti disgrazie del poeta, mi correva alla mente e per logica deduzione tentava di corrermi alle labbra, scacciai la scabrosa idea più d'una volta e finalmente azzardai:

—E ha lasciato da molto tempo l'Inghilterra....

—Non capisco.

Ripetetti la domanda; fu inutile.

L'inghilterra aveva dovuto agire in uno strano modo sul sistema nervoso del superuomo; dilatò gli occhi come se gli avessi domandato di quadrare il circolo, e se ne stette li, muto, immobile quasi inseguendo dei lontani ricordi da tempo sopiti.

Mi accorsi di averla fatta grossa, lo salutai e me ne andai. Egli mi fece un lieve cenno di testa o si retrasso.

Ma un po' di notiziario, diremo così, intimo del poeta e dell'amico suo, l'ho pure attinto e lo regalo ai lettori. Lo do per autentico, essendomi stato fornito da persone che sono presso i due viaggiatori.

L'appartamento dei due amici è composto di sei o sette camere arredate benissimo, i due amici, a quanto pare vi resteranno ancora per qualche tempo.

Al servizio di Wilde e di lord Douglas vi sono, un cuoco che i due portarono con loro da Capri e due servitori, due bei ragazzi dalle facce paffute e muliebri, di quei volti in cui l'estetica di Wilde tanto profondamente si compiace.

I malevoli vicini della villa del Giudice hanno voluto tessere delle calunnie sul conto di questi due poveri ragazzi, i quali con le loro belle guance paffute e i loro occhi ingenui, sembrano ridersene completamente di queste stupide dicerie.

Nulla è più facile che il vedere uscire, verso l'una, le due della notte, o Oscar Wilde o lord Douglas; si avviano soli per Posillipo tornando il mattino dopo.

I due amici passano il giorno in continue passeggiate per Posillipo e vengono a Napoli spesso, qualche volta restano in villa a conversare e allora la conversazione è spesso interrotta da abbondanti libazioni che si protraggono fino all'ora del pranzo.

Quando io vidi Oscar Wilde, l'amico suo non era in casa; era uscito la sera prima e non ancora—alle 10—era entrato.

E cosi, m'indugiai ancora qualche minuto per i bei viali; voltando a destra, da lontano, io vidi ancora la figura di Oscar Wilde; come le tende alla finestra erano un poco discoste da un lato, vidi il poeta presso il piccolo terrazzo, disteso su una poltrona a sdraio; le sue labbra indolenti tiravano il fumo dalla sigaretta e gli occhi di lui vagavano, vagavano in alto su pel cielo cinereo, ove fra i groppi di nuvole s'addensava la minaccia della pioggia imminente.

An Interview with Oscar Wilde

The news that Oscar Wilde—who was nearly named Poet Laureate of the Court of England and whose aesthetic theories instead landed him a sentence of hard labour—had, for several weeks, been here at Naples, in a remote and delightful villa in Posillipo, had moved in some artistic and journalistic circles, and had been commented upon rather excessively, with hints and allusions of Platonic and Socratic reminiscences.

This esthete against whom English hypocrisy is ferociously unleashed with a special fury by the judges, the newspapers of public opinion—however vicious and corrupt he might be—has ended up becoming an interesting fellow and winning that celebrity which, outside his homeland, his marvelous plays and novels, with their stylistic finesse and artistic fictions, never achieved. The man who stained himself with a sin all the more monstrous because some perverts wanted to idealize it almost as an aesthetic canon of life has suffered and atoned for it. Has he mended his ways?

He came down to Italy with that Lord Douglas [*sic*] whose name often came up during the unfolding of the trial and their union, alas! suggests that hard labour did not extinguish in the famous writer the aesthetic vice that the English consider a double incarnation of evil.

I, who was strangely curious to approach this superhuman and to attempt to interview him, cannot imagine the immeasurable magnitude of his selfishness, which makes him foreign to everything that has no relation to his person, seeking, as best he can, to realize an ideal of life that healthy and balanced people can only judge as monstrous.

Wilde is at the Villa Giudice in Posillipo. This will be known by most readers but the difficulty was in reaching him, as he had given strict instructions that he was not to be disturbed.

He has been in Naples for about a month: he first took a room at the Hotel Royal and then moved on to the Villa Giudice where there are splendid furnished apartments.

But how can one circumvent the strict rules that have been set out...

The caretaker—to whom I sincerely confessed my wish—could not answer me.

"Sir," said the good woman, "milord don't want to see nobody!"

But this first stumbling block did not put me off. I deployed all my skills of persuasion and finally managed to break through to the soul of the guardian.

"What to do... I'll call milord's servant and see if 'e'll let you in."

"Call milord's servant," I nodded as I entered the villa and passed down the beautiful shaded path that leads to the apartments.

Figure 20. Wilde and Lord Alfred Douglas in Naples, 1897.

The good woman motioned for me to wait near a door on the ground floor, a door with blue and white opaque glass: it was Oscar Wilde's apartment.[1]

"Wait a moment."

I waited. The place was beautiful, surrounded by flower beds kept with great care, long shaded paths, and between the trees the vastness of the calm sea, of a livid hue that stretched to the horizon. A profound silence.

"Who wants the gentleman?" It was the servant who brought me out of my reverie.

"I would like to know who is at home, Mr. Wilde or Lord Douglas?"

1. Wilde's name is spelt "Vylde" in this instance, but correctly elsewhere.

675

"Lord Douglas is out, Mr. Wilde is here. I am his servant."

"Would you care to announce me?"

"But... no one can be received, the orders are strict."

And here another dose of dialectical skill was required to convince this other who did not at all show the intention of being convinced.

Little by little the servant was persuaded. He left a tray that he had in his hands and went to his master. A few minutes later the glass door opened again and the servant beckoned me to enter.

———————————

I went in and sat down.

O gods of heaven! Who had that dog of a servant announced me as? I saw a white mass moving affectionately towards me and the prospect of the excessively cordial greeting did not—I swear to you, dear readers—give me much pleasure.

But suddenly the affection of the first moment disappeared completely. Wilde approached me again with a slow step and a glacial and questioning look.

And then I could see him well.

He is a man of about forty, tall, with a vigorous complexion, the clear eye of the Englishman, a noticeably ruddy face, and lip and chin shaved with the greatest care. His hair of a splendid blonde, kept with extraordinary care, falls around his very elongated face—one of those horsy faces that are often seen in the English type.[1]

The strange thing about this man is that when he speaks to you one of his upper incisors, the left middle incisor to be precise, is a single piece of gold secured in the gum, and which encloses some other corroded teeth. When the aesthete opens his mouth, the metal glitters strangely.

But Wilde's overriding characteristic is the elegance of his dress.

He had a perfect suit of white wool, of those unsurpassed English wools, a rich silk shirt with embroidered lapels, and under the collar of his shirt a bow tie, a vermilion streak on the whiteness of the suit.

"Mr. Wilde," I began, just to buy some time, "I beg your pardon; perhaps your servant did not repeat my name correctly."

"In fact... I thought..."

"But anyway, since your presence in Naples is already known, would you be kind enough to tell me how long you have been here?"

---

1. Wilde's hair is generally described as brown (see p. 519, note 2), although the 1895 portrait by Henri de Toulouse-Lautrec (1864–1901) shows Wilde with blonde hair. Wilde's hair had begun to grey in prison and it is likely that he was dying it.

"My friend and I have been in Naples for about a month; we took accommodation at the Hotel Royal des Etrangers; last Thursday we came here."[1]

"And will you stay for long?"

"Well… we don't know. The place is delightful, maybe we will stay a little more time, at least…"[2]

"And you, Mr. Wilde, wishing to work on your art, perhaps—is it not true?—preferred this sweet solitude in order to acquire that calmness of spirit so necessary for the writer?"

"Well… for now… not really. I have not yet decided what I will do, it depends on how long I will still stay here."[3]

Of his current life I knew enough. A few questions about the poet's previous misfortunes came to my mind and tried to make their way to my lips. I chased away the coarse idea more than once and finally ventured:

"And has it been a long time since you left England…?"

"I do not understand."

I repeated the question; it was useless.

England must have had a strange effect on the superhuman's nervous system; he widened his eyes as if I had asked him to square a circle, and stood there, mute, motionless, almost as if he were seeking distant memories that for some time had lain dormant.

I realized I had blown my chance, so bade him farewell and left. He gave me a slight nod and withdrew.

But I will also give my readers a little intimate news, as it were, of the poet and his friend. I take it as authentic, it having been provided to me by people who are with the two travellers.

The apartment of the two friends consists of six or seven beautifully furnished rooms. The two friends, apparently, will remain there for some time yet.

1. Douglas explains in his autobiography that, in mid-September, he "went on to Naples [from Aix-les-Bains], meeting Oscar on the train from Paris. We went to the Hôtel Royal, and I celebrated the occasion by running up a bill for £68 in the fortnight we were there." (Douglas, 152.) Wilde wrote to Robert Ross on 22 September that he and Douglas were moving to Posillipo, and by the 25th they had taken the Villa Giudice, but he was still writing on Hôtel Royal stationery on the 26th (CL, 948–9). Assuming that this interview was conducted in the days before 9 October (a Saturday), "last Thursday" must be either 23 or 30 September.

2. Douglas left for Rome early in December; Wilde remained at the villa until the end of the year, leaving Naples for Paris in mid-February (Page, 80–1).

3. While in Naples Wilde completed and arranged for the publication of *The Ballad of Reading Gaol*.

In the service of Wilde and Lord Douglas are a cook that the two brought with them from Capri and two servants, two handsome boys with plump and feminine faces, of those faces that so deeply please Wilde's aesthetics.[1]

The malevolent neighbours of the Villa Giudice wanted to weave slanders against these two poor boys, who with their beautiful chubby cheeks and their naive eyes seem to laugh completely at these stupid rumors.

Nothing is easier than seeing Oscar Wilde or Lord Douglas come out around one or two in the morning; they set off alone for Posillipo, returning the next morning.[2]

The two friends spend the day in continuous walks around Posillipo and often come to Naples. Sometimes they stay in the villa to converse and then the conversation is often interrupted by abundant libations that last until lunchtime.

When I saw Oscar Wilde, his friend was not at home; he had gone out the night before and—by 10—he had not yet returned.

And so, I lingered a few more minutes on the beautiful paths; turning right, from a distance, I again saw the figure of Oscar Wilde; as the curtains on the window were parted a little on one side, I saw the poet on the small terrace, stretched out on a deck chair. His indolent lips drew the smoke from his cigarette and his eyes wandered, wandered up into the ashen sky, where the threat of imminent rain thickened among the banks of clouds.

1. Wilde and Douglas had not come from Capri, though they spent a few days there in mid-October. Several decades later Douglas would remember that at Posillipo "we had a cook called Carmine, a maid, Maria, and two boys called Peppino and Michele, who waited on us." (Douglas, 158.)

2. There were other references in the local press to Wilde and Douglas's nocturnal exploits (Sturgis, 658–9/614). Wilde wrote to Ernest Dowson of the "lovely Greek bronzes" in the Naples Museum: "The only bother is that they all walk about the town at night. However, one gets delicately accustomed to that—and there are compensations." (CL, 958.)

[Clifford Millage], "The Late Oscar Wilde," *The Daily Chronicle* (London, UK), 3 Dec. 1900, 5[1]

[From Our Correspondent]

PARIS, Sunday Night[2]

About three weeks ago I was scouring Paris to discover the address of a M. Sebastian Melmoth for the purpose of verifying a statement that he had been unjustly deprived of certain dramatic rights of authorship.[3] At length a French literary friend informed me that the object of my search was lying ill at a little hotel in the far-off Rue des Beaux Arts. To save time he had called upon him in my name. M. Melmoth was Oscar Wilde. On the same evening I received a letter in answer to my petit bleu. I instantly answered this in person. The once brilliant and adulated poet-playwright, though in bed, looked well in the face. The first part of the conversation on his side was a mixture of defiance and bitterness. I did my best to console him, and he suddenly burst into tears. I felt deeply moved as he told the sad tale of blight and misery through which he had passed. Men who had been the recipients of sterling generosity had betrayed him and trodden him under their feet. Perhaps there was some justice in his wailing.

Then he turned to religious subjects, and muttered almost savagely, "Much of my moral obloquy is due to the fact that my father would not allow me to become a Catholic. The artistic side of the Church and the fragrance of its teaching would have curbed my degeneracies. I intend to be received before long." He spoke almost smilingly of his operation, saying that it would cost him £40,[4] adding that he owed nearly 2,000f. to the hotel.

1. Reprinted as "Oscar Wilde," *The Evening Telegraph* (Dundee, UK), 3 Dec. 1900, 4; and, without the final paragraph, as "The Late Oscar Wilde," *The Derry Journal* (Derry, UK), 5 Dec. 1900, 3. Excerpted in the *Northern Echo* (Darlington, UK), 4 Dec. 1900, 3; and *Sunderland Daily Echo* (Sunderland, UK), 5 Dec. 1900, 3. Quoted in Hyde, 368; Ellmann, 548/583; and Sturgis, 711/658. John Clifford Millage was the Paris correspondent of *The Daily Chronicle*.

2. 2 December. Wilde died at 13:50 on 30 November of meningoencephalitis secondary to chronic right middle-ear disease (Robins, A. H., & Sellars, S. L. (2000). Oscar Wilde's terminal illness: reappraisal after a century. *The Lancet, 356*, 1841–3).

3. Millage wrote to Wilde on 5 November on *Chronicle* stationery asking for an appointment to discuss Wilde's new play (Small, 95–6). Wilde had written the scenario for a play he called *Love is Law* and sold it to a number of people, including Frank Harris, who based his script for *Mr. and Mrs. Daventry* upon it. Harris's play was staged in London between 25 October 1900 and 23 February 1901 (Ellmann, 544/579; CL, 1205). Harris was obliged to pay off the other claimants and withheld most of Wilde's fee. Wilde wrote several letters to Harris demanding payment (CL, 1199–208).

4. In a letter dated [? 12 Oct. 1900] Wilde told Frank Harris that: "The operation I have had to undergo was a most terrible one. The surgeon's fee is 1500 francs (£60). This, by the aid of my doctor, I got reduced to 750 francs." (CL, 1200.)

The operation in question was intestinal, and then symptoms of cerebral meningitis set in.[1] Leeches were applied to the ears, but the patient sank away rapidly. Two kind friends, Mr. Robert Ross and Mr. Turner, nursed him, whilst Father Cuthbert Dunne, one of the British Catholic chaplains from the Avenue Hoche, administered the customary rites of the Church.[2] Oscar Wilde tried to articulate the prayers which accompany Extreme Unction, and his death bed was one of repentance.

Tomorrow morning the funeral service will take place at the Church St. Germain des Prés, after which the body will be interred in the Bagneux Cemetery. A small cross will surmount the grave, with the following inscription:—"Ci gît Oscar Wilde, Poéte et Auteur Dramatique. R. I. P."[3]

1. The operation was conducted on 10 October and was probably a radical mastoidectomy.

2. Reginald "Reggie" Turner (1869–1938) was an English journalist and author. Cuthbert Dunne (c. 1868–1950) was an Irish-born Passionist priest. His name is spelt "Dunn" in the source.

3. The inscription on Wilde's gravestone at Bagneux read: " † | OSCAR WILDE | OCT. 16TH 1854— NOV. 30TH 1900. | VERBIS MEIS ADDERE NIHIL AUDEBANT | ET SUPER ILLOS STILLABAT ELOQUIUM | MEUM. [After my words they spake not again; and my speech dropped upon them.] | JOB XXIX, 22. | R. I. P." (Gide, 11, 80).

Appendix A: Untraced Interviews

It is likely that Wilde gave interviews of which I am unaware. There are also interviews that are known or suspected to exist that I was nevertheless unable to trace. Some are the originals of reprinted interviews and may contain more or different content. Some have been referenced by other authors. Some may, on inspection, prove not to be interviews at all.

Here I list the interviews or possible interviews I was unable to trace. If readers are able to find these articles—or others not listed here—and provide them for use in a later edition, I would be grateful. I discourage readers from entering into correspondence with relevant local libraries about the articles listed here; this would replicate my own research and needlessly add to librarians' workloads. However, readers with physical access to library collections may wish to undertake more exhaustive searches themselves.

Please find my contact details on my website: https://robmarland.co.uk

1. Unknown [New York?] newspaper, c. 3 Jan. 1882. Hyde, 51, quotes an interview in which a reporter asks: "What did you come to America for, Mr Wilde?" Wilde replies: "To lecture at Chickering Hall and elsewhere, if the public approve of my philosophy [...] Also to produce a play on Nihilism." Because this material does not appear in the same form in any known interviews, it may originate from an unknown interview.

2. Unknown [Philadelphia?] newspaper, c. 17 Jan. 1882. The source of the first extract reprinted in "The Aesthete on His Travels," *Truth* (London, UK), 2 Feb. 1882, 175–7, p. 707. No interview was printed in the *Public Ledger* (Philadelphia, PA) 16–20 Jan. 1882.

3. Unknown Louisville newspaper, c. 22 Feb. 1882. Ellmann, 186/196, quotes Wilde saying "on 21 February in Louisville": "Yes, I am a thorough republican. No other form of government is so favorable to the growth of art. [...] Of course, I couldn't talk democratic principles to my friend the Prince of Wales." The quotation is not sourced. No interview was printed in the *Courier Journal* (Louisville, KY).

4. Unknown [Springfield/Chicago?] newspaper, c. 28 Feb. 1882. OWDA, 210: "[...] Wilde prepared to depart by Monday's [27 Feb. 1882] 7:30 morning train [from St. Louis] for Springfield. [...] The next time he would be interviewed Wilde would say, 'Several St. Louis citizens told me the city was not at its best. I

should have thought so, even though the information was lacking.'" The quotation is not sourced. Pearson, 68, appears to quote from OWDA. No interview was printed in the *Illinois State Journal* (Springfield, IL), or the *Daily Illinois State Register* (Springfield, IL).

5. *The Capital* (Washington, DC), early March. "Our Washington Letter," *The Daily Chronicle & Constitutionalist* (Augusta, GA), 9 Mar. 1882, 2, praises Don Piatt's editorials for *The Capital*: "The latest production of his is largely devoted to Oscar Wilde, with whom he had an interview of the raciest character". The Library of Congress website indicates that relevant issues are not held by any library.

6. Unknown [Chicago?] newspaper[s], c. 1 Mar. 1882. Lewis and Smith (OWDA, 216–17) quote several interviews Wilde gave in Chicago at the end of February 1882. Some of the quotations are not sourced. One interviewer apparently asked Wilde if he had "[m]ade much dust", and Wilde wondered if he meant money. Another asked if it was "true that tea made from the yellow fringe of sunflowers will cure smallpox", and if he believed in "the blue grass theory of curing rheumatism and baldness". Pearson, 67, appears to quote OWDA. The quotations suggest that Lewis and Smith's source may have been a burlesque interview, but further evidence of an genuine interview at this time comes from Wilde's correspondence. After Whistler had sent a gently mocking telegram to Wilde, which was printed in the *World* (London, UK) on 15 February, Wilde wrote to Whistler from Chicago: "I was so enraged that I insisted on talking about you to a reporter. I send you the result." (Holland and Hart-Davis, 147.) In a letter to Mrs George Lewis dated c. 20 March Wilde wrote: "Weary of being asked by gloomy reporters 'which was the most beautiful colour' and what is the meaning of the word 'aesthetic', on my last Chicago interview I turned the conversation on three of my heroes, Whistler, Labouchere, and Irving, and on the adored and adorable Lily [*sic*]. I send you them all." (Holland and Hart-Davis, 154.) Wilde mentions Labouchère, Irving, and Langtry in known interviews printed on 1 March, but there are no mentions of Whistler in the known Chicago interviews. It therefore seems probable that there was another, earlier interview in which Wilde referred to Whistler, with the most likely date being 1 March.

7. Unknown [Chicago?] newspaper[s], c. 1 Mar. 1882. Hyde, 65, quotes an interview or interviews with Wilde in Chicago. His quotations do not match those given by Lewis and Smith, so his source[s] may be different. Hyde writes that Wilde was asked what he thought of Chicago, and "he replied that the number of telephones impressed him, and he told his questioner how a fellow Briton, doing business in America, had said that the comparatively undeveloped device had saved him $8,000 a year, not to speak of time and worry." Note that Wilde's praise of the telephone was more cautious elsewhere (p. 161). Wilde was also

supposed to have asked his hosts: "Why don't you get some good public dwellings?"

8. Unknown Milwaukee newspaper, c. 6 Mar. 1882. Lewis and Smith (OWDA, 215–6) quote an interview Wilde gave in Milwaukee on 5 March. Wilde had arrived in the city having missed the celebration of the birthday of Irish patriot Robert Emmet on the 4th, and "said that if he had known it he would have given up his Racine lecture [on the 4th] to attend the exercises. He talked to reporters about the kinsman of Emmet he had met in Cincinnati and added that he was 'strongly in sympathy with the Parnell movement' for Irish Home Rule". The quotation is not sourced. No interview was printed in the *Milwaukee Daily Sentinel*. Lewis and Smith later indicate that they consulted the *Republican* (presumably *The Daily Republican and News*) and *The Evening Wisconsin*. Librarians checked both papers for 6 and 7 March (there were no issues on the 5th), but were unable to find the article.

9. *Chicago Herald* (Chicago, IL), c. 5 Mar. 1882. Reprinted (excerpted?) in "Oscar's Opinion," *Sedalia Weekly Bazoo* (Sedalia, MO), 14 Mar. 1882, 7. The microfilm for March 1882 is missing from the collections of the Chicago Public Library (checked June 2020), the University of Illinois at Urbana-Champaign (checked July 2020), and the Abraham Lincoln Presidential Library and Museum (checked May 2021).

10. *Denver Times* (Denver, CO), c. 13 Apr. 1882. OWDA, 310: "Wilde was worried enough to ask a *Denver Times* reporter what kind of an audience he would have." Lewis and Smith do not specify a date but, as the content appears to be about Wilde's impending visit to Leadville, 13 April 1882 seems most likely. Librarians were unable to find the article.

11. "The Art Aspect of Oscar Wilde in Nebraska," *The Daily State Democrat* (Lincoln, NE), 24 Apr. 1882. Possible interview excerpted in *Bruno's Weekly*, *3*(25), 16 Dec. 1916.

12. *Prairie City News* (Prairie City, IA), c. 27 Apr. 1882. Quoted in Hoeltje, H. H. (1937). The apostle of the sunflower in the state of the tall corn. *The Palimpsest*, *18*(6), 186–211: "A full half column was given to a writer for the Prairie City *News* who had heard Wilde lecture in Des Moines and thought him genuine. To this writer, who had interviewed the lecturer, Wilde explained the aesthetic movement more accurately than he had at Dubuque" (199). I also note that the author of "The World Wonder Wilde," *Iowa Daily Register* (Des Moines, IA), 27 Apr. 1882, 2, states that he was accompanied by a fellow newspaperman. He may have been referring to the author of the *Prairie City News* article or a reporter for an unknown Des Moines paper. The State Historical Society of Iowa and the Prairie City Public Library do not hold relevant issues (checked April 2021).

13. *Hesperian* (Lincoln, NE), [1 May] 1882. Possible interview quoted in *Prairie Schooner* (Lincoln, NE), *21*(1) (Spring 1947), 108–16. Wilde visited Lin-

coln on 24 April, so the article likely appeared in the next issue of the paper (issues on 1st and 15th of the month).

14. *New Orleans City Item* (New Orleans, LA), c. 15–23 (most likely 16–19) June 1882. Quoted in "Louisiana Gleanings," *The Lake Charles Echo* (Lake Charles, LA), 24 June 1882, 1. No 1882 issues are held by the New Orleans Public Library (checked September 2020). The Library of Congress website indicates that the relevant issues are not held by any library.

15. "Oscar Wilde," *Ottawa Daily Citizen* (Ottawa, ON), 17 May 1882, 1. H & S, b80. This article is not an interview with Wilde, but rather an account of his lecture in Ottawa on 16 May 1882. A librarian checked the reference for me; as I have not seen the newspaper myself, it is possible than an interview appears elsewhere in this or another edition.

16. *Philadelphia Press*, c. 31 Aug. – 4 Sep. 1882. Presumably identical or very similar to "A Chat With Oscar," *The Times* (Philadelphia, PA), 2 Sep. 1882, 5. A librarian checked the issues published on 28–31 August; none of these contain the interview. It remains possible that the interview appeared in another issue or that it appeared in the *Philadelphia Weekly Press*.

17. *Town*, c. 19 Sep. 1882. Reprinted (excerpted?) in "Pursuing a Venus," *The Chicago Daily Tribune* (Chicago, IL), 12 Aug. 1882, 6.

18. *Boston Home Journal* (Boston, MA), [1882], quoted in "The Trifler," *Musical Courier* (New York, NY), 26 Jul. 1893; which is quoted in Schwab, A. T. (2004). James Gibbons Huneker's critiques of Oscar Wilde. *The Wildean*, *24*, 2–24. Wilde is reported to have "said the dream of his life had been to play 'Hamlet,' and if he went to Australia he would; that he would like to write a comedy, but that he did not think he would get any manager to produce it; that as for marrying he did not think that he ever should." It is unclear whether this is an interview.

19. *Bangor Daily Commercial*, c. 1–12 Oct. 1882. Reprinted (excerpted?) in "Oscar Admires the American Autumn," *The Boston Daily Globe* (Boston, MA), 13 Oct. 1882, 5.

20. *The Daily Graphic* (New York, NY), c. 23 Oct. 1882. Reprinted (excerpted?) in "The Jersey Lily," *The Boston Herald* (Boston, MA), 24 Oct. 1882, 4. The interview does not appear in the first edition, but may be in later editions.

21. *The Daily Star* (New York, NY), c. 23 Nov. 1882. Reprinted (excerpted?) in "Persons and Things," *The New Haven Evening Register* (New Haven, CT), 24 Nov. 1882, 2. The Library of Congress website does not provide holding information for this title (checked December 2021), and the relevant issues do not appear to be held by any library.

22. *The Mail and Express* (New York, NY), 21 Aug. 1883. Reprinted (excerpted?) in "Oscar's Opinion of 'Vera,'" *Philadelphia Press* (Philadelphia, PA), 22 Aug. 1883, 3.

23. *[Lady's] World*, 19 Jan. 1884. Cited in Melville, 181. Wilde is reported to have answered a question, but it is unclear if this article is an interview. The title given by Melville may be incorrect; there was a New York magazine named *Ladies' World*.

24. Unknown Paris newspaper, c. 5 July 1892. The possible source of "Les Théatres," *Le XIXe Siècle* (Paris, France), 6 July 1892, 3.

25. Unknown newspaper, c. Jan.–Feb. 1894. The source of "Local Stage Gossip," *The Philadelphia Inquirer* (Philadelphia, PA), 4 Feb. 1894, 10.

26. Unknown newspaper, c. 4 Jan. 1895. The source of "Théatres," *Le Temps* (Paris, France), 5 Jan. 1895, 4. Wilde's remark that *An Ideal Husband* was "good—very good" appeared in *The Glasgow Herald* (Glasgow, UK), 4 Jan. 1895, 5. *The Era* (London, UK), 5 Jan. 1895, 12, prefixed Wilde's remark with "as is known, he said [...]". This suggests that these articles were drawing from an earlier, unknown article.

27. Unknown [London?] newspaper, c. 14 Feb. 1895. Hyde, 178: "Asked by a reporter next day [i.e. the day after the dress rehearsal of *The Importance of Being Earnest* on 12 February] whether he thought the play would be a success, he replied, 'My dear fellow, you have got it wrong. The play *is* a success. The only question is whether the first night's audience will be one.'"

Appendix B: Articles Not Original Interviews

I provide a list of the articles in Hofer and Scharnhorst's bibliography that do not qualify as original interviews according to my criteria.

b6. "Our New York Letter," *The Philadelphia Inquirer* (Philadelphia, PA), 4 Jan. 1882, 7. A burlesque interview, included in Appendix E, pp. 874–5.

b7, 8. "Oscar Wilde," *The Chicago Daily Tribune* (Chicago, IL), 4 Jan. 1882, 5; "Morning Dispatches," *Daily Evening Bulletin* (San Francisco, CA), 4 Jan. 1882, 1. Both are abbreviated reprints of "A Six-Feet-Four Young Man," *The Evening Telegram* (New York, NY), 3 Jan. 1882, 3rd ed., 5, pp. 46–8.

b9. "Of Gangling Gait," *The Atlanta Constitution* (Atlanta, GA), 5 Jan. 1882, 1. An abbreviated reprint of "Arrival of Oscar Wilde," *New York Tribune* (New York, NY), 3 Jan. 1882, 5, pp. 43–6.

b10. "Oscar Wilde," *The New York World, Semi-Weekly Edition* (New York, NY), 6 Jan. 1882, 2. Not an interview but included in Appendix C, pp. 691–4.

b13. Hall-Haynes, "Art's Apostle," *The Sunday Herald* (Boston, MA), 15 Jan. 1882, 8. Not an interview but included in Appendix C, pp. 696–9.

b16. "Wilde and Whitman," *The Philadelphia Press* (Philadelphia, PA), 19 Jan. 1882, 8. Not an interview with Wilde but included in Appendix D, pp. 757–9.

b18. "Wilde on Greek Drama," *Philadelphia Inquirer* (Philadelphia, PA), 20 Jan. 1882, 8. An abbreviated reprint of "Aesthete Wilde on Greek Plays," *The Evening Telegram* (New York, NY), 13 Jan. 1882, 1, pp. 69–70.

b21. "Art's Apostle," *The Evening Star* (Washington, DC), 21 Jan. 1882, 3. A reprint of b13.

b22. "New York Gossip," *The Sunday Herald* (Boston, MA), 22 Jan. 1882, 4. Not an interview but included in Appendix C, pp. 700-3.

b29. Lilian Whiting, "They Will Show Him," *The Daily Inter Ocean* (Chicago, IL), 10 Feb. 1882, 2. An abbreviated reprint, with additional commentary, of "Oscar Wilde in Boston," *Daily Evening Traveller* (Boston, MA), 28 Jan. 1882, pp. 114–17. Included in Appendix C, pp. 708–11.

b50. "Oscar Wilde," *The Saturday Review* (Indianapolis, IN), 11 Mar. 1882, 7. A burlesque interview, included in Appendix E, pp. 893–5.

b65. "Oscar Wilde," *The Denver Republican* (Denver, CO), 13 Apr. 1882, 4. A burlesque interview, included in Appendix E, pp. 907–8.

b78. "An Aesthetic Discussion," *Daily British Whig* (Kingston, ON), 16 May 1882, 1. Not an interview with Wilde but rather the transcript of a local government meeting written in mock aesthetic language.

b84. "Oscar Wilde," *The Globe* (Toronto, ON), 26 May 1882, 6. Not an interview but included in Appendix C, p. 716.

b88. "Oscar Wilde," *Columbus Enquirer-Sun* (Columbus, GA), 30 June 1882, 4. Not an interview, but an excerpt of "Over the Breakfast Table," *The Times-Democrat* (New Orleans, LA), 26 June 1882, 2, pp. 717–19.

b95. "Oscar Wilde Explains," Daily Transcript (Moncton, NB), 18 Oct. 1882, 2. An abbreviated reprint of "Oscar Wilde Explains," *The Boston Herald* (Boston MA), 16 Oct. 1882, 2, pp. 476–8.

b97. "Oscar Wilde Thoroughly Exhausted," *New York Tribune* (New York, NY), 27 Nov. 1882, 3. A reprint of "Oscar Wilde Prostrated," *The Cincinnati Commercial* (Cincinnati, OH), 26 Nov. 1882, 7, pp. 494–6.

b99. "Mr. Oscar Wilde and the Unutterable Wheel," *The Pall Mall Gazette* (London, UK), 7 May 1883, 11. An excerpt of "Paris Gossip," *The Chicago Daily Tribune* (Chicago, IL), 17 Apr. 1883, 7, pp. 529–32.

Articles cited elsewhere as interviews but which do not meet my criteria.

1. Lewis and Smith (OWDA, 32) quote a letter from Wilde to Sarah Bernhardt in which Wilde describes how he was "impudently interrogated" by an interviewer. The source is a volume of forged letters: Dorian, S. (1924). *Oscar Wilde's Letters to Sarah Bernhardt*. Haldeman-Julius.

2. Lewis and Smith (OWDA, 45) write that Wilde had said "[t]o reporters soon after his landing [...] 'I wish to see Clara Morris dressed all in white brocaded satin.'" The source is "A Reception in Miss Alcott's Honor," *New York Tribune* (New York, NY), 9 Jan. 1882, 5. Wilde may not have spoken with a reporter.

3. "Wilde's Lecture," *Philadelphia Press* (Philadelphia, PA), 18 Jan. 1882, 5. Quoted in OWDA, 73, where it is stated that "the poet told a Press reporter [...]". Not an interview but included in Appendix C, p. 700.

4. W. T. Mercer, "The Aesthetic Gospel," *New York Tribune* (New York, NY), 23 Jan. 1882, 5. Quoted in Fong, B. (1979). Oscar Wilde: five fugitive poems. *English Literature in Transition, 1880–1920, 22*, 7–16. A burlesque interview, included in Appendix E, pp. 888–90.

5. "En Passant," *The American Queen* (New York, NY), 18 Nov. 1882, 322. Quoted by Ellmann, 195/206. Not an interview: see p. 483, note 1.

6. "En Passant," *The American Queen* (New York, NY), 23 Dec. 1882, 402. Quoted by Ellmann, 195/206. Not an interview: see p. 495, note 6.

7. "Farewell to Oscar Wilde," *New York Tribune* (New York, NY), 28 Dec. 1882, 4. Sturgis, 268/256, describes this as a "valedictory interview". Not an interview but included in Appendix C, pp. 727–9.

Appendix C: Other Articles of Interest

In this appendix are collected articles that do not qualify as interviews according to my criteria, but may nevertheless be of interest.

"Oscar Wilde," *The New York World, Semi-Weekly Edition* (New York, NY), 6 Jan. 1882, 2[1]

The Aesthetic Apostle's First Appearance in New York Society.

Mr. and Mrs. A. A. Hayes, jr., of 112 East Twenty-fifth street, held a reception yesterday afternoon in honor Mr. Oscar Wilde. Mrs. Hayes's pretty suite of Japanese rooms furnished pleasant surroundings for the now famous apostle of English aestheticism. Their careless artistic grace must have commended them to Mr. Wilde's good opinion. Personally Mr. Wilde, not being a Japanese young man, suggests entirely different surroundings.[2] It is allowable to consider him in this light, since he is supposed more fully than anyone else to embody in his person his views of life, which is to say the relation of the man to his aesthetic environment.

Personally Mr. Wilde suggests Greek porticos and Doric columns, with open spaces looking towards the blue Aegean, and near by the Venus of Milo or a chaste Diana to furnish the necessary antithesis. To consider Mr. Wilde from an even more artistic point of view, he might fitly make a third of this calm group. His face is that of a colossal maiden untroubled by heated visions but over which at times beams a certain joyousness, wholly Greek, at the sight of the largeness or beauty of nature. In its lines it is essentially feminine, but these are on so large a scale that their soft curves indicate none of the weakness which might hastily attach to the adjective. Otherwise his broad sturdy physique is as English as if trained in athletics instead of aesthetics.

Practically Mr. Wilde accommodates himself with great amiability to the more contracted limits of modern life, at least in a foreign country, in spite of his physiognomy, and adopts without constraint the current coin of society. Not to mention with greater circumstance Mr. Wilde's personal appearance would be inconsistent with alluding to him at all. He wore a Prince Albert coat, tightly buttoned, and held in his hand a pair of light gloves. His broad collar was half hidden by his coat, though revealing a blithe blue scarf, but was not worn as low as that of Mr. Nicholas Smith,[3] nor was his hair of greater length than the cut usually

1. Printed simultaneously on page 6 of the daily edition (which is H & S, b10). Quoted in OWDA, 47; Ellmann, 153/160; and Sturgis, 230/220. This is an account of a reception at which Wilde spoke. He may have spoken directly to the reporter or only to other guests.

2. A reference to *Patience*. Bunthorne sings that he is: "A Japanese young man, | A blue-and-white young man, | Francesca di Rimini, miminy, piminy, | *Je-ne-sais-quoi* young man!"

3. Colonel Nicholas Smith (1847–1919) was the son in law of Horace Greeley and at one time reputed to be "the handsomest man in the world" ("Handsomest Man in World is Broke," *Los Angeles Herald* (Los Angeles, CA), 16 Mar. 1902, 2; "Col. Nicholas Smith Dies at Daughter's Home," *New York Tribune* (New York, NY), 17 Aug. 1919, 12). He is supposed to have claimed that his beauty was a "constant annoyance", and that "he did not dare to dress as well as he would like to,

adopted by the philosophers of the *Tribune*. In short, his manner exhibited the unconsciousness of a gentleman, and in that respect was unlike the indigenous aesthetic not to say asthmatic types with which we are familiar.

The lion of the occasion, he was very appropriately lionized, towering above all the women who clustered prettily about him, and above most of the men, but roaring very gently. He expresses himself very graciously concerning our country, and evidently expects more sympathy for his views in our broader, less crystallized opinions than he has found among the British Philistines. Of these views he speaks with great seriousness, as if their earnestness lay like a burden upon him, but he expresses himself with a rhythmical fluency, which shows he has long grown used to it, and this takes the edge off one's sympathies in admiring the literary form.

Mr. Wilde is enthusiastic in his admirations of others, and especially of Mr. Whistler, whom he declares to be the first painter in England, but he maliciously adds: "It will take England 300 years to find it out." In Paris Mr. Whistler finds appreciation, is at home; but Paris is artistic, and recognizes art when it reveals itself in whatever guise. Of Mr. Whistler's infantile simplicity of character Mr. Wilde is even more generous in praise. Such bits of conversation were tossed hither and thither among the crowd which surged about the stranger, although after yesterday the term is scarcely appropriate, and with Mr. Wilde at least the conversation rarely dropped below a certain level, lifted into a somewhat rarer air than is usual at afternoon teas. To Mr. Wilde this seemed to be native ether, and however short-breathed were those he conversed with, the circumstances of the situation did not allow it to appear, as group effaced group before him.

Wherever he moved the crowd naturally swayed, leaving breathing room behind, following him into the dining-room with well-bred curiosity, making a faint excuse over the punch-bowl, to see him quaff his tea. This attention the hero of the occasion received with that calm unconsciousness which distinguishes his actions, and if he perceived the agreeable impression he created, he did not let it appear.

During the reception Mr. Wilde stood in the middle parlor, and back of him was a gigantic Japanese umbrella covered with grotesque figures on gaily colored paper. The long, thick bamboo handle rested on the floor under a table at Mr. Wilde's left and protected him on that flank. On the other side was the partition dividing the two parlors, and in the enclosure thus formed Mr. Wilde remained, like a heathen idol, most of the time between 3 and 6 P. M. Daylight was excluded from the room by heavy dark curtains closely drawn and heavy portieres fell over the doors. The gas was lighted within, and but fell upon Mr. Wilde softened

---

because, when he was really well dressed, the women pursued him so." (Rowell, G. P. (1906). *Forty Years an Advertising Agent: 1865–1905*. Printers' Ink Publishing Co. 258–9.)

and tinged to a delicate pink by the colored shades fastened upon the globes of the chandeliers. This rosy light softened whatever there might be of harshness in Mr. Wilde's features and made more gentle the gentle expression of his smile. His posture was full of grace, and strongly brought to mind the pictures seen in *Punch*, with the element of caricature of course left out. The rooms were filled with articles of bric-a-brac, but not a lily or sunflower or anything else supposed to be intimately connected with Mr. Wilde's philosophy was to be seen. The dresses of the ladies were not more sad-colored than those seen at the receptions of people who are Philistine or indifferent. In all the rooms conversation was carried on between groups independent of Mr. Wilde, but whatever the latter said was eagerly listened to by the groups which stood around him. The parlors and the refreshment-room were crowded all the time the reception lasted.

✂ *A list of the guests at the reception.*

Mr. Wilde's abode has been kept somewhat of a secret. It is understood that this was done because a number of harmlessly insane persons wish to interview him, and his managers do not wish to have him bothered.[1] Since his arrival he has received many invitations to social entertainments from members of rival sets of society, but he has been protected against the designs of all, and has accepted none of the invitations. This is in accordance with the desire of his managers, who stipulated that his social as well as his lecturing engagements should be under their control, and who, well knowing the importance of his forming only the best social connections, have so far allowed him to go nowhere except to Mr. Hayes's.

Mr. Wilde's agent said yesterday that Mr. Wilde was about to have published at Philadelphia a poem explaining his philosophy which he brought over from England. "There are two or three things in that poem," added the agent enthusiastically, "which I think will go to the very bottom of things." At this a mild shudder of mingled delight and alarm ran around the room and agitated all the fans.[2]

At one happy moment Mr. Wilde advanced a little from the seclusion made by the rod of the Japanese umbrella and the partition, and was instantly surrounded by ladies, who stood grouped in the form of a horseshoe, with the heels of the shoe represented by Mrs. John Bigelow and the Marquise Lanza. Mrs. Bige-

1. Wilde's private address: see p. 53, note 1.

2. J. M. Stoddart had requested via transatlantic cable that Wilde "write poem, twenty lines, terms guinea a line; *subject—sunflower or lily*, to be delivered on arrival", for a new magazine. Two poems by Wilde, *Le Jardin* and *La Mer*, twelve lines each, appeared above a facsimile of his signature in *Our Continent*, 15 Feb. 1882, 9 (CW i, Nos. 94, 95). See also "Oscar Wilde's Visit," *The Scranton Republican* (Scranton, PA), 3 Jan. 1882, 2, p. 750; and "Oscar, The Aesthete," *Philadelphia Press* (Philadelphia, PA), 7 Jan. 1882, 8, p. 754.

low, with her characteristic hospitality, took occasion to secure Mr. Wilde for dinner on Sunday evening, and the young poet in promising to be prompt showed that he felt that in coming to New York he had come among a people who are hospitable and discriminating at once.

"Oscar Wilde Sees 'Patience'," *New York Tribune* (New York, NY), 6 Jan. 1882, 5[1]

THE POET AT THE STANDARD—HIS COMMENTS ON THE PART OF BUN-
THORNE.

Oscar Wilde, the poet and the apostle of aestheticism, went to see 'Patience' at the Standard Theatre last night. The party of which he was one arrived at the theatre about half-past 8. *Lady Jane* was telling *Patience* what love was. "In it," she was saying, "there is a transcendentality of delirium, an acute accentation [*sic*] of supremest ecstasy, which the earthy might easily mistake for indiges-tion."[2] The audience was pondering over this sentence, so that the entrance of Mr. Wilde and his friends was hardly noticed at first. A. A. Hayes led the way to the box, followed by Mrs. Hayes and Miss Gabrielle Greeley, Mr. Wilde bringing up the rear. The poet had on a heavy ulster, with fur cuffs and collar, a fur cap and white kid gloves. His faultless shirt front was relieved by one enormous stud, of some colored stone, in the centre, and a red silk handkerchief protruded from his waistcoat. He wore pumps. The other members of the party were Mrs. Sargent, of Boston, Miss Mack, Mrs. H. Curtis, Mrs. Lillie, Mr. and Mrs. Francis Willet, Colonel and Mrs. W. F. Morse, and Miss Helen Lenoir.[3] They occupied the two lower boxes on the south side of the theatre which connect with the stage.[4]

1. Quoted in OWDA, 54–5; Ellmann, 153/161; and in Sturgis, 204/197. As Friedman, 64, points out, Wilde's party was joined on their visit to the theatre by "a reporter from the *New York Trib-une*, so Wilde knew his words and actions were on the record." However, Wilde's only recorded comment is addressed to "one of the ladies" and not the reporter. Another account of the eve-ning identifies the woman to whom Wilde spoke as Miss Gabrielle Greeley and reports his quip as "This is the homage which mediocrity pays to that which is not mediocre" ("The 'Aesthete' Witnesses a Performance of 'Patience'," *Boston Daily Journal* (Boston, MA), 6 Jan. 1882, 4). "Oscar Goes to See 'Patience,'" *The Daily Picayune* (New Orleans, LA), 9 Jan. 1882, 4, reports the same phrasing as the *Journal*.
2. This moment occurs quite early in the first act. Wilde had missed the opening chorus and Patience's solo.
3. Helen Lenoir (1852–1913), born in Scotland as Susan Helen Couper Black, was D'Oyly Carte's assistant and, later, business manager. The pair married in 1888.
4. It had been announced in *The Daily Graphic* (New York, NY), 5 Jan. 1882, 447, that Wilde's party would occupy the two boxes to the right of the stage.

Mr. Wilde at first stood up in the rear box out of sight, but he finally took a seat where the audience had a good view of him. There were numberless opera glasses turned toward the poet, but he appeared genuinely unconscious of the scrutiny. Most of the time he chatted pleasantly with the ladies, but he watched the performance carefully, notwithstanding. When *Reginald Bunthorne* (J. H. Ryley) came on the stage the whole audience turned and looked at Mr. Wilde. He leaned toward one of the ladies and said with a smile, looking at *Bunthorne:*

"This is one of the compliments that mediocrity pays to those who are not mediocre."

After the first act the whole party, including James Barton Key, the original *Grosvenor* at the Standard, who had recently gone to the box, went behind the scenes. Mr. Wilde was introduced to Miss Burton and Miss Roche and other members of the company.[1] Mr. Ryley stayed in his dressing-room, although he is to meet Mr. Wilde today. There were some fifty persons who waited in the lobby to see the poet as he came out after the opera. After they had been there about fifteen minutes and the audience had gone and most of the lights were turned down, and the aesthete did not appear, they sent in a committee to see what had become of him. This brought word from W. F. Morse that Mr. Wilde had slipped out another way about ten minutes before.

✂ *An account of the Hayes reception.*

"Sunbeams," *The Sun* (New York, NY), 10 Jan. 1882, 2[2]

✂ *Several paragraphs that are unrelated to Wilde.*

Mr. Oscar Wilde has naturally since his arrival in New York accepted several invitations to dinner and on such occasions is announced to have appeared in evening dress suit. This seems to have been a cruel disappointment to some of his admirers who expected to see him clad after the manner of *Bunthorne*, in "greenery-yallery" velvet, and holding in his hand the familiar lily or sunflower. It may be interesting to slender women to know that Mr. Wilde's ideal of perfect beauty is Sarah Bernhardt's, whom he regards as the realization of all his aesthetic dreams. He says he would ask no higher earthly delight than to sit the livelong night on the doorstep of the house in which she sleeps.[3] Mr. Wilde is regarded as very like Henry Irving in appearance, and especially in pose.[1]

1. Carrie Burton played Patience; Augusta Roche played Lady Jane.
2. There is no indication that Wilde's remarks were made in the presence of the reporter.
3. This is reminiscent of the story Lillie Langtry would tell in her autobiography: "[...] although Wilde had a keen sense of the ridiculous, he sometimes unconsciously bordered thereon himself.

✂ *Several paragraphs that are unrelated to Wilde.*

Hall-Haynes, "Art's Apostle," *The Sunday Herald* (Boston, MA), 15 Jan. 1882, 8[2]

England's Aesthete at the Photographer's Gallery.

The Too-Too Reception Suit Accompanies Him,

And He Poses in a Score of Exquisite Styles.

(FROM OUR SPECIAL CORRESPONDENT.)

NEW YORK, Jan. 13, 1882. Oscar Wilde has been on exhibition since his arrival here at private receptions, and once on the lecture platform, and, perhaps, the stalwart but fair aesthete would himself admit that his person has been of much more interest than his philosophy. Of course, an object of so much feminine curiosity—for the mad infatuation of the lone, lorn maidens for Bunthorne in Gilbert's charming opera is only a caricature of the real admiration lavished on this apostle of the beautiful—could not escape the photographers. Some of them were so anxious to get sittings from him, that they began to negotiate with his managers before the young aesthete's departure from England. Sarony was the lucky one.

The poet has proved very tractable since he has been in this city, so, when he was told that he must go and sit for pictures, he attired himself in faultless raiment, packed up his reception suit—the "too too" one, which consists of a velvet swallow-tail coat, knee-breeches, silk stockings and pumps—and set out for Sarony's. The scenes at the studio were more amusing to those who had the fortune to be there, than any that have taken place since the poet began his career in this country. Sarony himself, when in good humor, is, as they say, as good as a show—with his very short stature and frisky ways. But first Postlethwaite's dress on this occasion.[3] To begin at the top, he wore a seal-skin cap, with the

---

For instance, one night he curled up to sleep on my doorstep, and Mr. Langtry, returning unusually late, put an end to his poetic dreams by tripping over him." (Langtry, 93.)

1. This comparison would not have been of much use to the readers of *The Sun* as Irving had yet to visit America.

2. H & S, b13. Reprinted, minus the last paragraph, as "Art's Apostle," *The Evening Star* (Washington, DC), 21 Jan. 1882, 3 (which is H & S, b21). This is an account of Wilde's photography session with Napoleon Sarony. The level of detail suggests that the reporter was present, but Wilde neither answers questions of him nor makes any comments.

3. Postlethwaite: see p. 40, note 2.

side-flaps tied across the crown. A cravat of sky-blue (a favorite color with him) hid from view what of his shirt front left bare by his waistcoat.

A BLACK VELVET JACKET,

a magnificent pair of brown trousers and patent leather shoes completed his dress, except the fur-lined and fur-trimmed ulster which envelops his tall form when he goes out, almost from top to toe.

Sarony was waiting for him in the reception room, momentarily expecting his arrival, his little figure (he is not much over four and a half feet high) crowned with a red Turkish fez. When the tall aesthete entered, the pair looked like the giant and the dwarf greeting each other.

"Ah, here is a picturesque subject, indeed!" exclaimed the artist, clapping his hands and dancing around the room.

The poet, who is much given to laughing and smiling, laughed and smiled in return. After standing around still more, Sarony asked the apostle of the beautiful and true if he had ever seen his (Sarony's) nose.

"Your nose?" asked Wilde, laughing immoderately.

Then it was told that years ago Sarony was caricatured by a rival photographer, who selected his very prominent nose as a particular feature to be developed. But the subject of the caricature was by no means crushed by this, in fact, he went on enlarging his maligned feature himself until it assumed enormous proportions, and portraits showing the result of his artistic endeavor in this direction are found on the walls of the gallery everywhere. Sarony went around, with his peculiar shuffling gait, and pointed some of them out. But there is something that he takes more interest in than his nose, and that is his wife. He has taken her picture in all possible attitudes and in all sorts of costumes; and these portraits are met with as frequently in his studio as those of his own nose. If a visitor manifests especial interest in

HIS WIFE'S PICTURES,

he will pull out still others from drawers and portfolios. They are without end. But this was not enough, for he must show some particularly fine studies of the nude. He was delighted when they were approved, and, in his good spirits, he fell to dancing around the room again.

When these preliminaries were over the artist turned his attention to manipulating the subject. The young apostle of aestheticism has a great stock of hair that falls down on his shoulders in folds and ringlets. That was a good point, giving a picturesque effect. It was observed that the ulster possessed beautiful lines. Therefore it must be kept on—at least for the first series of sittings. Turning out the edges of the ulster, turning back this corner, smoothing out a line here and a line there, turning the subject's hands this way and that way, putting him at side

697

view, full face, three-quarters standing, sitting, his legs disposed so, and again so, the little man in the red fez, backing off each time to see the effect, finally made up his mind what was best to do. He clapped his hands in anticipation, and, giving orders that all visitors should be kept at a distance, he went dancing ahead to the gallery. Postlethwaite and the others followed.

The artist's manner of conducting the sittings was much the same as usual, except that he took extraordinary pains in getting the postures to suit him. To keep the poet in a pleasant mood and from showing signs of weariness, he kept up a constant rain of small talk. When the subject was at last posed, Sarony turned his back, those present doing the same at his bidding, and, throwing his head back, looked up through the windows in the roof at the sky. He does this, whenever he takes a picture, like an automaton. The operator, at this signal, removed the screen from the camera, turned his back to the sitter and began to whistle. This was also part of the programme, and, through much repetition, has become as mechanical as Sarony's

LOOKING UP AT THE SKY.

After a few moments the whistling died away, and some commonplace remarks were exchanged between the artist and the matter-of-fact operator. These performances, from first to last, were gone through for the purpose of breaking the silence and to give the subject as much ease as possible in his strained position. This rigmarole was repeated eight or ten times, and then the aesthete exchanged his ulster and jacket and elegant brown trousers for a dress coat, knee breeches and buckles and silk stockings. About as many more sittings completed the second set, and the thing was done. But no celebrity gets out of Sarony's studio without first writing his autograph in an album. Still other pictures of Mrs. Sarony were produced and looked at, after which the party took its departure, Mr. Wilde with some of Mrs. Sarony's pictures in his pocket.

These photographs of Oscar Wilde are exceedingly interesting to anyone who has a curiosity to know something of his personal appearance. One of them is a panel, and represents the poet with his ulster on in a sitting posture. His hair is parted in the middle, and falls down at the side of his face on his shoulders. The elbow of his left arm rests on his knee, and his chin leans on his left hand: the right hands rests on the other knee, and clutches a pair of gloves. As his head is thrown considerably forward, his eyes are turned up, giving his face a rapt, ecstatic expression.[1] Another panel represents him as standing, holding his

---

1. Photographs from Sarony's sessions with Wilde are reproduced in Cooper, J. (2019). 'A picturesque subject indeed!' The Sarony photographs of Oscar Wilde. *The Wildean, 55,* 3–33; and at oscarwildeinamerica.org. The description corresponds to Sarony's plates 7 and 8. In the almost identical plate 2 Wilde does not appear to be holding his gloves.

698

gloves in one hand, and crumpling the border of his ulster in the other.[1] The cabinet size shows him at a three-quarter view, with the ulster buttoned up and his sealskin cap on. His head is inclined somewhat to one side.[2] The second set is more poetical, the most aesthetical attitudes having been taken. In one of these he holds a copy of the English edition of his poems, which he fondly cherishes as a mark of art, the elaborate design of the cover having been made by himself.[3]

Harry Hewitt, who is associated with the management of Oscar Wilde, was asked how the poet liked the pictures.

"HE IS DELIGHTED,"

was the reply. "Although many pictures have been taken of him, he says he has never had a satisfactory one before—that is, a good likeness, and artistic finish."

✂ *Several paragraphs about photographs taken of other celebrities.*

"We had faith in the commercial value of Oscar Wilde's pictures, and we would not accept the first offers made," said Mr. Hewitt. He was a man, to be sure, but one of unusual interest even in a mere pictorial sense. His tall figure, shock of flowing hair and peculiarities of dress were all points in his favor as a subject for a picture. It was also considered that the artistic ideas that he would have regarding his sittings would be of value. Sarony took this view and made a good proposition."

"How much did he pay the poet?"

"Not as much as Bernhardt or Patti, but the arrangement is very satisfactory."[4]

HALL-HAYNES.

---

1. Plate 5.

2. Plate 3.

3. Wilde holds a copy of *Poems* in plate 9A but the reference appears to be to plate 15 or 18, which are part of the "second series" (after Wilde had changed his clothes). The top outer corners of the front and back covers of *Poems* are decorated with a design in gilt of a prunus blossom. The design is reproduced in Mason, 287.

4. Hewitt had previously mentioned in a section of the interview excluded here that Sarah Bernhardt had, "through her native shrewdness, got $1500, which, through her shrewdness again, she nearly doubled by taking her pay in photographs and selling them on her tour through the country." Adelina Patti "was paid $1000, having been engaged before she left Europe. No pictures of her have appeared, and the reason is said to be that she claimed that each one (she had 30 sittings) made her look too old. It is also said that she refused to return the money."

699

"Wilde's Lecture," *Philadelphia Press* (Philadelphia, PA), 18 Jan. 1882, 5[1]

THE POET MEETS WITH WHAT HE CALLS A COLD RECEPTION

A Large and Fashionable Gathering in Horticultural Hall that Fails to Applaud the Limp and Lank Young Man.

✂ *An account of Wilde's lecture in Philadelphia.*

After the lecture a reception was tendered the poet in the house of J. M. Stoddart, No. 107 North Nineteenth Street. He expressed himself very much dissatisfied with the treatment he had received from his Philadelphia audience. He said his hearers were so cold that he several times thought of stopping and saying: "You don't like this, and there is no use in my going on," and then abruptly leave the stage.[2]

✂ *A summary of the content of Wilde's lecture.*

"New York Gossip," *The Sunday Herald* (Boston, MA), 22 Jan. 1882, 4[3]

Meeting of the Aesthetic Poet and Clara Morris.

"Squatter Sovereignty" at the Theatre Comique.

The Vanderbilt Mansion—Society Conundrum.

(FROM OUR REGULAR CORRESPONDENT.)

NEW YORK, Jan. 16, 1882. Something too much of Oscar Wilde! and yet he is quite worth a valedictory, in view of the fact that "all New York" is still talking of him, popular opinion in this regard not yet having reach that stage where the

---

1. It is unclear whether Wilde's comment was spoken in the presence of the reporter or only to another person (e.g. Stoddart), who later quoted him. Quoted in OWDA, 73; Hyde, 58; and Sturgis, 215/207. The comment was reprinted widely, beginning with "Personal," *New York Tribune* (New York, NY), 19 Jan. 1882, 4.

2. The *Press* reported that Wilde's monotonous delivery and lack of gestures caused his audience to sink "into sullen despair". Applause was not heard more than three times during the lecture. When Wilde paused to drink some water he was "met with the most vigorous applause of the evening, but applause of a kind that greets the 'super' when he confronts a waiting audience and straightens the carpet at the front of the stage." This caused Wilde momentarily to lose his composure and the audience laughed.

3. H & S, b22. Wilde is quoted but his remarks are made to Clara Morris and not to a reporter.

"mere mention of that hallowed name" will be greeted with the same emphatic protest that once attended the crack quotation from "H. M. S. Pinafore."[1] In the mean time, Oscar hies him to Philadelphia, where he has been unduly heralded; he gives his lecture one night only there, as here, his manager being shrewd enough to recognize the fact that once is a genteel sufficiency.

✂ *A defence of Oscar against the criticisms of another* Herald *correspondent.*

The past week has been an exhausting one to Oscar, but just how far he may be held to have penetrated into "society," in the sense that weds fashion and wealth to exclusiveness, may well be doubted. To be sure, he attended receptions at Mrs. McClellan's, Mrs. John Mack's and Mrs. Paran Steven's, dined at Mrs. John Bigelow's and called on several ladies, such as Mrs. John Sherwood and Mrs. Lester Wallack, who hold the open sesame to reunions of the élite,[2] but he was also a guest at half-way houses where the beau monde are conspicuous by their absence. It is reported that Oscar naïvely repeated an injunction that had been laid upon him, to the effect that he must not allow himself to be "Bigelowed," saying: "I have heard of being 'bulldozed,' but what is 'Bigelowed'?" To which came the reply, "If you don't know, Mr. Wilde, I can't tell you." The fair sex are disposed to be more courteous to Oscar than are men, as a rule, and Mr. D'Oyly Carte's poet passed a very *mauvais quart d'heure* at the Century Club on Saturday, where the members stared at him as though he were a freak of nature, and but few people requested an introduction. It is unquestionable that a very strong prejudice exists against Mr. Oscar Wilde, and this is generally deepened, on a sight of him, among men who despise affectation, and detest the humbug of advocating nature and sincerity, and yet all the time furnishing every evidence to the contrary. "There is but one consolation for this craze over Oscar Wilde," said a man the other day, "and that is the manner London society went mad over Mrs. Langtry." In artistic circles, Oscar has been adopted as a kindred spirit, actors and actresses receiving him as a

SUCCESSFUL FELLOW PERFORMER,

1. *H. M. S. Pinafore; or The Lass That Loved a Sailor* is a comic opera by Gilbert and Sullivan (1878). The allusion is presumably to the number "My gallant sailors, good morning … I am the Captain of the Pinafore", in which Captain Corcoran boasts that he never gets seasick or uses bad language. The exchange that followed was widely quoted: "CHORUS. What, Never? | CAPTAIN. No, never! | CHORUS. What, never? | CAPTAIN. Hardly ever!"
2. Ellen Mary McClellan née Marcy (1836–1915) was the wife of General George Brinton McClellan. Mary Elizabeth Sherwood née Wilson (1826–1903) was an American author and socialite. Emily Mary Wallack née Millais (c. 1826–1909) was a sister of John Everett Millais.

quite aware of the fact that "stage mask may cover honest faces, and hearts beat true beneath a tinsel robe!"[1] Sarah Bernhardt had told him that the two things she best remembered about America were "Clara Morris and the western slaughter houses," and Oscar is said to have been inquiring the way to Clara immediately on landing from the Arizona a fortnight since. The shortest route was ultimately found to lay through the residence of Mrs. Croly in Thirty-eighth street,[2] and thither Oscar proceeded with impressment, preceded by three separate messengers to beg Miss Morris not to leave until he arrived, detention having taken place at Mrs. John Bigelow's and Mrs. Paran Stevens en route. The meeting of the gifted actress and the *soi-disant* apostle of beauty was viewed with much curiosity by Mrs. Croly's assembled guests. Clara, arrayed in white, glistening with ornamentation and jewels, awaited the appearance of "the youth to whom is given so much of earth, so much of heaven!" with mixed emotions. Oscar, rejoicing in the most extraordinary composure ever vouchsafed to mortal man, repeatedly besought her not to "run away," saying that he could scarcely hope to convey to her how much this meeting meant to him. "I am nobody," he remarked, "but Mlle. Sarah Bernhardt is an authority; she has told me how greatly she admired your acting, all reports to the contrary notwithstanding. There are so many things I should like to say to you." An opportunity was found later in the evening, after Oscar had been duly introduced to others present, who, he likewise modestly remarked to Miss Morris, were not there to see him, but "because they love and honor" her. Oscar "grew upon" the actress, who, when she first saw him, felt surprised at having to raise her eyes so much higher than usual to look into a face that was lengthened, as though reflected in a tablespoon; the Medusa-like locks also arrested her attention. The actress and the poet spoke much of Oscar's play, which he touched up on board ship coming over, making, by a strange coincidence, a prophetic forethought, one alteration which Miss Morris afterward suggested on meeting him. The language is powerful and beautiful, in her opinion, but the play needs technical carpentry. The Nihilistic theme does not altogether appeal to Clara's sympathies. After seeing her in

"THE NEW MAGDALEN

Oscar said many complimentary things. One speech was: "Is it possible that you are guilty of an affectation? For it is one to persist in your refusal to act in London." The newspapers say that Oscar went to Booth's to see Mary Anderson's Galatea in company with Miss Morris and her husband, Mr. Harriott, but the newspapers also said that Clara was at Kate Field's luncheon, where she was

---

1. The author quotes *Masks and Faces*, an 1852 play by Charles Reade and Tom Taylor.
2. Croly's reception: see p. 67, note 2.

not,[1] and at Mrs. Fortescue's reception: instead of attending the latter symposium the actress occupied a box at the Theatre Comique, to see Harrigan & Hart's latest success, "Squatter Sovereignty." Somebody jestingly handed her a calla lily—the "arum" of aesthetic phraseology—whereupon spake the actress: "My name is C. Arum Morris from this moment." Oscar was not of the party; he mingled pensively with the throng [*illeg. wd.*] Fortescue.[2] As Wordsworth remarked—quotation all right this time:

> Society became my glittering bride,
> And airy hopes my children.[3]

✂   *Several paragraphs that are unrelated to Wilde.*

"The Aesthete Entertained," *The Washington Post* (Washington, DC), 23 Jan. 1882, 4[4]

Mr. Oscar Wilde was entertained by Mrs. Frances Hodgson Burnett at her residence on Saturday evening, where a number of woman suffragists and other prominent persons met and stared at him. He was arrayed in small clothes and silk stockings, with large buckles, a shabby old claw-hammer coat, two sizes too small for him, a soiled white vest and a flowing cravat. "Do you know," said the proper young man to a gentleman who conversed with him, "that the greatest man I have met in your country is Walt Whitman?"

"Don't you think Mr. Longfellow is the greatest poet we have?" was the response.

"Lord, bless you, no. We don't esteem Mr. Longfellow so much in England as we do Mr. Whitman."

"What is the thing you most desire to see? he was asked. "I think I shall most desire to see Spring in California." was the answer, "but I don't know as I will be able to stay here so long."

1. Wilde and Morris did attend the luncheon given by journalist and president of the Cooperative Dress Association Kate Field (1838–1896) on 11 January, and saw Anderson in *Pygmalion and Galatea* on 14 January with Morris's husband (Page, 18).
2. Possibly a reference to *Mr. Pope's Welcome from Greece*, a poem by John Gay (1685–1732).
3. The poem quoted is Wordsworth's *The Excursion*.
4. This may be an interview or a report of an overheard conversation.

"Oscar Wilde a Guest of the Wednesday Club," *The Sun* (Baltimore, MD), 26 Jan. 1882, 4[1]

Mr. Oscar Wilde, the poet, sentimentalist and lecturer, attended a musical entertainment at the Wednesday Club last night in all the glory of silk stockings and knee breeches. It is said that in one of his many attitudes, when he twined his left leg, which is a poem in itself, aroused his right leg, which is an acknowledged essay on beauty, and then placed the upper half of his body on a delicate, obtuse angle to the lower half, he presented a model which Phidias would have been proud to engage at almost any salary asked. He did not put in an appearance until eleven o'clock, however, and not a few of the audience who left early were deprived of the pleasure of seeing estheticism illustrated. It may have been admiration of Mr. Wilde and his teachings which drew together the large audience, or it may have been the entertainment itself, or, again, it may not be improbable that curiosity had something to do with it; but whatever the cause, certain it is a more intelligent, more fashionable, more elegantly-attired gathering has seldom been seen in this city. More stylish ladies it would be difficult to find anywhere, and Mr. Wilde gave undisputed evidence of his good taste in this respect by so expressing himself. While a large number of those present seemed delighted with what they saw of Mr. Wilde, others appeared to be undecided in their minds, but looked as if they would give anything for a secluded place where they could have a real good laugh. Mr. Wilde himself was bright and animated, and graceful, too, notwithstanding the slenderness and apparent unreliability of his spindle shanks. Before going to the Wednesday Club he dined at the residence of Mr. Benjamin F. Horwitz, No. 18 Cathedral street. Among those present were Judge Gilmor, Dr. H. J. Groesbeck, and Messrs. James Hodges, Richard Gittings, Richard J. Gittings and Wm. Read. Of Mr. Wilde's address and scholarship all of the gentlemen who were at the dinner speak in flattering terms of commendation, but are silent when questioned as to what they think of his style of dressing. One remarked casually, however, that it may be an eccentricity of genius. Another gentleman, who had a conversation with Mr. Wilde during the day, and who takes a practical view of things, said that Mr. Wilde's object in coming here was ostensibly to lift us out of the mud and to teach us to recline on a bank of roses, but really to make all the money out of us he could. We are very gullible, he continued. Mr. Wilde knows this, and dresses himself fantastically for the purpose of exciting curiosity and the satirical comments of newspapers, knowing that some of the fashionable people will believe that he is being ill-treated, and will sympathize and spend money accordingly. It's a clever game, and is being

---

1. The last lines of this article report Wilde's impressions of Baltimore, but the source of these impressions is unclear.

cleverly played. In the afternoon Mr. Wilde visited the Academy of Music, the Johns Hopkins University and the Peabody Institute, and said that he was pleased with all he saw. He thinks the dwellings of the city are sadly in need of architectural improvement.

"The Aesthete on His Travels," *Truth* (London, UK), 2 Feb. 1882, 175–7[1]

ANY European of note or of notoriety who goes over to America is sure of a hearty welcome. As a nation, the Americans are exceedingly hospitable, and they are, moreover, very curious to see in the flesh those whose names are familiar to them. Mr. Oscar Wilde is a cognate personage, not so much because he has written poems, but because he is one of the principal leaders of the social and artistic movement, which goes by the name of aestheticism. What that movement is I never exactly knew, except that it had to do with lilies, sunflowers, dados, frizzy hair, clinging garments, and angular movements. Lectures on aestheticism have never, to my knowledge, been given in England by any of its priests, nor have its arcana been revealed except by the jeers of its opponents. In America, they are more fortunate. They have the High Priest amongst them, and the newspapers are filled, not only with his views in the lecture-room, but with his more familiar outpourings to reporters and others, whilst his mode of life and his attire are dwelt upon exhaustively.

A few extracts from these newspapers will, I think, prove amusing and instructive.

Here is a picture of Mr. Wilde "at home," being interviewed:—

The apartment was intensely warm. A hot coal fire in the low-down grate burned fiercely, though the intense blaze was prevented from scorching the cheeks of the young aesthete by a screen of iron and brass. The sofa on which Mr. Wilde reclined was drawn up to the fire. An immense wolf-skin rug, bordered with red and stitched with the same colour, thrown negligently over the back and seat of the sofa, also served to half encircle the graceful form of the poet in

1. I am grateful to John Cooper for identifying this article. The author's first excerpt, beginning "The apartment was intensely warm", is taken from an untraced American article. This excerpt, like the others, may originate from a Philadelphia newspaper published c. 17 January. The excerpt was also reprinted, with minor variations, in "Oscar Wilde," *Lady's Pictorial* (London, UK), 18 Feb. 1882, 556; which was in turn excerpted in the Keystone Press (1906) edition of Wilde's lecture *Impressions of America*, edited by Stuart Mason.

its soft embrace.[1] Mr. Wilde was wearied. There could be no doubt about this, from the languid, half-enervated manner with which he gently sipped hot chocolate from a cup which stood on a chair by his side, or in the way he occasionally inhaled a long, deep whiff from a smouldering cigarette held lightly in his white and shapely hand. The aesthete was attired in a smoking-jacket of dark brown velvet, faced on the lapels with red quilted silk. The ends of a long dark necktie floated over the facing like seaweed on foam, tinged by the dying sun. Dark brown pants,[2] striped with red up the seam, and patent-leather shoes, with light-coloured cloth uppers, completed the rest of the poet's costume. The dress may be open to criticism, but the face of the poet disarms adverse opinion. Long masses of dark brown hair, parted in the centre, fell in odd curves of beauty over the broad shoulders of this super-aesthetical poet. The lines of the face are not marred by moustache or beard. The full, rather sensuous, lips, now parted in kindly smile, show to perfection the mobility of the countenance. A Grecian nose and the well-tinged flush of health on the poet's face add all that is required to make it a truly remarkable one. The eyes are large, dark, and ever-changing in expression. One thought of a lion when Mr. Wilde tossed back the thick hair on his head as it fell over his face when he reclined forward;[3] one thought of a woman when he waved his hand gracefully in the air, or sighed because he was so utterly wearied. Mr. Wilde is neither lion nor woman, but a particularly clever young man who is creating a sensation—which is more than one clever young man in a million is able to do.[4]

At parties, however, he adopts a different costume, for thus was he attired when he took part in an evening party got up in his honour by Mr. Davis, at Philadelphia:—

---

1. *Lady's Pictorial* has: "An immense wolf-skin rug, bordered with scarlet, was thrown over it and half encircled the graceful form of the hero in its soft embrace."
2. For "pants", *Lady's Pictorial* has "nether garments".
3. *Lady's Pictorial* has "leaned forward".
4. *Lady's Pictorial* continues: "IT is quite a mistake to suppose that because Mr. Wilde had a lily in his hand at the début of Sarah Bernhardt he always carries one about with him. Toujours perdrix implies satiety, and Mr. Wilde feels so absolutely pursued by the lily that he begins to regard it as his bête noire. | THE apostle of the new culture stands six feet one with his "socks on," so that being a goodly person he can afford to wear any style of dress he chooses. His favourite colour is something between brown and green, a tint "that never was on sea or sky," and he has both coat and trousers made of it. His walking-stick is a white one, presented to him at the Acropolis, and supposed to have been cut from the olive groves of the Academy. It is only in the evening that he dons knee breeches, but evening and morning alike find him neither more nor less than a man, and always a perfect gentleman. | THE aesthetic poet is a charming companion, and while he can tell racy stories and repeat bon mots of those whom society delights to honour, he can cap quotations from Greek authors, and show cause why Cleopatra should have lived to captivate Octavius."

Mr. Wilde wore a dress suit, the pants of which were cut off a little below the knee, the rest of the leg being encased in black silk stockings, low patent-leather pumps completing that portion of the attire. A loose rag of a white necktie was wound around the throat of the aesthetic expounder of high art and socialism. The full expanse of shirt front, which in an ordinary gentleman's evening attire cannot be too immaculate and rigid, in the case of the poet consisted of a wilted ribbed piqué.

Thus does he explain to a reporter what aestheticism is, and what are its aims:—

✂ *The paragraph in "Honors to an Aesthete," The Times (Philadelphia, PA), 17 Jan. 1882, 1, that begins "'The philosophy of aestheticism,' said Mr. Wilde, in conversation [...]" (see pp. 82–3).*

"What are your politics?" asks the reporter:—

✂ *The paragraph in "A Talk with Wilde," Philadelphia Press (Philadelphia, PA), 17 Jan. 1882, 2, that begins "'O, do you know, those matters are of no interest to me.'" (See p. 76.)*

My last extract is a conversation, in which he gives his views upon velvet coats, "Patience," the beauty of American women, and the sympathies of Mrs. Langtry.

✂ *An excerpt from "A Talk with Wilde," Philadelphia Press (Philadelphia, PA), 17 Jan. 1882, 2, that begins "'Do you not hope to bring back picturesque dressing [...]'" and ends "'She has an artistic house, deserves all her reputation for beauty, and sympathizes thoroughly with the aesthetic school.'" (See pp. 75–6.)*

Altogether Mr. Wilde seems to be having a "high time" in America, and I am by no means sure but that he will be able to do useful work there. The country is wealthy, because it is utilitarian, and, because it is the latter, too little attention is paid to art. There are rich Americans, who have filled their comfortable houses with artistic objects, but these they have purchased because they have been told that it is correct to have them. American women do not dress well as a rule; they only dress expensively. They are the slaves of milliners. That a human being should go about lecturing upon art in its relation to domestic life no doubt fills Americans with surprise, and it is very possibly owing to the desire to see so strange a creature that a good deal of Mr. Wilde's success is due on the other side of the Atlantic. But I would urge Americans to take note of what the Pontiff of aestheticism says. They are not likely to array themselves in velvet coats and knee-breeches at his bidding, nor will they worship lilies or sunflowers; but they should remember that, when a tree is bent too far one way, the only means to straighten it is to bend it too much the other way. To counteract hyper-utilitarianism there must be for a time hyper-aestheticism. In a land where the almighty dollar has such fervent adorers, no harm will be done by a creed being preached which, if it errs by its exaggerations, has at least the merit of teaching that those who care neither to heap up dollars nor to shine as political "bosses" have still something to live for. The wisest man, to my mind, is he who gets the most enjoyment out of life.

Lilian Whiting, "They Will Show Him," *The Daily Inter Ocean* (Chicago, IL), 10 Feb. 1882, 2[1]

Oscar Wilde Will Learn a Thing or Two About Art if He Remains in Boston.

The People Have No Idea of Being Humbugged by This Utterly Utter Young Man.

Anna Dickinson and Her Future—The Greek Play a Success—The Latest Literature.

Special correspondence of The Inter Ocean.

Boston, Mass, Jan. 29.—

✂ *A review of Oedipus Tyrannus at the Globe Theatre.*

THE POET OF THE AESTHETES

arrived at Hotel Vendome yesterday. I did not see the lily-laden lyrist make his entree in the portals, but I have the assurance of one of our Sunday morning papers of today that "Mr. Wilde arrived about noon and entered the Vendome like any ordinary person"—a statement that one must credit, considering the high local authority I quote, although I regret the fact, as I am sure something extraordinary was expected of Oscar in this important moment. The local historian

1. H & S, b29. Lilian Whiting (1847–1942) was an American journalist, newspaper editor, and poet. This article, reprinted in H & S, 51–3, is based on "Oscar Wilde in Boston," *Daily Evening Traveller* (Boston, MA), 28 Jan. 1882, pp. 114–17. *The Inter Ocean* quotes Wilde less and in-cludes more negative commentary than the *Traveller*. Whiting may be the author of both versions (she was on the staff of the *Traveller*), but the disparity in tone suggests that she took another's article and added her own commentary for *The Inter Ocean*. Wilde later told Mary Watson that she (Watson) was the first woman to interview him (Mary Watson, "Oscar Wilde at Home," *The Daily Examiner* (San Francisco, CA), 9 Apr. 1882, 1, p. 324); if correct, this interview cannot have been conducted by Whiting (although both articles were preceded by [Florence Duncan], "A Chat with Oscar Wilde," *Quiz* (Philadelphia, PA), 25 Jan. 1882, 4, pp. 83–5).

neglects to chronicle whether or no his manner was intense, and whether he appeared in good spirits thus separated from his "mamma." (For the full force of this last allusion, vide a Mrs. Gustafson's glowing eulogy on Miss Genevieve Ward.)[1] One would fancy, by the by, that Miss Ward's prayer to the gods would have been, "Save me from my friends," on the appearance of this amazing chronicle.

THE AESTHETE INTERVIEWED.

But to return to the aesthete: I chanced to meet Mr. Wilde for an hour or two before dinner last night, and found little of that eccentricity which has seemed so pronounced to his numerous interviewers. From some supremely poetical perception of the eternal fitness of things, I suppose, he proceeded to entertain me with tales of the atrocity of the American press. In the evening I was laughingly relating Mr. Wilde's power of natural selection, conversationally considered, to a musical artist—a prima donna, in fact—who assured me in return that half the people whom she met would regale her with unflattering allusions to her profession. However, I listened with equanimity to Mr. Wilde's tale of "the dangers he had passed" less moved than Desdemona, yet not without a sympathetic perception of truth in his strictures.

The fact is, he has been greatly misrepresented, his individualities caricatured, his tastes exaggerated, his appearance burlesqued. He is not great enough to merit so much attention, and he is not necessarily

AN OBJECT OF RIDICULE.

Mr. Wilde has more than the average intelligence, is a scholarly and sufficiently well-appearing young man, whose intellectual method is strongly flavored with the ideas of Ruskin, Swinburne, Morris, Rossetti, and who, without being at all an original genius, is yet remarkably assimilative of genius. He is one of those people who produce the right atmosphere for art. He is not an artist, but he is artistic; not creative, but intensely appreciative. The truly poetic mind is reverent. "Poets become such through scorning nothing."[2] Mr. Wilde is perceptibly egotistic, and in so far, is not a poet.

"My object in coming to America," remarked Mr. Wilde to me last night, "is to tell the American people what is the most important movement of thought in England, wishing that all should exactly understand what we artists intend to do.

1. Zadel Barnes Buddington Gustafson (1841–1917) was an American poet and journalist. The author refers to Gustafson's book, *Genevieve Ward: A Biographical Sketch* (1882), in which letters from Wilde to Ward are printed. In one, Wilde invites Ward to a gathering at which his "mamma" will be present (CL, 90–1).

2. A reference to *Aurora Leigh*, the 1856 epic poem by Elizabeth Barrett Browning (1806–1861). In 1899 Whiting published a biography of the poet.

709

Our object is to produce more concentration, more definite artistic movements of value than ever before.”

“Do you limit this movement to what are termed, distinctively, the ‘fine arts,’ or do you also include the decorative, Mr. Wilde?” I asked.

AN EPIGRAM.

“No one art is finer than any other,” he replied. “All true art is decorative.”

Now the avowed object of Mr. Wilde’s visit here indicates his ignorance of current life. The American people need no missionary to proclaim to them the latest thought in England. It is very probable that Mr. Wilde might learn, rather than teach, while here. We all take our pre-Raphaelitism—our Ruskin, Shelley, Keats, Swinburne, and Burne-Jones—at first hand, and need no apostle to translate or dilute it for us. However, we have contributed so largely to the growth of Mr. Wilde’s conceit that it is merely a bit of poetic justice that we should suffer from it. His goings-out and his comings-in have been chronicled, his dressing-gown, slippers, and neckties have figured in our newspapers, and he is quite justified in fancying himself to be

AN UTTERLY UTTER YOUNG MAN.

If you care to take a microscopic view of an unimportant subject, O, cosmopolitan INTER OCEAN, you will see that Boston will take the conceit out of Oscar. He will meet all the gentle courtesy of well-bred life, but he will not be regarded as an object d’art, to be placed under glass and gazed upon. He will neither be considered vaguely wonderful for some inexpressible reason, as he was in New York, nor will his really pleasant qualities be ignored.

Mr. Wilde’s greatest need is to be taught how to talk. He will make some commonplace statement with the air of an oracle, and ten chances to one his listener had known this same fact all his life, and is probably far more familiar with it than is this aesthetic young man.

I heard him expounding the ethics of Schools of Design last night to a lady who had visited them, studied them, and who had probably written more in the newspapers about them than Mr. Wilde had ever dreamed of.

HE SAYS SOME GOOD THINGS.

Yet, withal, he says some good things. For instance, he remarked that “The desire for beauty is the desire for life; for that enduring element in existence which is life. It is the essential part of all civilization,” he continued, “Without beauty civilization has no meaning, because industry without beauty becomes barbarism."[1]

The thought is derived from Ruskin, of course, yet it was well put, and many epigrammatic turns of thought expressed by Mr. Wilde are entertaining to the listener. I asked him about Burne-Jones, and he told me he considered him an artist "of the loftiest spiritual imagination, of a fervid type, of splendid range of vision, of a joyous color, and a wonderful fertility of design."

Mr. Wilde is to give his lecture on "The English Renaissance" in Music Hall on Thursday evening. No one expects to hear anything original or striking, yet it is anticipated that it will be a rather pleasant intellectual entertainment.

✂ *Several paragraphs that are unrelated to Wilde.*

Lilian Whiting

"Oscar's Departure," *Buffalo Commercial Advertiser* (Buffalo, NY), 9 Feb. 1882, 3[2]

Oscar Wilde changed his mind after his lecture yesterday afternoon, and instead of remaining in Buffalo over night, took the 6:10 train for Niagara Falls, where he took quarters at the Prospect House. After doing the Falls today, he will leave for Chicago, where he lectures on Monday evening next. Oscar was pleased to say that he was much gratified with Buffalo, and with the patient attention of his audience.

"Oscar Wilde," *The Chicago Daily Tribune* (Chicago, IL), 14 Feb. 1882, 7[3]

✂ *An account of Wilde's lecture in Chicago, 13 Feb. 1882.*

A SOCIETY EVENT.

Mr. Wilde was entertained yesterday afternoon by Mr. and Mrs. Franklin MacVeagh at their residence, No. 1823 Michigan avenue, in a very pleasant man-

---

1. Art and barbarism: see p. 117, note 1.
2. Wilde's comments may have been obtained directly or from a third party.
3. Wilde is quoted, but his remarks are not to a reporter.

ner.[1] At half-past 1 o'clock a lunch party was given in Mr. Wilde's honor, and there were present Mr. and Mrs. W. F. Whitehouse, Mr and Mrs. Leslie Carter, the Misses Alice and Kittie Arnold, Miss Gardner, Miss Hoteling, Mr. Ord, Mr. Wilde, and Mr. and Mrs. MacVeagh.

After lunch, Mr. MacVeagh drew Mr. Wilde out, and he talked very pleasantly on the subjects of dress, dancing, etc. He said that artificial flowers should never be worn: all ladies might wear lilies, but only an Oriental beauty could wear the sunflower. One dress made by an artist, he said, was worth five dresses made by a dressmaker. In speaking of dancing he said he believed that the minuet would be revived. When he gave large balls in England they used to dance the minuet and other old dances in the costumes of the time, and in this connection he stated that appropriate costumes should always be worn. He was told that the Americans thought they danced better than the English, and he acknowledged this to be a fact. In speaking of beautiful women he said he believed Mme. Christine Nilsson and Mrs. Langtry were the most beautiful women in the world. His conversation was very pleasant and agreeable, and he said many sensible and witty things.

✂   *An account of another reception Wilde attended that afternoon.*

"Decorative Art," *The Milwaukee Sentinel* (Milwaukee, WI), 6 Mar. 1882, 5[2]

Oscar Wilde's Lecture at the Opera House Last Evening.

A Small Audience and But Little Enthusiasm Manifested.

Appearance of the Aesthetic Gentleman and How He Talked.

The Lecture—Amusing Incidents—Several Allusions to Art—Wilde's Visit.

✂   *An account of Wilde's lecture in Milwaukee.*

1. Franklin MacVeagh (1837–1934) was an American wholesale grocer and lawyer. He served as United States Secretary of the Treasury between 1909 and 1913. His wife was Emily Sherrill MacVeagh née Eames (1842–1916).

2. An alleged interaction with a reporter that does not qualify as an interview. Quoted by Lewis and Smith (OWDA, 216), who believe the report to be false: "for while he [Wilde] had been undoubtedly less remarkable for good-humour since his St. Louis experience, the brusqueness and claims of noble birth ascribed to him were known to be entirely out of character."

At the close of the lecture the speaker made his bow and sought to leave the stage. He proceeded leisurely and failed to find the exit. Turning again he bowed awkwardly to the audience, and walked over behind the wings to where a Sentinel reporter was in waiting. Accosting the reporter he said: "Why did you not have that door so that it would open when I wished to go, and not compel me to make an ass of myself?" The reporter politely imparted the information that he was not the scene shifter, and, with a grumble, the aesthete started to leave. At this juncture a supe ejaculated: "Mr. Wilde, we thought it would open." The poor boy was directly crushed by the denunciatory shout: "Don't 'Mr. Wilde' me; I am of noble birth. Treat me as becomes my station—with respect." He then turned and walked away, shouting: "Come up stairs! Come up, will you!!" Who was meant no one knew, and accordingly no one responded to the lank aesthete as he strode off. Mr. Wilde will return to Chicago on the early train this morning. He took a ride yesterday afternoon, and was greatly pleased with Milwaukee.

"Wilde Under Ground," *Denver Tribune* (Denver, CO), 15 Apr. 1882[1]

The Great Aesthete Explores the Workings of the Matchless Mine at Leadville.

(Special Dispatch to THE TRIBUNE.)

LEADVILLE, April 14.—Last night between 1 and 2 o'clock Oscar Wilde went through the works of the Matchless, having been invited to do so by Governor Tabor. Some time after he finished his lecture he was driven to the mine with his agent and Mr. McDonald, a London correspondent.[2] He was politely received by Superintendent Charles Pishon. He arrived dressed in a slouch hat, corduroy coat, low shoes and rather tight pants. He was furnished in the Superintendent's office with Governor Tabor's underground suit, a complete dress of india rubber. He was then taken down No. 3 shaft, which is rather dryer than other Fryer hill shafts, but at the best is dirty and chilly. The Superintendent pointed out various ore bodies and the difference between high-grade and low-grade ores. He was struck with the fact that such rich ore bodies as the chlorides and the carbonates of the Matchless should be so common and somber-looking. He seemed to be very much pleased. He said it was the first mine he had ever seen, and said sev-

1. Quoted in OWDA, 316. It is possible that the author accompanied Wilde, but it seems more likely that he obtained his information from a third party (presumably Superintendent Pishon).

2. Wilde's visit to Leadville was briefly referred to in the London press. McDonald's article, assuming it was ever written, remains untraced.

eral times it was the finest sight in the world. He expressed himself as gratified that a chance had been given him to inspect a first-class Leadville mine, and thanked the Superintendent in grateful terms for escorting him around. He did not seem at all fatigued, but chatted incessantly.

The Evening Item (Richmond, IN), 2 May 1882, 4[1]

—Ye Oscar Wild [*sic*], he of the lily and sunflower fame, honored Richmond by a neighborly call this morning. His royal nibs, who is the original Jacobs and son in his own right of Old government Java, condescended, he having been dropped here at 5 o'clock, to remain until the 7 o'clock train to Dayton, and put in his time very enjoyably no doubt, in viewing our school buildings and other monuments of pioneer days. He took breakfast at the Arlington and it was observed broke his bread with his lily fingers and sucked his toast off the tines of a fork; meanwhile wiping his mouth with a napkin occasionally while casting eyes at the pretty waiter. The Item managed to get a word edgewise with the gentleman, and found him a very pleasant talker, and like a singed cat—not so hightoned as he looked. He was dressed neatly and plainly, looking much like the common man of the masculine species. His eyes were remarkably bright, his collar set well, his nose was clean, his coat fit like the proverbial "skin on a sausage," his hair flowed in waves to his shoulders, and his pantaloons fit tightly. After a short conversation in response to a question as to whether he would leave his autograph he replied, "certainly; with pleasure," and scrawled the name and date on a page of the reportorial note-book. He writes a very peculiar running hand, but it is beautiful and easily read; though from the way he spreads his letters and the width he leaves between his lines it is evident that if he says much in his love letters it renders his sweet heart round-shouldered to carry them in her bosom, for it takes quires of paper for the inscribing of his sentiments judging from the above. The few words he wrote, Oscar Wild [*sic*]; May 2, '82. Richmond, Ind."

1. On the front page of the following day's edition of the *Item* appeared an article claiming that the rumour that Wilde had been seen in Richmond was untrue. That article was followed by a clearly fabricated letter from Wilde: "I did not write [the autographs] but my valet, who did, is a good penman." Although Wilde joked in a letter to a friend in January 1882 that he had a secretary "to write my autograph and answer the hundreds of letters that come begging for it" (CL, 127), the idea that his African American valet would be mistaken for him is clearly intended to be humorous. However, the falsity of the follow-up article does not necessarily imply that the encounter described here did not occur. Wilde's route between Rock Island and Dayton meant that he certainly did travel via Richmond. The descriptions of Wilde's manner and of his handwriting (the generous spaces between lines, and his habit of appending the place and date to his autograph) are consistent with other reports. In any case, as Wilde makes no comment nor answers any questions, the article does not qualify as an interview.

Take up a whole page of a scratch book 3½x5½. Several other of our young people who were present secured his autograph also, all of which he gave willingly and pleasantly.

"Oscar at the Art Gallery," *Toronto Evening Telegram* (Toronto, ON), 25 May 1882, 4[1]

Visit of Mr. Oscar Wilde to the Gallery this Afternoon—What he thought of the Drawings—What he wore.

By invitation from the Society of Artists, Mr. Oscar Wilde this afternoon viewed the paintings now on exhibition at the rooms of the society, King-street west. He wore a pair of gray tweed trousers, somewhat shorter than usually worn. Just short enough to display the foot and ankle, mouse coloured velveteen coat and vest, a dark green tie, loosely fastened and handkerchief of the same colour. A flowing coat of black, trimmed with velvet, hung from his back, and was secured by a cord tied across the chest. Among those present were Capt. Geddes and a few members of the Lieut. Governor's family. His criticism of the drawings was keen, and the colour which attracted his attention the most was grey and its shades. The oil painting, No. 72, "Flitting Shadows," was gazed at by him very intently for some time. So much so, indeed, that he seated himself on a chair, and assumed an aesthetic attitude and looked with an intense longing at the dull grey sky. During his walk around the room he made use of the expression, "very clever," "very pleasing," and "beautiful." No. 29, "Ka-ka-be-kah Falls," is an oil painting, and in the background is a fall of water a great many feet high, with the waves rushing pell-mell over each other. The water in this picture he characterized as being "too happy."[2]

1. Quoted in OWDA, 352. Referenced in O'Brien, 102–3. The account of Wilde's visit as given in "Aestheticism's Apostle," *Toronto Evening News* (Toronto, ON), 25 May 1882, 4, pp. 408–9, suggests that Wilde was accompanied by one or more reporters. However, it is unclear whether the author of this article spoke with Wilde or merely overheard him talking to others or to himself.

2. This painting by Lucius Richard O'Brien (1832–1899) is now in the collection of the National Gallery of Canada. At 84 x 122 cm, it was probably among the more prominent pictures at the exhibition. It was listed for sale at $500.

"Oscar Wilde," *The Globe* (Toronto, ON), 26 May 1882, 6[1]

Lecture in the Grand Opera House Last Night.

The Leader of the Aesthetic Movement Discourses on "Art Decoration" to a Crowded House.

✂ *An account of Wilde's lecture in Toronto.*

THE AESTHETE AT THE ART EXHIBITION.

Mr. Oscar Wilde visited the exhibition of the Ontario Society of Artists yesterday afternoon, where he was shown around by Mr. T. M. Martin. The aesthete spent about an hour there, criticising the different works freely and with a quickness of perception which showed him to possess clear and well-defined ideas of true art. Portraits and object painting, containing nothing idealistic, he passed over as unworthy of notice. He especially admired Mr. Watson's works, finding in them considerable "soul" and "feeling," expressing the opinion that the artist was "an exceedingly clever fellow." Dull grey sky and rocks always attracted his attention. Upon glancing at a miniature painting of Mrs. Cornwallis West, he remarked that miniature painting was dead.[2] After enquiring as to the working of the Society, Mr. Wilde took his departure. He visited the University in the afternoon.

"Homicide at Vicksburg," *The Daily Picayune* (New Orleans, LA), 15 June 1882, 2[3]

Oscar Wilde Views a Coroner and Delivers an Aesthetic Lecture—He Leaves for New Orleans Today.

(SPECIAL TO THE PICAYUNE.)

---

1. H & S, b84. Reprinted in H & S, 155–6. The account of Wilde's visit as given in "Aestheticism's Apostle," *Toronto Evening News* (Toronto, ON), 25 May 1882, 4, pp. 408–9, suggests that Wilde was accompanied by one or more reporters. However, it is unclear whether the author of this article spoke with Wilde or merely overheard him talking to others or to himself.

2. Mary "Patsy" Cornwallis-West née FitzPatrick (1856–1920) was an Irish socialite, "professional beauty", and a mistress of the future King Edward VII. The miniature on ivory, which was not for sale, was painted by Ontario-born American artist Gerald Sinclair Hayward (1845–1926). Hayward trained at the Royal Academy between 1879 and 1883, and so was presumably not present to hear Wilde's remark.

3. Quoted in Mendelssohn, 198. It is unclear whether Wilde's comment, if genuine, was made directly to the reporter.

Vicksburg, June 14.—About half-past 11 o'clock this forenoon, Jessie McHaffee was shot in the head by John Ryan, and died of his wounds at 1 o'clock. The shooting occurred just beyond Glass Bayou, near the southern terminus of the National Cemetery road, and grew out of a dispute concerning a raft of timber in which the parties were jointly interested.

Ryan immediately surrendered himself to the authorities, but refuses to make any statement concerning the affair.

The jury of inquest found a verdict in accordance with the facts stated above.

While the coroner was holding the inquest Oscar Wilde passed by on his way to visit the National Cemetery, and remarked that this was the first instance of murder that had come under his observation in America.

A large audience greeted Oscar Wilde this evening, notwithstanding the hot weather. The sunflower was a prominent feature in the ladies' toilets. Everybody seemed delighted. The courtesies shown him are universal. A reception awaits Mr. Wilde tomorrow, after which he departs for New Orleans, where he lectures on Friday evening.

"Over the Breakfast Table," *The Times-Democrat* (New Orleans, LA), 26 June 1882, 2[1]

A Pleasant Chat on Art and Other Matters with Oscar Wilde.

Yesterday morning there was a little breakfast party at the Spanish Fort, beneath the cool shadows of its oaks, at which Mr. Oscar Wilde and a few other gentlemen were present. The occasion was *sans ceremonie* and most enjoyable throughout. The host, Col. Saiter, had prepared an ideal breakfast, for every dish was a study worthy of a much more pretentious *dejeuner*.

A delightful breeze was blowing from the east, and the sun was obscured by heavy rain clouds, making the temperature most pleasant.

During the discussion of the shrimp, fish and other toothsome dishes, the conversation drifted on art matters, of which Mr. Wilde is the new exponent. With a frankness which was charming, and a freedom from cant which was refreshing in one so well versed in the subject, Mr. Wilde gave his opinions quietly yet freely.

1. Reports a conversation, possibly overheard, rather than an interview. Reprinted as "Oscar at Breakfast," *The Daily American* (Nashville, TN), 28 June 1882, 3. Excerpted in "Oscar Wilde," *Columbus Enquirer-Sun* (Columbus, GA), 30 June 1882, 4 (which is H & S, b88).

Speaking of contemporaneous actors and actresses, he said that he thought there were only two that could be considered really great artists, and they were Sara Bernhardt and Salvini. No such a perfect artist [*sic*] as Sara had been seen on our stage for years. She was a wonderful woman in every way, and her personations were sometimes terrible in their truth to nature. She had studied nature itself, and followed it in every scene and act. Our age has not produced her equal, nor will it, for such great characters do not appear but at long intervals.

Referring to Salvini, Mr. Wilde said that he was the prince of actors. His remarkable appreciation of the true interest and meaning of the author, his delineation of this appreciation by perfect gesticulation and elocution will not be equaled for some time to come.

"Rossi?" said he in answer to a query, "Rossi is a nice gentleman and a good, good fellow, but then he don't compare with Salvini. He is a personal friend of mine, but as an actor he does not rank near Salvini. He, perhaps, is to be compared with your Booth nearer than with any other actor here, an excellent reader, graceful in action, but far short of Salvini."

As the peaches were brought on the table the subject turned on humor, when Mr. Wilde remarked that the English have now no caricaturists. They seem to have passed away. Maurier, of the London *Punch*, is a good draughtsman, but he lacks humor. So does Nast. He went on to tell the story of Herbert Spencer, whom he said was a very reserved man. Spencer had just completed his work on the human emotions, and had omitted humor.[1] He went to a well known author and asked him if there was such a thing as humor. His friend took down book after book from Joe Miller to the latest collection of jokes and read to the great sociologist.[2] His face grew larger and larger, and not a smile wreathed his set features. The friend gave up the effort, and even now the word humor is not to be found in Spencer's work.

Mr. Wilde admired Gavarni and Cham, of the French, as both possessed humor in the highest degree, particularly the former.[3] With a touch of his pencil, he could give a ludicrous effect to the mere art of putting one's handkerchief in the pocket.

1. Wilde is presumably referring to Spencer's series *Descriptive Sociology*, which the author began in 1873 and interrupted in 1881 due to a lack of public support. The work was completed by later editors in 1934.
2. Joseph Miller (1684–1738) was an English actor. After his death a book of jokes attributed to him was published by the English writer John Mottley (1692–1750): *Joe Miller's Jests, or the Wit's Vade-Mecum* (1739).
3. Paul Gavarni (1804–1866) was a French artist who produced satirical cartoons and illustrations for fashion magazines. In the source his name is spelt "Gavarini". Cham was the pseudonym of Charles Amédée de Noé (1818–1879), a French cartoonist. Both Gavarni and Noé published cartoons in *Le Charivari* for many years.

As the pleasant talk went on Mr. Wilde gave several interesting anecdotes of the great Thespian artists he had known, and then the subject drifted on to the esthetic and to the floral emblems of the newer school of art.

He said the sunflower had always been regarded with favor by the artistic, for the reason that its design was so suggestive. A circular disk emblematic of the sun with its surrounding rays presented a wonderful field of study to the artist. Its shape was so perfect that it naturally attracted the artist's eye.

The lily was the flower of station art. At that centre of the artistic Florence one enters its environs beneath gates adorned with carven lilies.[1] In fact, lilies were held to have had immaculate powers according to art traditions.

The lily has, on account of its color, erroneously been called the emblem of purity, but in art it is not so considered. It is not as the representative of purity, but from other traditions, that it had been for centuries adored by artists.

Of course it is impossible to give the ornate language, soft expression of the poet in speaking of these subjects. His voice in conversation is gentle, attractive and most interesting, and holds one a listener per force.

The breakfast was one not soon to be forgotten by those present.

"The State Camp," *The New York Herald* (New York, NY), 31 July 1882, 3[2]

POOR GUARD MOUNTING BUT AN EXCELLENT DRESS PARADE—THE TWENTY-SECOND REGIMENT AT WORSHIP—A LARGE CROWD AT THE SACRED CON-CERT.

(BY TELEGRAPH TO THE HERALD.)

STATE CAMP, PEEKSKILL, N. Y., July 30. 1882.

✂ *Accounts of the military parade and religious services.*

THE DRESS PARADE.

Dress parade this evening was a really magnificent effort on the part of the regiment. The men wore their white full dress uniforms and the companies came

---

1. This may be a reference to the gates of the Florence Baptistery, the frames of which are adorned with carvings of various plants, including lilies (Bioch, A. R. (2009). Baptism and the frame of the south door of the Baptistery, Florence. *Sculpture Journal, 18,* 24).

2. Wilde's comment given in this article may well be genuine, but is also of a type that might be fabricated by a reporter. Wilde was in Peekskill visiting Henry Ward Beecher.

on the line solidly and with precision. The ceremony was practically faultless from beginning to end and was witnessed by fully five thousand people, including Oscar Wilde, who expressed himself as being much pleased with the pale yellow effect of the setting sun on the utterly white coats. Oscar was in his usual uniform, and wore besides a particularly sweet smile, beside which the beam of Surrogate Rollins, who sat with him in the carriage, paled to insignificance.

✂ *Several paragraphs that are unrelated to Wilde.*

"The Saratoga Season," *The Times* (Philadelphia, PA), 13 Aug. 1882, 6[1]

People Who Have an Idea That it is Not Fashionable to Dance.

PHILADELPHIA GIRLS' TRUNKS

Amusements at the Springs—Some of the Guests—Personal Paragraphs.

Special Correspondence of THE TIMES

SARATOGA, August 10.

✂ *Several paragraphs that are unrelated to Wilde.*

Oscar Wilde arrived yesterday morning and in the five minutes walk from the depot along the piazzas of the United States Hotel to the Broadway front of that house he formed and expressed his opinion of Saratoga, which, being favorable, of course, assures the success of the remainder of the season here. I believe there has been a good sale of tickets to a first-class audience for his lecture this evening, and the fireworks in the park will not draw off many from his pyrotechnic oratory. A breakfast at Mount McGregor was given in his honor this morning. It was announced in advance that daisies and pond lilies would be in order and sunflowers eschewed. By a singular coincidence the gorgeous sunflowers which appear in Congress Park every summer did not begin blooming with their usual luxuriance this year until within the last three days, as if they had waited to greet the poet.

✂ *Several paragraphs that are unrelated to Wilde.*

1. It is unclear whether Wilde spoke directly to the reporter. If he had done so, it seems likely that his comments would have been quoted.

"The Jersey Lily," *The Boston Herald* (Boston, MA), 24 Oct. 1882, 4[1]

Arrival of Mrs. Langtry at New York.

Incidents of the Famous Beauty's Reception.

Her Hopes and Aims in Her New Field.

(SPECIAL DISPATCH TO THE HERALD.)

NEW YORK, Oct. 23, 1882. Mrs. Langtry, who comes to America under engagement with Mr. Henry E. Abbey, arrived on the steamship Arizona this morning, shortly after 8 o'clock. The news that the vessel had been sighted was received in this city last evening. By invitation of Mr. Abbey, representatives of the press and a number of other gentlemen went down the bay in the Laura M. Starin, which left the foot of West Twenty-second street before daylight. Among the invited guests, who came aboard about 5 o'clock, were Mr. Oscar Wilde and Dr. Charles Phelps. Mr. Wilde's toilet was a nocturne in a tender, dark green, as to his top coat, which had a heavy and altogether comfortable fur collar, with cuffs of the same material. Furthermore, he wore a dark brown hat, very nearly of the shape, and quite of the shade, of the sort of pot in which beans are baked in Boston.[2] His trousers were of a dark brown, and baggy at the knees, falling over well polished shoes of the conventional toothpick pattern. His coat was of black velvet, and his neck scarf an etherealized brick red or logwood claret, with a ring of malachite. His gloves were undressed kids of the shade of ruby, mellowed by several centuries of absence from the sunlight. Mr. Wilde and the brass band and a hot lunch were the only incidents connected with the trip down the bay. It should be mentioned that the English flag was displayed in honor of the lady friend of His Royal Highness the Prince of Wales. That the English flag was displayed, instead of the Turkish or Russian flag, is noteworthy for the reason that the steamer which went to meet the Bernhardt inadvertently astonished that lady by flaunting the German flag in her face.[3] It was 6:05 o'clock when the Laura M. Starin drew up alongside the Arizona, which was lying off the boarding station at quarantine. The band played "My Country, 'tis of thee," followed by "Rule Britannia," and then a quickstep, to the great delight of a crowd of immigrants and a

---

1. Excerpted in *The Buffalo Commercial* (Buffalo, NY), 26 Oct. 1882. As Wilde appears to have been overheard speaking to Langtry, Labouchère, and Abbey, this article does not qualify as an interview. Also present were the authors of "Mrs. Langtry Arrives," *The News and Courier* (Charleston, SC), 26 Oct. 1882, 1, pp. 478–83; "The Lily of Jersey Here," *The Times* (Philadelphia, PA), 24 Oct. 1882, 1, pp. 484–7.

2. The fur hat Wilde wore for Sarony's plate 3.

3. Sarah Bernhardt was French. Presumably the spelling of her name confused her American hosts (she was born with the name Bernard, adopting Bernhardt for the stage).

few first cabin passengers who were gathered on the deck. It was 6:30 before the health officer put in an appearance on the Gov. Fenton. Fifteen minutes later Mrs. Labouchère, the wife of the editor of London Truth, who was once an actress herself, and who accompanies

MRS. LANGTRY,

came on the upper deck and exchanged greetings with Mr. Abbey and Mr. Wilde in a voice several degrees removed from a stage whisper. Directly after Mrs. Langtry herself caught her first view of American shores and that peculiarly American institution, the interviewer. She smiled at Mr. Abbey, and, as she smiled, the band again played "Rule, Britannia." While the band was playing, and Mrs. Langtry was pulling on her brown Bernhardt gloves, one had time to notice what she wore. Her toilet was simple—a close fitting jacket and walking dress of dark blue, with trimming of narrow gold braid at the breast and on the sleeves; a hat of English straw, with a very narrow brim, trimmed with a ribbon of dark crimson and blue stripes. Mrs. Langtry is unmistakeably beautiful. Hers is a type of beauty that grows upon one. The lady appeared to be about 5 feet 3 inches in height, with a supple, willowy figure, which seemed to add a half-foot to her stature. Her features are extremely regular, and the outline of her nose is pure Grecian. Her lips are red and rich, forehead low but broad, and her hair is brown, with a golden tinge. Capt. Brooks invited Mr. Abbey, Mr. Tillotson, Mr. Wilde and party to come

ABOARD THE ARIZONA,

and the invitation was promptly accepted. Mrs. Langtry and Mrs. Labouchère appeared delighted to meet Mr. Abbey, and Mr. Wilde came in for no small share of attention. The band followed Mr. Abbey aboard the Arizona, and played national airs in the most pronounced sort of a way. The Graphic's representative was first presented to Mrs. Labouchère, who is a comely and altogether entertaining lady.

"I was seasick for a day or two—awfully sick—but Mrs. Langtry wasn't ill for a moment. She is a famous sailor. That comes from her yachting so much. I wouldn't have been surprised to see her climb the ladder and take a hand at furling the sails."

After expressing her delight that the voyage was over, she asked if the autumn scenery is really as gorgeous as has been represented. Just as the Graphic's representative was attempting to explain that the forest colors are hardly as brilliant this season as usual, Mr. Oscar Wilde clasped his hands, rolled up his eyes, and, with genuine aesthetic fervor, remarked:

"There's one thing in this country that will bother you awfully."

"What is that?" asked Mrs. Labouchère.

722

"Why they say 'deepo' here instead of station."

"They say what?" she asked in bewilderment.

"Deepo," repeated Mr. Wilde.

"Depot," interposed Mr. Abbey, giving the correct French pronunciation.

"Oh!" she said, in evident relief.

"Yes, but it's awfully depressing, do you know," persisted Mr. Wilde. "It took me a month to get over it, and it will take you at least a fortnight."

Meanwhile the band kept heroically at its work.

"I do wish they would play 'Yankee Doodle;' I like it so much," said Mrs. Langtry, and directly after "Yankee Doodle" was played, while she beat time with a very dainty foot. Mrs. Langtry expressed her gratification at being at last in America, of which she had heard so much, and concerning which she had the

MOST AGREEABLE ANTICIPATIONS.

"I only play in parts that I like," she said, in response to a question; "but I haven't yet got over my stage fright. I suffer from it every time I come out. It is awful. The public has no idea what frightful things we have to undergo to please it."

"It will be different here in many respects, so far as your performances are concerned," was suggested. "In England, for a time, of course, your appearance on the stage was looked on as something of an experiment. Here you come with an established reputation, and the public will expect much of you."

"And I shall certainly do my best not to disappoint it. I know I was considered something of an interloper by the profession at home, and it was only by sheer good luck that I won at once what others have to work for so long. But the professionals were very, very kind to me—all of them."

"I suppose that, since you have gone on the stage, you consider yourself out of society, do you not?" some one very rudely asked.

A slightly added tinge of color showed in her fair cheeks as she replied, without any tinge of offence:

"Since I have gone on the stage I try to devote myself wholly and faithfully to my work."

"With whom have you studied?"

"With Mrs. Labouchère only. She has been my sole teacher."

Something was said of the prospective fortune which awaits her in this country.

"I don't see why one should care so much for money when one hasn't time to spend it," she said; "still, I believe if one makes one fortune there is always the desire to go ahead and make two fortunes. During my first week here I intend to amuse myself by visiting your theatres. Is Mary Anderson playing here now? I want to see her."[1]

Mrs. Langtry was told that Mary Anderson is not playing here at present, and, in response to questions, was informed of the present programmes at the leading theatres. She was particularly entertained, apparently, by a description of the peculiarities of the double stage which is operated like a "lift" at the Madison Square Theatre.[2] In speaking further of her trip over, Mrs. Langtry said that two dramatic entertainments were given, one for the seamen's hospital in Liverpool, and the other for St. John's Guild in New York; and she expressed her delight that the receipts of the performance for the benefit of St. John's Guild were larger by several pounds than for the English institution. Mrs. Langtry

QUITE CHARMED ALL THE GENTLEMEN

who met her by the simplicity and easy grace of her manner. Her voice is remarkably agreeable, and she talks even more eloquently with her eyes than with her lips. The manner in which she submitted to the horde of interviewers who thronged around her, and her gracious responses to the most impertinent questions, showed her to be as heroic as she is clever. On reaching the dock she was driven to the Albemarle Hotel, where she and Mrs. Labouchère have the same suite of rooms as was occupied by Mme. Bernhardt. These rooms, which are on the first floor and look out on Madison square, have been newly furnished and tastefully decorated.[3]

Mrs. Langtry will make her first appearance as Hester Grazebrook, in "The Unequal Match," at the Park Theatre, on next Monday evening, Oct. 30. Her rehearsals with her company, which arrived on the Egypt yesterday, will begin at once.

Mrs. Langtry, when asked what her impression was of New York, said: "I am delighted with its appearance. It resembles Paris so much that I am sure I shall like it, for I love Paris. I am sure I shall like America and its people. They are so much more courteous than the English. The Americans I have met seem to me to resemble the French in regard to politeness, and that is why I like them, I presume, for you know I am French. We all speak French in Jersey, and I can talk easily in the Jersey patois, but at home we generally spoke English, because my mother was a Scotch woman."

1. Mary Anderson was touring *The Lady of Lyons* in the Midwest. Another interviewer recorded that Langtry also asked after Clara Morris ("I am very anxious to see her"), but she was not playing in New York either ("The Great English Beauty," *New York Tribune* (New York, NY), 24 Oct. 1882, 2).
2. Double stage: see p. 489, note 1.
3. First floor above ground level; what in America today would be referred to as the second floor.

724

As to how she expected to be received by an American audience Mrs. Langtry said: "I am very, very nervous; but I shall do the best I can. I shall make my début in 'The Unequal Match,' and shall afterward appear for the first time in 'The Honeymoon.' I never have played in it. My other rôles will be Rosalind in 'As You Like It,' and Miss Hardcastle in 'She Stoops to Conquer.'"

"Which is your favorite rôle?" was asked.

"Rosalind, I think," was the reply, "although I feel unworthy of it. My engagements last six months. I play in many of the large cities of the States. My present engagement in New York will continue for five weeks."

In the evening Mrs Langtry drove with Mrs. Labouchère and Mr. Abbey to the Park Theatre, where John T. Raymond is playing Col. Sellers. There was a crowd waiting at the entrance to see Mrs. Langtry. She eluded it by going in at the stage door. Her party occupied the left hand proscenium box, which resulted in a remarkable arrangement of the crowd of gentlemen professionally known as "standees." Usually these theatregoers stand behind the last row of chairs near the centre aisle, but tonight every man who was standing got over as far as possible to the right hand side of the theatre, so as to get a glimpse of Mrs. Langtry. It gave the house a remarkably lob-sided [*sic*] appearance, and was quite useless, for Mrs. Langtry sat so far back in her box as to be quite out of sight. Crowds remained about the entrance after the theatre had closed, but the actress was taken away through the stage door and driven rapidly back to her hotel.

"New York," *Boston Evening Transcript* (Boston, MA), 18 Nov. 1882, 10–11[1]

(Correspondence of the Transcript.)

New York, Nov. 17.

✂ *Several paragraphs that are unrelated to Wilde.*

Little has been said in print about the Wyndham breakfast, which was, in its way, the most enjoyable social event of last week. As last week's news is not good news in a daily journal, the fact that the breakfast was given by Mr. A. M. Palmer and eaten by seventy or more industrious men need not be insisted upon. The table was laid in the large dining room of the Hotel Dam; and it is hard to say whether the dining-room or the crowd seated at Mr. Palmer's hospitable board was more interesting to the observer. The rich and beautiful decoration of the

---

1. Reprinted as "The Wyndham Breakfast," *Buffalo Commercial Advertiser* (Buffalo, NY), 20 Nov. 1882, 4. It is unclear whether the reporter overheard or took part in the conversation.

apartment, with its fine tone of color and bronze adornments, and with its superb fireplace, delighted the eye. As to the crowd—I had never seen such a gathering at any previous breakfast or dinner. Journalists of the highest standing and journalists of unfortunately low standing elbowed each other. All types of the theatrical manager helped to devour an exquisite and highly indigestible repast. Men of fashion and men who have no reputation to lose sat side by side. Half of the crowd did not speak to the other half. Each guest could see, not a dagger, but an enemy before him. Imagine a table with Mr. George Jones, Mr. Oakey Hall and Mr. Whitelaw Reid seated at it.[1] Yet the occasion was a particularly happy one; for each person appeared to be in jovial humor, and Mr. Palmer smiled benignantly upon his complex family. On the whole, this was an exceptionally bright company; and not less interesting because it contained a queer variety of elements. If I were a reporter of other men's good or curious sayings, I might make a list of striking things said on Thursday afternoon. But one may be forgiven for quoting Mr. Oscar Wilde, who, in the course of conversation upon art, declared that "color is the keynote of nationality," that "a nation's dress makes its character," that "France is the only country where one does not find common people," that "Whitman is the great American poet," and that "Edgar Fawcett's poems are exquisitely perfect." Mr. Wilde is an entertaining and fluent conversationalist, and he utters wisdom or nonsense with an almost Jovian dignity and complacency. His manners—barring the complacent air which he assumes, and which is irritating—are gentle, courteous and unaggressive.

✂ *Several paragraphs that are unrelated to Wilde.*

"New York City Life," *The Brooklyn Daily Eagle* (Brooklyn, NY), 26 Nov. 1882, 1[2]

MARIE PRESCOTT AND OSCAR WILDE have put their stock of publicity together, and will try to sell it, with resultant fame and fortune. She will play the heroine in his drama of Nihilism. The contract has been signed by him in New York and was to have received her signature yesterday in Boston. The title of the piece is "Vera," and it is crowded with Nihilistic horrors.

---

1. George Jones (1810–1879) was an English-American actor and lawyer who was famously litigious in later life. A. Oakey Hall (1826–1898) was an American politician and writer. Whitelaw Reid (1837–1912) was an American politician and the editor of the *New York Tribune*.

2. This article may be based on interviews, but it seems more likely that Prescott provided written quotes to the press.

"It is the greatest, grandest play ever written," said Marie, after reading it, "and to create such a character as he has written for the heroine is the opportunity of a lifetime. I am proud to be selected as worthy to make the effort."

"I have seen no actress," said Oscar, after hearing her as Emilia, "denounce the faithless Iago with so exactly the right combination of passionate intensity and womanly fierceness that the heroine of 'Vera' demands."

Their mutual admiration seems sufficient for a society with a membership of two, with the public excluded. However, I have Steele Mackaye's judgment for it that Oscar's play is no laughing matter, and that, as likely as not, Miss Prescott will be as successful in it as she was in her suit against the American News Company.[1]

"It comes about in the play," says Mackaye, "that Vera's lover Alexis is crowned Czar of Russia. He has been a Nihilist, like herself; and for taking the throne his former companions in conspiracy doom him to death. The assassination falls by lot upon Vera, and she accepts the awful commission. The others send her into the Czar's bedchamber, armed with a dagger, which she is to throw to them from a window, stained with his blood, or else they will, after waiting five minutes, conclude that she has been foiled, and dash in to rescue her. Alexis awakes, protests his love for her and loyalty for the cause, and thus develops a situation for her exceeding in horror anything ever seen on the stage—if it can be acted as strongly as it is written. She hears the conspirators murmuring outside, and knows that they are about to break in. She cannot stab her ardent lover, and she cannot face them with a broken oath. But she throws to them a bloodied dagger, for she reddens it by a thrust into her own heart."

"Farewell to Oscar Wilde," *New York Tribune* (New York, NY), 28 Dec. 1882, 4[2]

Oscar Wilde took a sorrowful leave of America yesterday and set sail for England. He confessed before his departure that his mission to our barbaric shores had been substantially a failure. He came here to reform our taste and dress, but we had paid little heed to his admonitions. He has gone back with his knee-breeches, his long lank hair and his sunflower, leaving us to our fate. It can-

1. In October 1882 Prescott had won a case against the American News Company for publishing allegations that she was promiscuous. She was awarded damages of $12,500, although in January 1884 the judgement was overturned. See Dearinger, 79–103, 152–3.

2. Reprinted as "A Touching Farewell to Oscar Wilde," *The Chicago Daily Tribune* (Chicago, IL), 30 Dec. 1882, 9. Quoted in OWDA, 442; Hyde, 81; and Sturgis, 268/256. Wilde is quoted, but it seems unlikely that this article is based on an interview.

not be truthfully said that we shall miss him. The public never took any interest in him save as a curiosity, and that was satisfied long ago. For a time he was a mild source of amusement to a people who are continually on the watch for somebody or something to get some fun out of, but all the fun there was in him was speedily exhausted. It is amusing for a moment to see a man make himself ridiculous, even when he goes about it with deliberation and design, but the spectacle soon becomes wearisome. There was not variety enough about Mr. Wilde's exhibitions of himself to make the public interest in them at all enduring. One view of those breeches and that hair was enough to satisfy the curiosity of most people, and if by any chance a spectator cared for a further and more pro-longed acquaintance, the droning monologue on art, now universally known as "Ruskin and water," completely satisfied him. Our sources of information may be defective, but we have never chanced to hear of anybody who went to hear or see Mr. Wilde a second time.

This lack of staying quality in the public interest in him saddened Mr. Wilde, and he shook off the dust from his feet against us in sorrow if not in anger when he went away. He complained that the propensity of the American newspaper man to see something funny in everything caused him no little annoyance. His last hours among us were embittered by a cruel report that he, like a mere coun-tryman, had fallen victim to the "banco steerer" and had paid $3,000 for the ex-perience. Was this the final outcome of his labors for our aesthetic elevation? Did he, in return for assurance of handsome pecuniary remuneration, consent to come among us and instruct us in the "perceptibly intense and consummately utter," only to have it intimated that in personal garb and appearance he resem-bled the unsophisticated countryman? "Really," he remarked with a sigh, "you Americans are the most ingenious people in the world. Your newspaper report-ers invent the most remarkable stories about me." And with this tribute to our greatness he sailed away. We shall probably never see him again. At any rate let us hope for the best.

If we benefitted little by his visit, he has not stayed with us without gaining much valuable information for the enlargement of his mind. He knows a good deal more about the world than he did when he arrived here. He may return home and write a book about us and fill it with unamiable observations upon our manners and customs. He may call us crude, ignorant and young. But he cannot disguise the fact even from himself that we were neither young enough nor igno-rant enough to take him seriously. The oldest people in the world could not have estimated him more justly that the Americans have. He may speak slightingly of the Atlantic Ocean, may sniff at Niagara Falls, may speak contemptuously of America's fondness for cast-iron stoves, and may say that our architecture is "too utterly dreary," but when he has done all this he must admit that with all our defects we know a charlatan when we see one as quickly as any other nation in the world. We suspect it was this conviction which made him so sad when he left us.

"Keswick," *Cumberland and Westmorland Advertiser* (Penrith, UK), 26 Feb. 1884[1]

✂ *Several paragraphs that are unrelated to Wilde.*

MR. OSCAR WILDE'S OPINION OF DERWENTWATER.

—Mr. Oscar Wilde visited Keswick on Thursday, and was met at the station by Mr. H. I. Jenkinson and Mr. R. S. Cahill.[2] After paying a visit to Mr. Cahill's studio, where he seemed most interested in his water colour studies of Irish coast scenery, he proceeded to Friars' Crag and enjoyed the grey mystery of the scene before him. "This," said he, "is lovely. And that's Southey's Lodore.[3] The effect of the atmosphere is just right for seeing a picture of this sort. The lake is just large enough for beauty. In America the lakes are like seas, where you lose sight of land, and there are cruel storms which wreck vessels." He thought open footpaths should exist through all beautiful places everywhere, and that it was a mistake to think that the public were ruthless destroyers of property when admitted to private grounds. He inquired very closely into the subject of a railway being injurious to the effect of beautiful scenery, and said, without giving a direct opinion on the matter, "It must be a pleasant thing to look out of a first-class saloon carriage and see the beauties as you pass," and thought they would be better enjoyed when perfectly at one's ease.

1. Excerpted in Dibb, 95–6. Quoted in Sturgis, 304 (omitted from the American edition). It seems likely that a reporter accompanied Wilde on his visit, but it is possible that Wilde's hosts quoted him to the reporter afterwards.

2. Henry Irwin Jenkinson (1838–1891) was the author of *Jenkinson's Practical Guide to the English Lakes* (1872), taught at the Keswick Mechanics Institute, and served as secretary of the local Preservation of Footpaths Association. Richard Staunton Cahill (1827–1904) was an Irish artist who moved to Keswick in the early 1880s and who advocated against the construction of railways and roads through the Lake District.

3. Lodore Falls is a waterfall near Derwentwater, and was a popular visitor attraction during the Victorian era. English poet Robert Southey's *The Cataract of Lodore* (1820) describes the falls.

"Mr. Oscar Wilde," *The Standard* (London, UK), 30 June 1892, 5[1]

(FROM OUR CORRESPONDENT.)

PARIS, WEDNESDAY NIGHT.

The prohibition of his play, *Salome*, by the Lord Chamberlain, has cut Mr. Oscar Wilde to the heart, as he has informed a correspondent of the *Gaulois* that he is about to part with an ungrateful country, and have himself naturalised as a Frenchman. His statement to the representative of that journal is characteristic. He said:—

"Yes, my resolution is deliberately taken; since it is impossible to have a work of art performed in England I shall transfer myself to another fatherland, of which I have long ago been enamoured. There is but one Paris, *voyez-vous*, and Paris is France. It is the abode of artists; nay, it is *la ville artiste*. I adore Paris. I also adore your beautiful language. To me there are only two languages in the world, French and Greek. Here (in London) people are essentially anti-artistic and narrow-minded. Now the ostracism of *Salome* will give you a fair notion of what people here consider venal and indecorous. To put on the stage any person or persons connected with the Bible is impossible. On these grounds the censorship has prohibited Saint Saen's *Samson and Delilah* and Massenet's *Herodias*. Racine's superb tragedy of *Athalie* cannot be performed on an English stage. Really one hardly knows whether the measure is the more hateful or ridiculous."

Here the interviewer interposed, "Surely you have not such a bad opinion of your countrymen?" Mr. Oscar Wilde replied:—

"Of course, I do not deny that they possess certain practical qualities, but, as I am an artist, those qualities are not those which I can admire. Moreover, I am not at the present an Englishman. I am an Irishman, which is by no means the same thing. No doubt, I have English friends, to whom I am deeply attached, but as to the English I do not love them. There is a great deal of hypocrisy in England, which you, in France, very justly find fault with. The typical Briton is Tartuffe, seated in his shop behind the counter. There are numerous exceptions, but they only prove the rule."

Mr. Oscar Wilde intimated that he would bring out *Salome* in Paris with Madame Sarah Bernhardt. It would appear from the outline of this drama given by the *Gaulois* that St. John the Baptist is introduced, and that, owing to his rejecting Salome's love, she orders him to be beheaded. A wax effigy of the Saint's head is brought in on a salver, when "*Ivre de fureur et d'amour, elle prend cette tête,*

1. A translated reprint of Maurice Sisley, "La Salomé de M. Oscar Wilde," *Le Gaulois* (Paris, France), 29 June 1892, 1, pp. 607–12. Excerpted in Mason, 374; and Hyde, 141. Quoted in Pearson, 228–9; and Sturgis, 455/423.

qu'elle couvre de baisers."[1] If this be accurate, can Mr. Wilde be really surprised at the Lord Chamberlain's veto? I shall be more than astonished if it be allowed in Paris.

As to Mr. Oscar Wilde's naturalisation, it shows great fortitude on his part, as, on becoming a French citizen, he will have to serve in the ranks of the French Army, and his aestheticism will have to come into contact with the unpleasant realities of barrack life.

Arthur Howard Pickering, "Unknown Wives of Well-Known Men," *The Ladies' Home Journal* (Philadelphia, PA), Oct. 1892, 11[2]

XXII—THE WIFE OF OSCAR WILDE

The first meeting of Oscar Wilde with the beautiful Miss Lloyd, who afterward became his wife, had in it something of the dramatic. One afternoon while out calling with his mother, Lady Wilde, he was presented to a lovely young girl with whom he talked for some time and in whom he became very much interested, so much so that when leaving the house he turned to his mother and said:

"By the by, mamma, I think of marrying that girl."[3]

Lady Wilde laughed, for she was accustomed to her son's eccentricities and sudden fancies. This fancy, however, was buried deeper than any that had gone before. Oscar Wilde went to America; he lectured, posed, talked and wrote until his name was as familiar in the chief cities of the United States as in England. He returned home, he settled down to steady literary work, and—much to the amazement of Lady Wilde, as well as of his friends—he married "that girl."

Constance Lloyd was the daughter of Horatio Lloyd, Queen's Counsel, an English gentleman who had gained a great reputation as a lawyer for a very erudite opinion on certain railway bonds which were ever afterward known as "Lloyd's bonds." Constance was a beautiful girl, with masses of thick wavy chestnut hair, large blue eyes, beautifully pencilled eyebrows, a broad forehead and a figure full of grace. In their early married days, when Mr. Wilde was still practicing his gospel of the beautiful, and was himself the head and front of the aesthetic movement in England, his young wife was a willing and loving disciple, and wore

1. "Drunk with fury and love, she takes that head, which she covers with kisses."

2. Arthur Howard Pickering (1852–1904) was an elocutionist who gave popular readings from Greek and English dramas and poetry in his home town of Boston. "He is a model of fashionable dressing and strictly correct carriage and sartorially he may vie with Beau Brummel himself." ("Under the Rose," *The Boston Sunday Globe* (Boston, MA), 18 Oct. 1891, 12.)

3. According to Constance's brother, Constance and Oscar met at a tea party in London in the early summer of 1881 (Moyle, 45).

the aesthetic gowns and artistic colors approved of and designed by her husband. Walter Pater has written nobly on the subject of beauty; but Mr. and Mrs. Wilde were willing in their own persons to preach their sermon.

The first appearance of Mrs. Wilde in society was a marked success; her youth, her beauty, her freedom from affectation, her lovely aesthetic gowns, were the talk of the town. Few persons knew how bashful this lovely young girl really was, what an effort she had to make before she entered a drawing-room. Mrs. Wilde often says now that her first season, after her marriage, was torture to her; the constant meeting of new people, the knowledge that she must do her best to make a pleasing impression, hung like a pall over her whenever she left her pretty home. In her own house, on her reception days, it was even worse; and yet she always appeared perfect mistress of herself and of the occasion, and the very bashfulness from which she suffered lent a new and, as it were, a far-off charm to this pretty woman. In her own person she furnished an excuse and at the same a text for her husband's essays on beauty. No one, who saw her in those early days, in her clinging draperies of dull gray or blue, or in her graceful white Grecian gowns, can ever forget the beautiful pictures she presented.

Ultra-aestheticism in dress having gone out of fashion, and having accomplished its work, Mrs. Wilde today is only aesthetic enough to tinge the fashions of the season with her own personality. Her gowns are perfect examples of good taste in fold, harmony and color. She is still so aesthetic as to care for the beautiful; but she bends the fashions of the day to her own sweet will instead of clinging to the mediaeval forms re-introduced, some years ago, by her husband. Indeed, in no manner is Mrs. Wilde conspicuous today, excepting for her beauty and good taste, any more than is her husband, who has returned to the somewhat conventional costume of the latter portion of the nineteenth century, and only occasionally helps to make a new color or a flower "the rage."

To see Mrs. Wilde at her best, one should visit her at her pretty house in Tite Street, Chelsea. On one side of the hall is Mr. Wilde's "den," where books, periodicals, manuscripts and flowers are to be found on all sides. The dining-room is at the back, and is a study in ivory white; walls, ceiling, furniture and china all harmonize. Above stairs is the drawing-room, with its many beautiful panels of stamped Japanese leather, its few perfect specimens of bric-à-brac, its low, comfortable lounges, its graceful chairs, its pretty tea table with its delicate porcelain and old silver, its artistic etchings, and its full-length portrait of Oscar Wilde in an old-fashioned costume.[1] Here on Wednesday afternoons during the season, Mrs. Wilde can be found, with her two pretty boys clinging to her gown, dispensing "tea" to her guests and receiving them with gracious hospitality, while her husband assists with his ever-ready fund of witty talk.

1. Harper Pennington's portrait of Wilde in Regency dress.

There are two children, both boys, Cyril and Vivian. Oscar Wilde laughingly says that he has put them at a disadvantage with this modern age by giving them such romantic names; the names of Cyril and Vivian do seem out of place in the money-making, materialistic world of London; but yet it is hardly to be expected that the Wilde boys will ever become business men. With such a father and such a sweet, poetic and lovely mother, it almost goes without saying that the boys must develop into artists of some sort or other. They are attractive boys, with great masses of thick, wavy brown hair, thoughtful blue eyes, and the sturdy strength and rounded limbs of young Greeks.

Although Mrs. Wilde has always taken such a lively interest in her husband's pursuits, and has cared for all that is truly beautiful, she has by no means neglected the more homely duties of domestic life. She overlooks her household in almost an American fashion, and herself cares for the pleasures and necessities of her children.

Americans, especially those who have become famous in literature or art, are always sure of a hearty welcome from the Wildes. Mrs. Wilde has never yet crossed the Atlantic, but hopes to do so some day.[1] Her boy Cyril is an adventurous spirit whose ambition is to be a sailor and to sail to America, where he has promised to visit all his dear American friends and have some "tea and cake" with them. Edgar Fawcett, Edgar Saltus, Clyde Fitch and Jonathan Sturges are all friends of Mrs. Wilde, and are sure to find their way to her pretty home whenever they pass through London.[2] Any American who wishes to see London society and does not meet and visit Mrs. Wilde has lost one of the most delightful opportunities offered by that great metropolis, for her home proves that it is not alone unlimited wealth and gorgeous entertainments that attract interesting men and women. There is perhaps no house in London where more brilliant and delightful people congregate during the season, and where the talk is sure to be so effervescent, as in the little salon presided over by Mrs. Oscar Wilde. Poets, artists, sculptors, members of Parliament, scientific men, actors and actresses, ladies of high title, men of lofty position, and the gilded youth of the day, gather together around Mrs. Wilde's tea-table, attracted quite as much by the charm of the hostess as by the inimitable wit of her husband.

1. Constance never left Europe.

2. Wilde had met American author Edgar Saltus (1855–1921) in New York in 1882. Saltus inscribed Constance's autograph book in London, November 1889. He published a reminiscence of Wilde, *Oscar Wilde: An Idler's Impression*, in 1917. Clyde Fitch (1865–1909) was an American writer who appears to have had a brief affair with Wilde in the summer of 1889 (Sturgis, 383/354). He later became a prolific and successful dramatist. Jonathan Sturges (1864–1911) was an American writer. He and Wilde first met in the summer of 1890 (Sturgis, 404/374).

"'Five o'Clock' Played at Dinard," *The New York Herald, European Edition* (Paris, France), 8 Sep. 1893, 3[1]

Mme. Thénard, of the Comédie Française, Assists Miss Lowther in Producing It.

SUCCEEDED BY A LIGHT SUPPER.

Mr. Oscar Wilde Has Many Yachting and Dinner Parties Given in His Honor.

(FROM OUR SPECIAL CORRESPONDENT.)

DINARD, Sept. 6.

✄ *Several paragraphs about activities in Dinard, including parties attended by Wilde and the staging of the one-act comedy* Five o'Clock, *with Aimée Lowther in the lead role.*

IN AN OLD ROSE COSTUME.

When the curtain arose for "Five o'Clock," showing Miss Lowther seated at a table in an old rose costume of Parisian make, with a cherry-colored sash, the applause was spontaneous, and continued until the young lady was forced to smile. However, as Mr. Oscar Wilde remarked, "her self-possession was wonderful and her self-restraint most artistic, for Miss Lowther is a born actress. Everyone expected that she would be erratic and give free play to all sorts of mannerisms, while, on the contrary, she has truly been perfection."

✄ *Several paragraphs about activities in Dinard, including parties attended by Wilde.*

---

1. The context in which Wilde's remarks were given is unclear. It is plausible that he spoke directly to the correspondent (surely the author of "Mr. Oscar Wilde the Lion of Dinard," *The New York Herald, European Edition* (Paris, France), 3 Sep. 1893, 5, pp. 633–4; and "Mr. Oscar Wilde's Philosophy," *The New York Herald, European Edition* (Paris, France), 9 Sep. 1893, 1, pp. 635–6), but he may have spoken with someone else who quoted him to the correspondent.

"To Champion Sin," *The Clinton Public* (Clinton, IL), 6 Oct. 1893, 5[1]

Many Theorists Who Will Shortly Be Among Us.

Oscar Wilde's Unique Mission—Chamberlain's Vast Project—Why Clemenceau Will Visit America.

(COPYRIGHT, 1893.)

Of the many distinguished men who are to visit the United States very soon—and the names of Joseph Chamberlain, Emilio Castelar, Archbishop Walsh, Goldwin Smith, Dr. Franz von Rottenburg, Lord Randolph Churchill and others are on the list—not one comes to us upon a more unique mission than does Oscar Wilde. For the apostle of agnostic aestheticism, to employ his favorite verbal designation of himself, will open in America a new crusade, that of championing sin and demonstrating its general desirability.

Mr. Wilde is due in New York late this month or the beginning of next. Upon his arrival he will prepare for the stage a play in which Rose Coghlan is to star. The piece is all written, but Mr. Wilde's anxiety that it be correctly interpreted has brought him among us and incidentally led to the propagation of his new theory in our country first of all.

The statement that Oscar Wilde will endeavor to patch up a reconciliation between his brother and Mrs. Frank Leslie is authoritatively denied.[2] Once the staging of his play is accomplished, the Don Quixote of philosophy will devote all his leisure to the development of certain dogmas which as yet he has given but partial expression to. In "The Picture of Dorian Gray," and in certain metrical productions, in addition to the play which was suppressed because of a too daring moral radicalism,[3] Mr. Wilde has tried to evolve certain ideas relative to the virtue and general utility of sin. The abuse that has been heaped upon him, to quote his own words, "makes vindication sweet." The sunflower knight has not

---

1. This article was trailed in *The New York Herald* on 7 October and appeared as "Oscar Wilde's Unique Mission," *The New York Herald* (New York, NY), 8 Oct. 1893, 14. A few days after publication it was described as "a recent interview with a HERALD representative" ("Both False and Dangerous," *The New York Herald* (New York, NY), 15 Oct. 1893, 8). *The Clinton Public* version appears to be the earliest appearance of the article, which was reprinted widely. It is unclear whether it is a genuine interview. There were rumours at this time that Wilde would soon return to America, and he would later confirm that he had considered visiting New York to superintend the rehearsals of *A Woman of No Importance* (F. E. McKay, "A Clever Dramatist's Eccentric Views," *Kate Field's Washington* (Washington, DC), Vol. 9, 4 Apr. 1894, 220–1, p. 638).

2. Mrs Frank Leslie née Miriam Florence Folline (1836–1914) was an American publisher. She inherited her husband's business and took it from near collapse to a paying concern. In 1891 she married Wilde's brother, Willie, but divorced him within two years because he refused to work (Sturgis, 451/419).

3. The reference is to *Salomé*.

forgotten the vituperation of George Parsons Lathrop, who styled Wilde's writings "disgusting filth and a-reek with the atmosphere of unnatural debasement."[1]

Mr. Wilde's theory of sin, so far as he has given utterance to it by voice and pen, is this: The tendency to sin is inborn. Sin, therefore, enters ipso facto into the schemes of the universe as much as virtue. Now, there are variations of sin as well as shades of virtue. Since virtue carried to excess is nauseating and can only be praiseworthy when practiced from ethical motives, is not its antithesis, sin, also a means to certain ends? Cannot sin be studied, in other words, with a view to its utility as a servant instead of as a master? Has anyone ever made a study of the possibilities of sin? Has sin ever been dissected and experimented with from worthy motives? No. The physician who exposes himself to smallpox and consumption that he may better know and battle with those diseases is a hero in the cause of science. Similarly, the being who exposes himself to every temptation and yields his spotless soul to the debaucheries of a Tiberius at Capri or practices the exquisite wickednesses that have rendered the name of Heliogabalus synonymous with sensual slavery will, if prompted by worthy motives, retain every vestige of his innocence.[2] Here, then, is the germ of the Oscar Wilde theory: One may sin—sin knowingly and deliberately, from worthy motives.

In justice to Mr. Wilde, it should be pointed out that he draws a distinction between sin for the sake of sinning and sin committed in the line of scientific experiment on much the same basis as eating to live is the ethical antithesis of living to eat. Moreover those sins which involve vulgarity are entirely inexcusable. To steal another's purse is contemptible, because it is unrefined, but to investigate the elective affinity between hearts and souls which have come in contact too late for such a study from the conventional point of view, may be noble self-sacrifice. "There is a time for all things," says Solomon.[3] The great misfortune of the human race has been that never has it seemed able to tell when the time for sinning has arrived. The sins of the world have usually been so inopportunely committed as to afford no material for the scientific study of wickedness, a region in which Mr. Wilde would become the pioneer.

This explains, in Mr. Wilde's opinion, the strange attraction exerted by sin and sinners upon even the virtuous in all ages. How interesting is the handsome

---

1. George Parsons Lathrop (1851–1898) was an American poet, novelist, and newspaper editor. He had recently reviewed *The Picture of Dorian Gray* for the *New York World*, describing it as "disgusting and sickening [....] [Wilde] has committed an inexcusable offense against good morals, good art and pure minds." (Reprinted in "Fleshly Oscar Wilde," *The Minneapolis Tribune* (Minneapolis, MN), 21 Jul. 1890, 7.)

2. Tiberius (42 BCE–37 CE) and Heliogabalus (c. 204–222), or Elagabalus, were Roman emperors with reputations for depravity.

3. "To every thing there is a season, and a time to every purpose under the heaven:" (Ecclesiastes 3:1).

rascal who has broken scores of hearts and wrecked the happiness of those who unscientifically stooped to folly! What a wealth of material for investigation has thus run to waste! Society has long revolted against this conventional injustice to sin, but no one has yet had the courage to champion the cause. Upon Mr. Wilde has it devolved to become the parent of the science of sin in much the fashion that Adam Smith is now the father of political economy.

Whether the sunflower is to be retained as the cross of the new crusade seems yet unknown. Emile Zola's suggestion of a pair of horns has not been noticed.

✄ *Several paragraphs about other persons planning to visit America.*

"Oscar Wilde Scandal," *South Wales Daily News* (Cardiff, UK), 8 May 1895, 5[1]

BAIL ACCEPTED.

RELEASE OF WILDE.

The expected application for Mr Oscar Wilde to be released on bail was made at Bow street on Tuesday before Mr Vaughan. Mr Travers Humphreys appeared on behalf of the prisoner, while the Treasury was represented by Mr Angus Lewis.[2] Mr Humphreys briefly recapitulated the history of the case up to the application made yesterday to Baron Pollock, and said that he was now prepared with the necessary sureties. Both of them were persons of substance, and their names had been submitted to and approved by the Treasury. One was the Rev. Stewart Headlam, and the other Lord Douglas of Hawick, otherwise Viscount Drumlanrig, the eldest son of the Marquis of Queensberry.[3] Both these gentlemen men were called and swore that they were worth £1,250—the amount of bail fixed for each surety by Baron Pollock. Mr Vaughan said he was perfectly satisfied with the bail tendered, and he ordered Wilde's immediate release.

1. This report, which appeared in many newspapers around the country, describes Wilde's release from Holloway Gaol after the collapse of his first trial for gross indecency. It includes a refusal by Wilde to grant an interview.
2. Travers Humphreys (1867–1956) was a British barrister and, later, judge who served as junior counsel for Wilde in all three trials. He wrote a preface for H. Montgomery Hyde's *The Trials of Oscar Wilde.*
3. Headlam did not know Wilde personally before agreeing to stand his bail. Lord Douglas of Hawick is not to be confused with Lord Alfred Douglas, Wilde's lover. Hawick was Percy Sholto Douglas (1868–1920), the second son of the Marquess of Queensberry, and, since the death of his elder brother Francis in 1894, his father's heir apparent, and therefore more correctly styled Viscount Drumlanrig.

A later telegram states that Oscar Wilde left Holloway Gaol in the afternoon. He drove from the gaol in a four-wheeler to Bow street, where he went into the clerk's room and signed what is known as the bail book, after which (accompanied by Lord Douglas of Hawick) he re-entered the cab and drove off.

Detective Inspector Brockwell, Sergeant White (gaoler at Bow street), and a clerk of Messrs Humphreys and Son (Wilde's solicitors) arrived at Holloway Prison at 20 minutes past 1 o'clock, for the purpose of receiving Oscar Wilde and taking him to Bow street, so that he might enter under his own recognisance before being restored to liberty. The necessary formalities at the prison took some little time, but just before 2 o'clock the party emerged through the wicket door and took seats in a cab. Wilde wore a dark cloth overcoat, grey trousers and silk hat. There was a wearied expression about his pale features, strongly indicative of sleepless nights, and it could plainly be seen he was in anything but robust health. His body also seemed slightly bent. Neither at the prison gate nor at Bow street was there the slightest demonstration, and during the journey Wilde is stated to have maintained almost absolute silence, being seemingly intensely absorbed in thought. At Bow street the two sureties—Rev. Stewart Headlam and Lord Douglas of Hawick—were waiting, and the proceedings in connection with recognisances of £2,500 having been completed, accused was released. He immediately drove to the Midland Hotel, St Pancras, accompanied by his sureties, and it was subsequently stated he was suffering from extreme prostration and quite unable to undergo the fatigue of an interview.[1] It is expected he will leave London today, and his solicitors, at his own request, have offered to keep the authorities fully informed of his movements and precise whereabouts between now and the 20th instant, when he will in due course give himself up to the police. In course of the afternoon it was stated that Wilde had an interview at the Law Courts with Sir Edward Clarke.[2]

REV STEWART HEADLAM INTERVIEWED.

The Rev. Stewart Headlam, interviewed by a Press Association representative at the close of the proceedings as to his reason for becoming surety, said: "I have undertaken this responsibility on public grounds. I felt that the public mind had been prejudiced before the case began, and I was anxious to give Mr Wilde any help I could to enable him to stand his trial in good health and spirits."

---

1. Versions of this article printed over subsequent days further stated that "Mr. Wilde, in answer to inquiries addressed to him by a reporter, declared that he had nothing to say; but he seemed much relieved by the prospect of a little freedom and fresh air after so many weary days confinement," (see e.g. "Release of Oscar Wilde," *Harrow Observer* (London, UK), 10 May 1895, 6).

2. Sir Edward Clarke (1841–1931) was the barrister who represented Wilde in the libel trial.

"Oscar Wilde Released," *The Pall Mall Gazette* (London, UK), 19 May 1897, 7[1]

SMUGGLED FROM READING TO PENTONVILLE.

TO RESUME HIS LITERARY CAREER.

Just before eight o'clock last evening a private carriage drove up to the Governor's house at Reading Gaol. It held three ladies in evening dress. Two or three newspaper men who saw the smart coachman whip the pair into the enclosure concluded that Major Nelson was giving a dinner party.

There was a general air of festivity about the Governor's house. There was a good deal of light, and on the turret even were a couple of comely sewing-maids who whiled away their time dancing to the music discoursed by the town's band in the park hard-by.

At about a quarter past eight o'clock the private carriage left the ground surrounding the Governor's house. The blinds were drawn, and the wily coachman seemed in a great hurry. He was taking Oscar Wilde, the Deputy-Governor of Reading Gaol, and a stalwart warder named Harrison to the railway station at Twyford. Twyford is a wayside station about half an hour's drive from Reading. Express trains do not as a rule stop there. Last night the 8.43 express did ease up at Twyford, and took on board Oscar Wilde and his brace of guardians.

Oscar Wilde was looking remarkably well, and one may quite believe the statement of a confidant that when he left the prison he weighed exactly one stone more than he scaled immediately upon his sentence at the Old Bailey.[2] Moreover, the prison regulations or the exigencies of the particular sentence have obviated the necessity of clipping his Byronic locks. The razor is a thing of the past in prison life, and the beard of the erstwhile prisoner has been allowed to grow. It has been subjected, however, to periodical shearings with one of those diminutive instruments beloved of the "coster" barber and most suggestive of a lawn-mower.

---

1. This article contains a number of inaccuracies: Wilde's health in prison was not as good as the author suggests, and Wilde was not planning to settle in Paris. Upon his release Wilde was taken directly from Pentonville Prison to the London home of Stewart Headlam, but because this fact is not mentioned in the article it seems certain that the author, who clearly went to much trouble to investigate Wilde's movements, was unaware of it. Therefore, although Wilde is quoted towards the end of the article, it is unlikely that his comments were obtained by the reporter: there was no opportunity for him to give them between his release and the publication of the article. Another possibility is that they were paraphrased from Frank Marshall White [and Robert Batho], "Oscar Wilde to Write," *The Chicago Daily Tribune* (Chicago, IL), 17 May 1897, 2, pp. 655–60.

2. Wilde's weight upon reception at Pentonville was just under 14 stone, equivalent to 196 lbs or 88.9 kg (Hyde (1963), 4).

It would require more space than the *Pall Mall* cares to give to thoroughly describe the prison *régime* through which Wilde has had to go during the last two years.

When he was sentenced to two years' hard labour on May 20, 1895, he was taken at once to Wandsworth Prison. There he was put upon the treadmill—"the golden staircase," as it is known among old-time criminals.[1] There is nothing more demoralizing known to our punitive authorities than this particular form of punishment. Meanwhile the prisoner is subjected to what is known as fourth-class diet. This is the lowest fare which the medical men allow. It consists of 8 ounces of "black bread" in the morning; a fairly large quantity of suet pudding—varied now and then by a fare of haricot beans and eight ounces of bread, supplemented by a pint of "skilly" by way of collation. "Skilly" is a weak—nay, even a consumptive, preparation of oatmeal and boiled water.

Strange as it may appear, this particular form of nourishment seemed to suit Wilde.[2] It is a fact that since his incarceration it has been found necessary to allow him an extra hour's exercise each day in order to lessen his tendency to "run to flesh." This is the only special privilege he has been accorded during his term of punishment.

THE POLISHED DOOR KNOBS.

To set all doubts at rest in regard to the particular form of hard labour which has been meted out to Oscar Wilde since he left Wandsworth Prison and was taken in charge by the Governor of the Berks county penal establishment, he has been mainly engaged in the making or sewing of coal sacks.

In the early part of the day as a good conduct prisoner he has been detained in the polishing and furnishing gang, and during the latter part of his hard labour he has been mainly occupied with the repairing and re-binding of the prison hymn books, books of Common Prayer, and Bibles.

The evidence of the chaplain is that while extremely attentive to his religious ministrations, the notorious prisoner exhibited a profound indifference to the copies of the only three works allowed in prison cells; and which, by the

1. According to Hyde (1963), 8, "Wilde seems to have escaped" the treadmill.

2. In a letter to the editor of the *Daily Chronicle*, Wilde placed hunger top of his list of "permanent punishments authorised by law in English prisons," claiming that the "food supplied to prisoners is entirely inadequate. Most of it is revolting in character. All of it is insufficient. Every prisoner suffers day and night from hunger. A certain amount of food is carefully weighed out ounce by ounce for each prisoner. It is just enough to sustain, not life exactly, but existence. But one is always racked by the pain and sickness of hunger," (CL, 1045–6). Wilde complained to Frank Harris that the food was "not fit for dogs" (Harris, 332). However, in *De Profundis*, which was composed between January and March 1897, Wilde admitted "I get now sufficient food," (CL, 949). Sympathetic warders also gave him extra food, such as ginger biscuits, meat pies, and sausage rolls (CL, 798; Ricketts, 49).

irony of fate, he was called upon to overhaul in the course of duty. Wilde was somewhat fortunate in the matter of "the mill." It is customary to inflict this cruel task upon hard labour convicts for the first six months of their "time." Wilde, however, was going through the Bankruptcy Court during the fifth and sixth months of his detention,[1] and the constant interviews he had with his legal advisers rendered the wheel impossible for at least two months and induced the provision of a trifle better dietary. On his arrival at Reading, when the coal-bag making commenced, Wilde was placed upon a somewhat better footing in the way of food. That is to say, he had the advantage of a third-class diet, which is the same as that described above, with the addition of two ounces of meat once each week.

The gaol officials assert that the modern poet has been a most exemplary prisoner from the beginning. He has faithfully carried out his task, and it is noteworthy that in Reading Gaol, which is known technically as a "task gaol"—this means that after a certain hour the prisoner has a given quantity of work to do in his cell, and is only free for the day when he has finished it—he has always been in the front rank of those who have "completed" up to time.

His friends will be glad to hear that he has enjoyed excellent health through his enforced retirement. He has indeed been an absolute stranger to the infirmary, and has, according to the dispenser, cost the State no more than threepence in the matter of physic throughout the whole term of his imprisonment.[2]

His Future Movements.

In spite of the vigilance of the prison officials, Oscar Wilde's views of the situation and rough outline of his future movements were ascertained by the special correspondent of the *Pall Mall Gazette.* He will retire into suburban privacy for some considerable time, and he will then settle down in the neighbourhood of Paris—St. Cloud is the district he favours most and devote himself mainly to literary work of a poetic description. Fiction will also occupy his attention to a considerable extent in novel form, and for a time at least the drama will be left severely alone.

There was a good deal of difficulty in obtaining any information in regard to the special arrangements made for the release of the prisoner. For some inscrutable reason the ordinary custom was entirely abandoned, and arrangements of an extremely elaborate and exhaustive nature were made, upon the direct initiative of the Home Secretary himself. It was a matter of considerable comment in

---

1. Wilde was taken to Bankruptcy Court on 24 September 1895. The examination was adjourned until 12 November (Page, 69).

2. Wilde spent two months in the infirmary at Wandsworth and two days at Reading (Hyde (1963), 31, 39, 58).

741

gaol circles that a distinct privilege be granted to Oscar Wilde. However, this is a matter which is likely to attract the attention of some young and enthusiastic member of Parliament in want of a grievance, and may be safely left to such care.

Although bearing the reputation of being the most contented inmate of Reading Gaol, it is understood that Wilde was seriously agitated some five months ago. It occurred to him—probably owing to a smattering of knowledge gleaned during his journalistic experience—that he was entitled to a remission of sentence in respect of good conduct. The conduct was unquestioned, but the time limit was inexorable. Wilde twice appealed to the visiting justices on this subject, only to learn that not alone are hard labour criminals disentitled to any good conduct privilege, but the offence in regard to which he received his sentence was one of the few on the Statute-Book which did not allow, *under any circumstances*, of the slightest remission of time.

The ownership of the private brougham which conveyed Wilde from Reading is still a matter of doubt. It is a fact that no jobmaster in the immediate neighbourhood supplied either the horses or the vehicle, "the lot" was driven in from some distant part, and, after having dropped the party, as described, at Twyford, it disappeared. It was noteworthy also that neither at Reading nor Twyford were there any relatives or friends to greet the convict. The local authorities had expected quite a gathering at the gates of the prison. Certain intimate friends of Wilde who were looked for, from their declarations two years ago to have been present ready to receive their quondam friend did not appear. That Wilde was accompanied only by two law-appointed guardians may of course, have been the outcome of his own request, or on the other hand, it may be only one of the series of hard lessons which, although he has left the prison behind Mr. Wilde has still to learn.

From Twyford the prisoner still in custody was taken to Westbourne-grove, when he was conveyed in a closed carriage to Pentonville Prison. Shortly after nine o'clock this morning an unobtrusive private brougham drew in to the principal entrance of the Metropolitan House of Detention, and some five minutes later it left with Oscar Wilde—a free man. There was no one with him, and there were but a couple of people who witnessed his departure. Mr. Wilde has declined to make any statement for publication beyond the fact that he is "mentally tired."

It may be of interest to the gatherers of ill-considered trifles to learn that one of the first things Mr. Oscar Wilde did on regaining his freedom was to refuse an offer of £1,000 for a short description of his prison experiences.[1]

Wilde says that he has no intention of hiding himself, and will resume his literary career, writing over his own name.

1. Wilde refuses an offer of £1,000 for an interview: see p. 655, note 1.

"Oscar Wilde Released," *The Times* (Philadelphia, PA), 20 May 1897, 1[1]

The Apostle of Aestheticism Completes His Term of Imprisonment and is Now a Free Man.

LONDON, May 19.—To avoid probable demonstrations, Oscar Wilde, who, on May 25, 1895, was sentenced to two years' imprisonment with hard labor for immoral practices, was not released from Reading Jail, where he has served out his sentence, but was transferred last night to Holloway Prison, London, under a special arrangement made by the Home Secretary.[2]

He was liberated at 9 o'clock this morning. Contrary to expectations, there were no friends to meet him, either at Reading or at Holloway.

The prison fare seems to have suited him, as he weighs quite fourteen pounds more than when he entered jail. For several months the prison authorities have omitted the usual hair and beard clipping operation in his case, and during the whole term he has had less than the usual quantity of treadmill discipline. His principal prison duties have been to bind books and mark coal sacks. His conduct has been most exemplary, and his health uniformly good. Not once was he compelled to enter the infirmary.

About five months ago he became rather restless in the expectation that his good conduct would obtain some remission of sentence. He twice appealed to the visiting Justices, only to learn that remission was never granted in the case of the offense for which he had been sentenced.

Wilde has gone into the suburbs of London for a few weeks' rest, after which he will resume his literary work. He may go to France or Italy for a few months, but he says his present expectation is to return here at no late date.

He has not decided whether he will write under a pseudonym or over his own signature. He admits that he has several offers under consideration, and says that, so far as his movements in the future are concerned, he will covet neither notoriety nor oblivion.

---

1. This article contains a number of inaccuracies: see notes to "Oscar Wilde Released," *The Pall Mall Gazette* (London, UK), 19 May 1897, 7, pp. 739–42. Wilde's comments are unlikely to be genuine. Ellmann, 492/524, claims that Wilde spoke to a reporter who observed his departure from Reading, and quotes *The New York Times* of 19 May 1897. No article about Wilde was printed in that issue, and Ellmann must be referring to "Oscar Wilde Released," *The New York Times* (New York, NY), 20 May 1897, 7, which is an abbreviated and re-ordered version of the Philadelphia *Times* article. The Philadelphia *Times* version was printed simultaneously as "Oscar Wilde Gives His Liberty," *St. Louis Globe Democrat* (St. Louis, MO), 20 May 1897, 2.

2. Wilde was transferred to Pentonville, not Holloway.

Appendix D: Interviews about Wilde

Here are collected examples of interviews given about Wilde by members of his circle and others with whom he interacted. Also included are several interviews with Wilde's wife, Constance, and his mother, Lady Wilde; although they are not directly about Wilde, they provide insight into his family life.

"Return of Miss Blanche Roosevelt," *The New York Herald* (New York, NY), 10 Oct. 1881, 4[1]

A SOJOURN AMONG FOREIGN ARTISTS—WHAT OUR AMERICAN CANTATRICE SAW ABROAD—NILSSON AND PATTI BOTH COMING TO AMERICA—OSCAR WILDE AND OTHERS.

Among the passengers on the Mosel, which arrived on Saturday, was Miss Blanche Roosevelt, the well known prima donna, who has been spending the summer abroad, visiting old friends and utilizing her spare time in study with her former teachers. She returns in the fullness of health, and, as she says, with a voice so greatly improved that a few years ago she would have scarcely recognized it herself. A reporter of the HERALD yesterday found Miss Roosevelt at her residence in Twentieth street, and in a hurried conversation, frequently interrupted by visitors, she narrated the facts that follow:—

✂ *Several paragraphs that are unrelated to Wilde.*

"Another of my interesting evenings was spent at the house of a friend, where was present the famous Oscar Wilde, the leader of the aesthetic circles, and Mr. Gilbert's model of the hero in 'Patience.' His mother, Lady Wilde, was also present—a very attractive woman."

"How did he strike you?" queried the reporter.

"Well, he struck me," said Miss Roosevelt, laughingly, "as being very, very 'utter.' He has a languishing face, long, light hair, blonde complexion and was dressed in light pantaloons and a gray redingote buttoned so very tightly that it displayed a profusion of wrinkles. He looked as if he had hard work to get into it. He is a large sized man, with enormous feet and hands and makes a conspicuous feature in every throng, but his face has a decidedly animal like expression, which is only offset by the originality of his conversation in which, being a poet, he occasionally utters bright things. He told me he thought of coming to America to see what we are like, and referred with apparent pleasure to the flattering manner in which some of his poems had been received by a portion of the American press.

✂ *Several paragraphs that are unrelated to Wilde.*

1. Excerpted in "Blanche Roosevelt," *Memphis Daily Appeal* (Memphis, TN), 14 Oct. 1881, 2; "A Prima Donna's Talk," *The Daily Nebraska State Journal* (Lincoln, NE), 19 Oct, 1881, 1; and Sturgis (2020), 62. Blanche Roosevelt (1853–1898) was an American opera singer and journalist. In 1879 she played Josephine in Gilbert and Sullivan's *H. M. S. Pinafore* and created the role of Mabel in *The Pirates of Penzance.*

"Mr. Boucicault's Return" *The New York Herald* (New York, NY), 23 Dec. 1881, 4[1]

NO IRISH PLAYS TOLERATED IN LONDON—THE ACTOR'S OPINION OF THE PRESENT DRAMATIC TASTE OF NEW YORK—OSCAR WILDE AND MRS. LANGTRY.

✂ *Several paragraphs that are unrelated to Wilde.*

OSCAR WILDE AND MRS. LANGTRY.

"Did you meet the aesthetic hero, Mr. Oscar Wilde, while you were in London?"

"Oh, yes, I saw him constantly."

"What do you think of his idea of lecturing here?"

"Well, oddly enough, I was the first to suggest to him to give entertainments in this country in the form of lectures on modern aestheticism. He didn't take to the idea at first when I told him he would have to appear on a platform before perhaps one thousand or two thousand persons, as he said that whatever effect he could make would only be appreciated by a drawing room audience. But I am glad to see he has made up his mind to come, and I think that, as the leader of this present craze, he will be a fashionable success."

"What is your definition of modern aestheticism, Mr. Boucicault?"

"Well, I should say that aestheticism is the love and art of all that is beautiful. Modern aestheticism is the love and art of all that is grotesque of the beautiful."

✂ *Several paragraphs that are unrelated to Wilde.*

"A Chat with Genevieve Ward," *The Daily Picayune* (New Orleans, LA), 27 Dec. 1881, 8[2]

AN ACTRESS WHO SPENT SOME OF HER EARLY LIFE IN LOUISIANA.

✂ *Several paragraphs that are unrelated to Wilde.*

"Oscar Wilde? Oh, yes; I've known him since he was a boy. His mother is a charming woman, and a great friend of mine, highly accomplished she is, and

1. Excerpted in "Mr. Oscar Wilde at New York," *The Pall Mall Gazette* (London, UK), 4 Jan. 1882, 8. Boucicault was interviewed in New York shortly after returning to America on the SS *Bothnia*.
2. Ward was interviewed in her rooms in New Orleans's St. Charles Hotel.

Oscar was always very nice until he got this absurd aesthetic notion in his head. He began by wearing yellow cravats; sometimes he and Mrs. Langtry, who is really very beautiful, would come to see me play, and she generally carried a lily or two in her hand, frequently sending them behind the scenes to me and was always charmed if I carried them on the stage."

✂   *Several paragraphs that are unrelated to Wilde.*

"Oscar Wilde's Visit," *The Scranton Republican* (Scranton, PA), 3 Jan. 1882, 2

Philadelphia the Objective Point of the Aesthete's Journey—The Sun-flower Worshipper now Composing a Poem for a New Philadelphia Paper, and Preparing to Publish Two New Books.

✂   *An announcement of Wilde's imminent arrival in America and a brief biography.*

WILDE'S AMERICAN PUBLISHERS.

A *Press* reporter yesterday interviewed Jos. M. Stoddart, of the well-known publishing firm, in relation to Mr. Wilde's visit to this city.[1] Said Mr. Stoddart "Oscar Wilde is now on the steamship *Arizona*, and is due at New York about January 4th or 5th. He will stay in New York a few days, when he will come to this city. He has accepted an invitation to become my guest. While he is here, probably about the middle of January, a reception will be given him at the residence of Robert Stewart Davis, the former publisher, at the corner of Eighteenth and Spruce streets, to which the most prominent people of the city in literary and social circles will be invited.[2] Mr. Wilde will also deliver a public lecture while in Philadelphia, setting forth his theory of poetry and art."

"Has Mr. Wilde any specific object in his visit to Philadelphia?" asked the reporter.

"Oscar Wilde's general object in visiting the United States," replied Mr. Stoddart, "is to expound his aesthetic views. His special object in coming to Philadelphia—but I want to say right here," broke in Mr. Stoddart, interrupting himself, "that Oscar Wilde is no fool, and ought not to be prejudged as one. *Punch* is funny but not exact. The Reginald Bunthorne of 'Patience' is merely a friendly

1. Philadelphia.
2. See "The Aesthetic Bard," *The Philadelphia* Inquirer (Philadelphia, PA), 17 Jan. 1882, 2, pp. 80–1.

burlesque, and that it did not cut as deeply as did Dickens' picture of Leigh Hunt as 'Horace Skimpole,' for example, is shown by the fact that Gilbert and Sullivan are on excellent terms with Mr. Wilde.[1] He is by no means 'this most aesthetic, peripatetic, magnetic lover,' he is commonly supposed to be."[2]

"You bespeak, then, for Mr. Wilde, a hearing first and judgement afterward?"

"Certainly. He is to be taken for what he shows himself to be. To return to his visit here, it is for a very definite and important purpose. In the first place, a new weekly paper will be started here very soon. This paper is backed by heavy capital, and no expenditure will be spared to make it a marked departure in the literary world. Its illustrations will be drawn by the best artists in America, and engraved by the most skilled wielders of the graver. Its mechanical execution, its paper, type and general appearance, will be not merely unsurpassed, but absolutely unequaled in the world. The names of its publishers or editors I am not authorized to make public at present. This new publication will contain in its first number a poem by Oscar Wilde. This will be his first contribution in America. While he was at Liverpool, before embarking on the Arizona, he was engaged by cable to write this poem while on the passage, at a guinea a line. A good price, that. I fear his publishers hope he has been sea-sick."[3]

NEW BOOKS BY THE AESTHETE.

"Are any other productions of Mr. Wilde's to appear here?"

"Yes, indeed. In fact, the poem in the new paper is itself a minor matter. More important is the fact that a new book of new poems by Wilde is to appear from our press. This will be immediately followed by the publication of a prose book, treating in detail of Mr. Wilde's theories, and defining the doctrines of his school with more fullness and accuracy than has yet been done. In short, this prose work will cover the new aesthetic evolution."[4]

1. Horace Skimpole is a character in Charles Dickens's novel *Bleak House* (1852–1853). He claims to be ignorant of "worldly matters" and models himself on the butterfly that freely flits "from rosewood to mahogany, and from mahogany to walnut", but remorselessly sponges off his friends. Dickens admitted that he had based Skimpole on the English critic and poet James Henry Leigh Hunt (1784–1859).

2. In *Patience* Grosvenor sings of a "magnetic, | Peripatetic | Lover", a magnet in a hardware shop that attracts iron scissors, needles, nails, and knives, but loves a silver churn.

3. The new paper was *Our Continent*. The first number appeared 15 Feb. 1882 and included Wilde's poems *Le Jardin* and *La Mer*. The editor was Albion Winegar Tourgée (1838–1905). The paper was renamed *The Continent* in 1883 and ceased publication in 1884. See also "Oscar Wilde," *The New York World, Semi-Weekly Edition* (New York, NY), 6 Jan. 1882, 2, p. 693, note 2; and "Oscar, The Aesthete," *Philadelphia Press* (Philadelphia, PA), 7 Jan. 1882, 8, p. 754.

4. Wilde published neither a second book of poetry nor a book about aestheticism. Stoddart's plans evidently changed once he and Wilde met in New York.

"Will Wilde supervise in detail the publication of these works, as Walt Whitman did the printing of the 'Leaves of Grass' in Boston?"

"It is not likely that he will give so much personal attention to the technical work; but the editions will have his personal sanction, as well as his oversight to some extent. It is expected by both author and publisher that these books will meet with more remarkable success than has the book of his poems already published in Boston. When that work appeared Mr. Wilde was by no means so well known as he is now."

"What is to be the name of the new weekly paper?"

"That I am not at liberty to state.[1] I can only say that the capital behind this publication, and the liberal patronage it will give to literary workers for its contents, and to artists for its embellishment, are bound in time to make Philadelphia the American centre of literature and art. That result must come, and this weekly publication will be an important factor in bringing it about."

"Preparing the Poet for Work," *New York Tribune* (New York, NY), 5 Jan. 1882, 3[2]

HOW MR. MORSE STRUGGLES TO PUT OSCAR WILDE IN TRAINING FOR HIS
LECTURE.

The steamship Arizona, with its precious cargo, Oscar Wilde, the poet and apostle of aestheticism, left Quarantine at 7 a.m. Tuesday. Coming up the bay it was met by a tug on which was W. F. Morse, D'Oyly Carte's agent, who is going to manage Mr. Wilde—if he can. The Arizona arrived at its pier a little after 9 a.m., but it was two hours before the passengers were disembarked. Mr. Morse and Mr. Wilde went to the Hotel Brunswick, where the poet made way with a remarkably hearty breakfast.

"I want to get a suite of rooms," said Mr. Morse, to one of the utterly superb clerks of the Brunswick.

"I am sorry, but they are all engaged."

"But I want it for Mr. Wilde."

"We haven't rooms even for Mr. Wilde."

Mr. Wilde and Mr. Morse then went up Broadway slowly to Mr. Carte's office at No. 1,267, where the poet rested himself for an hour or two.

---

1. Stoddart would reveal the title of the paper a few days later: "Oscar, The Aesthete," *Philadelphia Press* (Philadelphia, PA), 7 Jan. 1882, 8, p. 754.

2. Referenced in Mendelssohn, 108. This article is included in the Robert Ross Memorial Collection album (Ross b.6, 81).

"Mr. Wilde explained to me the import of his lecture," said Mr. Morse to a TRIBUNE reporter in the afternoon, "and I think it will be a fine thing. It will be a definition and description of English culture as applied to social life. And there is no man that knows the subject more thoroughly than Mr. Wilde does. However, the lecture is far from being ready yet, and he will have to spend the next four or five days working on this. He found three invitations to dinner and any number of cards to receptions awaiting him and he will be obliged to decline them probably—he must. You see he is one of those men that cannot be interrupted by thoughts of where he will eat and where he will sleep when he had been wrought up to the proper pitch for work. Such things, if forced upon his notice, distract him from labor for three or four hours. I have taken apartments for him, therefore, in a private building and not a hotel.

"Tomorrow he will work all the time; Thursday he will go to a private dinner (it is the only one), and in the evening he will occupy a box at the Standard Theatre.[1] He isn't vain at all, or he wouldn't go to see what is supposed to be a caricature of himself. Mr. Wilde was somewhat surprised at the way the newspapers received him here, and was somewhat annoyed at first at their descriptions of his personal appearance. I explained to him, however, that journalism was not journalism here unless it had something personally descriptive about it, and he rather laughed after that."

"Oscar, The Aesthete," *Philadelphia Press* (Philadelphia, PA), 7 Jan. 1882, 8[2]

HIS NEAR APPROACHING VISIT TO PHILADELPHIA.

What His Publisher Thinks of Him After a Brief, but Close Acquaintanceship—
The Poet's Portrait—Poems by a Sunflower Disciple.

Oscar Wilde, who is still staying in New York, where he will lecture in Steinway Hall, Monday evening, on 'English Renaissance,'[3] will reach Philadelphia probably on Saturday next. He will, as already announced, be the guest of Joseph M. Stoddart, of the publishing firm. His visit here will be very brief, covering but a few days. While in this city he will deliver a lecture, at a time and place not yet definitely fixed, upon a subject similar to that of his New York discourse,

1. The Hayes reception and a performance of *Patience.*
2. Quoted in Cooper, J. (2019). 'A picturesque subject indeed!' The Sarony photographs of Oscar Wilde. *The Wildean, 55,* 3–33.
3. Wilde lectured on Monday 9 January 1882 in New York, not at Steinway Hall but at Chickering Hall.

but probably covering a somewhat different ground. He has accepted his invitation to give a reception at the residence of Robert Stewart Davis, which will probably be one of the principal social events of the winter.

A PRESS reporter yesterday called upon Joseph M. Stoddart, who had just returned from New York, where he met Mr. Wilde, and whose impressions of the poet were fresh and vivid. As soon as he was asked about his opinion of Oscar Wilde, Mr. Stoddart said emphatically: "Mr. Wilde has so far surprised every one who has seen him by his lofty removal from the false idea which the burlesques from over the water have given the American people. Aside from his poetic powers, he has keen perceptions, brilliant social qualities, an almost encyclopaedic grasp of facts, and a most happy readiness of expression. Nothing could be more unjust than to suppose him the extravagant combination of affectation and nonsense he has been pictured. Every one who has seen him has been quick to make this discovery. I have the utmost confidence that a general popular acquaintance can only make him universally esteemed."

"What is the personal appearance of the poet?" asked the reporter.

THE POET'S PHOTOGRAPH.

"I can best answer that by showing you his photograph," said Mr. Stoddart, taking from his desk a large cabinet picture, made by Sarony, Thursday. This photograph represented the poet in an easy, sitting posture. He wore an outer wrapping, too loosely cut to be called an overcoat, which fell in heavy folds to the floor. This was lined with fur and trimmed with otter. Its general color, Mr. Stoddart explained, was bottle green. Out of this wrapping rose a full, white neck, a rather massive face with prominent chin and sensuous lips. The beardless countenance was framed in long, brown hair, parted in the middle and tossed backward over his shoulders.[1] The face had an open, candid look. "The eyes, which are blue, look straight at you," said Mr. Stoddart, "and while they sometimes pierce you, they are also gentle; sometimes even melting. They are very expressive. When talking, he has a way of throwing his head back, closing his eyes in silence for a moment and then suddenly opening them. You can see the sparkle of the idea he is about to utter."

The rest of the dress of Mr. Wilde was a dark brown velvet coat, trimmed with braid of a rather lighter shade of brown. His linen collar, cut very low, displayed a swelling neck, and the tie—the poet is fond of a dash of color at his neck—flames in the triangle between the collar and the coat lapels. His trousers were of the "thoroughly commonplace" latest London cut, and he wore patent

---

1. Six of Sarony's photographs show Wilde seated and wearing his overcoat, but the description of his posture and neck suggest that this is plate 6.

leather shoes. His small sealskin cap, which he usually wears on the back of his head, was not shown in the photograph.

"How does Wilde like America?" asked the reporter.

"I have been struck with the fact that he is much more familiar with American affairs than one would think," was the reply. "He knew a great deal about prominent places in New York. He has been annoyed there by finding that people only knew him as burlesqued. They thought he was a kind of 'Bunthorne,' and some of them rushed to see him as if he were a wild beast on exhibition. He stayed at a hotel incognito when he first arrived, but people tracked him out, and those who did not understand that his purpose in coming to this country is not to make a furore were sometimes persistently obtrusive. We went to Booth's Theatre the other night to see Mary Anderson. The audience looked at our box so much, instead of at the stage, that we had to draw the curtains. Wilde was pleased, on the whole, with Mary Anderson's acting."[1]

POEMS BY AN AESTHETE DISCIPLE.

"What day will he come to Philadelphia?"

"That I cannot tell yet. I found that he had written, while on the passage over, the poem which I had engaged by cable, and which will appear in the first number of *Our Continent*, the new publication.[2] He also brought with him for publication by our firm, a manuscript volume of poems, written by a young disciple of his, which he looks upon as fondly as if they were his own, and which he will preface with a prose introduction of his own, introducing the new poet to the American public."[3]

"How does Oscar Wilde's lecture in New York promise financially?"

"The rush for seats is very great. Ten dollars premium was offered last night for choice places. His manager is D'Oyly Carte."

"How does the poet talk?"

"I was at a small dinner party given him the other evening, and his rattling comments on Ruskin, Rossetti, Browning, Mallock, Victor Hugo, Bernhardt and other celebrities of London and the continent kept the whole table entertained. He talked very fully, but I do not care to repeat what he said in private. He thinks a good deal of the 'Romance of the Nineteenth Century.'[4] He is an ardent admirer

---

1. Wilde was not pleased with Anderson's acting: see e.g. "Sunflowers and Lilies," *Fort Wayne Daily Gazette* (Fort Wayne, IN), 16 Feb. 1882, 6, p. 177.

2. *Le Jardin* and *La Mer*. See "Oscar Wilde," *The New York World, Semi-Weekly Edition* (New York, NY), 6 Jan. 1882, 2, p. 693, note 2; and "Oscar Wilde's Visit," *The Scranton Republican* (Scranton, PA), 3 Jan. 1882, 2, p. 750.

3. Rennell Rodd's *Rose Leaf and Apple Leaf*.

4. Wilde's opinion of Mallock's novel was more nuanced: see "A Talk with Wilde," *Philadelphia Press* (Philadelphia, PA), 17 Jan. 1882, 2, p. 77.

of Walt Whitman. He was given a reception Thursday at the residence of Augustus Hayes, Jr., on East Twenty-fifth street, when he spoke freely with all who were introduced to him. He wore a full dress suit of black, and carried no flowers. When he comes to Philadelphia he will certainly not walk down Chestnut street with a sunflower in his hand. People will be delighted with him—that's my prophecy."

"D'Oyly Carte and His Plans," *New York Tribune* (New York, NY), 12 Jan. 1882, 8[1]

R. D'Oyly Carte was one of the passengers by the steamship Servia which arrived yesterday afternoon. To a TRIBUNE reporter, who called on him last evening, Mr. Carte said that he had a very fair voyage with the exception of four or five days in which the steamship encountered head winds and high seas. Mr. Carte came alone.

"What do you think of Mr. Wilde's success?" asked the reporter.

"Well," said Mr. Carte, "I know nothing about it save what I've seen here in the papers. I thought he would make a stir. He's a clever young man and has lots to say to the people. Yes, I thought he'd be successful. He's an aesthete but, come to think of it, I believe he doesn't like that word—he's an art critic; that's better, you know. I don't consider it anything out of the way my bringing Wilde over here.[2] 'Patience' is only a good-natured satire."

"Do you intend travelling with Mr. Wilde?"

"In view of his success I think I shall take him around the country. He's to have a reception in Philadelphia on Monday and lectures there on Tuesday. He's going to Baltimore, Washington and Chicago. He will probably be here two or three months. He wants to see the country."

"What about Mr. Wilde's new play?"

"Nothing has been done yet in regard to it. It has never been produced. It was rehearsed at the Adelphi Theatre in London, but was stopped—that is, by the managers; they came to the conclusion that they daren't put it before the public."

"It is said that you have it in mind to build a permanent theatre here; is that true?"

1. Reprinted as "The Oily D'Oyly Carte," *The Atlanta Constitution* (Atlanta, GA), 14 Jan. 1882, 5. Excerpted in "D'Oyley [*sic*] Carte's Plans," *St. Louis Globe Democrat* (St. Louis, MO), 12 Jan. 1882, 3. Quoted in OWDA, 61; Hyde, 55; and Sturgis, 209/202.

2. D'Oyly Carte may be referring to *Patience* and its description of aesthetes Bunthorne and Grosvenor as "out of the way" young men.

"That's simply rumor."

"When do you expect to produce 'Claude Duval'?"

"Oh, I'm in no hurry about that. 'Patience' holds on pretty well, and I shall not interrupt it."[1]

"Are any new operas being written and composed for you?"

"Yes, Gilbert and Sullivan are at work on one now for me. I don't expect to produce it in London until next Fall. 'Patience' is having an immense run there. Sullivan is wintering in Cairo, Egypt. He's there for his health and to amuse himself, but is working on the new opera."

"What will be the title of the new opera?"

"That I can't tell you; we haven't got so far as that. It's an entirely new subject."[2]

"Have you made any engagement with Mrs. Langtry?"

"Well, I've made a proposition to her and that's as far as we've got. But if she comes to this country she will, no doubt, come under my management.[3] She's been very successful, I saw her first appearance, and she was very graceful. Naturally, being a debutante, you would expect her to be embarrassed, but she was very graceful. I don't mean to say she's a great actress; but she will be."

"Do you expect to stay here in New York some time?"

"No; I haven't had a holiday for five years. I'm going to take one now. I didn't come here for business."[4]

"'Patience' has been a great success, has it not?"

"Yes; we are playing in London to $9,000 houses every week, and it's been running since September 22.[5] I've got fifteen companies playing now in Europe, America and Australia—including, of course, Oscar Wilde and Archibald Forbes."

"Why don't you have Oscar Wilde give readings of his poems?"

"Well, I don't know why it wouldn't be a very good scheme, you know. I shall probably suggest it to him. I haven't seen him yet."[6]

1. *Claude Duval, or Love and Larceny* is a comic opera based on the life of the nineteenth-century highwayman, with music by Edward Solomon (1855–1895) and libretto by Henry Pottinger Stevens (1851–1903). Seeley, 82, suggests that, although D'Oyly Carte had agreed to produce *Claude Duval*, he was reluctant to replace *Patience* with an inferior piece. *Claude Duval* had a run in New York in March and April 1882, alternated with *Patience*.

2. Gilbert and Sullivan's comic opera *Iolanthe* opened simultaneously at D'Oyly Carte's Savoy Theatre in London and William Henderson's Standard Theatre in New York on 25 November 1882.

3. Langtry came to America under the management of Henry Abbey.

4. D'Oyly Carte holidayed in Florida and departed America on 11 March 1882 (Seeley, 58, 60).

5. *Patience* ran at London's Opera Comique between 23 April and 8 October 1881, and at the Savoy Theatre between 10 October 1881 and 22 November 1882.

6. Wilde had suggested during contract negotiations with D'Oyly Carte that he give readings of one of his lyric poems, but pressure was put on him to lecture on aestheticism instead (Sturgis, 193/186).

"Wilde and Whitman," *The Philadelphia Press* (Philadelphia, PA), 19 Jan. 1882, 8[1]

THE AESTHETIC SINGER VISITS THE GOOD GRAY POET.

He Asks the Advice of the Latter, and is Told to Go Ahead in His Mission to Shatter the Ancient Idols.

Oscar Wilde yesterday called upon Walt Whitman, at his home in Camden, where he has lived for the past nine years, and the two poets discussed men and letters for nearly the entire afternoon. Remembering the value it would have been to the world now, had a record been made of Emerson's celebrated visit to Carlyle,[2] a PRESS reporter last evening obtained Whitman's fresh impressions of the afternoon. The author of "Leaves of Grass," although partly an invalid, makes long jaunts, and has returned from his recent trip to New England in more vigorous physical health than since his paralysis of 1873. "Yes, Mr. Wilde came to see me early this afternoon," said Walt, "and I took him up to my den, where we had a jolly good time. I think he was glad to get away from lecturing, and fashionable society, and spend a time [*sic*] with an 'old rough.' We had a very happy time together. I think him genuine, honest and manly. I was glad to have him with me, for his youthful health, enthusiasm and buoyancy are refreshing. He was in his best mood, and I imagine that he laid aside any affectation he is said to have, and that I saw behind the scenes. He talked freely about the London literati, and gave me many inside glimpses into the life and doings of Swinburne, Dante Gabriel Rossetti, Morris, Tennyson and Browning.

Thus talking, Walt Whitman led the way to his "den," as he calls it, on the third floor. "Wilde and I drank a bottle of wine down stairs," he continued, "and when we came up here, where we could be on 'thee and thou' terms, one of the first things I said was that I should call him 'Oscar;' 'I like that so much,' he answered, laying his hand on my knee. He seemed to me like a great big, splendid

---

1. H & S, b16. Reprinted as "Wilde and Whitman," *The Daily American* (Nashville, TN), 22 Jan. 1882, 2; and in Mikhail, 46–8. Excerpted in OWDA, 75–7. Quoted in Pearson, 62; Hyde, 58; Ellmann, 160–2/168–70; and Sturgis, 216–7/208. Wilde is quoted briefly towards the end of the article, but it is unclear whether his comments were spoken in the presence of a reporter or only to Stoddart, who later quoted him. Wilde and Whitman met again in May 1882. Whitman also mentioned Wilde in an 1890 interview: "Yes, I have met a good many poets in my time, but I cannot talk at any length about them. The apostle, or rather the former apostle of aestheticism, Oscar Wilde, is a friend of mine. I like Oscar Wilde very much, and have had some genial, companionable hours with him. Outside of his long hair—he has it cut now—and his Bunthorne attitudinizing, I found him a whole-souled and natural fellow." (Foster Coates and Homer Fort, "Walt Whitman at Home," *Sunday Express* (Buffalo, NY), 25 May 1890, 3).
2. Thomas Carlyle (1795–1881) was a British historian. Emerson visited Carlyle's home in Craigenputtock, Scotland, in 1833, and the pair corresponded until Carlyle's death.

boy," said Whitman, stroking his silvery beard. "He is so frank and outspoken, and manly. I don't see why such mocking things are written of him. He has the English society drawl, but his enunciation is better than I ever heard in a young Englishman or Irishman before. We talked here for two hours. I said to him: 'Oscar, you must be thirsty. I'll make you some punch.' 'Yes, I am thirsty,' he acknowledged, and I did make him a big glass of milk punch, and he tossed it off, and away he went."

ADVISED TO GO AHEAD.

During the communion the representative of the aesthetes expounded freely the theories and intentions of his school, occasionally asking the old gray poet's opinions and views. The old man, however, evaded these inquiries with a smile. He said: "I wish well to you, Oscar, and as to the aesthetes, I can only say that you are young and ardent, and the field is wide, and if you want my advice, I say 'go ahead.'" Mr. Wilde made friendly inquiries about Whitman's own theories, and the mode and origin of his peculiar work. While answering freely, Walt wound up this part of the conversation by saying that those were problems he himself was always seeking to solve. Wilde described himself as having absorbed the Whitmanesque poetry from boyhood. He said that Lady Wilde bought one of the earliest copies of the poems some sixteen years ago, and was accustomed to read passages from it to him. He also spoke of the Oxford boys taking the book with them and reading it in [sic] their rambles. Thus he declared to Whitman: "I have come to you as to one with whom I have been acquainted almost from the cradle."

Wilde was very frank in his criticisms of British Philistinism, saying in substance: "One can hardly conceive how doubly and trebly bound literature and art and manners yet remain, even in the best society, in Great Britain. The poet or artist in any department who goes beyond beaten ruts and lines is pretty sure of a hard time. And yet there is a most determined class of the best people in England, not only among the young, but of all ages, both men and women, who are ready and eager for anything in art, science or politics that will break up the stagnation. He makes a great mistake who supposes that old England is abandoned entirely to conservatism. Young blood is pulsing yet in the veins of your old mother country."

THE ESTABLISHED IDOLS.

Wilde brought many cordial messages from the poets of England to Whitman, and received many to take back. Not the least part of his visit, it may be noted, is the intertwining, which is becoming closer and closer every year through sympathy and personal knowledge, of representative citizens in each country. At one time, in their two hours' talk, Wilde broke out, "I can't listen to anyone unless he attracts me by a charming style, or by beauty of theme."

"Why, Oscar," replied Whitman, "it always seems to me that the fellow who makes a dead set at beauty by itself is in a bad way. My idea is that beauty is a result, not an abstraction."

"Yes," was the quick response, "I remember you have said 'all beauty comes from beautiful blood and a beautiful brain;'[1] and, after all, I think so, too." Later on Whitman asked: "Are not you young fellows," scanning stalwart Oscar's big proportions, "going to shove the established idols aside, Tennyson and the rest?"

"Not at all," said Wilde, emphatically. "His rank is too well fixed, and we love him too much. But as for Tennyson, he has not allowed himself to be a part of the living world, and of the great currents of interest and action. He is of priceless value, and yet he lives apart from his time. We, on the other hand, move in the heart of today."[2] As for American poets, Mr. Whitman modestly acknowledged that Wilde had said many gushing things of himself, and had repeated the opinion he has more publicly expressed—"We in England think there are only two— Walt Whitman and Emerson."[3] Longfellow, he said, poet as he was, had contributed little to literature that might not have come just as well from European sources. Wilde also told Whitman that he was much impressed with the active life, the intelligence and the evident superiority of the masses of people in America, so far as he had seen them, over the common ranks in foreign countries. "That's nothing new," said Whitman, patriotically: "but it shows that the young man has his eyes open." As the aesthete departed, Mr. Whitman's farewell was: "Good bye, Oscar, God bless you."

During the ride over from Camden, in company with J. M. Stoddart, the publisher, Oscar Wilde was very silent, and seemed deeply affected by the interview. He spoke admiringly of "the grand old man," and of his struggles and triumphs.

Mr. Wilde was given a breakfast yesterday morning by Professor S. H. Gross. The others present were Mrs. Orwitz, of Baltimore, Professor Gross's daughter, William Henry Rawle, F. Carroll Brewster, Daniel Dougherty, Dr. Henson and J. G. Rosengarten. The poet wore his usual morning dress of brown velvet coat, and brown trousers of the ordinary cut. From the breakfast he went to Walt Whitman's, and in the evening he dined with George W. Childs.

1. From the preface to the first edition of *Leaves of Grass*.

2. Wilde had previously shared his assessment of Tennyson: see "The Aesthetic Bard," *The Philadelphia Inquirer* (Philadelphia, PA), 17 Jan. 1882, 2, p. 80.

3. "I think that Walt Whitman and Emerson have given the world more than anyone else." ("A Talk with Wilde," *Philadelphia Press* (Philadelphia, PA), 17 Jan. 1882, 2, p. 76.)

"Wilde's Experience," *The Topeka Daily Capital* (Topeka, KS), 23 Jan. 1882, 3[1]

Some Unpublished Things he Has Seen and Done in America.

From the Philadelphia Press.

Oscar Wilde, the apostle of the aesthetic school of art, dress, society and manner, is yet to make his definite and lasting impression on the American public. Already, however, he has attracted universal notice, and has at least succeeded in removing the grotesque idea of his personality and theories which existed before he touched America's shore. His advance agent, Henry Hewitt, was discovered at breakfast at the Continental yesterday morning, and told a *Press* reporter some interesting details of the poet's impression of the great republic, and of his contact so far with its practical people. The public interest in Mr. Wilde has shown itself so far, aside from the personal courtesies with which he has been favored in New York, in the demand for his photographs, his autograph and his book. Mr. Wilde's aesthetic notions were shocked when he saw the commercial and common way in which the American edition of his poems was issued. The English edition is a beautiful book, bound in white and gold, with uncut edges, and with an artistic design traced on the back and on the corner of the cover. But, though the American edition is less attractive, the publishers, Mr Hewitt says, have been unable to meet the demand which has sprung up since the author's arrival. Mr. Wilde has been deluged with requests for his autograph, of which he has so far answered nearly a thousand. But his stock of aesthetic green paper, which his eye can glide a pen with comfort, was soon exhausted, and he was obliged, to his chagrin, to write his name on common cream tint.

As a matter of course, Sarony, Mora, Mare, Gambier and Anderson, the New York photographers, were all anxious for Oscar Wilde's photograph, and the right to sell it.[2] Bernhardt was paid $1,500 for this right, which sum, by the way, she took out in pictures, which she peddled around the country, clearing $2,500—and Patti was paid $1,000 to pose before an exclusive camera. But the photographers all told Mr. Hewitt, who is the shield between Mr. Wilde's tender soul and sordid business arrangements, that no man's face would sell as largely

---

1. Referenced in Sturgis, 202/196.

2. Marc Gambier (1838–1900) was a French photographer. He had trained as a miniature painter and for several years in the 1870s was employed by Sarony to colour photographs. He operated his own studio from 1881. In 1884 he admitted to an interviewer that "[o]f late I have not taken the quantity of portraits among the [acting] profession which I formerly did". David H. Anderson (1827–1905) was an American photographer with a studio at 785 Broadway. In 1884 he boasted of repeat sittings from numerous well-known actors, including Laura Don, Margaret Mather, John McCullough, Marie Prescott, and Tommaso Salvini ("Theatrical Photography," *The New York Mirror* (New York, NY), 22 Mar. 1884, 10).

as a woman's, and that they could not pay so much. But they soon found out their error. All New York demanded the poet's picture, and Sarony was glad to pay as much for Wilde as for that of any woman.

POSED BEFORE SARONY.

Wilde's visit to Sarony's gallery was comical enough. The poet's stature of six feet three dwarfed ridiculously the artist's Liliputian [*sic*] height of three feet six. There were thirty sittings in all,[1] some of them in the poet's velvet knee-breeches suit; and Mr. Sarony was so delighted at the artistic possibilities of the poet's dress, the falling folds of his garments, the commanding grace of his stature and the marked individuality of his face that he exclaimed, when the sittings were finished, that he had never done such good photographic work before.

Wilde brought over many letters of introduction to prominent men and society people, among them Mr. Connery of the *Herald*, Whitelaw Reid of the *Tribune*, George Jones of the *Times*, William H. Hurlbert of the *World*, Mr. Fiske of the *Star*, Oscar Vezin, Mrs. Paran Stevens, whose daughter was recently married to young Paget, and many others.[2] Wilde says that there were two persons whom everybody recommended to him—Henry Longfellow, the poet, and Sam Ward, the club man, whose dinners are celebrated among *bon vivants* the country over. One of the editors, however, treated him rather shabbily.[3] Fiske of the *Star* published the private address which Wilde sent to him, with his letter of introduction, causing great annoyance to the poet, who wished to be personally secluded. And then Fiske printed a nondescript editorial on the aesthete, and sent it to Wilde with his compliments. The disgusted poet thought this conduct "very curious." Another editor used him more kindly. Mr. Hulbert gave him a dinner party, to which he invited a number of prominent men, and Wilde thought the experience one of the most "charming" he had ever met.

It will be a surprise to those who have looked on "Patience" as an extravagant burlesque to learn that Oscar Wilde himself declares that ladies' dresses in that opera are not in the least exaggerated. Of course the dresses are made for stage effect, and their decorations are a little larger in outline that those really

---

1. Sarony is known to have taken at least 29 photographs of Wilde in 1882. Most were taken in January, but four appear to have been taken later in the year (Cooper, J. (2019). 'A picturesque subject indeed!' The Sarony photographs of Oscar Wilde. *The Wildean*, *55*, 3–33; Holland, M. (2020). The Sarony photographs. *The Wildean*, *56*, 89–93).

2. Thomas B. Connery (c. 1838–1923) was editor of *The New York Herald* and later a novelist and diplomat. George Jones (1811–1891) co-founded the *New York Daily Times*, later *The New York Times*. Oscar Vezin (1838–1902) was secretary of the Pictet Artificial Ice Company.

3. Wilde complained to George Lewis about Whitelaw Reid: "Your friend Whitelaw Reid, to whom I brought two letters of introduction, has not been very civil—in fact has not helped me in any way at all. I am sorry I brought him any letters, and the *New York Herald* is most bitter. I wonder could you do anything for it?" (CL, 136.)

761

worn, but with this exception Mr. Wilde says that he has seen "very many lovely ladies in London drawing rooms garmented very like to Lady Jane and Angela." The aesthetic reform in woman's dress has banished the tight waist, and introduced flowing, clinging robes, which suggest natural outlines and half reveal curves of beauty, never meant to be concealed. As for men's dress, Mr. Wilde hopes to lead the movement of reform much further than he has yet gone.

MASCULINE AESTHETICISM.

His idea, apparently, is that men should not be so completely debarred from the beautiful fabrics which women adorn themselves, and that men's dress, instead of being after a uniform, stiff, conventional pattern, should be individualized, so as to express in some degree the inner nature of the wearer. So far, the masculine disciples of aestheticism have not departed widely from the despotism of the modern tailor. They have merely adopted new colors, such as green and brown, and yearn after odd but subdued tints for neck-clothes. It is hoped that as women have gone so far, men may have the courage to follow and throw off the yoke of the tyrannical tailor. Mr. Wilde's usual dress in the house is a plain brown cloth jacket, trimmed with red; brown trousers with red cord in the side, and invariably patent leather shoes. At morning receptions he wears a brown Prince Albert coat, and trousers of the same color. He has, so far in this country, worn his velvet knee-breeches only at his lecture. The velvet coat he wears with the costume is something like a swallow-tail, with very wide lapels, faced with silk.

As a lecturer, Mr. Hewitt thinks that Mr. Wilde will make a great hit. When he lectured in Chickering hall last week, he appeared on a stage for the first time in his life. He has a fine presence, an entrancing voice, with a peculiar inflection characteristic of Oxford men, and his natural gift of oratory is of high order.

Mr. Wilde is universally admired by the ladies he meets. But his "fatal gift of beauty" does not make him unsusceptible to the charms of American women, whom he thinks the most beautiful he ever saw. He was quite carried away at Jennie June Croly's the other evening by the focused radiance of Mary Anderson and Clara Morris.[1] And he is no less delighted with the New York society belles he has met. "I shouldn't be surprised," said Mr. Hewitt, "if Wilde carried back to England an American girl as his wife."

A pretty pamphlet of selections from the aesthete's poems is soon to be issued, and will be an effective document in the campaign of aestheticism in America.

1. Croly's reception: see p. 67, note 2.

"Oscar and the Barber," *The New York World, Semi-Weekly Edition* (New York, NY), 24 Jan. 1882, 2[1]

The German Artist Puzzled About "Dem Aesdetics," and the Apostle too "Lonely" to Speak.

"Vot is dot aesdetics?"

The above question was asked of a startled WORLD reporter yesterday afternoon by a placid-looking German barber, named Charley, who keeps a shop on Fourth avenue, in the neighborhood of Murray Hill.

"Why do you ask, Charley?"

"Vell, I see by dem papers all de time aesdetics. Nodings but aesdetics. Und also Oscar Vilde vos un aesdetics, ain't it?"

"What do you know about Oscar Wilde, Charley?"

"I know dot man. I haf me some bizness mit him vile he vas living around here."

"I suppose you shaved him?"

"No; I haf curled his hair."

"Curled his hair?"

"Yah! I haf! Von day about a week ago a black man comes in here and says he wants a parper to go by 46 Vest Twenty-eighth strett to see Oscar Vilde, who vants his hair dressed. I vent round, but he vasn't in. Den I vaited, and pretty soon Mr. Vilde came in. He had a big long sealskin coat, skin tight breeches dot ended by der knees und plack stockings und bumps on. He jumped into a chair and says, "Curl my hair!" und dot's all he said for five or six minutes. After a vile I says, 'It's a vine day,' and he says, 'My hair grows on der top so.'"

Here Charley imitated the action by raising his hands upwards on top of his head.

"Den pretty soon he says: 'Vot time it is?' I told him it is a quvarter to ten, and he says: 'Much obliged,' und dot's all."

"Has he nice hair? Easy to curl?"

1. It is possible that this is one of the many fabricated stories about Wilde that appeared in the American press in 1882. The article is included here because several details suggest that it may be genuine. It is plausible that Wilde's African American valet would have requested the barber attend Wilde's private address in West 28th Street. The address is given (although since it had been leaked in the *New York Star* it was perhaps common knowledge). Wilde's hair does appear to have been curled for the photographs taken by Sarony in January 1882; his hair is straighter in the photographs taken later that year (Cooper, J. (2019). 'A picturesque subject indeed!' The Sarony photographs of Oscar Wilde. *The Wildean*, *55*, 3–33, 10). The phonetic rendering of the barber's German accent, a common journalistic mannerism of the time, should not be taken as evidence that the story is false.

"No, sir! It vos as straight as a proom. But vot I vanted to know vos vot vos dem aesdetics—der hair or der short preeches? I don't catch on mit dem aesdetics, und I didn't ask Mr. Vilde, he vos so lonely like, all der time I vos at vork."

"Not Too Aesthetic to Eat," *New York Tribune* (New York, NY), 28 Jan. 1882, 8

Oscar Wilde arrived in this city yesterday morning from Baltimore. As the poet does not live by contemplating lilies when travelling he ate a hearty breakfast at the Grand Union Hotel. Then he took the first train for Albany, where he is to lecture tonight.[1]

"Mr. Wilde's lecture at Baltimore last night," said Colonel Morse, his agent, yesterday evening, "was a great success, notwithstanding all the talk there has been. Mrs. Carroll, whose reception he was to attend, you know, and Ross Winans were among those who occupied boxes.[2] There was a very large audience, and after the lecture Mr. Wilde had a supper with some Baltimore gentlemen. The night before he was given a reception by the Wednesday Club, the same which the newspapers said he had insulted. The whole trouble grew out of the error of one of my men, who made a mistake in delivering my instructions.[3] I have had about 200 applications for Mr. Wilde to lecture."

"Boucicault at Home," *The Sunday Herald* (Boston, MA), 29 Jan. 1882, 2[4]

Informal Chat with the Famous Author-Actor.

Something About His New Play.

His Ideas of Oscar Wilde's Management.

✂ *Several paragraphs that are unrelated to Wilde.*

1. Wilde lectured in Albany on 27 January and not the 28th as the article implies.
2. Ross Revillon Winans (1850–1912) was heir to the fortune amassed by his father Tom Winans (1820–1878), a railroad pioneer and early patron of Whistler.
3. Wilde had written to D'Oyly Carte a few days earlier to complain about "[t]he little wretched clerk or office boy you sent to me in Col. Morse's place" (CL, 130).
4. Quoted in OWDA, 117; and Pearson, 61. Referenced in Ellmann, 173/181. Boucicault was interviewed in Boston's Vendome Hotel, according to the reporter, "one day last week".

"By the way," said Mr. Boucicault, "speaking of American institutions,[1] reminds me that a friend of mine will be here shortly to study them.[2] Have you seen this?" He held up a New York paper, in which Mr. Oscar Wilde's portrait was printed. "This is a capital picture, and I am sending a number of these papers to mutual friends in London.[3] Have you met

MR. WILDE?

No? Then, of course, you know very little what sort of a man he is. The use to which those managing his American tour are putting him is simply disgraceful. He is a gentleman of refinement and eminently a scholar. They are making him a show. He is too simple and gentle in his nature to realize or even perceive his position. These speculators parade him as a kind of literary 'Dundreary,' endeavoring to persuade him that notoriety is reputation. The press seems to lend itself to this heartless exhibition, which may afford amusement to some, but will be fatal and ruinous to its object. Many are thus persuaded to believe that he is playing the fool's part, and is an accomplice in this showman's scheme. I wish to say emphatically this is a cruelly false impression. I have every right to say so, every right to feel hurt and indignant at the treatment he has suffered. There is no guile in him; he is the easy victim of those who expose him to ridicule and to the censure of the thoughtful. Those who have known him as I have, since he was a child at my knee, know that beneath the fantastic envelope in which his managers are circulating him, there is a noble, earnest, kind and loveable man."

"Miss Genevieve Ward," *Cincinnati Daily Gazette* (Cincinnati, OH), 3 Feb. 1882, 5[4]

HAS A CHARMING CONVERSATION WITH A GAZETTE REPRESENTATIVE.

One of the Most Brilliant American Women—Her Affectionate Regard for Cincinnati—What She Knows of Oscar Wilde and Mrs. Langtry.

✂ *Several paragraphs that are unrelated to Wilde.*

1. He had been speaking of American theatres.
2. Wilde had arrived in Boston early on the morning of 28 January and an interview with him appeared in the same edition: "The Aesthetic Apostle," *The Boston Sunday Globe* (Boston, MA), 29 Jan. 1882, 5, pp. 127–31.
3. Boucicault sent "a paper with a portrait [of Wilde]" to Mrs George Lewis, although it may have been a caricature rather than the "capital picture" he refers to here (CL, 135).
4. Ward was interviewed on 2 February in her suite at Cincinnati's Emery Hotel.

The conversation drifted, of course, to the aesthetic craze. Miss Ward knows Oscar Wilde well, and says he had a large following in London, though Whistler and Burne Jones, she thinks, outrank him as a leader in the Renaissance movement in which this utterly utter craze is but a fungus growth. Of Lady Wilde (Oscar's "mamma") she can not say too much in praise.[1] She is a woman of strong character, keen intellect, and has the most generous heart the world over. In personal appearance she is very tall, and has a long face, strongly marked characteristics which the aesthete inherits from her. Without being a fat woman, her arms and bust are something prodigious, and her costumes would have made Cruikshank or Cham die in aromatic delight.[2] In "Doblin's Swate city" Lady Wilde's house was a center of hospitality, and when she came to London with her sons her Saturdays were notable. She had at once, Miss Ward says, what an Englishwoman rarely attains to—a salon, and her society was sought by the brightest people in London. Willie Wilde, a very handsome man by the way, and the clever dramatic critic of Vanity Fair, lived with his mother, but Oscar set up his household gods with surroundings too too for any intuition but his own in Keats' house down by the shore of the Thames. Thence he sent invitations to the gay world and became the rage, realizing that imitation is the sincerest flattery. The professional beauties rallied about him, bringing their slaves with them, and when ladies disposed to be punctilious declined the young bachelor's invitations, then the billets ran "Mamma and I," and they came, of course, because all the world adored Lady Wilde. "They used to say he was a fool in London," Miss Ward says with a ripple of laughter, and now they say, "Ah, he is shrewd, been playing a part all this while to make money out of those Americans," and altogether he appears to be as little comprehended at home as he is in America.

✂ *Several paragraphs that are unrelated to Wilde.*

"The Question of the Hour," *The New York Herald* (New York, NY), 4 Mar. 1882, 9[3]

Shall the Homely Trousers be Superseded by Knee Breeches?

SOCIETY'S PEACE IN DANGER.

1. Oscar's "mamma": see p. 709, note 1.
2. British illustrator George Cruikshank (1792–1878), like his father Isaac (1764–1811) and Cham, caricatured outlandish fashions.
3. Kate Field had written a pair of articles for *Our Continent* (1 Mar. 1882, 47; 1 Mar. 1882, 63) advocating for men to adopt knee breeches.

A Lady Who Is in Favor of Oscar Wilde's Innovation.

"How do you suppose, from what you know of England, Oscar Wilde would have been received, if he went on a lecturing tour in that country, the same as he has done here? Would he be guyed and hooted?"

"I think not. The respect for caste over there is too strong. He would be listened to with respectful attention, though I recall the fact that when he appeared in the parquet of a theatre in London the first night "Patience" was produced the boys in the gallery poked fun at him. Delivering a lecture, however, would have been a different matter. Mr. Wilde became prominent entirely through *Punch*, the play of "Patience" and the newspapers, and no foreigner ever landed on these shores who had such full and free advertising. But for the press he would scarcely have been heard of."

"You have some hope, Miss Field, that the day will come when man, relinquishing his selfishness as well as his trousers and anxious to please woman, will kindly take to knee breeches?"

"I have. I don't despair. I have great confidence that the good things of the past which have been unwisely discarded will be revived, and that the poetry and beauty of life will yet be greatly enhanced."

"Gotham Gossip," *The Tribune* (Minneapolis, MN), 5 Mar. 1882, 1

Special correspondence of The Tribune.
　　New York, March 1, 1882.

OSCAR WILDE.

Col. Morse, who is D'Oyly Carte's business manager and who has had charge of Oscar Wilde's lecture tour in this country, was in jubilant spirits when I called to see him yesterday.

"Your aesthetic young man must be doing well in the West," said I.

"It's wonderful how he is drawing out there. Crowded houses everywhere he goes."[1]

---

1. This was true at the time the interview was conducted, when Wilde was boasting in a letter to Mrs George Lewis that "since Chicago [13 February] I have had two great successes: Cincinnati [23 February] where I have been invited to lecture a second time [...] and St Louis [25 Feb-

"How do they treat him?"

"Much better than he was treated here in the East. They don't guy him at all."

"Are any social attentions shown him?"

"He is invited out in every city he visits by the best society."

"Where is he to be this week?"

"Springfield, Ill.; Dubuque, Iowa; Rockford and Aurora. Next Sunday he will lecture in Milwaukee. Then he will take a run through Central Illinois. He may go to Minneapolis before his return."[1]

"Does he deliver the same lecture everywhere?"

"The subject is the same, but the matter is varied. He is very happy, I think, in this particular. He always incorporates something of local interest into his lectures. Next week he will lecture on a new subject at Chicago."[2]

"What is that?"

"'Art Decoration.' He prepared it at the suggestion of friends. It is devoted to what you may call a practical application of the principles of aesthetic art to everyday home life. In this he will give his views about ladies' dresses, the way men should dress, household furniture, tapestries, hangings, pictures, and all other forms of decoration."

"How does Mr. Wilde receive the fun that is poked at him, by this time?"

"He only laughs. He doesn't care a straw for it. Of course he bristles up when the fun-making degenerates to insult. That cartoon in The Washington Post, making him like a baboon was

SIMPLY OUTRAGEOUS."

"It is reported that Mr. Wilde paid for the printing of that. Is that so?"

"That statement is false straight through. The idea is simply preposterous!"[3]

---

ruary]" (CL, 143). By the time the interview was printed, however, Wilde was mid way through a less successful tour of smaller Midwestern towns, after which he wrote to Morse to complain that: "Such fiasco as the last ten days have given should be avoided" (CL, 146).

1. This is an accurate itinerary of Wilde's engagements in early March. He lectured in Minneapolis on 15 March. Before he returned to New York his tour was extended to California.

2. Wilde debuted *The House Beautiful* in Chicago on 11 March.

3. See "Oscar Wilde," *The Republican* (St. Louis, MO), 26 Feb. 1882, 13, p. 222, note 1. Morse wrote a letter of complaint to the editor of the *Post*, who declined to publish it. It appeared instead in *The Evening Critic* (Washington, DC), 23 Jan. 1882, 4:

WASHINGTON, Jan 22, 1882.

To the Editor Washington Post

SIR: I noticed in today's *Post* a cartoon which is an insult to a gentleman announced to lecture here under the management of Mr. R. D'Oyly Carte.

This seems to me to be a senseless exhibition of petty malignity and gratuitous malice which, both for the credit of your paper and American journalism, might well have been omitted.

When a speaker has declared himself before his audience then he becomes a legitimate subject for criticism, but an attempt like this to prejudice him in advance, without the shadow of a

The manager exhibited a scrap-book containing interviews with the apostle of beauty, editorial comments, reports of his lectures and cartoons and paragraphs from the comic papers. Taken all in all, it is the most remarkable scrap-book ever pasted together. It is seen that of late the poet has been the subject of much poetry—his admirers singing his praise in resonant lines, and the unappreciative Philistine indulging in good-humored satire that (the best of it) induces laughter at the end of every verse.

"What effect has Mr. Wilde's visit had on the sale of his poems?" I asked, resuming the conversation.

"It has increased it greatly. Three or four times as many are sold as there were before."[1]

"Is he going to publish anything in this country that has not been in print?"

"Rennell Rodd, one of his associates in England, is going to republish a book in a few days, called, I believe, 'Songs of the South [*sic*].'[2] It is to contain a preface written by Wilde. That will be all."

"When is Mr. Wilde going back to London?"

"Some time in April."

✂   *Several paragraphs that are unrelated to Wilde.*

"An Interview with Oscar Wilde's Brother," *The New Zealand Herald* (Auckland, NZ), 8 Apr. 1882, Supp. 2[3]

THE London Cuckoo prints the following amusing report of a chat with the brother of the long-haired esthetic who sits up with lilies and gazes soulfully at

---

reason, must merit and receive the condemnation of all who can comprehend that ill-taste and bad judgment do not improve the columns of any reputable paper.
Very truly yours,
W. F. Morse,
Business Manager for R. D'Oyly Carte.

In [late June 1882] Wilde wrote to Morse to take him to task for writing the letter: "No mention should have been made of the cartoon at Washington. I regard all caricature and satire as absolutely beneath notice." (CL, 174.) In fact, Wilde had already denied the rumour in an interview: see "Oscar Wilde," *The Dubuque Herald* (Dubuque, IA), 3 Mar. 1882, 4, p. 244.

1. Morse might be expected to say this, but his claim is borne out by an interview with a bookseller in Buffalo, where Wilde lectured on 8 February: "For several weeks before and after Oscar Wilde came here we had to continually order fresh consignments of his poems. The demand was something frightful; they went off like hot cakes." ("What Buffalonians Read," *The Buffalo Sunday Morning News* (Buffalo, NY), 5 Mar. 1882, 2.)

2. *Songs in the South*: the title of the English edition of Rodd's poems, republished in the United States as *Rose Leaf and Apple Leaf*.

3. Referenced in Sturgis, 173/168.

butterflies. It says:—While our reporter was turning over the leaves of a puerile production called Kottabos[1] a black-bearded, thick-lipped, almond-eyed, swarthy, satyr-like, Pan-all-over young man of about six feet high strode into the room, clad in a long dressing-gown, at the collar of which might be seen the slightest suggestion of a white unstarched garment, while at the nether end a pair of scraggy-looking naked ankles, the feet of which were encased in an old pair of red Turkish slippers, made their appearance. After a friendly appellation, "Will you have a brandy-and-soda, old boy, or a cigarette?" had been declined, we fell to work.

"I see you have been looking at Kottabos. It is very clever, is it not? My brother, Oscar, became a contributor at the age of 10, and even I myself have occasionally given them little things, all of which have been repeatedly reprinted and repaid for as original matter in several London journals—but mind that is a secret."

"Your brother, I understand, has received a prize for a copy of verses at the 'Maudlin' College;[2] is it worth much?"

"Not pecuniarily, but the *kudos* is great."

"Indeed, then I suppose all the Newdigate men have distinguished in literature?"

"Oh, no, indeed, *au moment*, I cannot recall any that have succeeded in literature except poor little Mallock, if you call his success, but socially it is of great advantage; you see, you go up to London labelled by the greatest university in the world 'a poet,' and people, whatever they may think, will not risk contradicting Oxford."

"I am to understand, then, that Oxford is warranted to supply the world with a real live poet every year, no matter at what level the brain power may be?"

"Exactly, but, you see, a great many Newdigate men don't understand the trick of advertisement, and so they drop out of sight. I had a letter from dear Oscar this morning to say that the Prince has been to tea with him."

"And has the Prince?"

1. *Kottabos, A College Miscellany* was a Trinity College, Dublin magazine named for the ancient Greek drinking game, the aim of which was to fling wine-lees at a target. It was edited by Robert Yelverton Tyrrell (1844–1914), a fellow of the college whom Wilde credited as one of his two most important tutors (the other was Mahaffy; Harris, 40). Both Wilde and his brother Willie published several works in *Kottabos*. Willie's first, a translation of a Victor Hugo poem, appeared in 1872 (Sturgis, 48/52); Oscar's was his poem *The Rose of Love, and with a Rose's Thorns* (later split in two and reprinted in *Poems* as *La Bella Donna della mia Mente* and *Chanson*; CW i, Nos. 9, 10), which was published in Trinity Term 1876 when he was aged 21.
2. The pun on Magdalen refers to the image of aesthetes as melancholy and world-weary.

"Ah, that I cannot say—but he says he has, and whether he has or not people will believe it and show Oscar the respect he deserves for being so clever. I would show you the letter, only I have just sent it to Lady Wilde."[1]

"And what does your brother mean to do for a livelihood?"

"Oh, he will probably marry an heiress."

"Then, if you had a son, and he did not happen to be as clever as your brother, but had sufficient knowledge of scansion to take the Newdigate, what would you do with him?"

"I would article him out to a good solicitor, so that the boy might not go off his head, and earn a tolerably honest livelihood."

"Is your brother really so fond of lilies and long matted hair as Mr. Du Maurier represents him to be?"

"Why, certainly, when their sex is feminine and they wear a red jersey; what do you think?"

Not knowing what to think, our reporter took up his hat to go.

"Well, goodbye, old chappie. I must go and dictate a political leader to Dr. Shaw for Saunder's tomorrow, and I dine Dr. Nedley in the evening. Take my word for it, my brother is no fool. I am going to perform at Carrie Nilson's benefit tomorrow. Give us a look in and a line—" And the door shut on our reporter, who wandered away thinking that Willy wasn't much of a fool, whatever his brother, whom he hasn't yet met, may be.

"The New Costume," *The New York World, Semi-Weekly Edition* (New York, NY), 5 May 1882, 6[2]

How the Aesthetic Young Men of New York Are Expected to Dress.

Mr. Oscar Wilde is coming back, like young Lochinvar, "out of the West" like a giant refreshed.[3] He has been so enthusiastically welcomed from Chicago to

1. The Prince of Wales: see p. 309, note 2.
2. Printed simultaneously as "The New Costume," *Daily Gazette* (Wilmington, DE), 5 May 1882, 3. Reprinted as "Oscar's New Clothes," *St. Louis Post-Dispatch* (St. Louis, MO), 8 May 1882, 3. Excerpted in "Oscar Wilde's New Clothes," *Hartford Daily Courant* (Hartford, CT), 13 May 1882, 6; "New Costume for Aesthetic Young Men," *The Pall Mall Gazette* (London, UK), 22 May 1882, 10; and "Charming Oscar," *Fort Wayne Daily Gazette* (Fort Wayne, IN), 4 June 1882, 3. Quoted in Ellmann, 177/186. The report also appeared in many small town papers in the United States and the United Kingdom.
3. Lochinvar is the romantic hero of the ballad *Marmion* (1808) by Sir Walter Scott. The stanzas telling the story of Lochinvar were the most popular and were widely anthologised. They contain the lines: "O, young Lochinvar is come out of the west, | Through all the wide Border his steed was the best; | And save his good broadsword, he weapons had none, | He rode all un-

Leadville as the apostle of a new era that he intends to grapple with the great clothes-question in deadly earnest. He has planned and furnished the drawings to a New York artist in toggery for two costumes not only "utterly utter," but lovely and exhilarating beyond all modern comparison, in which within a few days New York may expect to see him illuminate our public places.[1] Mr. Wirtz, the fortunate artist who has been intrusted with this commission, was kind enough yesterday to give a reporter of THE WORLD the following lucid and instructive sketch of the coming garb:[2]

"Well, I am making two suits for Mr. Wilde according to his order and drawings. One to be of black velvet and the other to be of the shade of a lake glistening in the moonlight. The shade is called *couleur du lac au clair de la lune*." This explanation seemed perfectly satisfactory, but rather general, and the artist was asked for details. These the artist gave. He said that there were two suits, one black and the other mouse-color. The black suit has a plain black velvet doublet fitting tight to the body, without any visible buttons, after the style of Francis I., the lower part of the sleeves being of embossed velvet, with embroidered field-flower designs, and fitting tight to the arm. The upper part of the arm is to be in large puffs of the same material, only of a larger pattern, and the body of plain velvet. The sleeves are of two designs of brocaded velvet edged with a delicate ruffle of *mousseline de soie*.[3] Around the neck is also a narrow frill in three rows of the same material as that which edges the sleeves. The breeches are to come to the knee and to be tight fitting, with two small buttons at the bottom. The stockings are to be of black silk and the shoes cut low and secured with a silver buckle. It may be interesting to know that the following are the dimensions of the costumes in inches: Trousers, 30 inches; bottom of doublet, 45¼; waist, 38½, and breast, 36½. The puffs at the upper part of the sleeves 32 inches, at the bottom 11 inches, the collar being 17 inches in size.[4]

Yesterday Colonel Morse received a telegram from his agent, who is with Mr. Wilde, informing Colonel Morse that Mr. Wilde had received an offer from Australia for the summer. Colonel Morse said he had several engagements for Mr. Wilde through the South, but if there was a better opening in Australia of course

---

armed, and he rode all alone. | So faithful in love, and so dauntless in war, | There never was knight like the young Lochinvar."

1. Wilde had written to Morse from St. Louis (c. 25 February) requesting that his manager have a theatrical costumier make two outfits in the style of Francis I: "They will excite a great sensation." He further instructed Morse not to mention his name, an instruction it appears Morse ignored (CL, 141).

2. "Mr. Wirtz" is presumably the John C. Wirtz Jr., dressmaker, who in 1882 operated premises at 25 East 20th Street, overlooking Gramercy Park.

3. A thin silk fabric with a texture like that of muslin (OED).

4. The *Courant* has the bottom of the doublet as 42¼ inches. The *Post-Dispatch* has the puffs at the upper part of the sleeves at 31 inches.

Mr. Wilde would go there. Colonel Morse said that Mr. Wilde's share of his lectures would amount to over $30,000.

"Oscar Wilde," *The Atlanta Constitution* (Atlanta, GA), 27 June 1882, 5[1]

A Talk With the Advance Agent of the Apostle of Aesthetics.

In conversation with Mr. Frank Gray, Oscar Wilde's advance agent, he said yesterday: "We could not give Atlanta the slip. In fact Mr. Wilde would hardly consent to return to his native land without first having planted his feet upon Atlanta soil. He will therefore lecture at DeGive's Opera house on the evening of next Tuesday upon the subject of "Decorative Art," one of his favorite themes. He is in New Orleans now and will lecture there tonight. He will spend tomorrow with Hon. Jefferson Davis, at Beauvoir, by special invitation.[2] He will be in Mobile Wednesday and at Montgomery Thursday. I will go down to Columbus tonight and make arrangements for him to lecture there Friday night. He never lectures on Saturday nights. Monday he will be in Macon and on Tuesday night he will be in Atlanta."

"Leaving Atlanta, where will he go?"

"His route from Atlanta will be by Augusta, Savannah and Charleston. He will sail from New York for Japan on the 31st of July."[3]

"How much will he carry with him?"

"The profits of his American tour, which commenced in January, will foot up about thirty thousand dollars, nearly all of which is net, as Mr. Wilde is not extravagant.[4] He has little chance to spend money as he is lionized everywhere."

"How much time does his lecture occupy?"

"From an hour and ten minutes to an hour and twenty-five. The titles of his lectures are "Decorative Art," and "The House Beautiful."

"Does he wear that knee breeches rig on the streets?"

"No. He calls that an evening dress and wears it only on evenings and at his lectures."

Mr. Wilde is about five feet and three to six inches high, has large features and a heavy mouth. He wears long hair, has brown eyes and is said by some of

1. Quoted in OWDA, 371–2.

2. This interview must have been given on 26 June. Wilde lectured for the second time in New Orleans on 26 June and visited Jefferson Davis the following day.

3. Gray describes Wilde's lecture dates correctly. Lectures in Wilmington, Norfolk, and Richmond were later added to the tour of the South. Wilde did not sail for Japan.

4. Wilde's extravagance: see p. 499, note 2.

his admirers to be a charming conversationalist.[1] He is travelling under the management of Mr. Peter Tracy, with Mr. Frank Gray as advance representative. He has a private secretary, Mr. J. S. Vale, and a valet. He will spend only one night in Atlanta.

"Theatrical World," *Truth* (New York, NY), 17 Sep. 1882, 5

✂ *Several paragraphs that are unrelated to Wilde.*

Colonel W. F. Morse is the gentleman who has the distinguished honor of piloting Mr. Oscar Wilde through America, and is now a sort of Mentor to the long-haired apostle of aestheticism. Colonel Morse relates some very harrowing experiences while en route with the unshorn Oscar. He says that Wilde was apparently not regarded by the American people as a gentleman, nor scarcely as a human being. They followed him about the streets and hooted at him, and paid him no more respect than they would have accorded to Barnum's "What-is-it."

"Of the herd I expected nothing more," said Morse, "for gamins is gamins, the whole world over; but I certainly expected better treatment from those who appeared to be ladies and gentlemen in every other respect. While we were at Saratoga elegantly dressed people of both sexes would form a circle about Mr. Wilde and examine him in much the same manner as they did Jumbo at the Madison Square Garden.[2] But they were not content with staring, and made all sorts of remarks, the majority of which, you may rest assured, were not complimentary. I used to git [*sic*] fighting mad, but Wilde took it philosophically, and coolly ignored everything."

Morse also told me that Wilde is now busily engaged in revising his play, "Vera," which he hopes to produce in America the present season. I had hoped that the time of Oscar's departure was drawing nigh, but as we have tolerated him as a lecturer, I suppose that we will give him audience as a dramatist. Morse says that the Apostle is the best informed man concerning stage matters that he ever met, either in this country or any other, and that if "Vera" is produced it will be found to be a remarkably strong play. This may all be true, but as Morse is Wilde's press agent, I am compelled by experience to accept his statements in this respect cum grano salis.

1. Wilde was over six feet tall and was said to have blue or grey eyes. It seems unlikely that Gray would have provided false information, so the reporter must have guessed at traits that could not be determined from photographs.
2. In 1882 P. T. Barnum brought the elephant Jumbo to America.

"Madame Christine Nilsson," *The New York Herald* (New York, NY), 25 Oct. 1882, 5[1]

Arrival of the Swedish Nightingale on the Gallia.

A CHATTY INTERVIEW.

The Popular Prima Donna Discourses About Herself and Others.

HER OPINION OF OSCAR WILDE.

Then some one remarked that Oscar Wilde had met Mrs. Langtry the day before.[2]

"Oh, is Oscar Wilde here?" she asked. I shall be delighted to see him. Has he cut his hair yet? What on earth is he doing over here?"

"Making money," was the response.

"What do you think of Mr. Wilde, madame?"

"Why, I think he is a— Oh, but you mustn't publish this."

"Why?"

"Well, I don't care if you do. I think he is not such a—"

"Fool as he looks," concluded an auditor as she hesitated.

"Oh, no!" she responded, laughing, "not really that you know, but something of that kind. Really now, you know, without joking, he can be very serious and very nice to talk to when he wants to."

1. Nilsson arrived in New York on her fourth visit to America after an absence of eight years. She was interviewed in her stateroom by a group of reporters who had sailed out to meet the SS *Gallia*.

2. Langtry had arrived in New York on the 23rd and Wilde had met her. See "Mrs. Langtry Arrives," *The News and Courier* (Charleston, SC), 26 Oct. 1882, 1, pp. 478–83; "The Lily of Jersey Here," *The Times* (Philadelphia, PA), 24 Oct. 1882, 1, 484–7; and "The Jersey Lily," *The Boston Herald* (Boston, MA), 24 Oct. 1882, 4, pp. 721–5.

"Mrs. Langtry's Visit," *The New York Herald* (New York, NY), 26 Oct. 1882, 6[1]

ACTIVE PREPARATIONS FOR HER AMERICAN DEBUT—SHE SEES "PATIENCE"
AND "THE RIVALS"—ENTHUSIASTIC OVER THE AUTUMN FOLIAGE.

✄ *Several paragraphs that are unrelated to Wilde.*

When a reporter accosted her [Langtry] as the theatre was cleared and the hum of the retiring audience died away she said:—"I am sorry I was not able to be here earlier. I only saw the end of the performance."[2]

"It pleased you then?"

"I liked all I saw of it very much indeed."

"Acting and singing both?"

"Assuredly."

"Miss Russell?"[3]

"Oh isn't she pretty?" exclaimed the English beauty with a charming sincerity that proved her eager to yield to others the praise of which she had been so lavishly the recipient.

"And Mr. Howson?"

"Bunthorne, you mean? Why, he dresses for Oscar Wilde, doesn't he?"

This naïve query being answered in the affirmative Mrs. Langtry with apparent surprise said:—

"Oh! yes. I remember now that I heard it was he who was imitated here in all the plays in which aestheticism entered."

"Such is not the case in England then?"

"No, it is not. Bunthorne as played there is dressed after a countryman of yours—Mr. Whistler, a very distinguished artist. The tuft on the forehead and some other peculiarities of the 'make-up' are characteristic of him."[4]

✄ *Several paragraphs that are unrelated to Wilde.*

1. Quoted in Schroeder, 250.

2. Langtry had been rehearsing for her American stage debut at Abbey's Park Theatre and had arrived at the Grand Opera House for the matinee performance of *Patience* just before the duet between Bunthorne and Lady Jane ("So go to him, and say to him").

3. Lillian Russell (1860/1861–1922) was an American actress and singer. She was playing the title role in *Patience*. Like Langtry she was reputed for her beauty.

4. Whistler had dark hair with a single lock of white. See also [John Black], "Interview with a Theatrical Manageress," *The South Australian Advertiser* (Adelaide, SA), 4 Aug. 1885, 6, p. 794.

"Mme. Christine Nilsson," *The Chicago Daily Tribune* (Chicago, IL), 5 Dec. 1882, 5[1]

Her Views on America, Chicago, Wilde, Langtry, and Patti.

✂ *Several paragraphs that are unrelated to Wilde.*

At this stage of the conversation Mme. Nilsson asked:

"Did Oscar Wilde visit you?"[2]

The reporter replied in the affirmative.

"He ought to have been taken by the ear and taken to the boat and driven out of this country. What right has he to come here and say that everything American is all wrong? I think that your people are too good-natured or they never would stand it. I know I shouldn't put up with his nonsense. You know in Europe he doesn't appear clad as he does here. That wouldn't be tolerated there. The ladies are taken by that lock of his on his forehead. The idea of a sunflower being pretty! It reminds me with its yellow color of paleness and sickness. I like the lilies, there is nothing more perfect than the lily-of-the-valley. But that sunflower—if that is estheticism, I am not esthetic. That craze has been the means of accumulating a mass of worthless rubbish in lots of houses. I met Oscar Wilde in London once, where we were both guests, and he was to take me down to dinner. He commenced to talk his nonsense and pose to me as were going to the dining-room. I said to him: 'Look here, Mr. Wilde, Mme. Nilsson will put up with no such stuff. This is all put on, and there is nothing in it but nonsense.' Mr. Wilde said: 'Thank you. You are the first sensible woman and true friend that I've met.' After that he acted as a man should and talked sensibly. Some days after he sent me a volume of his poems, appropriately inscribed. But he is not considered a poet in Europe. When I sang last Saturday in Steinway Hall I saw Mr. Wilde sitting in a front row in one of those affected positions of his, with his shoulders one way, his head another, and his body anywhere.[3] I was singing a little Swedish ballad, and it just occurred to me, I am so full of mischief, that it might be a good thing to imitate him, but I thought that the audience might not like it, so I didn't do it."

✂ *Several paragraphs that are unrelated to Wilde.*

---

1. Reprinted as "Christine Nilsson," *The Topeka Daily Capital* (Topeka, KS), 8 Dec. 1882, 2.

2. Nilsson is asking if Wilde visited Chicago.

3. Nilsson sang at New York's Steinway Hall on the evening of Tuesday 28 November and the afternoon of Saturday 2 December.

"Lily Langtry's Friend," *Buffalo Evening News* (Buffalo, NY), 15 Dec. 1882, 3

THE BOY GEBHARD WHO FOLLOWED HER TO BOSTON.[1]

The Facts of the Globe Theater Trouble—A Letter From the Prince of Wales That Did Not Open All the Doors of New York Society—Oscar Wilde with the Shakes.

✂ *An account of various scandals relating to Lillie Langtry: her inability to gain access to New York high society, and her association with Frederick Gebhard in Boston. An interview with Mrs Labouchère conducted by a representative of the* New York Star.

The *Star* tried to get the views of Mr. Oscar Wilde on the misconduct of his fair countrywoman, and with this intention went in search of a well-known poet who resides in the vicinity of the Gilsey House, and whose admiration for the aesthete and intimacy with him led the reporter to believe that he could furnish the present address of Mr. Wilde. The two gentlemen have become, if possible, warmer friends than were Mmes. Labouchère and Langtry.[2]

"Mr. Wilde is very much depressed; he is really ill," said the poet.

"Not on Mrs. Langtry's account, I hope?" said the reporter.

"No, I think not," continued the poet. "It is malaria that has taken hold of him. He had a chill yesterday, and another is expected tomorrow."

"This is very sad," said the reporter.

"Yes; he is naturally of a robust constitution, although he does not look so. He will probably soon return to England. The climate does not at all agree with him."

With his eyes "in a wild frenzy rolling" the poet dashed back upstairs,[3] and the reporter started for the temporary abode of the victim of malaria. Oscar is in apartments on East [*sic*] Eleventh street. The house is a common red brick one, and the hall has a desolate appearance—quite in keeping with the very too too [*illeg.*]tness of aestheticism. A faint [?perfume] of boiled cabbage floated out [?as a] servant opened the door.

1. In the source the name is spelt "Gebhart".

2. The anonymous poet may be Edgar Fawcett. Fawcett was among the literary men with whom Wilde "fraternized most freely" in the months before his departure from America ("From New York," *Buffalo Commercial Advertiser* (Buffalo, NY), 6 Oct. 1882, 1; "Oscar Wilde's Flight," *St. Louis Globe Democrat* (St. Louis, MO), 31 Dec. 1882, 6). Wilde had complimented Fawcett's poetry, and Fawcett would later visit Wilde's home in Tite Street.

3. The reference is to Shakespeare's *A Midsummer Night's Dream* (V, 1), in which Theseus describes how "The poet's eye, in fine frenzy rolling, | Doth glance from heaven to earth, from earth to heaven".

"Mr. Wilde is not at home," said she. The girl actually looked frightened, and repeated her assurances, so the reporter was obliged to depart.

"How They Took Oscar In," *The Sun* (New York, NY), 29 Dec. 1882, 1[1]

TONY DREXEL'S SON INTRODUCES THE POET TO GENUINE BUNCO.

Scarcely Any Money in the Operation—Mr. Wilde Stops his Checks for $3,700 and Some of Them Come Back to the Police by Mail—Hungry Joe Disappears, but Returns After Mr. Wilde's Departure and Gives a Childlike Version of the Sad Affair.

The bunco "joints," which are the headquarters of the confidence operators, closed with mysterious unanimity throughout the city on Dec. 14. and all the games with which the operators were wont to swindle their victims were stopped until Wednesday. The Cunarder Bothnia started for Europe with Oscar Wilde as a passenger on that morning at 7 o'clock, and by 9, when the Englishman had passed Sandy Hook, the bunco dice throwing and other devices were going on as usual.

The cause of this sudden cessation of very profitable business was an adventure of Mr. Wilde with one of the most successful of the bunco steerers in the metropolis, James Mitchell, alias Selleck, alias "Hungry Joe," and two confederates, who all left the city within a few hours after meeting Mr. Wilde. They thought he might get them arrested.

Mr. Wilde's experience with the bunco men was exceptional. The story as told by bunco men themselves is that Mr. Wilde was met on the morning of Dec. 14 as he was walking in Madison square, by a very well dressed and affable Englishmen. At least the stranger appeared to be an Englishman, for "Hungry Joe," who has been laying plans with his confederates for over a fortnight to catch the lover of the beautiful in art, and made use of his cleverest disguise and assumed the English accent and drawl to perfection. The stranger stopped and gazed earnestly at Mr. Wilde a few moments, and then, as if his doubts were set at rest, held out his hand with frank cordiality and said:

1. This article about Wilde's encounter with conmen in New York includes interviews with "Hungry Joe" and with Captain Williams, the police officer to whom Wilde allegedly reported the crime. Williams's interview also appeared in "Oscar Fleeced at Banco," *The New York Times* (New York, NY), 29 Dec. 1882, 5. The final two paragraphs, in which it is revealed that the person conned was not, in fact, Wilde, imply that the article was fabricated. However, it lacks many of the more outlandish elements of other burlesque interviews.

"Why, Mr. Wilde, how do you do? You have hardly changed a particle since I saw you in my father's office some months ago."

Mr. Wilde did not recognize the affable stranger. This was what was expected, however, and Hungry Joe, with perfect good nature, continued: "I see you do not recognize me. I am Tony Drexel, son of Mr. Drexel of Drexel, Morgan & Co.; don't you recollect?"[1]

He mentioned some circumstances connected with Mr. Wilde's visit to the banking house, incidents that he had got hold of only by weeks of patient investigation. They were recalled with such accuracy and the whole proceeding was so evidently in good faith that Mr. Wilde was disarmed of suspicion, and, returning the grip of "Hungry Joe's" hand, exclaimed with some vigor:

"I'm really glad to see you, sir. I am happy to meet an honest man in America."

Passing over this unexpected compliment to his calling, Hungry Joe talked on pleasantly and skilfully. They walked on down Broadway, chatting, until, when the proper moment came, Hungry Joe produced the usual bait in the bunco game.

"I have a lottery ticket here," said he, "which has drawn a prize, and if you'll come with me to the office I'll just get it cashed. It's right in the neighborhood."

By this time Hungry Joe had got Mr. Wilde to Fifteenth street, near Third avenue, where two confederates were waiting in a private apartment that had been engaged a long time before and fitted up expensively to represent a lottery office. When the two entered they found two men behind the counter engaged in sorting tickets and manipulating a roll of bank bills and loose silver, of which commodities there appeared to be a good deal in the drawer. Hungry Joe walked up to the counter and presented his lottery ticket. The confederates made a mock examination of their books as if to verify the number, and then counted out the money and paid it over to Hungry Joe. Then the latter explained to Mr. Wilde, who became deeply interested, that there was an opportunity for any one to make a large amount of money by investing in a similar lottery ticket. The risk was so very small, he said, that Mr. Wilde had practically every chance in his favor.

Mr. Wilde consented to try his fortune. The men behind the counter produced the large envelope with which bunco is played. In the envelope were placed a large number of tickets with black numbers on them. These it is the custom to slip into the envelope in the presence of the "guy" or greenhorn, who is allowed to pick out a number. Mr. Wilde's new-found friend bought a chance and

---

1. Wilde had visited the offices of Drexel, Morgan and Company earlier in the year (Friedman, 235). It is unclear why the conman would have affected an English accent as Anthony Joseph Drexel Jr. (1864–1934) had, like his father, been born and raised in the United States.

picked out a winning number, and then Mr. Wilde did the same thing, his friend volunteering to advance the money just to show him "how very easy it is to win, you know." Then Mr. Wilde was induced to play on his own responsibility, Hungry Joe playing "capper" and prompting him. The man behind the counter picked out a card that was number 135, and accidentally bent the edge a little.

"See that," whispered Hungry Joe. "He has bent that card. Watch it and pick it out when you take your choice and you'll win sure."

The man behind the counter, of course having bent the card in order to deceive Mr. Wilde, managed to straighten it again and bend the next number, 133, which he put into the envelope with apparent carelessness. Mr. Wilde saw it and thought it was 135. But the card had been deftly "flashed" upon him, and he was greatly amazed to find, on picking it out, that he had the wrong number.

The man behind the counter, however, appeared to be uneasy and exclaimed, "By gracious, you came mighty close to it, sir. It was the very next number to it."

Mr. Wilde paid the loss and consented to play several times. He paid in checks each time until he had been "caught" for $2,700.

By this time he began to be convinced that he had fallen into the hands of swindlers, and, without waiting to pick up his fur-lined overcoat, which he had thrown aside on the counter, he made a dash for the street.[1] The bunco men did not dare to intercept him, for fear that he would raise an outcry and bring the police and other occupants of the building, who do not appear to have been privy to the bunco swindle, to his assistance. He ran to the corner as swiftly as his feet could carry him, and, jumping into a cab, shouted to the driver to go to the Madison Square Bank as fast as his horses could travel.

The driver divined that something unusual had happened, whipped up his horses, and in ten minutes brought them to a stop in front of the bank. Mr Wilde sprang out, and, hurrying into the building, cried, with evident emotion, to the cashier:

"Stop payment on three checks that bear my signature. I have just been swindled into signing them."

The cashier promised to comply with his request, and Mr. Wilde reentered his cab and drove to the Thirtieth street station, where he asked to see Capt. Wil-

---

1. This element of the story seems improbable, as Wilde owned the fur-lined coat until he went into prison in 1895. In 1897 he wrote to Robert Ross from Reading Gaol to ask him to recover the coat, which, in his absence, his brother had pawned: "it was all over America with me, it was at all my first nights, it knows me perfectly, and I really want it," (CL, 785). It is possible that this is not the coat referred to in the article: John Cooper has pointed out that Wilde was photographed by Napoleon Sarony in 1882 wearing two different, but similar, fur-lined coats (Cooper, J. (2019). 'A picturesque subject indeed!' The Sarony photographs of Oscar Wilde. *The Wildean*, *55*, 3–33, 26–7). But it is perhaps more likely that the reporter fabricated the detail.

liams. After being introduced to the Captain by Sergeant Westervelt, Mr. Wilde asked for a private interview, and Capt. Williams admitted him to his private room. When the door had been closed Mr. Wilde with charming frankness said:

"I've just been making an ass of myself."

"You don't say so," said the Captain. "How?"

Mr. Wilde explained. He gave a description of the person calling himself Drexel, and when a picture of Hungry Joe was shown to him recognized it at once. Two of Mr. Wilde's checks were sent by mail to Capt. Williams on the following Monday. This last afforded Mr. Wilde great relief, as he was afraid some innocent person would lose money on the checks.

The companionable, smooth-faced, lantern-jawed young man who occupies a bench in Madison Square Park on sunshiny afternoons was there as usual on Wednesday. His silk hat was new and glossy, and his whole get up was spick and span. Best known as Hungry Joe,[1] he is also called John Jacob Astorhaus, Samuel Johnson, James John Smith, and other names. He had just come back from out of town.

Notwithstanding his good clothes, Hungry Joe wore an air of melancholy when he made room for a reporter upon his bench. He said in a confidential whisper: "Business is getting deuced dull. I haven't caught on to anybody for two hours. If this sort of thing is to last I shall have to hire rooms in the almshouse. I saw four black cats one morning last week, and again the same night. That means the worst sort of luck, and we made the worst sort of a mess of it with Oscar Wilde."

The reporter asked how that was. "Ask me no questions and you'll get no lies," said Hungry Joe. The reporter asked innumerable questions, and finally Hungry Joe told his story as the version of the Wilde affair that he desired to have live in fame:

"We don't know so much about Wilde as we do about the other fellow, and we know deuced little about either. The fellows had read so much about Oscar Wilde in the newspapers that they thought they must have a go at him. The first time the plan was thought of was when he came back to the city and stopped at the Fifth Avenue Hotel with an English lord—Lord knows who. The first report the man that was set to watch made was that Mr. Wilde was very close, and that it would take a hard pull to get any money out of him. One fine morning he moved over to the Brunswick. That was an advantage to us. Our man had got to be known in the Fifth Avenue. Then Wilde climbed up to the Windsor. We could

1. Note that in Williams's account it is Hungry Joe who impersonates Drexel and steers Wilde to the gambling den. The same is true in Williams's account as given in "Oscar Fleeced at Banco," *The New York Times* (New York, NY), 29 Dec. 1882, 5, pp. 784–6. Here, Hungry Joe gives a version of events in which another "young man" is the steerer.

not make out what was the matter. A plan to strike him was attempted at the Windsor. Somehow or other he had a dreadful lot of business on hand up there and was too busy to be sociable. In a short time he dropped down into West Eleventh street—48 I think was the number.[1] Someone said that he had lost a pile of money in Wall street. That was news to the boys, and they set about investigating the story. Of course, if Oscar Wilde spent his money in Wall street he was of no particular use to the boys. They discovered that he had not lost his money, but that his several removals were part of a plan of economy which Mr. Wilde had imposed on himself.

"When he got nicely settled in Eleventh street he had more time than usual on his hands. He had grown good-natured besides. Early one Friday forenoon a young man accosted Mr. Wilde on Fifth avenue, just below Delmonico's. Mr. Wilde seemed quite taken with the young man. There was a good deal of talk. I don't know on what tack the young man steered Mr. Wilde, but he took him into a house on Fifteenth street, near Third avenue. An actor that Wilde had known lived thereabouts, and Wilde mentioned the fact to his companion. When Wilde came in he commented upon the appearance of the room, saying that there was too much red. After a little shying of dice in which a great pile of money changed hands, Wilde was asked to take a hand in. At once he set to work, and won, I think, $150. He put that by in an inside pocket, in spite of the protests of the young man who had brought him in. The next time Wilde lost $50. Then followed another $50. From all accounts, it was thought better to play light, and, as Wilde became excited, to come in with the big licks. His next losses were $125, $200, and $300 in bills. It surprised everybody to find that he had so much money about him, and that he was so cool. He had recourse in the next game to the $150 stored in the inside pocket. He lost. Then he tossed back his hat, and accused the man who was playing with him of cheating. There was a long growl. Wilde apologized, and paid the $150 in bills. Next he lost $187, and gave us a check on the Fifth Avenue Bank. The boys knew he had no account there, and told him so, but he insisted that he had. The next loss he paid with a check on the Madison Square Bank. 'That's more like it,' said the boss bugler. The next was on the Madison Square Bank, and so was the next.[2]

"Just here the fellows began to suspect that a job had been put up on them, and that the police were somewhere around. But they consulted the sentinels outside and concluded to go ahead. The next play Wilde got terribly mad, and said that the boys were a gang of swindlers, and that he wanted his money and checks back. He was told that he would get them all back in time. He became

---

1. Wilde had rooms at 48 West 11th Street from November 1882 (CL, 189).

2. Wilde had an account at the Madison Square Bank. See "Mr Wilde Closes his Bank Account," *The Sun* (New York, NY), 27 Dec. 1882, 1, p. 500.

more excited then, and cried in a most piteous voice that the savings of his trip were gone. This made some of the fellows sad. Wilde was then for striking a bargain. He said that he did not know how much he had lost, but he would give his check for $3,200 for all the money we had got. He was told to keep his $3,200 check. Then he threatened us with arrest. He was told that publicity would be unpleasant for him. Then he wilted, and made no further efforts to get his money. All he wanted was to be free. He promised to make only ordinary efforts to get his money back, and after some more parley was allowed to go out. An account of stock was taken. The profits were found to be $3,937.

"It occurred to one of the boys that one of the greenbacks looked queer. Then the boys looked over the whole lot. They were all counterfeit. Even the boys' own $150 package that had passed a few minutes in Mr. Wilde's overcoat had come out counterfeits. The signature on the check was not Oscar Wilde's signature.

"This was very gloomy. The boys waited, but nobody sent them back their $150 by mail or express. The boys don't know who the bogus Oscar was. They wish they did."

"Oscar Fleeced at Banco," *The New York Times* (New York, NY), 29 Dec. 1882, 5[1]

HOW MR. WILDE LEARNED THE GAME FROM MR. DREXEL.

THE BANCO MAN IDENTIFIED AS "HUNGRY JOE"—WILDE'S VISIT TO CAPT. WILLIAMS—CHECKS FOR $1,160 RETURNED.

The story that Oscar Wilde fell an easy victim to "banco" operators was truer than many stories which come to New York by way of the country. Capt. Alexander S. Williams, of the Twenty-ninth Precinct, to whom Mr. Wilde applied for advice and related his adventure, said last night that Mr. Wilde having left America, it would do no harm to tell the facts which were bound to come out in time. It would also save him (Capt. Williams) some annoyance, as "a small million" of persons had asked him about the story and had been given evasive explanations. "Two weeks ago today, in the afternoon," said the Captain, "Oscar Wilde came to this station-house in a hack. He was ill at ease and in a hurry, and told the Sergeant he wanted to see the Captain privately. Well, he came into my room, sat down on that lounge, shook back his hair, threw open his coat so as to show an expanse of white shirt front, arranged his neatly cased legs to show their

---

1. Quoted in OWDA, 439; Pearson, 76–7; Ellmann, 190/200; and Sturgis, 268/255.

shape, stroked them with one hand, looked aesthetic, and said to me, 'You've had a long and various experience in Police business, Capt. Williams?' I replied that I had had a little experience during a long term of service. Then he continued: 'And I suppose you've seen and heard of people making fools of themselves?' I admitted that I had, and he said with an outburst of confidence: 'Well, I've been making a damned fool of myself!' Oh, he said 'damned,' and with emphasis. I asked him what was the trouble, and he told me the old story of a 'banco' swindle in which he figured."

The story Mr. Wilde told Capt. Williams is the stereotyped one. He was walking early in the afternoon in Fifth-avenue, near Fifteenth or Sixteenth streets, when a well-dressed man, whose manners were far from common, accosted him by name, said he was "young Drexel," and that, although he had often seen Mr. Wilde at the firm's office down town, he had never had the advantage of making his acquaintance. Mr. Wilde had had dealings with Drexel, Morgan & Co., and believed the fellow. They had a pleasant chat of a few minutes over ordinary topics, and Mr. Wilde was about to leave, when his friend, Mr. Drexel, spoke of an odd occurrence that he ventured to say had never happened to Mr. Wilde. Mr. Wilde was disposed to hear about it, and Mr. Drexel informed him that a few days ago, to get rid of a fellow who importuned him, he bought a lottery ticket. He was convinced that the money was thrown away—in fact, it was his first venture in such a chance—but, happening that morning to look over a list of the lucky numbers drawn in the lottery of which he had a ticket, he discovered that he had drawn a prize of $500. Mr. Wilde thought this extremely odd, and when Mr. Drexel asked him to see him draw his money, and then accompany him to friends in Fifth-avenue, Mr. Wilde consented and went to a house on the east side of the City, perhaps in Fifteenth-street. They entered a queer sort of office, in which were several very busy persons and a man who appeared to be a sort of cashier. He took Mr. Drexel's winning ticket, handed him what appeared to be $500, and asked him what he proposed to do about the "half ticket." This was the opening of the "banco" game. Mr. Wilde was not able to remember all that passed, but he had a jumbled recollection that the "half ticket" was a sort of bonus with the $500, that could be "played off" with a chance of winning much money; that "for the fun of it and the good of the house," Mr. Drexel played, that he was lucky and sure of winning a large sum, but that he had to make a show of a certain amount, and that the gambling infection seized on Mr. Wilde. First he lent Mr. Drexel his check for $60, then one for $100, and finally one for $1,000. The cashier, as soon as the last check was placed with Mr. Drexel's pile, and the other checks, made a "drawing," and announced that Mr. Drexel had lost. The stakes were seized and it was now time to get rid of Mr. Wilde. As is usual, a fuss was made by Mr. Drexel, who insisted that "his friend, Mr. Wilde," should receive back his checks. The "keeper of the joint," as the cashier is called in "banco" parlance, replied with asperity that the concern did not give back any checks, and that if Mr. Drexel had borrowed any money from Mr. Wilde to lose Mr. Drexel was well able to pay Mr. Wilde. Mr. Drexel left the house with Mr. Wilde, conducted him a safe distance, and went away saying he was "going to see about it." Then Mr. Wilde was convinced that he had been swindled by a trick just gotten up for countrymen, and in time so perfected as to scoop in Bunthornes. Mr. Wilde called a hack, told the driver to hurry to the Madison Square Bank, stopped the checks and called on Capt. Williams.

Mr. Wilde was looking at the Rogues' Gallery of the Twenty-ninth Precinct soon after he had told his story, and he picked out the portrait of John Jacob As-torhous, or "Hungry Joe," who had assumed the name of Drexel. A consultation followed, Capt. Williams advised Mr. Wilde to follow the matter up and prosecute the swindler. Mr. Wilde could not make up his mind to do this. He was alarmed at the possibility of some enterprising lawyer suing for the amount of the checks and terrified at the possibility of his adventure being made public. Capt. Williams suggested that publicity could hardly harm Mr. Wilde, but he said he had been advertised enough, and he did not want the American public to know that he had been taken in by a shark. That night Capt. Williams hunted for John Jacob Aster-hous, intending to arrest him and arraign him before a magistrate, even if Mr. Wilde declined to prosecute him, but he was not to be found, and all the men suspected of being "banco" operators appeared to have left New York. Capt. Wil-liams put a man to watch Astorhous's house, but he has not been seen in the City for two weeks. Last Monday week an envelope addressed to Capt. Williams at the Thirtieth street station-house and mailed in New York contained Mr. Wilde's three checks. Capt. Williams telegraphed to Mr. Wilde at No. 48 West Eleventh-street: "Checks are in my possession." It took Mr. Wilde but a few minutes to go to the station-house, and he was delighted when he tore up the evidences of his gullibility. He thanked Capt. Williams warmly, and appeared satisfied that the grave of his folly had been filled up and that the public would not know of his adventure.

"Theatrical World," *Truth* (New York, NY), 11 Feb. 1883, 5

✂ *Several paragraphs that are unrelated to Wilde.*

Mr. William Perzel, the husband of Miss Marie Prescott, has purchased the exclusive right to Mr. Oscar Wilde's play, "Vera," and Miss Prescott will star in it next season. I saw Mr. Perzel the other day, and he told me that the long-haired apostle of the sunflower had promised to return to this country and be present at all rehearsals of the piece.

"Mr. Wilde will not superintend the rehearsals, exactly," said Mr. Perzel, "but we think that his suggestions as the author will prove invaluable. And then he is to travel with us, too, and that will serve to attract public attention, I think."

I asked Mr. Perzel if Mr. Wilde was to be in the cast, or if he was to go in the capacity of a press agent.

"Oh, neither," the gentleman answered. "Nor will he be in any sense a side-show to the main attractions. He will neither pose nor lecture when he returns, and he has promised to leave off his breeches and don ordinary attire. In fact, he will become like Grosvenor, 'an everyday young man,' with the exception that he will not have his hair cut. But then, I shan't mind that, for Oscar without his hair would hardly be Oscar at all, and we must retain some of his characteristics or else the public will believe that we are imposing upon them." And Mr. Perzel rubbed his hands softly, one over the other, and smiled blandly and contentedly in the anticipation of the fortune that awaited his return.

———————

He then informed me that both he and Miss Prescott were delighted with "Vera," and were confident that the people of this country would be too when they had seen the play.

"You may know that I think a great deal of it," he said, "when I tell you that I had to give up several thousand dollars for the exclusive right of presentation. I have shown the manuscript to Mr. Steele Mackaye and to Mr. Lawrence Barrett, and both these gentlemen pronounced the work excellent."

After that I think the public may rest easy in the assurance that "Vera" is indeed a great play. Mr. Perzel also told me that he intended to rehearse the play three months before producing it. He thought the play would run easily through a season in the United States, and then he would take it to England, where he was certain it would prove a great success.

Altogether, Mr. Perzel was in high glee over his prospects, and drew quite a roseate picture of the success he expected to attain.

✂ *A synopsis of* Vera; or, The Nihilists, *followed by several paragraphs that are unrelated to Wilde.*

"D'oyley Carte," *The Chicago Daily Tribune* (Chicago, IL), 27 Feb. 1883, 5[1]

HIS VIEWS ON WILDE IN "IOLANTHE."

NEW YORK, Feb. 26.—(Special.)—D'Oyly Carte, who arrived today on the Alaska, when Oscar Wilde's name was mentioned, broke out rather sharply, saying: "Wilde, I think, has fulfilled his mission in America. I am through with him, at any rate. He called on me while I was in London, but I was not in, so I have not seen him since I left America.[2] In London, you know, he is comparatively a nonentity. Of his book and reported coming to America as an actor, I can say nothing, except that as an actor he must be a failure." In reference to his connection with Messrs. Gilbert and Sullivan and "Iolanthe," Mr. Carte said: "I made on Thursday a week ago a new contract with the composer and author of 'Pinafore' for all countries for five years. No one but myself has the right to produce any of their works, either already written or that may be prepared. The success of 'Iolanthe' in London has been wonderful, due, I think, to the high order of its music. In America it has succeeded beyond our fondest hopes."

"Oscar Wilde's Play Withdrawn," *The New York Times* (New York, NY), 28 Aug. 1883, 8[3]

NOT PAYING IN THE CITY, BUT BETTER LUCK EXPECTED IN THE COUNTRY.

"Vera" has been withdrawn from the Union-Square Theatre. Saturday night's performance was the last opportunity for New-Yorkers to see Oscar Wilde's drama. Mr. Perzel, the husband of Marie Prescott, who plays the title rôle, smiled a cheerful smile through the box-office window at the Union-Square yesterday, and informed everyone who inquired that he had yielded to dismal necessity and had withdrawn the piece. "It was no go," he said. "Of course, it is very melancholy to be obliged to accept the situation, but we lost $2,500 on the piece last week, and that is a great deal better than losing $25,000, which would very likely be the result if we kept it on a while longer. The play is withdrawn simply because it did not pay. I shall lose the forfeit which I deposited when I assumed a three weeks' lease of the theatre, and I shall pay the company in full for two weeks' work, as the members are entitled to a week's notice. The $12,000 or so I

---

1. D'Oyly Carte's name is spelt "D'Oyley Carte" in the title and in the body of the source.
2. Carte had left America on 11 March 1882 (Seeley, 60).
3. Quoted in Ellmann, 228/242; and Sturgis, 295/280. Wilde is quoted speaking to a reporter, but only to refuse an interview.

have spent on the play—costumes, scenery, &c.—I don't count as lost, for I expect that we shall meet with good success in other cities, and make up for our bad luck here. We shall reorganize the play a little, and start out on the road Oct. 15 with 'Vera' and 'Czeka.' Mr. Wilde doesn't lose a cent: he was paid a good price for the play." Mr. Perzel was unwilling to say much about Mr. Wilde and what the latter thought of the failure of "Vera," but implied that Mr. Wilde had declined his proposition to render the play more attractive by appearing himself in some way, by lecturing between the acts, or otherwise.

The distinguished aesthete himself seemed disinclined to say much on the subject of his play yesterday. A reporter found him smoking a cigar, but Mr. Wilde, who looked quite conventional with his short hair and a pair of white duck trousers, declined to say a word. He merely remarked, "Ah, but I am eating my breakfast, don't you see?"

Mr. Sheridan Shook said last night that "Vera" had been withdrawn simply because it did not pay and Mr. Perzel could not keep his contract. "In the first place," he said, "the present management of the Union-Square Theatre had nothing to do with Mr. Wilde or Mr. Wilde's play or with Miss Prescott. The contract made with Mr. Perzel, the husband of Miss Prescott, was a relic of Palmer's administration and handed down on us when he retired from the management of the theatre. All we could do was to sit by and see the play put on the stage. I had not seen the play, nor do I think Mr. Collier had until the theatre was opened. We were not consulted at all in the matter. This morning, according to the terms of the contract, Mr. Perzel was to pay us a certain sum of money. When we met him he said he did not have the money. I asked him if he had any money, and he said, 'barely enough to pay the people on the stage for the one week.' He then wanted to go on with the piece, and said if there was any difficulty he either would give a note indorsed by Miss Prescott, or Miss Prescott would give a note with his endorsement. This was not exactly satisfactory, so we thought we would shut up the house. The theatre will remain closed until Sept. 10, when Charles Wyndham's four weeks' engagement will begin. Joseph Jefferson will follow for six weeks. Then, probably, the theatre will be closed one week for rehearsals of 'Storm Beaten.'" Mr. Perzel, he understood, had paid up his actors for the week they had played. Now the company had been disbanded. The scenery, which was painted outside the theatre, Mr. Shook thought, did not cost more than $700 or $800, and was shabby to make the best of it. It all belonged to Mr. Perzel. According to the contract between Mr. Perzel and Shook and Collier the latter were to let the theatre for three weeks, receiving $1,650 per week for the first two and $1,800 for the third, and to furnish the orchestra and the attachés. The first week's rent was paid and a part of the money for another. Mr. Shook said he did not know what the receipts had been during the week. On the first night they were $800 or $900. Then they fell off rapidly, and on Saturday there could not have been taken in more than $150.

"'Vera' Withdrawn," *Truth* (New York, NY), 28 Aug. 1883, 1[1]

Oscar Wilde's Play Taken From the Metropolitan Boards—The Reason.

The illustration above represents Oscar Wilde as he appeared last year.[2] Unless Truth is greatly mistaken he wished yesterday that he was still like that. With his long tresses and short breeches Oscar made money. With his short hair and long pantaloons and longer play he has not accumulated much more wealth. "Vera," so far as the public is concerned, is dead, and Oscar is not happy.

After one brief week of existence the aesthete's play succumbed to the on-slaughts of the critics and gave up the task of endeavoring to attract the theatre-going public. The last performance was given Saturday night, but it was not until yesterday that the nurses formally threw in the sponge and decided that the dramatic offspring of Oscar could thrive better in the air of the Provinces.

Mr. William Perzel, the husband and manager of Miss Marie Prescott, yesterday sent the following letter to Truth:

✂ *The letter that also appeared in "The Failure of 'Vera,'" New York Tribune (New York, NY), 28 Aug. 1883, 5, p. 562.*

Before Truth received the letter, however, he had heard the news, and found Mr. Perzel at the Union Square Theatre. The manager took the matter very philosophically, and offered to state just how matters stood.

"It is simply this," he said. "I lost about $2,600 on the week. The people showed no inclination to come and judge for themselves in numbers sufficiently profitable. I saw no way of making up my losses here, and, in fact, there was considerable danger that I would lose more money. It was my original intention to run the piece in New York for three weeks, but I thought that it would be better to lose the rent for the remaining two weeks than to run the risk of losing $6,000 or $7,000 on the engagement, which seemed likely, judging by last week's business."

"What does Oscar think of the withdrawal?" Truth inquired.

Mr. Perzel shrugged his shoulders and remarked that if Mr. Wilde had been able to change the effect of the criticisms on Tuesday the piece would not have been withdrawn. He added that the piece would be reconstructed and pruned

---

1. Wilde is quoted speaking to a reporter, but only to refuse an interview.
2. The article is accompanied by a caricature of Wilde with long hair.

even more than it was last week and that he was certain it would take upon the road, but it would not be the only attraction, as Miss Prescott will also appear in Czeka. Mr. Perzel made a proposition to Oscar that he appear in one of the characters himself, but the aesthetic–poet–dramatist would not consent.

Truth hunted up Oscar. He found him in the cafe of the Brunswick, looking rather disconsolate as he smoked a cigarette and gazed vacantly at the empty dishes before him. It indeed seemed strange that Oscar, who has always eagerly seized the opportunity to be interviewed, should petulantly plead to be excused as he was at breakfast when approached on the subject of "Vera," but it was a fact, and as Truth's time was too valuable to await the pleasure of the apostle of sunflowers, he did not take advantage of the information volunteered by the gentleman who thought he surprised the world by having his hair cut, which was to the effect that he would be at the theatre at 2 o'clock.

"A Crushed Author," *Morning Journal and Courier* (New Haven, CT), 28 Aug. 1883, 3[1]

Oscar Wilde's Play a Flat Failure.

WITHDRAWN FROM THE BOARDS.

Heavy Financial Losses to The Manager.

A CONCERT IN A MAMMOTH CAVE.

The First Music Ever Rendered There.

NEW YORK

"Vera" Withdrawn—Oscar Wilde's Dramatic Effort a Failure.

New York, Aug. 27.—Oscar Wilde's play of "Vera" at the Union Square theater has ingloriously fizzled out of existence at the end of one week's run. This fate was foreseen for it from the first, although Miss Prescott declared in print that the public were, so to speak, crying for it. The piece will not be played tonight and Mr. Perzel publishes the following card in explanation:

1. Printed simultaneously, minus Perzel's letter, as "Fizzled Out," *The Daily American* (Nashville, TN), 28 Aug. 1883, 1; "Gotham Gossip," *The Cleveland Leader* (Cleveland, OH), 28 Aug. 1883, 2; and "Summer Dramatics," *The Daily Picayune* (New Orleans, LA), 28 Aug. 1883, 4. Excerpted in "Theatrical," *The Chicago Daily Tribune* (Chicago, IL), 28 Aug, 1883; and "'Vera' Busted," *The Courier-Journal* (Louisville, KY), 28 Aug. 1883, 2.

✂ *The letter that also appeared in "The Failure of 'Vera,'"* New York Tribune *(New York, NY), 28 Aug. 1883, 5, p. 562.*

Messers Sheridan Shook and A. R. Cazauran were met in the lobby of the Union Square theater musing over the uncertainty of worldly matters. "Just a week ago," said Mr. Cazauran, "at this hour people were fighting at the box office for tickets; today even the chronic deadheads pass the place without looking in. Mr. Wilde admits that the play does not suit the public. He says this is not the play's fault. I saw him yesterday at noon. He said that he could not understand the lack of interest shown by the public, but he does not blame the critics for saying what they believe to be true. There was a misunderstanding all around. Mr. Wilde did not understand the public, and the public and the critics did not understand Mr. Wilde's play. There was also a misunderstanding as to the extent of Mr. Perzel's financial resources. He was believed to have plenty of money—enough to run the play at a loss until 'Vera' could be taken on the road with a record of a New York season behind it. Now the prospects of the piece, even on the road, have not been improved by this fiasco. It turns out that Mr. Perzel cannot or will not furnish necessary money to continue playing at a loss. Mr. Perzel," added Mr. Shook,[1] "rented the theater for three weeks and paid us the usual forfeit amount. He is unable to go on. We are sorry for him, but we have nothing to do with 'Vera.'"

Among the habitues of the Union Square Theater it was said that the total expenses incurred by Mr. Perzel from the time he purchased 'Vera' has been about $10,000.

It was said by actors who have had nothing to do during the week but study the fortunes of 'Vera' that the loss during the last week has been about $1,200 on the seven performances. Even on the first night the house was not a paying one according to experts in such matters, for tickets had been lavishly distributed among the crowd of actors who make their headquarters in Union Square during the summer. On Saturday afternoon the receipts were less than $40, and at the evening less than $100 were received. The total receipts for the week were not $600 and the expenses, including rent, were at least $1,500. Among the Union Square philosophers the collapse of 'Vera' coming so soon after the failure of the George Edgar company last week in Chicago, and of 'Zenobia' at the Twenty-third street theater on Saturday night, was considered as specially unfortunate, and likely to deter managers with any money to lose from sending out companies on "the road." The hundreds of actors who depend upon such engagements for a living looked blue this morning in consequence.

---

1. There is no indication in the source as to where Cazauran's comments end and Shook's begin.

The rumor that Oscar Wilde would appear in 'Vera' himself was pronounced to be a hoax.

"Mrs. Langtry in Paris," *Birmingham Daily Mail* (Birmingham, UK), 12 Sep. 1883, 4[1]

>< *Several sentences that are unrelated to Wilde.*

Anxious to elicit her opinion as to Oscar Wilde, my friend referred to the failure of his last play in New York.[2] Mrs. Langtry roundly asserted that the play was by no means a failure, the comments of the American Press to the contrary notwithstanding. In her defence of the erratic "Childe of Song" and apostle of tootooism, the young lady became enthusiastically eloquent. "Oscar Wilde," she said, "has hosts of enemies on the other as well as on this side of the Atlantic, but he will live them all down, like other men of genius. He is a very clever writer, possesses remarkable ability, and is destined to do great things in the near future."

"Matthew Arnold's Opinions," *The Detroit Free Press* (Detroit, MI), 26 Oct. 1883, 7[3]

Afraid That American Audiences Will Not Appreciate Him—Oscar Wilde a Mushroom—Labouchere—The Lords.

What Matthew Arnold said to a New York reporter was this:

>< *Several paragraphs that are unrelated to Wilde.*

Speaking of English art or aestheticism, as represented by Oscar Wilde, Mr. Arnold said: "Poor fellow, I can't help feeling sorry for him. He was a kind of a goose, you know; and yet he is a clever fellow. But he has no solid reputation in England. In English art he was a kind of a —"

"Mushroom?" suggested the reporter.

"Well, yes. But I would rather you would not say that I said he was a goose. Oscar is a clever fellow, and I'm afraid he feels sore over his last venture in this

---

1. Printed simultaneously as "Mrs. Langtry in Paris," *Aberdeen Evening Express* (Aberdeen, UK), 12 Sep. 1883, 4.

2. The "friend" referred to is a Paris correspondent.

3. Reprinted as "Matthew Arnold's Opinions," *The Daily American* (Nashville, TN), 27 Oct. 1883, 6; and "Matthew Arnold's Opinions," *Weekly Public Ledger* (Memphis, TN), 6 Nov. 1883, 1.

country. Carried away a good deal of money for a balm? Well, not near so much. Twenty-five thousand dollars? Let's see: how much is that in pounds? Yes, £5,000. Oh, dear, no. He didn't make anything like that amount. I know it positively. It was but a small fraction of that sum."

>< *Several paragraphs that are unrelated to Wilde.*

[John Black], "Interview with a Theatrical Manageress," *The South Australian Advertiser* (Adelaide, SA), 4 Aug. 1885, 6[1]

One of the passengers to Adelaide by the R.M.S. Parramatta was Miss Helen Lenoir, who has for several years past managed an important part of the ever-extending business of Mr. R. D'Oyly Carte, the well-known owner and manager of the Savoy Theatre, London.

>< *Several paragraphs that are unrelated to Wilde.*

"Did you make the business arrangements for any other celebrities in America?"

"Yes, Oscar Wilde, among others. His lectures and appearance made a great sensation in America. It became the fashion with a number of ladies to follow him about, very much in the same way as the aesthetic maidens follow Bunthorne in the opera. They used to throng rapturously around him at receptions; I remember on one such occasion seeing a lady approach him with clasped hands, exclaiming 'Oh, Mr. Wilde, this is what I have longed for.' During his stay in America sunflowers became quite the rage, and ladies wore them everywhere in public."

"Is the general idea that Oscar Wilde was the original of Bunthorne correct?"

"As a matter of fact Bunthorne's personal appearance on the stage was modelled on that of Mr. J. McNeill Whistler, the well-known painter and etcher, whose original opinions on art keep him constantly at feud with the Academicians. He is the owner of the celebrated white lock in the centre of the forehead which is the distinctive mark of Bunthorne. In Mr. Whistler its effect is striking, because the rest of his hair is black. He is the author of such modern artistic terms as 'a nocturne,' 'a symphony in black and grey,' &c. Mr. Oscar Wilde and Mr. Whistler meet a great deal in the upper circles of London society, and outvie one

---

1. Reprinted in "Interview with a Theatrical Manageress," *The Express & Telegraph* (Adelaide, SA), 5 Aug. 1885, 7; and "Interview with a Theatrical Manageress," *The South Australian Weekly Chronicle* (Adelaide, SA), 8 Aug. 1885, 5 (which is quoted in Sturgis, 246/236). Quoted in Seeley, 54–5, where the interviewer is identified as Lenoir's brother.

another in the production of witticisms, and Mr. Wilde is sometimes accused of retailing [*sic*] his rival's good things as his own. At a large party not long ago Mr. Whistler achieved some *bon mot* before an admiring audience, and Mr. Wilde, who was lolling on a couch close by, could not help exclaiming—'I wish I had said that.' Turning towards the rival aesthete Whistler replied—'Never mind, Oscar, you *will*.' Mr. Whistler also makes his début in America as an art lecturer next year. He lately gave a brilliant address on that subject to a fashionable audience in London. He would not hear of his remarks being called a 'lecture,' but entitled them (from the hour of commencement) 'his 10 o'clock.'[1] Oscar Wilde always appeared before his American audiences in the celebrated knee-breeches, black silk stockings, and pumps. When the interviewers descended upon him on his first arrival, and asked him his opinion about America and the voyage across, he replied 'that he was disappointed with the Atlantic.' This was duly cabled over to the English papers, and as the passage had been a rough one it created some astonishment. Since his tour he has married a very charming American lady,[2] and he is not doing much at present beyond writing for the magazines and some of the newspapers.

✄ *Several paragraphs that are unrelated to Wilde.*

"An Amazon of Journalism," *The Pall Mall Gazette* (London, UK), 28 Aug. 1886, 1–2

AN INTERVIEW WITH MRS. FRANK LESLIE.

✄ *Several paragraphs that are unrelated to Wilde.*

THE SECRETS OF INTERVIEWING.

"All through my trials," she continued, "the press has been with me. The reporters are always looking me up and saying, 'Mrs. Leslie, you are worth ten dollars to us any day. Won't you give us an interview?' You in England, by the way, don't half appreciate the services of the interviewer. Mr. Oscar Wilde came into my office the day after he arrived in New York, and cried: 'Mrs. Leslie, do you see what they are saying about me? I never did such a thing. I never said that.'

"'What's the matter, Mr. Wilde?' I asked.

---

1. Given at Prince's Hall, Piccadilly, on 20 February 1885.
2. Constance was not American. She was born in London ("Births," *The Morning Chronicle* (London, UK), 6 Jan. 1858, 8, cited in Moyle, 14). Her father was English and her mother Irish. She was raised in London and Dublin.

"'Why, these horrible reporters. They swarmed on to the boat before I landed, and crowded around me, and—'

"'And what did you do?'

"'I turned my back upon them.'

"'There you made a mistake, Mr. Wilde,' I said. 'If you come to America you must recognize the interviewer as a powerful institution. You represent to him so much capital. His business is to interview, the same as it is yours to lecture. If you don't speak to him, he must earn his money all the same, and will write something which is certainly not likely to be complimentary.' With us" (she continued) "the best talent on the press is devoted to this branch of journalism. The interviewer is invariably a man of ability and education, but he is just inclined to be a little too personal at times. Women are the best interviewers."

✂ *Several paragraphs that are unrelated to Wilde.*

"Here and There," *The Omaha Daily Herald* (Omaha, NE), 4 May 1888, 4

Colonel Vale,[1] manager of Ragan's illustrated lectures, is the man who piloted Oscar Wilde through this country. The wonder is that he still lives. "Oscar Wilde was no fool, by any means," said the colonel. "He worked the United States 'for all there was in it.' He cleaned up $40,000 net, not counting the $3,000 he lost against Hungry Joe's bunco game in New York. Oscar was a genteel fakir. The 'Oscar Wilde' craze was his own invention. He worked the aesthetic rage for every dollar in sight. Whenever anybody used to call on him at his hotel, he always struck an attitude, arranged the lilies and sunflowers, and did everything possible for effect before the visitor entered; but the moment the visitor left he became another man, and was one of the b'hoys.[2] His aestheticism was all assumed. When he returned to England he cut off his long hair, got down to business, and gave the Yankees the grand laugh. The most amusement I ever had on the Oscar Wilde tour was in Denver, when Eugene Field got a wig and personated Wilde to perfection. Field in his makeup took in the town and fooled everybody. His imitation of Wilde was very deceptive, and was a great hit. Nobody enjoyed it more than Wilde himself, who was in the party. Wilde had his long hair tucked up

---

1. Vale's name is given as "Vail" in the source.

2. B'hoy was a slang word used to describe the pleasure-seeking working class denizens of Lower Manhattan in the mid-nineteenth-century. A modern equivalent might be "one of the guys."

under a cowboy hat, and nobody recognized him, while everybody took Field for Wilde."[1]

"Chats With Celebrities," *Hearth and Home* (London, UK), 30 June 1892, 219–20[2]

LADY WILDE

It is more than forty years since Lady Wilde first gained celebrity in the columns of the Irish *Nation* under her chosen pen-name of "Speranza." In that time the "Young Ireland" movement of which "Speranza" was the brilliant bard had been almost forgotten in England, cherished as its memories may be in the sister isle.[3] After an interview with Lady Wilde, however, one's impressions of that stirring time are of the most vivid; in her company one recalls the glowing words of Sir Charles Gavan-Duffy in describing the introduction of a new power into Irish politics, the poetic genius of its women. For in the half-darkened room of the house in Oakley Street, Chelsea—the afternoon sunlight being almost entirely excluded by the drawn blinds—one can easily picture to oneself in the tall, stately elderly woman the young Irish girl whose rebel muse roused the enthusiasm of a nation to fever pitch. There are the same flashing eyes, the same queenly grace which so impressed the editor of the *Nation* when he first called upon his fair and unknown contributor at her parents' house in Dublin. Of some of the weakness of age, however, Lady Wilde frankly makes confession—the visual weakness which shrinks from glaring light, and the physical weakness which shuns the fatigue of walking.

"Would you believe it," Lady Wilde exclaims, "I have not been out of doors for weeks. It's my indolence, I suppose, but I much prefer my friends coming to see me to going to see them. Then if I can only get a good book and a good fire I am perfectly happy—I want nothing more."

"Then you have the conditions of happiness constantly at command," I remark, looking at the bright fire in the grate and the books on the table and on some library shelves.

"In society you are never given the divine thoughts that great writers give you. Who is there that can speak as Ralph Waldo Emerson speaks to you?"

1. Eugene Field (1850–1895) was the managing editor of the *Denver Tribune*, and well known for his practical jokes. His impersonation of Wilde is also described in OWDA, 320–1, where it is claimed that Wilde was not present, having been delayed in Colorado Springs.
2. Quoted in Melville, 12, 14, 16, 55, 186, 218, 246.
3. Young Ireland was a political movement of the 1840s that sought an independent Ireland. It culminated in the failed 1848 Uprising.

"And in your youth, Lady Wilde, had you this feeling then?"

"I was always very fond of study and of books. My favourite study was languages; I succeeded in mastering ten of the European languages. Till my eighteenth year I never wrote anything. All my time was given to study. Then, one day, a volume of "Ireland's Library," issued from the *Nation* office by Mr. Duffy, happened to come in my way. I read it eagerly, and my patriotism was kindled."

"Till that time, then, you were neither poet nor politician?"

"No, I was quite indifferent to the national movement, and if I thought about it all [*sic*] probably had a bad opinion of its leaders. For my family was Protestant and Conservative, and there was no social intercourse between them and the Catholics and Nationalists. My grandfather was Archdeacon Elgee, the Rector of Wexford, and my great grandfather, Dr. Kingsbury,[1] was in his day president of the Irish College of Physicians and the intimate friend of Dean Swift."

Of Archdeacon Elgee, by the way, Lady Wilde tells a story illustrating his kindly character and the impulsive feelings of the Irish people. When the rebels entered in 1798, the Archdeacon fully expected death at their hands—for rebels and loyalists alike had been committing great cruelty—and had assembled some of his parishioners in the church to partake of the sacrament together. The rebels were, indeed, about to kill the Archdeacon, when one of them turned away their pikes, and related a great kindness which the clergyman had rendered to his family. It was at once resolved that the Archdeacon and all his belongings should be untouched and a guard was placed at his house for its protection."

"Is your family, Lady Wilde, a purely Irish one?"

"No, it migrated in the 16th century from Italy, and Elgee is an Irish corruption of the name.[2] But once I had caught the National spirit, and all the literature of Irish wrongs and sufferings had an enthralling interest for me. Then it was that I discovered I could write poetry. In sending my verses to the editor of the *Nation* I dared not have my name published, so I signed them 'Speranza' and my letters 'John Fenshaw Ellis' instead of Jane Francesca Elgee.[3] But after awhile Mr. Duffy wished me to call at the office, and again 'Mr. Ellis' had to excuse himself from doing so. One day my uncle came into my room and found the *Nation* on my table. Then he accused me of contributing to it, declaring the while that such a seditious paper was fit only for the fire. The secret being out in my own family there was no longer much motive for concealment, and I gave my editor permission to call upon me. Even then, as Sir Charles Duffy has since told me, he

1. In the source the name is spelt "Kingbery".

2. Lady Jane liked to claim that Elgee was a corruption of Alighieri, thereby implying kinship with Dante. In truth, the Elgees hailed from County Durham (Fitzsimons, 16).

3. Jane signed her letters "John Fanshawe Ellis" (Melville, 18).

scarcely knew who 'Speranza' might be, and great was his surprise, therefore, when I stepped out from an inner room."

After twenty years of London life Lady Wilde can still speak with animation, if not enthusiasm, of these episodes of her remarkable girlhood. Of the failure of the Young Ireland movement, of the fate of its leaders we do not speak. Yet "Speranza" had sung:—

> We stand in the light of a dawning day,
>   With its glory creation flushing;
> And the life-currents up from the pris'ning clay
>   Through the world's great heart are rushing.
> While from peak to peak of the spirit land
>   A voice unto voice is calling;
> The night is over, the day is at hand,
>   And the fetters of earth are falling![1]

To the over-wrought spirit of the poetess, who had been brimming over with hope and faith in many such verses, the after-time of despair must have been terrible. Happily for her love came to fill the soul, and in 1851 "Speranza" was married to the man of her choice, a physician who achieved professional fame as Sir William Wilde.[2] Sir William had apparently something of his wife's patriotism, for his leisure was employed in studying the ancient lore of Ireland.

"He would employ very many people—schoolmasters in the villages chiefly—who could speak both Irish and English, to investigate and collect all the local traditions, superstitions, etc. of the peasantry. When he died a great amount of material had been collected, much of which I have published in the last year or so in the volumes entitled, 'Ancient Cures, Charms, and Usages of Ireland,' and 'Ancient Legends of Ireland.' Sir William had a passion for such research, and in recognition of his services the Royal Irish Academy gave him its gold medal."

"Did you continue to write, Lady Wilde, after your marriage?"

"Oh, yes; but I then turned to prose, and wrote papers on various subjects for the *Dublin University Magazine*. Some of them have been republished in the volume—'Notes on Men, Women, and Books'—which Ward and Downey brought out for me last year. Then I translated a great deal, both poetry and prose, and of translation I have always been very fond. Some of these translations— 'Driftwood,' from Scandinavia, two books from the German, and one of the works of Dumas—have been published at different times since I have resided in London, and many of the shorter poems from different European languages are, of course,

---

1. These are the opening lines of Lady Wilde's *The New Path*.

2. In the source the name of Lady Wilde's husband is incorrectly given as "Sir Thomas", but only in this paragraph. The correct name is used thereafter.

included in my little volume of collected poems, but I have still a great deal unpublished."[1]

After the death of her husband in 1871 Lady Wilde came to London, she tells me, for the sake of her sons, Oscar and William.[2] In London she has many devoted friends, as the photographs on the crowded overmantel will tell you, although probably quite unknown personally to most of the literary and musical "sets," and I suspect from her talk that she has notwithstanding patriotic sentiment, a sneaking love for the cockney city. Italy is one of the few themes which moves her to enthusiasm, and with her Italian origin and poetic nature it would be strange indeed if she were not eloquent regarding the land of song. Her poetic nature, too, leads Lady Wilde to take a delightfully unpractical view of the great woman question.

"If I were Dictator," she exclaims, "no girl should be taught to read and write. It is a woman's mission to adorn life, to impart beauty to the commonplace. And I think with Sir James Crichton Browne, that learning hinders rather than helps this mission. No woman, if I had my way, should have to work for her livelihood; it is simply terrible to think of girls wasting youth and beauty in hard toil."[3]

In all this there is, of course, a vein of exaggeration, but in more deliberate language Lady Wilde has expressed the same opinions in some of her essays. Although so much of her own life has been given to intellectual activity, she has none of the zeal of those whom Mrs. Lynn Linton dubs "the Wild Women."[4]

1. Judging from the punctuation, it seems that the reporter thought *Driftwood from Scandinavia* (1884) a translation. It is Lady Wilde's memoir of her 1858 trip to Denmark, Norway, and Sweden with Sir William.

2. Sir William died on 19 April 1876.

3. Sir James Crichton-Browne (1840–1938) was a Scottish psychiatrist. His name is given in the source as "Crichton Brown". On 2 May 1892 he delivered "The Annual Oration on Sex in Education" before the Medical Society of London (*British Medical Journal*, 7 May 1892, 949–54). He argued that "intellectual disparities" between men and women were due to sex differences in the biology of the brain, and that high schools for girls, in their attempt to imitate schools for boys, were overworking their pupils. This overwork, he claimed, caused headaches, insomnia, and anaemia, and increased a girl's risk of permanent insanity and "debility". He also thought that over-educating girls negatively affected their physical appearance: "Genuine education contributes to beauty, but triple-condensed high pressure education must be ultimately destructive of it." (*British Medical Journal*, 21 May 1892, 1110–11.)

4. Eliza Lynn Linton (1822–1898) was an English journalist and novelist, and a critic of early feminism. Her series on "The Wild Women" (i.e. women who disdained "the duties and limitations imposed on them by nature") for *Nineteenth Century* began in July 1891; "The Partisans of the Wild Women" appeared in the number for April 1892 (455–64).

"The Censorship and 'Salome,'" *The Pall Mall Gazette* (London, UK), 6 July 1892, 1–2[1]

INTERVIEWS WITH MDME. SARAH BERNHARDT AND M. A. DARMONT

THE interest that attaches to the views of Mdme. Bernhardt and M. Darmont on the artistic questions raised by the prohibition of "Salomé" is hardly less than that belonging to those of Mr. Oscar Wilde. The interpreters are in even more direct touch with the public than the author, and may be held to have quite as weighty reasons for not running counter to the tastes of playgoers as the latter.

"I don't read newspapers," said Mdme. Bernhardt to a representative of the *Pall Mall Gazette*, "and seldom see what is written about me. I know that Mr. Oscar Wilde is pleased that I like Salomé, and I really am very taken with it; it is an artistic work in every sense of the word. Unfortunately it is off for London, but I shall play the piece in Paris at some time or another; I cannot say when, as my season is not fixed there yet."

"Would it not be possible to do as Mr. Wilde hoped to have done when he first heard of the prohibition—bring it out at an invitation performance?"

"Oh, I wouldn't do that. It has been refused by the Censor, and I respect the decision. It is not my style to take advantage of the opportunities afforded by private representation to perform what has been suppressed. I don't think it has ever happened to me before to accept a play and a rôle, and to have been refused permission to act.

"Religion is not outraged in this piece; you know me—you know I am a Christian woman, and it is not likely that I would consent to be the medium of an insult to religion."

Our representative pointed out to Mdme. Bernhardt that the Censorship might have been influenced by the fact that when once the play was licensed it might be wrongly interpreted by others who did not hold religion in so high respect as she did. Once licensed, the play was always licensed.

"But the rôle is mine; Mr. Oscar Wilde has given it to me, and nobody else can perform it. No, no, no; that's an error. If the Censor had that contingency in mind, he might have consulted me.

"The Censor didn't even communicate with the author. I understand, however, that in this the regular course was followed in treating with the administration of the theatre, by whom the play was submitted for licence. A play is licensed to the theatre and not to individual persons."

1. Excerpted in "Mme. Bernhardt an Upholder of Religion," *The New York Herald, European Edition* (Paris, France), 7 July 1892, 1. Quoted in Sturgis, 455/423. This is the "unidentified interview with Bernhardt, 8 July 1892 (Hyde)" referenced in Ellmann, 250 (574, note 13)/371 (610, note 13).

We spoke for some time on Censorship and its works, not only in England but in France, and after having endeavoured in vain to find a parallel case Mdme. Bernhardt again maintained that religion was not outraged in the interpretation that it was proposed to give to "Salomé":—

"It's not a religious play. It deals with love, passion, nature, the stars, the moon—"

"Yes, that reminds me, Mr. Oscar Wilde told me himself that the moon played the principal rôle."

"C'est vrai, c'est tout à fait vrai. Mais...."[1] and with a gesture indicating that what has been done could not be undone Mdme. Bernhardt rose, and the interview was at an end.

M. Albert Darmont, the charming young *premier* who has accompanied Mdme. Sarah Bernhardt round the world, was even more enthusiastic about the play and his own rôle:—

"It is a fine piece," he said. "I should have liked very much to have created the part of Yokanaan [*sic*]. Mdme. Bernhardt was to have played Salomé, M. Rebel Hérode, and Mdme Jane Méa Hérodias."[2]

"Yokanaan disguises the personage of St. John the Baptist, does it not?"— "Yes, but there is nothing in the character to offend the most religious. Salomé falls in love with Yokanaan; she wishes to place her hand on his hair, and he puts her back sternly and with dignity. She becomes more enamoured with the saint—begs to be allowed to kiss his forehead, his eyes, his lips. Still he resists. Had Yokanaan (or John the Baptist, if you will) succumbed, and been represented as entering into the spirit of a great love scene, I could understand the objections that have been raised. But he does not. His attitude is always saintly and dignified. And then, when Salomé obtains possession of Yokanaan's head as the price of her dance before Herod, she fulfills the vow she had made to kiss the lips of the man with whom she has fallen so deeply in love. If, as it appears, religious subjects are not permitted on the English stage, I cannot understand how it was that 'Leah' passed the Censorship.

"So long as you introduce nothing scandalous or against received faith in the work, I fail to see why St. John the Baptist, or even Christ and the Holy Virgin, should be banished from the stage. The theatre was formed by the priests with

1. "It's true, it's absolutely true. But..."
2. William Tydeman and Steven Price, based on the roles played by members of Bernhardt's company in other plays of this time, speculate that Darmont was to play Herod; Jane Méa, Herodias; and M. Fleury, Jokanaan (Tydeman, W., & Price, S. (1996). *Wilde: Salome (Plays in Production)*. Cambridge University Press. 21). Holland and Hart-Davis (CL, 529, note 1) and Joseph Donohue (CW v, 468) concur as regards Darmont. Wilde told Maurice Sisley that Bernhardt and Darmont had been cast in "the two main roles" (Maurice Sisley, "La Salomé de M. Oscar Wilde," *Le Gaulois* (Paris, France), 29 June 1892, 1, p. 611).

mysteries based on sacred history, and as long as scandal is not to be feared this form of teaching is quite as much to the glory of the Evangile as the book that one reads—as the New Testament itself. It cannot *froisser* the public;[1] on the contrary. That is my opinion. The moment the actor says something religious, something that strikes the spirit and the conscience of his audience, I don't see why you should forbid him to say it. What is the difference between the comedian and the curé? There is none. If the comedian, then, can say anything high, sacred, and inspiring, which tends to the glory of the Lord and sacred ideas, do not forbid him. Prevent those pieces which raise dissention among the people or tend to brutalize them, but the moment the Censorship goes against those plays which elevate I find it incomprehensible—especially here in London, where the artist is so appreciated."

Adele Marroc, "Oscar Wilde's Children," *The Philadelphia Inquirer* (Philadelphia, PA), 5 Nov. 1893, 23[2]

A Chat With Their Mother on Their Training.

Within a stone's throw of the house once inhabited by the Sage of Chelsea and Jane Welsh Carlyle,[3] stands the quaint Queen Anne mansion in which Mr. and Mrs. Oscar Wilde have elected to dwell.

Even the most casual visitor cannot but notice how strangely different to the average British house is the interior of the home of the one-time apostle of aestheticism.

To begin with there is an utter absence of so-called artistic coloring; dirty greens and mouldy yellows are absent. Everything is dainty, neat, and clean-

---

1. Offend.

2. Printed simultaneously as "Oscar Wilde's Children," *Sunday World-Herald* (Omaha, NE), 5 Nov. 1893, 11; "Oscar Wilde's Boys," *St. Louis Republic* (St. Louis, MO), 5 Nov. 1893, 18; and (without images) "Oscar Wilde's Boys," *The Los Angeles Times* (Los Angeles, CA), 5 Nov. 1893, 20. Reprinted as "Oscar Wilde's Children," *The Scranton Republican* (Scranton, PA), 8 Nov. 1893, 6; and "Oscar Wilde's Better Half," *The Kansas City Times* (Kansas City, MO), 12 Nov. 1893, 19. Marroc contributed signed columns to various major American newspapers between 1892 and 1895. Most are profiles of famous European women but there are also occasional notes on literature and fashion. They were sent from London, Paris, and Berlin. Marroc does not appear in census records and it seems likely that she wrote under a pseudonym. In the source the byline is "Adelle Marroc"; her name is spelt "Adele" elsewhere. The article is accompanied by images of Constance and the two boys, with Cyril in indoor dress and Vyvyan in outdoor dress.

3. Thomas Carlyle and his wife resided at 5 (now 24) Cheyne Row, Chelsea, about half a mile from the Wilde's Tite Street home.

looking. A cream paneling forms the base of the whole scheme of decoration and makes a delicate background to the beautiful things placed against it.

Mrs. Oscar Wilde received me in the drawing room, a lofty apartment which has been graced at divers times with many cosmopolitan gatherings of English and French, to say nothing of American celebrities.

A prettier room could scarce be found in London. The Louis Quinze furniture is upholstered in a soft blue brocade over which lingers a gray sheen. Above the high cream-colored dado which runs round the room a dead-gold fabric has been stretched. The few choice proof engravings and signed etchings hanging thereon are framed in plain white wood.

Most of the pictures bear in the margin the dedication to Mrs. Oscar Wilde. First comes the working proof of Noel Kenealy's engraving of the Gainsborough "Mrs. Siddons," the famous picture hanging in the British National Gallery;[1] then an exquisite pen and ink drawing by Walter Crane, illustrating a little poem written by his own daughter;[2] a proof of Bastien Lepage's Sarah Bernhardt, with an inscription from the artist; a set of Venetian drawings by the great Whistler himself;[3] and a drawing of Rubinstein by Moscheles.[4] Above the white carved marblepiece a gilt copper bas-relief by Donoghue translates Oscar Wilde's exquisite poem Requiescat.[5] Opposite the fireplace, leaning against the wall, is a narrow full-length of the master of the house, in gray and brown, by a young American artist.[6]

1. Noel Byron Kenealy (1867–1918) was a British artist. Marroc refers to the portrait of the actress Sarah Siddons (1755–1831) by Gainsborough. Kenealy also made an engraving of a portrait of Siddons by Sir Thomas Lawrence (1769–1830).

2. Wilde printed the poem and illustration in the February 1888 number of *The Woman's World* (177). Wilde wrote a letter thanking Crane that is not included in CL (see Crane, W. (1907). *An Artist's Reminiscences*. Methuen & Co. 195).

16 Tite Street, Chelsea, S. W.

My dear Crane,—Many thanks for the charming design and for Beatrice's pretty little poem. I will have it reproduced at once.—Very truly yours,

Oscar Wilde
(A horrid pen.)

Beatrice Crane (b. 1873) later wrote for the children's periodical *Little Folks* (CW vii, 387).

3. Whistler was commissioned by the Fine Art Society to produce a series of etchings of Venice in 1879. A set of twelve was published in 1880 and a further set of twenty-four in 1886. It is unclear how many the Wildes owned; three that belonged to them were sold at auction in 1900 (Moyle, 323).

4. Felix Moscheles (1833–1917) was an English painter and writer and the son of Bohemian pianist Ignaz Moscheles. Anton Rubinstein's name is given in the source as "Rubenstein".

5. Wilde was given the bas-relief by Donoghue in Chicago. See e.g. "Truly Aesthetic," *The Daily Inter Ocean* (Chicago, IL), 13 Feb. 1882, 2, p. 166.

6. Harper Pennington's portrait of Wilde in Regency dress.

Figure 21. Legend of the Blush Roses, *a poem by Beatrice Crane, illustrated by Walter Crane. Wilde published the page in* The Woman's World *and hung the original in the drawing room of his Tite Street home.*

805

Faded Eastern carpets form a harmony in themselves. The only touches of bright color in the apartment are the two Japanese leather panels let into the otherwise plain panelled ceiling.

Mrs. Oscar Wilde, though still quite a young woman,[1] has won a place for herself in her husband's brilliant circle. Her masses of brown hair, deep blue eyes and fair skin would mark her anywhere as an English woman, and an hour's talk with her shows she has read and thought on the modern problems of the day. Entirely to her, Oscar Wilde has left the training of their two sons, Cyril and Vivian, two singularly-gifted children, who bid fair to carry on both the literary and artistic traditions of the family.

"I have never been interviewed before," remarked Mrs. Wilde smiling; "but if you will ask me what you wish to know I will do my best to answer you clearly."

"I should like to begin by a very prosaic question," said I. "Have you and your husband any special theories about how children should be clothed?"

"I think that above all," answered Mrs. Wilde, "a child's garments should have usefulness rather than beauty for their first object, for the one will generally bring the other. My little boys for rough-and-tumble wear are clothed in blue sailor suits. You see this kind of clothing has been designed by a necessity. Long experience must surely have taught seamen the most practical and easy mode of dressing. When acting as page to Lady Harberton's daughter, on the occasion of her marriage, Cyril wore a green plush suit,[2] but I prefer him, when he has to be dressed up," she added, brightly, "in tan-colored cloth."

"I suppose that as regards underclothing you also delight in the modern fad of combination suits?" I queried.[3]

"No, indeed! I consider them very uncomfortable and sometimes dangerous for little children, for they are apt to shrink out of their size and proportion in washing. My children have worn flannel next their skin since the day they were born, and always sleep in blankets. Indeed, Cyril can't bear sheets, and declares he cannot sleep between linen."

"And do you prefer bringing up a child at home or sending it when quite young to a day school?"

1. At this time Constance was 35.
2. Florence Wallace Pomeroy, Viscountess Harberton (1843–1911) was a British campaigner for dress reform. In 1883 she became President of the Rational Dress Society. Her daughter Hilda Evelyn Pomeroy married Thomas Arthur Carless Attwood at St Jude's, South Kensington, on 5 October 1892.
3. A combination suit, known in the United States as a union suit, is a type of one-piece underwear. It originated as women's wear and later gained popularity among men, who wore suits with long arms and legs that buttoned up the front and had a button-up flap at the rear. Gustav Jaeger advocated combinations made from wool.

Figure 22. Images of Constance, Cyril (left, in indoor dress), and Vyvyan Wilde (right, in out-door dress) that accompanied Adele Marroc's 1893 interview with Constance.

807

Mrs. Wilde hesitated. "My eldest don goes to a kindergarten school every day, for I have a great belief in kindergarten methods; although one of the youngest, he is now captain, or, as they call it, Prime Minister of his school; and I discovered to my great amusement that the other day they had a trooping of the colors in honor of his birthday.[1] But, of course, I do all I can to keep his education in my hands; for instance, I read to him a great deal."

"And what do you find are his favorite books?"

"Robinson Crusoe, Thackeray's Rose and Ring and Stevenson's Treasure Island.[2] Indeed, any book of adventure, with plenty of fighting, is what he most enjoys at the present time. Then, you know, I am a great believer in the Quaker method, keeping a child perfectly quiet occasionally; I think it does a child good. He generally goes to church with me on Sunday, and takes the greatest interest in everything he hears there and delights in having Stanley's Children's Sermons read to him—one of the best collections of the kind ever issued, I think.[3] These sermons have a curious history. The late Dean of Westminster, who was extremely fond of children, always preached a special sermon to them in the Abbey on the Holy Innocents' day, and after death these were gathered together and prove a lovely book.

"I ought to add," she continued, after a moment's pause, "that I quite agree with the clergyman who once said that it was far worse to force a child's spiritual growth than even his mental growth; but still I think religious aspirations should be fostered. It is greatly a question of temperament, for my younger boy cannot be kept quiet for a minute in church; in fact, taking him to service is a veritable penance."

"And do you intend to send your sons to a public school?"

"It will be a case of 'must' with them, for, of course, later on, they will have to earn their own living," replied Mrs. Wilde. "My husband is anxious that they should ultimately get good scholarships, and to have a chance of that a boy must go through the regular mill.

"My ideal would be for a child to always spend six months of the year in the country. There I would teach him elementary botany and all about flowers and animals. I have now in my mind a little Londoner I know who can tell you in a moment what a bird is by his voice; his father takes him out for long country walks, and together they watch through a field glass the flight of birds. I would do everything I could to take a child out of itself. Still, I do not believe in only a

1. Cyril turned eight on 5 June 1893, so the interview may have been conducted in the summer.
2. *Robinson Crusoe* (1719) by Daniel Defoe (c. 1660–1731); *The Rose and The Ring* (1854) by William Makepeace Thackeray.
3. Arthur Penrhyn Stanley (1815–1881) was an English Anglican priest and Dean of Westminster from 1864 to his death. His *Sermons for Children* was published in 1887.

country life, for I think the more intelligent and good people young folks see the better."

"And I suppose a good deal of what you say would apply equally to your theories on the education of girls?"

"Yes and no. The problem with girls assumes very different proportions; for instance, vanity is nearly entirely absent from boys, while it is one of the most predominant traits in the character of most girls. A curious proof of this came to my notice the other day. My boys gave a little party to their young friends, and among their guests came a very pretty little girl somewhat daintily dressed. She walked in, and, after glancing round, ran out on the landing and called out: 'Nurse! Nurse! I said I should be the smartest little girl here, and I am!' Now I do not think a boy would ever have thought of such a thing.

"But it is impossible to lay down general rules on education, for children differ so much; what would be advisable in one case would be very injurious in another. My own ideal of the beginning of a child's education is that he should find out his own place in the world's organization; therefore he should be taught religion in order that he may find his place in relation to the divinity of spirituality; science, that he may place himself in relation to the laws that govern the material world; history, geography, and languages, that he may find his place in his work for humanity; and with religion I place mathematics as being in the region of pure thought, and the only means we have of grasping the actuality of other worlds besides our own."

After a short pause she continued, "Theoretically, I would have education take some such form. Actually, things work themselves out pretty much according to the child's natural temperament and character. And the pressure of material things is so strong that it is hard to keep up ideals; harder for a woman than for a man, men being much more independent in their lives. Also, besides requiring great pliancy on the child's part, a theory of education requires perfection on the part of the educator.

"Very little can be done in reality except in some small way of guidance. Take my two boys; Cyril has a much greater love of color than Vivian, but somehow to Vivian has certainly been given the appreciation of art in its forms of poetry and painting. Vivian likes the rhythm of poetry, Cyril the ideas expressed by it—if one can say anything so decidedly about two babies," she concluded, smiling.

"One last question, Mrs. Wilde; do you think any special kind of feeding influences a child?"

"As for food," she replied thoughtfully, "I have no theories whatsoever; for some children oatmeal is not only good, but almost necessary—the difficulty is to make them take it. If any mother were to ask me for advice on the subject I would answer, give your child plenty of milk, if possible, plenty of variety in food and plenty of fruit; and never, never use 'deprivation of food' as a punishment, as was too often done in old days."

ADELLE MARROC. [*sic*]

"Mrs. Oscar Wilde at Home," *To-day* (London, UK), 24 Nov. 1894, 93–4[1]

Like her husband, poet, playwright and wit, Mrs. Oscar Wilde may be truly called an apostle of the beautiful. She has in a quiet and unobtrusive manner made everything that concerns the beautifying of the home a special study, and her exquisite embroidery and needlework is appreciated by a large circle of friends and acquaintances, although she has never yet been persuaded to exhibit anything in one of the many yearly "shows" which make a speciality of the blending of the arts and crafts.

Mr. and Mrs. Wilde have set up their household gods in one of the prettiest corners of old Chelsea, within a stone's-throw of the Walk once paced by the Sage of Chelsea and Jeannie Welsh Carlyle, by Dante Gabriel Rossetti, and George Eliot.

There is an utter lack of so-called aesthetic colouring in the house of which Mrs. Oscar Wilde is mistress; the scheme consisting, as it does, of faded and delicate brocades, against a background of white or cream painting, is French rather than English.

Rare engravings and etchings form a deep frieze along two sides of the drawing-room, and stand out on a dull gold background, and the only touches of bright colour in the apartment are lent by two splendid Japanese feathers let into the ceiling, while, above the white, carved mantelpiece, a gilt-copper *bas-relief*, by Donoghue, makes living Mr. Oscar Wilde's fine verses, "Requiescat."

To most of Mrs. Oscar Wilde's visitors not the least interesting work of art in this characteristic sitting-room is a quaint harmony in greys and browns, purporting to be a portrait of the master of the house as a youth; this painting was a wedding present from Mr. Harper Pennington, the American artist, and is much prized by the wife of the original.

Even apart from this picture, Mrs. Wilde can boast of an exceptionally choice gallery of contemporary art. Close to a number of studies of Venice, presented by Mr. Whistler himself, hangs an exquisite pen-and-ink illustration by Walter Crane. An etching of Bastien Le Page's portrait of Sarah Bernhardt con-

---

1. Referenced in Pearson, 262. *To-Day* was edited by Jerome K. Jerome (1859–1927), an English writer best known for his comic novel *Three Men on a Boat* (1889).

tains in the margin a few kindly words written in English by the great *tragedienne*.

"I scarcely think myself competent to say much on decoration," observed my hostess, modestly. "Of course, those matters are so much questions of sentiment and feeling. I am, personally, often struck by the amount of over-decoration that is now the rule, rather than the exception in many houses."

"Then you think that the amateur decorator should always aim at simplicity?"

"Certainly," she replied, thoughtfully; "no one who has not tried them knows the value of uniform tints and a quiet scheme of colouring, One of the most effective effects in house decoration can be obtained by leaving, say, the sitting-room, pure cream or white, with, perhaps, a dado of six or seven feet from the ground. In an apartment of this kind, ample colouring and variety will be introduced by the furniture, engravings, and carpet; in fact, but for the trouble of keeping white walls in London clean, I do not think there can be anything prettier and more practical than this mode of decoration, for it is both uncommon and easy to carry out. I am not one of those," continued Mrs. Wilde, "who believe that beauty can only be achieved at considerable cost. A cottage parlour may be, and often is, more beautiful, with its unconsciously achieved harmonies and soft colouring, than a great reception-room, arranged more with a view to producing a magnificent effect. But, I repeat, of late, people, in their wish, to decorate their homes, have blended various periods, colourings, and designs, each perhaps beautiful in itself, but producing an unfortunate effect when placed in juxtaposition. I object also to historic schemes of decoration, which nearly always make one think of the upholsterer, and not of the owner of the house."

"I believe that flowers are now playing a very great part in decoration?"

"Yes, but it is possible to have too many flowers in a room, and I think that scattering cut blossoms on a table-cloth is both a foolish and a cruel custom, for long before dinner is over the poor things begin to look painfully parched and thirsty for want of water. A few delicate flowers in plain glass vases produce a prettier effect than a great number of nosegays, and yet, even though people may see that something is wrong many do not realise how easily a charming effect might be produced with the same materials, somewhat differently disposed."

"And what do you think of the present craze for Japanese art?"

Mrs. Wilde smiled.

"I wonder how many people know that the greater number of cheap Japanese fans and screens, to say nothing of trays, etc., etc., sold in this country, are specially made for the English market. That this is so, is easily proved to anyone who knows anything of Japanese life. The Japs have a horror of a black background, and all their work is done in light, pale colourings. Again, a Japanese native room is furnished with dainty simplicity, and one flower and one pot supply the Jap's aesthetic longing for decoration. When he gets tired of his flower and his pot, he puts them away, and seeks for some other scheme of colour produced by equally simple means. As for fans, they are, of course, in Japan made for use and not for show. I think that even if people would only try to see that the articles they have in daily use are beautiful, and devoted a little less time to simply buying useless nick-nacks, whose only *raison d'être* is their supposed artistic worth, the problem of many a would-be House Beautiful would be solved."

"I believe, Mrs. Wilde, that you do a good deal of embroidery."

"Yes, but I do not claim to have any special ideas on the subject. I am, just now, anxious to learn Chinese needlework, such very beautiful effects seem to be produced by its means."

"And do you think that such an exhibition as the Arts and Crafts is of much use from a practical point of view?"

"The Arts and Crafts Exhibitions seem to serve two purposes. They produce emulation amongst the workers, and awaken curiosity and latent artistic instincts among the general public, and I should imagine that the exhibitions are of unmixed good, if sufficient time is allowed for the production of new and original work. I speak as an entire outsider, one to whom all decorative work, whatever form it may take, is intensely interesting, and who consequently thoroughly enjoys these exhibitions."

An interesting glimpse into Mrs. Oscar Wilde's tastes and surroundings is afforded by a glance through her autograph-book, a plain little volume cased in a charming book-cover made by herself.[1] From the dedicatory verses on the first page, written by the author of "Salomé" to his wife:—

> "I can write no stately proem,
>   As a prelude to my lay;
> From a poet to a poem,
>   That is all I say."[2]

to the last of the many characteristic utterances contained therein, every signature gives food for thought, and, oftener than not, reveals something of the writer.

"Our greatest happiness should be found in the happiness of others," declares Mr. G. F. Watts, the great painter, whose work has brought joy to so many.[3] Sir Edwin Arnold drops into poetry with some pretty lines.[4] George Meredith

1. Constance's autograph book: see also William Theodore Peters, "Oscar Wilde at Home," *The Sunday Inter Ocean* (Chicago, IL), 16 Dec. 1894, 31, p. 619.

2. The first four lines of a 12 line poem Wilde inscribed in a copy of *Poems* he gave to Constance. First published in the 1893 anthology *Book-Song: An Anthology of Poems of Books and Bookmen from Modern Authors* (CW i, No. 102).

3. Watts's inscription is dated August 1892.

4. Arnold's inscription is dated 1 August 1889.

writes his little poem, "Love is winged for two." Sturdy independence is equally shown in the round, frank caligraphy of Robert Browning,[1] and the more delicate American handwriting of Mark Twain;[2] and under some ardently patriotic forecasts signed T. P. O'Connor,[3] Mr. Arthur James Balfour dryly remarks, "Of all exercise of the human intelligence political prophecy is the most vain." Mr. Swinburne must have had his hostess's two boys in his mind when he transcribed in their mother's book his beautiful lines on childhood,[4] and Mr. Walter Crane is represented by —

> "From your book I take a leaf,
> By your leave to leave and take;
> Art is long if life be brief,
> Yet on this page my mark I'll make."

And then comes John Bright's favourite quotation, "In peace sons bury their fathers. In war fathers bury their sons."[5] Mr. Whistler contributes his long-suffering "Butterfly broken on the wheel," and the simple signatures of Oliver Wendell Holmes, Sargent, the American painter, John Ruskin, Henry Irving, Miss Ellen Terry, and many other familiar and unfamiliar names, evokes a vision of what should be a unique gathering of notable men and women.[6]

1. Browning inscribed his autograph on 16 May 1889.

2. Twain inscribed a few lines from his novel *Pudd'nhead Wilson* (1894) in Florence, March 1893. Constance was in Florence while Oscar was in London for rehearsals of *A Woman of No Importance* (Page, 52).

3. In the source there is a full stop here but a comma was surely intended because in Constance's album Balfour's inscription appears directly below that of the politician and journalist Thomas Power O'Connor (1848–1929), which reads: "There is something almost bewildering in the thought that this generation of Irishmen is about to see the close of a struggle that has gone through seven centuries." O'Connor's inscription is dated 24 July 1888.

4. Swinburne inscribed his poem *Children*, first published in 1882.

5. Bright inscribed this on 21 April 1887.

6. Holmes signed the album in London, 3 June 1886; Sargent (the name is spelt "Sergeant" in the source), in May 1894.

Baroness von Zedlitz, "Some Famous Stage Lovers: No. 1.—Mr. George Alexander at Home," *The Englishwoman* (London, UK), Mar. 1895, 33–8[1]

"When did you first undertake the management of a theatre?" I asked presently.

"In February, 1890, I opened the Avenue Theatre with *Dr. Bill*, which absurdity, you perhaps remember, had a great success."[2]

When the Avenue Theatre lease expired, Mr. Alexander, somewhat riskily, people thought, entered upon an agreement to take over the St. James's Theatre, which at that time had achieved the reputation of being an unlucky house.

Here Mr. Alexander's admirable tact and managerial faculties soon turned a consecutive run of bad luck into a succession of successful productions, for "*Lady Windermere's Fan*," followed by that delightful and sublimely-acted domestic idyll, "*Liberty Hall*," then "*The Second Mrs. Tanqueray*," and later, "*The Masqueraders*," have proved for themselves that the actor-manager had always considered the public and its requirements above all things.[3]

When asking him his opinion of his audiences, Mr. Alexander spoke with his usual characteristic good feeling and sound judgment.

"There is nothing half-hearted in their appreciation," he said, "they either like or dislike, and convey their opinion to the stage without hesitation.

"The difference between reading a book which bores you, or going to see a play which fails to interest you, is this: In the case of a book, why, you simply put it down if you don't like it, and pick up another one more suited to your taste and

1. Marie Antoinette Cécille von Zedlitz née Beatty-Kingston (1867–1944) was an American-born journalist who wrote for several British and German periodicals. Her other interviewees include Lawrence Alma-Tadema, Arthur Sullivan, Adelina Patti, and Ellen Terry. In 1896 she "edited and compiled" the memoirs of Italian violinist Luigi Arditi (1822–1903).

2. Alexander leased the Avenue Theatre in January 1890. *Dr. Bill* was a farce adapted by Charles Hamilton Aide (1826–1906) from Albert Carré's *Le Docteur Jojo* (1888). It opened at the Avenue on 1 February and ran for nine months, after which it was replaced with *The Struggle for Life* by Alphonse Daudet. That play closed after one month. (Sutherland, 31–2.)

3. *Lady Windermere's Fan* ran from 20 February to 29 July 1892 and was given a second run between 31 October and 30 November that year. R. C. Carton's *Liberty Hall* opened on 3 December 1892 and closed on 20 May 1893. The two plays shared a number of cast members, including Alexander, Fanny Coleman (1840–1919), Nutcombe Gould (1849–1899), and Marion Terry (1853–1930). *The Second Mrs. Tanqueray* by Arthur Wing Pinero opened on 27 May 1893 and was still attracting sizeable audiences when Alexander closed it on 21 April 1894. *The Masqueraders* by Henry Arthur Jones (1851–1929) opened on 28 April 1894 and closed on 22 December. (Sutherland, 262–3.)

mind; but if you go to the theatre and cannot follow the play with interest or pleasure, you feel that you are morally bound to 'see it through,' notwithstanding, and of course you are thoroughly dissatisfied with everything and everybody. I am sorry that 'Guy Domville' failed to give satisfaction, but there can be no doubt that the public is right, and that I am wrong.[1]

"It is a poetic little play, and one which took us a long time to prepare; however, we have another new piece in rehearsal now, by Oscar Wilde, which I hope will meet with undivided approbation."[2]

Hereupon Mr. Alexander read me one or two scenes which, I have every confidence in predicting, will elicit many a hearty smile. Although I may not speak largely on the subject, one scene took my fancy greatly. Of course the whole play is *Wild-ish* [*sic*] to the core, and contains a conglomeration of topsy-turvyisms *mêlée* with many startling truisms. Illustrative of one of the huge jokes Mr. Oscar Wilde launches forth, the heroine's mamma, a wide-awake match-making dame, enters the room in which her daughter is being proposed to by a young gentleman who is kneeling at her feet in an attitude of adoration. The daughter seeing her mother, says in a lofty tone:

"Mamma, please leave the room, this is no place for you. Besides, Mr. So-and-so hasn't finished yet."[3]

✂ *Several paragraphs that are unrelated to Wilde.*

---

1. *Guy Domville* by Henry James opened on 5 January 1895 (two days after *An Ideal Husband*) and was performed thirty-two times before it was closed on 5 February (Sutherland, 263).

2. *The Importance of Being Earnest* opened on 14 February.

3. Gwendolyn's line is: "Mamma! (*He* [Jack] *tries to rise; she restrains him*) I must beg you to retire. This is no place for you. Besides, Mr Worthing has not quite finished yet." (CW x, 779.382–3.)

"Lord Queensberry in the Dock," *The New York Herald, European Edition* (Paris, France), 3 Mar. 1895, 1

Charged with Unlawfully and Maliciously Libelling Mr. Oscar Wilde.

LEFT A CARD AT HIS CLUB.

Reasons for His Lordship's Resentment—Estrangement Between Father and Son.

DETAILS OF THE ARREST.

Evidence Given by the Club Porter—Remanded on Heavy Bail.

INTERVIEW WITH THE MARQUIS

(BY THE HERALD'S SPECIAL WIRE.)

LONDON, March 3.—

✂ *Several paragraphs describing the circumstances leading up to the arrest of the Marquess of Queensberry. A judge grants the Marquess bail.*

LORD QUEENSBERRY EXPLAINS.

I saw the Marquis of Queensberry last night at Carter's Hotel and, though he was naturally in a somewhat nervous and excited condition, he talked freely concerning the case, so far at least as it affected Mr. Wilde alone. "I sent that card," said he, "to Mr. Oscar Wilde to bring matters to a head.[1] For the past two years I've been hunting for him in order that I might have an opportunity of assaulting him in consequence of what I believe to be well founded rumors in connection with persons in whom I am interested.

"About a year ago I called upon him at his house, but could not get hold of him.[2] In fact, he always manages to elude me, and I think he must employ detectives to keep him posted with regard to my movements. I wished to assault him so that he should be forced to bring an action against me, and thus give me the opportunity of stating what I believe to be the truth about the matter. I am delighted at the result of my action in leaving that card, and feel much easier in my mind now. In regard to the words I wrote upon that card the reports in the papers are incorrect. I did not apply an offensive epithet to him directly, for that would have been libellous. I prefaced them with the words 'Posing as,' which renders them, from a legal point of view, entirely different.

---

1. Queensberry had left a card for Wilde at his club that read: "To Oscar Wilde, [?posing as] somdomite [*sic*]". The unclear words may be "ponce and".

2. At the libel trial Wilde testified that Queensberry had come to his house some time at the end of June 1894 and accused Wilde of "disgusting conduct" (Holland, 56–9).

"Into the exact reasons for the strong action I have taken I do not care at present to enter very fully, for you must remember that the case has still to be heard of in Court, but I may tell you that for the last ten days I have hardly been able to contain myself, so enraged was I by certain statements which have reached my ears. I can only regret that unfortunately duelling is not now permitted in England. Of course if a man of my size were to assault Oscar Wilde, a man of fifteen or sixteen stone, he would have no chance against him, but it would have effected my object, which was to bring the matter before the public.

TO GET HIM OUT OF THE COUNTRY.

"There is another thing you may say, and that is, that I desire, more than anything else, to get him out of the country. Some time ago he talked of going to live in France,[1] but he has not yet gone there, or, at all events, has not taken up his residence there permanently. Of course I have no direct proof of Wilde's guilt, for under the circumstances that would be impossible. It is enough for me to know that the matter has been of late so generally known that it may be fairly termed 'a topic of common gossip.'"

Mr. Wilde was said not to be at home when I called at his house in Tite-street, nor had he returned up to a late hour last night.

"Finished!" *The Sun* (London, UK), 5 Apr. 1895, 3[2]

END OF THE LIBEL CASE.

QUEENSBERRY VINDICATED.

Sir Edward Clarke Withdraws.

THE VERDICT AGAINST WILDE.

THRILLING SCENE IN COURT.

LETTER TO THE PUBLIC PROSECUTOR.

✂ *Several paragraphs about the outcome of the Marquess of Queensberry's libel trial.*

---

1. See "The Censure and 'Salome'," *The Pall Mall Gazette* (London, UK), 29 June, 1892, 1–2, p. 606; and Maurice Sisley, "La Salomé de M. Oscar Wilde," *Le Gaulois* (Paris, France), 29 June 1892, 1, p. 610.
2. Quoted in Sturgis, 558/520–1.

WILDE AT A HOTEL.

THE DOUGLAS FAMILY STILL HAVE FAITH IN HIM.

Mr. Oscar Wilde was this afternoon at the Holborn-viaduct Hotel, where, with Lord Douglas of Hawick and Lord Alfred Douglas, he had a suite of rooms during the trial. A representative of The Sun called at the hotel soon after the collapse of the suit, with the object of obtaining from Mr. Wilde his own statement as to why he had decided to withdraw the prosecution and consent to a verdict against himself. Lord Douglas of Hawick said Mr. Wilde felt quite unable at the moment to bear seeing anyone. The young lord, however, added that on Mr. Wilde's behalf he was willing to answer any questions he could. He was, he said, himself, together with his brother Lord Alfred,

UNDER SUBPOENA FOR THE PROSECUTION.

He himself would have been quite willing to go into the box, and his brother was most anxious to be allowed to do so, and was exceedingly grieved that Mr. Wilde had prevented him. It was to prevent that—and because he felt that "no man could bear to have every little act and indiscretion of his life, and every word and thought produced against him they perverted in the basest way and placed in their worst possible light [*sic*]," that Mr. Wilde had resolved to retire from the prosecution.

"You may say from me myself," went on Lord Douglas of Hawick, "that I, and

EVERY MEMBER OF OUR FAMILY,

excepting my father, disbelieve absolutely and entirely the allegations of the defence.[1] It is, in my opinion, simply a part of the persecution which my father has carried on against us ever since I can remember. I think Mr. Wilde and his counsel to blame for not showing, as they could have done, that was the fact."

---

1. In the next day's edition the following letter to the editor was printed: "Sɪʀ,—My nephew, Lord Douglas of Hawick, was certainly not authorised by my mother, my sister, or myself, to say as reported in your evening issue—'Every member of our family, except my father, disbelieves, absolutely and entirely, the allegations of the defence.' We do most certainly believe them, and must repudiate any sympathy with the statement of my nephew.—Yours faithfully, Aʀᴄʜɪʙᴀʟᴅ Dᴏᴜɢʟᴀs." ("Hon. and Rev. A. Douglas," *The Sun* (London, UK), 6 Apr. 1895, 3.) Reverend Lord Archibald Edward Douglas (1850–1938) was the son of Archibald Douglas, the previous Marquess of Queensberry. Lord Alfred Douglas, describing 34 years later the events that precipitated the libel trial, stated that: "I am entitled to say (and in this I am supported by my mother and also by my uncle, my father's now sole surviving brother, the Very Reverend Canon Lord Archibald Douglas, who is a Catholic priest) that the main responsibility for the trouble must rest with my father." (Douglas, 100.)

His lordship cited several alleged circumstances in support of his statement, and concluded by asserting, with considerable emotion that scandal after scandal had been heaped upon them till he felt utterly unable to hold up his head.

Then in answer to a question, Lord Douglas added that with Mr. Wilde's full authority he could state that Mr. Wilde had no thoughts of immediately leaving London, and would stay to face whatever might be the result of the proceedings.

"Oscar Wilde Imprisoned," *The New York Times* (New York, NY), 6 Apr. 1895, 5

Worse Than Failure Comes of His Suit for Vindication.

QUEENSBERRY'S ACTION JUSTIFIED

Jurors Decide in a Subsidiary Verdict that the Marquis's Accusation Was Made for the Public Good.

✂ *Several paragraphs about the outcome of the Marquess of Queensberry's libel trial.*

The Marquis of Queensberry said to a representative of the United Press:
"I have sent this message to Wilde: 'If the country allows you to leave, all the better for the country; but if you take my son with you I will follow you wherever you go and shoot you.'"

✂ *Several paragraphs about Wilde's movements immediately after the close of the trial.*

A United Press reporter visited the Haymarket and St. James's Theatres, where Oscar Wilde's plays are running.[1] Mr. Morrell, one of the managers of the Haymarket, in reply to the question how the result of the case would affect future business, said he would rather not express an opinion. He would say, however, that Mr. Wilde's name had been taken out of the bills and advertisements of "An Ideal Husband," and from this the public could form its own conclusions.

Mr. George Alexander, manager of the St. James's Theatre, where Oscar Wilde's play, "The Importance of Being Earnest," is running, said:

---

1. *An Ideal Husband* was transferred from the Haymarket to the Criterion Theatre, as per a long-standing arrangement, on 13 April, running there until the 27th. Wilde's name was restored to the programme. *The Importance of Being Earnest* ran at the St James's Theatre until 8 May (Seeney, M. (2015). *From Bow Street to the Ritz: Oscar Wilde's Theatrical Career from 1895 to 1908*. Rivendale Press. 9–10).

"When the scandal was first rumored business here was slightly affected, but it is now normal. Mr. Wilde's name has been withdrawn from the bills and advertisements of his comedy, which is the most innocent play in the world. It does not contain a line that could hurt the most tender susceptibilities. Whether the trial will cause a change in the business of the future remains to be seen."

He said also that "The Importance of Being Earnest" would be kept on the stage pending the public verdict. If he should be compelled to withdraw it, some 150 persons would be thrown out of work, as he had nothing ready to replace it.

It is reported that the Criterion, to which "An Ideal Husband" was to be transferred from the Haymarket, has declined to put the play on its stage.

The audiences at the Haymarket and St. James's Theatres, where Mr. Wilde's plays are being given, were rather small this evening, but they made no hostile demonstration. At the St. James's there were few persons, excepting those who had bought their tickets in advance. The gallery was somewhat critical, and two or three audible comments confused the players slightly.

The Daily Telegraph will say tomorrow in a leader on Wilde's case:

"It was a just verdict, and must be held to include with Wilde the tendency of his peculiar career, the meaning and the influence of his teachings, and all the shallow and specious arts by which he attempted to establish a cult and even set up new schools of literature and social thought."

Daniel Frohman, manager of the Lyceum Theatre, where Oscar Wilde's drama, an "Ideal Husband," is being played, said last night, when asked what action he would take regarding the use of Wilde's name in connection with the play, that he had ordered Wilde's name erased from the programmes and advertisements, and that he had just canceled a lot of contracts for printing matter relative to the piece upon which the author's name figures.

The play itself, he said, was a moral one, and there was nothing in it that would shock even the most sensitive. The play will be continued at the house, he said.

Rose Coghlan Abandons Wilde's Play

DETROIT, Mich., April 5.—Mr. Leslie, the manager of Miss Rose Coghlan, who has been playing Oscar Wilde's "A Woman of No Importance" here this week, was asked this evening by a representative of the United Press if the play would be shelved because of the scandal affecting Wilde.

He said it would be impossible, under the contract, to take Wilde's name off the play bills, and out of advertisements of "A Woman of No Importance," and therefore it had been decided that the play should be taken out of Miss Coghlan's repertoire.[1]

"Mr. Oscar Wilde in a Cell in Bow Street," *The New York Herald, European Edition* (Paris, France), 6 Apr. 1895, 1[2]

Trial of the Marquis of Queensberry Ends in a Verdict of "Not Guilty."

PROSECUTION WITHDRAWN.

Arranged Between the Opposing Counsel Last Thursday—A Mysterious Cable.

LETTER TO THE TREASURY.

Lord Queensberry Tells His Story to the "Herald"—Threats to Shoot.

ARRESTED AT HIS HOTEL.

Detective Sergeants Find Their Man Chatting with the Douglas Boys.

TO APPEAR THIS MORNING.

(BY THE HERALD'S SPECIAL WIRE.)

✂ *Several paragraphs about the outcome of the Marquess of Queensberry's libel trial.*

"DONE MY DUTY."

"I think," said Lord Queensberry to me later in the afternoon when I found him at Carter's Hotel, Albemarle-street, his table littered with congratulatory telegrams which continued to arrive in batches at intervals, "I think I have done my duty, not only to my family and myself, but also to the community. It has cost

---

1. *A Woman of No Importance* was performed in Detroit on 4 April to positive reviews and had made such "a distinctly favourable impression on the public mind" that it was predicted it could run for a week ("The Stage," *The Detroit Free Press* (Detroit, MI), 5 Apr. 1895, 4; "The Stage," *The Detroit Free Press* (Detroit, MI), 6 Apr. 1895, 4). Leslie and Coghlan decided to withdraw the play, placing an advertisement in *The Detroit Free Press* on the 6th stating that that day's matinee and evening performances would be the last. In the event, even these performances were cancelled: after the performance on the evening of the 5th Coghlan announced "That is the last time I will ever present that piece. I cannot take Wilde's name off the bills without breaking my contract, and I shall simply drop the play entirely. The opinion of the people is against the play since the publication of the scandal, as is shown by the falling off in advance sales." ("Play under the Ban," *The Boston Daily Globe* (Boston, MA), 6 Apr. 1895, 2.)
2. Quoted in Stratmann, 236; and Sturgis, 560/523.

me £1,200 and now if the law of England does not step in I must make my own
law. I have sent a message to this creature Wilde that if he chooses to leave the
country, I, for one, shall certainly not lift a finger to stay him, but he must distinctly understand that if he takes my son with him I shall follow him and shoot
him like a dog. But I think he ought not to be allowed to leave the country; I think
he ought to be placed where he can ruin no more young men.

"For the part I have taken myself in this matter I can only say I acted absolutely and entirely from a sense of duty. Many of my friends have said, as many of
these telegrams received also say, that I am to be commended for my pluck. I do
not see that pluck had anything to do with it.

"I do not see that I could have acted otherwise than I have done and have
preserved my self-respect. I may tell you that the full measure of this man's
baseness was not revealed to me until after my own arrest at his instance.

DEPTHS OF IMMORALITY.

"Then the evidence which accumulated and the voluntary confessions
which were made to us showed us a depth of immorality which is almost incredible. But I have come to the conclusion that the man, if man you can call him,
must be demented. No sane man could have adopted the tone he did on the witness stand; no sane man could have made the ridiculous assertion you tell me he
has concerning the reason of his counsel's withdrawal.[1]

"Why he has not long since fled the country I cannot imagine, for he knew of
our defence and our witnesses days ago, and must have anticipated the only result possible. I may tell you that our evidence was irrefutable, peculiarly so, indeed."

✂ *Several paragraphs about Wilde's arrest.*

---

1. Sir Edward Clarke had asked to withdraw from the prosecution because he and his colleagues felt that a verdict of not guilty was unavoidable, given that Queensberry had only accused Wilde of "posing" as a sodomite, and that the evidence presented thus far seemed likely to
be perceived to justify that accusation.

"Charge Against Oscar Wilde," *The Birmingham Daily Post* (Birmingham, UK), 8 Apr. 1895, 8[1]

✄ *Several paragraphs about the proceedings at Bow Street Police Court on the morning of Saturday 6 April 1895, after which Wilde was taken to Holloway Gaol, and about the arrest of Alfred Taylor.[2]*

Lord Alfred Douglas told a reporter in the course of an interview on Saturday evening that he did not think he would be one of the witnesses for the defence in the case of Wilde, but that at any rate he would "be on hand if wanted."[3] He is anxious to deny the statement that on Friday he went to the bank and drew money for Wilde. "The only foundation for the story," he says, "is that Mr. Wilde sent a friend of his down to enquire at the bank what balance he had, and to draw a very small sum of money." He accuses the press generally of having "deliberately suppressed" letters read in court which fully explain the attitude he takes up with regard to his father. "I refused to acknowledge that my father had any right over me, inasmuch as he never treated my mother as his wife nor me as his son." "As to Mr. Wilde," he added, "he has been grossly abused by the press. But the conduct of journalists is, after all, very English—'once a man is down, kick him.'" Questioned as to what he was going to do now, his lordship replied, "If Mr. Wilde should be locked up, I shall get a house near the prison, and live there till he comes out."[4]

Up to ten o'clock last night no further arrest had been made in connection with the case.

1. Printed simultaneously as "The Society Scandal," *The Northern Echo* (Durham, UK), 8 Apr. 1895, 3. Reprinted as "The Oscar Wilde Case," *Western Mail* (Cardiff, UK), 9 Apr. 1895, 5; and "A Call for the Author," *The Weekly Standard and Express* (Blackburn, UK), 13 Apr. 1895, 3.

2. Alfred Taylor (c. 1862–?) introduced Wilde to several young men who later testified against Wilde. On 21 May he was found guilty of committing improper acts. He had also been charged with procuring, but that charge was dropped after the jury failed to agree.

3. In his *Autobiography* Douglas would write that, prior to the libel trial, "Sir Edward Clarke was pledged to fight the case according to my ideas and to put me into the witness-box immediately after his opening speech." (Douglas, 91.) Clarke denied that he had made any such promise, pointing out that "[t]he question of Lord Queensberry's character was quite irrelevant to the case, and was never mentioned in my instructions or in consultation, and if an attempt had been made to give such evidence, the judge would of course have peremptorily stopped it." (Hyde, 208.) It therefore seems unlikely that Clarke ever contemplated calling Douglas as a witness at Wilde's trials, although in a later interview Douglas would suggest that he had (see Georges Docquois, "Entretien avec Lord Alfred Douglas," *Le Journal* (Paris, France), 25 May 1895, 1–2, p. 841).

4. Although Douglas visited Wilde regularly in Holloway, he left for Rouen on 25 April and lived in France and Italy during Wilde's imprisonment (Page, 66).

"His Oscars," *The Cincinnati Enquirer* (Cincinnati, OH), 8 Apr. 1895, 1[1]

Has Some Friends Left.

Mrs. Frank Leslie, Who Married His Brother,

Knows the Aesthete Well and Thinks Him a Model.

Mrs. Langtry Believes He Is Being Persecuted,

While Mrs. Grannis Wants Him Made "an Example."

Inspector Williams Tells How Wilde Was Once Bunkoed By Hungry Joe.

SPECIAL DISPATCH TO THE ENQUIRER.

NEW YORK, April 7.—Oscar Wilde, during his visits to this country, found the doors of society wide open. Mrs. Frank Leslie, who married the harum-scarum brother of Oscar, and cast him aside after a joyless honeymoon, was asked for her opinion. She said:

"I have visited Mr. Wilde at his home on Tite Street. I have met his venerable mother, Lady Wilde. I also know Mr. Wilde's wife, Constance, who is a model of all that is pure and womanly, and a most devoted mother to their children, two boys, called Vivian and Clarence [*sic*]."

"Do you believe that the charges made against Mr. Wilde are true?" asked the reporter.

"No. I cannot credit them. I speak of Mr. Wilde as I know him, my acquaintance extending over a period of 14 years. During that time I have considered him a model. His tastes are most refined, and it is difficult to associate his admirable character with such a scandal."

"Will society receive him if he is acquitted of the charge?" was asked.

"With open arms, with acclamation. You have no idea how highly it regards him. I hope that Mr. Wilde will be able to vindicate himself and emerge triumphant."

---

1. Printed simultaneously as "Startling," *The Kentucky Leader* (Lexington, KY), 8 Apr. 1895, 1, 8.

Mrs. Langtry was asked for her opinion of Wilde. She said: "I think him one of the most brilliant and polished men London society possesses."

"What do you think of his present predicament?"

"I assure you I can not credit it. I have great admiration for the man as a writer and wit, as well as for his social qualities. I am forced to believe that he is in this case a victim of persecution."

Inspector Williams, who was Captain of the Tenderloin Precinct when Oscar Wilde was first in this city, met him more than once. One of these occasions was when Oscar was introduced to an American trick by Hungry Joe, the famous bunko man.

Wilde was fleeced out of about $2,500 by Hungry Joe and his pals, who declared after the game had been played that Wilde was "dead easy."

The big Inspector told how the esthete had fallen into the bunko trap and handed over, besides what money he had, two checks on the Madison Square Bank, one for $1,000 and one for $1,200, which, fortunately for Wilde and thanks to the Inspector, were stopped before the bunko workers could cash them. Hungry Joe fled, and when he returned Oscar was in London.

"Do you think Wilde ought to be convicted?"

The Inspector thought deeply for a minute and replied: "There are some very strange people in this world, and quite a few in this city. I know of two messenger boys who were arrested on the charge of stealing $500 worth of clothes from a man almost as prominent as Oscar Wilde, although in a different line. The boys told me before they were taken to Court that the charge would not be pressed, and it was not."

EMPHATIC DENUNCIATION.

Mrs. Elizabeth Grannis, President of the Society for the Promotion of Social Purity, was emphatic in her denunciation of Oscar Wilde.[1]

"I am in a position," said she, "to know the extent of this evil, which is fast becoming prevalent in New York. The attention of our society has been called repeatedly to the existence of this abomination."

"What do you consider the best method of combating the evil?" was asked.

"To make public examples of those in high life who follow low practices. We may thus set up a warning to the masses. Let their crimes be made public, as was

---

1. Elizabeth Bartlett Grannis (1840–1926) was an American editor, suffragist, and advocate of dress reform and eugenics. She founded the National Christian League for the Promotion of Purity in 1887.

done in the case of Breckinridge.[1] The trouble in combating evil is that families hesitate to make known the reality. When the culprit invades the home circle every effort is made to hush it up."

Superintendent Byrnes smiled sarcastically when asked if he had anything to say on the Oscar Wilde matter.[2]

"I met Wilde in this city once, purely on business. I don't think our dispositions were such that our acquaintanceship could have advanced beyond mere business."

"Do you know anything interesting about him?"

The Superintendent lighted a fresh cigar, and, banishing the interesting smile he had worn, he said: "Doctors do not tell all they know about their patients, lawyers keep secrets from their clients, and at times policemen have information regarding persons they are bound to protect which should not be disclosed." And the Superintendent refused to discuss the matter further.

MAYOR STRONG SILENT.

Mayor Strong,[3] when asked if he would express an opinion wrinkled his face up tight. "No, sir;" he replied, with his peculiar Ohio emphasis, "I have nothing to say on such a subject." Then he ejaculated "Ah-h-h!"

✂ *An account of the Mary Travers libel case, including the mistaken claim that Travers was the mother of Sir William's illegitimate son, Henry Wilson.*

Many stories were told today of Oscar Wilde when he was in this country. At that time he became well acquainted with an artist who lives here. "Wilde," remarked this gentleman, "often said that the ambition of his life was to write an obscene novel on an artistic line. This was long before he ever attempted to write a story. So it is quite evident that the novel 'Dorian Gray' was the product of a long cherished hope, and secretly it must have gratified Oscar immensely to have put forth the production."

1. William Campbell Preston Breckinridge (1837–1904) was an American lawyer and a Democratic member of the United States House of Representatives between 1885 and 1895. In 1894 Madeleine Pollard, with whom he had had a decade-long relationship, sued him for breach of promise after he married his cousin. The trial began on 8 March 1884 and lasted 28 days. The jury ruled in Pollard's favour and awarded her $15,000. Breckinridge's reputation was destroyed and the following year he failed to win re-election.

2. Thomas F. Byrnes (1842–1910) was an Irish-born American police officer who served as head of the New York City Police Department's detective department between 1880 and 1895.

3. William Lafayette Strong (1827–1900) was the Mayor of New York City from 1895 to 1897.

"Oscar Wilde," *Le Gaulois* (Paris, France), 10 Apr. 1895, 1–2[1]

JUGE PAR LE

DOCTEUR MAX NORDAU

L'exemple de dégénérescence des facultés littéraires les plus fines et les plus pénétrantes en un ésotérisme abject, que le cas de M. Oscar Wilde vient de nous offrir, nous a donné l'idée d'interroger M. Max Nordau sur ce cas particulier. L'avis de l'auteur de *Dégénérescence*, le livre remarquable qui paraissait naguère dans la bibliothèque de philosophie contemporaine d'Alcan et qui eut un si vif succès, était assurément très précieux à recueillir.

— Mais, je l'avais presque prévue cette fin de M. Oscar Wilde, nous dit M. Max Nordau, en nous accueillant avec sa bonne grâce accoutumée. Et vous me voyez même fort embarrassé pour vous parler de lui, car l'ayant attaqué comme je l'ai fait quand il était triomphant, j'ai des scrupules à revenir sur les doctrines détestables d'un homme qui a fini par en être la propre victime.

— Cependant, répliquons-nous, le fait ne change rien à la théorie. Puisque vous avez vu juste de prime-saut, dites-nous ce que vous aviez vu.

— Eh bien ! nous répond M. Max Nordau, je disais, car nous n'avons plus qu'à mettre au passé ce que je mettais alors au présent, je disais textuellement que le décadentisme n'était pas resté limité à la France et qu'il avait aussi fait école en Angleterre. L'égotisme du décadentisme, son amour de l'artificiel, son aversion contre la nature, contre toutes les formes d'activité et de mouvement, son exagération du rôle de l'art, avaient retrouvé leur représentant anglais dans les « esthètes », dont le chef était Oscar Wilde.

» Oscar Wilde avait plus agi par ses bizarreries que par ses œuvres. Il s'habillait de costumes étranges, qui rappelaient en partie les modes du moyen-âge, en partie les formes rococo. Il prétendait avoir renoncé au vêtement actuel parce que ce vêtement offensait son sens de la beauté, mais ce n'était là qu'un prétexte auquel, très probablement, il ne croyait pas lui-même. Ce qui réellement déterminait ses actes, c'était l'envie hystérique d'être remarqué, de faire parler de lui. On assure qu'il s'est promené en plein jour dans Pall Mall, la rue la plus fréquentée du West-End de Londres, en pourpoint et en culotte, avec une toque pittoresque sur la tête, et, à la main, un soleil, fleur adoptée en quelque sorte comme symbole héraldique des poètes.

» L'amour des costumes étranges est l'aberration pathologique d'un instinct de l'espèce... Quoi qu'il en soit, M. Oscar Wilde obtint, dans le monde anglo-saxon tout entier, par son déguisement de paillasse, la notoriété que ses poésies ou ses

---

1. See below for an annotated English translation. Quoted in Erber, N. (1996). The French trials of Oscar Wilde. *Journal of the History of Sexuality*, 6, 549–88.

drames ne lui auraient jamais acquise [*sic*]. Je n'avais aucun motif pour m'occuper de ceux-ci, faibles imitations de Rossetti et de Swinburne, et d'une nullité désespérante. Ses articles, au contraire, méritaient l'attention, parce qu'ils accusaient tous les traits qui laissent reconnaître dans l'esthète le congénère du décadent.

» M. Oscar Wilde méprisait la nature, comme le font d'ailleurs les maîtres français. Voici quelques-uns de ses paradoxes. « Toutes les mauvaises poésies sortent de sentiments vrais. Être naturel veut dire être évident, et être évident veut dire être antiartistique. Ah ! ne dites pas que vous êtes d'accord avec moi. Quand les gens sont d'accord avec moi, je sens toujours que je dois avoir tort. » Son idéal de la vie était l'inactivité : « Que l'on cherche à être quelque chose, non à faire quelque chose... Les élus sont ceux qui sont là pour ne rien faire... Le sûr moyen de ne rien savoir de la vie est de se rendre utile. » *Et cætera.*

« Enfin M. Oscar Wilde aimait l'immoralité, le péché et le crime. Dans une caressante étude biographique sur l'assassin Thomas Griffith Wainewright, dessinateur, peintre et auteur, il dit : « C'était un faussaire de talent exceptionnel, et comme empoisonneur délicat et discret il n'a presque pas son pareil dans ce siècle ou dans un autre. Cet homme remarquable, si puissant par la plume, le pinceau et le poison, etc. Ses crimes semblent avoir exercé une action considérable sur son art. Ils ont donné à son style une empreinte fortement personnelle, un caractère qui manquait sûrement à ses premiers travaux. »

» Pour en revenir aux aphorismes, continue M. Max Nordau, en voici d'autres d'une originalité tout aussi caractéristique : « Il n'y a pas de péché, excepté la bêtise. Une idée qui n'est pas dangereuse ne mérite même pas d'être une idée. » M. Oscar Wilde en arrive à cultiver le mysticisme des couleurs : « L'amour du vert est chez les individus toujours un signe de disposition artistique délicate, et, chez les peuples, il indique le relâchement et même la dissolution des mœurs ». Qu'en pensez- vous ?

» Et puisque nous sommes sur le chapitre de la couleur, voici un autre enseignement de M. Oscar Wilde : « L'esthétique est supérieur au moral ; il appartient à une sphère plus intellectuelle. Percevoir la beauté d'un objet est le point le plus noble auquel nous puissions parvenir. Même le sens de la couleur est plus important dans le développement de l'individu que le sens du juste et de l'injuste. »

» Ainsi, continuais-je à dire dans mon livre, la doctrine des « esthètes » affirme, avec les parnassiens, que l'œuvre d'art est son propre but ; avec les diaboliques, qu'elle n'a pas besoin d'être morale, qu'il vaut mieux qu'elle soit immorale ; avec les décadents, qu'elle doit éviter le naturel et la vérité et leur être directement opposée, et avec toutes ces écoles égotistes de dégénérescence, que l'art occupe un rang plus haut que toute autre fonction humaine. J'ai démontré toute l'absurdité de ces thèses.

» Et je reviens à ma conclusion que je vous répète très volontiers, puisque nous sommes venus à parler de ces choses à propos de l'arrestation de M. Oscar Wilde. Ces gens-là ne sont d'aucun profit pour la société et nuisent à l'art véritable par leurs productions, dont la quantité et l'importunité cachent à la plupart des hommes la vue des véritables œuvres d'art de l'époque. Ce sont des débiles de volonté, impropres à une activité qui exige des efforts réguliers, uniformes, ou des victimes de la vanité qui veulent être plus célèbres qu'on ne peut le devenir comme casseur de pierres ou tailleur. Le manque de sûreté, de compréhension et de goût de la majorité et l'incompétence de la plupart des critiques permettent à ces intrus de se nicher dans les arts et de vivre là en parasites pendant toute leur vie…. Ils appartiennent aux portions les plus antisociales de l'espèce. Privés de sens pour les tâches et les intérêts de celle-ci, inaptes à comprendre une idée sérieuse, une action féconde, ils rêvent seulement à la satisfaction de leurs plus vils instincts, et nuisent autant par l'exemple de leur existence de parasites que par la confusion que jette dans les esprits insuffisamment avertis leur abus du mot « art » envisagé comme synonyme de démoralisation et d'enfantillage. Les dégénérés égoïstes, les décadents et les esthètes ont rassemblé au grand complet sous leur bannière ce rebut des peuples civilisés, et marchent à sa tête.

» Voilà ce que j'ai dit quand M. Oscar Wilde était triomphant. Aujourd'hui qu'il est, comme je viens de vous le dire, victime de ses propres doctrines, je forme le vœu que son aventure serve d'exemple à d'autres. Mais je crains fort que nous ne soyons qu'au commencement ! ... »

PAUL ROCHE

Oscar Wilde

JUDGED BY

DOCTOR MAX NORDAU

The example of the degeneration of the finest and most penetrating literary faculties into an abject esotericism lately offered by the case of Mr. Oscar Wilde prompted us to question Mr. Max Nordau on this particular case. The opinions of the author of *Degeneration*, the remarkable book which was recently published in Alcan's contemporary philosophy library and was so successful, were undoubtedly worth gathering.[1]

---

1. Max Simon Nordau (1849–1923) was a Hungarian physician and social critic. His two volume book *Entartung* was published in 1892–1893; English (*Degeneration*) and French (*Dégé-*

829

"But I had almost foreseen this end of Mr. Oscar Wilde," said Mr. Max Nordau, welcoming us with his usual good grace. "And I am even rather embarrassed to speak to you about him because, having attacked him as I did when he was triumphant, I am reluctant to revisit the detestable doctrines of a man who ended up their victim."

"However," we reply, "the fact does not change the theory. Since you saw it right off the bat, tell us what you saw."

"Well!" replies Mr. Max Nordau, "I said—because we only have to put in the past tense what I then put in the present—I said, verbatim, that decadentism had not been confined to France and that it had also established a school in England. The ego-mania of decadentism, its love of the artificial, its aversion to nature, and to all forms of activity and movement, its exaggeration of the role of art, had found their English representatives among the 'aesthetes', whose leader was Oscar Wilde.[1]

"Oscar Wilde had expressed himself more by his eccentricities than his works. He dressed in strange costumes, partly reminiscent of the fashions of the Middle Ages, partly the Rococo modes. He pretended to have abandoned the dress of the present time because it offended his sense of the beautiful, but this was only a pretext which, most likely, he himself did not believe in. What really determined his actions was the hysterical craving to be noticed, to be talked about. He is said to have walked in broad daylight in Pall Mall, the busiest street in London's West End, in doublet and breeches, with a picturesque cap on his head, and, in his hand, a sunflower, the flower adopted as the quasi-heraldic symbol of the poets.[2]

"The love of strange costumes is the pathological aberration of a racial instinct...[3] Anyway, Mr. Oscar Wilde obtained, in the whole Anglo-Saxon world, by his clownish fancy dress, the notoriety that his poems or his dramas would never have acquired for him. I had no desire to deal with these feeble imitations of Rossetti and Swinburne, hopelessly inane. His articles, on the contrary, deserved attention, because they exhibited all the features that make us recognise in the aesthete the conspecific of the decadent.[4]

"Mr. Oscar Wilde despised nature, as do his French masters. Here are some of his paradoxes. "All bad poetry springs from genuine feeling. To be natural is to

---

nérescence) translations appeared in early 1895. Nordau identified "degeneration" as a mental illness characteristic of the age. He supported his theory with case studies of various artists, including Wilde.

1. As Nordau points out, his responses are quoted almost verbatim from *Degeneration* (Nordau, 317).

2. Nordau, 317.

3. Nordau, 318.

4. Nordau, 319.

be obvious, and to be obvious is to be inartistic.[1] Ah! don't say that you agree with me. When people agree with me I always feel that I must be wrong."[2] His ideal of life was inactivity: "That we seek to be something, not to do something...[3] It is to do nothing that the elect exist...[4] The sure way of knowing nothing about life is to try to make oneself useful."[5] *Et cetera.*

"Finally, Mr. Oscar Wilde loved immorality, sin and crime. In a sympathetic biographical study of the assassin Thomas Griffiths Wainewright, designer, painter and author, he says: 'He was a forger of no mean or ordinary capabilities, and as a subtle and secret poisoner almost without rival in this or any age. This remarkable man, so powerful with "pen, pencil and poison", etc.[6] His crimes seem to have had an important effect upon his art. They gave a strong personality to his style, a quality that his early work certainly lacked.'"[7]

"To return to the aphorisms," continues Mr. Max Nordau, "here are others of equally characteristic originality: 'There is no sin, except stupidity.[8] An idea that is not dangerous is unworthy of being called an idea at all'.[9] Mr. Oscar Wilde came to cultivate the mysticism of colours: 'The love of green is in individuals always a sign of a subtle artistic temperament, and, in peoples, denotes a relaxation and even a dissolution of morals'.[10] What do you think about that?

"And since we're on the subject of colour, here's another lesson from Mr. Oscar Wilde: 'Aesthetics are higher than ethics. They belong to a more intellectual sphere. To discern the beauty of a thing is the finest point to which we can arrive. Even a colour-sense is more important, in the development of the individual, than a sense of right and wrong.'[11]

1. *The Critic as Artist* (CW iv, 195.26–7).
2. *The Critic as Artist* (CW iv, 199.17–18).
3. Nordau paraphrases Wilde's essay about the English painter, forger, and suspected murderer Thomas Griffiths Wainewright (1794–1852), *Pen, Pencil, and Poison* (1889, revised 1891): "This young dandy [Wainewright] sought to be somebody, rather than to do something." (CW iv, 108.6–7.) Gilbert in *The Critic as Artist* expresses a similar sentiment: "Yes, Ernest: the contemplative life, the life that has for its aim not *doing* but *being*, and not *being* merely, but *becoming*—that is what the critical spirit can give us." (CW iv, 178.27–9).
4. *The Critic as Artist* (CW iv, 175.4).
5. *The Critic as Artist* (CW iv, 180.5–6).
6. *Pen, Pencil, and Poison* (CW iv, 105.17–19).
7. *Pen, Pencil, and Poison* (CW iv, 120.19–21).
8. *The Critic as Artist* (CW iv, 204.13–14).
9. *The Critic as Artist* (CW iv, 183.10–11).
10. *Pen, Pencil, and Poison*: "He [Wainewright] had that curious love of green, which in individuals is always the sign of a subtle artistic temperament, and in nations is said to denote a laxity, if not a decadence of morals." (CW iv, 108.19–21.)
11. *The Critic as Artist* (CW iv, 204.20–3). Wilde has "spiritual" rather than "intellectual".

"So, as I continued to say in my book, the doctrine of the 'aesthetes' affirms, with the Parnassians,[1] that the work of art is its own goal; with the diabolics, that it doesn't have to be moral, that it is better that it be immoral;[2] with the decadents, that it must avoid what is natural and true and instead directly oppose them, and with all these egotistical schools of degeneration, that art ranks higher than any other human function. I have demonstrated the absurdity of these theories.

"And I come now to my conclusion which I will repeat to you very gladly, since it happens that we are talking about these things due to the arrest of Mr. Oscar Wilde. These people are of no benefit to society and injure true art by their productions, the quantity and importunateness of which obscure from the view of most men the genuine works of art of the epoch. They are weaklings in will, unfit for an activity that demands regular, uniform effort, or else victims to vanity who wish to be more famous than one can become as a stonebreaker or a tailor. The uncertainty of comprehension and taste among the majority and the incompetence of most critics allow these intruders to make their nest among the arts and dwell there as parasites for their entire lives…. They belong to the most antisocial elements of the species. Insensible to its tasks and interests, incapable of understanding a serious thought, a fruitful deed, they dream only of the satisfaction of their vilest instincts, and harm as much by the example of their existence as parasites as by the confusion they cause in minds insufficiently forewarned by their abuse of the word 'art', seeing it as synonymous with demoralisation and childishness. Selfish degenerates, decadents, and aesthetes have gathered together under their banner the scum of the civilised peoples, and are marching at its head.[3]

"This is what I said when Mr. Oscar Wilde was triumphant. Now that he is, as I just told you, a victim of his own doctrines, I hope that his adventure will serve as an example to others. But I am afraid that we are only at the beginning!…"

PAUL ROCHE

1. A school of French poets active during the latter half of the nineteenth-century. The Parnassians rejected Romanticism in favour of emotional detachment and formal structure.

2. "'Diaboliques' and 'décadents' are distinguished from ordinary criminals merely in that the former content themselves with dreaming and writing, while the latter have the resolution and strength to act." (Nordau, 261.) d'Aurevilly had published his collection of short stories, *Les Diaboliques*, in 1874; the stories dealt with crime and debauchery.

3. Again, this paragraph is quoted almost verbatim from *Degeneration* (Nordau, 337).

"Marquis and Son Come to Blows," *The New York Herald, European Edition* (Paris, France), 22 May 1895, 1[1]

Extraordinary Scene in Piccadilly—Lord Douglas of Hawick Attacks His Father.

"ONE OF WILDE'S ANCESTORS."

Conviction of Taylor—Further Revolt of the Scotch Members in the House.

(BY THE HERALD'S SPECIAL WIRE.)

LONDON, May 22.—This morning the Marquis of Queensberry will for the second time in the last three months appear in a police-court. This time, however, he will be attended by his eldest son, Lord Douglas of Hawick, both father and son being charged with disorderly conduct.

As to the events which led to this unpleasant conclusion rumors of the most erratic character were floating around the London clubs last night, no two of the stories agreeing in detail. I am able, however, from the testimony of a disinterested eye-witness to give the exact facts as they will be revealed before the magistrate this morning.

INSULTING LETTERS AGAIN.

At about a quarter-past five last evening Lord Queensberry crossed over Piccadilly in the direction of Albemarle-street, where his hotel is situated. As he reached the corner of the latter street and Piccadilly he was met by his son, Lord Douglas of Hawick, who appeared to be in an excited condition and who apparently, without any preliminary beyond asking his father how he dared to send insulting letters to Lady Douglas, pushed rather than struck the elder man.

The latter staggered somewhat and his hat fell off, but recovering himself almost instantly he struck out at his son. At this juncture a policeman appeared upon the scene and putting his arm between the two requested them both to refrain from making a scene.

LORD DOUGLAS STRIKES THE POLICEMAN.

Lord Douglas, however, in returning his father's blow struck the policeman violently on the mouth, though of course only accidentally. After a short discussion the gentleman in blue somewhat wisely retired from the scene, but the

---

1. Reprinted as "According to Queensberry," *The New York Herald* (New York, NY), 22 May 1895, 9. Quoted in "Tribunaux Étrangers," *Le Temps* (Paris, France), 23 May 1895, 3; and in "Wilde Tit-Bits," *Reynolds's Newspaper* (London, UK), 9 June 1895, 8 (which is quoted in Hyde, M. (1973). *The Trials of Oscar Wilde*. Dover. 233–4).

combatants, a few yards further along Piccadilly, resumed their verbal altercation and eventually came again to actual blows.

In the short but sharp encounter which followed the author of the Queensberry rules put his pugilistic theories into practice, and when the police, who by this time had reappeared, separated them, Lord Douglas of Hawick was the possessor of a scientifically discolored eye.

TAKEN TO THE POLICE STATION.

Both representatives of the house of Douglas were then incontinently marched off to the Vine Street Police Station, where a charge of disorderly conduct was preferred against them by the constable and entered on the charge sheet by the sergeant in charge of the station.

As they were perfectly well known they were allowed to depart when they had entered into their own recognizances in the sum of £2 to appear in court this morning.

These are the facts of the actual encounter. As to the preliminary matters which led thereto, I cannot do better than quote Lord Queensberry himself, whom I saw in the evening, and whose account of the occurrence, by the way, tallies perfectly well with the above.

LORD QUEENSBERRY SPEAKS OUT.

"I should like, first of all," said he, "to impress upon you that, as I shall have an opportunity of putting upon record tomorrow morning, I was not the aggressor. I had just returned from the Old Bailey, where I heard the jury find Taylor guilty, and had sent away my cab opposite St. James's Palace.

"I then walked up St. James's-street and was crossing over to Albemarle-street, when, by a coincidence which seems almost fateful, I saw my son some hundred yards away. He caught sight of me at the same time and at once charged down upon me and after a few angry words attempted to assault me.

"Even after we were first separated by the police my son was for the second time the aggressor. However, this is a matter which I suppose I shall have to explain to the satisfaction of the magistrate tomorrow morning.

WHAT LED TO THE CONFLICT.

"As to the reason for this attack by my son, I can only imagine that he was annoyed by the events of the day and felt foolishly exasperated against me. As to the letter which he accused me of sending to his wife, that was on my part in the nature of a joke.

"I was struck with a certain resemblance lurking in this picture," and the marquis held up to my view a drawing from one of the weekly illustrated papers depicting a huge iguanodon as it is supposed to have appeared to its prehistoric

834

Figure 23. Drawing of an iguanodon by Alice B. Woodward, with annotations in the hand of the Marquess of Queensberry (for a transcription, see p. 836, note 1).

contemporaries. There was a distinct touch of the humorous about the dinosaurian's attitude, and the marquis could not refrain from chuckling as he drew my attention to it. "I sent a copy of the picture," he continued, "to my son's wife, endorsing it as well as I remember 'a possible ancestor of Oscar Wilde' and intending it more as a good-natured joke than anything else.[1]

BAD BLOOD FOR SOME TIME.

"Of course I regard this evening's affair as very painful from one point of view, but from another I am rather glad of it. There has been bad blood between my son and myself for some time, and I think this encounter has probably let some of it out. At all events I feel more kindly disposed towards him than I have been for some years past, and I think very possibly he may think all the better of me."

And I left the marquis chuckling anew over this comic picture of the iguanodon.

1. The drawing of the iguanodon, by English artist Alice Bolingbroke Woodward (1862–1951), was printed in *The Illustrated London News* (London, UK), 18 May 1895, 614. A copy pasted into a scrapbook once owned by Stuart Mason has a typed note in the upper left corner: "This leaf, with comments in his own handwriting, was sent by the Marquess of Queensberry addressed to Oscar Wilde at the Old Bailey in May 1895" (No. 268, Oscar Wilde Scrapbook Vol. 5, Honma Hisao Collection, Jissen Women's University Rare Books). The comments in Queensberry's hand are as follows. Above the illustration: "Original ancestor | of Oscar Wilde | on the war path | of the madness of kissing | young males" (in a letter to Lord Alfred Douglas that was read out in court during the trials, Wilde had written: "it is a marvel that those red rose-leaf lips of yours should have been made no less for music of song than for madness of kisses", CL, 544). To the right of the illustration is a stick figure in the act of running, with two arrows pointing in the same direction, and a comment reading: "To Rouen | Flight of the slim gilt | soul" (in the same letter quoted above, Wilde had written: "Your slim gilt soul walks between passion and poetry"). Beneath the illustration is a standing stick figure holding what may be a spear, and a comment reading: "H of shitters with bail | Birds of a feather | flock together". The caption under the illustration reads: 'The animal is shown in the attitude in which it usually walked. The fore limbs are much shorter than the hind limbs, which are very powerful, having three toes to each foot and the same number of joints as in a bird's foot. The ponderous tail no doubt gave support to the animal when in an erect position, and was also used in swimming." Queensberry has appended "& copulating" and underlined the final instance of "the animal". The illustration was reprinted in *The New York Herald* (New York, NY), 26 May 1895, 9; and other American newspapers. See Tsuchiya, Y. (2022). Wilde iguanodon: what happened behind the trial. *Journal of Jissen English Department*, 74, 5–17.

Ballard Smith, "Father and Son Fight," *The Philadelphia Inquirer* (Philadelphia, PA), 23 May. 1895, 1

Marquis of Queensberry's Row With Lord Douglas Ventilated in Court.

DOUGLAS WAS THE AGGRESSOR

The Old Man's Letters to His Daughter-in-Law Caused All the Trouble.

CROWDS CHEER THE MARQUIS

Both Prisoners Held Under Bonds to Keep the Peace for Six Months.

Special Cable to The Inquirer, Copyright, 1895.

LONDON, May 22.—While Oscar Wilde's trial was proceeding at Old Bailey this morning two of the eccentric Queensberry family—The Marquis and his heir apparent, Lord Douglas of Hawick, whom he hates almost as furiously as he does his younger son, Lord Alfred Douglas—were in the Marlborough Street Police Court explaining about their fight in Piccadilly yesterday afternoon.

✂ *An account of the trial.*

A TALK WITH THE MARQUIS.

The Marquis of Queensberry talked with the utmost freedom to The Inquirer correspondent this evening. He said:

"The cause of my son's anger was this: Before Wilde was released on bail I went to Holloway Prison and left a note saying if he went about with my younger son, Lord Alfred Douglas, after his release he would do it at serious risk.[1] He sent no reply. I accordingly put detectives on him and called at the hotel after his release, but he refused to see me. My other son, Lord Douglas, took him and his lawyer to dine, but just as they were sitting down to dinner I appeared, and Wilde forthwith fled out of the house.[2]

"I heard next day that Wilde had gone to stay at Lord Douglas' country house at Kingston on the Thames and that Alfred was there. I presented myself at the house and was received by Lady Douglas, who refused me admission and said I should not come there.[3] Subsequently I learned that Alfred was at Rouen,

1. Stratmann, 242, states that Queensberry went to Holloway on 4 May.

2. The Midland Hotel, St Pancras, and the Great Northern Hotel, by King's Cross (Sturgis, 577/537).

3. Queensberry visited Chalcott House, Long Ditton on 11 May. The next day he wrote to Lady Douglas: "If I had not thought Wilde was there, as I believe he is or was, I should not have come." In fact, Wilde was staying with his friends Ada and Ernest Leverson in Kensington. (Stratmann, 244–5.) Lord Alfred had certainly been at Chalcott House before departing for Rouen: he sent a

Oscar Wilde having frightened him into leaving the country by falsely stating that a warrant had been issued for his arrest."

"Do you believe Wilde will be convicted?"

"A million to one on it, though I was scanning the jury today and I think there are a couple of queer looking fellows among them."

"Do you believe the authorities want a conviction?"

"It looks as if they didn't. They have got no fresh evidence, as they might have done. By the way, there is one matter I would like you to mention—that is the shabby way the authorities have treated me. They are relying altogether on the case prepared at my expense. It has cost me £2000, and when I applied to the Treasury for compensation they offered me £35. I protested against this meanness and they offered me £100, but I told them they might keep it.[1] I intend to get a question put in Parliament on the subject when the case is concluded, and have already seen Labouchère about it. I am a poor man and can't stand this expense.

"My sole object was to keep Wilde and Alfred apart, so I hope Wilde will be convicted. Should he escape, I will pursue him until I am satisfied the intimacy between them is stopped."

BALLARD SMITH.

Georges Docquois, "Entretien avec Lord Alfred Douglas," *Le Journal* (Paris, France), 25 May 1895, 1–2[2]

(PAR DEPECHE DE NOTRE ENVOYE SPECIAL)

Rouen, 24 mai 1895.

Je viens de converser longuement avec lord Alfred Douglas, dans la manière de jardin au fond duquel s'élève l'hôtel de la Poste, rue Jeanne-d'Arc.

---

letter from that address dated 19 April to the London *Star* ("The Wilde Case," *Western Mail* Cardiff, UK), 23 Apr. 1895, 5).

1. Sir William Vernon Harcourt (1827–1904), the Chancellor of the Exchequer, refused to compensate Queensberry for his "bribes to blackmailers" (Stratmann, 253).

2. See below for an annotated English translation. Quoted, 444/472, and referenced, 433/461, in Ellmann. Also referenced in the French translation of *The Autobiography of Lord Alfred Douglas*, published as *Oscar Wilde et Quelques Autres* (1930), for which Douglas wrote an additional chapter not in the English edition (Donald Mead's English translation of the chapter is printed in Douglas, A. (2022). *Oscar Wilde et Quelques Autres*: some additions to the text of *The Autobiography of Lord Alfred Douglas* for the French edition. *The Wildean*, 60, 29–36). In this additional chapter Douglas remembers that Docquois (1863–1927) interviewed him and "wrote a very kind article", although he incorrectly states that Docquois "was sent by *L'Echo de Paris*". Douglas adds that, shortly afterwards, Docquois introduced him to Eugène Tardieu, a journalist on the staff of *L'Echo de Paris* (Schroeder, 183), who translated Douglas's poems into French prose.

Le fervent ami d'Oscar Wilde a vingt-quatre ans. Comme dirait ma concierge, il ne les paraît pas. On lui donnerait vingt ans, tout au plus. Il est grand. Au premier coup d'œil, des pieds à la tête, il m'apparaît blond : blond de cheveux, blond de peau, blond d'habits. Très en harmonie avec cette générale impression blonde, trois teintes tendres : le bleu céleste des yeux ; le rose, au cou, de la cravate de linge ; le mauve, au bord de la poche du veston, d'un petit mouchoir fin.

Bien que s'y accusent un peu fortement le nez et la bouche, le visage — long — est celui d'un mystique. Cela ne va pas pourtant, jusqu'à de l'extase dans le regard. La physionomie d'Alfred Douglas n'a rien de très particulier que sa douceur absolue et son calme. Mais, pour celui qui ne cherche pas midi à quatorze heures, cet adulte a simplement l'air d'un parfait bon petit jeune homme.

Et rien d'anormal dans la démarche ; des allures tout à fait naturelles.

— Je suis ici depuis le commencement du procès, me dit-il. L'avocat de M. Wilde m'avait dit que j'y pourrais être appelé comme témoin, et je ne voulais pas cela. J'ai été à Paris, il y a trois jours; mais j'avais fait en sorte que les journaux ne connussent point ma présence.

— Est-ce donc que vous fuyez l'occasion de vous expliquer ?

— Mais, pourquoi parler ?

— Plutôt écrire, n'est-ce pas ?

— Pas davantage.

— Cependant, votre lettre au *Temps*, hier ?

— Il convenait de rectifier...

— Savez-vous bien que vous vous y montrez définitivement un fils bien extraordinaire ?

— Aoh ! Voilà. Il faut donc vous expliquer que ma conduite vis-à-vis de mon père n'a rien que de très logique.

— Ho ! ho !

— Oui, vous ne savez pas. Vous ignorez quel homme entièrement abominable est le marquis de Queensberry. Probablement, vous avez un bon père, vous ? Oui, n'est ce pas ? Moi, non. Jusqu'à l'âge de douze ans, peut-être j'ai vu le mien à peine vingt fois, et je ne savais pas du tout, observant quelles manières il avait avec moi, si j'étais le fils de cet homme.

Et, comme je me taisais, songeant, Alfred Douglas reprit :

— Ne pensez pas que je ne suis pas son fils. Sûrement, il est mon père, car ma mère est la créature la plus noble. C'est elle qui, sans le vouloir, me le fit voir tel qu'il avait été et comme il est. Je questionnai ma mère, en effet, après qu'elle eut obtenu le divorce. Il y a huit ans, je crois, de cela. Moi, j'avais seize ans. Je voulais savoir les choses. Ma mère me dit seulement une partie des souffrances que le marquis lui avait fait endurer. Après le divorce, il continua, du reste. Encore il continue. Il n'a cessé, il ne cesse d'adresser à la marquise des lettres ignobles et insultantes, et, souvent, il est allé, le soir, frapper dans la porte, pendant des heures, quand il savait que ma mère était malade et que le repos lui était indispensable.

— Avait-il de meilleurs procédés pour lord Douglas of Hawick, votre frère ?

— Non. Mon frère déteste le marquis tout comme moi. Et il est vrai qu'il a dû être parfaitement satisfait de le corriger il y a quelques jours.

Lord Alfred Douglas disait ces choses sans passion, avec la plus stupéfiante tranquillité.

— Néanmoins, ajouta-t-il, je ne crois pas que rien de désastreux eût dû survenir entre le marquis et moi, s'il ne s'était un jour avisé de regarder de trop près dans ma vie, à laquelle il n'avait jamais contribué que par son argent, et s'il n'avait eu la prétention de détruire mon amitié pour Oscar Wilde. Je lui écrivis nettement qu'il n'avait pas de droits sur ma conscience, et que je trouvais mauvais qu'il se mêlât de mes affaires, lui qui, pendant vingt ans, s'y était montré si peu attentif. Il me répondit que si je n'interrompais mes relations avec Wilde, il me couperait les vivres (j'étais alors à Oxford et il m'envoyait trois cent cinquante livres par an). Je lui écrivais : « Gardez votre argent. » Plus tard, pourtant, il voulut connaître Wilde, et s'arrangea pour déjeuner avec lui et moi. Durant ce déjeuner, il fut charmant et s'excusa d'avoir méconnu mon maître. Mais il ne devait pas persister dans ces bonnes dispositions... Vous savez, comme tout le monde, ce qu'il fit.

— Votre frère était aussi à Oxford ?

— Non. Après avoir désiré entrer dans la marine, il avait renoncé à cette carrière, et il était parti pour l'Australie. Il eut la chance d'y trouver de l'or, et, il y a six mois, il est revenu assez riche pour pouvoir fournir la caution de Wilde, ces temps derniers.

Alfred Douglas se tut.

Je cherchai comment je pourrais lui poser, sans le blesser, la question délicate sur les façons d'être de Wilde et sur les siennes propres, en dehors de leurs habitudes de pur esprit.

Je finis par trouver une formule, et je sus me faire entendre du jeune lord qui, toujours fort tranquille et très doux, me dit, dès que, relativement confus, j'eus achevé de m'exprimer :

— Wilde n'a pas les passions anti-physiques qu'on lui prête. C'est, seulement, un être original et fantastiquement artiste. Il recherche toutes les émotions, mais ce n'est que par singularité morale. Ainsi, il adorerait causer avec un assassin et lui offrirait avec joie à dîner dans sa chambre. Cela comporterait un danger. Il estime que ce serait véritablement amusant. Vous me dites que dans son roman: *le Portrait de Dorian Gray*, il a montré son héros courant à des aventures contre nature : cela veut-il dire que, lui, Wilde, ait les mêmes préoccupations et qu'il s'abandonne aux mêmes actes ? Votre grand romancier Balzac a peint, dans

Une Passion du désert, l'amour d'un soldat pour une panthère ; et je ne crois pas, pourtant, que Balzac ait jamais couché avec une panthère (*sic*).

— Alors, pour ce qui vous concerne, l'amitié que vous avez vouée à Wilde...

— Cette amitié, fit Alfred Douglas s'animant soudain, je ne dis pas qu'elle n'ait pas un côté exceptionnel. J'avoue même, vous entendez, que l'affection que j'ai pour lui est extraordinaire. Appelons-la romantique. Il n'y a pas, pour moi, de plus grande joie que celle de dîner avec Oscar Wilde, quand il est en *good form*. Nos deux âmes communient réellement dans le Symbole. Cela a quelque chose d'extraterrestre. Ici, cela peut sembler louche, et cela n'est que nous avons tant souffert l'un à cause de l'autre, que nous songerions le moins à nous séparer. Avant, j'étais lié à lui par une sorte d'unique plaisir de dilettante ; je suis maintenant lié à lui, plus sûrement, par la persécution.

GEORGES DOCQUOIS.

An Interview with Lord Alfred Douglas

(BY DISPATCH FROM OUR SPECIAL CORRESPONDENT)

Rouen, 24 May 1895.

I have just had a long conversation with Lord Alfred Douglas, in a garden of sorts at the end of which stands the Hôtel de la Poste, rue Jeanne-d'Arc.

The devoted friend of Oscar Wilde is twenty-four years old. As my concierge would say, it doesn't show. We would say he was twenty, at the most. He is tall. At first glance, from head to toe, he appears blonde to me: blonde in hair, blonde in skin, blonde in clothes. Very much in harmony with this general blonde impression are three subdued shades: the celestial blue of the eyes; at his throat, the pink of his linen tie; at the edge of the jacket pocket, the mauve of a small, fine handkerchief.

Although the nose and the mouth are slightly accentuated, the face—long— is that of a mystic. However, it does not fit well with the ecstasy in his eyes. The physiognomy of Alfred Douglas has nothing very particular about it other than absolute gentleness and calm. But, for those who prefer a simple description, this grown-up looks just like a perfect, good little young man.

And nothing abnormal in the approach; completely natural looks.

"I've been here since the trial began," he told me. "Mr. Wilde's lawyer told me that I could be called as a witness, and I didn't want that.[1] I was in Paris three days ago; but I made sure that the newspapers did not know of my presence."

"So are you running away from the opportunity to explain yourself?"

"But why talk?"

---

1. Douglas a possible witness: see p. 823, note 3.

841

"You'd rather write, would you?"

"Not any more."

"However, your letter to *Le Temps* yesterday?"[1]

"It was appropriate to rectify…"

"Do you know that you are really showing yourself to be a very extraordinary son?"

"Ah! Here we go. So I must explain to you that my behaviour towards my father is nothing but very logical."

"Ha! ha!"

"Yes, you don't know. You don't know what a completely abominable man the Marquess of Queensberry is. You probably have a good father, do you? Yes, right? I do not. Until the age of twelve, I saw mine no more than perhaps twenty times, and I could not have had any idea, from observing his manner towards me, that I was this man's son."

And, as I was silent, thinking, Alfred Douglas continued:

"Don't think I'm not his son. He is surely my father, for my mother is the noblest creature. It was she who unwittingly made me see him as he had been and as he is. He questioned my mother, in fact, after she got the divorce. I believe it was eight years ago. I was sixteen. I wanted to know things. My mother only told me part of the suffering the marquess had made her endure. After the divorce, he continued, however. He still continues. He never ceased, he never ceases to send the marchioness despicable and insulting letters, and in the evening he often hammered on the door for hours, when he knew that my mother was ill and that rest was essential to her."

"Did he behave better towards Lord Douglas of Hawick, your brother?"

"No. My brother hates the marquess just as I do. And it is true that he must have been perfectly satisfied to chasten him a few days ago."

Lord Alfred Douglas said these things without passion, with the most astonishing tranquility.

"Nonetheless," he added, "I do not believe that anything disastrous should have happened between the marquess and me, if he had not one day taken it upon himself to look too closely into my life, to which he had never contributed

---

1. Douglas's letter, dated 22 May [*sic*], Hotel de la Poste, Rouen, was printed in *Le Temps* (Paris, France), 24 May 1895, 3. In it Douglas corrects a number of errors in "Tribunaux Étrangers," *Le Temps* (Paris, France), 23 May 1895, 3. That article had stated that Queensberry had fought in Piccadilly with Lord Alfred over a difference of opinion about the result of Taylor's trial. Douglas pointed out that "unfortunately" it was Lord Douglas of Hawick who had fought with the Marquess, and the reason was that their father had, "for two months, not stopped writing letters of incredible obscenity and coarseness to my brother's wife." Douglas also took *Le Temps* to task for referring to his mother as Queensberry's "divorced wife" ("sa femme divorcée"), when she had divorced him "because of his cruelty and adultery for eight years."

except by his money, and if he had not attempted to destroy my friendship with Oscar Wilde. I wrote to him plainly that he had no rights over my conscience, and that I found it perverse for him to care about my affairs, he who for twenty years had been so inattentive to them. He replied that if I didn't end my relationship with Wilde, he would stop my allowance (I was at Oxford at the time and he sent me three hundred and fifty pounds a year). I wrote to him: 'Keep your money.' Later, however, he wanted to become acquainted with Wilde, and arranged to have lunch with him and me. During this lunch he was charming and apologised for having misjudged him.[1] But he was not to persist with this pleasant disposition... You know, as does everyone else, what he did."

"Was your brother at Oxford too?"

"No. He once wished to join the navy, and after giving up on that career he left for Australia. He was lucky enough to find gold there, and six months ago he came back rich enough to be able to provide Wilde's surety."

Alfred Douglas fell silent.

I tried to work out how, without hurting him, I might introduce the delicate question of Wilde's manner of being and his own, outside of their pure-minded ways.

I finally found a method, and I knew how to make myself understood by the young Lord who, always very calm and very gentle, said to me, as soon as, relatively confused, I had finished speaking:

"Wilde doesn't have the anti-physical passions he is credited with. He is only an original and fantastically artistic being. He seeks all emotions, but it is only out of moral unconventionality. So he would love to chat with a murderer and happily offer him dinner in his room. This would entail a danger. He would think it very amusing. You tell me that in his novel, *The Picture of Dorian Gray*, he showed his hero partaking of unnatural adventures: does that mean that he, Wilde, has the same concerns and that he abandons himself to the same acts? Your great novelist Balzac painted, in *A Passion of the Desert*, the love of a soldier for a panther; I don't believe, however, that Balzac ever slept with a panther" (sic).[2]

"So, as far as you are concerned, your friendship with Wilde..."

1. Presumably the lunch that Holland and Hart-Davis (CL, 696, note 1) date to circa 1 April 1894, and which Wilde describes in *De Profundis*: "Two days after we [Wilde and Lord Alfred] had returned to London [from Paris], your father saw you having luncheon with me at the Café Royal, joined my table, drank of my wine, and that afternoon, through a letter addressed to you, began his first attack on me."

2. *Une passion dans le désert* (*Passion in the Desert*; 1830) is a short story by Balzac. In an article for *The Pall Mall Gazette* Wilde described it as an "extraordinary romance" (13 Sep. 1886; CW vi, No. 37, line 65). The "(sic)" here is present in the source.

"This friendship," said Alfred Douglas suddenly livening up, "I am not saying that it doesn't have an exceptional side. I even admit, you hear, that my affection for him is extraordinary. Let's call it romantic. There is no greater joy for me than having dinner with Oscar Wilde, when he is on top form. Our two souls really commune in the Symbol. There is something extraterrestrial about it. Here, this may seem peculiar, but having suffered so much for each other we could not dream of separating. Before, I was bound to him by a sort of singular dilettante pleasure; now, the persecution has reinforced our bond."

GEORGES DOCQUOIS.

"O. Wilde is Guilty," *The Sunday Tribune* (Minneapolis, MN), 26 May 1895, 1

THE NOTED AESTHETE CONVICTED BY THE JURY.

The Judge Follows Up the Verdict by Imposing Sentence of Two Years Imprisonment at Hard Labor Upon Both Wilde and Taylor—Wilde Makes a Statement in Which He Asserts His Innocence.

LONDON, May 23.

✂ *An account of the final day of the second trial.*

Immediately after the verdict was rendered, C. Gill,[1] of counsel for the prosecution, said to a representative of the Associated Press:

"I am somewhat surprised at the verdict myself; not that I doubted Wilde's guilt, but that I thought that surely one member of the jury would stand out."

When Mr. Gill was asked if there was any chance of a new trial he replied:

"No, indeed; it is now disposed of forever, thank heaven."

Travers Humphreys, of counsel for Wilde, also told the representative of the Associated Press that the verdict was a surprise to him. He added:

"The sentence is for two years on all the counts of the indictments and not on each count separately. Now that they have hit their man, I am certain his health will break down, and possibly the authorities will favorably entertain the idea of a pardon."

✂ *An account of Wilde and Taylor's movements immediately after the conclusion of the trial.*

---

1. Charles Frederick Gill (1851–1923) was a British barrister who appeared for the prosecution in Wilde's two trials.

"Oscar Wilde in Prison," *Reynolds's Newspaper* (London, UK), 9 June 1895, 5

STATE OF HIS HEALTH.

DAILY ROUTINE OF WORK.

✂ *A brief summary of the reports that had been circulating for a few days of Wilde's deteriorating physical and mental health in Pentonville Prison, followed by several paragraphs about an investigation into the same.[1]*

The rumour that Oscar Wilde was suffering severely from the rigour of his present treatment and that his mental condition was such as to cause grave anxiety, induced a reporter to visit Pentonville and ask the governor if the report was true. Mr. Manning, the governor, said, "None whatever. The whole thing is a cruel fabrication—cruel to the friends of the prisoner and to everybody else concerned."[2]

"Is there anything else that you care to add to that statement?" queried the reporter.

"Only this: that both the prisoners are going on very satisfactorily.[3] We have had no trouble whatever with them. I do not know who is responsible for the rumours that have got about, but they have put me to a lot of inconvenience—answering letters, and inquiries, and so forth. I need scarcely assure you that I am as anxious as anybody can be for the health of the prisoners."

"Is Wilde on the treadmill?"

"I am afraid," Mr. Manning replied, "that I must not answer that question. But you may be perfectly certain that no prisoner is put to any work here until he has been thoroughly examined and certified fit for it by the medical staff."[4]

1. See also Sturgis 591–2/551.
2. John Burgess Manning (1829–1908) was appointed Governor of Pentonville in 1890 and retired in 1899 ("The Late Mr. J. B. Manning," *Acton Gazette* (London, UK), 18 Sep. 1908, 7).
3. Wilde and Alfred Taylor.
4. In 1895 Manning gave evidence to the Departmental Committee on Prisons (the Gladstone Committee), acknowledging that two years' hard labour was the hardest punishment a prisoner could undergo (Hyde (1963), 2). Wilde and the treadmill: see p. 740, note 1.

Georges Docquois, "Les Poèmes de Lord Alfred Douglas," *Le Journal* (Paris, France), 8 May 1896, 2[1]

Lord Alfred Douglas est de passage à Paris.

Peut-être se souvient-on de la conversation que j'eus avec lui, à Rouen, dans le jardin de l'hôtel de la Poste, le 24 mai de l'an dernier, quelques heures avant que ne fût prononcée, à Londres, la condamnation d'Oscar Wilde.

Depuis ce triste jour, flétri tout ensemble dans son sentiment puissant et trouble d'amitié et sans l'estime de l'hypocrite Angleterre, il avait dû se résoudre à exiler son désastre, et la douce Italie des Bucoliques avait été son refuge.

Et, pareil — j'imagine — au Francisco de sa tragédie *When comes the King, he is welcome* (1), à la question de tel autre Giovanni :

> But thou, Francisco, say how hast thou fared
> In this gray city of Padua? (2)

lord Alfred Douglas ferait volontiers, aujourd'hui, cette réponse :

> Oh! as well
> As a sunflower when the sun shines out,
> As a moonflower when the moon is coy.
> As a lute-player who has lost his lute,
> I have been sad and sick, and like a plague
> I have infected nature... (3)

Néanmoins, hier, au *Journal*, il m'apparut bien portant.

— Je suis venu vous trouver ici, me dit-il, pour vous demander si vous ne pourriez pas m'aider à trouver un éditeur pour ces choses.

Ce disant, il déposa sur ma table une assez forte liasse de papiers habillée d'une chemise de carton bleu au beau milieu de laquelle brillait ce simple mot: *Poems.*

Pendant que je jetais un premier coup d'œil d'ensemble sur le manuscrit, Alfred Douglas, avec sa voix hésitante et légère de timide, reprit.

— Avant les événements que vous savez tous ces poèmes, moins seulement quelques-uns que j'ai écrits depuis, devaient être publiés à Londres. Mais, après le procès, l'éditeur qui s'était engagé a pris peur, et il m'a renvoyé mes vers. Il paraît que, par-delà le détroit, j'ai cessé d'être une personne respectable. J'espère qu'à Paris, où une traduction du *Portrait de Dorian Gray* d'Oscar Wilde et une représentation de sa *Salomé* ont eu ; récemment, un si grand succès, je pourrai trouver une maison assez libérable et amie du seul Art pour couvrir mon livre de son pavillon. Ne croyez-vous pas que je pourrai trouver cette maison ?

---

1. See below for an annotated English translation. Quoted in Lee, L. (2020). To Oscar Wilde in prison. *The Wildean*, *57*, 76–90.

Je lui répondis, toujours feuilletant et fort curieux, que je croyais qu'il la pourrait trouver assez facilement.

— Oh ! vous lisez ? fit-il, soudain. Est-ce que, vraiment, vous voulez prendre cette peine ? Oui ? Oh ! alors, laissez-moi, d'abord, vous dire que, comme poète, je ne suis pas un disciple de M. Oscar Wilde, à qui vous voyez que tout ceci est dédié. J'ai une autre manière d'écrire que lui, et je n'ai jamais cherché à l'imiter. Je suis son disciple seulement en ceci que je m'efforce constamment vers la beauté et que, comme lui, je ne vois dans l'Art que l'Art. Et c'est ainsi que je ne trouve rien de plus détestable que toute espèce de *propagande* dans l'art. J'écrit seulement ce que je veux écrire et seulement ce qui me semble beau. Et je n'ai donc pas à m'excuser d'avoir écrit sur ce sujet à la fois si grandiose et si tendre qu'est l'amour dit hellénique. Je crois que tout le monde est d'avis qu'un jeune poète ne peut mieux faire que d'imiter les meilleurs modèles dans la poésie et dans l'art en général. Eh bien ! en choisissant ce sujet de l'amour hellénique (et pourquoi plutôt hellénique qu'anglais, par l'exemple, ou européen ?) je suis l'exemple de Shakespeare dans ses sonnets et celui de Marlowe, l'aïeul poétique de Shakespeare, et, à mon avis, plus grand que lui. Ne trouvez vous pas ?

— Je connais beaucoup mieux Shakespeare.

— Marlowe, dans sa superbe et « incorporelle » tragédie d'*Edward II*, est plus grand que lui. Et ne connaissez-vous pas sa phrase mémorable : *The man that loveth not tobacco and boys is a fool* ?

— J'avais le malheur de l'ignorer. Je la trouve, en effet, parfaitement mémorable.

— Qu'on pense seulement, reprit Douglas, tandis que s'animait sa pâleur, à ce qu'aurait perdu le monde si ce sujet de l'amour hellénique avait été défendu à ces artistes !

— Vous avez raison, dis-je alors. Mais il me parait qu'au point de vue moral, vous n'avez rien à gagner à la publication de vos *Poèmes*.

Très calme, le jeune lord me répondit :

— Vous pensez qu'en lisant mes poèmes, on dira que toute cette histoire du procès Wilde est décidément vraie en ce qui me concerne ? Je vous avoue que je n'en éprouve pas, à l'avance, un ennui même léger. D'ailleurs, il sera bien téméraire d'en juger ainsi. Et puis, je suis très résigné dès maintenant à tolérer qu'on pense de la sorte, pourvu, toutefois, qu'on n'oublie pas que, pour le moment, c'est de ma poésie qu'il s'agit et non pas de ma vie particulière. Au moins, je ne pense pas qu'on me taxera d'hypocrisie ; et c'est surtout de l'hypocrisie que j'ai horreur, ce qui est tout naturel, puisque je suis né d'un père hypocrite dans un pays d'hypocrites, et que je suis la victime d'une moralité hypocrite.

Et, s'échauffant un peu pour la deuxième fois :

— Je voudrais vous exprimer clairement cette idée que, selon moi, l'artiste recherche avec une égale ardeur deux choses : la première, c'est l'admiration des hautes intelligences ; la deuxième, c'est le mépris des personnes médiocres. Or, je trouve que tout homme qui est capable de l'indignation morale (ce qui consiste en l'indignation contre les faiblesses que soi-même on n'a pas) *est sur une basse plaine intellectuelle*. C'est ainsi que je recherche le mépris de tous ces gens qui ont bavé sur mon cher ami Oscar Wilde, et je les prierai, ceux-là, de regarder mon volume comme une poignée de boue jetée dans leur face avec le plus absolu dédain.

Ayant ainsi parlé, lord Alfred Douglas se tut. Pendant une grande demi-heure que j'employai à parcourir son recueil, il demeura silencieux.

Ce recueil comporte quinze cents vers environ.

Le morceau capital en est ce *When comes the king, he is welcome*, auquel j'ai emprunté quelque chose au début de cet article. C'est une tragédie. Elle occupera un bon tiers du volume. Deux jeunes hommes s'y empoisonnent l'un près de l'autre, double holocauste à ce fameux amour « hellénique ». Je ne dois point omettre de dire que ce Giovanni et que ce Francisco meurent en parfait état de chasteté physique.

Un autre morceau important du livre, c'est le monologue de Perkin Warbeck, lequel prétendit au trône d'Angleterre, s'il faut s'en rapporter à une histoire à moitié légendaire. Perkin Warbeck est un jeune Flamand du quinzième siècle. Il ressemblait, dit-on, extraordinairement au roi Edouard IV. Lord Alfred Douglas nous le montre en sa prison, le veille de son exécution à Tyburn.

Les autres poèmes sont de courte haleine. Les plus longs n'ont guère plus de trente vers. Il en est de purement descriptifs. Il y a aussi une quinzaine de sonnets. Trois de ces sonnets ferment le livre, sous ce titre : *Oscar Wilde en prison*.

Je me rappelle ce vrai joli vers du dernier :

I loved you as a child loves sleep.

— Comme poètes anglais, me dit lord Alfred Douglas en prenant congé, j'admire plus que tous les autres Milton et Keats. Pour écrire ma petite tragédie en vers blancs, j'ai essayé d'échapper à l'influence presque tyrannique de Shakespeare en lisant beaucoup de ce superbe poète — incomplet mais titanique — Webster!

GEORGE DOCQUOIS.

The Poems of Lord Alfred Douglas

Lord Alfred Douglas is passing through Paris.

Perhaps you remember the conversation I had with him, in Rouen, in the garden of the Hôtel de la Poste, on May 24 of last year, a few hours before the conviction of Oscar Wilde was announced in London.[1]

From that sad day, withered all together in his powerful and troubled feeling of friendship and, lacking the esteem of hypocrite England, he has had to resolve to banish his catastrophe, and the gentle Italy of the Bucolics has been his refuge.

And, similarly—I imagine—to the Francisco of his tragedy *When Comes the King, He is Welcome* (1),[2] to the question of one Giovanni:

> But thou, Francisco, say how hast thou fared
> In this gray city of Padua? (2)

Lord Alfred Douglas would gladly give this answer today:

> Oh! well
> As a sunflower when the sun shines out, [*sic*]
> As a moonflower when the moon is coy.
> As a lute-player who has lost his lute,
> I have been sad and sick, and like a plague
> I have infected nature ... (3)[3]

However, yesterday at *Le Journal* he appeared to me to be in good health.

"I came to find you here," he said, "to ask if you could help me find a publisher for these things."

So saying, he placed on my table a fairly large bundle of papers enclosed in a blue cardboard folder in the middle of which shone this simple word: *Poems*.

As I took a first look over the manuscript as a whole, Alfred Douglas, with his hesitant, light, and timid voice, continued.

1. Georges Docquois, "Entretien avec Lord Alfred Douglas," *Le Journal* (Paris, France), 25 May 1895, 1–2, pp. 838–44.

2. Numbers in parentheses, which are present in the source, indicate footnotes in which the English quotations are translated into French. All such footnotes are given below.

    (1) Quand le roi vient, il est le bienvenu.

    (2) Mais, toi, Francisco, dis-moi comment tu t'es porté dans cette blanche cité de Pardoue.

    (3) Oh! comme une fleur de soleil quand a disparu le soleil, comme une fleur de lune quand la lune se cache, comme un joueur de luth quand il a perdu son luth, j'ai été triste et malade, et comme une peste j'ai infecté la nature...

3. Douglas's *Poems / Poèmes* was published in 1896 by the Mercure de France, with the English text printed on the versos and French translations on the rectos. The title of this "tragedy in one act", a dialogue between Giovanni and Francisco set in sixteenth-century Padua, was given as *When the King Comes he is Welcome / Quand vient le roi, il est le bienvenu*. Docquois has accurately transcribed the quotations from Douglas's manuscript, except that "sun shines out" should be "sun shines not". Docquois's translations into French do not match exactly those that appear in the book, suggesting that they are his own.

"Before the events you know of, all of these poems, except a few that I have written since, were due to be published in London. But, after the trial, the publisher who signed me up became scared, and returned to me my verses.[1] It seems that, across the channel, I have ceased to be a respectable person. I hope that in Paris, where a translation of Oscar Wilde's *Picture of Dorian Gray* and a performance of his *Salomé* have recently had such great success, I will be able to find a fairly liberal publisher and a friend of the only Art to put its insignia on my book. Don't you think I will be able to find such a publisher?"

I told him, while still leafing through his manuscript with great curiosity, that I thought he would find a publisher quite easily.

"Oh! you are reading it?" he said suddenly. "Do you really want to take the trouble? Yes? Oh! so, let me first tell you that, as a poet, I am not a disciple of Mr. Oscar Wilde, to whom you see all this is dedicated.[2] I have a different manner of writing than he, and I've never tried to imitate him. I am his disciple only in that I constantly strive for beauty and that, like him, I only see Art for Art. And it's for that reason that I find nothing more loathsome than any kind of *propaganda* in art. I only write what I want to write and only what seems beautiful to me. And therefore there is no need for me to apologise for writing on a subject so grand and so tender as so-called Greek love. I believe everyone agrees that a young poet can do no better than imitate the best models in poetry and art in general. Well! by choosing this subject of Greek love (and why Greek rather than English, for example, or European?) I follow the example of Shakespeare in his sonnets and that of Marlowe, the poetic grandfather of Shakespeare, who is, in my opinion, greater than him. Don't you find?"

"I am much more familiar with Shakespeare."

"Marlowe, in his superb and 'incorporeal' tragedy of *Edward II*, is greater than he is.[3] And are you aware of his memorable line: 'The man that loveth not tobacco and boys is a fool?'"[4]

1. Douglas had corresponded with William Heinemann about publishing his poetry in 1894. Heinemann thought that it would be "inadvisable to publish" some of the poems, presumably those that were most explicitly about what Douglas refers to here as "Greek love". Douglas himself had asked Heinemann to return the poems in the wake of the "accidental death" of his (Douglas's) eldest brother, Francis, who may have had a romantic relationship with the Prime Minister, the Earl of Rosebery. See Lee, L. (2020). To Oscar Wilde in prison. *The Wildean*, *57*, 76–90.

2. Wilde had agreed to accept the dedication during what he would later term his "days of [...] greatness and fame", but when he received the news in prison that Douglas's *Poems* would soon be published and would include the dedication, he was overcome with "a sort of nausea of life" (CL, 721). The book appeared with no dedication.

3. Marlowe's *Edward II* is about the relationship between the English king and his favourite, Piers Gaveston. In prison Wilde requested Marlowe's *Works* (Wright, 319–20).

4. The informer Richard Baines (1568–1593) attributed the opinion "they that love not Tobacco and Boies are fools" to Marlowe in a note denouncing the playwright.

"I had the misfortune not to know it. Indeed, I find that perfectly memorable."

"Just think," said Douglas, his pallor increasing, "of what the world would have lost if the subject of Greek love had been forbidden to these artists!"

"You are right," I then said. "But it seems to me that from a moral point of view, you have nothing to gain from the publication of your *Poems*."

Very calmly, the young Lord replied:

"Do you think that reading my poems, one will say that this whole story of the Wilde trial is decidedly true as far as I'm concerned? I confess that I am not in the least worried about it. Besides, it would be very reckless to judge so. And then, I am very resigned from now on to accept that people think in this way, provided, however, that they do not forget that this is all about my poetry and not about my life. At least I don't think I will be called a hypocrite; and it is hypocrisy especially that I hate, which is only natural, since I was born of a hypocritical father in a land of hypocrites, and I am the victim of hypocritical morality."

And, warming to his theme for the second time:

"I would like to express to you clearly this idea that, in my opinion, the artist seeks with equal ardour two things: the first is the admiration of great intellects; the second is the contempt of mediocre people. Now, I find that any man who is capable of moral indignation (which consists of indignation against weaknesses that one does not have oneself) is on a low intellectual plane. This is why I seek the contempt of all those people who spat at my dear friend Oscar Wilde, and I would ask that they consider my book a handful of mud thrown in their faces with absolute disdain."

Having thus spoken, Lord Alfred Douglas was silent. For a full half hour, while I went through his book, he remained silent.

His collection contains about fifteen hundred lines.

The key piece is *When Comes the King, He is Welcome*, which I quoted at the start of this article. It's a tragedy. It will occupy a good third of the volume. Two young men poisoning themselves together—a double holocaust to this famous "Greek" love. I must not fail to say that this Giovanni and Francisco die in a perfect state of physical chastity.

Another important piece of the book is the monologue of Perkin Warbeck, a pretender to the throne of England if one relies on a half-legendary story. Perkin Warbeck is a young Fleming from the fifteenth century. He was said to resemble King Edward IV extraordinarily. Lord Alfred Douglas shows him to us in prison the day before his execution at Tyburn.

The other poems are brief. The longest are no more than thirty lines. They are purely descriptive. There are also about fifteen sonnets. Three of these sonnets close the book, under the title: *Oscar Wilde in Prison*.[1]

I remember this very pretty line from the last one:

> I loved you as a child loves sleep.[2]

"Among English poets," said Lord Alfred Douglas to me, taking his leave, "I admire Milton and Keats above all others. To write my little tragedy in blank verse, I tried to escape Shakespeare's almost tyrannical influence by reading a lot of that superb poet — incomplete but titanic — Webster!"[3]

GEORGE DOCQUOIS.

Adolphe Possien, "Oscar Wilde," *Le Jour* (Paris, France), 28 May 1897, 2nd ed., 1[4]

CHEZ LORD DOUGLAS

Une nouvelle controuvée. – Oscar Wilde est à Dieppe. – Les lamentations d'un jeune lord.

Le *Figaro* annonce que sir Oscar Wilde est à Paris.

Cette nouvelle, qui pourrait intéresser un grande nombre d'esthètes parisiens, est fausse : le trop célèbre écrivain anglais n'a pas quitté Dieppe, où il est en villégiature depuis son départ de Londres.

---

1. The poems to Wilde were not included in the book.

2. This line appeared in Douglas's *Sonnets* (1909) under the title *To Olive* (Douglas married Olive Custance in 1902).

3. John Webster (c. 1580–?1638) was a Jacobean playwright, best known for his revenge tragedies *The White Devil* (1612) and *The Duchess of Malfi* (1614).

4. See below for an annotated English translation. Ellmann, 511/544, describes how Douglas had disclaimed this interview and, after reading it, challenged Possien (1861–1906) to a duel. Possien insisted that he had quoted Douglas accurately. No duel took place. In a letter to Lord Alfred dated [? 2 June 1897] Wilde wrote: "I hear the *Jour* has had a sort of interview – a false one – with you. This is very distressing: as much, I don't doubt, to you as to me." (CL, 873.) By the next day Wilde had obtained a copy of the interview and wrote again to Lord Alfred: "My dear Boy, I have just received three copies of *Le Jour*, that I ordered from Dieppe; not knowing what day the supposed interview with you had taken place, I had ordered the numbers for Friday, Saturday, and Sunday. The interview is quite harmless, and I am really sorry you took any notice of it." He asked Lord Alfred to let him see anything written about him (Wilde) in the Paris papers: "All mystery enrages me, and when dear More [Adey] wrote to say that a false interview with you of no importance had been published, I hired a *voiture* at once and galloped to Dieppe to try and find it, and ordered, as I have told you, three separate numbers. It wrecks my nerves to think of things appearing on me that are kept from me. If More had enclosed it in his letter, I would have been happy and satisfied. As it was, I was really unnerved." (CL, 876–7.)

Nous avons vu ce matin son ami intime, lord Alfred Douglas, à l'hôtel qu'il habite, boulevard des Capucines, 25.

Malgré l'heure matinale, lord Alfred Douglas n'était pas dans sa chambre ; il causait déjà avec un de ses camarades qui demeure à l'étage supérieur.

Lord Alfred Douglas veut bien se déranger, cependant. Il arrive à nous, vêtu d'un maillot de soie richement brodée, d'un pantalon de soie également et de couleur tendre.

Le visage de lord Douglas est doux et mélancolique ; il est de ces Anglais atteints de spleen qui ne trouvent plus de distraction dans la fréquentation de leurs semblables et cherchent dans le rêve la consolation de la vie.

— Sir Oscar Wilde est-il à Paris ?

— Mais cette nouvelle est dénuée de fondement. Mon ami n'a pas quitté une plage que je ne veux pas nommer, et où il se repose des horribles tortures que lui infligea la loi anglaise, bien dure, ne vous semble-t-il pas ?

Nous opinons de la tête.

— En effet, reprend le jeune lord, quelle faute avait donc commise mon malheureux ami ? On a répandu sur son compte une foule de calomnies, et les magistrats n'ont pas voulu se souvenir qu'il était avant tout un poète exquis, un homme de lettres de haute valeur, dont un jour l'Angleterre devra retenir le nom comme celui d'une de ses gloires.

» Les Français ne sont pas hypocrites à ce point ; votre Verlaine n'aura-t-il pas bientôt son buste au Luxembourg ? »

Lord Douglas paraît très convaincu. Il est loin de paraître se douter que le nom d'Oscar Wilde est, à Paris, synonyme d'un cas de pathologie passionnelle.

Nous nous permettons de lui demander si l'opinion en Angleterre est plus favorable à Wilde depuis sa libération.

— Certainement ; elle n'a jamais été défavorable au sens propre du mot. Beaucoup de nos concitoyens se sont laissé aussi tromper sur le compte du maître.

» Je puis vous dire qu'à Londres même, parmi toute la jeune génération littéraire, composée en grande partie de ses disciples, Oscar Wilde est tenu en spéciale admiration et sympathie. » [*sic*]

Nous prenons congé de lord Douglas, et, sans partager son enthousiasme pour le poète forçat, nous ne pouvons nous empêcher de reconnaître que, s'il fut coupable, il expia durement son erreur.

Il est donc superflu de démentir le bruit qui courait de l'arrivée de Wilde à Paris ; notre interview avec son plus intime ami et défenseur prouve surabondamment qu'il n'en est rien.

Adolphe Possien.

Oscar Wilde

AT LORD DOUGLAS'S PLACE

A baseless story. – Oscar Wilde is in Dieppe. – The lamentations of a young lord.

Le Figaro announces that Sir [*sic*] Oscar Wilde is in Paris.

This report, which may interest a large number of Parisian aesthetes, is false: the infamous English writer has not left Dieppe, where he has been holidaying since leaving London.[1]

This morning we met his intimate friend, Lord Alfred Douglas, at the hotel where he lives, at 25 Boulevard des Capucines.

Despite the early hour, Lord Alfred Douglas was not in his room; he was already chatting with one of his pals who lives upstairs.

Lord Alfred Douglas is willing to be disturbed, however. He comes to us dressed in a richly embroidered silk shirt and silk trousers of a light hue.

Lord Douglas's face is sweet and melancholic; he is one of those Englishmen who suffer from despondency and who no longer find diversion in the company of their fellows and seek in dreams the consolation of life.

"Is Sir Oscar Wilde in Paris?"

"But this story is without foundation. My friend has not left a beach resort that I do not wish to name, where he rests from the horrible tortures inflicted on him by English law, which is very hard. Don't you think so?"

We nod in agreement.

"Indeed," resumed the young lord, "what fault had my unfortunate friend committed? A host of slanders was spread about him, and the judges chose not to remember that he was above all an exquisite poet, a man of letters of high value, whose name England must one day remember as that of one of her glories.

"The French are not that hypocritical; will your Verlaine not soon have his bust in the Luxembourg Garden?"[2]

Lord Douglas seems very convinced. He is far from appearing to suspect that the name of Oscar Wilde is, in Paris, synonymous with a case of a disease of passion.

We allow ourselves to ask him if opinion in England is more favourable to Wilde since his release.

"Certainly; it has never been unfavourable in the proper sense of the word. But many of our fellow citizens have also allowed themselves to misjudge the master.

1. Wilde had relocated from Dieppe to Berneval on 26 May (Page, 75).
2. Verlaine's bust: see p. 668, note 3.

"I can tell you that in London, among the whole of the young generation of writers, composed largely of his disciples, Oscar Wilde is held in special admiration and sympathy."

We take leave of Lord Douglas, and, although we do not share his enthusiasm for the convict poet, we cannot help recognising that, if he was guilty, he atoned for his error the hard way.

It is therefore unnecessary to deny the rumour that circulated of the arrival of Wilde in Paris; our interview with his most intimate friend and defender proves overwhelmingly that this is not the case.

Adolphe Possien.

Robert Sherard, "At Oscar Wilde's Grave," *Reynolds's Newspaper* (London, UK), 21 Jun. 1903[1]

(Written for "REYNOLDS'S NEWSPAPER.")

BY ROBERT H. SHERARD.

✂ *An account of Sherard's visit to Wilde's grave at Bagneux in the company of Jean Dupoirier, the proprietor of the hotel in which Wilde had died.*

After we returned to the hotel—the Hôtel d'Alsace, in the Rue des Beaux-Arts—we visited the room where he died, a small bedroom on the first floor, looking out on a damp courtyard. From his bed his eyes had for horizon a gray and dripping wall. The hangings of the bed, the window curtains, the upholstery of the furniture were of the colour of the lees of wine. Behind a ricketty table a maculated couch squatted like a toad. All was faded and threadbare. The impression was that of poverty masquerading as comfort. Chatterton's garret in Brooke-street must have presented a sight less poignant. Nero could not have died amidst such surroundings.

"There he lay," said the landlord, pointing to the bed, "with ice on his head, and in his delirium he swore at his pain. He kept raising his hands to his head to try to ease the torture. The doctors said that they ought to cut into the head, but that there was no sign to guide them where to cut, and so no operation could be tried. He must have suffered greatly for he swore and swore. And there he died—in my arms. It was at two o'clock in the afternoon."

---

1. The copy text is a clipping in a scrapbook once owned by Stuart Mason (Nos. 198–9, Oscar Wilde Scrapbook Vol. 3, Honma Hisao Collection, Jissen Women's University Rare Books). Excerpted in Sherard, R. H. (1915). *The Real Oscar Wilde*. T. Werner Laurie. 410 (which is reprinted in Mikhail, 455–6).

The man spoke in short, gasping sentences, under evident emotion, and I recalled pointing out to Wilde that where a deep tragedy is to be described the short sentence has always been used by artists. It depicts the breathless emotion of the writer. It is like the words of a messenger of evil tidings, who has run a long way to tell them and can find but gasping utterance. So Goethe in the last lines of the "Sorrows of Werther," and so Wilde also at the end of "Dorian Gray."[1]

We heard that before he became ill of his final illness—the meningitis which killed him, and which is only the scientific name for the "broken heart"—he had worked hard. What he wrote was given to others, who published it as their own work.

"He used to work at nights, all night long. As a rule he would come in at one o'clock in the morning and sit down to his table, and in the morning he would show me what he had written, and 'I have earned a hundred francs tonight,' he would say. And he seemed pleased and proud to think that he had earned a hundred francs in one night."

At these words a rapid calculation passed through my head. It underlines the pathos of his pride. His plays used to be written in a fortnight or three weeks. There was more earned there than twice £100 in any night.

"But," continued the landlord, "the man who employed him was irregular about sending him money, and this used to vex Monsieur Wilde very much, and he was always very *inquiet*[2] until the payment came and used to rail against his employer.[3] Towards the end it became very difficult for him to write, and he used to whip himself up with cognac. A litre bottle would hardly see him through the night. And he ate little. And he took little exercise. He used to sleep till noon, and then breakfast and then sleep again till five or six in the evening. But, *il se soi-*

1. *Die Leiden des jungen Werthers* (*The Sorrows of Young Werther*; 1774, revised 1787) is an epistolary novel about the unrequited love of a young man for a girl, Charlotte, who is engaged to an older man, Albert. At the end of the novel an old bailiff rushes in with the news of Werther's suicide. The final lines are: "Der Alte folgte der Leiche und die Söhne, Albert vermocht's nicht. Man fürchtete für Lottens Leben. Handwerker trugen ihn. Kein Geistlicher hat ihn begleitet." ("The old man and his sons followed the corpse to the grave, Albert couldn't. Charlotte's life was despaired of. The body was carried by labourers. No priest attended.") The comparison with *The Picture of Dorian Gray* is not exact, although there are several short sentences in the last two paragraphs. For example: "They [Gray's servants] knocked, but there was no reply. They called out. Everything was still." (CW iii, 357.27–8.) The last sentences are: "He was withered, wrinkled, and loathsome of visage. It was not till they had examined the rings that they recognized who it was." (357.34–6.)
2. Worried, uneasy.
3. In a letter to the *St. James's Gazette* (9 Mar. 1905, 6–7) Sherard would describe Wilde's employer as "a taskmaster in London". The editors of Wilde's journalism have not attributed any articles to Wilde after 1895 (CW vii).

The landlord of this hotel will be remembered hereafter. He was very good to the poor poet. At first he had been suspicious and indeed had forced him to leave his house, the bill being unpaid. He afterwards met him in the street, and heard that he had been forced to leave his new hotel also, because he could not pay, and was literally without a shelter. Thereupon this kindly man bade him return to his old room in God's name, and, more than this, went and fetched away his things from the hotel where they were detained and paid the bill. It was a bill for £5. He has the receipt still and shows it with some pride. When Wilde died he was heavily in this man's debt, and the debt remains. Meanwhile, men are making money by trading on Wilde's name, exploiting his fatal notoriety. There has recently been published in Paris, as a translation by his pen, a version of a French novel, which in the original its style alone saved from the charge of obscenity.[2] The style of the English version is that which distinguishes the publications of certain booksellers in the lenocinia of Amsterdam or the purlieus of Leicester-square. The very grammar is faulty. It is an outrage on the poet's memory that such a book should be issued under his name. It has the horror of sacrilege. And it is being done for money.

My English friend asked the landlord if he had any little thing which had belonged to the poet which he would care to sell him as a souvenir.

"I have something interesting," said the landlord, leaving the room. He presently returned with a little packet in his hand. Unfolding this, he disclosed the poet's false teeth. As they were set in gold plates, they had not been buried with the rest. He had left so little property that had any value; his wardrobe was almost depleted. His false teeth and a score of masterpieces; that was all his legacy.[3] The touch of the macabre and the sinister crowned the horror that held me.

But there was the ink bottle that he had used, a trumpery little china thing, worth a few pence, perhaps. The Englishman was glad to pay a louis for it.

Of many evil days that day will ever be remembered by me as the very worst. There are things which one should not know, there are things that one

1. "But, he treated himself well when he could. Oh yes! He treated himself with Champagne and required Veuve Clicquot at eight or ten francs a bottle."

2. d'Aurevilly's novel *Ce qui ne meurt pas* (1883) had been privately published in an English translation (*What Never Dies*; 1902) spuriously attributed to Sebastian Melmoth, Wilde's alias. Sherard, 264, had claimed that the translation was "the last work he [Wilde] did before he died", but later told Stuart Mason that he regretted his mistake ("Oscar Wilde's Works," *The Evening Standard and St. James's Gazette* (London, UK), 29 Apr. 1905).

3. In his letter to the *St. James's Gazette* Sherard notes that Dupoirier had the teeth "on sale", and that they "were left him as slight dédommagement [compensation] by the people who settled Wilde's affairs". Also "on sale" was "the Pravaz syringe which was used to allay his [Wilde's] agony". Dupoirier still possessed the teeth and syringe in 1930 (Mikhail, 454–5).

ought not to know. And the punishment that results from seeking out the knowledge of them, bitter as it is, is only too well deserved. This also is one of those faults which, as Goethe says, avenge themselves on earth.[1]

Desda Cornish, "Oscar Wilde Redivivus," *Boston Evening Transcript* (Boston, MA), 16 Dec. 1908, 22[2]

HONORS PAID HIS FRIEND AND LITERARY EXECUTOR

A Dinner in London a Tribute to Robert Ross, Who in the Face of Overwhelming Odds Won His Battle and Sold Enough of Wilde's Works to Pay off His Debts—To Germany Is Due the Credit for Recognizing "De Profundis" and "Salome," and in General for the Restoration of Wilde's Fame—Some of the Details of Mr. Ross's Fight in the English Courts

BY DESDA CORNISH

✂ *A report of the dinner given in honour of Ross at London's Ritz Hotel on 1 December 1908, including a list of guests and a transcript of Ross's speech.*

WHO MR. ROSS IS

I have just had a conversation with Robert Ross, who, by the way, is a well-known art connoisseur, a director of the Carfax Art Gallery, and is also on the staff of the Morning Post. He has undoubtedly shown much cleverness in bringing Wilde's literary estate out of bankruptcy and made it a paying concern in the comparatively short period of eight years. He tells me of his gratitude to Messrs. John W. Luce & Co. for issuing the authorized copyrighted edition of Wilde's Works, they having arranged with Putnam, who hold the rights of "De Profundis,"

---

1. A reference to the last line of a poem in Goethe's novel *Wilhelm Meister's Apprenticeship* (1795–1796), "Denn alle Schuld rächt sich auf Erden." ("Then every offence is avenged on Earth.") Thomas Carlyle had inscribed his translation of the first four lines of this poem in a volume of Goethe he gifted to Lady Wilde (Melville, 255–6).

2. Reprinted as "An Oscar Wilde Redivivus," *The Nebraska State Journal* (Lincoln, NE), 14 Jan. 1909, 6–A. Desda Cornish was a British journalist who had been born in Ceylon. Other interviews with Ross that focus more on Wilde's works than on Wilde himself are not collected here. Interested readers are directed to "De Profundis," *The Evening Standard and St. James's Gazette* (London, UK), 14 Mar. 1905 (see Nos. 247, 249, Oscar Wilde Scrapbook Vol. 7, Honma Hisao Collection, Jissen Women's University Rare Books); and "Play's Strange History," *The Tribune* (London, UK), 4 June 1906 (about the loss and rediscovery of the manuscript for *A Florentine Tragedy*; see No. 221, Oscar Wilde Scrapbook Vol. 2).

and Lippincott, who hold the rights of "Dorian Gray."[1] For a long time it has pained him to think that America has no authorized edition, and has had foisted upon it not only an unauthorized version, but also spurious work which Wilde never wrote. That those spurious works should have received the imprimatur of Mr. Le Gallienne, an old friend of Oscar Wilde, has been an added annoyance to Mr. Ross.[2] The Le Gallienne edition not only contains false works by Oscar Wilde, but a false text. His version of "De Profundis" is merely a translation from the German, Messrs. Putnam having the only authorized version.[3] "The Duchess of Padua" is issued in the Le Gallienne edition in the form of a prose translation from the German.[4] The first version in blank verse is to be issued by John W. Luce & Co. Mr. Ross tells me of his hopes of the new edition insuring for Oscar Wilde the same appreciation in America that England has for Nathaniel Hawthorne, Edgar Allan Poe, Walt Whitman, Henry James and other literary artists.

Oscar Wilde died bankrupt in 1900. In 1895, the year of his imprisonment, the bankruptcy amounted to £6000. In 1901 Mr. Ross made inquiries as to the possibilities of getting hold of the copyrights which had been pirated in both England and America, and though he was not allowed to handle them he was told they were of no value whatever. The creditors had then been paid two shillings in the pound. In 1904, owing to the German performances of Wilde's plays, principally "Salome" (not the opera) the creditors were being paid 10 shillings in the pound and four per cent interest.[5] In 1905 Mr. Ross produced "De Profundis"

1. The Methuen *Collected Edition* of Wilde's works was published in the United Kingdom in 1908 under Ross's editorship (Mason, 459–60). The John W. Luce & Co. American edition appeared in 1910 (Mason, 491). Under the title of *De Profundis*, Ross had in 1905 published an expurgated version of the long document that Wilde had written in prison.

2. The Keller–Farmer *Uniform Edition* was published in the United States in 1907. It included an introduction by Le Gallienne and the frontispiece was a portrait of him. Ross and Le Gallienne's correspondence about this edition was printed in *The Times Literary Supplement* (London, UK). On 28 June 1907 Ross took Le Gallienne to task for putting out an edition that included the spurious translation of d'Aurevilly's *Ce qui ne meurt pas*, and John Bloxam's (1873–1928) *The Priest and the Acolyte* (at the Queensberry libel trial, Wilde had said that the latter, published in 1894 in *The Chameleon*, to which Wilde had contributed his *Phrases and Philosophies for the Use of the Young*, "violated every artistic canon of beauty"; Holland, 70). Le Gallienne responded on 3 October, claiming that his only connection with the edition was his introduction. He was not responsible for the editing, but insisted that the publishers "would be glad to know to whom they can pay a royalty on their edition." Ross replied on 10 October, pointing out that the Keller prospectus promised that the edition would include facsimile Wilde letters and texts that Ross suspected could not be published "even under American copyright law."

3. A German translation of *De Profundis* by Max Meyerfeld (1875–1940) had been published two weeks before Ross's English edition.

4. Max Meyerfeld had translated *The Duchess of Padua* and staged the play in Germany, although without much success (CW v, 16–17).

5. Richard Strauss (1864–1949) was a German composer and conductor. His opera of *Salome* premiered in Dresden on 9 December 1905 and was afterwards performed widely.

which was an unprecedented success in England and Germany. Three months after the publication, the official receiver in bankruptcy, who had told Mr. Ross that Wilde's works were of no value, obtained an order of court to seize the proceeds of the book, which at that moment, upwards of three months after publication, amounted to £1000 which Mr. Ross had intended handing to Oscar Wilde's children. Then followed the long and acrimonious correspondence between Mr. Ross's solicitor and the official receiver, which lasted about a year.

THE LONG LEGAL BOUT WITH THE GOVERNMENT

Mr. Ross then offered the official receiver the following terms, that he, Ross, would not go into litigation concerning the proceeds of "De Profundis," if he would allow him to be the administrator of Wilde's literary property on behalf of the English creditors, and when, as he boasted, he had paid off every English creditor twenty shillings in the pound with the four per cent interest demanded by the bankruptcy, that he, the official receiver, should support his application to the court of bankruptcy, that he should be made administrator and executor of Wilde's literary estate for the benefit of his children. The official receiver accepted these terms after much needless expense and correspondence, but which one must however expect at the hands of British officials. On August 14, 1906, Mr. Ross was appointed legal administrator and executor of Wilde's literary estate, which appointment should have been made five years before. Within one year all the English creditors were paid twenty shillings in the pound out of the receipts of Wilde's plays and books, and there was a surplus sufficient to satisfy the French creditors, whom Wilde on his death bed had asked Robert Ross to see paid in due time. Since that date Mr. Ross has managed the estate of the two surviving children who live under another name. One of the sons of Wilde is now a distinguished officer in the English army and a famous athlete. The younger son, who is only twenty-two years of age, was educated at the Roman Catholic College of Stonyhurst, and is now at Cambridge. He shows a decided literary promise.

Mr. Ross appeared indignant and distressed at the foolish and vulgar reports appearing in an American newspaper, purporting to say that Oscar Wilde still lives. He died on Nov. 30. 1900, at the Hotel d'Alsace, the only persons at his deathbed being Robert Ross, Reginald Turner and Dupoirier, the proprietor of the hotel.

On the other hand, it is a source of enormous gratification that people are beginning to appreciate Wilde in his work. Mr. Ross appears to be deeply touched by the people who have come to his dinner, but cannot conceal his disappointment at the absence of some of those younger men who have helped in the lifting of Wilde's work without any acknowledgment, and also at the absence of some of those men who were his contemporaries.

Hayden Church, "The Facts About Oscar Wilde Scandal Are Coming Out at Last," *The Atlanta Constitution* (Atlanta, GA), 3 Aug. 1913, G6[1]

(Lord Alfred Douglas, Involved With Wilde, Is Now Writing a Statement in Regard to the Matter.

Lord Douglas Wants World to Know the Truth in Order to Clear Name of His Little Son.

London, August 2.—Lord Alfred Douglas is going to speak out at last. The man who, as Oscar Wilde's most intimate and best loved friend, knew him better than anybody else ever did, and whose name, since Wilde's downfall, has been coupled with his in evil notoriety, at last is going to tell the full story of their acquaintance in a book which, when published, is likely to provide one of the biggest literary sensations of recent years.[2]

This book, which its author declares, will reveal Wilde in an entirely new light, will be, he asserts, the first biography of Wilde that has been written by one who had his confidence, or whom, by the remotest chance, would have been selected by him as his Boswell.[3] Incidentally, Lord Alfred lays claims to the distinction of being about the only biographer of Oscar Wilde in whose arms the author of "Lady Windermere's Fan" did not die.

It will not be surprising, by the way, if one of the bitterest and most sensational controversies in literary annals follows the publication of Lord Alfred's book, for in it he will make some pretty severe comments on the administration of Oscar Wilde's literary estate by the writer, who, according to Lord Alfred, constituted himself Wilde's executor without a shadow of authorization from the writer, who left no will.[4]

In this connection, too, Lord Alfred will tell for the first time what he claims to be the secret history of the suppressed portion of Wilde's "De Profundis," the passionate human document written by Wilde in prison, which was addressed by him to Douglas. This was first made public in the libel action recently brought by

1. I am grateful to Laura Lee for identifying this article.

2. The book was *Oscar Wilde and Myself* (1914), which was ghost-written by Douglas's friend, T. W. H. Crossland (1865–1924).

3. James Boswell (1740–1795) wrote the *Life of Samuel Johnson* (1791).

4. The reference is to Robert Ross. Wilde wrote to Ross from prison on 1 April 1897: "I want you to be my literary executor in case of my death, and to have complete control over my plays, books and papers. As soon as I find I have a legal right to make a will I will do so. My wife does not understand my art, nor could be expected to have any interest in it, and Cyril is only a child. So I turn naturally to you, as indeed I do for everything, and would like you to have all my works. The deficit that their sale will produce may be lodged to the credit of Cyril and Vyvyan," (CL, 780).

Lord Alfred against Arthur Ransome, an English writer, and to gain possession of it the former has already begun proceedings against the authorities of the British Museum, to whom it was handed over without his knowledge.[1]

When He Met Wilde.

Lord Alfred Douglas, who was 21 when first he met Oscar Wilde, and is now 42, is, of course, the second son of the eighth Marquis of Queensberry,[2] and the younger brother of the present marquis who recently spent some time in America, and it was the effort made by his father to put an end to Lord Alfred's friendship with Oscar Wilde that led to the famous trial which ended in the latter's imprisonment and disgrace. The two men first met in 1892, or while Lord Alfred Douglas, who already had become known as a poet, was still an undergraduate at Magdalen college, Oxford.[3] For the three years that intervened before the exposure that wrecked Wilde's career the young sonneteer and the brilliant dramatist and poet, then at the top of his powers and at the apex of his fame, were inseparable, often sharing the same establishments and meeting regularly for dinners, suppers and similar entertainments, and it has been asserted more than once that if justice had been done, many of Wilde's most famous works would bear on their title pages the legend, "By Oscar Wilde and Alfred Douglas."

Lord Alfred is writing his book about Wilde in a comfortable, but far from luxurious house, which he has inhabited for some time in Church row, Hampstead, a little, old-world street in London's most "literary," historic and, incidentally, most beautiful suburb which, until quite recently, also was the abiding place of another literary celebrity in the person of H. G. Wells, the novelist. Shelley also lived in this street.

Almost ever since one can remember, Lord Alfred has been mixed up in one litigation or another—generally in connection with the old Wilde scandal, and one confidently expected to find him an embodiment of fussiness and petulance, with the most insecurely balanced of chips on his shoulder.

Good-Humored Boy.

He proved, however, to be just a tall, clean-shaven, well-dressed, pink-skinned, simple and good-humored "boy," who looks the runner and skillful horseman that he was before he took to literary work, and who generally gives

---

1. Arthur Ransome (1884–1967) wrote *Oscar Wilde: A Critical Study* (1912) with the cooperation of Robert Ross. The book was critical of Douglas, who sued Ransome and his publishers for libel. Unexpurgated portions of *De Profundis* were read out in court to justify the statements made against Douglas, and were widely reproduced in the press. Douglas lost the case and was bankrupted. An account of the Douglas vs. Ransome and Others trial is given in Lee, 242–57.

2. Lord Alfred Douglas was the third son.

3. Wilde and Douglas first met towards the end of June 1891 (Sturgis, 419/387).

the impression of having lived out-of-doors most of his life and of having less than his share of the worries of this existence. Besides his sonnets which a pretty prominent literary critic declared the other day entitled him to a place beside the finest of British bards, Lord Alfred has, of course, published no end of light verse and parody under the pseudonym of "The Belgian Hare," and for three years, or until quite recently, he was editor and sole owner of that really distinguished literary weekly, The Academy.

Lord Alfred's forthcoming book will not be a confession; he declares that he has nothing to confess. When questioned as to his motive, after so many years of silence, of at last making public the story of his association with Wilde, he lost his expression of tolerant good humor, and there was a hard look in his eyes and bitterness in his tone as he replied:

To Clear His Name.

"I am writing this book," he said, "to clear my name and that of my little son, because the allegations against me in connection with Oscar Wilde, which, hitherto, had been circulated by means of irresponsible gossip and innuendo, have at last found men with at least some literary standing—though not the authority of having known either Wilde or myself—to father them, and because they have been set down as facts in works that purport to be critical studies of Oscar Wilde as a man of letters, I suppose the details of the libel action which I recently brought against Arthur Ransome for repeating in his 'Life of Oscar Wilde' the oft-repeated diction [*sic*] that I lived on Wilde, and that the evil influence exercised over him by me was the cause of Wilde's downfall, are still fresh in most people's minds. I lost that case. I knew I should lose it, though I was then ignorant of the existence of the suppressed portion of 'De Profundis,' the savage denunciation of me which Wilde wrote while in prison in a fit of what he himself called 'mischievous madness.' The reading of this document, discovered by Wilde's self-appointed literary executor among his effects,[1] and, though addressed to me, bequeathed by him to the British museum with the stipulation that it should not be made public until 1960, told powerfully against me, as I was not able to bring out facts which would have deprived that document of its force. However, that action had the result which I hoped to gain when I brought it, for it revealed for the first time the whole case of my detractors, knowing which I can now proceed to demolish it with proofs.

---

1. Ross claimed that Wilde had handed him the manuscript as he stepped off the steamer in Dieppe, the day after his release from prison, saying: "This, my dear Bobbie, is the great manuscript about which you know." (Sturgis, 629/586.) Wilde had previously written to Ross about the letter with instructions to have it copied (CL, 780–2.)

"In my book I shall make a full statement regarding the mistaken attitude toward me, afterwards acknowledged by Wilde, which prompted the writing of the unpublished part of 'De Profundis,' and of his own attitude toward it after he came out of prison. I also shall reveal the details of a deliberate plot, inspired by desire for revenge, to vilify me while living and to besmirch my name and memory when I was dead, a plot engineered by persons of some supposed standing in the literary world and carried out remorselessly.

"Of all those who surrounded Oscar Wilde," Lord Alfred went on, "I practically alone maintained a disinterested attitude. Time after time since his death I have been approached with offer of my own price for a book about Wilde, but invariably I have refused to consider such offers. Of course, those who made them hoped for the material for fresh scandals, whereas the association between Wilde and myself was the friendship of two literary men, and nothing more. Why, I asked myself, should I tell the world of what passed between us? Why rake up a past that was being forgotten? I have sat silent under countless attempts to blackmail me while enemies have been engaged in blackmailing my name, merely taking legal steps, and always before, successfully, when statements reflecting on me were made in books with any literary pretensions. The revelation of a plot to defame me after my death is, however, too much for flesh and blood, and has goaded me at last into abandoning my policy of silence.

"The story of my acquaintance with Wilde," Lord Alfred went on, "will be told in detail, and the picture I shall draw of him will differ vastly from the mythical figure that has been conjured up by biographers who either did not know him at all or who had barely a nodding acquaintance with him. I shall be able to tell a great number of sayings and anecdotes of Wilde which have not before been printed, and I shall throw an entirely new light upon his own attitude toward his various works.

Ballad of Reading Gaol.

"In this connection I may say that he felt something like contempt for his own 'Ballad of Reading Gaol,' which was written almost entirely at my villa at Naples, and in which, he declared, he was 'bordering on the realm of George R. Sims.'[1] There will also be a chapter, which I think will prove rather a staggering one, on that much discussed work, 'The Picture of Dorian Gray,' which Wilde de-

1. George Robert Sims (1847–1922) was an English journalist, dramatist, novelist, and poet. He wrote comic verse for the magazines *Fun* and *The Referee*. His *In the Workhouse: Christmas Day* (1877), a ballad that criticises the harsh conditions of English workhouses, was hugely popular.

scribed as 'poisonous, but perfect.'[1] Likewise a full account of my relations with the Wilde circle, which included Verlaine, Walter Pater, Dr. Warren, John Addington Symonds, Zola, Daudet, Whistler, John Davidson, W. E. Henley, William Morris, De Maupassant, Huysmans, Sir Henry Irving, Sarah Bernhardt, Marcel Schwob and a host of other celebrities.[2]

"Of course," he added, "I shall deal with the Wilde scandal, but this I propose to do as briefly and as delicately as possible. Probably it will surprise the public to be told that, close as was my acquaintance with Oscar Wilde, I was absolutely ignorant of his perverse practices until they were revealed to all the world at his trial. My book will show how vital it was to him to keep them from my knowledge, and how rather than confess his guilt to me, even at the eleventh hour, he gave up the chance that was offered him of escape from imprisonment and infamy."

The slim young man in blue serge lighted another cigarette and inhaled a long draught from it before continuing.

Introduced to Wilde.

"Wilde and I," he said, "first met in 1892 in London while I was still at Magdalen college, Oxford, where he had been. As a young poet, who had been editor of one paper at Winchester school and of another at Oxford, I was taken to meet Wilde by the late Lionel Johnson, the poet,[3] and he at once adopted me as an intimate. Remember that I was barely 21 and ready to accept friendship as disinterested. Frankly I don't believe Wilde was sorry to become acquainted with the son of a marquis. No one can read his writings without realizing that he loved to write of duchesses and other members of the aristocracy—his plays are full of them. Through me he met the late George Wyndham, my cousin, who was certainly one of the most brilliant men in English society, and I also introduced him to my mother and my father, the late Marquis of Queensberry, who at first liked him immensely. He was a frequent guest at my mother's houses in London and in the country where he had the opportunity of studying a social rank which he would not otherwise have met.

"At the top of his fame," Lord Alfred added, "Wilde thought himself the greatest man that ever lived, and he very nearly succeeded in making me believe the same. For three years or until his disgrace, we were on the most intimate of

---

1. Wilde wrote a letter to the *Daily Chronicle* to protest against the newspaper's review of *The Picture of Dorian Gray*, which had described the novel as "poisonous": "It is poisonous if you like, but you cannot deny that it is also perfect, and perfection is what we artists aim at," (CL, 436).

2. John Addington Symonds (1840–1893) was an English writer and advocate of sexual reform. Mayer André Marcel Schwob (1867–1905) was a French Symbolist writer.

3. Lionel Pigot Johnson (1867–1902) was an English poet and literary scholar and a friend of Douglas.

terms, and during this time he produced some of his finest work. Of what assistance I was to him in this I do not care to speak now. It is enough to say that we were flint and steel, two literary craftsmen living together and sharing their inspiration. It is in this period, I suppose, that I am accused of having 'lived on him.'

Gave Wilde Money.

"My answer is that I never had so much as a sixpence from Oscar Wilde, though I gave him thousands of pounds, and that when one of us was the host of the other it was oftener I than he that played that part. We actually lunched and dined together very frequently and he appears to have kept a strict ledger account of his bills without the least set-off with regard to mine. For myself I kept and keep no accounts, but I know where the money went. When my father died I came into $250,00, and all my life I have thrown money out of the window. The idea that the son of a wealthy marquis with the family funds always more or less at his disposal could possibly be dependent upon a bohemian of slender and uncertain income is too preposterous for serious discussion. Wilde, on the contrary, who was of humble birth and had risen to affluence from poverty, rejoiced in these entertainments which were the fruits of his success."

"What is your answer to the charge that you were an evil influence in Wilde's life?" Lord Alfred was asked.

"My answer is that it is ludicrous to suggest that a boy of 20 corrupted a man of nearly 40," replied Lord Alfred. "My answer is that we lived as two artists, that ours was one of the truest literary comradeships in the history of letters, and that Wilde's three most successful plays were written at Goring and Worthing and Babbacombe, where we shared homes.

Never Led Wilde Astray.

"This preposterous tale that I led Oscar Wilde astray has no shadow of foundation save for the 80,000-word diatribe which Wilde addressed to me in prison when, mistakenly, he imagined himself abandoned and neglected by me."

"Was it not your father, the Marquis of Queensberry, who prosecuted Oscar Wilde for the sake of ending your friendship with him?" was queried.

"It was my father who was prosecuted for libel by Oscar Wilde," answered Lord Alfred, quietly. "My father, you must understand, was extremely eccentric. My mother had been obliged to divorce him, so you can imagine that I was not likely to take any advice of his too seriously. My father had heard rumors regarding Wilde's vices—the vices of which I was absolutely ignorant, and he urged me to break with him. I refused, declining to believe in Wilde's guilt. Then my father embarked on a systematic persecution. Once, when Wilde was at the theater, he sent him a 'bouquet' made, I believe, of carrots and turnips, with a card attached accusing him of indecency.[1] In every fashion he hounded him, and eventually Wilde appealed to me. 'Your father is slandering me right and left,' said he, 'what am I to do?'

Wilde Refused to Escape.

"What could I say? Soon after, Wilde sued my father for libel, only to change places with him in the dock. The authorities, I may say, had no wish to imprison him. Bail was granted him and his friends implored him to escape. His motives for refusing I explain in my book.[2] I never even was called as a witness in the Wilde trials. I blundered in not insisting on having my say, but I had no heart for it. I suppose one might call it supineness.

"When Wilde came out of prison," Lord Alfred went on, "he was a pauper. He came to me and told me he was in need, and I gave him money. I housed him at Giudice, my villa at Naples. Between this time and that of his death, two years later, he had over 4,000 pounds sterling from me. Wilde was extravagance personified. He could not keep money. All his tastes were luxurious. If there were ortolans to be had, he would have them. When he died, I was in Scotland on a visit, and thus may claim to be the only one of Wilde's biographers in whose arms he did not expire. Robert Ross notified me of his death and I returned to Paris and paid the expenses of his funeral and his debts. Then I was told that Wilde had left various valuable manuscripts, of which someone else offered to take charge. At this time I was carrying on a racing stable at Chantilly, and did not want to be bothered, so I consented to this arrangement. Among these manuscripts was, it appears, the document that Wilde addressed to me in prison, as well as some of my letters to Wilde. The document was recently handed to the British museum to be published after my death, and it was used at the recent trial in London to blacken my name before all the world."

HAYDEN CHURCH

1. This was on the opening night of *The Importance of Being Earnest* (14 February 1895). Queensberry was denied admittance to the theatre and left his "bouquet" at the box office (Sturgis, 537/501).
2. "There was never any question of [Wilde's] leaving the country until the time when he was out on bail. According to his own showing, he had no reason for leaving the country other than to avoid the inconvenience of a criminal trial. In any case, he could not have left, because he was shadowed by detectives from the moment he had left the Old Bailey that morning," (Douglas (1914), 93).

Appendix E: Burlesque Interviews

"Your newspapers are comic without being amusing," said Wilde to a representative of *The Chicago Daily Tribune*. "English papers are founded on facts, while American papers are founded on imagination."

It is certainly true that journalists—on both sides of the disappointing Atlantic—were happy to conjure interviews with Wilde entirely from their own imaginations. This appendix collects examples of these burlesque interviews. Each presents a caricature of the "utterly utter too-too" aesthete, cultivated by Du Maurier's cartoons and Gilbert and Sullivan's *Patience*.

"Wilde Interviewed," *The Daily Graphic* (New York, NY), 31 Dec. 1881, 422[1]

The aesthetic representative of THE GRAPHIC, having chartered a special tug, boarded the Arizona far outside of Sandy Hook, and introducing himself to Oscar Wilde, stated to him that the New York press and public were feverishly hungering for his first impression and expressions consequent on his visit to the New World.

"Did the ocean strike you as being too-too?" he asked of the aesthete. "Did you upon its swelling bosom realize all that vast expansiveness of the roll on, thou dark, blue ocean, roll, 10,000 fleets shall cover thee in vain; man marks the earth with ruin and even from the slime the monsters of the deep are made; each zone obeys thee; thou goest forth dread fathomless alone, while man, with bubbling groan, sinks in thy depths unknelled, uncoffined and unknown?[2] Did you, Oscar?"

"It was billow sublime and divinely pea greenery at times," said the aesthete, "but over boisterous, disorderly, turbulent—a physical condition with which the coarser part of my materiality at times sympathized, to my great disgust and disquiet."

"You mean," said THE GRAPHIC aesthete, "that your stomach—"

"Hush!" said Oscar. "I never admit the existence of such an organ. I have not heard the word before for fifteen years. Excuse me, sir, I must go below."

The poet soon returned, looking pale, holding in his hand his lily, in the other his smelling salts, and took alternate sniffs of either, being supported meantime by two young ladies, who glared indignantly at our reporter, and one was heard to whisper:

"He has given Oscar a dreadful shock!"

"Bear with me, dear sir," said the poet, "I presume your American usages of speech have not as yet touched that high plane of perceptive sentiment which involves even fatal injury to the more delicate organization by the mere utterance of a lacerating or bludgeon headed word like the one you but now pronounced. Bear with me, I shall be better presently. Miss Matilda, fan me just below the organ of delicate perception. Glognelda, rub my perturbed brow. There! I recuperate. Now, sir, I am ready. Please, however, be careful in the future. I am accustomed only to the gentlest expressions. A boisterous word is as a blow to me, a blow, dear kind sir."

---

1. I am grateful to John Cooper for identifying this article. Reprinted as "Oscar Wilde Interviewed," *The Cincinnati Enquirer* (Cincinnati, OH), 2 Jan. 1882, 4; and "Oscar Wilde's Sea Voyage," *The Detroit Free Press* (Detroit, MI), 8 Jan. 1882, 10.

2. The reference is to canto iv of Lord Byron's *Childe Harold's Pilgrimage* (1812–1818), a narrative poem about the travels of a world-weary young man.

THE GRAPHIC aesthete internally consigned the term stomach to the waters of oblivion.

The steamer was now near the Battery.

Said the aesthetic apostle: "I had pictured New York as situated in the primeval forest, with Indians and herds of deer and buffalo scattered about and an occasional hairy hunter of the white species surrounded by his dogs, standing on some bold promontory leaning upon his rifle, and as he gazed upon the noble Hudson thinking to himself wild, unwrit poetry—the genuine fervor and natural distillation of thought sentiment which evolves spontaneously in the free, untaught, uncultured breast of the rover of the hills and plains."

Said our native aesthete: "O, you've come too late for that, Oscar, by about 200 years. We've improved on all that. But just look at what we have in its place. Look at our graveyards. There's a regular string of 'em all around the city. And for monuments, sculptured urns and statues, there's nothing to compare with them on the other side of the Atlantic. If you want to see grief, sympathy and affection froze into marble by the stonecutter, just go into one of 'em. And everybody gets a funeral here—twelve coaches at least—gilt-edged coffin, free ride to the grave, and flowers! Bouquets a yard long. O, Oscar! we let our friends die sometimes of starvation just for the pleasure of pilin' flowers on 'em when dead."

The poet spoke.

"What a post-mortem sepulchral expression of refined charity, eschewing that material grossness which would devour coarse pabulum, waits but for the loosening of the silver chord that it may express its deeper sentiment by these beautiful expressions of Nature."

Said our aesthete:

"Smellest thou not something, Oscar, strong, as if indicative of the vigorous life of our young and great Republic?"

"A perception of the beautiful does seem to be invading my olfactories," said the apostle. "It seems a robust expression of your fair land—yes, rather robust," said he, dreamily.

"Yes; it is robust. But we do nothing by halves here, Oscar. When we get up a smell we mean business. That's the olfactory expression of Hunter's Point, Oscar.[1] It's prosaic manufacture serialized and sublimated. But it's refinement. That's Castle Garden, Oscar. Originally an art gallery built by Tammany, Chief of the Manhattans and a great patron of the fine arts, a great friend of the 'Early English' in America. It's now used as a reception room for the millions coming to

---

1. A district in Queens, across the East River from Midtown Manhattan.

our shores, the poor and oppressed of other nations. The Mayor meets each emigrant in person there and presents him or her with a bunch of lilies."[1]

"Beautiful," murmured the poet. "It seems like a dream of the Hesperides. But your wharves look rather bare and unsightly."

"Oh, that's because we've just taken down their Christmas decorations. Ordinarily they're covered with wreaths and garlands of evergreens—pots of roses and pinks, too, stuck all about on the piles. You should have seen them day before yesterday."

Wishing to divert Mr. Wilde's attention from the wharves our aesthete remarked:

"That towering pinnacle over there is the sky end of one of our great newspaper offices. The editor, when the moon is at her full, derives all his physical sustenance from gazing on her face and is not seen of men till she quarters. The editorials during that period are just phosphorescent with genius.

"And near by is another newspaper office. Once its editor disappeared from the world's gaze. His friends sought him far and near in Central Park, over yonder in Hoboken, in the Tombs, in the green rooms of all the theatres, everywhere, but they found him not. Some said he had gone to Europe. The common herd believed he had. Finally, he appeared. It was believed he had returned from abroad. Oscar, the truth is that gentleman was discovered in a conservatory, where for six months he had lived on the fragrance of a pink he held to his lips. Oh, he's an aesthete, too. He can beat you at your own game and give you points besides, he can."

"O let me see him," said the apostle: "let me sit at his feet. Let us buy two roses and shut ourselves up together, out of sight of the lower orders—out of sound of your elevated road roar and rattle—and there commune in those higher, more rarefied and beatific regions of thought accessible only to the few whose minds are so sublimated as to be able to attune themselves to the melody of the calyx, the rhythm of the stamen and the harmonies of the pistol."

"You'll get enough of the harmonies of the pistol if you stay a fortnight in New York, Oscar. Every boy, every burglar, every thief carries one, and uses it, too, first pop!"

The steamer being made fast to the pier the interview ended, THE GRAPHIC representative remarking:

"I am sorry I can't stay with you longer, Oscar. But I must attend the symposium of our city truckmen and car drivers, in Steinway Hall, this morning.

1. Castle Garden, previously and subsequently Castle Clinton, is a sandstone fort located in Battery Park. It was built in 1808 on what was then a small artificial island. It served as an exhibition hall and theatre until 1855 when it became an immigration station. Tammany or Tammanend (c. 1625–c. 1701) was a chief of the Lenni-Lanape nation.

They're discussing a new form of verse wherewith to greet each other when they get in a jam down town. They're a poetic lot. You ought to hear the hexameters they sing out to each other when they're full of inspiration, and see them pelt each other with five dollar bouquets."

"Our New York Letter," *The Philadelphia Inquirer* (Philadelphia, PA), 4 Jan. 1882, 7[1]

Changes at the Sub-Treasury—Counting the Government's Cash—Many Tons of Gold and Silver to be Handled—A Talk With Oscar Wilde—His Views on Esthetic Subjects—General Items.

New York, Jan. 3.

Correspondence of The Inquirer.

✂ *Several paragraphs that are unrelated to Wilde.*

Oscar Wilde, the young English poet and apostle of aestheticism, reached this city this morning. He came in the Arizona, which arrived last night, but anchored off quarantine until this morning. Mr. Wilde is a smooth-faced young man, twenty-six years of age and six feet four inches in height. His hair is long, his face is large and flat, and he dresses in an aesthetic costume, of which the most con-

1. H & S, b6. Reprinted in H & S, 17–18. Wilde's language is uncharacteristically high-flown, suggesting that this interview has been fabricated or embellished. Much of the content is similar to that of "Oscar Wilde Interviewed," *The Stage* (London, UK), 20 Jan. 1882, 12, pp. 886–7; and some material is shared with "Oscar Wilde," *The Evening Post* (New York, NY), 4 Jan. 1882, 4, pp. 48–50. "Oscar Wilde," *The Detroit Free Press* (Detroit, MI), 7 Jan. 1882, 5; and "The Esthete Talks," *The Atlanta Constitution* (Atlanta, GA), 8 Jan. 1882, 2, were published later but with more content. The *Constitution* begins with a report of Wilde's attendance at the performance of *Patience* at the Standard Theatre, similar to that given in "Oscar Wilde Sees 'Patience,'" *New York Tribune* (New York, NY), 6 Jan. 1882, 5, pp. 694–5. The interview section in both the *Free Press* and *Constitution* begins: "After a few introductory remarks about his voyage across the ocean, which he seemed to enjoy exceedingly, he said to a reporter present that he was sorry to read in the American papers alleged interviews with him, which, if true, were exaggerated unjustly and unreasonably. 'I don't mind being caricatured and made fun of, sir; but I do object to being lied about. I only saw two reporters, and as they were apparently gentlemen, I treated them as such. Although I have not had much of an opportunity to see your city, I am delighted with its magnificent sky and atmosphere. I am already convinced that I shall thoroughly enjoy it and that it will keep me here for a considerable time. I came to this country, sir, as a stranger, but yet as a public man. I am confident that I shall succeed, because I am in earnest and am determined to achieve my object. You are aware already that one of those objects is a lecture tour, and as art is steadily growing in America I am assured that it will be successful. One cannot readily converse with a stranger about subjects in which his whole life is interested.'" Both then continue with the interview as given here.

spicuous parts this morning were a long bottle-green overcoat trimmed with fur, a sky-blue necktie, yellow kid gloves, patent leather boots, and a sealskin cap several sizes too small for him.[1] The most noticeable peculiarities about his talk were a sing-song division of words into a species of blank verse of his own, and a vacant smile which seemed to be part and parcel of the spoken lines.[2] When talking of aestheticism the smile seemed to suggest that he looked upon the whole business as an absurd farce, and his arrival in New York upon a lecturing tour as its most ridiculous incident. He talked freely, and said among other things:

"My philosophy, about which I have been so grossly ridiculed, is the appreciation of the beautiful, and coarse, indeed, must be the intelligence of the man who will knowingly sneer at that which makes the world about us so glorious. I have always loved nature in its wild, magnificent beauty. When I can meet her in the wilderness amid towering cliffs and hanging cataracts, then I love her and become her slave. I have since I can remember been impressed by the intensity of nature; but, alas, for the past few years I have been unable to gratify my longing. I have been a London man, and have been surrounded by naught but smoke and fog. It is in the midst of the city life that I first saw the follies of the present society and the grotesqueness of modern customs. I admire the Middle Ages, because their social life was natural and unharassed by petty rules. I approve of the mediaeval costumes, because they are graceful, because they are beautiful. The surroundings of art, no one doubts, enhances one's existence and makes life worth living. This talk of the sunflower and lily is nonsense, sir, especially as I am represented gazing fondly over it. I love flowers, sir, as every human being should love them. I enjoy their perfume and admire their beauty.

"I saw *Patience*, the comic opera, while it was played in London. I fail to see its point, sir, but think it a very pretty opera with some charming music. As a satire on the philosophy of the beautiful, sir, I think it is the veriest twaddle. Before I had made my mind up to come to America I had been informed that the Americans were very impressionable. I find them so, sir, and am extremely gratified. Grand ideas, sir, are more likely to attain the fullness of their foliage in the soil of a new civilization than in the wasted energies of effete governments. The cultivation of estheticism, sir, is a grand idea, and I am ready to sacrifice my 'life, enmity and amity' in its successful development. Estheticism has not an enervating influence on society, it redeems it from gross errors and cleanses it from the accumulation of the scraps of ages. I do not know, sir, whether or not I shall make an extended lecture tour. It will all depend on circumstances. Good morning!"

---

1. This description of Wilde is similar to that given in *The Evening Post*, p. 49.
2. This and the following sentence also appear in *The Evening Post*, p. 50.

"After an Interview," *The Brooklyn Daily Eagle* (Brooklyn, NY), 8 Jan. 1882, 4

One of the enterprising reporters of the great *Never Get Beat Daily* was lazily scanning the heavens with a marine glass at Sandy Hook, on Monday evening last, when he suddenly exclaimed, "That must be the ship," and a moment later he added, "Yes, I'm right, I can tell the Arizona at any distance. Is the boat ready?"

"All ready, sir," said an old sailor, standing at the reporter's elbow.

"Then we'll put off at once, and get a beat on the quarantine craft," and a little tug was soon puffing its way through a very lively sea, while the hull of the great steamer loomed up more plainly on the horizon.

"We'll just about strike the channel in time to bring her to," said the pilot of the tug.

"Correct," said the reporter, as he stretched himself in a camp chair forward and proceeded to light a cigarette. It was blowing whole batteries of great guns, and the little tug burled her nose deep in every wave, while the spray fell in thick showers over the ulstered knight of the quill.

"Let's see," said the reporter, taking out a lavender silk covered note book and a gold pencil. "I might as well jot down a few leading questions." And he proceeded to write, regardless of his somewhat unique situation.

"She's coming head on for us," said the pilot.

"Ah, yes, everything works nicely. Lie to," said the reporter, and he proceeded to blow vigorously upon a pipe connected with the breast lining of his ulster, until his back and shoulders puffed out to an enormous size. "It's a little invention I picked up in England," said the reporter, answering the astonished gaze of the pilot. "Life preserver and overcoat in one, you understand?"

By this time the tug had stopped directly in the channel.

"I say," shouted the pilot. "If we stay here she'll knock us into fire wood," but it was too late; the great prow of the steamer struck the tug amidships, and the latter went to the bottom in sections: but not so the reporter. He cleared everything and could just be distinguished bobbing up and down on the long waves and busily engaged in taking notes on the accident. "Ship ahoy," he shouted as the steamer stopped her engines, "Throw us a rope, somebody. It's rather chilly bathing this time of year," and then he went on with his writing.

"You're a cool 'un," said a sailor, as they hauled the scribe on board.

"Decidedly so, just at present," said the reporter, as he took a long pull on his pocket flask. "Save any of the other fellows?"

"No, you are the only one picked up."

"Thanks," said the reporter, as he jotted down "entire crew lost," and then, putting up his note book, he followed a sailor to the captain's cabin.

"You have a passenger on board named Oscar Wilde, I believe?" said the reporter, seating himself in an easy chair, and lighting up one of the captain's cigars.

"Yes. Tall, rather peculiar looking gentleman," said the captain. "Like to meet him?"

"Yes, that's my purpose in coming aboard," said the reporter.

"We'll have him in at once," said the captain. "But you'll excuse me. He's the most everlasting talker," and the captain left. Soon a tall gentleman in a Russian overcoat entered the cabin.

"Wilde, I believe," said the reporter.

"That is my name, sir, and you wish—"

"To have a little chin with you, old boy. That's all. Plant yourself over there and take a fly at the captain's brandy. I suppose you know the quality of it by this time."

"Sir, I am not acquainted—"

"Yes, to be sure. I represent the *Never Get Beat Daily*, and I'm here for the purpose of interviewing you. Catch on?"

"Catch what, sir?"

"Do you twig? Do you tumble to my racket?" asked the reporter.

"I do not understand you, sir."

"Well, this beats the deck," said the reporter. "Why I thought you were up in everything, invented languages and never got left in the meaning of words. I see you have yet to learn United States."

"I did not come over here to be taught, but to teach," said Oscar, lighting a Chinese cigarette and puffing out the fragrant smoke in artistic curves and circles.

"I understand," said the reporter, "you are going to work all the cities with the grand lyceum act?"

"I am going to lecture, if that is what you mean," said Oscar, throwing one long leg over the other, and looking indifferently toward the deck.

"Yes, you have come over here to spring that esthetic business on us," said the reporter. "Well, you haven't struck a sinecure, old man, and don't you forget it. You may have pretty easy sailing in the East, but when you get on your Western route you will have the hardest kind of soil to break."

"How is that?" asked Oscar.

"Well, you see they go in for hard pan common sense out there," said the reporter, pouring out another pony of brandy. "There is Chicago, for instance. If you can convert Chicago to your lily worshiping business, you can sweep the whole deck this side of the Rocky Mountains; but when you strike San Francisco you will have about the toughest work you ever attempted; and there are Detroit and St. Louis. If you knock any of your languishing business into them, may I be—. Well, they won't have it, that's all."

"Then you think the East will look favorably upon my teaching?" said Oscar.

"Oh, yes; New York and Boston will tumble at once," said the reporter. "They are like sheep. Let the first animal leap over the fence into your sunflower patch, and the rest will follow. You'll rake in a stock of shekels in New York, and don't you forget it."

"But I'm not after money," said Oscar, with an injured air. "I came to your country purely for the sake of my religion. The religion of art. The religion of the beautiful. The—"

"Oh! that's solid, old man," said the reporter. "We understand all that. But you can't live on lilies and sunflowers. America is rich. She is willing to put up the dust liberally for being amused."

"But I'm not an actor, Mr.—"

"Of course you're not," said the reporter. "You are the high priest and grand lum tum leader of the intense school. Keep it up my boy, keep it up. The older you are the better you will make the thing pay. Hello, the engines have stopped, and we are at Quarantine. Well, I must leave you, old man. Just time to get my copy ready for tomorrow's paper."

"But I thought you wished to interview me," said Oscar.

"Just what I've been doing," said the reporter.

"But you have not asked me a question about my mission in coming over, or—"

"Oh, I'll do all that at the office," said the reporter. "Run in a lot about your high aim in visiting us, and make you say all sorts of good things about America, and how happy you are to arrive at last among your free born cousins. Oh, I'll do you up brown, never fear. Ta ta," and the reporter bowed himself out and reached the dock just in time to go ashore with the Government officers.

"Where the Poet is Kept," *Truth* (New York, NY), 8 Jan. 1882, 4[1]

HOW HE IS PROTECTED AND GUARDED FROM ENNUI.

Discovering Symptoms of Good Fellowship—He Says He will Talk Simply and Plainly—Will He be able to Express His Ideas?—A Western Journalist.

Yesterday afternoon TRUTH called upon Mr. Oscar Wilde of England. Mr. Wilde was in the sanctum of Mr. R. D'Oyly Carte's office on Broadway, and was guarded by Mr. W. F. Morse, whose society stands between the poet and *ennui*. Young Mr. Wilde was standing uncovered. He was posed in an expectant attitude.

1. Excerpted in "Oscar of Ould," *Helena Weekly Herald* (Helena, MT), 19 Jan. 1882, 2. Wilde's comments to the *Truth* reporter may well be genuine, but the interaction with the Butte City reporter is clearly a burlesque and must therefore call the whole article into question.

From previous descriptions that TRUTH had read of Mr. Wilde's personality in various of the metropolitan journals, he thought that perhaps the stranger in a strange land hoped and expected at last to meet a representative of a newspaper who would describe him as he is. Indeed, Mr. Morse, before conducting TRUTH into the presence chamber, had first cautiously put the question:

"Is there any particular point you want to make?"

A weaker natured being might have assumed an expression of great sagacity, or an impenetrable front, that might lead to an inference of wily, Machiavellian, diplomatic reserve behind it. TRUTH—as always—in his candor was almost stolid. He said: "I wish to see Mr. Wilde."

PRESENTED TO A POET.

Then Mr. Morse, with an apologetic nod, went in and broke the news to Mr. Wilde. The details of Mr. Wilde's apparel TRUTH refers to, because they will not form a portion of this article, further than that his broad neck scarf, loosely tied in a sailor, or some similar knot, was of the shade which belongs peculiarly to crude carbon oil as it is pumped from nature's tanks, with its incompatible accompaniment of salt water.

Mr. Wilde's expression, as he shook TRUTH'S hand, was beaming. There was in his look—the conviction was transmitted over a psychological private wire to his new acquaintance—that if he would only give a little more play to some portions of his nature, even if he had to put the check-rein upon the untamed Pegasus of his idealism, if he would let up on poesy, occasionally, and perambulate a little more with the boys, TRUTH would not mind running with him. There will be plenty of fellows think the same thing, if they can just get Mr. Wilde on the strict q. t., away from [*illeg. wd.*]— contaminating influences.

After all, TRUTH immediately recognised Mr. Wilde as an Irishman. He knows more than a good many of them about poetry. And there was a good many of his fellow-countrymen here who know more than he does—about politics. TRUTH, after a good, square look at Mr. Wilde, felt as resigned with him [*illeg.*] purposes.[1] He had not prepared for the interview by "faking" a new vocabulary or phrase book of aestheticisms, so he asked him how he liked the country.

PRETTY WELL FOR A TENDER FOOT.

Mr. Wilde's smile seemed to express pleasure at his experience in the country to date. Still it was slightly tinged with ghastliness. As Mr. Morse had previously remarked to TRUTH:

"He's a tenderfoot, you know, and didn't quite know what to make of the racket he got from you newspaper fellows."

---

1. In the copy text one or two lines are obscured here by a fold.

879

Mr. Wilde said he hoped that he would like it better when he became a little more inured to the people's ways. He said:

"I am going to tell them simply and in a plain way, at my lecture, of the origin and progress of this new movement for the cultivation of the beautiful. If I can suggest to them ways to make life and home pleasanter, I shall be satisfied. The satire has preceded the reality here, and I understand perfectly well how quick the American perception of humor is. All I hope is that I shall make my meaning plain. As I am in earnest, I am confident that I can do that."

MR. BRODY FROM BUTTE.

Mr. Wilde's interchange of thought with TRUTH, who was an appreciative listener, was rudely interrupted by a slight scuffle at the door of the sanctum. A stranger with chin whiskers, a black soft hat and very loose pantaloons had evaded the grasp of Mr. Morse and had succeeded in entering the sanctum. He presented a card with the upper-left corner bent over and flattened down, as if he had pounded it to make it stay. This was done in deference to the supposed requirements of fashion.

"My name is Mister Joseph Brody, an' I 'spose you're Mister Oscar Wilde. Well, look here, I'm the editor of the Butte City *Mountain Echo*,[1] and my special correspondent here got a prospectus of your lecture. I just told Mr. Townley—he's my correspondent—that I'd come up an' interview you for the *Echo*."

"I am pleased to meet another journalist who I hope will prove another friend."

"Well, now, I like that Os, an' if the other young man's through, I'll ask you a few questions, an' I know your answers will satisfy the Butte City folks: they'll be boilin' over to hear about your new interpretation of nature, because there's so much of it out our way that I'll be hanged if we can do it."

A DARNED GOOD DEFINITION.

"I simply wish to tell that Beauty, Mr. Brody, whether in art or nature, in the form of woman, or as seen in the lily, is paramount to all materialism."

"Well, that's a darn good definition of the aesthetic craze. I wonder I never thought of that before. I say, Os, did your father never show no indications of insanity? I'm speakin' aesthetically now, an' don't make no mistake."

"Well, no, sir, I cannot say that he did," said Mr. Wilde, smiling good-naturedly at TRUTH and his guardian. "He was particularly devoted to physical science and archaeology."

---

1. The Butte City, MT newspaper was the *Miner*. Newspapers titled *The Mountain Echo* had previously been published in Johnstown, PA and Keyser, WV.

"Heap of head work, eh? and never struck it very rich, either. That's the way it is with the scientists that ride out our way, and walk back. Your mother, probably, is where you get it from. I see that she kept the only literary saloon [*sic*] there was in Dublin."

TOUCHING FILIAL GRATITUDE.

"Yes, indeed, I am blessed with a mother who is one out of thousands, and I have always felt deeply indebted to her, I may say, for my being what I am."

"Bully for you, Os. That's the way I like to hear a young fellow talk. I see that when you and Ruskin were pards you used to break stones and make roads.[1] Well, now comes out to Butte an' see us 'fore you go over the briny again. We've all had to work out there for the proud positions we now occupy, an' we don't look down on no one on that account."

Here Mr. Morse broke in impatiently, and said:

"But, really, Mr. Brody, Mr. Wilde is going to rehearse his lecture this afternoon, and he is hungry."

"Well, as long as you can eat ox, you'll be all right; but don't stay too long in this effete eastern civilization. Shake it early, and strike for Montana. Ask for John Brody of Butte, and I'll be there to promote the festivities."

Mr. Morse quietly whispered to Mr. Wilde as they all left:

"What we call a 'cranky' kind of a newspaper man. Good fellow and all right if you know how to take him." Mr. Wilde looked as if he was minded to be pleased with every phase of character that he might encounter.

As Truth neared 20th street the Butte City journalist ranged up alongside of him and said: "Os is a kind of a cranky poetical young man. He'd be a good fellow though and pan out all right if you just struck the right lead."

"Fitznoodle in America," *Puck* (New York, NY), 11 Jan. 1882, 295[2]

No. CCVI.

OSCAR WILDE.

Ya-as, aw, young Wilde, whom I used to wemembah as a b-b-boy, has arwived he-ah, I believe, faw the purpose of lecturwing, or pwoducing a play, or doing some of the othah things by which literwarwy fellahs usually gain their bwead and buttah.

---

1. Ruskin's road: see p. 27, note 3.
2. "Fitznoodle" had a regular column in *Puck*. He also "reviewed" Wilde's first New York lecture in the 18 Jan. 1882 issue.

I am not a gweat admiwah of this kind of business, ye know; faw if a fellaw belongs to a wespectable family, and has enough money to live like a gentleman, I cahn't, faw the aw life of me, undahstand why he should worwy himself about mattahs that othah individuals twy to derwive an income fwom.

This young Wilde, of course, bwought lettahs of intwoduction to me, and I couldn't vewy well do less than listen to what he had to say, as the intwoductions were fwom fellaws with whom I wish to continue to wemain fwiendly.

He called at my wesidence, the othah morning, while I was sitting in the lobwarwy smoking my pipe aftah bweakfast.

"Aw, Mr. Wilde, I'm verwy glad to see you," I wemarked, aftah having wead one of the lettahs he presented to me.

"Ya-as," he weplied: "awfully obliged, I'm sure. Do you think you would have known me fwom my portwaits?" he asked.

"What portwaits?" I inquired.

"I mean," he said: "those widiculous carwicatures of me in *Punch* by that Du Maurwi-er fellow."

"Aw, don't fancy I should have wecognized you."

"I'm wathah glad of that," he wemarked: "because it would be so deuced awkward he-ah to have everwybody starwing at you as you walked the stweet."

"You have certain aesthetical pwoclivities, I believe, and occasionally aw pass the night in the society of a lily of sunflowah or violets or wosebuds or othah varwiety of florwiculture. To a fellow like me, I am fwee to confess that it seems quee-ah."

"Ya-as," said he, with a wathah stwange laugh: "it is twue I wejoice with everwything beautiful, but my peculiarwities have been gweatly exaggerwated. Beside, Mr. Fitznoodle, you have aw no conception how things have altered since you were a conspicuous figure in Bwitish society. The taste for art has imp-woved—I may say, it has made gigantic stwides. Have you wead any of my po-etwy?"

"Aw I have looked thwough it, but I nevah wead poetwy; it is too gweat a baw aw. Hasn't a Mr. Gilbert parwodied some of your work in an operwa called 'Patience'?"

"Ya-as."

At this moment Mrs. Fitznoodle entered, and I pwesented Wilde to her. I nevah saw a woman so interwested with anybody in my life. 'Pon my life, I cahn't say whethah it was weal or pwetended interwest. She invited him to dinnah, pwomised to take a numbah of seats faw his lecture and to patwonize his play, all in the same bweath. But I am not desirwous of having my boy bwought up in aesthetic fashion. Perwhaps I may like the ide-ah bettah when I compwehend Wilde's charwactah, though I must say that at pwesent he stwikes me as being odd, quee-ah, unnaturwal and devilishly widiculous.

"Oscar Interviewed," *Punch* (London, UK), Vol. 82, 14 Jan. 1882, 14[1]

New York. Jan. 1882.

DETERMINED to anticipate the rabble of penny-a-liners ready to pounce upon any distinguished foreigner who approaches our shores, and eager to assist a sensitive Poet in avoiding the impertinent curiosity and ill-bred insolence of the Professional Reporter, I took the fastest pilot-boat on the station, and boarded the splendid Cunard steamer, *The Boshnia* [*sic*],[2] in the shucking of a pea-nut.

HIS AESTHETIC APPEARANCE.

He stood, with his large hand passed through his long hair, against a high chimney-piece—which had been painted pea-green, with panels of peacock-blue pottery let in at uneven intervals—one elbow on the high ledge, the other hand on his hip. He was dressed in a long, snuff-coloured, single-breasted coat, which reached to his heels, and was relieved with a seal-skin collar and cuffs rather the worse for wear. Frayed linen, and an orange silk handkerchief gave a note to the generally artistic colouring of the *ensemble*, while one small daisy drooped despondently in his button-hole..... We may state, that the chimney-piece, as well as the seal-skin collar, is the property of OSCAR, and will appear in his Lectures "on the Growth of Artistic Taste in England." But

HE SPEAKS FOR HIMSELF.

"Yes; I should have been astonished had I not been interviewed! Indeed, I have not been well on board this Cunard Argosy. I have wrestled with the glaukous-haired Poseidon, and feared his ravishment. Quite: I have been too ill, too utterly ill. Exactly—seasick in fact, if I must descend to so trivial an expression. I fear the clean beauty of my strong limbs is somewhat waned. I am scarcely myself—my nerves are thrilling like throbbing violins,—in exquisite pulsation.

"You are right. I believe I was the first to devote my subtle brain-chords to the worship of the Sunflower, and the apotheosis of the delicate Tea-pot. I have ever been jasmine-cradled from my youth. Eons ago, I might say centuries, in '78, when a student at Oxford, I had trampled the vintage of my babyhood, and trod the thorn-spread heights of Poesy. I had stood in the Arena and torn the bays from the expiring athletes, my competitors."

---

1. Reprinted as "Oscar Interviewed," *The Albany Times* (New York, NY), 28 Jan. 1882, 1; "Oscar Interviewed," *New York Tribune* (New York, NY), 29 Jan. 1882, 4; and, omitting the final paragraph, in Hamilton, 111–13.

2. Wilde arrived on the *Arizona*. He returned to the United Kingdom on the *Bothnia*.

"Precisely—I took the Newdigate. Oh! no doubt, every year some man gets the Newdigate; but not every year does Newdigate get an OSCAR. Since then— barely three years, but centuries to such as I am—I have stood upon the steps of London Palaces—in South Kensington[1]—and preached Aesthetic Art. I have taught the wan beauty to wear nameless robes, have guided her limp limbs into sightless knots and curving festoons, while we sang of the sweet sad sin of SWIN- BURNE, or the lone delight of soft communion with BURNE-JONES. SWINBURNE had made a name, and BURNE-JONES had copied illuminations e'er the first silky down had fringed my upper lip, but the Trinity of Inner Brotherhood was not complete till I came forward, like the Asphodel from the wilds of Arcady, to join in sweet antiphonal counterchanges with the Elder Seers. We are a Beautiful Family—we are, we are, we are!"

LECTURE PROSPECTS.

"Yes; I expect my Lecture will be a success. Do does DOLLAR CARTE—I mean D'OYLY CARTE. Too-toothless Senility may jeer, and poor, positive Propriety may shake her rusty curls; but I am here, in my creamy lustihood, to pipe of Passion's venturous Poesy, and reap the scorching harvest of Self-Love! I am not quite sure what I mean. The true Poet never is. In fact, true Poetry is nothing if it is intelligi- ble. She is only to be compared with SALMACIS, who is not boy or girl, but yet is both."[2]

HIS NEOPHYTES.

"Who are my neophytes? Well, I fancy the Lonsdales and the Langtrys would have never been known if I hadn't placed them on a pedestal of daffodils, and taught the world to worship."[3]

HIS KOSMIC SOUL.[4]

"Oh, yes! I speak most languages; in the sweet, honey-tinted brogue my own land lends me. *La bella Donna della mia Mente* exists,[5] but she is not the Jersey

1. Not a royal residence, but the South Kensington Museum.
2. In Greek mythology Salmacis was a naiad who refused to take up hunting or archery, pre- ferring idleness. She fell in love with a son of Hermes and Aphrodite, Hermaphroditus, and prayed that they should be together forever. A god answered her prayer by combining the two in one androgynous body.
3. Gwladys Robinson, Lady Lonsdale (later Lady de Gray and the Marchioness of Ripon; 1859– 1917), was a Professional Beauty and close friend of Wilde. He dedicated *A Woman of No Impor- tance* to her.
4. A reference to *Panthea*. See p. 137, note 4.
5. "The beautiful woman of my mind." Wilde's poem *La Bella Donna della mia Mente* describes a beautiful nameless woman.

Lily, though I have grovelled at her feet; she is not the Juno Countess, though I have twisted my limbs all over her sofas; she is not the Polish Actress,[1] though I have sighed and wept over all the boxes of the Court Theatre; she is not the diaphanous SARAH,[2] though I have crawled after her footsteps through the heavy fields of scentless Asphodel; she is not the golden-haired ELLEN, more fair than any woman VERONESÉ looked upon,[3] though I have left my *Impressions* on many and many a seat in the Lyceum Temple,[4] where she is the High Priestess; nor is she one of the little Nameless Naiads I have met in Lotus-haunts, who, with longing eyes, watch the sweet bubble of the frenzied grape. No, Sir, my real Love is my own Kosmic Soul, enthroned in its flawless essence; and when America can grasp the supreme whole I sing in too-too utterance for vulgar lips, then soul and body will blend in mystic symphonies; then, crowned with bellamours and wanton flower-de-luce, I shall be hailed Lord of a new Empery, and as I stain my lips in the bleeding wounds of the Pomegranate, and wreathe my o'ergrown limbs with the burnished disk of the Sunflower, Apollo will turn pale, and lashing the restive horses of the Sun, the tamer chariot of a forgotten god will make way for the glorious zenith of the one OSCAR WILDE."

At this moment *The Boshnia* gave a sudden lurch, and the grand young Poet fell prostrate on the rabbit-skins, worshipping Poseidon, and calling feebly for the Steward. Seeing that he would be incapable of receiving any other interviewers, I quitted the cabin, drank the brandy-and-soda which the Steward was bringing, and then returned to shore as quickly as possible. So here is the First Intelligence!

1. Helena Modjeska.
2. Sarah Bernhardt.
3. Ellen Terry.
4. The Lyceum Theatre. "*Impressions*" is a reference to "*Impressions du Théatre*", a group of five poems on theatrical subjects in *Poems.*

"Oscar Wilde Interviewed," *The Stage* (London, UK), 20 Jan. 1882, 12[1]

Mr. Wilde had a lively time the day following his arrival in New York. The reporters were out after him early, the smartest being the *New York Dramatic News* man, who caught the poet in a tram-car with this effect:—"I object to being lied about," Mr. Wilde said, "and my experience of a few hours in America has taught me that your reporters exaggerate most unjustly and unreasonably. If they had caricatured—in a word, made fun of me—I might have been pleased with their skill and laughed at their wit, but to be described and misrepresented in the language of the police court reporter, that is a little hard."

"Your misfortune in that respect was owing to climatic influences, perhaps," the reporter suggested. "The climate is glorious," Mr. Wilde replied with energy. "I am delighted with your magnificent sky and crisp, breezy atmosphere. I have long been a London man, enveloped in smoke and fog. It was there, in the midst of the busy life of the world's great capital, that I first saw all the follies of modern society, and the grotesqueness of the customs of this generation." The reporter, glancing at Mr. Wilde's queer outfit, was in doubt whether the philosopher meant customs or costumes. As gently as possible the scribe hinted as much. "Either or both," Mr. Wilde replied, smiling. "I admire the middle ages because their social life was natural. It was not harassed by the tyranny we call society—foolish customs limited by petty rules. On the other hand, their costumes were graceful, and I approve of them because they were beautiful."

"I see by some of the papers that you claim for aestheticism that it is a philosophy," the reporter said, as he and Mr. Wilde exchanged straps. "It is," the aesthete answered, "the philosophy of beautiful in art and nature. The surroundings of art enhance existence, and make life worth living. Aestheticism is the study of truth in art. Whatever there is in all art which represents the eternal truth is the expression of the great underlying truth."

"That is clear," the reporter gasped. "Very," the philosopher answered. "I knew that in America my philosophy would be readily understood and appreciated. Before I came here I was told that you were an impressionable people. I have found you so. I am glad, gratified to find a nation ready to accept grand ideas and glorious ideals. The cultivation of aestheticism is a grand idea, sir, and its results will be the glorious ideal after which I am striving." The reporter ventured to inquire if *Patience* reflected in any way the aims and objects of aestheti-

---

1. It does not seem likely that Wilde would have travelled on a tram when Morse was attempting to limit his public appearances ahead of his first lecture. Compare with "Our New York Letter," *The Philadelphia Inquirer* (Philadelphia, PA), 4 Jan. 1882, 7, pp. 874–5; and "The Esthete Talks," *The Atlanta Constitution* (Atlanta, GA), 8 Jan. 1882, 2, which have similar content but make no mention of the tram. The article's source in the *New York Dramatic News* is untraced.

cism. "*Patience*, sir, is twaddle," Mr. Wilde replied, indignantly. "As a satire on the philosophy of the beautiful I fail to see its point. Coarse, indeed, must be the nature of the man who would sneer at what makes the world so glorious, and in so far as *Patience* is a satire on aestheticism, it is only a sneer at what is beautiful in art, at the intimate study of the correlation of all arts." It was getting to be deep water for the reporter, and so he ventured to change the subject, inquiring about Mr. Wilde's proposed lecture. "Yes, I lecture at Chickering Hall next Monday evening," he said, "on the English Renaissance. I do not know whether I shall lecture in other cities besides New York or not. That will depend upon the encouragement which is shown to my school of philosophy. But I do not want to produce my tragedy in America."[1]

"Tragedy seems played out with us," the reporter began, but Mr. Wilde looked at him with an aesthetic stare that stopped his unaesthetic tongue. "Mine has not been played out at all yet," he said gently, and the Apostle of Aestheticism left the humble vehicle in which he had been riding to look for the office of Mr. D'Oyly Carte, in the Gilsey Building.[2]

"The Latest," *Moonshine* (London, UK), 21 Jan. 1882, 34

Not wishing to be behind our contemporaries, we instructed our own correspondent to interview Mr. Oscar Wilde, and we have now much pleasure in publishing our representative's account of the interview. He says:—

I entered the poet's apartment and found him with a large jack knife in his hand whittling the leg of the table which he had broken off. Beside him stood a tumbler of toe tickler, his favourite beverage; between his lips rested an immense cigar; and in the distance reposed a salivarium, to use which with propriety he was assiduously practising. "Ah! Poet of the higher life," I said, "what a mind must yours be thus to adapt itself to circumstances." I paused for the great one's reply. He removed the cigar, laid down his knife, refreshed himself from the goblet, took a careful but erring shot at the distant salivarium, and thus commenced—

"Wall, stranger, I guess I'm in it, this show. I was tarnation queer on that there ditch, and you bet your last dollar if you'd seen nothing but the inside of a sleeping berth for ten days, the Atlantic would have disappointed you. But now I reckon I'm about free from that twisted long-haired crew that waltz around me in town, and, old hoss, I'm on for lark. What's your pison [sic]?" I shook my head.

---

1. This statement is at odds with apparently genuine interviews at the time: that Wilde would stage the play if he found suitable actors.
2. Gilsey House, a former hotel located at 1200 Broadway at West 29th Street.

"No, siree, you wet, or—" and his hand drew a six shooter from among his coat tails. I accordingly suggested a gin sling, which was promptly brought. "I'm darned if I can plug that cussed thing nohow," he continued, after three or four ineffectual shots. "Wall, sonny, I just feel at home here, none of your bunkum round me now, I've dropped the *slap*. I'm just plain O. Wilde. I'll play you at poker, eucre, or what you like. I'm game to go tobogganing, skating, dancing, or what the deuce you give a name to. But answer questions I will not."

"But oh, Poet," I gasped, "for the sake of—"

"Now quit!" was the only reply, and out came the six shooter again. I fled, and descending the stairs I heard—"By thunder, I've done it!" followed by a metallic ring.

W. T. Mercer, "The Aesthetic Gospel," *New York Tribune* (New York, NY), 23 Jan. 1882, 5[1]

A PROFESSION OF FAITH AND AN UNPUBLISHED POEM BY OSCAR WILDE.

To the Editor of The Tribune.

Sir: When in London, through the kindness of William Morris I was introduced to our present guest Oscar Wilde, and on calling upon him, the following dialogue occurred, which may be of interest to your readers:

"Mr. Wilde, do you intend delivering more lectures in New York to explain fully your ideas and views on aestheticism, and try to create a school of your particular philosophy?"

"Well, that question I can hardly answer, as it depends largely on the receptive nature of the Americans, and their desire to understand our unwritten philosophy."

"Well, I hardly understand your answer. Do you mean that you have no particular laws or tenets of your philosophy?"

"Oh, no. We have a positive, special, independent metaphysical science; but the mind of the average Philistine Briton is incapable of understanding it. Consequently we have never published it, but transmit orally to the members of our society. But if I thought the American people desired, I would gladly give a few of them, as they have treated me so kindly and seem to welcome all advanced ideas on religion, art, philosophy or aestheticism."

1. Quoted in Fong, B. (1979). Oscar Wilde: five fugitive poems. *English Literature in Transition, 1880–1920, 22*, 7–16. Fong credits the interview as genuine, but it is similar to other burlesque interviews that ascribe uncharacteristically high-flown language to Wilde.

"Suppose you give me a few condensed ideas of your subject, so that I could somewhat prepare the minds of the people, and, as it were, feel the pulse of public sentiment."

"Oh, I shall be glad of your kindly assistance, and will try to give you merely an outline of our metaphysical science, as we believe it our duty and mission to the world to have it study the creation of the beautiful, its relation to color, tones, lights, shadows, and have perfect harmony by exquisite blendings, so that man may have a higher and nobler appreciation of what is beautiful and true both in nature and art. In the first place, we believe there is no actual difference between the world of matter and space, because matter is the part or portion of space; that God had made Himself manifest to us through what we call Form; or, in other words, matter is space with Form; Space is matter without Form. Form is the manifestation of God to us. Therefore, Form is the essence of all matter, or God. Now, our views on this subject are, the nearer we approach the beautiful and graceful in the form of things, the more God-like it is, and, consequently, the more perfect pleasure it gives. When the creative hand of man has built or moulded a beautiful thing, the portion of his mind which created it becomes his soul; but when it is destroyed, its form or beauty is gone, just as when a man dies his form has left us. So in poetry; the more beautiful its creation, the more enjoyable it is; and as I must bring our interview to a close, I will give you one of my unpublished poems, which partly illustrates my views on the longing of the soul for the beautiful and unattainable:

> "Our soul is like a kite,
> That soars with ease to heavenly height,
> Held by a thread invisible.
>
> On earth through nature see,
> But only feel when reaching toward infinity
> The link that binds this life.
>
> So frail the thread of life,
> Our souls could not endure the strife
> Without this link with heavenly heights.
>
> We droop as blighted things
> If clouds but touch our earthly wings,
> Too human yet for heaven.

Our soul longs for new life,
Breaks the frail thread by constant strife,
Nor ceases in unending flight."[1]

Yours truly, W. T. MERCER

New York, Jan. 16, 1882.

"The Stage," *Bell's Life in London* (London, UK), 28 Jan. 1882, 11[2]

(BY D. A.)

✂ *Several paragraphs that are unrelated to Wilde.*

Byrne's Dramatic Times, of New York, gives an amusing, though I should say imaginary, interview with Mr Oscar Wilde, just now the lion of that city. Sarony, the famous photographer, accepting Mr Wilde as an undoubted celebrity, has paid the poet of "cultchaw" a sum of money for the sole right of publishing his likeness in America. "When," says the *Dramatic Times*, "our representative entered the august presence of the aesthete, Mr Wilde was busily engaged in eating his breakfast. His heavy under-chin wagged at an appalling rate, and the table fairly rattled with the energy of the brawny poet of the senses, as he fell upon the viands piled before him. Next in interest to a description of what Mr Wilde looks like, comes, of course, an illustration of Mr Wilde's dietetic fancies. When visited by the representative of the *Dramatic Times* his breakfast consisted of six poached eggs on toast, a dish of English bacon, half a pound of country sausages, cold beef and piccalilli, broiled oysters, devilled kidneys, half a partridge cold, frizzled ham, lyonnaise potatoes, *roth-kraut*, mutton-hash, head-cheese, liver-and-onions, cold ham, galantine of turkey, lobster salad, succotash, cold roast pork, broiled quail, a cup of milk, hominy, Scotch porridge, cracked wheat, grapes, coffee and brandy."

1. *"Our soul is like a kite"* was attributed to Wilde in Fong, B. (1979). Oscar Wilde: five fugitive poems. *English Literature in Transition*, *22*, 7–16, and included in the OET *Complete Works* (CW i, No. 93). However, that it appeared beneath this interview is evidence against its having been authored by Wilde. As Fong notes, the poem does not fit easily into Wilde's oeuvre: "There is nothing else in his work quite like it." No manuscript survives. It also does not seem plausible that Wilde would have gifted "Mercer" an unpublished poem when he had recently received a guinea a line for *Le Jardin* and *La Mer* (see "Oscar Wilde's Visit," *The Scranton Republican* (Scranton, PA), 3 Jan. 1882, 2, p. 750; and "Oscar, The Aesthete," *Philadelphia Press* (Philadelphia, PA), 7 Jan. 1882, 8, p. 754). See also Marland, R. (2022). 'Our Soul is Like a Kite': a poem misattributed to Oscar Wilde. *Notes and Queries*. doi:10.1093/notesj/gjac023
2. The article's source in *Byrne's Dramatic Times* is untraced.

Asked how the people of New York affected Mr Wilde's sense of the beautiful, that gentleman is made to reply:—"Superlatively! To the visual and sensuous Perception you are utterly consummate—just as to the analysis of Reason, you are supremely Absolute and Complete! I see, I recognise, for example, in your buildings the immutable, infrangible, and limitless wedlock of the Useful with the Exquisite. Your factory chimneys, for example—shafts that pierce the very sky— indicate the upper ether in one sense—carry off your surplus smoke, in the other. Your streets are not mere rigid utilitarian canals for the ebb and flow of your traffic. On the contrary, while they accommodate your foot passengers and your omnibuses, they delight him who revels in the formless, who suns his soul in the blaze of colour, who loathes the crude and the commonplace, who wears upon the drapery of his spirit the Marigold-and-Lily emblems of inner perceptiveness, and to whom the key is not so sweet or so fraught with delicious sustenance as the parable which it supplements. Ah! dear friend!" observes Mr Wilde, intently eyeing his cold ham, "the pensive mission of the Lily and the joyous gospel of the Marigold must be sweetly and consummately preached, and heard, too, with rick brooks, in sylvan nooks, by foamy lakes, in ferny brakes, where lilies grow and poppies blow, from shores of seas, from knotted trees and marsh and mere and fens where rocking rushes rear their tufted heads, from violet beds and scented dells, and brown and heather-plumaged fells, from silent corners of the wood, where soft-eyed does but lately stood, and tortured by their senseless fears, pricked up their ears and trembled at the very wind, from shining pools, where dace, in schools, flashed silver, and the shrew mouse, blind, wept for his too too eyeless kind! Her they have carried off, while the brown Fauns stood in hiding, while the Dryads hushed the whisper of the oak leaves, while the Satyrs crouched low in the shaggy underwood and Great Pan himself was silent in his pain—her they carried off to make her the faint, wan, sorrowful, pining handmaid of grim Utility!" Certainly, that is "admirable fooling," funny, and at the same time good-natured.

Mr. Arthur Sullivan is staying at Cairo, Egypt, busily engaged in the composition of the music of the comic opera to follow "Patience."

"Oscar Wilde," *The Sunday Oregonian* (Portland, OR), 19 Feb. 1882, 6

The Prototype of Bunthorne Keeps his own Counsel and the Conundrum Merchant gets Taffy

I had actually been suffering for an interview with Oscar Wilde, and so, while in New York, I went one morning to see him. I sent up my card, and soon received word to follow my pasteboard. I found Oscar with his long hair done up in papers, and looking about as unaesthetic generally as a moose in a menagerie. He came toward me and threw his head slightly forward, and then a good deal to the right side, and thrust out his hand and took my little lily-white one in his, all in a sort of two-dollar-chromo-departing-hero style, and issued one of his seven-by-nine smiles for me. I said that I hoped I had not intruded, and I asked Oscar if he had breakfasted. The imported sunflower rolled his eyes in a sort of absconding-bank-cashier-trying-to-calculate-the-deficiency fashion, and said he had just taken his breakfast by feasting his eyes on a bird's-eye view of a too-but-soulful-dado. I ventured to suggest that for a man who was so largely engaged in the soulful business, he was in rather good flesh. He here presented me with another copy of his smile and murmured in a gentle whisper, which must have reached the mosquito foundries of New Jersey, that he was growing thinner every day. I said, perhaps, he'd better change boarding-places, but he assumed a kind of tombstone advertisement or graveyard prospectus look, and said he was getting more ideal every hour; he would gradually drift into the truly ideal, and his soul would float in an atmosphere of true art. I changed the conversation by asking him if he liked America. He cheered up and said he did. He loved the east and yearned for the west, I said it took considerable of a yearn to cover it. He asked if Chicago was a fast town. I said yes, it was fast; there were so many mortgages on it that it couldn't get away. He wanted to know if the Indians in Chicago were troublesome now. I said no; the cigar signs has [*sic*] been very quiet of late. Oscar said he pined for a sight of the noble red man. There was a hidden poem in him; there could be nothing more beautiful than the dusky maiden stealing with the grace of a moonbeam through the perfumed air of a great forest looking shyly for the little flowers that first put forth their sweet faces to be kissed by the gentle zephyrs of spring. I said, I liked his exotics of speech, but the only thing he would find secreted about the red man would probably be a flask of whisky, strong enough to open a mine, hidden in the top of the remains of a once plug hat; and as for the maidens, they were fond of stealing anything,—even a forest, if it wasn't so large and wasn't fastened down,—but that moonbeams, especially the American brand, didn't wear government pants and sport a complexion greasy enough to shame a last season's ham into an early grave, or the incurable ward of a lunatic asylum. He said the current of the r.m.'s life must flow on smoothly to the end. I said it did; the current of life and conflagration water were about equal, odds if any in favor of the water. Oscar said he would like to live near the great lakes. He longed to try the waters of Lake Michigan, one of the great inland seas. I told him that unless he used a filter, the water not being pure might affect his liver and aggravate his aestheticism. He said he merely referred to a residence near the lake, where he could go out when the sun had gone to distribute a few cases of sunstroke among the blest inhabitants of the Orient—go out after the moon rose. I told him the moon-rose was scarce here, the moss-rose being more common.

I asked the wandering hair store if he had written anything new lately; he said he had written an ode to winter. I asked him how much he owed Mr. Winter, but he didn't say. I think perhaps he can compromise though. He then showed the beginning of a poem he intends having constructed in a boiler-shop. I will give it as I remember it:

> The intensely much and saleratus plambago,
> Oh, much! Oh, more! Oh, less!
> With north winds from the southwest,
> Direct reports every twenty-four hours,
> And several counties yet to hear from.

Oscar said it was blank verse: I agreed with him. I thought it was the —est verse I ever saw. He said this effort would be in about 175 lines, but he didn't know what to call it. I suggested that he christen it "One Hundred and Seventy-five Attacks of Hydrophobia and the Author Still Lives." But he won't do it, I know. Some persons have no idea of the eternal fitness of things.

I felt that I must now cut the tendrils of love that had entwined themselves about my heart and make my escape from this Colossus of culture. He saw me getting ready to depart, and he came and laid his mattress on my coat-collar and his bosom heaved heavily. He said he hoped I would become soulful.

And then I reached the fire-escape and got away.

SO-FULL.

"Oscar Wilde," *The Saturday Review* (Indianapolis, IN), 11 Mar. 1882, 7[1]

At the Governor's Reception—Positively the Last.

Governor Porter's miscellaneous reception has not drifted so far away towards the shoreless past, that a story about it, especially with Oscar Wilde as the central figure, will be altogether uninteresting.[2] It will be remembered that the greenbackers, who were at that time playing at holding a convention, had fin-

---

1. H & S, b50. Quoted in OWDA, 197-8. It seems likely that this article is part burlesque, part report from a third party. Wilde did attend the reception at Porter's residence on 22 February 1882 ("City News," *The Indianapolis News* (Indianapolis, IN), 23 Feb. 1882, 3).

2. Albert Gallatin Porter (1824–1897) was a Republican politician who served as the nineteenth Governor of Indiana between 1881 and 1885. He was originally a Democrat, but was expelled in 1856 by the pro-slavery faction of that party.

ished nominating a state ticket, and, on invitation, attended the reception in a body. To these sons of toil, who wandered through those halls of dazzling light, by "particular request," where all was gas and gaiters, all seemed as an enraptured dream. The host, however, was dissatisfied. There was something lacking. He could not think what it was, but there was something that had escaped the bill of fare, without which the menu was incomplete.

Mr. Roberts, recently of Sullivan county, now of the governor's office, is as ready an interpreter as was Joseph before Pharaoh. He suggested Oscar Wilde. "The very thing," said the governor, resuming his wonted smile and animation, and Mr. Roberts, albeit the clock was on the stroke of eleven, was sent for the missing link.

Mr. Roberts went to the New-Denison hotel. Oscar had retired for the night. Mr. Vale, the agent, was found and with Mr. Roberts ascended to Oscar's dormitory.

"Wha-a-t is it?" asked the voice behind the oak.

Mr. Vale answered.

"Wait a moment."

There was a rustle of bed clothes, a long pause, and the voice inside with great deliberateness intoned, "Come-in-Mr.-Vale-I-am-now-prepared-to-receive-you."

Mr. Roberts stiffened all his joints and prepared for a formal reception. He was taken quite off his legs when Mr. Wilde rushed at him from behind the bed, both arms extended as if to embrace him, saying: "How-do-you-do-my-deah-fellah; will-you 'ave-some-wine-with-me?"

The wine was Spanish, and was in a goat skin—the genuine article. Mr. Roberts, who is no bigot, but on occasion, a four-finger Hoosier,[1] drank a great deal of it. He thought Mr. Wilde didn't look well and the wine might not be good for him.

"How far does the governor-general live from here?"

"About ten squares," said Mr. Roberts.

"Ten squares; and is that a league?"

Explanation was made that it was about a mile, and that they could ride there in a hack. They did so; Mr. Wilde insisting upon calling the vehicle a "ca-ab."

Mr. Roberts asked Oscar what he had come here for—his real motive.

"For recreation and pleasure," said Oscar, "and I am finding both bounteously. But I have not, as yet, found any Americans. There are English, and French, and Danes, and Spaniards in New York, but I have yet to see an American."

"I notice," he drawlingly continued, "the men shake hands a great deal here. Do the ladies shake hands, too?"

1. Hoosier: a person from Indiana.

He was told they did.

"Aw, I think I should like that. I believe I will—aw—familiarize myself with the custom a little tonight."

They were nearing the governor's residence, and noticed a number of men on the sidewalk. "Who are the populace?"

He was told that they were greenbackers going to pay their respects to the governor.

"Greenbackers—aw—are they the class you call grangers?"[1]

Mr. Roberts answered affirmatively.

"Aw, I must shake hands with some of them and talk to them. They must be quite a study."

The governor's residence was a disappointment to Mr. Wilde. He asked if the people gave it to him to live in, and entering into a discourse on architecture, concluded with the opinion that it was a very inferior house for a governor to inhabit.

The governor met him at the door. Their salutations soon were o'er, and then they mingled with the throng inside. The hack was to call for Mr. Wilde at half past twelve. After the reception was over he was invited to remain and lunch with the governor and family. Mr. Wilde is not an animated feeder. He placed the small of his back in the seat of the chair, and spooned in the ice cream with the languor of a debilitated duck. At the conclusion he rose suddenly to his feet, shook hands with great solemnity, and strode sorrowfully away. Perhaps ice cream disagrees with him.

The hack was not at the door. Mr. Roberts uncorked a choice selection of anathemas which the hackman was not there to receive. Mr. Wilde was shivering in his knee breeches and thin stockings, for he wore his lecture suit to the reception.

"Is the c-a-ab gone?" his teeth chattered.

"Yes, it is gone."

"Oh, the stewpid villain!"

1. The Greenback Party was active between 1874 and 1889. It opposed the return to gold-backed currency, thinking it would lead to deflation in the prices paid to farmers. It emerged from the policies of The Grange, an agricultural advocacy group.

Kate Crombie, "Aunt Ruth Goes to Hear Oscar Wilde," *Godey's Lady's Book and Magazine* (Philadelphia, PA), Apr. 1882, 352–4[1]

No. 9.

BY KATE CROMBIE.

Yes, I went to hear Oscar when I was in Boston; and I was a good deal surprised at the way they treated him. You see I knew there was lots and lots o'folks in Boston that hain't got nothin' ter dew, and that are jest spilin', as it were, for somethin' to occerpy their minds; and I did think that there was enough on 'em ter give Oscar a gratifyin' recepshun or a respeckful hearin at least.

But 'twa'nt so; they come there that night in their seal skin sacks and dimonds—money enough on their backs ter build a railroad from here to Chiny—the best and most "*culchewered*" folks in the city—but they didn't come ter honor Oscar; fur from it. Judgin' by their actions they jest come to make fun and have a good time; and I dunno's I blamed 'em much.

Ye see in the fust place, they'd heard how he was rigged out in knee breeches, with a sunflower in his button hole and so on, when he'd lectured at other places, so the college boys, about sixty of 'em, dressed themselves up ter take him off, and marched in as big as life jest afore Oscar put in his appearance.[2]

They did look killin' that's a fact! They was all decked out in great shape, and every one on 'em carried a big lily or sunflower in his hand, and lopped along, looking as silly and holler heded as they knew how.

I asked a man settin' beside o' me, if he didn't think it was kinder insultin' to Oscar; I told him I thought it was real mean ter treat a stranger so.

He laughed and says he "Don't you worry; he knows all about it—and he likes it. He calls it, 'the 'omage that *mediockrity* pays to genius.'"[3]

"Is that so?" says I "Wall, then I s'pose it's all right; but I should think he'd ruther they'd pay him some other way."

"So they have tonight, madam;" says the man lookin round him. "This crowded house represents to Oscar a pocket full o' money and that's all he cares about it."

"Oh I guess not, sir;" says I "fur he speaks a good many times, I notice, in his poems, about everything bein' holler and good for nothin' except art and beauty and so on. Now *I* think he'd a ben dretful well pleased if we'd all clubbed together and persented him with a harnsome chromo tonight."

The man had a bad caughin' spell jest then so he didn't say no more.

---

1. Quoted in OWDA, 128.
2. A reference to the Harvard incident: see p. 134, note 2.
3. Wilde had used this phrase in *The English Renaissance* (*Miscellanies*, 250). See also e.g. "Oscar Wilde's Views," *The Morning Call* (San Francisco, CA), 27 Mar. 1882, 4, p. 293.

There was one arrangement a little different from anything I ever see afore.

When I went to see the Siamese twins and the two-heded girl and the five-leggid calf they didn't try to give no effecks in color—didn't have no background nor nothin', you know. S'pose they never thought on't.

But Oscar, he had a red curtin' drawed behind him, and it did set him off wonderful! I should most a' thought some o' them show men would a' got hold o' that kink before!

I wonder though, that he didn't put that statu of Bethoven behind the orgin or out o' the way somewhere. There it stood jest the other side o' the curtin' right in plain sight—towerin' up above everything; and bein' so big and rough lookin' he made quite a contrast to Oscar. It was pooty hard on Bethoven; for he had on his everyday clo'es ye know and Oscar was all dressed up in his swoller tail and white kid gloves.

I felt bad ter see a statu we all set so high by, so kind o' put in the shade—as it were. I don't know's Oscar meant ter cut anybody out; still, it looked a little like it. His fixin' that curtin' so and wearin' them gloves and all.

Wall, I'd read his lectur' beforehand and I was glad I had, for I couldn't understand one word he said that night; nobody couldn't nuther. They was all complainin'. Folks like ter hear the words if they can't ketch the idee, don't you know?

I've ben to school exhibishions, and heard the boys speak their Latin and Greek pieces, and if I hadn't a' known, I should a' thought that Oscar was speakin' one o' them kind.

I 'spose he never had nobody ter tell him how to speak a piece, and I most made up my mind afore he got through that it was *my* dooty to see him myself and tell him about that a little in a friendly way, and mention some few other pints wherein I could see he might improve.

But I wan' ter tell ye how that aujence treated him that night: they didn't seem ter be happy 'less they was clappin' their hands and stompin' and makin' a noise.

They was so chuckin' full o' mischief that they couldn't hold in, and every time that poor feller stopped ter take a long breath or drink a swaller o' water, they'd begin and make sech a dretful rumpus as I never heard anywhere afore; no, not even at a minstrel show! And I will say, that he appears ter be oncommon patient and good natered, for he jest stood still and carm as a baby through it all, and waited till they got ready to stop, and then begun where he left off—though nobody'd a' known if he hadn't—and went on as if nothin' had happened.

Yes, whatever other faults Oscar may have, I'm sure he'd got a *ral good disposishion!*

If you want to read his lectur', you'll find it at most any bookstore printed 'long with his poems.[1]

I've read it over a few times and I'm goin' ter read it agin. I allers feel kinder mixed up in my mind when I git through, as if I didn't really *sense it*, as it were, but it's awful interestin' the way them sentences is constructed together.

I shouldn't wonder if readin' the dictionary so much has 'fected his stil; its his favorite book and he speaks on't in his lectur' as bein' the only book fit for a poet ter read.

To wind up with, he tells us why he sets so much by the lily and the sunflower; as nigh as I can make out, it aint because sunflower seeds is good ter feed to chickens, nor because the lily smells so sweet, but because the sunflower looks somethin' like a *lion*, and the lily is *perfeckly lovely!*[2]

Wall, that's all right: I'm fond o' flowers myself, but I can't see wherein them two is so much better 'n all the rest.

It was pooty bad weather the next mornin' arter the lectur, but I never 'low nothin' ter stand in the way o' dooty. So I spunked up, and set out afoot and alone to call on Oscar.

I sent up my card, and he didn't keep me waitin' long. He came a tiptoein' inter the room, with a flower in his buttonhole—though he wore a mornin' gownd—a silk one, all embroidered off and hangin' clear down to his heels.

"How do ye do, my young friend?" says I, as cordial as could be.

He bowed very graceful and smiled, and says he "How do you do, madam? It is bad weather for a lady to be out."

"Oh la," says I "I don't mind it."

He looked out the winder and shivered, and takin' out his white handkercher brushed a snowflake that I had brought in, off'n a chair next to him. Then he seemed ter be waitin' for me to speak, so I begun.

"Oscar," says I "I went to hear ye lectur last night, and I didn't by no means approve of the way they 'bused ye; and knowin' that you was away from all your folks—a stranger in a strange land, as it were, I felt as if I wanted ter come and see if I couldn't dew a little suthin' ter kinder help ye along.

"If you're goin' ter get your livin' in this way—make it your bizness ye know—there's some few pints you'd orter tend tew."

He coughed behind his hand and bowed very perlite.

"Ye see," said I "you're young and you can't be expected to know everything yet; and perhaps you hain't had advantages—if so you ain't so much ter blame.

---

1. A reference to the Seaside Library's pirated edition of *The English Renaissance* and *Poems*.

2. In *The English Renaissance* Wilde spoke of "the gaudy leonine beauty" of the sunflower and the "precious loveliness" of the lily (*Miscellanies*, 276). Wilde had also referred to "[t]he gaudy leonine sunflower" in *Le Jardin* (CW i, No. 94, line 5).

"Another thing your looks is agin ye; it's a pity you're so awful homely. A harnsome man can git along most anywheres specially with women; but never mind, don't ye feel discouraged. You can fix yourself up ter look considerable better, and I'm a goin' ter tell you how ter dew it; that's one thing I came for.

"In the fust place you must cut off that ere long hair—'taint the fashion here—and I'll show ye how ter fix your necktye; and then if you could *take in* your lips a little, and try to look a little more wide awake, not so resigned ye know. We like *live* folks."

I stopped here, for he had riz up and was fumblin' with his watch chain kinder narvous and lookin' at me most as ef he was mad at what I was sayin'.

"Set down, set down Oscar," says I "I ain't a goin' for some time and you might as well take it easy."

"Madam," says he, "this is very extraordinary conduct, *very!*"

"Oh la," says I, laughin' "you know it's only the tribute mediockrity pays to genius!"

Upon that he laughed quite natural and hearty and sot down agin and looked at me as good natered as you please.

"Now Oscar," I goes on "I think you mean well and I know somthin' how you feel—specially 'bout nater and flowers and birds and sech things.

"Why, bless your heart," says I warmin' up, "sometimes of a summer's mornin' to home I've gone to our back door and opened it and stood there. I've looked off on the grand old hills and way down 'cross the green medders with the dew a sparklin' on the grass, and the daisies and buttercups a noddin' good mornin' to each other; and p'r'aps if its early, a thousand birds is a splittin' their little throats a singin' so beautiful, and the air is all so sweet and fresh—Massy sakes!" says I "I can't begin ter tell ye how I feel," and I had ter wipe my eyes, "but I guess," says I, "that I feel same as you do, when you tell about treadin' the golden hights and so on."

"Why, bless you, dear lady," says Oscar, rizin' up and ketchin' hold o' my hands "you are, in your way, an *estheet—*a *poet;* and I love to meet sech souls!"

"Oh, no I ain't," says I calmin' down. "I'm a commonsensicle woman, and when I say a thing I ginerally say it so common folks can understand, without runnin' ter the dictionary. The great fault with you, ain't in your idees nor your feelin's; and I dunno' but your morals is well enough, only you've writ some o' your poitry in sech a way that it don't *read* exactly moral. Now, why not write things and say things right end tew, with the sense—if there is any—right out plain in words we can all understand? Good land! I've got mad enough ter eat ye up 'fore now, a sweatin' over some o' your sentences, tryin' ter make out what you was drivin' at. Did you ever hear o' Dan'l Webster?[1] Wall, he never 'lowed ter use a big word, nor an outlandish one, when a simple common one would dew. So if you've really got anything ter say to rashional creeters, dew, for pity's sake, say it so we can understand! I ain't the only one to complain on ye in this respeck. I've heard several speak on't, and I mention it fer your good. Then agin men and women must forgit themselves and their hair and so on, before they can really 'complish much in any great work. And you'll excuse me for sayin' it, I hope, but it does seem to me somehow, as if you was all the time tryin' ter git admiration and a big name for yourself, a good deal more'n you're tryin' ter teach folks about beauty and art. If I's you I'd leave my hair and clo'es pooty much to the barber and tailor hererarter; they know what's what and then you can give all your time to your 'great movement' you know, and you'll git along better, and in time be respected and make money tew."

Oscar bit his lips and looked as if he felt hurt.

"Come Oscar," says I "don't be mad at me. I'm Aunt Ruth—perhaps you've heard on me? I'm most as much of a public charicter as you be; and I was a goin' ter speak a favorable word for you to Mr. GODEY and tell him what a good dispersishun you've got, and I mean tew yet," says I.

Upon that he smiled agin and put out his hand; he is amiable that's a fact, and I couldn't help kinder takin' tew him.

"All right," says he "let us be friends."

"With all my heart," says I "and if I can ever dew anything for ye I will and be glad to."

Then an idee struck me all to once. "Oscar," says I, "you're away from home, and I think's likely your *mendin'* is all behindhand—now if you'll lemme take a little bundle o' your stockin's along with me, I'll mend 'em up for ye and welcome. I'm a master hand ter mend."

He's got a bad cough—I believe I mentioned it before—and he put his little white hand up to his mouth and coughed a number o' times, then he spoke up real soft and gentle, and says he, "Dear Aunt Ruth, you are most kind and I thank you; but my wardrobe is in good order, so far as I am aware." So sayin' he took the little bokay out of his buttonhole and gave it tew me, and we parted the best o' friends.

1. Daniel Webster (1782–1852) was an American politician who served as the 14th and 19th United States Secretary of State.

"Oscar," *The Idaho Avalanche* (Silver City, ID), 1 Apr. 1882, 2

An Ogden *Pilot* reporter gives the following interview with the sunflower and lily man, Oscar Wilde:

P.R.—How have you enjoyed your trip, Mr. Wilde?

O.W.—Very much, indeed, sir. The thrilling ecstasy of my peregrinating experience could scarcely have been enhanced by a tour through the blissful realms of Paradise.

P.R.—How long do you intend to remain on the Pacific Coast?

O.W.—About three weeks. I am under an engagement to Mr. Locke to lecture in San Francisco and a number of other prominent towns in California, after which I shall return to the East, resuming the lecture field at Kansas City, sometime next month.

P.R.—Will you lecture in Utah on your return?

O.W.—Probably at Ogden, but decidedly not at Salt Lake.

P.R.—Why not there?

O.W.—Because my friend, Senator Jones, of Nevada, whom I met in New York, gave me a shocking account of the local reporter of the *Tribune*.[1] If there is anything in the world I utterly abhor, it is being interviewed by a newspaper man who washes down his onions and garlic with gin.

P.R.—We received today the mournful intelligence of the death of Longfellow.

O.W.—Ah! I've heard of the 'orse. A fair American hack, but not to be compared with the poorest of our English cracks, you know.

P.R.—How are you impressed with America, generally, Mr. Wilde?

O.W.—It is decidedly the finest country I ever visited. I've made over a thousand pounds here already.

P.R. (hesitatingly)—Will you take a drink, Mr. Wilde?

O.W. (promptly)—Yes, thank you. A noggin of whisky tapster. Sunflower brand, if you have it.

P.R. (lifting his glass)—Here we go.

O.W. (after drinking)—A blarsted funny custom, that of yours in America. A lot of men will stand around a bar and touch their glasses and say "'ere we go," but they don't go at all. They keep standing there all the time. A very paradoxical and absurd custom, sir.

Just then a Salt Lake man interrupted the interview by asking Mr. Wilde for his pocket handkerchief as a souvenir, and before the latter had complied with

1. John Percival Jones (1829–1912) served as a Republican United States Senator from Nevada between 1873 and 1903.

the request, he was again surrounded by a crowd and the reporter jostled to the rear.

A number of his fellow-passengers say that Oscar is a pleasant fellow to travel with; always cheerful and agreeable, and puts on no "airs." He is generous, and responds to every appeal for charity that is made to him. He has some cockney mannerisms,[1] but they probably serve to render him more popular among the American snobs who profess to be the most utterly utter of his following.

"A Distinguished Arrival," *The Daily Picayune* (New Orleans, LA), 1 Apr. 1882, 3[2]

THE APOSTLE OF HIGH ART IN THE CITY—HIS RECEPTION AND ENTERTAIN-
MENT.

Oscar Wilde, the poet, lecturer and aesthete, was among the arrivals at the St. Charles Hotel last evening. He came in on the Mobile Road, having left Louisville on Thursday. Mr. Wilde was on his way to California, where he has an engagement to deliver a series of lectures on art to the artless denizens of the Far West. His object in visiting New Orleans is a two-fold one.

Mr. Wilde, who is a nephew of the late Judge Elgee, thinks his claims to the vast estate left by the deceased jurist are well founded, and only need pressing to result in a handsome pecuniary return.[3] His attorneys, Messrs. Richardson and Magruder have been in constant communication with the young claimant ever since his arrival in this country, and they have the case in such a favorable condition now that his presence alone is necessary to complete the legal chain of facts which, it is thought will change the worshiper of the sunflower into a full-blown millionaire. The second and most important cause for his appearance is his de-

1. "Cockney": see p. 138, note 1.
2. A week after this article appeared the *Picayune* gloated that "The Oscar Wilde April fool hoax in the Picayune sold [i.e. deceived] a great many good and worthy people. The St. Charles Hotel rotunda was visited all day long with curious sight-seers who gazed in every nook and corner for the leonine Oscar, without seeing him, however. The Woman's Christian Exchange, where the apostle of aestheticism was announced to visit at noon, was crowded with open-eyed lunch eaters who were not, however, afforded a chance to feast on the loveliness of the Early-English-Irishman. Even the press of Mobile lamented in sorrowful tones that Oscar gave the Gulf City the go-by; while the rural journalists are still announcing the presence of the sunflower-worshiper here," ("Society," *The Daily Picayune* (New Orleans, LA), 9 Apr. 1882, 3). Wilde was in California at the beginning of April and would visit New Orleans in mid-June.
3. Judge John Kingsbury Elgee.

termination to travel to the California coast by the newly completed Southern Pacific Road.[1]

On his arrival at the hotel Mr. Wilde was shown to Parlor D, as he had telegraphed from Nashville for quarters. This, with the sleeping apartment adjoining, will constitute his rooms during his stay. It took the poet some time to perform his ablutions after the dusty journey, and to swallow the unesthetical meal ordered by his valet, which was served under the name of supper. The main constituents of the frugal feast were a plate of cold oatmeal, two eggs slightly fried on the side, and a half bottle of champagne. The wine was not *frappéd*, as the poet prefers to dilute it with small particles of ice.

A reporter of the Picayune was granted an interview with the leader of the Early English movement, after several well-known gentlemen had paid their respects. Among the callers were Col. A. P. Mason of the Boston, and Mr. Edward Fenner of the Commercial Club, who extended invitation to their respective club houses, courtesies which seemed to please the young Irishman greatly.

When the reporter entered he found the object of his visit half reclining on a lounge of hazy red color, and vigorously puffing away at a common clay pipe, such as children blow soap bubbles with. Mr. Wilde's attire showed the aesthetic sympathies of his nature. His gown or robe was a combination, the outer side being a leopard skin, soft to the touch and glowing in color, while the inside was of velvet in blue and gold. Instead of knee breeches, which the poet usually wears when lecturing, he wore a very comfortable pair of Turkish trousers of crimson colored cloth flecked with bars of gray.[2] For a smoking cap he wore a turban of yellow, streaked with gold filligree, from under which his long, curly hair fell with indescribable confusion.

The visitor received a warm clasp of the aesthete's huge palm, and heard a languid request to be seated. Evidently Mr. Wilde has been through the interviewing process so often since his arrival in this country that he takes the visit of a newspaper man quite as a matter of course.

"May I ask what you think of New Orleans?" began the reporter, remembering that this is the usual query put to all strangers.

"It is a revelation to me," answered the aesthete quickly and enthusiastically. "I was prepared for something. I know not what, but the reality is beyond that. What a marvelous place, to be sure, and what wonderful tints of varied existence you must see around you every day! When in Venice I sighed for Naples,

---

1. The Southern Pacific Railroad ran from New Orleans to Los Angeles via Houston, San Antonio, El Paso, and Yuma. Wilde travelled to and from California on the Overland Route. In June, after visiting New Orleans, he travelled west on the Southern Pacific route as far as San Antonio.

2. Perhaps a reference to the opening line of *Impressions I. Les Silhouettes*: "The sea is flecked with bars of grey" (CW i, No. 87).

but here I shall gaze at those idyllic currents which harmonize and round a life under a sensuous and mellow climate. You have a type of civilization so different from what I saw in New York and Chicago. I fail to realize that one country embraces them all. Yours is a city for one to dream, to paint, to chisel and to plan in. Here one may live for one's own best nature and the development of that infinite innerness which all must feel and acknowledge. I feel sure," said the speaker after a meditative pause, "the art spirit must flourish here. Love art for its own sake, and then all things you need will be added to you. This devotion to beauty and to the creation of beautiful things is the test of all great civilization; it is what makes the life of each citizen a sacrament and not a speculation.

"New Orleans has been encompassed by many troubles in the past," resumed Mr. Wilde, sympathetically, "but she has the sublime content of feeling that while philosophies fall away like sand, creeds follow one another, but what is beautiful is a joy for all seasons, a possession for all eternity."

"How did the scenery along your journey impress you?"

"It was weirdly strange," was the reply. "What particularly appealed to me was the fantastic lines [*sic*] of picturesqueness between here and Mobile. I assure you we have nothing in modern England to compare with it. The moss hung swamp, with its background of dancing waters, shining like myriad stars under the moon's reflection, were wonderful realizations of nature. It seemed to me a scene where

> To outer senses there is peace.
> A dreamy peace on either hand,
> Deep silence in the shadowy land.
> Deep silence where the shadows cease.[1]

I was intensely interested in observing the line of alligators we passed after leaving the Bay of St. Louis. What hideous, scaly monsters they must be! In the Royal Aquarium, at home, we have some puny specimens, which are dwarfs to these leviathans. I have given an order," and here the aesthete laughed in his loud, odd way, "to purchase several of these crocodiles to carry home with me."

"By the way, Mr. Wilde, if it is not too personal a question, have you seen the play of 'The Colonel,' which purports to be founded on the idiosyncrasies of your school of thought?"

"Oh, cert'nly; my friend Burnand invited me specially to see it when it was brought out first in London. It is a harmless composition, a burlesque in which satire pays the usual homage that mediocrity yields to genius. These things like 'The Colonel' and 'Patience' are horrible distortions of truth and intensely stupid.

---

1. The opening lines of Wilde's *La Fuite de la Lune*, first published in *The Irish Monthly* in February 1877 (CW i, No. 88).

But what can you expect? Both Burnand and Gilbert would write anything for money—"

"While you only lecture for that purpose," mildly hinted the listener.

Mr. Wilde laughed his own peculiar laugh at this, and muttered something about his being on a proselytizing mission instead of a coining expedition.

"You have been in this country some time and are able to form an opinion of our public characters; let me hear what you think of them."

"In New York the greatest man is Vanderbilt, who has a caricature of an art gallery, where the pictures are hung according to size. Kate Field is a kleptomaniac of other people's ideas. I think she is wrong in urging women to wear knee breeches; what they should put on are turkish trousers, something like these I have on.[1] Clara Morris is good but weak, and puts one's nerves out of joint when she comes to pieces. The young men in Washington are very useful; they make them dance at receptions and entertainments. You will oblige me," requested the poet, "by denying that I received $150 for attending a dinner party in Chicago, although I am certain that what one suffers at such gatherings is worth that much and more."

The conversation was here interrupted by the entrance of Mr. John Crickard, of the Art Union, who came to invite Mr. Wilde to attend a reception at the rooms of the Union, on Canal street, this evening. The pictures which have been on exhibition for the few past weeks will remain hanging, and the reception will be on the same order as that given on last Saturday night. The managers of the Art Union have decided to make no charge, and those who feel an interest in art matters are invited to be present. The reception will last from 8 until 11 o'clock. Mr. Crickard was very anxious to induce the poet to deliver a lecture, but Mr. Wilde declined on the score of fatigue, but promised to make a short address on the subject of "The Tendency of Modern Art." Mr. Wilde informed the reporter that his forenoon would be taken up by a consultation with his lawyers. He has promised to visit the Christian Woman's Exchange at noon, from which place he will go to the Jockey Club grounds under the care of President Simmons. In the evening he will dine with Mrs. Judge E. T. Merrick, and afterwards will proceed to the Art Union rooms. His address on "The tendency of Modern Art" is said to be very instructive and entertaining. He leaves on Sunday for California.

1. For Field's comments on knee breeches, see "The Question of the Hour," *The New York Herald* (New York, NY), 4 Mar. 1882, 9, pp. 766–7. Field advocated for men but not women to wear knee breeches. Needless to say, Wilde did not wear "Turkish trousers."

"Bill Nye and Oscar Wilde," *The Daily Inter Ocean* (Chicago, IL), 8 Apr. 1882, 11[1]

The aesthetic editor of the *Boomerang*, Bill Nye, had an interview with Oscar Wilde, and he gives his experience:

We went down to the overland train Thursday evening to see the great aesthete. We picked him out without any trouble and tackled him for a quiet talk all by ourselves.

Mr. Wilde is very tall, with a face like a broad ax. We told him that our name was Nye, the great Wyoming aesthete. He smiled like the rolling-mill and shook hands.

He wore a soft hat and a kind of steel-colored velvet sack coat. He also wore his hands in his pockets clear up to his elbow joint. He wears a kind of Byron collar and a necktie the color of a diseased liver. His pants were of a gray material and held in place with pale pink gum suspenders. These were shown as he stooped over, his coat being cut just below the shoulder blades. His shoulder blades are high and intellectual.

He wears his hair long, with hay and little mementoes from the sleeping-car in it. His face is thin, and when buried in a piece of pie must be a ghastly sight.

Mr. Wilde's teeth are evidently his own. Nobody could make teeth like them and escape the vigilance committee. They are broad and prominent, with a tendency to go out and look for air. He does not seem strong, but his breath proves this impression to be erroneous. Mr. Wilde wore a silk handkerchief the color of the illustrations found in public documents describing the cattle plague.

He spoke of various topics with a seductive drawl, wiggling his limber, angle-worm legs as he spoke and posing like a giraffe with the colic, for the benefit of the ladies who stood near. He wipes his nose in a languid yet soulful way, that makes you wish he would do so again.

We asked him when he would return to England, and he tossed his hand in the air and said:

"Ah! I don't know whether I shall survive or not."

"You get a good deal of free advertising, I see," said the *Boomerang* man, gnawing a little fragment from an irregular piece of navy and thoughtlessly stepping on the patent leather shoe of the great aesthetic.

"Oh, yes!" said Os., as he straightened up and extended his neck up through his collar till you could see the scolloped edge of his chemise. "Yes, sir. Much too

---

1. Edgar Wilson "Bill" Nye (1850–1896) was an American writer. In 1881 he founded the *Boomerang*, a humorous newspaper, which he edited until 1884. Reprinted as "Bill Nye and Oscar Wilde," *The Topeka Daily Capital* (Topeka, KS), 19 Apr. 1882, 3; "Nye and Wilde," *The Chicago Daily Tribune* (Chicago, IL), 20 Apr. 1882, 5; "Bill Nye and Oscar Wilde," *The Sporting Times* (London, UK), 3 June 1882, 7; and many small town newspapers.

much of it. Still it pays moderately well, he, he, he. However, it is absolutely stupid of them to make such beastly and peculiar little jokes upon me, you know."

We had a good deal more confidential talk with him before the train left, which we may give to the public after awhile, but at present space forbids.

Mr. Wilde's complexion is very pallid, with here and there a little pimple that relieves the monotony some. He wears no beard or mustache at all, but makes up for that with a large growth of hair on his head, which falls in graceful festoons over his shoulders like a horse's tail over an olive green dashboard. He is just as full of soul as he can be, and walks, and breathes, and exists like a 2-year-old steer in a cabbage grove. He smiles every little while like a collicky baby in its sleep, and sighs and places himself in statuesque positions, as though something had given away in his apparel and he was trying to keep his ethereal pantaloons on till people looked the other way.

"Oscar Wilde," *The Denver Republican* (Denver, CO), 13 Apr. 1882, 4[1]

The Apostle of the Lily and the Sunflower Arrives in Denver.

He Delivers His Lecture at the Tabor Opera-House Before a Large Audience.

✂ *An account of Wilde's lecture in Denver.*

Oscar Interviewed

The reporter met Mr. Wilde on the train about forty miles out and introduced himself. He beheld a man who hardly answers to the descriptions printed or the pictures which have been published. After making himself known and receiving a pleasant greeting, which had much of the physical in it, he sat down beside the apostle of the beautiful and asked him how he liked the free, bounding West.

"I am much pleased with it," he replied, gazing dreamily out upon the plain, which, covered with cactus and sagebrush and beautiful cows and dugouts, reaches to the land of sunrise.

"Do you take much interest in aesthetics in Denver?" asked Mr. Wilde.

"Very much," replied THE REPUBLICAN. "We have just experienced a revival.

"Ah!" he sighed with a show of interest. "How is it?"

---

1. H & S, b65. Quoted in OWDA, 285, 287. This interview appears to be fabricated.

"In this way. Estheticism was worshipped in a quiet way until a week or so ago when a demi-monde queen appeared upon the street with a large sunflower under her hat rim. The Chief of Police had the wearer arrested."

Mr. Wilde straightened up and asked "Why?"

"He said it was a meretricious display," replied THE REPUBLICAN.

Mr. Wilde gasped three times and then said, with indignation, blazing with a greenery, gallery [*sic*] glare in his eyes, "He considered a sunflower meretricious. My beautiful sunflower? What kind of a man is this chief!"

"As pleasant a gentleman as you could meet in a day's walk," responded the reporter warmly; "but let me continue. The Chief is an ascetic, and very pro-nounced in his opinion—

"'One of those beings grim of face,
"Who in all beauty see no beauty's trace.'

"But he could not keep up his dreadful war. He went out to 'The Heights'"—

"Where is that?" asked Mr. Wilde.

"It is a place outside of the city where the aesthetics most do resort," replied the reporter.

"I must go there," said Mr. Wilde.

"All right," replied the reporter. "I'll take you out there myself next Sunday. But to continue. The Chief went there last Sunday to suppress the sunflower and lily."

"Oh horrors!" said Mr. Wilde.

"Yes," continued the reporter.

"'But there he met a Waterloo,
"Whose victory was just too-too.'

"The esthetics surrounded him and pinned the lily and sunflower upon him. He relented, and heaven be praised, became converted."

"He did?" ejaculated Mr. Wilde. "The lovely man. I will incorporate this with my new lecture. This is sweetly utter."

Just then the conductor informed Mr. Wilde that he was within five miles of Denver, and he went into the baggage car and dressed himself.

"Oscar Wilde in Atchison," *The Atchison Globe* (Atchison, KS), 22 Apr. 1882, 1

A reporter who called at the Otis House this afternoon and asked for Oscar Wilde, was shown at once to a room on the third floor, where he kicked down the door, and asked a person bearing a marked resemblance to the drunken women seen occasionally in the police court, if he could see "the poet."

The person addressed was engaged in trimming his corns with a razor—it turned out to be a man, although at first glance the figure might have been mistaken for a woman, as he wore long hair and a flowing but soiled dressing gown—and for the purpose had removed from his feet a pair of cheap British hose, which were lying on opposite sides of the room.

The man did not immediately reply, but kept on cutting at his toe in a manner indicating that the corn was tender and the razor dull, for he lolled out his tongue, and there was a scowl on his face.

"I am Oscar Wilde," the man replied, finally, tossing the razor to his valet, and drawing on his socks, "What do you want?"

There was a negligee about the room amounting almost to disorder, old coats and hats being scattered about in confusion, and on a chair which had been drawn up to the window was the remainder of a lunch originally composed of dried beef, sliced onions, mustard, Holland herring, New York dairy cheese, and rye bread. On the window sill was a cigar which apparently did not burn well when lighted, but which had been rolled about in the mouth until it resembled the weed a drunkard brings home with him on returning from a night's debauch. The wash basin had been taken from its place on the commode, and was being used as a spittoon, and on the dressing case stood a bottle half filled with beer, with the cork pushed in. From the circumstance that no glasses could be seen, the reporter imagined that the missing beer had been drank out of the bottle, and some of it having been spilled on the marble, it was foul, sticky and wet.

"It is not of the slightest importance to anyone," the reporter said, removing a soiled shirt from a chair, and occupying it, "but I came up to ask you—the merest idle curiosity; this is a free country, and you are at liberty to do as you choose—why you persist in making a jackass of yourself by lecturing to audiences which only assemble to make fun of you. Are you really crazy on the subject of art, or do you consent to make a spectacle of yourself for money? We are familiar with this sort of thing because the Governor of Kansas is worse on the subject of temperance than you are on aestheticism, but he frankly acknowledges that it is a matter of personal gain,[1] and I ask in the great name of THE PRESS that you tell the honest truth, and admit as much. Out with it; is it lunacy or money which induces you to exhibit yourself over the country like a wooly horse or hairy elephant?"

1. John Pierce St. John (1833–1916) was a Republican politician who served as the 8th Governor of Kansas between 1879 and 1883. Under his tenure Kansas enacted a state-wide prohibition of alcohol that remained in place until 1948.

Mr. Wilde took from a very deep pocket in his pants a plug of black navy tobacco, and after biting off a hunk of it, chewed it meditatively awhile, and replied:

"You are entitled to two for one; you have called the turn. I confess to you, but in the greatest confidence—it must go no further (Reporter—Certainly; never to be mentioned to any one;) that I am, as Artemus Ward would say, hogging the public.[1] I usually receive reporters lying on a velvet lounge, holding a book of poems in my hand, but by accident at the hotel office you came upon me while I was enjoying myself, and the only thing I can do is to throw myself at your feet, and solicit the charity of your silence."

"Then you admit," the reporter said, sternly, "1. That you are a plagiarist, for every passable idea advanced in your lecture is stolen; 2. That you are a jackass to appear before intelligent audiences in knee breeches, (a style of dress, by the way, which does not become your bow legs), and advocate that they give up the honest business of making a living, and turn their attention to art, which has made every nation poor which has ever been noted for it, and, 3. That you are no poet, for though this is a reading people, a bookseller in this town has advertised your complete poems for sale for months at ten cents, and has not sold a single copy."

"I admit it all," Mr. Wilde said, "and more. I am an English adventurer, and having heard that Americans are easily humbugged, I came over to humbug them. I have made $25,000 at it, but I will shortly return to my own country again, as the attendance at my lectures is falling off. In Kansas City, St. Joe, Leavenworth and Topeka we scarcely paid expenses, and in a few weeks I will pretend that this country does not appreciate art, and shake its dust from my feet. In short, I will return home, and live at my ease with the money I have made. I really know no more about art than you do; I doubt if as much, as I believe the commonest paper hanger would scorn to put my ideas into practical use,[2] for except long hair and bandy legs, I do not amount to much. Every candid man says that who has seen me. When I see the beautiful homes everywhere in the West, and remember the squalid cottage in which I live when at home, I feel very guilty, but it is business; I must make money in America, since I cannot do it at home, for I could not even rent a hall in England unless I paid the price in advance. When I return home, I intend to build a house after the style of those I have seen in America, and furnish it in the fashion common here, for though I make fun of your buildings and architecture, they are the best I have ever seen. There are

1. Charles Farrar Browne (1834–1867), better known by his pseudonym, Artemus Ward, was an American humourist and lecturer. His comic articles about his own fantastical adventures were written phonetically. In writing of his decision as a young man to become a humourist, he quoted his father: "'Go,' he sed—'go, my son, and hog the public!' (he ment, 'knock em,' but the old man was allus a little given to slang)."

2. Paper hanging is a type of cheque fraud.

handsomer buildings in New York, Chicago, St. Louis, etc., than can be seen in London, but sneering at everything American to American audiences pays, though I can't understand it, and I must keep at it until I am found out. That's the long and the short of it. Must you go so soon?"

The reporter answered that he must, as the "first side" would go to press in an hour, and it was a part of his business to turn the wheel.

"Well, remember what I have said about this confession being in the greatest confidence," Mr. Wilde said, coming to the door. "It is never to be mentioned."

Reporter—"Never."

Mr. Wilde—"Never?"

Reporter—"Never."

Mr. Wilde—"What, n-e-v-e-r?"

Reporter—"Well, hardly ever."[1]

At this moment the hotel fell down, and the poet and reporter were killed. There will be no lecture tonight, and no paper will be issued from this office tomorrow.

There is good reason for believing that Oscar Wilde went among the merchants today offering to mention their business during his lecture tonight for fifty cents each, but as far as we can learn only two or three invested. The idea is not new with Mr. Wilde; it was invented by a circus clown.

"The Two Too," *The Topeka Sunday Capital* (Topeka, KS), 23 Apr. 1882, 2

A MOST HISTORICAL CONFAB.

The Meeting Between Oscar Wilde and the Aesthetic Editor of the "Commonwealth"—The Pupil and the Master—What was Talked About—Kansas Politics.

When Oscar Wilde was here, last Thursday, the aesthetic editor of the *Commonwealth* had an interview with him, the report of which has been crowded out for the past two days owing to a press of other matter.[2] As soon as the Topeka aesthete's card was taken to the great apostle the latter ordered him to be at once shown up, which was done, and pupil and master were at last face to face.

1. The author quotes *H. M. S. Pinafore* (see p. 701, note 1).
2. *The Commonwealth* was a rival Topeka paper, published and edited by Floyd Perry Baker (1820–1909), an American lawyer and Republican politician. An account of Wilde's lecture in Topeka appeared, without interview, in *The Commonwealth* (21 Apr. 1882, 1). It was generally positive, although, in common with most other accounts, criticised Wilde's delivery.

"I have heard of you," said Oscar sweetly as he extended his hand in greeting, and the crimson coloring which flew to the visitor's cheeks outrivaled the gorgeous hues of the necktie at his throat.

"You got those marked papers then?" asked Bent. in an anxious ecstasy.

"Yes," replied Oscar, "I have been receiving the *Commonwealth* pretty regularly since I have been in the West. I presume those pieces enclosed in red ink were yours?"

Bent. acknowledged that they were, and after a few other casual remarks about things in general the talk became more confidential.

"How do you like our little country, anyway, Os?" asked Bent. "Good deal of extreme boundlessness, so to speak, about some parts of it eh? Sort o' makes you feel that there is a co-existent far-reachedness in all this which is pleasant to a man born, like you, on a two by four island, don't it?"

Oscar said it was something like that, only perhaps, it was more so in places.

"Yes, that's about how it strikes foreigners on the average. There's Aleck, he's one o' them Russian grand dukes you know, and the Duke of Sutherland. They were here some time ago, but there ain't anything soulful about them fellers. They're sordid and inclined to be nifty, too, though Aleck was—"

"You were telling about the great extent of your country. I should like to spend more time in the West, viewing the beauties of the scenery, the grandeur of your mountains and the much—"

"For the true realization of excessive muchness," broke in Bent., who had been listening with his mouth and eyes wide open, "you ought to come to Topeka on a windy day. History records nothing like it. Of course it's better now since they have begun sprinkling the streets. Now, for instance, the wind starts at about the corner of Tenth, we'll say, and by the vigorous application of the cohesive forces characteristic of the Kansas zephyr, will take up enough dust to freight an ocean steamer, and charge down the avenue to the bridge, we'll say, and then back again, and then once more for the beer, leaving enough on the way to ruin several thousand dollars' worth of dry goods and give everybody his peck of dirt. I can't describe it."

"It must indeed be soul-inspiring," murmured Oscar, lying back on the cushions and looking at the ceiling.

"Well, you can bet just about three-fourths of all you'll make on your lecture trip that it is," replied Bent. "I know, because I've been there. Now when it gets there the third time—"

"Will he be able to make it for the third time, then?" inquired Oscar, sitting up.

"Make what the third time?"

"You said something about the third time, and I see a good deal in the Kansas newspapers about the third time, or the third term, whichever it is, and it's applied to the Governor, I believe."[1]

"Oh, yes; you mean the third-term book. Well, he won't make it."

"I think your Governor is a noble man and a man of principle. He is doing a grand work. He is working for the benefit of humanity, and no obstruction should be put in his way."

"Of course; we take the other side because we got left on coming out for him first—or rather the CAPITAL got in its work in the Monday morning issue, and we—that is to say we had everything ready to declare for St. John for a third term when that d—d paper over on the avenue came out and—and—well, as it stands now we have got to do some bucking, or we don't stand anywhere; that's about all there is of it."[2]

Bent. kept getting redder and redder as his explanation progressed and was not exactly reassured when Oscar asked: "What do you mean by buck? It's a Western term I should judge."

"In the majority of cases the average Westerner would take it to be the gentle beverage which cheers, but not inebriates about the first of the coming month; but in this instance it is applied in the sense of to kick—to—"

"To kick? What's that?"

"When we say kick we mean to expostulate; when a man gets left in Kansas he usually kicks, unless he gets some sort of a hold on his man that he can work him for enough to make the racket a remunerative one."

"In this case did you work the Governor, as you call it, and make the racket pay?"

Bent. blushed again and changed the subject by asking the great aesthete what he thought of American architecture in general.

"I find little to remind me of the early English here, of course," replied Oscar. "I know very little of the architectural features of Topeka, for instance, but judging from the people of the town I have met I should infer that it was at least unique."

Affecting not to notice this the visitor said Mr. Wilde would find little early English style in Topeka. "The latest we have is about 1856; or rather I should

1. John St. John (1833–1916) was a Republican politician and the eighth Governor of Kansas. He served two terms of two years each between 1879 and 1883. He sought a third term in the 1882 election (held on 7 November) but lost to Democratic candidate George Washington Glick.

2. "After mature deliberation and carefully considering the arguments advanced by the press of the State, we have decided to advocate the renomination of John P. St. John for Governor. Not for the reason that he is sure to be the winning candidate, but that we are convinced it will be for the best interests of the State." ("That Boom," *The Topeka Sunday Capital* (Topeka, KS), 17 Apr. 1882, 2.)

have said the earliest. There are still a few of the old duffers of that period floating around. They, however, are a good deal behind the times. They don't care for
renaissance and sunsets and things like that, as we do. They are more apt to care
for beer and politics."

"The study of the truly beautiful is an ennobling one," said Oscar, relapsing
into a sort of a reverie. "No man should be permitted to advance in years without
having acquired some knowledge of the art of searching after the beautiful. In
fact, if the people of the present day are unwilling to accept the beautiful in nature and art they should be forced—"

"You could mandamus 'em," broke in Bent. "That's about the best way to do.
It might not always work, but then it's worth trying."

"Mandamus the study of art? I do not understand."

"That was only a hint. They may seem a little rough to you European fellers,
but here in the West where we want anything we drive ahead and get it."

"But compulsion is used by me in a restricted and not a literal sense."

"In our case," replied Bent, "it was used to keep our hold on the State printing. The executive council gave it to the Capital, and we ought to have had it. You
can bet your sweet life we'll make it sultry for the Supreme court and the State
House, unless we get our fingers at least part way into the pie."

Oscar showed that he was interested, and said when he got back to London
he would be pleased to carry with him recollections of how they did things in
Kansas.

The conversation then turned upon the subject of dress, and Oscar, looking
at the aesthetic editor's neck-tie, said red was a favorite color of his; it was a
grand Venetian inspiration, and carried him back to the time of the doges when
the art of Italy was in its prime and had not suffered from the fingers of enervating decay.

"Did the old doges carry canes?" asked Bent.

Oscar said he didn't know.

"That is a subject of a good deal of controversy out here," said Bent, "and
may possibly decide the coming State campaign."

"Do they run political campaigns on the color of a man's neck-wear and the
manner in which he carries his cane, in Kansas?" queried Mr. Wilde

"They are apt to. You can't tell much about it until the time comes. Political
campaigns have changed a good deal in complexion and character since I came to
Topeka. I can't put on a white necktie or change the style of my plug hat without
all the papers in the State notice it. I'm a good deal like you in that regard. Everything I do is noticed."

"I care nothing for criticism," proudly exclaimed Oscar, tossing his mane
back and smiling. "Small souls do a good deal of caviling. I do not call that criticism."

"That's me," rejoined Brent [*sic*]. "I don't care for sneers and things like that. I shall continue my search after the beautiful all the same. I am not discouraged. But—well, old man, I must be going. I've got an article to write on irrigation. We're running that heavy now. Got quite a boom on it in fact. Ta, ta. Over the river. I'll see you in the immediate to come;" and taking the great aesthete's right hand in both of his he pressed it warmly, helped himself to a cigar from among the pile lying on the table, and was gone like a sweet perfume.

"Wilde Witticisms," *The Daily Nonpareil* (Council Bluffs, IA), 27 Apr. 1882, 5

The Champion Ass-thete Passes Through Council Bluffs.

While at the Union Pacific depot yesterday, a NONPAREIL news-gather was unfortunate enough to run across Oc. Wilde, Esq., the most [?assthetic] esthete the world has lately produced or the country knows anything about. Had we known Oc. was going to pass through at an early morning hour we should have permitted the visiting Odd Fellows to set sail for Omaha unaided and alone. But seeing the Wilde Englishman gliding artistically over the platform, he having arrived from Lincoln and was here waiting for the Rock Island to proceed to Des Moines, the news-gatherer considered it a duty he owed posterity and the fools of the present day, to tap Oc. and see what he knew or thought he knew.

"Ahem, excuse me, but is this Mr. Wilde?" the reporter asked.

"Ah, uh, he, he, it *is* the same," was the ass-thetic reply, and THE NONPAREIL man went at him.

"What do you think of this country, Mister Wilde?" he inquired by way of a feeler.

"Well, I regard it as a great and somewhat aesthetic country," was the reply.

"Does your trip through America convince you that Barnum had the thing down to a fine point when he said that the American people believe in humbuggery and the bigger the humbug the better they liked it?" put in the newspaper man, who thought this question would certainly floor the cheeky Wilde man—if he grasped the drift of the remark.

"Ah, he, he; well, I have found it easy to make from $300 to $500 per night talking to them on the artistic things of life, but, he, he, I never thought the people here were such fools until I tackled them," was the cute rejoinder.

Evidently the English poet and lecturer regarded the people of America easily duped, and probably concludes that the best way to make money rapidly in this country is to get up some fool scheme; get the papers to blow about it, and then let the fool originator start out and a fortune is assured him.

There are to be found people scattered through this land who will crowd a public hall to suffocation to hear a man spout his little spout on some subject that interests or benefits no one, simply because the spouter has been liberally and extensively spouted about through the columns of the press, and heralded by all manner of advertisement, even down to bills of fare on dining cars, signs for "cheep cloding houses," and in the make up of female wearing apparel.

It is said that when Oscar Wilde enters a hotel dining room at a railway station, he either doesn't know enough or hasn't sense enough to remove his hat and feminine cloak. Yet such a man can make from $200 to $500 per night talking nonsense and bosh, while legitimate and really intellectual speakers have trouble, sometimes, getting a society out "even" on a $50 lecture.

"Aestheticism," *Georgia Weekly Telegraph and Journal & Messenger* (Macon, GA), 14 July 1882, 5

An Interview with Oscar Wilde on the Night of His Lecture.

"Goodnight, Mr. Wilde; pardon my intrusion. I really was so much impressed by that divinely beautiful lecture tonight that I could not think of losing sight of you forever."

"By what name may I call thee," said he, placing the small ends of his little fingers in my hand.

"I'm Crabtree—Timothy Crabtree, and I assure you, Mr. Wilde, none, no, not one of the vast audience who listened to the silvery music of your voice tonight was more interested—ah, more enraptured with the sweet morsels you gave us. Brain food, Mr. Wilde, is what we Americans greatly need, and I, with the many who heard your lecture, received an abundant supply. Do you know, sir, that this subject of esthetics has been a day dream of mine for many long years? Until I read of you and heard your ideas on the subject of Decorative Art, I have wandered alone, like a solitary guest in a banquet hall deserted. How transcendentally beautiful was your description of the scenes which pleased the eyes and beautified the tastes of those workmen who erected the cathedral at Pesa. I always spelt it with an 'i' until you gave me its correct orthography."

"I am delighted, Master Crabtra, that oo was so well pleased with my leetle lecture, and oh, sir, it causes me heart to pulsate as sweetly as the gentle tapping of the petals of the sunflower upon its parent stem, to know that there was one kindred spirit in the theatre this after eventide who could accompany me into the bread fields of art out into the great labyrinth of nature, the greatest master of art, the primeval mother of all our conceptions of the beautiful. Me tenderest, me most patient teachers, Master Crabtra, are the leetle burds of the forests, and the daisies and buttercups of the meadows. From which school of art do you derive your sweetest blessings, Master Crabtra?”

“I’m a wood carver, Mr. Wilde. The tenderest recollections of my childhood are intertwined with the tendrils of the beach [*sic*], and my first lessons in my art were learned while whittling the bark from and making circular incisions on a beach switch, but when maturer years increased my experience and improved my taste, I became a designer, and now, sir, my life, my soul, has become a part of my art.”

“May I call thee brother? Me heart turns to you; me soul pants after thee like the wounded kine panteth for the water-brook. How me days of gladness would lengthen if I could pass an hour or more with thee, but me tired nature seeks repose; me soul’s longing must remain languishing. Have you Master Crabtra, a school of design in this leetle city? How many moments I could consume peregrinating through its arcades! Do you pass the days feasting among its beauties, Master Crabtra?”

“Most generally I do, Mr. Wilde. You never spoke a greater truism in your life than you did this night, when you asserted the fact that we Americans knew nothing of nor did we appreciate art. I was forced sir, to abandon the art of wood engraving and devote my time and energies to the house carpenter’s trade.”

“By the soul of St. Patrick and all the calendar of saints, am I in the presence of a man of toil and sweat! Begone sir, or I will do unto you violence.”

He struck an attitude, and I left, more of an ass-thete than I ever was.

T. C.

“Eli Perkins in Saratoga,” *Nashville Banner* (Nashville, TN), 16 Aug. 1882, 3[1]

A Huge Joke Perpetrated on Oscar Wilde.

Saratoga Correspondence of New York Star.

✂ *A paragraph unfavourably comparing Wilde to eccentric celebrities.*

I have had several long private talks with Oscar here. I have been anxious to see what was in him. He has no new ideas. His theories would make Indians of us if we should try to adopt them. He would give us the costumes and colors of the Astecs [*sic*]. He would give us the barbarian music of the Chinese. He is an utter

---

1. Melville De Lancey Landon (1839–1910) was an American humourist who went by the pen name Eli Perkins.

sham. Still he is a clever fellow—insane though harmless. Once in a while he strikes quite a pretty idea. In talking about American names yesterday, he said:

"I du not altogether quite like your American names, Mr. Perkins. Once day you will ride alow, you kneow, and come to Waneta. That is bootiful. The next station is Los Angeles. Very bootiful again, very! Then you come to Griggs. Now I do not quite like Griggs. It is quite shocking—this Griggs. Awfully unmusical, you kneow. Perfectly dwedful! Hawid Griggs!!"[1]

✂ *A burlesque account of the breakfast at Mount McGregor given for Wilde on 10 August.*

ELI PERKINS.

"Mrs. Langtry in America," *Funny Folks* (London, UK), 25 Nov. 1882, 372

[CABLED BY OUR OWN SPECIAL INTERVIEWER.]

I found the beauty deep in conversation with Mr. Oscar Wilde, who seemed to be busy at his favourite occupation, for he was indubitably engaged in "worshipping the 'Lily.'"

"Well, and what did you think of the fire the other day?" I commenced, bluntly, after I had stated my mission.[2]

"It was a beautiful fire," dreamily put in Oscar.

"While it was in progress I could only think of my unhappy manager," Mrs. Langtry replied, without heeding Oscar's interruption. "I said to myself, if it ruined Abbey"—

"Some ruined abbeys are distinctly precious," observed the aesthetic nuisance.

"But it didn't you see," I hastened to interpose. "And now pray tell me has your welcome by our people come up to your expectations?"

"It has far exceeded them. I may, indeed, be said to 'boom,' as you funny Americans have it."

"The 'boom' of a most charming *belle*," I put in. I could see that I had hit Oscar hard. He writhed to think that this delicate and witty compliment had not occurred to him. Following up my advantage, I next inquired what Mrs. Langtry thought of her audiences.

---

1. An allusion to the reports of Wilde's dislike of the name of Griggsville. See p. 292, note 1.

2. The fire at Abbey's Park Theatre. See "Mrs Langtry's Disappointment," *New York Tribune* (New York, NY), 31 Oct. 1882, 1, pp. 491–2.

918

"They charm me!" the lady exclaimed, "they are so fresh and responsive. I seem to possess the Yank-*key*, so to speak, which is able to unlock their hearts."

"Beauty jests!" cried that idiot Oscar, upstarting. "O ineffable quip! O consummate crank!"

"The last consummate 'crank' we had over here was Guiteau," I put in severely; and before he could recover I had asked Mrs. Langtry how she accounted for the comparatively chilly reception accorded to Patti on the same evening when her own had been so ardent.[1]

"Oh, you see her success was in the past, while mine"—

"In other words, madame, the Patti success was yesterday, but the Langtry-umph is today."

Again had I distanced the servile Oscar. I rose to go with the air of a victor.

"Mind!" I said, playfully, "no more fires! Take care what you are about with that 'Unequal *Match*' of yours. And so I wish you good-day. Do"—

I was about to say "Don't ring for my carriage," when Oscar, catching at my last words, rose from his reverie in all his might.

"Dado!" he commenced; but I heard no more, for, seeing that I had opened the floodgates of aestheticism, I fled.

"The O. W. Vade Mecum," *Punch* (London, UK), 23 Feb. 1895, 85[2]

Question. Is it easy to become a dramatist?

Answer. As easy as anything else.

Q. What are the requisites?

A. A West-end theatre, a first-rate troupe of artists, a trained audience, and a personality.

Q. What do you mean by a trained audience?

A. An assembly accustomed to accept everything as wit, and to laugh at everything.

Q. Would such a gathering consider it amusing for someone to say "Flirting with one's husband is quite indelicate: it is like washing one's clean linen in public"?[1]

---

1. On the evening of 7 November 1882, while Langtry was making her American debut at Wallack's Theatre, Patti was performing a mile away at the Academy of Music. Both shows were sold out. Patti received positive reviews but Langtry's were mixed (see e.g. "Record of Amusements," *The New York Times* (New York, NY), 7 Nov. 1882, 5; "At the Theatres," *The New York Mirror* (New York, NY), 11 Nov. 1882, 2).

2. Quoted in CW x, 983.

A. Certainly; and would find much to admire in a dialogue given over for something like ten minutes to an exhaustive consideration of muffins.[2]

Q. And what do you mean by a personality?

A. More or less—an *insouciant* manner, and a rather startling button-hole.[3]

Q. Does the personality require a speech or a cigarette?[4]

A. Neither now, as both have ceased to be in fashion.[5]

Q. Given the requisites you have specified for creating a dramatist, what is the product?

A. A trivial comedy for serious people.[6]

Q. Why give a play such a title?

A. Why not?

Q. Can a comedy occupying two or three hours in representation be entirely trivial?

A. Not to the members of the audience.

Q. And are they serious people?

A. That depends upon the condition of their brains and their capacity of enjoyment.

Q. Does the trivial comedy require a plot?

A. Nothing to speak of.

Q. Or characterisation?

---

1. Algernon in *The Importance of Being Earnest*: "The amount of women in London who flirt with their own husbands is perfectly scandalous. It looks so bad. It is simply washing one's clean linen in public." (CW x, 771.206–8.)

2. Act II of *The Importance of Being Earnest* ends with a lengthy tussle between Jack and Algernon over a plate of muffins. The reviewer for *Truth* (London, UK) noted that, at the first performance, "[t]he people in the humbler parts of the house" most thoroughly enjoyed the muffin scene (CW x, 713).

3. Wilde always gave careful thought to his button-holes. He and his male friends wore dyed green carnations on the first night of *Lady Windermere's Fan* (Sturgis, 442–4/411–2). In his *Phrases and Philosophies for the Use of the Young* Wilde asserted that: "A really well-made buttonhole is the only link between Art and Nature." (*Miscellanies*, 176.) Act III of *An Ideal Husband* begins with Lord Goring questioning whether the buttonhole brought for him by his butler is sufficiently "trivial".

4. Wilde came on stage after the first performance of *Lady Windermere's Fan* with a lit cigarette in his hand. Reviewers were generally unimpressed by this breach of etiquette. Afterwards *Punch* printed a cartoon of Wilde as "Shakespeare Sheridan Oscar Puff, Esq.", cigarette in his mouth, speech in his pocket, and fan in his hand (*Punch* (London, UK), 5 Mar. 1892, 113).

5. Wilde did not give a speech on the opening night of *The Importance of Being Earnest*.

6. The subtitle of *The Importance of Being Earnest* as it appeared in the first-production programme and the 1899 reading text. In Wilde's original four-act version of the play, and the three-act typescripts prepared for the production, the order of the adjectives is reversed (CW x, 855).

A. No, for the same kind of dialogue will do for all the company—for London ladies, country girls, justices of the peace, doctors of divinity, maid-servants, and confidential butlers.[1]

Q. What sort of dialogue?

A. Inverted proverbs and renovated paradoxes.

Q. Is this kind of dialogue entirely new?

A. Not entirely, as something rather like it has been heard at the Savoy for the last ten or twenty years.[2]

Q. But is it good enough for a British public?

A. Quite good enough. They will laugh when a London lady expresses surprise at finding flowers growing in the country, and roar when they hear the retort, that plants are as common in the provinces as people are in town.[3]

Q. But surely this vein of sarcasm, satire, or whatever it is, will some day be worked out. What can the dramatist then do?

A. Act upon precedent, and try something else.

1. Descriptions of the characters in *The Importance of Being Earnest.*
2. That is, in Gilbert and Sullivan's comic operas staged at D'Oyly Carte's Savoy Theatre.
3. *The Importance of Being Earnest*: "GWENDOLYN. I had no idea there were any flowers in the country. | CECILY. Oh, flowers are as common here, Miss Fairfax, as people are in London." (CW x, 819.595–7.)

Index

Abbey, Henry E., 298, 487, 491–92, 756
   and Lillie Langtry's arrival in America,
      478–86, 721–25
Absalom, 221
Adey, More, 659, 660
Aeschylus, 69
African Americans, 361, 417–19, 422, 425,
   432, 581–82
   OW's valet, 93, 131, 142, 173, 177, 178,
      181, 208, 236, 265, 298–99, 312, 323,
      350, 356, 389, 438, 465, 473, 582
Albani, Emma, 290
Aldrich, Thomas Bailey, 130, 331, 526
Alexander, George, 652, 654
   interviewed, 814–15, 819–20
Allen, Alsatia. *See* Allen, Virginia Ball
Allen, Virginia Ball, 454, 580–81
Alma Tadema, Lawrence, 444
Almy, Percival W. H., OW interviewed by,
   622–31
Anderson, David H., 760
Anderson, Mary, 555, 558, 724, 762
   beauty, OW praises, 51, 528
   Pygmalion and Galatea, OW sees in, 702
   Romeo and Juliet, OW criticises
      performance in, 51, 177, 754
Arabi. *See* 'Urabi, Ahmed
Archer, William, 651
The Argus (Albany, NY), 113–14
Argyll, Princess Louise, Duchess of, 397,
   412
Aristotle, 469
Arnold, Matthew, 583
   interviewed, 793–94
Arnold, Sir Edwin, 812
Arthur, Chester A., 358, 384
The Atchison Globe (Atchison, KS), 355–57,
   908–11
The Atlanta Constitution (Atlanta, GA),
   434–38, 773–74, 861–67

Atlantic Ocean, OW disappointed by, 35,
   39, 42, 51, 160, 201, 518, 521–22, 546,
   657, 795
l'*Auberge des Songes*, 599
Austin, Alfred, 625
Australia, OW's intention to visit, 357, 359,
   386, 463, 466, 475, 478, 482, 488, 490,
   493, 494, 496
Aynesworth, Allan, 652
Babbacombe, OW interviewed in, 622–31
Bacon, Francis, 586
Bad Homburg, 612, 617, 634
Balfour, Archibald, 619
Balfour, Arthur James, 619, 813
The Ballad of Reading Gaol (OW), 677, 864
*Baltimore American and Commercial
      Advertiser* (Baltimore, MD), 88–90, 109–
      10, 112–13
Balzac, Honoré de, 64, 78, 214
   Comédie Humaine, 64, 616
   Une passion dans le désert, 843
banco or bunco, bunko. *See* Hungry Joe
Barnes, General William, 320
Barnum, P. T., 246, 774
Barrett, Lawrence, 126, 553, 565, 787
   Yorick's Love, OW sees in, 110
Bastien-Lepage, Jules
   Sarah Bernhardt, 618, 804, 810
Batho, Robert, OW interviewed by, 517–23,
   583–88, 655–60
Bauer, Henry, OW interviewed by, 593–99
Bayard, Thomas F., 99, 111, 581
Lord Beaconsfield. *See* Disraeli, Benjamin
Beecher, Henry Ward, 259, 381–82, 445,
   555, 581, 719
   OW meets, 259, 260
   OW's resemblance of, 81, 204
Beerbohm Tree, Herbert, 636, 640
Beethoven, Ludwig van, 390
Bell's Life in London (London, UK), 890–91
Bellew, Kyrle, 242

Bemberg Ocampo, Herman Emanuel, 610
Benson, Frank Robert, 69
Bernard Beere, Fanny, 127, 636
Berne, Ed., OW interviewed by, 271–74
Bernhardt, Sarah, 70, 172, 234, 242, 480,
    490, 530, 602, 636, 721, 754, 865, 885
    Albemarle Hotel, Lillie Langtry takes
        rooms once occupied by, 486, 724
    Bastien-Lepage's portrait of, 618, 804,
        810
    Clara Morris, praises to OW, 75, 235,
        239, 258, 379, 702
    La Dame aux Camélias, not allowed to
        play in London, 234
    interviewed, 801–2
    letters by OW to, forged, 688
    Macbeth, OW sees in, 570–72
    Niagara Falls, writes in album at, 151
    OW praises
        acting, 379, 669, 718
        beauty, 695
        figure, 576
        voice, 448, 465
    OW writes poem for, 30
    photographed in America, 699, 760
    Salomé
        asks to play, 611
        dance of the seven veils, rehearses,
            614
        not allowed to stage, 601, 603–6
        OW reads script to, 606
Besant, Walter, 213
"*The Best Story in the World*" (OW), 669
Bigelow, Jane Tunis (née Poultney), 85,
    701–2
Bigelow, John, 693
The Biograph and Review (London, UK),
    25–31
Birmingham Daily Mail (Birmingham, UK),
    793
The Birmingham Daily Post (Birmingham,
    UK), 823–24
Black, William, 213
Blaine, James Gillespie, 107, 111, 121, 458
Blake, William, 27
    Songs of Innocence and of Experience, 74
Blunt, Wilfrid Scawen, 599
Boniface, George, 560
Booth, Edwin, 126, 143, 239, 262, 718
    OW praises, 235
    and the Prince of Wales, 453
The Boston Daily Globe (Boston, MA), 473

Boston Evening Transcript (Boston, MA),
    725–26, 858–60
The Boston Herald (Boston, MA), 253–54,
    410–16, 476–78, 721–25
The Boston Sunday Globe (Boston, MA),
    127–31
Boucicault, Dion
    interviewed, 748, 764–65
    interviewed with OW, 117–27
Boyle, Patrick, 405
Bradlaugh, Charles, 242
Brady, Judge John Riker, 450
Brawne, Fanny, 623
Breckinridge, William Campbell Preston,
    826
Breuer, H. J., 192, 195, 198, 379, 414
Bright, John, 813
Brodrick, William St John Fremantle, 555
Brontë, Charlotte, 625
The Brooklyn Daily Eagle (Brooklyn, NY),
    136, 534–36, 589–92, 726–27, 876–78
Brooklyn Union (Brooklyn, NY), 445
Brooks, Phillips, 128, 463
Broome, Isaac, 374, 377–78
Brown, Ford Madox, 225
Brown, Henry Billings, 457
Brown, Joseph, 464
Browne, Charles Farrar. *See* Ward,
    Artemus
Browning, Elizabeth Barrett, 518, 623
    Aurora Leigh, 623, 709
Browning, Robert, 322, 533, 623, 754, 757,
    813
Brown-Potter, Cora Urquhart, 619
Buckle, Henry Thomas, 419–20
"Buffalo Bill" (Cody, William Frederick),
    619
    OW's resemblance of, 310, 377, 439
Buffalo Commercial Advertiser (Buffalo,
    NY), 711
Buffalo Daily Courier (Buffalo, NY), 145–47
Buffalo Evening News (Buffalo, NY), 778–
    79
Buffalo Morning Express (Buffalo, NY),
    147–51
Bulwer-Lytton, Edward, 65, 402
Bulwer-Lytton, Edward Robert
    Lucile, 86
Bunthorne, Reginald. *See Patience* (Gilbert
    & Sullivan)
Burdette, Robert Jones, 382
Burgess, Gilbert, OW interviewed by, 643–
    47

Burke, Thomas Henry, 386
Burnand, F. C., 394
  The Colonel, 58, 95, 904–5
Burne-Jones, Edward Coley, 293, 314, 463,
    619, 710, 884
  OW decorates college rooms with works
    by, 27
  OW praises, 117, 287, 711
Burnett, Frances Hodgson, 108, 526
  Little Lord Fauntleroy, 638
  OW attends reception given by, 703
Burns, Robert, 333
Burton, Carrie, 695
Byrnes, Thomas F., Superintendent,
    interviewed, 826
Byron, George Gordon, Lord, 82, 125, 126,
    130, 139, 185, 521, 545
  Don Juan, 126
Cable, George Washington, 423, 426, 526
  The Grandissimes, 425
Cahill, Richard Staunton, 729
Camden Daily Courier (Camden, NJ), 488
Canada
    Amherst, NS, 473
      OW interviewed in, 466–72
    Charlottetown, PEI, 473, 474
    Fredericton, NB, OW interviewed in,
      465–66
    Halifax, NS, 473
    Kingston, ON, OW interviewed in, 399–
      401
    Moncton, NB, 476
      OW's "arrest" in, 476–77
    Montreal, QC, 397, 399, 406, 411
      OW interviewed in, 388–96
    Niagara Falls, ON, 152, 156, 160, 263,
      490, 494, 550, 711
      OW interviewed in, 150
    Ottawa, ON, 400, 411, 415, 427
      OW interviewed in, 396–99
      Parliament, OW visits, 398
    Quebec, 406, 410, 411, 412
    Saint John, NB, 474
      OW interviewed in, 473–76
    Toronto, ON, 410
      lacrosse, OW attends match, 403–5
      Ontario Society of Artists, OW attends
        exhibition of, 408–9, 715–16
      OW interviewed in, 403–9
Canadian Illustrated News (Montreal, QC),
    395–96

Carlyle, Thomas, 361, 419, 757, 803, 810
Carpenter, Frank George ("Carp"), OW
    interviewed by, 542–43
Carroll, Mrs Charles, 98, 100, 105–6, 764
The Catholic Union and Times (Buffalo, NY),
    62–64
Cavendish, Lord Frederick, 386
Cayley, Arthur, 112
Cazauran, Augustus R.
    interviewed, 792
    OW interviewed by, 67–68
Cellini, Benvenuto, 521
Cham (Charles Amédée de Noé), 718
Chase, Champion Clement, OW
    interviewed by, 360–63
Chase, William Merritt, 532
Chatterton, Thomas, 620, 624
Chaucer, Geoffrey, 116, 290
The Cheyenne Daily Leader (Cheyenne,
    WY), 332–33
Chicago Daily News (Chicago, IL), 162–65
The Chicago Daily Tribune (Chicago, IL),
    158–62, 169–73, 236–40, 445–48,
    529–32, 655–60, 711–12, 777, 788
Chicago Evening Journal (Chicago, IL), 226–
    29
Chicago Morning News (Chicago, IL), 173–
    75
The Chicago Sunday Tribune (Chicago, IL),
    249–51, 386–88
The Chicago Times (Chicago IL), 241–43
Childs, George W., 89
China
    art of, OW on, 289, 306
    beauty of the people of, 306, 576
    See also United States; San Francisco;
      Chinatown.
    See also Wilde, Oscar; political opinions;
      Chinese Exclusion Act.
Church, Hayden, interviews Lord Alfred
    Douglas, 861–67
Churchill, Caroline M., 349
The Cincinnati Commercial (Cincinnati,
    OH), 60–62, 197–99, 202, 494–96
The Cincinnati Commercial Gazette
    (Cincinnati, OH), 540
Cincinnati Daily Gazette (Cincinnati, OH),
    187–93, 765–66
The Cincinnati Enquirer (Cincinnati, OH),
    194–96, 824–26
Clarke, Sir Edward, 738, 822, 823
Classical Unities, 472

Claude Duval (Edward Solomon & Henry
Pottinger Stevens), 756
The Cleveland Herald (Cleveland, OH),
183–87
The Cleveland Leader (Cleveland, OH),
180–83, 542–43
The Clinton Public (Clinton, IL), 735–37
Cody, William Frederick. *See* Buffalo Bill
Coghlan, Rose, 638, 735, 820–21
Coleridge, Samuel Taylor, 193
Collier, James. W., 564
Collins, Wilkie, 213
The Colonel. See F. C. Burnand
Congreve, William, 624
Conkling, Roscoe, 460
Connery, Thomas B., 761
Constable, John, 587
Conway, Harry B., 242
Cook, Edward Tyas, 618
Corelli, Marie, 619
Cornish, Desda, interviews Robert Ross,
858–60
Cornwallis-West, Patsy, 716
Corot, Jean-Baptiste-Camille, 521, 646
Crane, Beatrice, 804
Crane, Walter, 541, 804, 810, 813
Crawford, Francis Marion, 596
Crichton-Browne, Sir James, 800
The Critic as Artist (OW), 322, 545, 572,
597, 641, 645
Max Nordau, quoted by, 830–31
Crocker, Hattie, 453, 581
Croly, Jane Cunningham ("Jennie June")
OW attends reception hosted by, 702–3,
762
Crossley, Sir Savile Brinton, 555
Cryder, William Wetmore, 500
Cumberland and Westmorland Advertiser
(Penrith, UK), 729
Curtis, David A., OW interviewed by, 40–
42
Curtis, M. B., 536
d'Aurevilly, Jules Barbey, 615, 832, 857,
859
d'Orsay, Alfred Guillaume Gabriel, Comte,
538
D'Oyly Carte, Richard, 37, 47, 71, 88, 100,
101, 103, 175, 216, 244, 258, 701, 754,
764, 884, 887
interviewed, 755–56, 788
Da Vinci, Leonardo, 150
The Daily Chronicle (London, UK), 679–80

Daily Evening Traveller (Boston, MA), 114–
17
The Daily Examiner (San Francisco, CA),
285–90, 313–14, 322–28
The Daily Graphic (New York, NY), 871–74
The Daily Inter Ocean (Chicago, IL), 64–66,
151–55, 165–69, 229–35, 251–53,
708–11, 906–7
The Daily Leader (Bloomington, IL), 261–
63
The Daily News (Kingston, ON), 399–401
The Daily Nonpareil (Council Bluffs, IA),
915–16
The Daily Picayune (New Orleans, LA),
422–24, 426–28, 431–33, 716–17,
748–49, 902–5
The Daily Record-Union (Sacramento, CA),
275–84
The Daily Report (San Francisco, CA), 304–
9
The Daily Sentinel (Fort Wayne, IN), 178–
80
The Daily Sun (Saint John, NB), 465–66,
473–76
Daily Witness (Montreal, QC), 391–94
The Damnation of Faust (Hector Berlioz),
526
Dante Alighieri, 190, 287, 321, 627, 798
Inferno, 662
OW sees prison inmate reading, 362
Darmont, Auguste Albert, 601, 603, 611
interviewed, 802–3
Darwin, Charles, 451
Daubigny, Charles-François, 521
Daudet, Alphonse, 442–43, 865
Daurelle, Jacques, OW interviewed by,
593–99
Davenport, Fanny, 487
Davis, Jefferson, 420, 426, 432–33, 433,
435–36, 581
*The Rise and Fall of the Confederate
Government*, 420, 436
Davis, Robert Stewart, 80–81, 749, 753
Dayton Daily Democrat (Dayton, OH), 369–
76
Dayton Daily Journal (Dayton, OH), 376–80
Dayton, OH, 374–76, 377–79
de Maupassant, Guy, 865
De Profundis (OW), 76, 461, 518, 740, 843,
859, 862, 867
publication of, 858–60
read in court, 863–64
de Régnier, Henri, 596

The Decay of Lying (OW), 77, 161, 598, 600, 619
The Decorative Arts (OW), 27, 146, 161, 232, 245, 251, 261, 267, 337, 383, 521, 768
Defoe, Daniel, 808
The Denver Republican (Denver, CO), 907–8
Denver Tribune (Denver, CO), 338–45, 713–14
The Detroit Free Press (Detroit, MI), 793–94
Dickens, Charles, 53, 64, 77, 144, 213, 214, 218, 227, 402, 478, 631
Bleak House, 750
Martin Chuzzlewit, 218, 382
Dickinson, Anna, 262
Diplomacy (B. C. Stephenson & Clement Scott), 646, 650
Disraeli, Benjamin, 420
Divorçons (Victorien Sardou & Émile de Najac), 234, 240, 605, 611
Dobson, Austin, 624
Docquois, Georges, interviews Lord Alfred Douglas, 838–44, 846–52
Donelly, Ignatius L., 586
Donoghue, John Talbott, 166, 189–90, 356, 358, 393, 413–14, 804, 810
Douglas, Lord Alfred ("Bosie"), 658, 663, 666, 674, 677, 818, 837–38
    interviewed, 823–24, 838–44, 846–55, 861–67
Jonquil and Fleur-de-lys, 653
Douglas, Percy (Lord Douglas of Hawick), 658, 737–38, 842–43
    interviewed, 817–19
    Marquess of Queensberry, fight with the, 833–38
Douglas, Reverend Lord Archibald Edward, 818
Dousman, Hercules Louis II, 209, 215
Dowson, Ernest, 670, 678
Drake, Sir Francis, 628
Dress (OW), 438, 464, 575
Du Maurier, George, 40, 54, 58, 61, 81, 188, 193, 208, 289, 291, 394, 718, 771
The Dubuque Herald (Dubuque, IA), 243–44
The Duchess of Padua (OW), 454, 537, 544, 555, 556, 557, 560
    plans to produce, 45, 528
    publication of, 528
Duffy, Sir Charles Gavan, 518, 797–99

Dumas *fils*, Alexandre, 652
    La Dame aux Camélias, 234, 614
Dunbar, Frederick A. T., 411
Duncan, Florence, OW interviewed by, 83–87
Dunfermline, OW interviewed in, 580–83
Dunne, Father Cuthbert, 680
Dupoirier, Jean, 860
    interviewed, 855–58
Duveneck, Frank, 373, 414
L'Écho de Paris (Paris, France), 593–99, 593–99
Edison, Thomas, 154, 157
Elgee, Judge John Kingsbury, 416, 582, 902
    property in Louisiana, 96, 423
Eliot, George, 77, 810
    OW's resemblance of, 339, 377
Emerson, Ralph Waldo, 31, 76, 220, 281, 331, 361, 384, 463, 757, 759, 797
Emmet, Robert, 683
The English Renaissance (OW), 27, 34, 36, 63, 71, 84, 117, 132, 133, 136, 141, 145, 188, 245–46, 245, 246, 265, 277, 279, 281, 284, 291, 293–96, 308, 383, 521, 711, 887, 896–99
The Englishwoman (London, UK), 814–15
L'Ermitage (Paris, France), 632–33
The Evening Item (Richmond, IN), 714–15
The Evening Light (San Antonio, TX), 428–31
Evening News and Star (Glasgow, UK), 574–79
The Evening Post (New York, NY), 48–50
The Evening Star (Kansas City, MO), 350–52
The Evening Star (Washington, DC), 94–96
The Evening Telegram (New York, NY), 46–48, 69–70, 527–28, 538–40, 557–58
The Evening Telegram (Providence, RI), 462–65
Farjeon, Benjamin Leopold, 213
Fawcett, Edgar, 471, 726, 733
    [?interviewed], 778–79
Field, Eugene, 797
Field, Kate, 703, 905
    interviewed, 766–67
Fiske, Harrison Grey, 638
    OW interviewed by, 492–93, 497
Fiske, Stephen Ryder, 53, 638, 761
Fitch, Clyde, 638, 733
Flaubert, Gustave, 443, 615, 639, 653
    Salammbô, 669

The Temptation of Saint Anthony, 662
Florence. *See* Italy
Florence, William Jermyn, 491
Forbes, Archibald, 88, 90, 93, 95, 97, 98, 99, 100, 104–6, 107, 213
    interviewed, 102–4, 104–5
Forbes-Robertson, Johnston, 242, 537, 652
Forbes-Robertson, Norman, 242, 343, 413, 501, 502, 652
Ford, John, 624
Fort Wayne Daily Gazette (Fort Wayne, IN), 175–77
Fort, Paul, 560
Fra Angelico, 28
France, 374, 455, 638, 726
    Dieppe, OW interviewed in, 660–70
    Dinard, 734
        OW interviewed in, 633–34
    Paris, 63–64
        International Exposition of 1867, 290
        OW interviewed in, 527–32, 569–74, 593–99, 616, 679–80, 730–31
        Salon, OW visits, 544
    Rouen, 666
France, Anatole (l'*Orme du mail*), 662
Francesca da Rimini (George Henry Boker), 553
Freake, Eliza, Lady, 533
Freake, Sir Charles James, 533
The Free Trader and Journal of Progress (Memphis, TN), 416–21
Fresh Air Fund, 461
Frith, William Powell (*A Private View at the Royal Academy, 1881*), 112, 469, 676
Frohman, Daniel, interviewed, 820
Froufrou (Ludovic Halévy & Henri Meilhac), 242
Fuller, Loie, 637
Fulton, Robert, 164
Funny Folks (London, UK), 918–19
Gainsborough, Thomas, 231, 232, 237, 238, 804
Gambier, Marc, 760
Garfield, James. A., 358
Garrison, William Lloyd, 164
Le Gaulois (Paris, France), 602, 607–12, 827–32
Gautier, Théophile, 193, 597, 650
Gavarni, Paul, 718
Gebhard, Frederick, 501, 778
Georgia Weekly Telegraph and Journal & Messenger (Macon, GA), 916–17

Gide, André, 14
Gil Blas (Paris, France), 663–70
Gilbert, W. S., 291, 295
    See also H. M. S. Pinafore, Iolanthe, and *Patience.*
Gill, Charles Frederick, interviewed, 844
Giotto, 231
Gladstone, William Ewart, 76, 232, 238, 388, 450, 533, 661, 662
Glasgow, OW interviewed in, 574–79
The Globe (Toronto, ON), 396–98, 403–5, 716
Godey's Lady's Book and Magazine (Philadelphia, PA), 896–900
Goethe, Johann Wolfgang von, 26, 77, 116, 193, 294, 521, 660, 661
    The Sorrows of Young Werther, 856
    Wilhelm Meister's Apprenticeship, 858
Goncourt, Edmond de, 443, 615, 669
Goncourt, Jules de, 669
Gough, John Bartholomew, 382
Gould, Jay, 122
Gower, Lord Ronald, 583–88, 657
Graham, Arthur J., OW interviewed by, 395–96
Grannis, Elizabeth Bartlett, interviewed, 825–26
Grant, Ulysses S., 445, 451
Gray, Frank, interviewed, 773–74
Greece, 29, 127
    Ancient Greeks, 161, 289, 293, 469, 530, 598
    art of, 122–23, 167, 372, 576, 578
    Athens, 29
    Olympia, 29
    Parthenon, 123, 415
Greenaway, Kate, 541
Grenet, Louis Edward, 429
Grosvenor Gallery, 30, 36, 215, 242, 450
Grosvenor Gallery, 1877 (OW), 30, 36
Guido Ferranti (OW). *See The Duchess of Padua* (OW)
Guiteau, Charles, J., 358
H. M. S. Pinafore (Gilbert & Sullivan), 911
Hague, John, OW interviewed by, 401–3
Hale, Sarah Josepha (née Buell), 282
Halifax Morning Herald (Halifax, NS), 466–72
Hall, A. Oakey, 726
The Happy Prince and Other Tales (OW), 76, 542

928

Harberton, Florence Wallace Pomeroy, Viscountess, 806
Harcourt, Sir William Vernon, 838
Harris, Frank, 655, 659
    Mr. and Mrs. Daventry, 679
Harrisburg Telegraph (Harrisburg, PA), 380–84
Harrison, Frederic, 418, 419
Harte, Bret, 378, 581
Hawthorne, Nathaniel, 859
    Scarlet Letter, 121
Hay, John Milton, 190
Haydon, Benjamin Robert, 231, 237
Hayes, Augustus A., 66, 694
    OW attends reception at home of, 51–52, 691–94, 752, 755
Headlam, Reverend Stewart, 660, 737–38, 739
    interviewed, 738
Hearth and Home (London, UK), 641, 797–800
Heine, Heinrich, 26
Heinemann, William, 850
Henley, W. E., 865
Henry François Farny, 195
Henry VIII, 627
Henry, Patrick, 436
Hermes and the Infant Dionysus (Praxiteles), 617
Hérodiade (Jules Émile Frédéric Massenet), 605, 610, 614, 730
Herrick, Robert, 623
Hewitt, Henry or Harry, interviewed, 699, 760–62
Higginson, Thomas Wentworth, 295, 460
Hoey, John, 458
Holland, 374
Holman Hunt, William, 125
Holmes, Oliver Wendell, 118, 128, 130, 192, 218, 358, 813
    OW criticises poetry of, 315
The Honey Moon (John Tobin), 486
Horwitz, Benjamin F., 112
    interviewed, 113
The House Beautiful (OW), 337, 383, 521, 575
Howe, Maud, 441, 452, 495, 581
Howells, William Dean, 110, 176, 192, 204, 331, 412, 526
Howson, John, 283, 303, 776
Hughes, Thomas, 213
Hugo, Victor, 420, 615, 653, 754
Humphreys, Travers, 737, 844

Hungry Joe, aka Joseph Sellick (OW conned by), 497–500, 525, 527, 728, 779–86, 796, 825
Hurlburt, William Henry, 53, 761
Huxley, Thomas Henry, 419
Huysmans, Joris Karl, 615, 668, 865
    À rebours, 570
    En Route, 662
    Le Rouge et le Noir, 570
Ibsen, Henrik, 652
The Idaho Avalanche (Silver City, ID), 901–2
An Ideal Husband (OW), 640, 641, 643, 646, 648, 649, 651, 652–54, 654, 815, 819–20, 819, 920
    first night, 642
The Iliad (Homer), 471
The Importance of Being Earnest (OW), 395, 629, 651, 654, 815, 819–20, 866, 920
Ingersoll, Robert, 214, 243, 244
Iolanthe (Gilbert & Sullivan), 756, 788
Iowa Daily Register (Des Moines, IA), 365–69
Ireland, 162, 289, 326
    Illaunroe, 26
    Lough Corrib, 26, 578
    Portora Royal School, Enniskillen, 26, 578
    Trinity College, Dublin, 26, 471
    See also Wilde, Oscar; political opinions; Irish Home Rule.
Irish Poets and the Poetry of the Nineteenth Century (OW), 383, 521
Irving, Henry, 233, 235, 262, 611, 619, 636, 657, 682, 813, 865
    OW praises, 233–34, 238, 239
    OW visits home of, 606
    OW's resemblance of, 695
Italy, 28, 57, 61, 182, 185, 200, 281, 282, 347, 374, 441
    Florence, 28, 54, 189, 383, 453
    Naples, 393, 666, 867
        OW interviewed in, 670–78
    Rome, 30
    Venice, 115, 189, 330, 343, 367
    See also Poetry (OW); *Ravenna*.
The Jacksonville Daily Journal (Jacksonville, IL), 259
Jaeger, Gustav, 577
James, Henry, 190, 192, 331, 443, 526, 859

James, Jesse, 413
Japan, 441, 443–44, 616
   art of, Constance Wilde on, 811–12
   art of, OW on, 123, 290, 359, 398–99,
     410, 437, 475
   OW's intention to visit, 303, 355, 359,
     365, 368–69, 397, 398–99, 410, 416,
     431, 433, 437, 445, 454, 455, 463, 466,
     475, 478, 496
Jefferson, Joseph, 235, 239, 490, 537
Jefferson, Thomas, 436
Jenkinson, Henry Irwin, 729
Jerome, Jerome, K., 810
Jesus Christ, 627, 669–70
Jews, 620, 629
Joel, Alfred, interviewed, 563
Johnson, Lionel Pigot, 865
Jones, George, 726, 761
Jones, John Percival, 901
Jonson, Ben, 624
Le Journal (Paris, France), 838–44, 846–52
The Kansas City Daily Times (Kansas City,
   MO), 352–54
Kate Field's Washington (Washington, DC),
   638–40
Kean, Charles, 234, 238
Keats, John, 30, 36, 41, 45, 53, 79, 82, 83,
   84, 125, 130, 139, 143, 185, 193, 287,
   293, 294, 361, 400, 545, 620, 623, 653,
   710, 852
   Endymion, 363
   Fanny Brawne, letter to, OW buys, 623
   Ode to a Nightingale, 279
   Sonnet on Blue, manuscript given to OW,
     617
Keifer, J. Warren, 92
Kenealy, Noel Byron, 804
Kerns, James, N., 457
Keswick, 729
Key, James Barton, 695
Kingsley, Charles (*Yeast*), 79
Kottabos (college literary magazine), 770
La Farge, John, 532
la Jeunesse, Ernest (l'*Imitation de notre
   maître Napoléon*), 662
Labouchère, Henrietta, 480, 482, 484, 485,
   489, 501, 721–25, 778
Labouchère, Henry, 214, 233, 241, 242–43,
   682, 838
   criticism of OW, 539, 546–47

Lady Windermere's Fan (OW), 490, 599,
   600, 606, 618, 619, 637, 640, 649, 654,
   814, 920
   The School for Scandal, compared with,
     624
The Lake Charles Echo (Lake Charles, LA),
   431
Lamb, Edward, 560
Landon, Melville De Lancey. *See* Perkins,
   Eli
Langtry, Lillie, 44, 241–42, 262–63, 298,
   450, 465, 488–92, 493, 495, 527, 533,
   541, 682, 701, 749, 775, 778, 918–19
   acting, OW describes, 234, 239, 241, 465
   aesthetic tastes, 75
   America
     arrival in, 478–87, 721–25
     intention to visit, 234, 262
   American debut, OW reviews, 492
   beauty, OW praises, 234, 239, 241–42,
     445–48, 449–50, 465, 470, 712
   D'Oyly Carte, Richard, on, 756
   friendship with OW, 445–48
   interviewed, 481–82, 776, 793, 825
   interviewed with OW, 486–87
   London stage debut, 234, 262, 448, 482,
     756
   OW defends, 85, 501–2
   voice, OW praises, 234, 239, 448, 465
Lathrop, George Parsons, 736
Le Gallienne, Richard, 15, 618, 859
Leadville Daily Herald (Leadville, CO), 345–
   47
Lecture to Art Students (OW). *See Modern
   Art Training* (OW)
Leigh, William Henry, Lord, 657
Leighton, Sir Frederic, 521
Leland, Charles Godfrey, 392
Lemaître, François Élie Jules, 670
Lenoir, Helen, 694
   interviewed, 794–95
Leslie, Mrs Frank (Miriam Florence
   Folline), 15, 735
   interviewed, 795–96, 824
Lewis, Angus, 737
Lincoln, Abraham, 420
Linton, Eliza Lynn, 800
Liverpool, 537, 657
   OW interviewed in, 517–23
Liverpool Daily Post (Liverpool, UK), 517–
   23

Lloyd, Constance. *See* Wilde, Constance (née Lloyd)
Locke, Charles E., 296–98, 303, 304, 313, 316, 339, 349
The Logan Leader (Logan, UT), 274
London, 54, 58, 61, 65, 177, 354
    OW interviewed in, 523–27, 533–34, 589–92, 601–16, 617–21, 636–54
    See also Tite Street.
Longfellow, Henry Wadsworth, 130, 358, 451, 761
    OW criticises poetry of, 759
        "A poem, not a poet", 192, 212, 315, 331, 361
        prefers Whitman to, 703
    OW's visit with, 190–92, 218
Loring, George Bailey, 107
Louisville Commercial (Louisville, KY), 199–202
Louÿs, Pierre, 669
Love is Law (OW), 679
Lowell, James Russell, 130, 331, 471
    Commemoration Ode, 471
Lowther, Aimée Constance Anne, 634, 734
Lugné-Poé, Aurélian, OW interviewed by, 660–63
Macaulay, Thomas Babbington, 63
MacDonald, Sir John, 472
MacKaye, Steele, 454, 489, 490, 565, 726–27, 787
Mackenzie, Ross, 404
Macmillan, George A., 29
Macpherson, David Lewis, 398
Macready, William Charles, 234, 238, 650
MacVeagh, Emily Sherrill (née Eames), 712
MacVeagh, Franklin, 712
Maeterlinck, Maurice, 605, 611, 615, 653
Magdalen College. *See* Oxford University
Mahaffy, Professor John Pentland, 28
    Rambles and Studies in Greece, 29
Le Maître de forges (George Ohnet), 572
malaria (OW suffers from), 495, 778
de Malesherbes, Guillaume-Chrétien de Lamoignon, 64
Mallarmé, Stéphane, 596, 668–69
Mallock, William Hurrell, 63, 770
    Romance of the Nineteenth Century, 77, 754
Manchester, 354, 378
The Manchester Weekly Times (Manchester, UK), 357–59
Manning, Cardinal Henry Edward, 28

Manning, John Burgess, interviewed, 845
Marlowe, Christopher ("Kit"), 624
    Doctor Faustus, 533
    Edward II, 850–51
Marroc, Adele, Constance Wilde interviewed by, 803–10
Martin, Thomas Mower, 409, 716
Massenet, Jules Émile Frédéric. *See* *Hérodiade*
Massinger, Philip, 624
Mathieson, Kenneth, Jr., 580
McCarthy, Justin Huntly, 213, 214, 224
    History of Our Own Times, 213
McClellan, Ellen Mary (née Marcy), 701
McClellan, George Brinton, 111, 701
McCullough, John, 126, 187, 235, 239
McDonald, Sir John A., 466
McKay, F. E., OW interviewed by, 638–40
McLaughlin, Mary Louise, 192
Mefistofele (Arrigo Bolto), 444
Melmoth, Sebastian (OW's pseudonym), 661, 679
Mendum, Charles Albert, 484
Meredith, George, 619, 812
    The Egoist, 625
Meredith, Owen. *See* Bulwer-Lytton, Edward Robert
Meriwether, Lee, OW interviewed by, 416–21
Merrill, Stuart, 596
Merrivale, Herman, 176
Mexico, OW's intention to visit, 47, 62, 126, 148, 168, 212
Meyer, Marcus R., interviewed, 298, 301, 304, 307
Meyerfeld, Max, 859
Michelangelo, 115, 153, 157, 372
Miles, Frank, 447, 453
Miles, John Christopher, 476
Mill, John Stuart, 420
Millage, Clifford, OW interviewed by, 679–80
Millais, Sir John Everett, 125, 231, 232, 237, 238, 521, 636, 701
    A Jersey Lily, 447
    The Black Brunswicker, 232, 238
    Chill October, 232, 238
    The Order of Release, 1746, 232, 238
    William Ewart Gladstone, 232, 238
Miller, Joaquin, 135, 175, 216, 218, 264, 315, 320, 328, 331, 361, 378
    Arizonian, 471

OW's resemblance of, 377
With Walker in Nicaragua, 328
Miller, Joe, 718
Milton, John, 219, 220, 852
Paradise Lost, 624
The Milwaukee Sentinel (Milwaukee, WI),
712–13
Milwaukee Sunday Sentinel (Milwaukee,
WI), 255–58
The Minneapolis Tribune (Minneapolis,
MN), 263–64
Mitchell, Berry, 207, 210
The Model Millionaire (OW), 629
Modern Art Training (OW), 163, 378, 537,
550
Modjeska, Helena, 52, 242, 490, 501
The Montgomery Advertiser (Montgomery,
AL), 580–83
The Montreal Daily Star (Montreal, QC),
388–91, 398–99
Moonshine (London, UK), 887–88
Moore (manager of OW's tour of New
England), 462
Moréas, Jean, 668–69
Mormons, 271, 428
See also United States; Salt Lake City, UT.
The Morning Call (San Francisco, CA), 291–
96
Morning Journal and Courier (New Haven,
CT), 131–33, 791–93
The Morning News (Paris, France), 569–74
Morrell, Henry H., interviewed, 819
Morris, Clara, 343, 724
The New Magdalen, OW sees in, 67–68,
75, 258
OW meets, 702–3, 762
OW praises, 126, 176, 235, 239, 379
and *Vera; or, The Nihilists*, 258, 702–3
Morris, William, 77, 80, 84, 116, 121, 287,
293, 389, 463, 624, 757, 865, 888
The Earthly Paradise, 331
Morrison, Lewis, 560, 567
Morse, Colonel W. F., 47, 71, 100, 101, 421,
475, 694–95, 772
interviewed, 106, 751–52, 764, 767–69,
772–73, 774
Morse, Samuel Finley Breese, 164
Moscheles, Felix, 804
Mount-Temple, Lady Georgina, 618, 622
Naples. *See* Italy
Nashville Banner (Nashville, TN), 917–18
Nast, Thomas, 318, 718

The Nation, 518, 797–99
The National Republican (Washington, DC),
91–94
Native Americans, 127, 205, 352, 378,
404–5, 406, 407, 422, 872, 892
Neilson, Julia, 641
Neilson, Lilian Adelaide, 234
Nelson, James Osmond, 657, 659, 739
Nero, 533, 542, 545–46
The New Haven Evening Register (New
Haven, CT), 493–94
The New York Herald (New York, NY), 40–
42, 67–68, 99–104, 248, 488–91, 545–
47, 567–69, 719–20, 747, 748, 766–67,
775, 776
The New York Herald, European Edition
(Paris, France), 583–88, 633–34, 635–
36, 734, 816–17, 821–22, 833–36
The New York Mirror (New York, NY), 492–
93, 497, 555–56
The New York Times (New York, NY), 35–
38, 51–52, 135, 554–55, 784–86, 788–
90, 819–21
New York Tribune (New York, NY), 43–46,
52–56, 133–34, 461–62, 491–92, 497–
98, 543–45, 562–64, 694–95, 727–29,
751–52, 755–56, 764, 888–90
The New York World (New York, NY), 771–
73
The New York World, Semi-Weekly Edition
(New York, NY), 31–35, 56–59, 104–6,
384–86, 763–64
The New Zealand Herald (Auckland, NZ),
769–71
New Zealand, OW's intention to visit, 478,
494
Newdigate Prize, 27, 29, 36, 63, 320, 579,
770
Newman, Cardinal John Henry, 28
The News and Courier (Charleston, SC),
438–41, 478–83, 561
Nichols, Maria Longworth (née Storer),
192, 195, 197
Nilsson, Christina, 298, 444, 712
interviewed, 775, 777
Nordau, Max, interviewed, 827–32
Norton, Charles Eliot, 360
Nye, Edgar Wilson "Bill", 906–7
O'Brien, Lucius Richard, 715
O'Connell, Daniel, 320
O'Connor, Thomas Power, 813
O'Reilly, John Boyle, 131, 498

Oakland Daily Evening Tribune (Oakland, CA), 310–13
Oedipus Tyrannus (Sophocles), 69–70
Ogden Daily Herald (Ogden, UT), 271–73
The Omaha Daily Bee (Omaha, NE), 270, 364–65
The Omaha Daily Herald (Omaha, NE), 267–70, 360–63, 796–97
Omaha Daily Republican (Omaha, NE), 359
Oscariana (OW), 635
Our soul is like a kite (attributed to OW), 890
Owen, Sir Philip, 584
Oxford University, 26, 28, 30, 36, 57, 60–61, 143, 178, 185, 256, 579
    tramway, 53, 154, 157
The Pall Mall Gazette (London, UK), 601, 603–6, 739–42, 795–96, 801–3
Palmer, Augustus M., 492, 564, 569, 638, 725–26
Palmer, General William Jackson, 51
Paris. *See* France
Paris Fin de Siecle (Ernest Blum and Raoul Toche), 617
Parnell, Charles Stewart, 224
Pater, Walter, 653, 865
Patience (Gilbert & Sullivan), 37, 39, 44, 82, 215, 283, 377, 454, 534, 589, 636, 747, 749, 755–56, 794, 875, 886, 887
    costumes, 55, 59, 61, 75, 257, 761–62
    Lillie Langtry sees, 776
    OW on, 75, 257–58, 887
    OW sees, 54, 58, 694–95, 752, 767
    referenced by reporters, 32, 39, 54, 81, 82, 111, 138, 142, 165, 194, 198, 199, 216, 263, 404, 439, 495, 534, 536, 553, 658, 691, 695, 696, 753
Patti, Adelina, 158, 193, 198, 298
    OW hears in concert, 196, 444
    photographed in America, 699, 760
Pen, Pencil, and Poison (OW)
    Max Nordau, quoted by, 831
Pendleton, George H., 581
Pennington, Harper (*Portrait of Oscar Wilde*), 618, 732, 804, 810
Perkins, Eli, 917–18
Personal Impressions of America (OW), 13, 47, 150, 170, 210, 221, 273, 282, 292, 313, 329, 337, 344, 370, 382, 415, 432, 435, 459, 464, 490, 493, 521, 528, 531, 532, 537, 539, 546, 550, 575, 582

Perzel, William, 553
    interviewed, 562, 565–66, 567–68, 786–87, 788–89, 790–91
Peters, William Theodore, OW interviewed by, 617–21
Pharaoh (OW), 663
Phelps, Elizabeth Stuart, 526
Phidias, 287
The Philadelphia Inquirer (Philadelphia, PA), 78–81, 637, 803–10, 837–38, 874–78
Philadelphia Press (Philadelphia, PA), 70–78, 558–60, 700, 752–55, 757–59
Phillips, Wendell, 164, 168, 357, 400
Piatt, Don, 682
The Pictorial World (London, UK), 600–601
The Picture of Dorian Gray (OW), 35, 66, 289, 313, 395, 444, 450, 573, 615, 635, 640, 653, 735, 736, 826, 843, 850, 856, 859, 865
Pigott, Edward F. Smyth, 183, 601, 614, 730–31
Plato, 469
Poe, Edgar Allan, 46, 315, 420, 436, 471, 545, 859
    The Raven, 139
Poems (OW), 31, 36, 172–73, 180, 219, 282, 751, 760, 769, 812
The Poet and the Puppets (Charles Brookfield and James Mackey Glover), 606
Poetry (OW)
    Ave Imperatrix, 287, 321, 537, 555
    Ave Maria Plena Gratia, 231
    La Bella Donna della mia Mente, 307, 770, 885
    Chanson, 770
    Charmides, 287, 306
    Chorus of Cloud Maidens, 30
    The Conqueror of Time, 30
    A Fragment from the "Agamemnon" of Aeschylos, 30
    La Fuite de la Lune, 904
    The Garden of Eros, 61
    Graffiti D'Italia, 28
    Humanitad, 137
    Impression de Voyage, 307
    Impression du Matin, 307
    Impressions I. Les Silhouettes, 217, 903
    In the Gold Room (A Harmony), 137, 321

Le Jardin, 467, 693, 750, 754, 890, 898
Liberta Sacra Fames, 288, 309
Louis Napoleon, 151
Madonna Mia, 480
Magdalen Walks, 321
La Mer, 693, 750, 754, 890
The New Helen, 30, 36, 480
OW's proposed second volume of, 130–
    31, 327, 342, 542, 547
Panthea, 137, 217, 306, 884
Queen Henrietta Maria, 30
Ravenna, 27, 29, 36, 63, 320, 363
Requiescat, 189, 804, 810
Rome Unvisited, 28
The Rose of Love, and with a Rose's
    Thorns, 770
Salve Saturnia Tellus, 30
[To] Sara Bernhardt, 30
Sonnet on Approaching Italy, 30
Sonnet to Liberty, 150, 288, 309
Sonnet on the Massacre of the Christians
    in Bulgaria, 76
Sonnet. On the Sale by Auction of Keats'
    Love Letters, 623
Sonnet Written at Turin, 30
The Sphinx, 542, 621
Vita Nuova, 472
ΓΛΥΚΥΠΙΚΡΟΣ ΕΡΩΣ, 328
ΘΡΗΝΩΙΔΙΑ, a translation from Euripides,
    30
Πόντος Ἄτ ν τος?, 472
Pope, Alexander, 278, 306
Porter, Albert Gallatin, 893
The Portrait of Mr. W. H. (OW), 590
    See also Ricketts, Charles; *Portrait of*
    Willie Hughes.
Postlethwaite. *See* du Maurier, George
Poynter, Edward, 124
Pre-Raphaelite Brotherhood, 80, 125, 136,
    139, 231, 238, 287, 294–95, 372–73,
    373, 597, 710
Prescott, Marie, 497, 537, 543, 544, 545,
    552, 553, 554, 562–64, 567–69, 726–27
    letter defending *Vera*, 561
    Othello, OW sees in, 549, 556
    performance in *Vera*, OW on, 560
The Press (New York, NY), 636–37, 640–
    41
La Presse (Paris, France), 660–63

The Prince of Wales, 85, 309, 330, 453,
    533, 721
Prinsep, Valentine Cameron "Val", 314
Puck (New York, NY), 881–82
The Pueblo Daily Chieftain (Pueblo, CO),
    347–49
Punch (London, UK), 32, 61, 81, 95, 188,
    208, 219, 289, 454, 517, 590, 693, 718,
    767, 883–85, 919–21
Il Pungolo Parlamentare (Naples, Italy),
    670–78
Queensberry, Marquess of, 16, 658, 842–
    43, 865, 866–67
    fight with Percy Douglas, 833–38
    interviewed, 816–17, 819, 821–22, 834–
        36, 834–36, 837–38
    leaves card at OW's club, 816–17
    libel trial, 817–19
Quiz (Philadelphia, PA), 83–87
Racine, Jean, 472
    Athalie, 610, 730
Ransome, Arthur, 862, 863
Raphael, 294
    OW's resemblance of, 49, 519
Raymond, John T., 536, 725
    interviewed, 540
Reade, Charles, 213
Reading Gaol, OW interviewed in, 655–60
Récamier, Madame de, 401
Rehan, Ada, 586, 636
Reid, Whitelaw, 726, 761
La reine de Saba (Charles-François
    Gounod), 605
The Relation of Art to Other Studies (OW),
    521
Renan, Joseph Ernest (*Vie de Jésus*), 627
Reni, Guido (*St. Sebastian*), 231
Reno Evening Gazette (Reno, NV), 328–29
The Republican (St. Louis, MO), 215–22
Reynolds, Sir Joshua, 231, 237, 377
    Penelope Boothby, 232, 238
Reynolds's Newspaper (London, UK), 845,
    855–58
Rice, James, 213
Richardson, Henry Hobson, 463
Richepin, Jean, 572
Ricketts, Charles, 86, 621
    Portrait of Willie Hughes, 617
Rider Haggard, Henry, 625
Ring, Mrs Zebedee, 476
The Rise of Historical Criticism (OW), 31
Robert Elsmere (Ward, Mrs Humphry
    Ward), 625-26

Robertson, Graham (*Ellen Terry*), 618
Robeson, George Maxwell, 107
Robinson, Augusta Louise, 404
Roche, Augusta, 695
Rochester Democrat and Chronicle
    (Rochester, NY), 142–45, 409–10
The Rockford Daily Gazette (Rockford, IL),
    247–48
The Rockford Daily Register (Rockford, IL),
    245–46
Rocky Mountain News (Denver, CO), 333–
    38
Rodd, Rennell, 35, 283, 326, 754, 769
Roland, Madame, 518
Rome. *See* Italy
Roosevelt, Blanche, interviewed, 747
Ross, Robert, 603, 643, 662, 677, 680, 781,
    861, 867
    interviewed, 858–60
    OW intveriewed by, 648–54
Rossetti, Dante Gabriel, 76, 77, 84, 231,
    293, 472, 517, 519, 597, 605, 612, 636,
    646, 709, 754, 757, 810, 830
    Christ in the House of His Parents, 231,
        238
    *Dante's Dream at the Time of the Death
        of Beatrice*, 522
    Ecce Ancilla Domini! (The Annunciation),
        231, 238
    poetry, OW praises, 116, 287
Rossi, Ernesto, 530, 718
Rousseau, Jean-Jacques, 226, 227, 621
Rousseau, Théodore, 294
Rubinstein, Anton Grigoryevich, 804
    Judas Maccabaeus, 605
Ruskin, John, 63, 71, 84, 116, 124, 279,
    301, 364, 372, 378, 400, 417, 418,
    419, 420, 522, 533, 587, 619, 709,
    710, 711, 728, 754, 813
    Fors Clavigera, 71
    A Joy For Ever, 128
    Lillie Langtry, OW praises to, 449
    lectures, OW attends, 27, 28, 53, 57, 453
    Modern Painters, 124
    OW disciple of, 57, 61, 185
    The Poetry of Architecture, 71
    road building, 27, 54, 360, 881
    warns OW against lecturing in America,
        206
Russell, Lillian, 776
Ryan, Abram Joseph, 423
Ryan, Patrick, 144

Ryder, Taylor, Henry, OW interviewed by,
    428–31
Ryley, J. H., 695
La Sainte Courtisane (OW), 635
Sainte-Beuve, Charles Augustin, 420
Sala, George Augustus, 469, 584–87, 657
    America Revisited, 478
Salomé (OW), 560, 599, 600, 617, 651, 735
    Germany, staged in, 859
    London
        cast for production in, 802
        refused licence for performance in,
            601–16, 649, 730–31, 801–3
        rehearsals for production in, 604
    OW hopes to stage in October 1892, 616
    OW's intention to publish, 605, 620
    Paris
        OW's intention to stage in, 730
        staged at the Théâtre de l'Oeuvre in,
            660, 663, 667, 850
    See also Bernhardt, Sarah; *Salomé*.
Salt Lake Daily Herald (Salt Lake City, UT),
    329–31
The Salt Lake Daily Tribune (Salt Lake City,
    UT), 331–32
Saltus, Edgar, 733
Salvini, Tommaso, 235, 239, 379, 549, 556,
    718
Samson and Delilah (Charles-Camille Saint-
    Saëns), 610, 730
San Francisco Chronicle (San Francisco,
    CA), 296–303
San Jose Daily Herald (San Jose, CA), 314–
    16
Sappho, 221
Sargent, John Singer, 813
    Portrait of Madame X, 573–74
Sarony, Napoleon, 49, 197, 317, 462, 495,
    696, 698, 721, 752, 763, 781, 890
    interviewed, 485
    on Lillie Langtry, 485
    OW photographed by, 696–99, 753–54,
        760–61
    OW regrets contract with, 327
The Saturday Review (Indianapolis, IN),
    893–95
Schiller, Friedrich, 77
Schopenhauer, Arthur, 418
Schwob, Marcel, 865
Scott, Sir Walter, 402, 625, 771
The Scranton Republican (Scranton, PA),
    749–51
Sedalia Weekly Bazoo (Sedalia, MO), 259

Sellick, Joseph. *See* Hungry Joe
Sérizier, Louis. *See* Spilett, Gedeon
Shairp, John Campbell, 363
Shakespeare, William, 51–52, 177, 190, 220, 239, 321, 322, 420, 472, 620, 652, 850, 852
    As You Like It, 234, 483, 486, 725
    Gower Memorial, 583–88, 657
    Hamlet, 262, 402, 572
    Julius Caesar, 192
    Macbeth, 570–72
    A Midsummer Night's Dream, 778
    Othello, 549
    Romeo and Juliet, 532, 560
Shannon, Charles (*Ashtoreth*), 618
Shelley, Percy Bysshe, 82, 126, 130, 139, 143, 185, 193, 219, 362, 623, 710
    Archy's Song, 193
    Hymn to Intellectual Beauty, 60
Sherard, Robert, 16, 492, 617, 626
    Jean Dupoirier interviewed by, 855–58
Sheridan, Richard Brinsley
    The Rivals, 490, 624
    The School for Scandal, 477, 624
Sherwood, Mary Elizabeth (née Wilson), 701
Shook, Sheridan, interviewed, 564, 569, 789–90, 792
Shorthouse, Joseph Henry, 394
Sickert, Helena, 413
Siddons, Sarah, 804
Sims, George R., 864
The Sioux City Daily Journal (Sioux City, IA), 265–67
Sisley, Maurice, OW interviewed by, 602, 607–12
The Sketch (London, UK), 643–47
Smith, Ballard, The Marquess of Queensberry interviewed by, 837–38
Soldene, Emily, 346, 485
Ye Soul Agonies in ye Life of Oscar Wilde (illus. Charles Kendrick), 134, 309
The Soul of Man Under Socialism (OW), 76, 80, 117, 164, 650
The South Australian Advertiser (Adelaide, SA), 794–95
South Kensington Museum (later the Victoria and Albert Museum), 266
South Wales Daily News (Cardiff, UK), 737–38
Southey, Robert (*The Cataract of Lodore*), 729

Spencer, Herbert, 418, 419, 451, 469, 718
Spilett, Gedeon, OW interviewed by, 663–70
Spinoza, Baruch, 629
Springfield Daily Republican (Springfield, MA), 108–9
St. James's Gazette (London, UK), 648–54
St. John, John Pierce, 909
St. Louis Daily Globe-Democrat (St. Louis, MO), 207–15, 222–25
St. Louis Post-Dispatch (St. Louis, MO), 203–7, 498–99, 500–502
St. Paul Pioneer Press (St. Paul, MN), 265
The Stage (London, UK), 886–87
The Standard (London, UK), 730–31
Stanley, Arthur Penrhyn, 808
Stendhal, 570
Stevens, Mrs Paran, 71, 85, 701–2, 761
Stevenson, Robert Louis, 625
Stewart, Alexander Turney, 459
Stewart, Cornelia Mitchell (née Clinch), 459
The Stockton Daily Evening Mail (Stockton, CA), 316–21, 321–22
Stoddard, Charles Warren, 301
Stoddart, J. M., 693, 700, 759
    interviewed, 749–51, 752–55
Stokley, William Strumberg, 457, 460–61
Stowe, Harriett Beecher, 581
Stratford-upon-Avon, 657–58
    OW interviewed in, 583–88
Strauss, Richard, 859
Strong, William Lafayette, 826
Sturges, Jonathan, 733
Sullivan, Alexander Martin, 225, 518
Sullivan, Arthur
    See H. M. S. Pinafore, Iolanthe, and *Patience.*
Sullivan, John Lawrence, 144
Sullivan, Timothy Daniel, 224
The Sun (Baltimore, MD), 110–12, 704–5
The Sun (London, UK), 817–19
The Sun (New York, NY), 38–39, 134–35, 454–55, 500, 536–38, 564–67, 695–96, 779–86
The Sunday Herald (Boston, MA), 117–27, 442–45, 448–54, 533–34, 696–99, 700–703, 764–65
The Sunday Inter Ocean (Chicago, IL), 617–21
The Sunday Oregonian (Portland, OR), 891–93

The Sunday Tribune (Minneapolis, MN), 844

Swinburne, Algernon Charles, 54, 76, 77, 90, 221, 287, 293, 517, 597, 615, 709, 710, 757, 830, 884
  Children, 813
  The Garden of Proserpine, 219
  Hymn to Proserpine, 219
  Laus Veneris, 219
  A Match, 219
  OW praises, 219–20, 420, 624
  OW's alleged imitation of, 219
  Songs before Sunrise, 219
  Songs of Democracy, 219
  on Walt Whitman, 415
Swing, Reverend David, 227–29, 249–50, 251–52, 253–54
Switzerland, 318, 343, 374
Symonds, John Addington, 865
Tabor, Horace, 342, 348, 713
Tardieu, Eugène, 838
Tartuffe (Molière), 611, 667, 730
Taylor, Alfred, 834
Taylor, John, 344, 520
Le Temps (Paris, France), 642
Tennyson, Alfred, Lord, 63, 80, 220, 351, 418, 624, 757, 759
  Promise of May, 540
Terry, Ellen, 234, 238, 576, 618, 619, 636, 813, 885
  OW writes poem for, 30
Thackeray, William Makepeace, 77
  The History of Henry Esmond, 625
  The Rose and The Ring, 808
The Chicago Times (Chicago, IL), 155–58
Theatre (London, UK), 622–31
Thomson, James (*The Seasons*), 624
Thresher, Sarah Bliss, 379
Tiffany, Louis Comfort, 532
Tilton, Theodore, 46, 65, 382
The Times (Philadelphia, PA), 81–83, 456–61, 484–87, 523–27, 720, 743
The Times-Democrat (New Orleans, LA), 424–26, 717–19
Tintoretto, 115
Tite Street (OW and Constance Wilde's home in), 617–21, 638, 732–33, 803–13
Titian (Tiziano Vecelli), 28
  Assumption, 231
Titus, Tracy, 493
To-day (London, UK), 810–13

The Tomb of Keats (OW), 30, 36, 231
The Topeka Daily Capital (Topeka, KS), 354–55, 760–62
The Topeka Sunday Capital (Topeka, KS), 911–15
The Toronto Daily Mail (Toronto, ON), 406–8
Toronto Evening News (Toronto, ON), 401–3, 408–9
Toronto Evening Telegram (Toronto, ON), 715
The Toronto World (Toronto, ON), 405–6
Toulouse-Lautrec, Henri de, 676
Townsend, Mary Ashley (Xariffa), 426
Townshend, C. J., 469
Tracy, Peter, 774
Traguier, W. M. (aka Traquair), 208
  See African Americans; OW's valet.
The Tribune (Minneapolis, MN), 767–69
Trinity College, Dublin. *See* Ireland
Trublet, Nicholas Charles Joseph, 621
Truth (London, UK), 705–8
Truth (New York, NY), 551–54, 774–75, 786–87, 790–91, 878–81
The Truth of Masks (OW), 327, 549
Turner, J. M. W., 161, 279, 587
Turner, Reginald, 680, 860
Twain, Mark, 461, 581, 813
Tyrrell, Robert Yelverton, 770
United States
  Albany, NY, OW interviewed in, 113–14
  Atchison, KS, OW interviewed in, 355–57
  Atlanta, GA, 441
    OW interviewed in, 434–38
  Baltimore, MD, 101, 102, 162, 174, 183
    Johns Hopkins University, 112, 125, 705
    OW interviewed in, 109–13
    OW's alleged snubbing of, 88–90, 90, 93, 95, 97–99, 100–101, 104–6, 111, 113, 129, 135, 143, 206, 213, 227, 764
    Peabody Institute, 112, 705
    Wednesday Club, 94, 98, 100, 105, 113, 124, 704
  Bangor, ME, 473
    OW interviewed in, 473
  Bloomington, IL, OW interviewed in, 261–63
  Boston, MA, 131, 132, 162, 179, 183, 192, 212, 218, 248, 335, 358, 463, 475, 521, 582

Harvard, 125, 131, 132, 134, 140, 143,
  159, 167, 201, 248
Literary Club, aka Saturday Club, 118
Oedipus Tyrannus, performance of,
  131
OW interviewed in, 114–31, 410–16,
  476–78
St. Botolph Club, 118, 131
Brooklyn, NY, OW interviewed in, 133–
  36
Buffalo, NY, OW interviewed in, 145–49
California, 329, 358, 370, 397, 400
  "Italy without its art", 343, 367, 393,
    410, 412
  OW interviewed on arrival in (on
    train and ferry between
    Sacramento and San Francisco),
    275–313
  OW's intention to visit, 72, 96, 126,
    148, 168, 266, 272, 703
Cape May, NJ, OW interviewed in, 456–
  61
Charleston, SC, OW interviewed in, 438–
  41
Cheyenne, WY, OW interviewed in, 332–
  33
Chicago, IL, 166, 170–72, 174–75, 176,
  179, 183, 186, 200, 201, 212, 218, 245,
  248, 266, 269, 335, 356, 358, 385,
  413–14, 422, 425, 482, 520
  OW interviewed in, 151–75, 226–43,
    249–54, 259
  water tower, 170, 250, 252, 254, 415,
    531
Cincinnati, OH, 201, 212, 233, 237, 241,
  259, 269, 335, 358, 444
  Art Museum, 188
  OW interviewed in, 187–99, 202
  pollution in, 378
  Rookwood Pottery Company, 188,
    192, 195, 196, 197, 198, 356
  School of Drawing, 188, 192, 266, 414
Cleveland, OH, 190
  OW interviewed in, 180–87
Colorado, 397
  OW's intention to visit, 168, 266
Corinne, UT, 283, 303, 304, 312
Dayton, OH, OW interviewed in, 369–80
Denver, CO, 359, 413, 469, 796
  OW interviewed in, 333–45
Des Moines, IA, OW interviewed in, 365–
  69

differences between East and West, 152,
  153, 156, 163, 167, 174, 183, 189, 201,
  212, 218, 226, 233, 237, 245, 258, 264,
  266, 268, 287, 302, 329, 345, 370–71,
  463
differences between North and South,
  436, 440
Dubuque, IA, OW interviewed in, 243–
  44
Fort Wayne, IN, 180
  OW interviewed in, 175–80
Galveston, TX, 428, 431
Griggsville, IL, 292–93, 301, 307, 378,
  918
Harrisburg, PA, OW interviewed in, 380–
  84
Jacksonville, IL, OW interviewed in, 259
Kansas City, MO, OW interviewed in,
  350–54
Kansas, OW interviewed in, 357–59
Leadville, CO, 63, 168, 342, 348, 359,
  364, 382–83, 385, 412–13, 416, 464,
  469–70, 521, 713–14
  OW interviewed in, 345–47
Lincoln, NE, 359
  OW interviewed in, 360–65
  Penitentiary, OW's visit to, 361–62
  State Hospital for the Insane, OW's
    visit to, 362–63
Long Branch, NJ, 458
Louisville, KY, OW interviewed in, 199–
  202
Memphis, TN, OW interviewed in, 416–
  21
Milwaukee, WI, OW interviewed in, 255–
  58
Minneapolis, MN, OW interviewed in,
  263–64
Mississippi River, 232, 240
Mobile, AL, 441
New England, 266
New Haven, CT, OW interviewed in, 131–
  33
New Jersey, 71
New Orleans, LA, 96, 210, 452, 582
  OW interviewed in, 422–28, 431–33
New York City, NY, 85, 95, 101, 110, 129,
  162, 183, 212, 266, 335, 356, 358, 459,
  463, 525, 582
  The Lotos Club, 527

OW interviewed in, 31–70, 384–88,
445, 461–62, 478–87, 488–502,
534–69
Delmonico's, 497–99
Madison Square Bank, 500
Newport, RI, 442, 458, 464
OW interviewed in, 442–45
Ogden, UT, OW interviewed in, 271–74
Omaha, NE, OW interviewed in, 267–70,
359
OW's intention to return (after 1882),
502, 527, 528, 530, 638, 735–37, 786
OW's lecture tour earnings, 131, 168–69,
181, 259, 264, 330, 461, 502, 773, 794,
796
OW's proposed book on the, 292, 449,
451, 456, 478, 528, 530–31
Philadelphia, PA, 95, 111, 162, 183, 335,
488, 521, 700
OW interviewed in, 78–87
School of Design, 122
Stewart Davis reception, 82
Portland, ME, 475
Providence, RI, OW interviewed in, 462–
65
Pueblo, CO, OW interviewed in, 347–49
Racine, WI, OW interviewed in, 248
Reno, NV, 304, 312
OW interviewed in, 328–29
Richfield Springs, NY, OW interviewed
in, 448–54
Rochester, NY, 167, 168, 201, 248, 355,
382, 410
OW interviewed in, 142–45, 409–10
Rockford, IL, OW interviewed in, 245–
48
Salt Lake City, UT, 272, 344–45, 385,
413, 428
OW interviewed in, 329–32
San Antonio, TX, 428
The Alamo, 429
Mission San José y San Miguel de
Aguayo, 429, 431–32
OW interviewed in, 428–31
San Francisco, CA, 335, 358, 359, 364,
367, 378, 384–85, 393, 414, 452
Bohemian Club, 320
Chinatown, 336–37, 359, 368, 384–85
OW visits, 313–14
tea cups, 336–37, 368, 371, 313–14
OW interviewed in, 322–28

San Jose, CA, OW interviewed in, 314–16
Saratoga, NY, 450–51, 458, 720
Sioux City, IA, 355
OW interviewed in, 265–67
St. Louis, MO, 207–12, 259, 336
Crow Museum of Art (later the Saint
Louis Art Museum), 208, 211, 215,
216, 231, 237
OW interviewed in, 203–25
St. Paul, MN, OW interviewed in, 265
Stockton, CA, OW interviewed in, 316–
22
Texas, 432
Topeka, KS, OW interviewed in, 354–55
Utica, NY, OW interviewed in, 137–41
Washington, D. C., 121, 183
OW interviewed in, 88–109
'Urabi, Ahmed, 470
Utica Daily Observer (Utica, NY), 137–41
Utica Morning Herald and Daily Gazette
(Utica, NY), 445
Vale, J. S., 131, 144, 150, 178, 208, 270,
290, 298–99, 304, 313, 339, 350, 376,
424, 429, 774
interviewed, 796–97
The Value of Art in Modern Life (OW), 575
Van Dyck, Anthony, 618
Vanderbilt Triple Palace, 459
Vanderbilt, William Henry, 459
Venus de Milo, 419, 445
Vera; or, The Nihilists (OW), 36, 86, 176,
183, 461, 528, 726–27
costumes, 537, 543, 551, 552, 553–54,
554
D'Oyly Carte, Richard, on, 755
Lillie Langtry on, 793
OW revises script, 774
OW talks with Clara Morris about, 702–
3
OW's "press junket" before the New
York opening of, 534–55
plans to produce, 31, 34, 45, 126, 162,
177, 258, 343, 496, 497, 566, 786–87
rehearsals of, 550, 554
response to first night of, 557, 558–60,
561, 573
scenery of, 550, 552, 554, 564
withdrawal of, 562–69, 788–93
Verlaine, Paul-Marie, 668, 854, 865
Il Pleure dans mon Coeur, 668
Verrocchio, Andrea del, 620

Vezin, Hermann, 330
Vezin, Oscar, 761
Victor Emmanuel II, 367
Voltaire, 227, 418, 472
Wainewright, Thomas Griffiths. *See Pen,
    Pencil, and Poison* (OW)
Walker, William, 328
Wallack, Joe Johnstone "Lester", 492
Waller, Lewis, 640, 641, 652
Ward Howe, Julia, 132, 441, 492, 596
Ward, Artemus, 910
Ward, Genevieve, 176, 180, 709
    interviewed, 748–49, 765–66
Ward, Mrs Humphry (Mary Augusta)
    Robert Elsmere, 625
Ward, Samuel Cutler, 85, 442, 495, 761
The Washington Post (Washington, DC),
    90–91, 96–99, 107–8, 703
Washington, George, 436, 455
Watson, Homer Ransford, 409, 411, 715
Watson, Mary, 708
    OW interviewed by, 322–28
Watson, William, 625
Watts, G. F., 812
Webster, John, 852
The Wedding Feast at Cana (Paulo
    Veronese), 528
West, Benjamin, 231, 237
Whistler, James McNeill, 56, 63, 244, 373–
    74, 544, 574, 618, 682, 692, 764, 776,
    794–95, 804, 813, 865
    *Arrangement in Grey and Black, No. 2:
        Portrait of Thomas Carlyle*, 574
    *Harmony in Grey and Green: Miss Cicely
        Alexander*, 574
    Three Figures: Pink and Grey, 374
    The White Symphony: Three Girls, 374
White, Frank Marshall, OW interviewed by,
    655–60
Whiting, Lilian, [?OW interviewed by],
    114–17, 708–11
Whitman, Walt, 76, 89, 130, 213, 218–19,
    315, 331, 361, 414–15, 471, 488, 703,
    726, 755, 859
    interviewed, 757–59
    Leaves of Grass, 219, 414, 751
    OW hopes to meet, 76–77
    OW prefers to Longfellow, 703
    OW's visit with, 84, 95, 124–25, 190,
        757–59
    To a Locomotive in Winter, 415
Whittier, John Greenleaf, 581

Wilde, Constance (née Lloyd), 118, 544,
    569, 570, 579, 592, 618–19, 635, 638,
    731–33, 795
    autograph book, 619, 733, 812–13
    interviewed, 803–13
Wilde, Cyril, 618, 732–33, 806–9, 860
Wilde, Jane Francesca, Lady ("Speranza"),
    26, 34, 36, 70, 255, 326, 518, 592, 593,
    731, 765–66, 799, 858
    interviewed, 797–800
    Jacta Alea Est, 76, 518
Wilde, Oscar
    on advertising, 111, 245, 257, 329
    on aestheticism, 34, 37, 39, 41, 45, 49,
        53, 82, 116, 156–57, 244, 256, 269,
        293, 372, 389–90, 541–42, 590–91
    on architecture, 62, 109, 111, 113, 123,
        127, 147, 148, 154–55, 157, 166, 176,
        179, 180, 186, 189, 200–201, 201,
        266, 268, 279, 282, 318, 336, 344, 360,
        366, 377, 378, 405, 406, 409, 411, 429,
        431–32, 458–59, 463–64, 475–76,
        525, 577–78, 705
        See also United States; Chicago, IL;
            water tower.
    on art in North America, 72, 94, 101,
        122, 140, 141, 143, 147, 166, 174,
        185–86, 189–90, 231, 233, 287, 315,
        347, 367, 374, 393–94, 399, 413–14,
        437, 501, 526, 547, 582
        Americans' preference for French
            over English art, 231, 237, 521, 547
    signs his autograph, 48, 114, 141, 216,
        247, 325, 348, 349, 381, 429, 714–15,
        760
    beauty and artistic ability of people
        linked by, 161, 269, 306, 385
    on beauty of women, 75, 84, 111, 113,
        124, 149, 162, 174, 258, 269, 338, 344,
        379, 405, 409, 431, 441, 449, 454–55,
        470, 581, 637, 639
        See also Langtry, Lillie.
    on censorship, 234, 239–40
        See also Salomé (OW); London;
            refused licence for performance in.
    character, 32, 164, 284, 349, 353, 363,
        364, 365, 376, 395, 401, 403, 456, 623,
        630–31, 726
    conversation, 84, 159, 199, 260, 262,
        267, 275, 291, 325, 335, 354, 442, 444,

456, 466, 530, 621, 629–31, 692, 710–11, 719, 754–55
    aesthetic slang, use of, 221, 283, 357
on criticism, 192, 206, 549, 566, 643–44, 650–51
  on decorative art, 55, 61, 146, 147, 162, 174, 193, 220, 240, 278, 368, 371–72, 385, 427, 440, 495, 521, 532, 541, 578, 590–91
    cast iron stoves, 317, 368, 371–72, 466, 728
  on dramatic art, 51–52, 196, 233–35, 238–40, 241–42, 278–79, 336, 379, 495, 549, 556, 570–72, 624, 626, 639, 651–54, 718
on dress reform, 39, 55–56, 59, 66, 75, 83, 116, 133, 315, 330–31, 336, 337, 425, 438, 464–65, 538, 541–42, 575–77, 579, 591, 762
on education, 62, 146, 147, 390–91, 398, 400, 411–12, 427
effeminacy, 65, 110, 137, 156, 158, 184, 188, 198, 200, 204, 236, 256, 261, 265, 266, 267, 276, 283, 284, 314, 315, 339, 349, 351, 354, 364, 366, 370, 377, 409, 530, 539
on flowers, 74, 85–86, 140, 182, 204, 284, 295, 359, 365, 372, 379, 383, 424, 436–37, 440–41, 449, 461–62, 712, 719
and food and drink, 71, 100, 107, 158, 177, 183, 184, 209, 238, 248, 341, 342, 348, 354, 440, 444–45, 465, 856–57
imprisonment, 655–60, 668, 845
    release, 739–43
  on interviewing, 129, 152, 179, 195, 221, 324, 520, 544, 575, 638, 655, 660, 670
on journalism in Britain, 233, 469, 502, 598
on journalism in France, 598, 667
on journalism in North America, 100, 101, 111, 117, 120, 129, 134, 135, 136, 139, 143, 147, 149, 159, 163, 172, 173, 179, 186, 205–7, 213, 221, 222, 226–27, 243, 244, 280, 295, 309, 221, 324, 221, 332, 337, 345, 354, 381, 452, 468, 474, 502, 524, 525–26, 752

on lecturing, 135, 136, 289, 320–21, 338, 356, 360, 382, 383, 520–21, 591
on manners, 144, 339–41, 385, 422, 425, 451–52, 455, 469–70, 474–75, 651, 713
    See also United States; Saratoga, NY.
on marriage, 175, 452–53
on music, 200, 290, 390, 531
on novelists, 77, 204, 213–14, 331, 442–43, 526–27, 569–70, 625–26, 662–63, 668–69
on painting, 124, 195, 200, 231–32, 237–38, 281–82, 343, 372–74, 521, 715–16
on poetry, 77, 82, 182, 218–19, 287–89, 295, 315, 320, 321–22, 325, 331, 342–43, 343, 361, 471–72, 623–24, 624–25, 703
  political opinions, 76, 79, 121–22, 140, 214, 225, 233, 243, 386–88, 420–21, 432–33, 435–36, 629, 633, 639
    Chinese Exclusion Act, 384
    Irish Home Rule, 222–25, 302
    Italy, 367
    land ownership, 577–78
    protectionism and free trade, 397, 399, 421, 456, 460
    Russia, 544, 548
on pollution, 77, 201, 232, 240, 378, 400, 427, 463
on rail travel, 72, 111, 135, 136, 148, 155, 161, 176, 188, 212, 341, 532, 729
and religion, 28, 276, 418, 452, 626–28, 667, 669–70, 679
on scenery
    of Britain, 729
    of Canada, 397, 400, 410, 411, 466
      See also Canada; Niagara Falls, ON.
    of the United States, 74, 114, 120, 148, 160, 205, 226, 240, 263, 265, 270, 273, 286, 292, 296, 299, 301, 305, 315, 318, 320, 335, 343, 348, 370, 378, 384, 400, 410, 417, 425, 431, 436, 440, 473, 494
on science, 77
on smoking, 114, 158, 248, 378, 459, 554, 597
trials of, 838, 867
    conviction, 844
    released on bail, 737–38

voice, 32, 37, 38, 39, 42, 44, 50, 62, 79,
91, 93, 138, 152, 159, 165, 194, 200,
204, 217, 236, 263, 270, 286, 288, 310,
314, 328, 335, 346, 349, 351, 353, 392,
408, 417, 425, 548, 667, 719, 875
on writing, 639, 646
Wilde, Richard Henry, 582
Wilde, Sir William, 25, 36, 255, 517, 799
*The Beauties of the Boyne, and its
Tributary, The Blackwater*, 468
Wilde, Vyvyan, 618, 732–33, 806–9, 860
Wilde, William Charles Kingsbury
("Willie"), 524, 592, 735, 766
interviewed, 769–71
William and Susan (W. G. Wills), 442
William III, 626
Williams, Captain Alexander S., 497, 499
interviewed, 781–82, 784–86, 825
Winans, Ross Revillon, 764
Wirtz, John C., interviewed, 771
A Woman of No Importance (OW), 66, 144,
560, 638, 640, 641, 649, 651, 735, 813,
820–21, 821, 884
The Woman's World, 47, 590, 804
Woodberry, George Edward, 360
Worcester, Joseph Emerson, 31

Wordsworth, William, 82, 185, 471, 472,
627, 703
The Excursion, 471, 624
Idiot Boy, 471
London, 1802, 472
The World Is Too Much with Us, 472
The World (New York, NY), 547–51, 691–
94
Worth, Charles Frederick, 59
Wyndham, Charles, 492, 564, 567
breakfast for, 551, 725–26
Wyndham, George, 865
Xariffa. *See* Townsend, Mary Ashley
(Xariffa)
Le XIXe Siècle (Paris, France), 616
Yates, Edmund, 30, 233, 243, 478
Yeats, William Butler, 669
Yonge, Charlotte Mary
The Heir of Redclyffe, 362
Young Mrs. Winthrop (Bronson Howard),
489
Young, Brigham, 344
Zaniboni, Eugenio, OW interviewed by,
670–78
Zola, Emile, 442–43, 600–601, 865
Germinal, 600–601
La Terre, 600–601